INDUSTRIAL AND ORGANIZATIONAL MARKETING

MICHAEL H. MORRIS

University of Central Florida

Merrill Publishing Company
A Bell & Howell Information Company
Columbus   Toronto   London   Melbourne

Published by Merrill Publishing Company
A Bell & Howell Information Company
Columbus, Ohio 43216

This book was set in Garamond

Administrative Editor: Pam Kusma
Production Coordinator: Rex Davidson
Art Coordinator: James H. Hubbard
Copyeditor: H. E. B. Anderson
Cover Designer: Cathy Watterson

Library of Congress Catalog Card Number: 87–61944
International Standard Book Number: 0–675–20519–0
Printed in the United States of America
1 2 3 4 5 6 7 8 9—92 91 90 89 88

To my wife, Lois,
and my saintly mother

PREFACE

The discipline of marketing has grown in many diverse directions over the past two decades. There are now courses, seminars, books, and journals devoted to high-tech marketing, nonprofit marketing, social marketing, international marketing, sports marketing, health care marketing, and financial services marketing, among others. Many of these represent new fields, or new applications of marketing. One of the most rapidly growing areas, however, is the field of industrial marketing, or marketing to organizations. This is an interesting development, because industrial marketing has been around for quite a long time. Yet, many business schools have only recently added industrial marketing courses, and some have yet to create such a course.

Why has industrial marketing come of age? One of the leading reasons involves industrial companies themselves. Marketing has traditionally been underemphasized by the managers of these firms, while technical and production-related concerns have received priority. Marketing was equated with personal selling and sales promotion. But the challenges and opportunities confronting these organizations have undergone great change in recent times, and with this has come a general recognition of the important contributions modern marketing has to offer.

These times are exciting for those who work with industrial products/services and markets. The rate of new product and service introduction is high, as companies rush to implement the latest technologies. Entirely new markets are appearing and old ones are being redefined. Meanwhile, industrial firms are devoting more resources to finding customers, studying customer needs, communicating with customers, and keeping customers satisfied. Many are creating marketing departments, appointing marketing vice-presidents, developing marketing plans, and implementing marketing strategies. At the same time, new concepts and tools are being developed to aid the efforts of the industrial marketer.

The purposes of this book are threefold: to provide an introduction to the distinctive nature of the marketing task when the customer is an organization; to provide an appreciation for the growing role of marketing within industrial companies; and, to provide insights into ways in which a number of marketing principles, concepts, and techniques can be used by the industrial marketing manager. The book is intended for undergraduate students who have completed at least a basic marketing principles course, as well as for M.B.A. students with some background in marketing.

ORGANIZATION

The book is structured around five major sections, and includes fourteen chapters and nineteen case studies. The five sections represent the rudiments of the marketing management process.

Part I introduces the reader to industrial marketing. The marketing philosophy is explained as it relates to the rapidly changing environment of industrial firms. Differences between consumer and industrial marketing are analyzed. Detailed attention is given to the nature of industrial products and markets, including international markets, and an overview of the procurement practices of organizations is presented.

Part II focuses on how to examine or analyze the industrial marketplace. This includes a detailed assessment of organizational buying behavior, industrial marketing research, demand analysis (including sales forecasting), and market segmentation. The abilities and insights of the marketer in each of these four areas often represent the difference between market success and failure, because they determine his or her ability to identify and serve customer needs.

Part III investigates the development of marketing strategies and tactics. Each component of the marketing mix is covered. Separate chapters are devoted to strategic marketing, product development, pricing, advertising, personal selling, and distribution. Importantly, these chapters build on the market analysis foundation established in Part II.

Part IV discusses the need to monitor, evaluate, and adjust marketing programs after they have been implemented. A number of problems and approaches are reviewed. Also included here are some of the ethical issues that industrial marketers continually face in managing the marketing mix.

The final section, Part V, consists of a variety of case studies. These cases require the student to analyze actual company situations and develop marketing solutions that address the opportunities and/or threats confronting the firms.

Rather than simply focus on identifying, defining, and providing examples of key concepts, this text attempts to integrate these concepts into a logical managerial process. A process approach is used to explain many of the major subject areas, including buyer behavior, marketing research, segmentation, strategic planning, product development, pricing, advertising, sales management, distribution channel management, and control. Approaching the management of such key areas as a process provides the student with a practical framework that can then be applied to industrial products, markets, and firms of all types in the real world.

HIGHLIGHTS

Some of the distinctive features of *Industrial and Organizational Marketing* include the following:

A detailed and systematic breakdown of how industrial markets differ from consumer markets, including a mini-situation that challenges students to cite the differences;

treatment of some of the newer technological developments in organizational purchasing and production, including just-in-time inventory, electronic data interchange, materials requirement planning, and flexible manufacturing systems;

two comprehensive chapters on the buying behavior of the industrial customer, including an extensive treatment of the buying center concept and simplified versions of the leading buying models;

a discussion of marketing intelligence systems and decision support systems as they relate to the traditional marketing research function in organizations;

a cost-benefit method for segmenting markets and targeting customers, based on a comprehensive set of managerial criteria;

a separate chapter devoted to industrial marketing strategy, types of strategies, and the meaning of a *strategic orientation* for industrial firms;

an examination of the role of marketing in corporate entrepreneurship;

contribution analysis as a marketing tool is stressed throughout the book, encouraging students to incorporate profit considerations in their analyses of marketing decisions;

a value-based approach to pricing; extended discussion of probabilistic bidding and transfer pricing;

emphasis on the two-way dyadic relationship in sales management;

detailed treatment of the importance of marketing control, and of techniques which can be used to monitor marketing performance, including spreadsheets;

nineteen real-life cases covering a wide range of products (including high-tech and defense-related) and services, and a variety of markets (including governmental, nonprofit, and international).

Also, the book includes chapter-by-chapter objectives, chapter summaries, end-of-chapter discussion questions, and an index of names as well as a subject index. Most chapters contain two or three exhibits that include real examples of successful marketing practices, examples of industrial advertisements or promotional materials, and summaries of the findings of major research projects on industrial marketing-related issues.

ACKNOWLEDGEMENTS

The author would like to thank all those who made this project a reality. Chief among these are Gordon Paul and Al Burns, both of the University of Central Florida, whose encouragement and helpful insights substantially improved the text. Much appreciation also goes to the case contributors, especially Roger Calantone and Tony di Benedetto of the University of Kentucky, who coordinated most of the case section. A number of reviewers made invaluable suggestions for revisions and additions, including P. Renee Foster, Delta State University; Robert R. Harmon, Portland State University; Dr. Jon Hawes, University of Akron; Richard Hise, Texas A & M University; C. Boyd Johnson, Central Washington University; Ramnath Lakshmi-Ratan; University of Wisconsin-Madison; Michael J. Messina, Gannon University; Dr. Charles O'Neal, University of Evansville; David Reid, Clarkson University; Marti J. Rhea, North Texas State University; John K. Ryans, Jr., Kent State University; William A. Staples, University of Houston–Clear Lake; Joe W. Thompson, Michigan State University; Lewis R. Tucker, University of Hartford; Wayland E. Vaughn, Slippery Rock University; and Gary G. Young, University of Massachusetts-Boston.

Finally, personal thanks to Joy Tatlonghari, Ceceile Lindo, Nathelle Gross, Jeanne Holman, Karla DeSousa, and Sarah Gorman for their many hours of high quality word processing and research assistance.

CONTENTS

PART I INTRODUCTION

The initial section of the book, consisting of the first two chapters, provides an overview of the nature and scope of industrial marketing and the industrial market-place. A foundation is laid for understanding the diverse set of institutions and activities involved, and the challenging tasks confronting the marketing manager in today's industrial environment. An attempt is also made to dispel some of the common misconceptions regarding industrial markets—such as the belief that they consist primarily of declining smokestack industries, or that the technical nature of the products being sold means that little marketing is required.

Chapter 1 defines industrial marketing and illustrates how the task of the industrial marketer differs significantly from that of the consumer goods marketer. This chapter sets the tone for the entire book, in that many of the key points introduced here are emphasized and elaborated upon throughout the subsequent chapters. The chapter also establishes the basic philosophy of the book; namely, that marketing is a creative, managerial process that serves to enhance the *value* that a firm is able to provide to customer organizations.

Chapter 2 introduces the reader to the many different types of goods and services sold by industrial marketers, and the wide array of customers who purchase these items. Ways are suggested for grouping industrial products and markets so that better insights can be drawn regarding how both can best be managed. Because the customer is an organization, usually with a formal procurement operation, some basic purchasing practices and procedures are also introduced in this chapter.

CHAPTER 1

THE BASICS OF INDUSTRIAL MARKETING

Key Concepts

Characteristics of industrial demand
Customer orientation (Marketing concept)
Customer value
Environmental turbulence
Exchange process
Industrial marketing
Information revolution

Marketing mix
Marketing myopia
Organizational environment
Product attribute bundle
Production chain
Product life cycle
Product orientation
Technological orientation

Learning Objectives

1. Define *industrial marketing* and the *industrial marketing mix.*
2. Establish the critical need for industrial firms to adopt a customer orientation.
3. Describe the size and importance of the industrial marketplace.
4. Discuss the dynamic environment facing industrial marketers.
5. Identify key differences between consumer and industrial marketing management.

*The knowledge—of inventors, entrepreneurs,
producers, and consumers—which accumulates
through the ongoing waves of human experience is the
most crucial curve and capital of industrial progress.*

GEORGE GILDER

Industrialized countries are in the midst of a marketing revolution. Everywhere we see a renewed emphasis on market segmentation, specialization, need assessment, product differentiation, and market research. Historically conservative institutions such as banks and hospitals are transforming themselves into aggressive competitors seeking creative means to maintain and expand their market niches. The trend is so prevalent that the 1980s have been dubbed the *decade of marketing* (*Marketing News*, 1984). Social observers such as Alvin Toffler and John Naisbitt have coined terms such as *de-massification* and the *multiple-option society* to describe a move away from an economy built upon mass production, centralization, mass marketing, uniform technologies, standardization, and homogeneity (Toffler 1980). Theodore Levitt (1983) suggests that the modern marketer is finding ways to differentiate such traditionally homogeneous products as isopropyl alcohol, strip steel, pork bellies, and plastics. New marketing techniques are being developed and applied to political, social, and economic problems.

These trends suggest that companies must become more knowledgeable in their understanding of marketplace demands, and more sophisticated in their attempts to reach and satisfy their target audiences. A superior product or production process is no guarantee of market success. The implications are perhaps greatest for companies that compete in industrial markets, where changing growth patterns and environmental turbulence are a way of life. These markets are the focus of this book. They represent a distinctly different challenge, one that presents major opportunities for the application of marketing principles and concepts.

DEFINING INDUSTRIAL MARKETING

Marketing is concerned with exchange processes between and among buyers and sellers. It is an attempt to match supply with demand. The subject of this exchange might be goods, services, technologies, business systems, people, concepts, or ideas. The buyer is traditionally viewed as some household member purchasing finished goods through a retailer or wholesaler, or directly from a manufacturer. In many instances, however, a company or institution is doing the buying. When this is the case, where both parties to the exchange are organizations, our focus becomes industrial marketing, also referred to as *business marketing* or *organizational marketing.*

Industrial marketing can be formally defined as the performance of business activities that facilitate exchange processes between producers and organizational customers. The focus is on a flow of goods and services which produce or become part of other goods and services, or which facilitate the operation of an enterprise. This enterprise can be a private firm, a public agency, or a nonprofit institution.

The essence of industrial marketing is creating value for customers with goods and services that address organizational needs and objectives. This idea is the marketing *concept.* As a philosophy of doing business, it has three major components. First, all marketing activities should begin with, and be predicated upon, the recognition of a fundamental customer need. Second, a customer orientation should be integrated throughout the functional areas of the firm, including production, engineering, finance, and research and development. Third, customer satisfaction should be viewed as the means toward long-run profitability goals. As Peter Drucker (1977) has explained, "the aim of marketing is to know and understand customers so well that the product or service fits them and sells itself."

This orientation is especially critical with industrial customers, for the goods and services they buy impact upon the performance of day-to-day business operations, and thus the viability of the enterprise. The buyer-seller relationship tends to involve mutual interdependence, with each party attempting to satisfy organizational objectives through the other.

An industrial firm that characterizes the marketing orientation is The Boeing Company, which transformed itself from a company dependent upon government contracts to a successful commercial competitor. The customer is placed at the top of the Boeing organizational chart, with customer needs stressed throughout the functional areas of the firm. Only those new product opportunities that can be matched with a customer need are pursued, and then in close partnership with user firms. When customers develop difficulties, it is not unusual for Boeing to send out engineering teams to tackle the problem directly. In production, cost objectives are emphasized, but not to the detriment of quality and reliability. Production schedules have been altered to accommodate a customer experiencing pressing needs. The company is structured so that management can adapt quickly when new market opportunities are identified. A project management approach is used, permitting both managerial autonomy and interfunctional coordination. The result is that customer concerns receive much greater weight than a preoccupation with engineering or technical issues might produce. All of this led Peters and Waterman to label Boeing as one of the select few so-called excellent American firms (Peters and Waterman 1982).

Boeing's customer orientation represents an exception to the rule. While few managers in companies today will disagree that customers are important, most do little more than pay lip service to customer needs. The marketing concept is a simple idea, but it requires commitment, hard work, and a financial investment on the part of the industrial firm. This is an effort many are unwilling to make.

CUSTOMER NEEDS AS THE DRIVING FORCE

Because many industrial products are fairly complex, technical people such as engineers and manufacturing managers tend to play a dominant role in marketing-related activities. They usually bring a technical orientation to managerial decision making. As a result, companies have to be wary of what has been called *marketing myopia,* which is a tendency to see one's business in terms of products or technologies rather than customer needs. This indicates a narrow-minded view of business purpose. For example, is a maker of glue in the glue business or the industrial adhesives business? The marketer might insist that such a company is in the business of making things stick together. While the distinction may seem insignificant, or even silly, how one defines the business boils down to a question of just how flexible and innovative the firm will be in satisfying the needs of a changing market. Ultimately, then, there is only one valid definition for any business—to create and keep a customer.

Products, as a rule, cannot sustain market growth indefinitely. This fundamental is the lesson of the product life cycle. The company that defines itself in terms of a specific product will fade as the product inevitably fades. The firm must adapt to changes in technology, competition, and especially customers. It must develop, over time, new technological applications, new products, and new markets to meet these opportunities. By defining the firm in terms of needs, change and adaptation become normal parts of business operations.

The National Cash Register Corporation (NCR) of Dayton, Ohio, is an example of a company almost destroyed by marketing myopia. By defining itself in terms of mechanical and electromechanical (key-driven) cash registers and accounting machines well after these products were mature, the company faced a disastrous situation in the early 1970s. Not only had its management ignored the signs of inevitable technological change, but also they had lost touch with the operations of their customers. The needs of major banks, and such retailing giants as Sears Roebuck and J.C. Penney, had evolved beyond NCR's capability to fulfill them. Many investment analysts openly predicted imminent company failure.

New management, in spite of a huge, outdated manufacturing complex and increasingly obsolete products, was able to turn the company around, but only at great cost. A $60-million loss was experienced in 1972. More than 13,000 manufacturing jobs were eliminated, creating havoc in the Dayton economy. A metamorphosis took place, as NCR became a major player in computer-based systems. Changes included decentralized manufacturing, streamlined product lines, new technologies, greater reliance on vendors, and increased R & D (with an applied orientation). Most importantly, the sales and service organizations were restructured from a geographic and product focus to one based on customer groups. NCR grew to dominate the market for point-of-sale terminals used by banks and retail food establishments and developed its own lines of business and personal computers.

THE INDUSTRIAL MARKETING MIX

Some of the specific activities performed by the industrial marketing manager include the following:

identifying customer needs

researching buyer behavior

segmenting users into manageable groups

developing products and services

setting prices

ensuring proper delivery, installation, and servicing of products

making products available at the right time and place, and in the right quantity

allocating marketing resources across product lines

communicating with target customers before, during, and after a sale

evaluating and controlling ongoing marketing programs

The major decision areas confronting the marketer have been conveniently grouped into a general framework called the marketing *mix*. This mix consists of four components: product, price, promotion, and distribution. Each of these is a category consisting of interdependent decisions.

Product decisions concern the specific attributes designed into a product, its packaging, warranties, adjunct services, customer training, and installation, among others. These decisions represent the core element of the mix in industrial markets, around which everything else revolves. Pricing involves terms of sale, establishing discounts, trade-ins, rebates, bidding strategies, and, possibly, financing. Promotional concerns include such areas as personal selling, sales management, trade advertising, free samples, trade shows, demonstrations, direct mail campaigns, and publicity. It is the communications component of the mix. Distribution decisions are those pertaining to the number and types of middlemen used, market coverage, delivery time, and inventory policies.

Note that each of these components is a *variable* that can be manipulated, not a *constant*. Each requires a strategy. While not all of these activities are necessarily performed by someone called a *marketer* in any given firm, each can play a key role in the marketing function. Collectively, they combine to determine the value received by a customer from a given product or service. For this reason, decisions in any one of these areas must be closely coordinated with those in the other three areas. Specific questions must be considered in formulating the industrial marketing mix. (See Table 1.1.) The relative importance of the different components of the mix within a particular industry is likely to vary. Table 1.2 provides an example.

WHY STUDY INDUSTRIAL MARKETING?

The field of industrial marketing is fairly underdeveloped. Only moderate progress has been made in determining what works, and why, in terms of industrial marketing strategy. The quantity and quality of research performed on industrial customers is limited. Compared to consumer products and markets, industrial products and markets tend to receive much less attention in textbooks, journals, and educational programs that deal with marketing. There is an overriding need to change this state of affairs.

Table 1.1   Questions Facing the Industrial Marketing Manager

1. How are my customers' markets changing? What changes can I expect in my customers' product lines and production processes?
2. Who are the key members of the decision-making unit in customer firms?
3. When should market research be performed, how much should I spend, and who should be the subject of this research?
4. What new forms of competition are impending, given anticipated technological, economic, and regulatory changes?
5. Are there more effective ways to segment my markets? Should I be focusing on industries, organizations, or specific individuals within organizations in my segmentation plan?
6. What is the profit-maximizing service level for each target segment?
7. How long can I keep the customer organization sold after the sale?
8. Should I organize our marketing effort around products, territories, customers, functions, or some combination?
9. What is the total amount my product will cost a customer over its useful life?
10. Are there gaps in my product line? Is it too broad? When do I decide to drop a product?
11. What products are in joint demand with mine? How will changes in their prices or availability affect my sales?
12. Are long-term contracts in our interest? Should I finance my customers' purchases?
13. Could discounts be used more effectively to achieve marketing objectives?
14. What effect will increased advertising have on the effectiveness of my sales force?
15. How do I evaluate the effectiveness of trade shows?
16. When should I use industrial distributors? Manufacturers' representatives?
17. How should commission structures be designed to ensure product line objectives?

Table 1.2   How Top Managers in Biotechnology Companies Rank the Importance of Strategic and Operational Factors to Their Companies' Market Success

1. Having state-of-the-art technology
2. Product image reputation
3. Price competitiveness
4. Reputation of the company's distributors
5. Having a strong service organization
6. Completeness of product line
7. Personal selling efforts
8. Having strong patent protection
9. Use of marketing research
10. Creativity of advertising message
11. Advertising media employed
12. Employing a competent advertising agency

Source: W. L. Shanklin and J. K. Ryans, Jr., *Essentials of Marketing High Technology* (Lexington, Mass.: Lexington Books, D. C. Heath and Co., 1987), 3. Reprinted with permission.

The need to develop a better and more complete understanding of industrial marketing management stems from three factors: (a) the markets are quite sizable; (b) the markets are growing; and (c) the environments faced by the firms involved are becoming more dynamic, turbulent, and complex. Let us examine each of these areas.

The Size of the Industrial Market

While a market economy ultimately depends upon the final consumer, the purchases of these consumers are actually equal to less than half of those of industrial customers. If we add up the dollars spent and the number of transactions that take place, the totals are higher on the industrial side of the market. Of course, much of this activity concerns the raw materials and components that eventually become part of consumer goods.

In 1986, there were more than 350,000 manufacturing establishments in the United States, employing over 20 million people. These firms were responsible for $2.5 trillion in sales. Another 300,000 firms provided services to businesses and other organizations. In addition, over 400,000 firms served as assemblers, resellers, wholesalers, manufacturers' agents, and brokers.

The productive output of these organizations is the foundation that enables the entire U.S. economic system to function smoothly. Table 1.3 provides comparative sales figures for manufacturing, wholesaling, and retailing establishments in the United States, while Table 1.4 is a general breakdown of major manufacturing industries, a $2.3-trillion market.

To better understand the vast array of economic activity that comprises the industrial market, consider the development of a consumer product such as a lawn mower. Before a lawn mower can be sold to a consumer, it has to be assembled, wholesaled, and retailed. Prior to assembly, someone had to manufacture a frame, a motor, a blade, a starter system, wheels, a grass bag, and a variety of elements. Any

Table 1.3   U.S. Manufacturing and Trade Sales for 1985 *(in millions of dollars)*

Manufacturing	2,341,220
Durable goods industries	1,243,793
Nondurable goods industries	1,097,427
Retail trade	1,373,941
Durable goods stores	514,207
Nondurable goods stores	859,734
Merchant wholesalers	1,373,926
Durable goods establishments	626,749
Nondurable goods establishments	747,177

Source: *1986 Survey of Current Business.*

Table 1.4   U.S. Manufacturers' Sales for 1985 *(in millions of dollars)*

Stone, clay, and glass products	57,255
Primary metals	125,777
Fabricated metal parts	168,953
Machinery, except electrical	212,620
Electrical machinery	185,514
Transportation equipment	313,427
Instruments and related products	56,743
Food and kindred products	296,142
Tobacco products	20,606
Paper and allied products	97,565
Chemicals and allied products	214,345
Petroleum and coal products	194,030
Rubber and plastic products	48,246

Source: *1986 Survey of Current Business.*

number of firms were involved in making such component parts—each of which, in turn, required machines, presses, tools, chemicals, lubricants, and paints for its manufacture. Again, these inputs had to be manufactured and marketed by someone. And finally, had not a variety of raw materials been developed, processed, and marketed in sufficient quantities, the entire process would never have begun.

This process is called the *production chain.* It concerns the process by which companies transform raw materials into components, parts, tools, and machines; and by which these components are used to produce other products; and which, ultimately, enables the production of consumer goods from industrial products.

Figure 1.1 illustrates the production chain. For simplicity, six major stages in the process are presented, with examples of firms involved at each stage. There are, in addition, a number of facilitating firms that provide vital support services to companies throughout the process. In our lawn mower example, the manufacturer requires insurance, telecommunications, auditing, marketing research, and a host of other ancillary services. While the consumer marketer focuses primarily on the link from manufacturer, wholesaler, or retailer to the consumer, industrial marketing includes a multiplicity of transactions leading up to this final link. This strategy involves an often complex network of interactions among many firms operating at different points in the production chain. Excluded from the domain of industrial marketing are the wholesaler and retailer of the final consumer product.

Despite the size and scope of these markets, many marketing-related decisions are made by engineers and technicians who have little formal understanding of marketing principles and strategies. In fact, many industrial firms have no marketing department or marketing manager, and fail to embrace the marketing concept in their operations. This situation must change, however, as firms find themselves unable to keep pace with new developments in their markets and the surrounding environment. In the meantime, programs and policies based on misconceptions regarding the marketing function often result in mediocre performance or outright failure. Table 1.5 highlights some of these misconceptions.

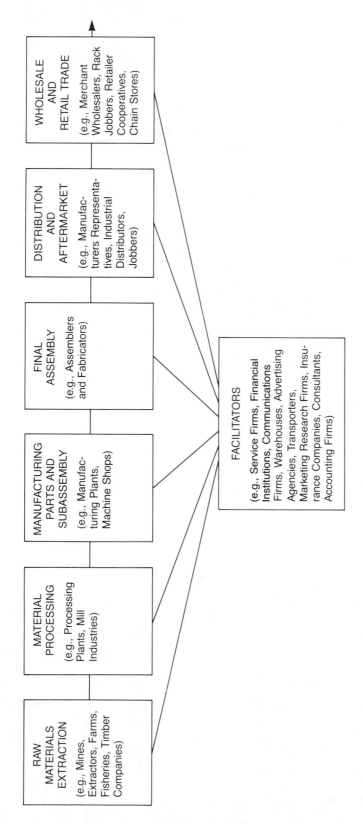

Figure 1.1 Types of Firms Involved at Various Stages in the Production Chain

Source: Adapted from Robert W. Haas, *Industrial Marketing Management* (Boston: Kent Publishing, 1982) and B. Charles Ames and James D. Hlavacek, *Managerial Marketing for Industrial Firms* (New York: Random House, 1984).

Table 1.5   Marketing Misconceptions Held by Managers of Industrial Firms

---

The industrial manager is apt to make certain untrue assumptions about customers, products, and marketing. Some of these mistaken notions, or myths, are summarized below.

Myth: Purchasing behavior is economically rational.
Reality: Subjective judgments and personal motives guide the behavior of organizational decision makers.

Myth: New technology sells.
Reality: Many technologically superior products fail in the marketplace, while many technologically obsolete products continue to be purchased.

Myth: The right product will sell itself.
Reality: One must have the right product at the right time; its benefits must be effectively communicated to the right people; and it must be made available through the right channels of distribution.

Myth: "We can't waste time on marketing, we don't have the product designed yet."
Reality: Failure to perform market research throughout the product development process is likely to result in exaggerated estimates of market potential, in product features of little value to customers, and in prices that are too high or low.

Myth: Sales and marketing are the same thing.
Reality: *Selling* is part of promotional strategy, which in turn is part of overall marketing strategy. *Marketing* includes product, price, promotion, and distribution activities that contribute to customer value.

Myth: Purchasing can be ignored—focus on the engineers.
Reality: Those in purchasing can be instrumental in helping the marketer understand how buying decisions are made in a particular organization; they can also work to ensure that the firm does not buy from a particular vendor. Also, after a buying decision is made, the vendor must deal directly with purchasing.

Myth: Low price is the customer's main concern.
Reality: Price is often a secondary concern to engineers and production managers, who will pay more for quality and reliability.

Myth: Bookings and sales are the same thing.
Reality: Industrial customers rarely pay in advance; a booking or purchase order represents a potential sale, but orders are often cancelled or changed, and revenue comes later.

Growth Markets of Today and Tomorrow

At first glance, one might conclude that industrial markets, regardless of their size, are on the decline. One has only to picture closed steel, automobile, and rubber plants, and recall the numerous obituaries that have been written for so-called smokestack industries. While such dire predictions hold true for industries built on obsolete technologies and aging capital equipment, they hardly describe the overall industrial market. In fact, many of the major growth opportunities would appear to fall on the industrial side of the ledger. This is the case, in part, because many industries are retooling and adapting to the future—a process that stimulates demand for goods incorporating the newest technologies, and goods that reduce production costs.

The post-industrial world holds much promise for producers of products and services intended for organizational customers. As AT&T closes plants that manufacture outdated telephone equipment, it opens plants that make computer chips. Developed nations are growing primarily in such areas as computers, environmental and energy controls, optical instruments, electronic connectors, telecommunications equipment, robots, office machines, business forms, lithographic processes, aerospace propulsion, plastics, electromedical equipment, and process control instruments. These are products sold, in large part, to organizational users—to factories, offices, hospitals, hotels, schools, and to the government.

The immense industrial potential represented by newer technologies is exemplified by the laser field. It seems that new applications for lasers are found daily, from their use in delicate ophthalmic surgery to the machining of extremely complex shapes within fine tolerances. The Fisher Body Division of General Motors cut the labor time for making steel rule die boards (used to cut cloth and vinyl for automobile interiors) from 32 hours to 4 hours using a laser. Product development can be aided by laser-produced holograms (three-dimensional photographic images) for simulation purposes in product testing. Laser technology can even assist in industrial espionage, enabling a company to eavesdrop in another room without having to enter and place a bugging device (Mullins 1982, 76).

The much-heralded "information revolution" also presents growth opportunities for industrial marketers. Companies are springing up to provide turnkey computer systems, video cassettes (e.g., for sales presentations), communication systems, telemarketing services, financial data bases, market research services, technological and market forecasts, computer software, word processing, and much more. John Naisbitt (1982, 38) explains, "In the computer age we are dealing with conceptual space connected by electronics, rather than physical space connected by the motor car." He points to the $400-billion electronics industry as positive proof that the new information age is upon us.

At the same time, many consumer markets are maturing. Makers of soft drinks, blue jeans, and automobiles increasingly look to international markets for growth, and segment the domestic market into smaller and smaller niches. Other consumer product categories, such as jewelry, lawn equipment, leather goods, and food utensils face zero growth or actual decline. This is not to say there are no dynamic opportunities on the consumer side—consider personal computers, bicycles, and specialty frozen foods. Rather, what is suggested is the need to broaden our focus in marketing to include organizational products and markets.

The attractiveness of opportunities on the industrial side can lead a firm with an established market position in consumer products to completely reposition itself. The Singer Company is a household name as the number one producer of sewing machines for consumer (and industrial) use. This traditional giant found itself in great difficulty as major demographic, social, and economic changes eroded its customer base. Singer's response was to redirect its resources and technologies toward aerospace and military markets, to become a major factor in the flight simulator and navigation system businesses. Exhibit 1.1 is an advertisement that illustrates the new directions the firm took.

In a related vein, more than half of today's college graduates are finding employment in organizations that operate in industrial markets. There has been a boom in entrepreneurial activity taking place in the U.S. economy. Some 600,000 new businesses are being created each year, many due to the technological opportunities just mentioned. These firms account for virtually all the employment gains taking place. College graduates work predominantly in white-collar jobs, the majority of them as professional and technical workers, managers, or salespeople. Through 1995, growth in professional and technical workers will increase at a faster rate than total employment. Most of these people will work for manufacturing or service firms. Of the occupations projected to grow the fastest, a number involve industrial firms. Examples include electronic technicians, technical sales representatives, engineers (electrical, civil, mechanical), mold machine operators, and office machine technicians, as well as computer programmers, systems analysts, service technicians, and operators.

Accompanying this growth in industrial markets are a number of profound changes in the environments surrounding these firms. Historically, customers may have seemed virtually captive, while a firm's sales growth was fairly easy to extrapolate. Managers could afford to focus their efforts on product line extensions and production efficiencies, and a solely technical orientation could prevail. This situation is no longer the case; companies must plan for a future as different from today as today is from yesterday. These changes represent the most compelling reason for an enhanced understanding of industrial marketing management. Let us elaborate on some of these environmental issues.

THE EXTERNAL ENVIRONMENT OF INDUSTRIAL FIRMS

Providing the customer with a better product at a lower price is, despite conventional wisdom, no guarantee of market success. A failure to anticipate and act on changes in customer needs, technology, resource availability, regulation, market structure, competitor moves, or economic variables can doom even the most innovative of companies. These components are part of a firm's *external environment,* defined as everything outside the organization itself. The environment also includes any social, political, geographic, and climatic developments that might affect the firm. Figure 1.2 illustrates a situation where the ability of the industrial firm to profitably meet customer needs, using the elements of the marketing mix, is directly affected by a number of environmental influences.

Organizational environments can be characterized by their degree of stability, complexity, market diversity, and hostility. As a generalization, industrial firms must increasingly cope with instability, significant complexity, more diversification in their customer base, and a number of hostile forces in their surroundings. The experience of Digital Equipment Corporation (DEC), one of the largest American computer manufacturers, provides an example. As this giant entered the mid-1980s, it found rapid technological change was undermining environmental stability, while the demands of new high-growth fields (such as office automation and computer-

Exhibit 1.1 Advertisement Illustrating Singer's New Directions

Reprinted by permission of the Singer Company.

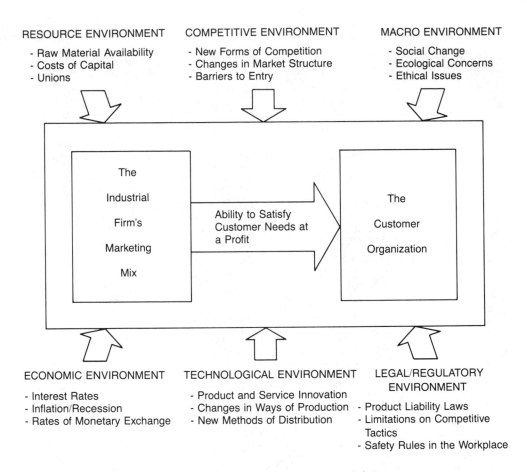

RESOURCE ENVIRONMENT

- Raw Material Availability
- Costs of Capital
- Unions

COMPETITIVE ENVIRONMENT

- New Forms of Competition
- Changes in Market Structure
- Barriers to Entry

MACRO ENVIRONMENT

- Social Change
- Ecological Concerns
- Ethical Issues

The Industrial Firm's Marketing Mix

Ability to Satisfy Customer Needs at a Profit

The Customer Organization

ECONOMIC ENVIRONMENT

- Interest Rates
- Inflation/Recession
- Rates of Monetary Exchange

TECHNOLOGICAL ENVIRONMENT

- Product and Service Innovation
- Changes in Ways of Production
- New Methods of Distribution

LEGAL/REGULATORY ENVIRONMENT

- Product Liability Laws
- Limitations on Competitive Tactics
- Safety Rules in the Workplace

Figure 1.2   The Environmental Challenges Confronting Industrial Firms

aided design and manufacturing) contributed to environmental complexity. It was forced to seek a broadened, more diverse customer base as growth opportunities shifted toward small business markets and desktop workstations. The presence of strong traditional competitors (e.g., IBM), together with aggressive upstarts (e.g., Elxsi) suggested a more hostile environment.

Industrial firms attempt to survive and prosper in what Drucker (1980) has termed the *age of discontinuity*. Environmental turbulence creates unplanned change divergent from past and present trends. Marketing strategy can play a major role in anticipating where the major changes will occur, and in providing action plans for exploiting these changes or adapting to them. The next few pages elaborate upon some of the specific changes taking place in the areas of technology, customers, competition, government regulation, and the economy—changes that represent both threats and opportunities for industrial marketing.

Technological Environment

The suggestion has been made that virtually all the innovations developed in the twenty-five years following World War II, excepting computers and pharmaceuticals, were actually based on technologies developed prior to 1920. In the sixty years between 1856 and World War I, a major invention resulting in an entire new industry was developed about every fourteen to eighteen months. The final few years of the twentieth century, and beyond, would appear to evidence a return to the dynamic pace of this earlier era.

Such technological change is especially relevant for industrial firms, where advances in product, process, and materials technologies frequently determine market success or failure (see Exhibit 1.2 for an example). Technical obsolescence poses a distinct threat, especially for more sophisticated industrial products. This fact of life has led some to conclude that the best way for industrial firms to remain competitive is by actively participating in the development of the latest technologies, and by continually using these technologies in new products to satisfy ever-changing customer needs. For instance, Cincinnati Milacron, a company that manufactured screws and taps 100 years ago, and milling and grinding machines forty years ago, has prospered more recently as a maker of machines to form plastics, silicon exitaxial wafers used in integrated circuits, and computer-controlled robotic arms used in production lines.

Marketing can play a key role in identifying likely changes in a customer's production process or in its delivery and service needs. Successful innovation requires the matching of a technological opportunity to a market need. Moreover, many industrial innovations originate in the customer firm, suggesting the need for a strong and continuous process of buyer-seller interaction. Marketing can also identify potential technological developments through competitive analysis, interaction with suppliers and distributors, and trade show forums, among others.

As new technologies are developed, countless opportunities for applying these technologies to products or processes become available. The firm must pick and choose from among these opportunities. Too often, projects are pursued simply because they are technically interesting. One of the major reasons for new industrial product failure is the so-called better mousetrap that nobody wanted. This means a truly innovative product for which there is little real market potential. Marketing inputs can help ensure that technical projects properly reflect the demands of the marketplace.

Customer Environment

The industrial marketer has faced, historically, a geographically concentrated customer base. This situation is changing as transportation, communication, and labor force developments enable companies to locate farther from their suppliers. Industries are becoming more widely dispersed, with a general shift from the Midwest to the Southeast and Southwest. In addition, many industrial firms find their customer base is expanding as pressure for new products or product applications forces them

Exhibit 1.2   A Marketing Strategy Built around Technological
Leadership

Northern Telecom, a designer and manufacturer of telecommunications equipment, provides an excellent example of how market aggressiveness combined with technological prowess can prove successful in the industrial marketplace. Edmund B. Fitzgerald, named president of the company in 1982 and its chairman in 1985, describes the strategy as follows: "to be the technological leader and, further, to seek out markets that have a high internal rate of what we call *discontinuity,* meaning those that are changing rapidly."

When Fitzgerald took over Telecom's U.S. division in 1979, he turned the company's operations around by refocusing the corporate energy on basic fundamental strengths. These strengths centered around the company's digital equipment technology. In the mid 1970s, Telecom decided to concentrate on developing digital telecommunications systems. They felt, from a customer perspective, that these systems are more faithful in the transmission of voices, offer the advantage of transmission of voice, text, graphics, data, and video over the same system, allow for much heavier packing of lines, and, most importantly, permit more economical transmission over the long haul. This decision and Telecom's ability to develop a superior product subsequently enabled them to capitalize on the discontinuity of the telecommunications market.

By positioning itself as the leader in digital technology, Telecom was able to exploit the opportunity created by the divestiture or break-up of AT&T. Some units of the Bell System had already begun to install Telecom digital systems before divestiture. Because of this, they were able to establish a track record, and when demand increased, Telecom was ready to satisfy it. They were not only in the right place at the right time with the right product, but had begun massaging the market well before it was ready to buy.

The Japanese market has always seemed closed to the products of U.S. manufacturers. However, this did not discourage Telecom. As a result, they installed the first American-made digital central office switching system into the Nippon Telegraph and Telephone Network, beginning in 1986. The contract was for $250 million over seven years and was accomplished by being patient and persistent. But it could not have happened without a well-designed and coordinated marketing strategy.

The financial results have been nothing short of outstanding. Revenues from U.S. operations jumped from $410 million in 1979 to $2.7 billion in 1985. To maintain and improve its technological advantages, Telecom has moved to accelerate capital expenditures for expanded plant capacity and continues to invest in research and development.

Source: R. Schweid, "Leadership Profile Series: Edmund B. Fitzgerald," *Sky Magazine* (April 1986), 44–49.

to consider markets and segments with which they have had little previous experience.

Another significant change has to do with the buyer's training and qualifications. For a variety of reasons, the industrial buyer is increasingly a more sophisticated, technically trained individual. Better than one-half of the revenues earned by the average industrial firm are spent on purchases. In turbulent times, pressure is brought for more cost-effective practices for managing these expenditures. The buyer may well have earned the certified purchasing manager (CPM) designation—a professional certification granted by the National Association of Purchasing Management to an experienced buyer who has passed a battery of examinations and has attended a series of professional development seminars. He or she may have received training in materials planning, value analysis, contractual terms, negotiation strategy, financial analysis, bid appraisal, inventory management, and computer applications in purchasing and materials management. Organizations themselves are elevating purchasing management to a senior-level position. In many instances, firms are reorganizing so that purchasing, materials handling, inventory, storage, and related activities are organized under one materials manager.

There is also some evidence that the future will bring more decentralized organizational structures and a greater demand for specialized goods and services. As these trends affect organizational buying, the industrial marketer must develop new strategies for need assessment, product management, and organizing the sales effort. Companies such as Hewlett-Packard, IBM, McDonnell Douglas, Westinghouse, ITT, General Electric, and Exxon are experiencing shifts to smaller production runs and customized items in certain product areas.

The customer environment is also becoming much more international in nature. In fact, many industrial products produced in the United States are sold to firms abroad, where they are processed or incorporated into other products that are, in turn, sold back to U.S. producers and distributors. Industrial marketers can play a key role in deciphering the social, political, cultural, and economic systems within which foreign customers operate.

Other trends in the customer environment include just-in-time purchasing and reverse reciprocity. Just-in-time purchasing is an attempt by the buyer to synchronize receipt of materials or components with production, so as to minimize resource inventories. Reverse reciprocity is a situation where, in times of shortage, two firms come to an agreement to sell vital resources to one another. In the absence of these special arrangements, adequate supplies of such resources may not be available to either firm.

Competitive Environment

A company's competitive position is defined, in part, by the number, size, and rivalry among competing firms in the industry. Other important factors include the availability of substitute products, the existence of barriers to market entry, and the bargaining power of the firm's suppliers and buyers (Porter 1980). Basic changes in each of these areas indicate a much more threatening competitive environment for many industrial firms.

Attractive growth opportunities and the sizable increase in new entrepreneurial activity suggest more competition in the industrial markets of the future. Some of these entrepreneurial ventures will come from established companies setting up semi-autonomous divisions in high-growth fields. Further, the rapid economic development taking place in a number of nations poses a major competitive threat. The market leaders of tomorrow may well be firms that are nonexistent or insignificant today.

Rivalry among companies will intensify—especially where competitors are diverse, fixed costs are high, products are homogeneous, exit barriers are high, and production capacity tends to be increased in fairly large increments. Each of these conditions is frequently found in industrial markets. Levitt (1983), for example, provides evidence of marketers increasingly trying to differentiate traditional industrial commodities in an attempt to establish some kind of competitive advantage in the minds of customer firms.

Competition may be further enhanced by diseconomies of scale resulting from smaller production runs and less standardization in certain product areas, and by attempts at global standardization (and large cost reductions) in others. Similarly, new technologies are both eliminating and creating barriers to entry. They are also providing new types of product substitutes and alternative methods of production and distribution, undercutting a firm's competitive position. Vertical and horizontal integration of firms at different levels in the production chain is changing the bargaining power of the industrial firm in negotiations with its suppliers and buyers. Such integration may also be a tactic pursued by the firm's competitors, further undermining its competitive position.

Legal/Regulatory Environment

The restrictions placed on the corporation by the government have multiplied dramatically in the past fifty years. One could argue that virtually no major marketing decision can be made without consulting a lawyer, or at least carefully considering legal ramifications. The marketing challenge is not only to satisfy customers' needs in a manner that provides the firm with a true competitive advantage, but also to meet legal and regulatory constraints.

These constraints on business decision making include economic and social restrictions—both of which reduce the manager's flexibility. Economic regulation affects such customer-sensitive areas as pricing, discount policies, advertising practices, arrangements with distributors, and tax considerations. Social regulation defines corporate responsibilities in such areas as health and safety, product ingredients, pollution control, energy efficiency, and product liability. This type of regulation can drive costs up and make product or production processes obsolete.

Importantly, government regulation in industrial markets affects both buyer and seller. The marketer must increasingly play a key role in assessing the impact of regulation on a customer's operations, and on how and what that customer buys. With time, a customer's needs may be entirely reshaped.

Economic Environment

Turbulence is pervasive in the economies of the industrialized nations of the world, both socialist and capitalist. Business cycles bring alternating recessionary slow-downs and inflationary booms every few years, while interest rates and money exchange rates vary daily. These trends impel companies to build down or build up inventories, creating a magnified effect on industrial demand. Unemployment and inflation rates will also periodically reach and maintain relatively high levels at the same time. Underlying such developments is a relative decline in the productivity of resources, especially labor.

Productivity problems are due, in part, to aging machines and equipment in industrial plants. This fact, of course, represents a major opportunity for the marketer, as industries retool and adapt the latest technologies, such as robotics. This fact also means that many industries will simply cease to exist, given the costs of reindustrialization. Such a development is all the more likely in an inflationary environment, where the replacement costs of capital are far greater than those allowed for by the depreciation account.

Labor force demands and government regulations also affect productivity. Unions bring pressures on management to limit the introduction of new technologies. Because of inflationary expectations, workers demand wage increases that outstrip increases in labor productivity. This, in turn, drives up the cost of finished goods, raising inventory costs of the buyer. Often, the most efficient production methods cannot be used, because of government regulation, making some industrial opportunities much less attractive.

Another key economic development is resource shortages, which affect not only costs, but also vendor relationships and contract terms. Shortages occur for a variety of reasons, including industrial cartels, international politics, war, and the nationalization of a domestic company's holdings in foreign countries. The major problem, though, is that natural resources are being depleted, creating demand for equipment and processes that conserve resources. This problem also encourages the birth of entirely new industries and markets, such as those for synthetic materials.

Up to this point, we have stressed that a greater understanding of marketing management is required in order to deal with the opportunities and threats facing industrial organizations. One might question, however, whether industrial marketing is really any different from consumer marketing, and whether separate attention is warranted. As will be seen, these differences are actually quite profound when it comes to the *practice* of marketing.

DISTINCTIVE ASPECTS OF INDUSTRIAL MARKETING

What is different about marketing to an organization? Marketing might seem to be basically the same, regardless of the type of customer or what is being sold (Fern and Brown 1984). This point is true to a certain extent because the basic tools and concepts—marketing concept, marketing mix, market segmentation, or the product life cycle—apply equally in both consumer and industrial markets. What *differs* is the design and implementation of marketing strategies and tactics to meet organizational versus consumer needs.

In fact, industrial marketing represents quite a distinct challenge. The major distinguishing elements concern the importance of technical product characteristics, the fact that these products directly affect the operations and economic health (e.g., profitability) of the customer, and the fact that the customer is an organization rather than an individual consumer. Differences related to these three characteristics can be further broken down into several categories: the product itself, the nature of demand, buyer behavior, communication processes, and economic/financial factors (see also Table 1.6).

Product Characteristics

In its simplest form, a product is a bundle of properties or attributes. The extensive focus placed on consumer goods in marketing texts is due, in part, to the fact that students can more easily relate to the relevant properties of these products (e.g., style, color, performance, size). All of us have extensive daily experience with consumer goods. Industrial products tend to be more complex, and the relevant properties are typically more technical in nature. Webster (1984, 15) explains, "The same man who, as a consumer, settles for plain shaving cream if he cannot find lemon lime, will be unwilling as an industrial buyer to accept a bolt with 30 threads to the inch when his specifications call for 28." In fact, the industrial product represents a multiplicity of physical and job performance specifications.

Many industrial goods carry a large unit dollar value, and most are sold in large quantities. Often they are custom-made or tailored to the specific application needs of the customer organization. Further, these products are marketed at different stages of completion, with much of what is sold taking the form of raw and semifinished goods. The buying firm may be purchasing for inventories as well as immediate usage. It may well purchase a given product for a number of differing uses. In some instances, the buyer has the option of making or leasing products rather than purchasing them.

The industrial product attribute bundle may also include technical assistance for installation and operation of equipment, service before and after the sale, and an emphasis on prompt, reliable delivery. The buyer organization may focus not just on a product's price, but also on all the costs that will be incurred over its useful life, including installation, maintenance, and servicing. This viewpoint can be evident for even the simplest of products, such as the lamps in Exhibit 1.3, which are priced higher, but save the customer $15.20 in energy costs. Packaging requirements have more to do with protection than with product information; promotional packaging is usually not needed. Finally, industrial products are distinctive because the daily operations and longer-term economic viability of the customer organization are directly affected by their satisfactory performance.

Table 1.6 How Industrial Marketing is Different

Major Distinguishing Characteristics	What This Means to the Industrial Marketer
Importance of technical product characteristics	Customer needs must be clearly understood, closely monitored
	Marketers must consider all costs a customer will incur with a product over its useful life
	Product life cycle is shorter due to technological change, necessitating continual product innovation
	Product quality is critical
	Distribution channels are shorter, more direct
	Need for technically qualified sales personnel and knowledgeable, specialized middlemen
	Importance of aftersale service, training, and technical assistance
	Packaging is more functional, less promotional
Products being marketed affect the operations and economic health of the user	Importance of buyer/seller negotiation skills
	Use of formal contracts
	Strong vendor loyalty exists; marketers should strive to develop long-term relationships
	Conservative attitudes are encountered in purchase decision making; marketers need to lower the buyer's perceived risk
	Formal product and vendor evaluation occurs
	Purchases are for inventory as well as use; inventions may need to be financed
	Delivery reliability is critical
	Industry demand is fairly inelastic
	Size and cost of purchases are large
	Price bidding is used
	Discounts are prevalent
Customer is an organization rather than an individual consumer	Fewer customers, often geographically concentrated
	More people are involved in buying decisions
	Longer, more complex buying process
	Promotion is more focused, using personal selling over advertising
	Marketing research is more difficult
	A major customer can have a strong bargaining position, placing the marketer in a vulnerable position
	Make-or-buy option exists
	Reciprocity arrangements develop
	Tax and accounting implications of products and services being purchased affect what is bought, when, and how it is bought

Exhibit 1.3   An Advertisement Selling Cost Savings Over the Product's Useful Life. Reprinted with permission of GTE Corporation.

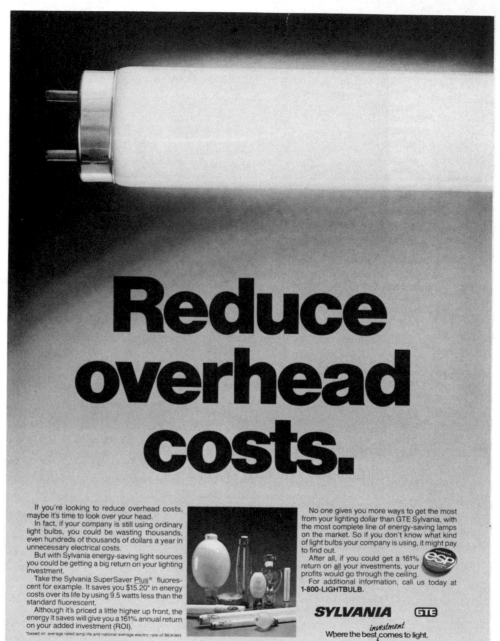

The Nature of Demand

Industrial goods contribute directly or indirectly to the manufacture of consumer goods, either as part of a consumer product, or as part of the production process. As a result, the demand for industrial goods is ultimately *derived* from the demand for consumer goods.

For example, a maker of electrical components sells the components to a producer of small motors, who in turn sells the motors to a windshield-wiper assembler, who then sells these assemblies to a truck manufacturer. Each of these firms will find its demand dependent upon the number of trucks being purchased. This situation creates an interesting marketing opportunity. The marketer may be able to affect sales by appealing not just to direct customers, but also to the ultimate consumer, or anyone in between. Market activity must be analyzed at all levels of the marketing channel.

Fluctuations in demand at the consumer level can, as will be shown in the next chapter, result in magnified changes at the industrial level. Keep in mind that industrial demand is affected by the inventory policies of each organization in the distribution chain. Inventory levels and the timing of purchases tend to reflect economic conditions, expectations, prices, and financial conditions. Industrial demand may, correspondingly, be quite volatile.

A related characteristic is termed *joint,* or *shared, demand.* Many industrial products can be used only in conjunction with other products, so the sale of one is dependent upon the other. Particle board used in construction requires wood chips, resins, and glue for its manufacture. The maker of gasoline products requires additives such as boron and lead. In each case, without any one of these components, the manufacturer does not need the others. Thus, such components have a joint demand.

The industrial marketer must be knowledgeable about the products that involve joint demand. For example, the manufacturer of computer terminals and printers may find that sales are markedly affected by changes in the prices or advertising of computer mainframes. Similarly, supply shortages of joint demand products can erode sales.

A third characteristic of industrial demand is that it is frequently concentrated; a handful of companies may account for a disproportionate share of a firm's sales. Economists refer to this type of situation as *oligopsony.* There are important implications for the degree of interdependency experienced between buyer and seller.

Finally, industrial demand is relatively inelastic. Where the product represents a key component, perhaps made to exact specifications, the buyer may be less sensitive to price changes. This result is because the item is more of a necessity, and there are fewer substitutes available.

Buyer Behavior

Developing successful marketing strategies is difficult without a fundamental understanding of customers and their needs. The most important point of departure between consumer and industrial marketing is buying behavior. The two types of buying behavior differ in terms of who buys, why, how, when, where, and what.

Organizational purchases typically involve a number of individuals. A given decision might include inputs from the engineering, production, finance, marketing, R & D, and purchasing departments. While the goal is to make purchases that best fulfill organizational needs and objectives, various departments may find their individual interests conflict when it comes to selecting a product or vendor. The manner in which these conflicts are addressed can create a very political buying process. The salesperson is placed in the difficult position of trying to figure out where to concentrate efforts in the buying firm to reach the key decision makers.

Industrial buying also involves a degree of formalization not found in consumer purchasing. Organizations can have formal policies regarding the determination of product and vendor specifications, the solicitation of bids or proposals, and the evaluation of available alternatives. Purchase requisitions, invoices, and contracts are used to specify the terms of sale. These terms are frequently negotiable.

The decision to purchase a product from a given industrial supplier may take a long time, because many such decisions last anywhere from six months to two years. Once sold, a customer is likely to be source-loyal unless significant problems develop. At the same time, the customer's interest is better served if orders are spread between or among a few suppliers.

The economic performance (e.g., profitability) of the buying organization may hinge on the quality of its purchasing decisions. Keep in mind that customers are working people, responding to an evaluation and reward system. As a result, products may represent significant risks and opportunities from the buyer's perspective.

Communication Processes

Given the complexities of industrial products and organizational buying, the communication process between seller and buyer also differs from that typically found with consumer products. Much less if any mass media advertising is used. Personal selling becomes the thrust of one's promotional efforts. In fact, frequently the seller goes to the buyer—not the other way around, as in consumer shopping. These contacts are supported with trade journal advertising, catalogs, industrial directories, trade shows, direct mail appeals, and other promotional tools.

The sometimes lengthy and involved buying decision produces a need for personal contact, with the sale taking on the appearance of a social negotiation process. Two-way (dyadic) interaction between buyer and seller over time will determine the outcome. Further, different media may be more or less effective depending on the stage of the buying process.

The marketer's message must address the needs and orientations of technical people and specialists. Appeals are often more factual and descriptive, with less emotional or symbolic content. Exhibit 1.4 is an example of an advertisement that stresses functional product benefits, such as quality, price, service, and warranty, but also appeals to the buyer's sense of pride. A related problem is to ensure that a given message reaches the intended member of the buying organization, and does so at the intended time.

Exhibit 1.4 An Advertisement Appealing to the Buyer's Sense of Pride. Reprinted with permission.

Economic/Financial Factors

Industrial marketing encompasses a number of interesting economic and financial aspects. For example, the marketer is likely to find an oligopolistic market, characterized by few competitors. In this situation, company strategies are much more interdependent, with whatever one firm does being strongly influenced by the anticipated reaction of its competitors. The result is often a strong competitive emphasis not based on price. Oligopolistic structures also give rise to price leadership.

In addition, the earlier-mentioned concentration among buyers (oligopsony) suggests the possibility of considerable relative economic power on both sides of the market transaction. This economic concentration can be envisioned by considering the negotiation process between U.S. Steel and General Motors. The outcomes are likely to follow from the nature of power/dependence relationships between buyer and seller. Does the seller need the buyer more than the buyer needs the seller?

Another aspect of industrial market structure is termed reciprocity. The customer may also be a key supplier to the marketer's firm. The existence of such reciprocal relationships may indirectly affect either party's willingness to significantly change the terms of the sale.

The dollar value of the product, and the need for customers to maintain inventories, make economic variables such as interest rates, inflation, and the business cycle critical concerns for industrial marketing. Inventories must be internally or externally financed, with the cost of money exceeding twenty percent at times in recent years. Inflation undermines the valuation of inventories and the replacement cost of capital, and may encourage buyers to look for new, creative financing alternatives. They may seek inflation protection through longer-term contracts. Leasing is often a viable alternative to purchasing. So, too, might be the option of making the products instead of buying them.

Now that we have identified some of the distinctive characteristics found in industrial markets, let us apply some of these differences to a specific case example. Exhibit 1.5 presents the case of Wheeler Specialties, an industrial products firm considering a new product.

WHERE ARE WE GOING FROM HERE?

This text is concerned with the challenges and opportunities confronting the marketer in industrial/organizational markets. It is organized so that the reader can develop a logical approach to the planning, design, implementation, and control of marketing programs. The chapters ahead will follow the framework outlined in Figure 1.3.

The body of this book is divided into five parts. Part I, consisting of the initial chapters, is an introduction to the field of industrial marketing. It attempts to define the nature and scope of the field. Part II is concerned with the types of analyses performed by the marketer to properly understand and evaluate the product/market opportunities available. The tools of analysis are developed to enable one to deal with the information needs of industrial marketing decisions. The focus in this section is on organizational buying behavior, industrial market segmentation, marketing research, the assessment of competitors, and demand analysis.

With these tools in hand, Part III takes a strategic approach to industrial marketing management. The nuts and bolts of developing specific strategies and tactics to meet customer needs profitably are examined. Individual chapters are devoted to

Exhibit 1.5   Industrial versus Consumer Marketing: The Case of
Wheeler Specialties

Bill Wheeler owns and manages Wheeler Specialties, a rapidly growing industrial chemical company located in the Southeast. The company produces and sells a variety of chemical products to manufacturing firms in the region. Mr. Wheeler personally invented all of the products sold. They are mixed entirely in the company plant. Examples include a treatment chemical sold to textile manufacturers to help soften fabrics, one that helps reduce static electricity when applied to synthetic fibers, and a cleansing liquid used in industrial spray-wash machines for cleaning company vehicles.

The plant is located outside a major metropolitan area in North Carolina. Finished product is shipped directly to customer locations, either in fifty-five-gallon metal drums or tank trucks. Wheeler owns a small fleet of delivery trucks. Minimal inventory is kept, as Wheeler can respond to orders virtually on demand.

The major sales are made by Mr. Wheeler himself. He maintains a close relationship with clients, often finding them to be important sources of new product ideas. A pilot, with his own jet airplane, Bill can be at any customer plant within a matter of hours. When not in his laboratory or overseeing plant operations, he can usually be found visiting with purchasing, production, or engineering managers from customer firms, often taking them to lunch.

In late 1983, Mr. Wheeler recognized a new chemical process that might be used to produce a suntanning product. Intrigued with the possibilities, he began to devote spare time to the idea. By mid-1985, he had perfected a process to produce a tanning oil that would provide varying amounts of sun protection, depending solely on how much oil was applied by the user. The product also blocked the ultraviolet rays of the sun that cause skin cancer. Further, it could be worn in the water without washing off, but soap and water would remove the oil. During 1986 and 1987, Wheeler commissioned a number of dermatologists and laboratory testing agencies to run safety and performance tests on the product; all proved highly successful. Wheeler has been awarded a patent for the process.

In recent discussions with a marketing consultant, Mr. Wheeler was advised to either sell the patent or license the product to the highest bidder. It was pointed out that suntan oil, a consumer product, required skills and marketing strategies completely different from those used to sell specialty industrial chemicals. Wheeler disagreed, arguing that chemicals are chemicals, and that the differences were insignificant.

From a marketing perspective, identify the major differences between marketing these two types of products.

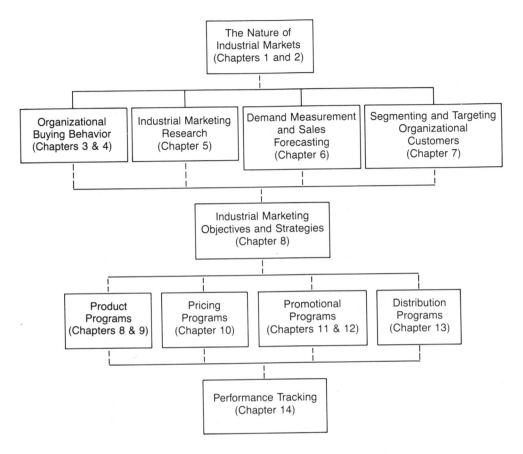

Figure 1.3   Flow Diagram of the Organizational Structure of This Book

product development strategies, approaches to pricing, issues in advertising and promotion, managing the industrial sales force, and the design of distribution channels for industrial products. Part IV addresses the control or tracking aspects of individual marketing programs, attempting to answer the question, "Which process do I use to make sure my plans are implemented correctly?" This last step should also alert industrial marketing managers to needed changes in objectives, strategies, or programs.

Finally, Part V consists of several case studies that explore actual industrial marketing problems. These provide hands-on practice and training in thinking like an industrial marketer.

SUMMARY

Industrial marketing is concerned with exchange processes among organizations. The industrial marketer is trying to create value for organizational customers by satisfying their needs—at a profit. This goal is accomplished by manipulating a set of variables commonly referred to as the marketing *mix:* product, price, promotion, and distribution.

In most of the economically developed nations, industrial markets make up the most significant sector of the economy. In the United States, for example, these markets represent not only a sizable number of transactions, but also a major source of economic growth. As a case in point, many so-called hi-tech industries are primarily involved in developing and marketing products and services sold to other organizations.

Firms that compete in industrial markets have only begun to adopt a marketing orientation in their approach to producing and distributing goods and services. These organizations traditionally have been dominated by technically oriented and production-oriented managers. The change in orientation is due to a number of fundamental changes in the technological, customer, competitive, legal/regulatory, and economic environments facing industrial firms.

As these companies place more emphasis on marketing skills, it becomes increasingly apparent that industrial marketing represents quite a distinct challenge when compared to consumer marketing. Major differences exist in product characteristics, the nature of demand, buyer behavior, communication processes, and economic characteristics. These differences are investigated in more depth in the chapters to come. Each has important implications for the development of successful industrial marketing strategies and tactics.

QUESTIONS

1. Bob King is president of a medium-sized firm (200 employees) that manufactures and sells customized electronic components to companies that make sophisticated consumer electronic products (e.g., advanced home alarm systems, high-quality home stereo systems). Although Mr. King employs five salespeople, he has little use for marketing. Explain to Mr. King what the role of marketing should be in a firm such as his, and how sales is different from marketing.

2. "Industrial marketing is the same as consumer marketing." Argue pro and con.

3. "The post-industrial era holds much promise for producers of products and services intended for organizational customers." Agree or disagree? Support your position.

4. At a recent management seminar, a marketing vice-president with thirty years of experience argued that "most industrial firms do not understand, and certainly do not practice, the marketing concept." What are some possible reasons for (a) their lack of understanding, and (b) the failure to implement or follow the marketing concept?

5. What are some problems in measuring customer satisfaction when the customer is an organization?

6. How can industrial organizations avoid marketing myopia? Identify specific problems in defining one's business too narrowly, or defining it in terms of

products. Can a company define itself too broadly? What, if any, is the relationship between the marketing concept and marketing myopia?

7. Many of the activities we claim to be part of marketing are not actually performed by someone called a *marketer*. For example, prices may be set by those in finance; distribution decisions made by those in production; and a product's design, features, and packaging determined by design engineers. What are some possible implications?

8. Consider the four elements of the industrial marketing mix. Why do we call it a *mix*? What are some ways in which each of the elements of the mix affects (or is affected by) each of the other elements?

9. Using the five components of the environment discussed in the chapter, discuss some of the environmental opportunities and threats facing industrial firms in the next five years. How can marketing improve an organization's ability to face these challenges?

10. In Table 1.5, p. 12, a number of common myths related to industrial marketing were discussed. Why do you think such myths exist? Examine each of them, and identify possible reasons that such misconceptions might be held by many people.

11. Separately, illustrate the concepts of joint demand and derived demand, using products with which you are familiar. Can you draw some implications for the marketing mix used with each of these products?

CHAPTER 2

INDUSTRIAL MARKETS, PRODUCTS, AND PURCHASING PRACTICES

Key Concepts

Acceleration effect
Commercial enterprise
Derived demand
Distributor
Global marketing
Government sector
Just-in-time inventory
Life-cycle costing
Materials management concept
Materials requirement planning (MRP)
Multidomestic marketing

Nonprofit and institutional sector
Original equipment manufacturer (OEM)
Product classification scheme
Purchasing procedures
Time-based buying strategies
User time-based buying strategies
Value added
Value analysis

Learning Objectives

1. Identify distinctive characteristics of the three major types of industrial customers: commercial firms, the government, and institutions.
2. Outline the opportunities and difficulties in international markets.
3. Discuss the nature of industrial products and services, and introduce practical approaches for classifying those products and services.
4. Provide an overview of the structure and operation of the procurement function in customer organizations.
5. Describe the tools and techniques used in industrial purchasing.

The factors that make the work of an industrial marketing manager different from that of his or her counterpart in the consumer goods field are fundamentally the nature of industrial products and the wide-ranging characteristics of industrial customers.

E. RAYMOND COREY

Chapter 1 introduced the reader to the field of industrial marketing and to the increasing role that marketing plays in business. Chapter 2 continues this introduction. It provides a more in-depth picture of the nature and scope of industrial markets, the products and services sold in these markets, and the purchasing organizations that buy these services.

THE NATURE OF INDUSTRIAL MARKETS

The most striking characteristics of industrial or organizational markets are their size and diversity. These markets consist of organizations of all types. We can draw a distinction, at a very general level, between first-, second-, and third-sector organizations. The first sector, consisting of private, profit-seeking organizations, constitutes the largest share of the industrial market. These organizations, referred to here as commercial enterprises, include both manufacturing and nonmanufacturing firms. The second sector includes all government-owned or government-controlled organizations, ranging from municipal airports and the postal service to regulatory agencies and penitentiaries. The third sector comprises all public and private service organizations and institutions, such as universities, museums, private hospitals, trade associations, and church organizations.

There is, in fact, no single statistic available to describe the total size and scope of these markets. Some insight can be gained, however, by considering a few key industrial market facts and figures—first, from commercial enterprises, and then from institutions and government.

Commercial Enterprises

There were 350,000 manufacturing firms in the United States in 1985, of which 150,000 had twenty or more employees, and only 43,000 had more than 100 workers. Almost 20 million people, earning a payroll in excess of $460 billion, worked for these companies. Total shipments by these firms generated revenues of $2,341 billion, of which about 53 percent was for durable goods. At the same time, they spent $1,200 billion to buy materials, and $75 billion for capital expenditures.

There are three major types of commercial enterprises: original equipment manufacturers (OEMs), users, and distributors. OEMs purchase industrial goods and services and incorporate them into the items that they, in turn, manufacture and sell. The maker of forklifts who purchases electric starters from an industrial marketer is an OEM from the perspective of that vendor, because the starter becomes part of the forklift. Users, alternatively, buy industrial goods and services for use in producing other goods and services. When a weighing machine or a cutting machine is sold to a leather goods manufacturer, this customer would be labeled a user. The machines are used in making leather goods, but do not become part of those goods. Distributors, then, are companies that do not actually produce a product, but rather, resell the goods of a manufacturer. They are middlemen who take title to the items that they sell. Keep in mind that the industrial marketer could, however, sell the same product to OEMs, users, and distributors. Similarly, a given industrial customer could be an OEM in terms of some products, a user in terms of others, and act as a distributor in terms of still others.

Selected data concerning establishments, employment, and shipments for some of the key 4-digit SIC groups which operate in industrial markets appear in Table 2.1.[1] Manufacturing industries experiencing the most rapid growth rates are summarized in Table 2.2. These industries are identified by 4-digit SIC code. While many of these are high technology or computer-related, a number are more traditional industries such as aluminum, tools and dies, and automotive stampings.

A sizable market also exists for industrial services. Intermediate services are provided by establishments whose output is used as input for production in other industries (e.g., accounting, engineering, and business services). Distributive services, alternatively, include transportation, communications, and utilities, among others. Such services have undergone consistent growth in recent years, and this trend should only accelerate. Table 2.3 provides some comparative information on these services. Overall demand for business services grew at a 12.1 percent rate between 1972 and 82, and even more dramatically for computer and data processing services, management consulting services, and leasing services. These trends reflect the general shift towards a service-based economy which has been taking place for some time. As the management problems facing even small businesses have grown in complexity, the demand for specialized services has greatly expanded. Moreover, as providers have recognized opportunities for economies of scale in service provision, the delivery costs for many services have become affordable for many small and medium-sized organizations.

Commercial Enterprises and Value Added

As shown in Figure 1.1 (Chapter 1) end products can evolve through a number of stages in the production chain (e.g., raw materials extraction, processing, manufacturing, assembly, and distribution). At each of these stages, value is added to the

---

1. The Standard Industrial Classification (SIC) system is explained in further detail in Chapters 5, 6, and 7. It is basically a numbering system for classifying different types of businesses, based on their major product or service.

Table 2.1 Largest Producers of Industrial Products

SIC	Industry	Shipments ($ mil)	Total Plants	Large Plants	Total Employees	% Shipments in Large Plants
2911	Petroleum refining	$140,200.8	299	166	90,885	93.94
3573	Electronic computing equipment	51,634.8	1,144	572	372,547	93.08
3714	Motor vehicle parts & accessories	38,236.6	1,234	628	358,137	91.80
3662	Radio & TV communication equipment	33,751.6	1,188	546	354,765	92.57
2869	Industrial organic chemicals, n.e.c.	31,895.0	525	231	113,623	86.99
3312	Blast furnaces & steel mills	29,592.5	319	191	230,563	96.71
3721	Aircraft	28,921.3	102	63	208,385	99.34
3079	Miscellaneous plastic products	23,823.9	4,303	1,414	438,886	71.08
2821	Plastic materials & resins	21,305.1	458	184	83,809	83.90
3441	Fabricated structural metal	20,819.7	1,436	308	107,424	53.04
2621	Paper mills	20,096.5	344	252	155,041	96.67
3679	Electronic components, n.e.c.	19,560.9	1,789	742	300,157	84.73
3661	Telephone and telegraph apparatus	19,031.6	239	139	120,847	96.56
2819	Industrial inorganic chemicals, n.e.c.	17,036.4	573	218	113,262	83.31
3585	Refrigeration & heating equipment	15,557.9	518	254	137,083	91.18
3443	Fabricated plate work, boiler shops	13,590.3	1,023	283	103,310	66.58
3761	Guided missiles & space vehicles	13,209.4	60	38	97,832	99.26
2752	Commercial printing, lithographic	12,924.6	2,022	394	148,879	57.19
3531	Construction machinery	12,104.1	470	209	92,294	87.18
3728	Aircraft equipment, n.e.c.	12,062.9	644	260	164,047	88.74
3444	Sheet metal work	11,850.7	1,686	295	109,504	48.73
3469	Metal stampings, n.e.c.	11,678.6	1,236	305	154,964	74.01
3599	Machinery, except electrical, n.e.c.	11,444.9	2,971	332	159,196	41.04
3579	Office machines, n.e.c.	11,378.5	186	71	45,475	89.38
3494	Valves & pipe fittings	11,338.4	672	285	94,285	82.07
3674	Semiconductors & related devices	10,938.5	397	212	152,207	95.78

Source: Reprinted by permission of *Sales and Marketing Management.* "1987 Survey of Industrial & Commercial Buying Power; 32.

item. Table 2.4 provides a simplified example of the production chain for copper wire used in commercial and residential telephone service. In this case, five different companies each make a contribution to the end product. The amount of these contributions is reflected in the value added at each stage, while the sum total of value added is equal to the income generated by the five firms. From this hypothetical example, one can see that industrial firms are a major source of economic value. In 1983, for example, U.S. manufacturers accounted for $882 billion in value added.

Almost 80 percent of the value added in manufacturing is provided by 10 percent of the country's manufacturers, primarily firms with 100 or more employees (Statistical Abstract 1986). This level of economic concentration suggests that, in

Table 2.2 Growth in Constant Dollar Industry Shipments for the Twenty-Five Manufacturing Industries Experiencing the Most Rapid Growth in 1987

1987 Rank Order	SIC Code	Industry	Annual Growth Rate		Compound Annual Growth Rate
			1986–87	1985–86	1973–87
1	3674	Semiconductors & related devices	26.5	28.6	30.0
2	3675	Electronic capacitors	11.5	2.4	4.2
3	3832	Optical instruments & lenses	11.0	11.0	15.4
4	3693	X-ray & electromedical apparatus	10.9	9.9	11.5
5	3825	Instruments to measure electricity	10.0	5.0	5.2
6	3465	Automotive stampings	9.4	2.8	2.8
7	3842	Surgical appliances & supplies	8.8	3.0	7.0
8	2891	Adhesives & sealants	8.3	4.0	3.8
9	2492	Particleboard	8.6	5.0	3.3
10	3761	Guided missiles & space vehicles	8.0	5.8	3.5
11	3333	Primary zinc	7.2	4.8	−7.1
12	3662	Radio & TV communication equipment	7.1	6.2	7.7
13	3661	Telephone & telegraph apparatus	6.8	10.0	5.7
14	2084	Wines, brandy, & brandy spirits	6.7	1.3	3.9
15	3694	Engine electrical equipment	6.2	6.2	2.7
16	2038	Frozen specialties	6.0	9.0	3.0
17	3769	Space vehicle equipment, n.e.c.	6.0	6.2	4.4
18	3592	Carburetors, pistons, & rings, etc.	5.8	5.5	2.5
19	2016	Poultry dressing plants	5.7	5.0	4.9
20	2022	Natural and processed cheese	5.6	1.7	3.1
21	3764	Space propulsion units & parts	5.4	6.2	2.9
22	3841	Surgical & medical instruments	5.4	2.2	6.1
23	2647	Sanitary paper products	5.0	4.0	4.1
24	2491	Wood preserving	4.7	4.0	3.5
25	2017	Poultry & egg processing	4.6	3.2	4.1

Source: *U.S. Industrial Outlook,* 1987.

many industries, a handful of firms is responsible for a disproportionate amount of output and, correspondingly, a sizable number of purchases. Such large buyers are in a position to dictate terms of sale to the marketer. At the same time, industrial marketers may be tempted to concentrate all of their efforts on a few large custom-ers, due to their significant sales potential. This approach can be a prescription for

Table 2.3   Receipts for Selected Intermediate Service Industries[1] for Years 1972, 1977, and 1982, and Annual Growth Rates *(millions of dollars except as noted)*

SIC	Industry	1972	1977	1982	Compound Annual Rate of Growth 1972−82
	Gross national product (billions of dollars)	1,185.9	1,918.3	3,069.3	10.0
73	Business services	35,493	49,999	111,414	12.1
736	Personnel supply	2,238	4,624	10,230	16.4
737	Computer and data processing	3,411	7,476	22,737	20.9
7392	Management, consulting and public relations	3,549	6,653	17,969	17.6
7394	Equipment rental and leasing	2,205	4,729	10,919	17.3
81	Legal services	9,724	17,147	34,338	13.4
891	Engineering, architectural, and surveying	7,186	14,048	33,532	16.7
893	Accounting, auditing, and bookkeeping	N.A.	7,277	14,596	14.9(77−82)

[1]Includes receipts for establishments with payroll only.

N.A.—Not Available

Source: *U.S. Industrial Outlook,* 1985.

failure, however, because large buyers are often less flexible and more demanding in their purchasing patterns, and less willing to consider unproven alternatives. While many more small and medium-sized accounts are needed to equal the potential of one large customer, serving a wide client base is often the more sound approach to establishing a company in a market and building long-term market success.

Commercial Enterprises and Derived Demand

The concept of derived demand argues that the demand for the products sold by commercial enterprises is actually derived from the consumer marketplace. Thus, while industrial markets may be more sizable, economic activity is ultimately driven by the end consumer. Of course, many industrial products are far removed from the consumer, and the linkage is difficult to see. Such is the case in the relationship

Table 2.4   Value Added in a Five-Stage Production Process
(hypothetical)

Stage of Production	Sales Value of Materials or Product	Value Added
Company A, copper mine	$25⎤	$25
Company B, metals refining and processing	75⎦⎤	50
Company C, copper wire manufacturer	100⎦⎤	25
Company D, cable and wire wholesaler	140⎦⎤	40
Company E, telephone company	200⎦	60
	Total Sales Value $540	
	Value Added (total income)	$200

Source: Adapted from C.R. McConnell, *Economics,* 8th ed. (New York: McGraw-Hill Book Co., 1981), 149.

between the demand for bauxite ore and sales of new homes, or the connection between production of some farm products and cosmetic sales. This separation becomes more apparent as the number of steps or stages increases between a given manufacturer and the end user. In other cases, the linkage is quite clear, such as the impact of automobile sales on the steel industry. Thus, if consumers are not buying homes, autos, clothing, stereos, educational or medical services, there will be less need for lumber, steel, cotton, plastics, computer components, and hospital forms. Consequently, industry will require less energy, fewer trucking services, and not as many tools or machines.

Industrial marketers must be cognizant, then, of conditions in their own markets, but also must be aware of developments in the markets served by their customers, and their customers' customers. Of course, this can become quite complex when a manufacturer's output is used in a wide variety of applications, such as with petrochemicals (see Table 2.5).

Derived demand is of further significance, however, because of the existence of what is known as the *acceleration effect.* When the demand for a consumer product increases by some amount, this rise does not translate into a one-to-one increase in the demand for the industrial products used to make that consumer item. Rather, demand changes will be magnified further back through the production chain. Figure 2.1 demonstrates how a 20 percent increase in final consumption of an item can lead to a 34 percent increase in the demand for a raw material used to manufacture that item. The reason for this acceleration of demand has to do with the inventory policies of the organizations involved in the production chain. There is a continual inventory adjustment process among industrial organizations. With a change in demand, a supplier will need to adjust his required inventory levels. This, in turn, leads to an adjustment in his purchases to meet new sales requirements as well as new inventory level requirements. The increase in purchases, then, exceeds the increase

Table 2.5 End Products Which Affect Demand for Petrochemicals

These Petrochemical Inputs	Supply these Industries	To Make these End Products
Plastics	Coatings Construction Electrical Housewares Packaging Transportation	Containers Plywood Paints Seat covers Wire coating Engineering material
Synthetic fibers	Apparel Carpets Home furnishings Tires	Clothing Rugs Upholstery fabrics Tire cord
Solvents	Dry cleaning Toilet preparations Printing	Cleaning fluids Personal care items Inks
Surface active agents	Soaps and detergents Mining	Household products Industrial cleaners Copper and zinc
Additives	Petroleum refining Transportation	Gasoline Lubricants
Synthetic rubber	Tires Fabricated rubber products	Tires Belting, hose, footwear
Fertilizers and agricultural chemicals	Agriculture	Foodstuffs

Source: U.S. Department of Commerce, *1979 U.S. Industrial Outlook with Projections to 1983 for 200 Industries* (Washington: U.S. Government Printing Office, January 1979), 124.

in consumer demand. This effect also can be created by a reduction in demand; orders fall off at an accelerated rate further back through the production chain.

Derived demand poses a number of difficulties for the industrial marketer. Sizable fluctuations in demand add to the difficulty of forecasting sales volume which, in turn, poses problems in planning manpower, materials, inventory, and distribution requirements. A manufacturer's sales can be dramatically affected by uncontrollable events (such as strikes) in the organizations from which demand originates. If derived demand is considered within the context of the cyclical nature of the economy, with the corresponding problems of inflation, unemployment, and stagnation in growth and productivity, the potential for volatility in the demand for industrial goods and services becomes apparent.

Derived demand also has implications for the development of marketing strategy. For example, marketers may want to determine if their efforts are best concentrated on the immediate customer, or if they should be targeted toward users further

Figure 2.1   Sales and Inventory Implications of Industrial Derived Demand
Source: Adapted from A.A. Kuehn, and R.L. Day, "The Acceleration Effect in Forecasting Industrial Shipments," *Journal of Marketing*, (January 1963), Copyright American Marketing Association. Reprinted with permission.

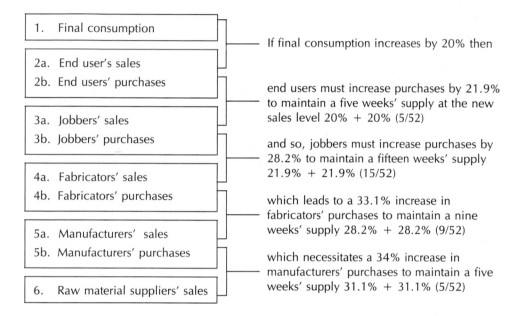

1. Final consumption	If final consumption increases by 20% then
2a. End user's sales 2b. End users' purchases	end users must increase purchases by 21.9% to maintain a five weeks' supply at the new sales level 20% + 20% (5/52)
3a. Jobbers' sales 3b. Jobbers' purchases	and so, jobbers must increase purchases by 28.2% to maintain a fifteen weeks' supply 21.9% + 21.9% (15/52)
4a. Fabricators' sales 4b. Fabricators' purchases	which leads to a 33.1% increase in fabricators' purchases to maintain a nine weeks' supply 28.2% + 28.2% (9/52)
5a. Manufacturers' sales 5b. Manufacturers' purchases	which necessitates a 34% increase in manufacturers' purchases to maintain a five weeks' supply 31.1% + 31.1% (5/52)
6. Raw material suppliers' sales	

down the production chain. Thus, Dupont has advertised to business travelers the benefits of luggage which is made from a particular proprietary material. In this case, its goal may be two-fold: first, to encourage these end users to place demands upon various luggage manufacturers (via retailers) to begin using the Dupont ingredient in their production process; and second, to provide promotional support for luggage makers currently using Dupont's product. If the marketer is trying to spur demand by focusing efforts further down the chain, this approach is a *pull strategy*. Alternatively, incentives such as promotional support provided directly to the immediate customer (luggage manufacturers in this instance) represent an example of a *push strategy*.

Another implication of derived demand is that marketers may find that they are competing with some of their own customers. Assume that company A sells an unfinished version of its primary product to company B, which then treats, adds finishing work, or adds a feature to the product, and sells it to companies C, D, and E. Circumstances such as a business downturn, excess capacity, or product line extensions may find company A deciding to sell some unfinished goods directly to C, D, and E, or to add the feature or the finishing work themselves, on demand. This places company A in direct competition with its customer, company B.

Geographic Dispersion of Commercial Enterprises

A final characteristic of the commercial enterprise market relates to its geographic structure. In addition to the earlier-mentioned economic concentration, the industrial market has historically been fairly geographically concentrated—especially in specific product categories. The U.S. automobile industry and its suppliers were historically concentrated in the Great Lakes states, the steel industry around Pittsburgh, the textile industry in the Northeast, and silicon chips and laser technologies in northern California. Companies involved in raw material extraction have located near natural resources.

While concentration has become less the rule for specific industries, it continues to apply to overall manufacturing activity. For example, the Great Lakes states were the source of 24.1 percent of total U.S. shipments in 1986, with the Southeast generating 21.4 percent, and the middle Atlantic states producing 17.4 percent. In addition, the top fifty counties in manufacturing activity accounted for 36.0 percent of all shipments by counties in the U.S. (*Sales and Marketing Management* 1987). Similarly, as illustrated in Table 2.6, the twenty-five leading metro markets in manufacturing activity accounted for 48.67 percent of total U.S. shipments.

Where markets are geographically concentrated, the marketer can be more efficient in the use of key resources, such as the sales force. Further, dealing directly with customers is easier, as is providing them with better service and more timely deliveries. The latter is especially important to customers trying to minimize inventory levels. At the same time, concentration in markets does not eliminate differences among individual customers within a given industry. The marketer may still need to tailor sales efforts to distinct and often diverse customer requirements within a given geographic locale. Concentrated markets are also likely to attract large and aggressive competitors.

As a generality, however, industrial markets are in the process of becoming more dispersed, due to a number of key environmental changes. Inflating costs, especially those related to property and organized labor, have made some geographic locales unattractive places to do business, especially as international competition has intensified. So, too, have onerous tax and regulatory restrictions applied by state and local governments. Population shifts, such as that to the Sunbelt, have been both a cause and a result of increasing mobility among industrial firms. As a result of these shifts, businesses can often find a sizable qualified labor force in regions which historically had insufficient labor resources. Technological developments in communications, electronic data processing, and transportation have also provided management with much more flexibility in site location; close physical proximity to suppliers or customers is less important to the organization.

Also, where industrial companies have diversified into new products and markets, advantages of traditional locations may become less meaningful. Geographic dispersion has also become more typical as the products and services which constitute the industrial market change. High technology industries, for example, may not require the same kinds of economies of scale in purchasing and manufacturing found in such traditional smokestack industries as steel. Moreover, where the markets for products have developed specialized needs and have become more highly

Table 2.6 The Twenty-Five Leading Metro Markets in Manufacturing Activity

1986 Rank	Metro Market	1986 Shipments ($Mil)	% of U.S.	Total Establishments	Average Shipments per Plant ($000)
1	Los Angeles–Long Beach	75,740	3.51	4,475	16,925
2	Chicago	71,478	3.31	5,653	12,644
3	Detroit	70,817	3.28	3,549	19,954
4	Philadelphia	52,280	2.42	3,113	16,794
5	New York	45,640	2.12	5,292	8,624
6	Boston–Lawrence–Salem–Lowell–Brockton	39,155	1.82	2,845	13,763
7	Houston	35,814	1.66	1,394	25,692
8	San Jose	30,499	1.41	806	37,839
9	Minneapolis–St. Paul	28,077	1.30	1,578	17,793
10	Newark	26,501	1.23	1,716	15,443
11	St. Louis	23,283	1.08	1,412	16,489
12	Cleveland	22,360	1.04	1,866	11,983
13	Cincinnati	20,000	0.93	948	21,097
14	Dallas	19,929	0.92	1,240	16,072
15	Nassau–Suffolk, NY	19,750	0.92	1,800	10,972
16	Milwaukee	19,361	0.90	1,227	15,779
17	Oakland	18,366	0.85	739	24,852
18	Atlanta	18,189	0.84	1,192	15,259
19	Pittsburgh	18,001	0.83	963	18,693
20	Greensboro–Winston-Salem–High Point, NC	17,613	0.82	816	21,584
21	Bergen–Passaic, NJ	17,347	0.80	1,656	10,475
22	Baltimore	17,102	0.79	929	18,409
23	Anaheim Santa Ana	17,071	0.79	911	18,739
24	Kansas City	17,029	0.79	936	18,194
25	Middlesex–Somerset–Hunterdon, NJ	16,860	0.78	779	21,644

Source: Reprinted by permission of *Sales and Marketing Management,* "1987 Survey of Industrial & Commercial Buying Power," 22.

segmented, industrial firms have found some advantage in decentralizing their operations.

Institutional Markets

The institutional market—all those organizations that do not fit into the commercial or government categories—represents a broad opportunity for the industrial marketer. Most of them are classified as nonprofit organizations for tax purposes. Insti-

Table 2.7 Types of Nonprofit Organizations

Health Care Organizations	Public Service Organizations
—hospitals	—police departments
—HMOs	—blood banks
—mental health centers	—sanitation services
Knowledge Organizations	Professional Organizations
—universities and colleges	—unions
—private secondary schools	—trade associations
—research organizations	—professional societies
Political Organizations	Religious Organizations
—political parties	—churches
—consumer groups	—church associations
—environmental groups	—evangelical movements
Cultural Organizations	Human Service Organizations
—museums	—Red Cross
—symphonies	—groups serving the infirm
—zoos	—family planning organizations

tutions can be publicly or privately owned, and include an extremely diverse collection of organizations (see Table 2.7).

Because of the variety of institutions, data regarding these organizations is fragmentary and sketchy at best. Even determining their absolute numbers and the size of their assets is difficult. However, a glimpse of some of the available information reveals that such organizations constitute a sizable portion of the economy. For example, California has over 990,000 business corporations, but also has more than 86,000 nonprofit corporations. Both Ohio and Michigan have approximately 170,000 business corporations, and have 30,000 and 40,200 nonprofits, respectively.

Most of these organizations are quite small, and many are not major purchasers of industrial goods and services. Others, such as hospitals, schools and universities, or credit unions, are an important market for a variety of products—business forms, environmental control devices, copiers, data services, and office furniture.

Marketing to institutional customers requires consideration of a number of distinguishing features of the procurement process within these organizations: weak cost control, limited purchasing expertise, the nature of relationships with vendors, uneconomical price behavior, and isolated purchasing operations, among others.[2]

Historically, institutions have not had the same level of concern with purchasing cost control as have commercial enterprises, nor have they implemented the

---

2. This discussion and that regarding distinctive aspects of governmental purchasing are drawn from D.W. Dobler, et. al., *Purchasing and Materials Management,* (New York: McGraw-Hill Book Co., 1984), 616–670.

same cost control mechanisms. In the absence of a profit motive or clearly specified financial objectives, there may be less incentive for efficiencies in purchasing. This attitude is changing, however, as the environments of these organizations change. For example, health care costs have come under close governmental scrutiny—in part due to the sizable public monies which defray these costs. Public universities, in some cases, have found state budgets frozen, while private universities find competing with lower tuitions at state-supported institutions increasingly difficult. Charitable organizations find the competition for philanthropic contributions greatly intensified. As a result, such organizations are more open to vendors who can provide them with greater economies or value.

Institutions tend to purchase a broad array of products and services. As a result, their purchasing personnel may lack the expertise to properly evaluate product quality or understand product specifications provided by vendors. This problem is all the more critical because institutions often do not—or cannot—hire experienced purchasing professionals; the salaries they offer frequently are not competitive with those paid by commercial enterprises.

An institution also may tend to favor vendors with whom members of its staff have formal or informal ties, or vendors preferred by members of its board of directors, as well as vendor organizations which have provided financial support to the institution. For example, members of the institution may serve as directors of, or as consultants to, companies that are potential sources of supply, creating a potential conflict of interest. In addition, companies that donate money, products, or services to an institution may do so with the expectation that the institution will reciprocate and buy from them.

Institutions frequently rely on purchasing practices that result in their paying higher prices than otherwise might be necessary. Inflexible policies requiring competitive bids, and the selection of the lowest bid, preclude one-on-one negotiation that could lead to more favorable terms. Also, institutions will attempt to get better prices by openly making price comparisons with other institutions. The marketer will be hesitant to provide an institution with a price deal, knowing that other institutions will learn about, and demand, the same deal.

The formal purchasing operation in institutions tends to operate at a fairly low level in the organizational hierarchy. This positioning creates problems in attracting qualified purchasing personnel, in coordinating functional needs throughout the organization, and in establishing strong centralized purchasing operations. Further, salespeople do not face the same problems of access to key decision makers (outside the purchasing department) found when selling to commercial enterprises, because institutions typically do not exert as much control over vendor representatives. This attitude leads to "back-door selling" by salespeople who will bypass the purchasing department and call directly on potential users and others in the organization thought to exert influence on the buying decision.

Institutions will frequently not have a well-established materials management function. For example, there may not be a traffic specialist or department. Receiving and inspection are given scant attention, sometimes resulting in unusable inventories. Similarly, expediting and delivery are under-emphasized, in part because institutions do not have daily production schedules to meet.

Government Markets

The third major market for industrial goods and services is the government. This market is so substantial, in fact, that many companies derive the largest proportion of their revenues from sales to the government.

This market can be logically divided into federal, state, and local governments as well as into international and domestic governments. Domestically, the federal government represents one unit, with ninety-six major subunits. There are fifty state governments, and approximately 82,300 local governments, including counties, municipalities, and townships. This domestic government sector was responsible for over \$366 billion worth of purchases in 1985, an amount which is growing by over six percent annually. Of this expenditure, \$201 billion was spent by the federal government, and \$165 billion by state and local governments (Survey of Current Business, July, 1986). These governments purchase a vast array of items, ranging from space shuttles, weapons systems, and major construction projects to personal computers, hand tools, and coffee makers.

Some of the distinguishing features of government purchasing include budget inflexibility, standardization, the public nature of government operations, the importance of social and economic objectives, competitive bidding, extensive paperwork requirements, long lead times, and regulatory constraints on a number of professional purchasing tactics.

Government budgets for a given fiscal year are usually fixed by legislative action. Further, transferring funds from one budgeted account to another is often difficult. As a result, government purchasers may be unable to take full advantage of one-shot deals or temporary price cuts. Funds may be budgeted in such a way that the flow of monies does not allow the purchaser to take advantage of economic order quantities, but instead necessitates smaller, more frequent purchases, regardless of current inventory levels. In addition, a given year's budget is generally based on the previous year's spending—which encourages heavy spending at the end of a fiscal year, often for unneeded items at unnecessarily high prices.

In many instances, government purchasing departments that buy for several different government agencies will attempt to increase efficiency through the use of standardization. Here, purchasing requirements of various users are consolidated by establishing standards and specifications for all equipment and supplies that are purchased. This practice discourages the purchase of different versions of a given item, thus reducing purchasing and storing costs.

The public exposure of government operations also has implications for purchasing. Purchases are paid for with public monies, and the public demands accountability. Voters resisting tax increases place pressure on government purchasers to buy goods and services which save money in the short run, but which deliver less value over time, requiring more frequent replacement. In addition, laws usually require that government organizations reveal pricing information to the public. This restriction limits the ability of purchasers to negotiate lower prices on a case-by-case basis, as vendors know that any price concessions they make can become public knowledge.

Government purchasing also contains a mix of objectives. In addition to the concern with efficiency found in commercial enterprises, governments often emphasize equity goals in purchasing. Thus, policies may require that certain amounts of purchases be made from minority vendors, from small businesses, or from businesses located in economically depressed areas.

Competitive bidding, or formal advertising, is strongly favored over negotiation for government purchases which exceed a minimum dollar amount. As a general rule, formal bidding is much less flexible than negotiation. Policies and procedures tend to require that initial bids be final bids, that bidder identities and offers be public information, and that bidding be open to any number of potential suppliers. The bidding process tends to overemphasize low price, when in fact there may be important trade-offs between higher price and product performance or useful life. The result can be less value for the purchasing dollar.

The volume of paperwork in government purchasing easily exceeds that for purchasing by a business firm, especially for large-ticket items. The government will place heavy paperwork demands on industrial marketers as well, that will raise the cost of doing business. Some of this red tape can be due to overly detailed product specification requirements for items that are relatively standardized and simple (e.g., a pair of pliers).

For some of the reasons discussed above, governments require more lead time in making purchases, again especially for large-dollar items. Because of this, they may sometimes be forced to maintain larger inventories than would otherwise be necessary. There is, further, a tendency to maintain stocks in excess of a level that is reasonable for current and ongoing operations.

Buyers for the government, in general, are not free to rely on a number of effective purchasing practices used by commercial enterprises. For example, government buyers do not have the corporate buyer's prerogative to withhold future business from vendors who do not strive to meet performance goals. Similarly, government purchasers are restricted in their use of multiyear contracts, life-cycle costing (discussed later in this chapter), and source loyalty.

This overview of the three major categories of industrial markets suggests varying needs and purchasing behavior on the part of each. At the same time, the three markets share numerous characteristics. Let us now turn to the question of the products sold in industrial markets, concentrating our focus on commercial markets.

THE INTERNATIONAL INDUSTRIAL MARKET

The large and rapidly growing international market is an additional market arena within which industrial companies compete for customers. Actually, there are numerous international markets, and most include all three types of customer organizations discussed up to this point. While it is difficult to capture the size and scope of these markets, a few statistics are illuminating (Survey of Current Business, 1986). The United States exported $362.3 billion worth of goods and services in 1985, and over $368 billion in 1986. Of these dollars, about 60 percent purchased merchandise, and 40 percent paid for services. The leading region, in terms of sales, is North America (excluding the U.S.), followed closely by Asia and Europe, and then South America, Africa, and Oceania (including Australia). Top nations in purchases of U.S. goods are Canada, Japan, Mexico, Great Britain, and West Germany.

There are substantial international markets for a wide range of industrial goods and services—everything from barley and lumber to organic chemicals, aircraft engines, and printing machinery (see Table 2.8). The fastest growth is coming in engineering services, design of computer and telecommunications systems, construction project management, financial and banking services, advertising services, and professional consulting. There are, in addition, a variety of more specialized service offerings, such as oilwell capping and meteorological forecasts. And, the demand is growing for so-called high-tech products, such as diagnostic imaging equipment in medicine, advanced radar systems, microwave components and robots.

Marketing in foreign countries is like marketing domestically, only different. While the basic function and concepts of marketing apply, the differences have to do with the environment confronting the marketer in each of the global markets entered. A common error when going abroad is to rely on the same strategies and tactics that have proven successful in domestic markets. Conditions are not the same, so why should the marketing program be the same? Cateora and Hess (1983, 437) explain, "Ironically, U.S. companies in the domestic market are very consumer-oriented, producing what the market wants, yet in foreign marketing, they are highly production-oriented." In addition, domestic companies face competitors abroad who have lower expectations for return on investment, whose employees have different expectations for their standard of living, and whose governments see their businesses' economic success as a national goal (McNally 1986).

Virtually every international marketing textbook emphasizes the distinctive cultural, political, legal, commercial, and economic characteristics that exist in the regions and countries of the world. Not only must these characteristics be recognized (e.g., through marketing research), but also implications must be drawn for the marketing of industrial products and services. Table 2.9 highlights sixteen of the major marketing-related problems resulting from differences between domestic and international industrial markets.

All four elements of the marketing mix are affected. For instance, in the product area, cultural differences can lead to variations from country to country in the importance placed on certain product features. Because nations are at differing stages of economic development, perceptions of quality in a given product are likely to vary. What is appropriate in a highly industrialized country may be inadequate in lesser-developed nations. This may also be true due to the climates, terrain, and infrastructure in various countries. The marketer also encounters a customer base that is sometimes unqualified to install, operate, or maintain products.

Pricing policies are vulnerable to rapidly fluctuating currency exchange rates. In response, marketers may demand payment in dollars, and offer no credit, but this policy frequently undermines their competitive position. Because hard currencies are often in short supply, many countries emphasize counter-trade, which is a kind of barter. A vendor sells goods in a foreign market in exchange for goods of that country. Price is further affected by the need to pay bribes and import tariffs.

Promotional efforts are hindered by the limited availability of specialized advertising media. There is also the problem of communicating technical product features and benefits, given the nuances of foreign languages and customs. Personal sales appeals must reflect the norms of dealing with managers from another culture, such as the need to engage in "small talk" or to respect a religious custom.

Table 2.8   Domestic Exports, from Selected Commodity Groups, 1985

	Value (million $)
FOOD AND LIVE ANIMALS	19,267.9
Meat and Meat Preparations	1,152.5
Dairy Products and Birds' Eggs.	388.0
Fish and Fish Preparations.	1,015.8
Grain and Cereal Preparations	11,050.2
Vegetables and Fruit	2,377.1
Feeding Stuff for Animals, Excl. Unmilled Cereals . . .	1,890.8
BEVERAGES AND TOBACCO	2,953.2
Tobacco-Unmanufactured.	1,520.6
Cigarettes	1,179.9
CRUDE MATERIALS, EXCEPT FUELS-INEDIBLE	16,939.5
Hides and Skins, Except Fur Skins-Undressed	1,088.0
Soybeans, Except Roasted as Coffee Substitute. . . .	3,906.1
Rubber Latex-Synthetic, and Synthetic Rubber	583.6
Logs and Lumber.	2,036.6
Paper Base Stocks-Pulpwood, Woodpulp, etc..	1,945.6
Raw Cotton, Excluding Linters and Waste.	1,633.2
Metal Ores, Concentrates, and Scraps	2,692.3
MINERAL FUELS, LUBRICANTS, AND RELATED MATERIALS. .	9,970.9
Coal, Coke, and Briquettes	4,553.6
Petroleum and Petroleum Products	4,707.1
OILS AND FATS-ANIMALS AND VEGETABLE.	1,434.0
Tallow, Animal Not Suitable for Human Consumption . .	538.1
Soybean Oil-Crude and Refined	439.3
Cottonseed Oil-Crude and Refined	126.3
CHEMICALS AND RELATED PRODUCTS, N.S.P.F.	21,756.7
Chemical Elements and Compounds	9,290.1
Medicinals and Pharmaceutical Preparations.	2,708.2
Fertilizers and Fertilizer Materials, N.S.P.F.	2,160.3
Synthetic Resins and Rubber of Plastic Material	3,777.2
MANUFACTURED GOODS CLASSIFIED CHIEFLY BY MATERIAL .	14,008.9
Tires and Tubes for Tires-Rubber or Plastic	342.9
Paper, Paperboard, and Manufactures	2,328.5
Textile Yarns, Fabrics, and Made-up Articles.	2,366.1
Nonmetallic Mineral Manufactures, N.S.P.F.-Cement	
Iron and Steel, Incl. Pig Iron and Ferroalloys.	1,234.3
Copper, Aluminum, Nickel, Lead, Zinc, Tin, and their Alloys-Wrought or Unwrought. . . .	1,471.6
Metal Manufactures, N.S.P.F.—Containers, Wire Cable and Household Ware, etc. . . .	3,253.3
MACHINERY AND TRANSPORT EQUIPMENT	94,278.4
Machinery	59,488.2
Power Generating Machinery Incl. Engines and Parts, N.S.P.F.	9,271.5
Machinery—Special Purpose	9,962.2
Tractors—Tracklaying Wheel Type Except Industrial Type . .	747.1
Construction, Excavating and Mining Machines, and Related Machinery and Parts . . .	820.0
Coal-Cutting, Mining, and Well-Drilling Machines and Parts . .	2,921.5
Textile, Sewing, and Leather Machinery	498.3
Paper and Pulp Mill Machinery-Making or Finishing Cellulosic Pulp, Paper, Paperboard, etc.. .	241.3
Printing and Bookbinding Machinery and Parts	439.2
Food Processing Machines and Parts (Excl. Domestic) N.S.P.F . .	270.6
Machinery and Mechanical Appliances Specially for Particular Industries and Parts, N.S.P.F. .	2,831.7
Metal Working Machinery.	1,249.2
General Industrial Machinery and Equipment, N.S.P.F. and Parts, N.S.P.F. .	7,421.1
Heating and Cooling Equipment and Parts	1,790.5
Pumps for Liquids, Parts, and Attachments	933.2
Centrifuges, Filtering, and Purifying Machines for Liquids, Air, and Gases and Parts . .	536.7
Industrial Trucks, Tractors, Portable, Elevator & Parts . .	252.3
Air and Gas Compressors and Parts.	279.1
Office Machinery and Computers	14,927.9
Telecommunications and Sound Recording and Reproducing Apparatus and Equipment . .	4,176.3
Electrical Machinery, Apparatus, Appliances, and Parts, N.S.P.F.. .	12,489.0
Transport Equipment	34,790.2
Automobiles and other Motor Vehicles and Parts (Parts Excl. Tires, Engines, and Electrical Parts) .	19,364.0
Other Transport Equipment.	15,345.5
Rail Locomotives and Rolling Stock.	428.6
Aircraft and Spacecraft and Parts	14,373.1
Ships, Boats, and Floating Structures.	305.7
MISCELLANEOUS MANUFACTURED ARTICLES, N.S.P.F.. . .	15,338.4
Furniture	559.8
Clothing, Excl. Footwear.	754.8
Professional, Scientific, and Controlling Instruments and Apparatus, N.S.P.F.. .	6,505.2
Photographic Supplies	1,313.1
Watches and Clocks and Parts	84.0
Printed Matter.	1,279.0
Miscellaneous Rubber and Plastic Articles	1,246.7
Baby Carriages, Toys, Games, and Sporting Goods. . . .	579.3
Office and Stationery Supplies	136.6
Numismatic Coins	14.3
Musical Instruments Parts and Accessories	897.7

Source: U.S. Bureau of the Census, *Highlights of U.S. Export and Import Trade*, Report 990.

Table 2.9 Significant Problems Confronting Industrial Marketers in International Markets

1. The need to identify and adapt to the cultural imperatives in dealing with purchasing decision makers in different countries;
2. Cultural differences can result in variations in the relative emphasis on service, dependability, performance, and costs;
3. Lack of secondary information sources for market analysis and research purposes (e.g., to estimate potential of forecast sales);
4. Customers lacking the technical skills required to install, operate, or perform maintenance on products;
5. The need to provide timely delivery of spare and replacement parts to distant markets; customers may substitute parts from other vendors, often causing equipment malfunctions;
6. Required accessory or complementary equipment used with a vendor's product (usually supplied by other domestic vendors) may be unavailable in foreign markets;
7. The lack of universal or common standards for use in specialized equipment manufacturing; the need to convert to the metric system;
8. Good quality as interpreted by a highly industrialized market may be inadequate when interpreted by standards of less industrialized nations;
9. Products are not priced competitively, as they are of higher quality than is actually required in lesser-developed nations;
10. Products that work well under the physical conditions (e.g., climate, terrain, transportation and utility systems) of one region may break down quickly in another region;
11. Shortage of hard currencies finds those in some countries emphasizing counter-trade, where goods are exchanged for goods rather than cash; the U.S. company must then find a market for the foreign goods;
12. Fluctuating exchange rates make it difficult to maintain control over prices unless payment is made in dollars; this is even more a problem with longer-term contracts;
13. A lack of specialized industrial advertising media in many parts of the world;
14. Partners, agents, and middlemen operate under different sets of rules and expectations than their domestic counterparts;
15. Heavier government involvement in production, promotion, pricing and distribution;
16. Expectations regarding bribes and payoffs in certain countries.

Distribution is a major problem for the international marketer, so a strategy must be developed for entering a particular market. Possibilities include exporting from the home country through local distributors, licensing, joint venturing with foreign firms, and establishing manufacturing facilities within the host country. When local distributors are used in any capacity, difficulties arise because these distributors do not always provide the same functions or perform at the same standards as domestic distributors. Another problem concerns the ability of the marketer to deliver spare and replacement parts after the sale. When these are not available on a timely basis, customers are likely to substitute other vendors' parts that do not meet specifications or that hinder equipment performance. This, in turn, hurts future sales and gives these other vendors access to customers.

One of the more controversial issues regarding international marketing strategy has to do with the distinction between *multidomestic* and *global* business (Hout, Porter, and Rudden 1982). A multidomestic approach finds a company carrying on separate strategies through subsidiaries in each diverse market. Operations are fairly independent and autonomous, with each subsidiary acting as a profit center. The company is able to tailor strategies and tactics to compete with other multinational vendors and local firms on a market-by-market basis.

A global approach focuses on developing a worldwide system of interdependent subsidiaries that emphasizes standardization and economies of scale. Operations within any one country are viewed in terms of how they fit into the overall global strategy. Thus, subsidiaries may specialize in parts of the total product line, and exchange them with other subsidiaries. Profit goals will vary by country. Operations are centralized or decentralized, depending on which is more cost-effective. Attempts are made to respond to local market needs, but only to the extent that the result does not adversely impact on overall global system efficiency.

Neither of these two approaches is necessarily better. Honeywell and Alcoa have successfully used the multidomestic approach, with controls and aluminum, respectively. At the same time, Caterpillar and General Electric have followed the global approach for their large construction equipment and heavy electrical equipment.

Regardless of their approach, industrial firms will be paying greater attention to the world marketplace in the future. This will happen, among many reasons, because of the dramatic inroads made by foreign competitors into the domestic marketplace.

THE NATURE OF INDUSTRIAL PRODUCTS

The products and services that are bought and sold in industrial markets may seem more difficult to picture than those in consumer markets. As consumers, we are familiar with such regularly purchased items as toothpaste, home furnishings, medical services, automobiles, clothing, and fast food. Industrial products may seem somewhat more obscure, especially for consumers who do not regularly buy or sell such goods. In reality, though, industrial products can be found all around us. Not only are they component parts in many of the consumer goods we buy (such as the fluoride in toothpaste or steel in automobiles), but they also include the forms we fill out at a hospital, the overhead projector used in a classroom, the computer that generates bank statements, and the truck that picks up the garbage. In addition, many goods are sold in both consumer and industrial markets, such as telephones, pencil sharpeners, and personal computers.

Just these few examples demonstrate that there is a wide assortment of industrial products, most of which would seem to have little in common. In fact, the one characteristic shared by all of these products is that they are sold to an organization. The task, then, is to come up with a means for organizing the wide array of industrial products into a meaningful classification scheme. In doing so, it will be possible to achieve a better understanding of industrial products. Also, the marketer is provided with a starting point from which to develop product strategies.

A good product classification scheme is one that is based on underlying characteristics of the product and/or the buyer. For example, we could classify goods as durable (e.g., an oil drill), nondurable (e.g., printer's ink), or services (e.g., marketing research), based on their tangibility and the expected product life (e.g., number of uses). The most popular approach classifies goods based on how they enter the production process and their relative costs—the *product use scheme*. This scheme consists of eleven different categories combined into three general groups—capital investment items, manufacturing materials and parts, and operational items and services. Keep in mind that the categories in this and most other classification schemes are not mutually exclusive. Also, a company's use of a particular product may change over time, which means that product could subsequently fit into a different category in the scheme.

1. Capital investment items:
   a. Equipment. Removable items with a depreciable life. Examples: cash registers, construction equipment, counters, desk calculators, electric typewriters, farm machinery, furniture and fixtures, and trucks.
   b. Installations. Items not readily removable and typically part of the office building, plant, or store. Examples: air conditioning, automated machines, computers, cranes, elevators, escalators, blast furnaces, and safes.
   c. Real estate, plant, and buildings. The real property of the enterprise. Examples: offices, plants, warehouses, parking lots, facilities for employee relaxation, and housing.
2. Manufacturing materials and parts:
   a. Raw materials, primarily from agriculture and the various extractive industries. Examples: cacao beans, corn, livestock, logs, minerals, ores, petroleum, and scrap, as well as dairy products, fruits, and vegetables sold to a processor.
   b. Semifinished goods and processed materials. Some work has been applied. The goods are finished only in part, or may have been formed into shapes and specifications to make them readily usable by the buyer. These products and materials lose their original identity when incorporated into other products. Examples: castings; chemicals; metals in many forms such as bars, sheets, tubing, wire, etc.; leather; salvage; sugar; and paper.
   c. Component parts. Completely finished products of one firm which can be used as a part of a more complex product by another firm. They do not lose their original identity when incorporated into other products. Examples: bearings, buttons, controls, dials, gauges, lenses, pulleys, spark plugs, transistors, radio and TV tubes, and automobile windshields.
3. Operational items and services:
   a. Operating supplies. Consumable items used in the operations of the business enterprise. Examples: typewriter ribbons, cutting oil, fasteners, insecticides, fuels, office supplies, small tools, packaging, and wrapping materials.
   b. Maintenance, repair, and overhaul (MRO) items. Items which are needed repeatedly or recurrently to maintain the operational efficiency of the business. Typically of relatively low unit cost, they would not include major machine installations or similar items more properly classified under capital investment.

Examples: electrical supplies, janitorial supplies, lubricants, paint, plumbing materials, and a wide variety of repair parts for plant and equipment.

c. Manufacturing services. The growing number of highly skilled and specialized services performed by one firm for another as a part of the latter's total manufacturing process. Examples: brazing and welding, casting, dyeing, finishing, glazing, and many applications of special forming and shaping services.

d. Business services. Somewhat parallel to the manufacturing services, except that these are business services provided to offices rather than manufacturing-process services to plants. Examples: copying and reproducing services, EDP maintenance, repair services on business machines and equipment, protection services, technical product research, trade shows, travel agents, and window cleaning.

e. Professional services. A wide range of professional services marketed to industry. Not generally recognized, they well deserve inclusion as part of the complex of industrial goods and services. Examples: accounting, advertising, consulting—both business management and engineering, educational, financial, insurance, legal—general corporate counsel and both patent and process-right protection, psychological testing, and tax.

SOURCE: Adapted from G. Risley, *Modern Industrial Marketing* (New York: McGraw-Hill Book Co., 1972), 24–25.

In this product use scheme, capital investment items can be depreciated by the customer as they wear out, and are treated as such from an accounting standpoint. These items are usually relatively costly. Manufacturing materials and parts are treated as expense items purchased on a repeat basis and maintained in inventory. Operational items and services are treated as business expenses, but are not typically assigned to the costs of production because they do not become part of the production process. Goods that fall into this category are commonly referred to as MRO—maintenance, repair, and overhaul items.

Kotler (1984) has suggested that the categories in a product classification scheme can be redefined, based on the degree to which an item actually enters into the production process of a company. This approach results in three distinct categories—foundation goods, entering goods, and facilitating goods. Foundation goods, used to make other products or services, include all capital investment items. Entering goods become a physical part of the finished product, and include all manufacturing materials and parts. Facilitating goods, which support the operations of the enterprise, are not used to actually produce products, and do not become part of other products. This category includes operational items and supplies.

Related to this scheme is one developed by Hillier (1975) that differentiates production services, production facilities, product constituents, and product transformers. Production services (e.g., insurance, advertising, repairs, welding) are background services that augment the production process. Production facilities (e.g., machines, tools, testing equipment) include plant and equipment that constitute the means of production for the purchasing organization. Product constituents (e.g., iron ore, copper, processed chemicals, nuts and bolts) are incorporated into the final product being made by the purchasing organization. Product transformers (e.g., fuel, abrasives, packaging, containers) help transform the initial product supplied by man-ufacturers into the product actually sold in the marketplace, but do not become a part of the product.

In the same vein, Corey (1983) explains that industrial products are marketed at different stages of completion and at different levels of the marketplace. He distin-guishes between new materials, semiprocessed materials, finished materials, com-ponents, subassemblies, and end products. Some firms operate at a number of lev-els, such as the paper company that makes and sells paperboard, corrugated fiberboard, and corrugated boxes—each of which is used in the manufacture of the next.

Another approach classifies products according to buying assignments within the customer firm. Companies may have different procedures and assign responsi-bility to different individuals, depending on what is being purchased. Based on this method, it may be logical to segregate products into several categories—standard product parts, custom product parts, machinery and equipment, raw materials, MRO, and internally sourced products. This last category includes products made some-where else within the customer firm, and "sold" to the requisitioning department or division at a transfer price.

Many industrial products are, in effect, commodities. That is, the customer does not perceive any appreciable differences in the specifications and performance characteristics among the various suppliers of a particular product (e.g., paint, ham-mers, copper wire, paper). We can draw a distinction, then, between differentiated and undifferentiated industrial products.

Finally, a commonly used and very detailed approach to classifying products is the Standard Industrial Classification (SIC) system. This fairly comprehensive num-bering system was developed by the Office of Management and Budget. Organiza-tions are assigned to one of ten major classes, depending on the type of economic activity in which they are engaged. Within these ten categories, a seven-digit number is assigned to individual products. The system is discussed in further detail in Chap-ters 5, 6, and 7.

While this discussion of product classification has sought to provide some in-sights into the nature of industrial products, it must be stated that the differences among many of these items are greater than the similarities. Although many indus-trial products tend to be more technical in nature and more costly than consumer products, there are many nontechnical and relatively inexpensive industrial items, such as nails, ashtrays, and bulletin boards. Wide variations also exist in the signifi-cance of each individual purchase to the user, time and effort spent purchasing, need for service, frequency of purchase, and the extent and variety of usage for individual industrial products.

THE PURCHASING FUNCTION

An industrial marketer selling to customers is operating in a formal and professional purchasing environment. A more complete understanding of the nature of this en-vironment can be achieved by considering how purchasing professionals approach the market transaction. Of course, this approach will vary from company to company, and so discussion will be fairly general. There are a number of excellent books on purchasing available that provide a much more detailed treatment of the subject, and nicely complement an industrial marketing textbook.

Purchasing Procedures

While the marketer can have an important influence on the buying process and buyer behavior within the customer organization (discussed in the next two chapters), a set of formal purchasing procedures and documentation requirement must be recognized and complied with. Some of these are described below and illustrated in Figure 2.2 (Bornemann 1974; Dobler, Lee, and Burt 1984).

Once a need has been identified for some product or service, usually by a user department in the buying organization, that department will initiate a purchase requisition. Only authorized personnel can originate and sign off on such requisitions, which often are numbered to identify the originating department. The form must describe the needed item as specifically as possible, and include information on the quantity required, when and where it is needed, and the account to be charged. Assuming the purchase requisition has been properly filled out and approved, and that sufficient stocks are not already on hand, the next step is the issuance of a written purchase order—usually by the purchasing department. However, if the purchase is for something minor, the item may be obtained using the petty cash fund.

Before issuing a purchase order for a more substantial purchase, the buying organization will investigate potential sources, negotiate with suppliers or solicit bids, establish price-related terms, and select a supplier. The buyer may maintain a list of approved suppliers for certain items.

The purchase order will provide the company name as well as the name and signature of the purchasing individual who is acting as agent. The order will specify the quantity, item description, and terms of purchase—including discounts, F.O.B. points, date of order, and desired delivery date. For many products, including catalog items, an item number or code is required. Terms and conditions (e.g., governing quality approval, cancellation clauses, or price changes) will often be preprinted on the purchase order.

The purchase order represents a formal offer, and is the first step toward establishing a legal contract between buyer and seller. Upon receipt of this form, the vendor will acknowledge acceptance of the order, the second ingredient for a legal contract. This acceptance can involve immediate shipment of the requested goods, the return of an approved copy of the purchase order, the return of an acknowledgement form sent by the buyer along with the purchase order, or the completion of a standard acceptance form designed and used by the vendor. The vendor can alter the terms of the purchase order by writing in changes on whatever acceptance form is used. This counter-offer now must be accepted by the buying organization.

After sending out the purchase order, the purchasing department will follow up to ensure that the contractual relationship has been established, to check the status of the order, and to expedite production and delivery. Also, if the vendor has subcontracted any part of the order, the buyer may want to monitor the progress of these subcontracts.

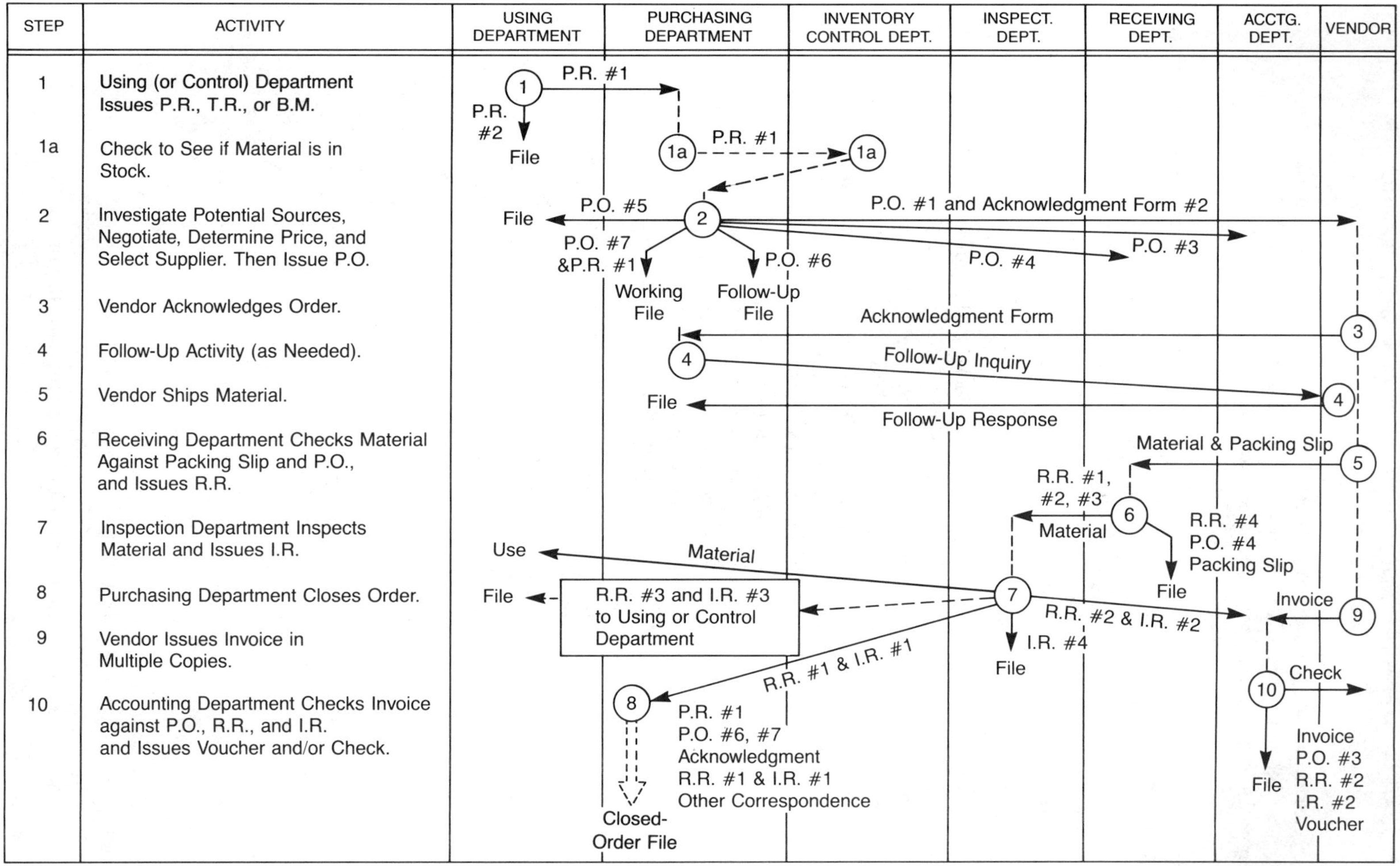
STEP
ACTIVITY
USING DEPARTMENT
PURCHASING DEPARTMENT
INVENTORY CONTROL DEPT.
INSPECT. DEPT.
RECEIVING DEPT.
ACCTG. DEPT.
VENDOR
1
Using (or Control) Department Issues P.R., T.R., or B.M.
1a
Check to See if Material is in Stock.
2
Investigate Potential Sources, Negotiate, Determine Price, and Select Supplier. Then Issue P.O.
3
Vendor Acknowledges Order.
4
Follow-Up Activity (as Needed).
5
Vendor Ships Material.
6
Receiving Department Checks Material Against Packing Slip and P.O., and Issues R.R.
7
Inspection Department Inspects Material and Issues I.R.
8
Purchasing Department Closes Order.
9
Vendor Issues Invoice in Multiple Copies.
10
Accounting Department Checks Invoice against P.O., R.R., and I.R. and Issues Voucher and/or Check.
P.R. #1
P.R. #2
File
P.R. #1
P.O. #5
File
P.O. #7 &P.R. #1
Working File
P.O. #6
Follow-Up File
P.O. #1 and Acknowledgment Form #2
P.O. #4
P.O. #3
Acknowledgment Form
Follow-Up Inquiry
File
Follow-Up Response
Material & Packing Slip
R.R. #1, #2, #3
Material
R.R. #4
P.O. #4
Packing Slip
File
Use
Material
File
R.R. #3 and I.R. #3 to Using or Control Department
R.R. #2 & I.R. #2
I.R. #4
File
Invoice
R.R. #1 & I.R. #1
Check
P.R. #1
P.O. #6, #7
Acknowledgment
R.R. #1 & I.R. #1
Other Correspondence
Closed-Order File
File
Invoice
P.O. #3
R.R. #2
I.R. #2
Voucher

Figure 2.2 Flow chart for a typical purchasing cycle.
Source: D.W. Dobler, L. Lee, and D. Burt, *Purchasing and Materials Management,* 4th Ed., (New York: McGraw-Hill Book Co., 1984), 491. Reprinted with permission.

P.R. = Purchase Requisition; T.R. = Traveling Requisition; B.M. = Bill of Materials;
P.O. = Purchase Order; R.R. = Receiving Report; I.R. = Inspection Report

Upon shipment of the order from the vendor, the receiving department will examine incoming materials and prepare a receiving report. Responsibility for inspection will typically rest within either the purchasing or the production departments. The vendor's invoice is audited for accuracy, and compared to the purchase order and the receiving report. This auditing function is usually done by the accounting department, but sometimes by the purchasing department. The invoice is paid, at a time that depends on the discounts offered by the vendor. In some cases, invoices are prepaid (i.e., before delivery) in order to take advantage of vendor incentives. The last step in the process is order-closing, which involves consolidating the documentation and correspondence pertaining to a given order in a closed-order file for future reference.

Much of the paperwork involved in this process (called the purchasing cycle) is replaceable by computerized communication systems. In fact, for routine and repetitive purchases, computer interface between buyer and seller organizations can eliminate the need for human interaction. The new technologies can dramatically reduce order and delivery time, and decrease errors in accounting and control.

Organizing the Purchasing Operation

The purchasing process used by a particular organization will depend, in large part, on how the purchasing operation is set up. Where is the purchasing function located within the organizational structure? This positioning will vary considerably among industrial firms, the government, and institutional organizations. For the purpose of example, our focus will be on industrial organizations.

Although each department or functional area in a firm could conceivably handle its own purchasing needs, this approach is generally viewed as inefficient. As a result, a formal purchasing or procurement function is established in most industrial firms, with responsibility for making commitments in the name of the company for the materials, tools, supplies and services needed by all user departments (Bornemann 1974). The purchasing department is, in a sense, an intermediary between these user departments and vendors.

The major tasks facing the purchasing department can include identifying and evaluating sources of supply, negotiating prices and terms, establishing the purchase contract, ensuring delivery arrangements compatible with production scheduling, expediting orders, handling returns of unacceptable merchandise, establishing vendor files, and maintaining ongoing relationships with suppliers. The department is further charged with monitoring changes in markets, prices, and regulations.

Traditionally, purchasing has not been a top-level function in the organizational structure. Rather, purchasing activities usually have been subordinate to the manufacturing function, as illustrated in Figure 2.3. Over time, however, most industrial companies have moved toward the establishment of purchasing as a distinct functional area on the same level as production, marketing, finance, and R&D. This change is demonstrated in the organizational chart found in Figure 2.4.

The enhanced role and status of purchasing have developed for a number of reasons. For most industrial firms, more than 50 percent of sales revenue is spent on purchases. Combine this fact with inflationary cost trends, raw material shortages,

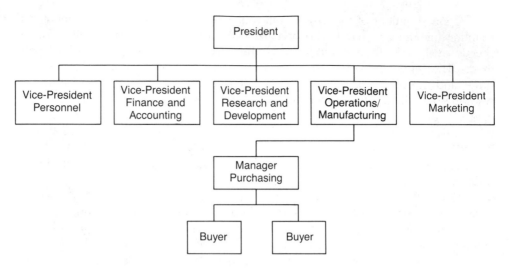

Figure 2.3   Simple Functional Organization Structure with Purchasing as a Subordinate Department.

high financing costs, and intense competitive pressures, and it is not surprising that increased attention is devoted to achieving efficiency and effectiveness in purchasing operations. Not only is purchasing a potential source of major material cost savings, but it is also a contributor to the operational efficiency of the organization. Purchasing is an important source of value, and can affect significantly the firm's competitive position in the marketplace.

The organization of the purchasing department might resemble the structure found in Figure 2.5, which is appropriate for a medium-sized company with a centralized department located at a single site. Companies with multiple site locations may maintain a single centralized purchasing department such as the one in Figure 2.4, they may add local purchasing officers at each location, or they may completely decentralize purchasing with fairly autonomous departments at each site. There are numerous structural alternatives available, each with different implications for the industrial marketing effort.

As seen in Figure 2.5, the purchasing department can include a considerable amount of specialized expertise. For example, buyers may concentrate in particular

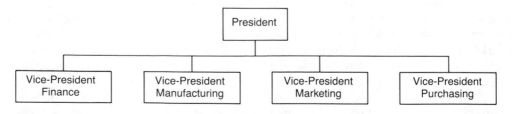

Figure 2.4   Purchasing as First-Level Function

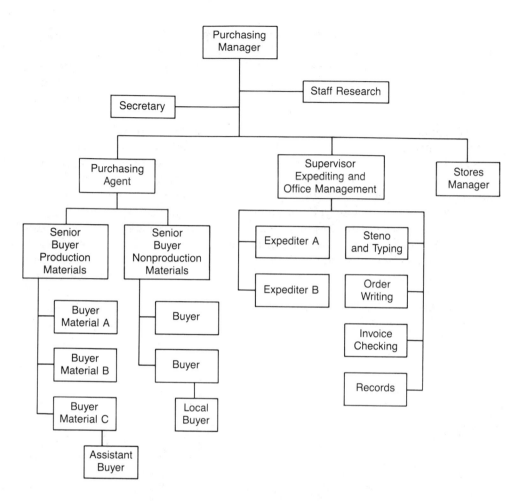

Figure 2.5 Organizational Structure of a Hypothetical Purchasing Department

product categories, and the department can include members whose sole function is to write orders or to work with vendors to expedite production and delivery. Staff assistants may be employed to perform studies on ways in which a purchased product's costs can be reduced, to assess economic trends, or to evaluate and forecast conditions in various commodity markets.

More recently, the procurement function has been integrated into what has been labeled the *materials management concept*—a systems approach to managing the total materials flow in an organization. The flow begins with the purchase of materials, and ends with the delivery of finished product to a warehouse, ready to be marketed. Activities such as receiving, incoming inspection, stores, materials handling, production planning and control, inventory management (raw materials, goods in process, finished goods), inbound and outbound traffic, shipping, warehousing, and customer services are integrated into a materials management division (see Figure 2.6). The three functions which are integrated, then, are buying, storage, and movement. Often the manager of this department is a vice-president, and professional purchasing managers can use this position to enhance their influence and control within the organization. Some service organizations, as well as a large number of manufacturing companies, have adopted the materials management concept.

The major benefit of this concept is the coordination which can be achieved within the materials area. In the absence of such an approach, decisions on purchasing, inventory, or shipping may be made in isolation. Webster (1984) provides the example of a purchasing agent who buys larger quantities than currently required so as to negotiate a favorable price. However, the savings may be illusory if this purchase creates storage problems due to insufficient warehousing capacity, or if the costs of managing this inventory (e.g., costs of space, capital investment, taxes, obsolescence and deterioration) exceed the apparent price savings. The materials management concept is intended specifically to address such problems. Also, better coordination is possible in satisfying the material needs of other functional areas in the organization.

The marketer trying to sell a product to a company organized around a materials management philosophy should recognize that the buyer is likely to assess the

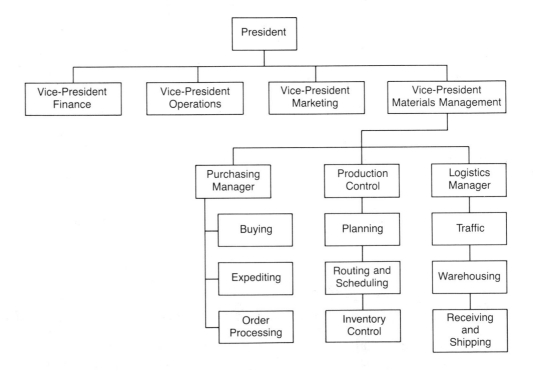

Figure 2.6 Hypothetical Materials Management Organizational Structure

product from a total materials perspective. While a purchasing agent may be attracted by a lower price, a materials manager may be willing to pay more for a product that offers greater use value in terms of storage, installation, maintenance, servicing, and disposal costs.

KEY ANALYTICAL TOOLS IN PURCHASING INDUSTRIAL GOODS

Successful marketing practices will reflect the concepts and tools used by customer organizations to evaluate and manage the products they buy. Five of the most important of these purchasing tools are life-cycle costing, value analysis, time-based buying strategies, just-in-time inventory, and materials requirement planning.

Life-Cycle Costing

As our discussion of materials management has suggested, products can cost more than just the initial purchase price. Delivery, installation, plant modification, training, maintenance, and servicing are among the costs that can be incurred over a long period of time for certain products. The marketer will find it helpful to consider the useful economic life of a product to a particular customer, and then to determine all of the costs that will be incurred during that time period—the *life-cycle* costs of the product.

There are three categories of life-cycle costs: initial cost (i.e., purchase price), start-up costs, and postpurchase costs (Forbis and Mehta 1981). The purchase price is defined as the total dollar amount paid to a vendor for an item, including freight costs, insurance, and any technical training provided by the supplier for a fee. Start-up costs are initial costs that are not paid to the vendor from whom the product was purchased, but must be incurred to make the product operational or usable. These costs are either paid to other suppliers, or absorbed by the customer. Examples include the costs of modifying physical facilities, meeting power requirements, or establishing the temperature control necessary to satisfy product requirements, as well as lost production time during installation, or any training not provided by the product vendor. Postpurchase costs are generated to keep the product in working condition after it has been put into use. Such ongoing expenditures as repair, servicing, financing costs, power consumption, inventory costs, and space requirements related to the usage of the item represent postpurchase costs. To get a complete picture of a product's total cost over its useful life, the purchaser may also want to subtract any salvage value which can be recovered when the item is disposed of.

The calculation of life-cycle costs can be difficult, requiring technical expertise and insight. The expected life of a product must be estimated, and reasonable judgments made regarding expected product performance, wear and tear, and use requirements. Past experience and value analysis studies can be useful here. Costs which are incurred over a number of years must be discounted and expressed in present value terms. To do so, a reasonable discount rate must be determined.

Life-cycle costing can have important meaning for the marketer. If company A's product has lower start-up and postpurchase costs than does company B's competing product, and both firms are charging the same price, company A is delivering more economic value to the customer (EVC). This value factor can be a major source of competitive advantage. Further, the company providing more EVC has a justification for charging a higher price.

Value Analysis

Another purchasing tool having important implications for the industrial marketer is *value analysis* (also called value engineering, value control, or value assurance). It was developed by General Electric during the 1940s as an approach to cost reduction in a period of material shortages. Value, in this context, is defined as "the relative cost of providing a necessary function or service at the desired time and place with the essential quality" (Fram 1974).

Value analysis is the organized study of a product after it has been developed, to identify unnecessary costs that do not add to the reliability or to the quality of the item, and to determine if the product can somehow be improved while achieving desired cost reductions. The components of an end product are analyzed in detail to determine if they can be redesigned, standardized, or manufactured by a less expensive means of production (see Figure 2.7 for examples). A key point in value analysis is that, although cost reduction seems to be the main focus, maintaining quality, satisfactory functional performance, and customer satisfaction are critical. The analysis consists, then, of an appraisal of cost/benefit trade-offs.

If one carefully assesses the design of a product, it is not unusual to find that 80 percent of the total cost is attributable to 20 percent of its component parts and materials. Because of the pressures on purchasing departments to save money without sacrificing quality, purchasers often look for substitute products or product components that will deliver the same value at lower cost. This approach provides an opportunity for the marketing organization that can produce functionally identical products more efficiently. Also, the marketer who pays close attention to customer value analysis programs can find such studies to be a valuable source of new product ideas. Astute marketers may want to develop their own value analysis program, or get involved directly with those of customer organizations. Marketers also may perform value analysis on their competitors' products, in a process called *reverse engineering*.

While there are various approaches to value analysis, some of the key questions that are addressed are listed in Table 2.10. To conduct the actual analysis, the value analysis team will proceed through five stages: information, speculation, analysis, execution, and reporting (Fram 1974; Zimmerman and Hart 1982). These stages, taken together, constitute a *job plan*. In the information stage, the concern is with describing the product, its cost, and its functions. Information is gathered regarding the materials used in manufacturing the product, the production process, the vendor's true costs, and what makes the product work. The speculation stage involves creative thought regarding how the product and its functions can be altered. Ideas such as substituting new materials or parts, reversing procedures, combining procedures, eliminating features that are not functional, and reducing or increasing

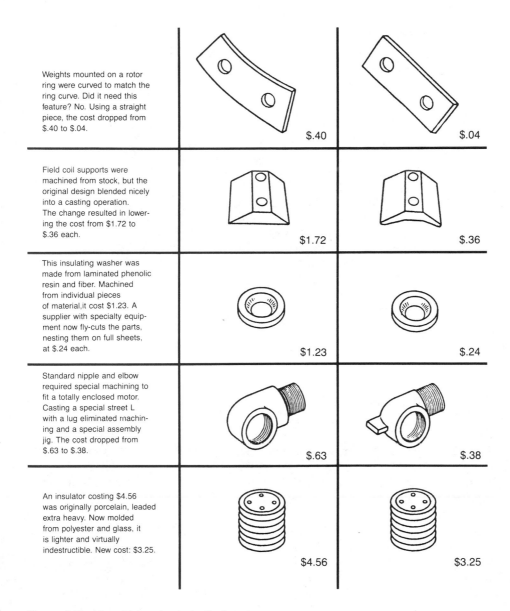

Weights mounted on a rotor ring were curved to match the ring curve. Did it need this feature? No. Using a straight piece, the cost dropped from $.40 to $.04.

$.40 $.04

Field coil supports were machined from stock, but the original design blended nicely into a casting operation. The change resulted in lowering the cost from $1.72 to $.36 each.

$1.72 $.36

This insulating washer was made from laminated phenolic resin and fiber. Machined from individual pieces of material, it cost $1.23. A supplier with specialty equipment now fly-cuts the parts, nesting them on full sheets, at $.24 each.

$1.23 $.24

Standard nipple and elbow required special machining to fit a totally enclosed motor. Casting a special street L with a lug eliminated machining and a special assembly jig. The cost dropped from $.63 to $.38.

$.63 $.38

An insulator costing $4.56 was originally porcelain, leaded extra heavy. Now molded from polyester and glass, it is lighter and virtually indestructible. New cost: $3.25.

$4.56 $3.25

Figure 2.7 How Value Analysis Slashes Costs
(Source: Lamar Lee, Jr., and Donald W. Dobler, *Purchasing and Materials Management, Text and Cases* (New York: McGraw-Hill Book Co., 1977), 265. Reprinted by permission of *Business Management* magazine.

product size, are all results of speculative brainstorming sessions among the members of the value analysis team. The feasibility and cost of these ideas are evaluated in the analysis or judgment stage. Some proposals involve detailed testing, such as

Table 2.10   Checklist of Standard Questions in a Value Analysis Study

1. Can the item be eliminated?
2. If the item is not standard, can a standard item be used?
3. If the item is standard, does it completely fit the application or is it a misfit?
4. Does the item have greater capacity than required?
5. Can its weight be reduced?
6. Is there a similar item in inventory that could be substituted?
7. Are tolerances specified closer than necessary?
8. Is unnecessary machining performed on the item?
9. Are unnecessarily fine finishes specified?
10. Is commercial quality specified? (Commercial quality is usually most economical.)
11. Can the item be manufactured cheaper in-house than purchased? If it is being manufactured in-house, can it be bought for less?
12. Is the item properly classified for shipping to obtain lowest transportation rates?
13. Can cost of packaging be reduced?
14. Are suppliers being asked for suggestions to reduce cost?

Source: *Basic Steps in Value Analysis*, a pamphlet prepared under the chairmanship of Martin S. Erb by the Value-Analysis-Standardization Committee, Reading Association, National Association of Purchasing Management, New York, 4–18.

replacing a critical component with an untried substitute. Others are more straightforward, such as eliminating gloss paint on an interior machine part where paint may not be necessary at all. In the execution stage, the proposals for change and evidence of their utility must be sold to management. Resistance to change of any sort, especially change regarding how a job is performed, is not unusual. A useful strategy is to include on the value analysis team those individuals thought to be most resistant. Lastly, those who are involved in the reporting stage are concerned with implementing and following through on the changes. Success depends on organizational commitment to value analysis as a philosophy.

The value analysis team will consist of a group of functional experts, and may have representatives from purchasing, design engineering, product engineering, accounting, and marketing, among others. The industrial salesperson often plays a role by providing data and technical assistance. The team approach is critical both in achieving a creative environment and in soliciting organization resources and support for the value analysis effort.

While this work can be performed at any time before or after a product is purchased, value analysis is especially relied upon in the maturity stage of a product's life cycle, or when technologies change. Usually by this time, other competitors have entered the market with less expensive replicas, while the original producer is attempting to solidify and maintain market share. Moreover, after a product has been on the market several years, customer organizations have seen what works and what does not, and are more likely to pursue cost-saving measures.

Time-Based Buying Strategies

The industrial marketer should be cognizant of the various objectives and strategies which underlie the way in which an organization buys. Traditional approaches to purchasing involve strategies that consider current usage or volume requirements, and existing and anticipated market conditions. Depending on how these factors are viewed, the purchaser will usually use one of the following three types of buying strategies: speculative buying, forward buying, and hand-to-mouth buying (Dobler, Lee, and Burt 1984). These strategies are time-based; the length of time that coverage of needs is provided (number of days' supply kept in stock) is the variable which distinguishes each approach from the others.

With *speculative buying,* the organization is purchasing quantities of goods in excess of projected or foreseeable requirements. The expectation is that a large purchase at current market prices will, over time, generate a profit for the organization. This is appropriate during periods of prolonged inflation, or when the market drops temporarily due to excess supply or a short-term decline in demand. The purchasing profit should be realized as changing conditions drive market prices higher. Of course, the apparent savings to the buyer are somewhat offset by the added inventory costs. There is a degree of risk involved in speculative buying. First, the organization's needs may change such that the excess quantities purchased are never used. While this excess could conceivably be sold, this alternative places additional demands on the buying organization. Second, prices may not move in the anticipated direction, or at least not as much as expected.

Forward buying also involves purchasing an amount of materials in excess of what is currently required, but not beyond anticipated future requirements. The need for what is being purchased can be clearly foreseen, and so forward buying does not entail the risk found in speculative buying. Reasons to engage in forward buying might include taking advantage of quantity discounts or volume freight rates, providing security against unstable supply conditions, and buffering against unreliable transportation or delivery performance by vendors.

When the buyer purchases in quantities that just satisfy immediate operating requirements and that are smaller than what would usually be considered economical, *hand-to-mouth buying* is in operation. This short-term strategy is intended to minimize inventories when prices are falling, when engineering design changes are imminent, or when the firm is experiencing temporary cash flow problems.

Alternatively, the organization may establish an ongoing program with vendors where ordering and delivery are tailored to daily production needs, as discussed below.

Just-in-Time Inventory

Industrial marketing is also affected by a trend in purchasing toward minimizing inventories, and away from an orientation where large, overstocked inventories are seen as an asset to the firm. Many efforts in this regard aim to create a situation where purchased materials and parts arrive at a user's location only as they are needed. Such an arrangement is commonly referred to as JIT (just-in-time) inventory. Waters (1984) explains, "As a philosophy, JIT targets inventory as an evil presence that obscures problems that should be solved, and that, by contributing significantly to costs, keeps a company from being as competitive or profitable as it might otherwise be." Ample inventories represent protection against human error, machine breakdowns, and defective parts; correspondingly, these inventories provide management with less incentive to eliminate production inefficiencies.

For JIT to be successful, the concept must be integrated into both the production and purchasing operations of the organization (Hahn, Pinto, and Bragg 1983). The production control system will seek to keep work-in-process and raw materials inventories to a minimum by scheduling delivery of the precise amount of materials or parts needed at each work station only as they are required. The production rate must be made fairly level or smooth, which typically leads to smaller production lot sizes for each item, and more frequent production setups. At the same time, the purchasing department must persuade suppliers to deliver small quantities of needed items as they are demanded—which may necessitate deliveries on a daily basis, if not more often. Delivery schedules must be extremely reliable, lead times for ordering must be very short, and deliveries can contain few, if any, defective parts. Correspondingly, the buyer will often sign long-term purchasing contracts with vendors.

Results can be dramatic. JIT can lead to reduced purchase costs, reduced inventory costs, faster response to product design changes, fewer delivery delays and production slowdowns, simplified receiving, fewer inspections, and more efficient administrative procedures due to a reduction in the number of suppliers required. Further, as demonstrated in Table 2.11, JIT can enable the buying organization to improve the quality of its own products.

American companies began to implement JIT largely in response to the inroads made into U.S. markets by efficient Japanese competitors. For example, Waters (1984) credits JIT as a principal reason why Toyota Motor Company could import all of its raw materials, produce a quality car, ship it 7,000 miles and still have a cost advantage over its American competitors of up to $1,500. U.S. companies are beginning to realize the same kinds of benefits. Omark Industries, a diversified corporation based in Portland, Oregon, saved an estimated $7 million in inventory carrying costs in one year. Their system is called ZIPS (zero inventory production system). A much smaller firm, T.D. Shea Manufacturing of Troy, Michigan, which sells automotive plastics products, uses a similar system, called Nick-of-Time. The Harley-Davidson Motor Company's engine plant in Milwaukee, Wisconsin, calls its version of the system MAN, for Material-as-Needed. Using JIT, A.P. Parts, of Toledo, Ohio, was able to reduce finished goods (exhaust systems) inventory by 32 percent, eliminate 460,000 square feet in warehouse space, and consolidate two plants.

General Motors integrated the just-in-time concept into production plans for the state-of-the-art Saturn project. Using advanced production management techniques, executives thought they could save about $2,000 in costs per car manufactured. To illustrate how automobiles may be made one day, consider the proposed approach. A consumer specifies the exact set of options desired on a yet-to-be-manufactured car. This data is entered on a computer terminal at the dealer location,

Table 2.11   How Just-in-Time Inventory Can Impact on Product Quality

Purchasing Activities	JIT Practice	Effect on Quality
Lot size	Purchase in small lots with frequent deliveries	Fast detection and correction of defects
Supplier evaluation	Suppliers evaluated on ability to provide high quality products	Suppliers put more emphasis on their product quality
Supplier selection	Single source in close geographical area	Frequent on-site visits by technical people; rapid and better understanding of quality requirements
Product specification	Fully specify only essential product characteristics	Suppliers have more discretion in product design and manufacturing methods, which results in specifications that are more likely to be attainable
Bidding	Stay with the same suppliers; do informal value analysis to reduce bid price; no annual rebidding	Suppliers can afford cost of long-term commitment to meet quality requirements, and they become more aware of buyer's true requirements
Receiving inspection	Vendor certifies quality; receiving inspections are reduced and eventually eliminated	Quality at the source (the supplier) is more effective and less costly
Paperwork	Less formal system; reduced volume of paperwork	More time available for purchasing people to devote to quality matters

Source: R. J. Schonberger and A. Abdohossein, "Just-in-Time Purchasing Can Improve Quality," *Journal of Purchasing and Materials Management,* 20, (Spring 1984), 4.

and sent electronically to the Saturn automobile plant. From here, computer messages are sent to Goodyear Tire and Rubber (ordering four tires) to Champion (six spark plugs), to PPG Industries (one windshield), and so on. The suppliers make these parts when ordered, maintaining virtually zero inventory, and deliver them immediately. The car is, in effect, made to order on the assembly line.

Materials Requirement Planning

Materials requirement planning (MRP) is an important approach to the systematic determination of current and foreseeable needs for materials and parts. Based on sales forecasts and minimum desired inventory levels, the MRP technique performs the detailed calculations necessary to translate these projections into precise order,

Exhibit 2.1   Implications of New Purchasing and Production Systems for Industrial Marketers

---

Just-in-time (JIT) and materials requirement planning (MRP) are but two of a number of new techniques for improving efficiencies and lowering costs in purchasing, inventory control, and production. Other new production/operations systems, all of which are made possible through advances in computer software, include manufacturing resource planning (MRP II), optimized production technology (OPT), distribution resource planning (DRP), and flexible manufacturing systems (FMS). As industrial customers adopt these systems, there are important implications for the marketer. Some possibilities include:

a) closer, longer-term relationships between buyers and sellers, leading to more source loyalty and the use of fewer sources;

b) a change in the power relationship between buyer and seller, initially in favor of the buyer;

c) a greater emphasis on product simplification, quality, and tailoring of products to customer requirements;

d) higher costs of products to the marketer, but stable prices;

e) more complex price-setting;

f) greater emphasis on company attributes, and less on product attributes, when making sales;

g) changes in the salesperson's role, with more stress on servicing and consulting activities;

h) shorter, more direct distribution channels, and higher logistical service levels;

i) a reliance on production scheduling patterns, service requirements, and geographic location in market segmentation and target group selection.

Source: Adapted from M. Morris and J. Dailey. "Implications of Trends in Materials Management for the Industrial Marketer," *AMA Educator's Proceedings,* 52, (Chicago: American Marketing Association, 1986), 212–217.

delivery, and inventory schedules (Ammer 1980). Numerous planning tools are incorporated, such as economic order quantity (EOQ) models, probability theory for establishing safety stocks, and statistical demand forecasting. Because of the complexity of the calculations and considerations that must be taken into account, MRP is heavily reliant on the computer.

Ammer (1980) provides an example of the usefulness of MRP:

> For example, suppose that item A is used in several dozen end products. The demand for these end products is changing constantly. How does this affect demand for item A? Before MRP, about all the average manufacturer could do was

carry a fat inventory of item A and just hope that it proved adequate. With MRP, each change in end product demand can be instantly reflected in inventory and production planning for each component, including those that are several stages away from the final production process.

The typical MRP system consists of three key informational inputs: a master production schedule, a bill of materials, and an inventory record file (Dobler, Lee, and Burt 1984). The production schedule indicates week-to-week output of finished products over the planning time horizon. A bill of materials identifies the materials needed to manufacture an item at each stage in its production process. The inventory record file monitors an item's current inventory balance on hand, the timing and sizing of outstanding orders for that item, the necessary lead time involved, and any related planning information. Working backward from these information sources, the MRP system spells out precise material needs for a given period of operation.

MRP is not without its drawbacks. The technique is less applicable for purchases that require long order lead times, large volume buying, and which are irregular or infrequent. A trade-off is involved between the benefits of reduced inventory carrying costs, and the burdens of more complicated operating problems and higher acquisition costs (Dobler, Lee, and Burt 1984).

As MRP is adopted by more organizations, the marketer's approach is affected. Materials requirement planning impacts upon the industrial marketer by managing buying practices in the areas of specifications, design, annual requirements, sources, quality, and price. When customer organizations use MRP, the marketer will most likely find key purchase decision makers to be involved with the MRP function. Such customers are also likely to be more open to vendors who are interested in developing long-term planning programs for material needs. Exhibit 2.1 presents additional implications of MRP and related technologies for the industrial marketer.

SUMMARY

Chapter 2 completes the introduction to industrial marketing. The chapter has focused on the nature and scope of industrial markets, characteristics and types of industrial products and services, and formal organizational approaches to managing the task of purchasing industrial goods. Throughout this discussion, implications for the marketer have been drawn.

The industrial market is so large and complex that differences among industrial organizations are often greater than differences between industrial and consumer markets. Despite this fact, the industrial marketer's task is generally quite different from that of the consumer goods marketer. The diversity of industrial markets makes this task all the more challenging. Three types of organizations constitute the industrial market: commercial enterprises, governments, and institutions. While commercial firms produce and consume most of the goods and services that are sold, the government purchases a sizable volume each year, and institutional demand is growing rapidly.

A wide range of industrial products is sold to these organizations, both domestically and internationally. A helpful way to characterize these goods is by the manner in which they are used in the customer's operations or production process. A distinction can be drawn, for example, between foundation, entering, and facilitating goods. There are, in addition, a number of other ways in which industrial goods and services can be classified.

The chapter also examined the role of purchasing departments in buying industrial products. While there are a number of approaches to structuring the purchasing department, increasing importance is placed on the materials management concept. These departments frequently rely upon a number of key tools and techniques in managing the organizational purchasing function, including value analysis, life-cycle costing, just-in-time inventory, and materials requirement planning.

The next section in the book will provide a framework for use by the marketer in assessing the industrial marketplace. Such an assessment, if properly conducted, will generate the inputs necessary for designing and implementing successful marketing strategies.

QUESTIONS

1. Provide examples of a foundation good, an entering good, and a facilitating good. How might the same product fit into two, or all three, of these categories? How could this product classification scheme be useful to the industrial marketer?

2. Is the demand for major equipment likely to be more or less price-sensitive than the demand for component parts? How about compared to the demand for MRO items? Why or why not?

3. Automobiles represent a product that is sold in both consumer and industrial markets. How is the marketing mix likely to differ between selling a sedan to a middle income family and selling a fleet of fifteen cars to a company for use by its sales force?

4. What are some ways in which industrial services differ from industrial products? Separately, think of three examples of industrial services. What are some ways in which these three services differ from one another?

5. What, if any, differences would there be between selling beds to hospitals and selling them to hotels?

6. Assume you were a U.S. manufacturer of hand trucks and were considering entering the overseas market. You've found that there is immense potential for your product line in South American countries. What are some of the marketing obstacles you are likely to encounter?

7. What are some reasons that a company whose products are profitable when sold to commercial firms might find it unprofitable to sell the same products to the federal government?

8. How do the purchasing procedures and the forms used by a company (such as those illustrated in Figure 2.2) affect the vendor? Are there any possible marketing implications?

9. Evaluate this statement: The industrial firm is threatened when its customers start performing value analysis studies, and should discourage customers from instituting such programs.

10. Identify possible marketing implications of a customer adopting (a) the materials management concept, (b) a just-in-time inventory system, and (c) an electronic data interchange system (making it possible to place orders to vendors via a computer terminal).

PART **II** EXAMINING INDUSTRIAL MARKETS

Part I examined the nature and scope of industrial products and markets, and attempted to define the tasks confronting the industrial marketing manager. The diversity found within the industrial marketplace is such that there is no single formula for marketing success. Success in business today requires, more than anything else, an ability to respond quickly and effectively to market conditions. What works in any one market at a given point in time is often ineffective in other markets or in subsequent time periods. This likelihood suggests a need to continually examine and reexamine the marketplace, an undertaking which will be our focus in Part II.

Managers are frequently guilty of putting the cart before the horse when developing marketing strategies and tactics. They implement a particular program because that program appears to be creative, is similar to what they think the competition is doing, or simply takes advantage of some available resource. This kind of approach produces programs based on little more than the manager's instincts and judgment.

The most effective marketing programs, however, are based on a detailed, comprehensive assessment of the marketplace. This assessment requires quality information, analytical skill, and human insight in such areas as customer needs and behavior, market size and growth, and competitor strengths and strategies.

Part II begins with a focus on the customer. Chapters 3 and 4 examine what takes place inside organizations as they attempt to make buying decisions for industrial goods and services. Chapter 3 focuses on the problems involved in determining who actually makes the buying decision. Buying is approached as a logical process during which a number of issues must be resolved within the customer organization, and a number of different individuals become involved.

Chapter 4 delves deeper into the behavioral complexities that come into play when organizations address and resolve their needs for products and services. The most theoretical chapter in the book, it is perhaps the most challenging. Its depth of treatment reflects the single most distinctive characteristic of industrial marketing: *the customer is an organization*.

Chapter 5 deals with the problems involved when performing marketing research in organizational markets. A logical research process is presented and applied to an industrial marketing situation. Distinctions are drawn between basic marketing research, marketing intelligence, and decision support.

Building on this research foundation, Chapter 6 investigates issues and approaches involved in analyzing industrial demand. Two demand-related topics are focused upon: estimating market potentials and forecasting company sales. Techniques for accomplishing each of these are reviewed.

Chapter 7 completes Part II of the book. Addressing the role of segmentation within industrial markets, it is a transitional chapter to Part III, which focuses on marketing strategy and tactics. Segmentation represents both a means for analyzing markets, and, when combined with targeting, a strategic decision area. The chapter examines the reasons for segmenting, establishes criteria for evaluating segments, and proposes a method for effectively implementing segmentation.

CHAPTER 3

MARKETING TO THE ORGANIZATIONAL CUSTOMER

Key Concepts

Buyer rationality
Buygrid
Buying process
Buystages
Dyadic perspective
External publics
Interfunctional involvement

Internal publics
Modified rebuy purchase
New task purchase
Straight rebuy purchase
Tactics of lateral relationships
Vendor attributes
Weighted-attribute approach

Learning Objectives

1. Emphasize the need to build all marketing programs around customers and their needs.
2. Describe the technical, commercial, and behavioral complexities involved when marketing to organizations.
3. Raise questions about the apparent rationality of industrial buying decisions.
4. Explain buying as a process, and identify the major stages and activities in that process.
5. Introduce the dyadic perspective as an approach for understanding buyer behavior.

MARKETING STARTS WITH THE BUYER

One of the most serious, and yet common, mistakes made by marketing practitioners is to develop creative marketing programs consisting of innovative products, exciting promotional efforts, and expensive distribution arrangements, while demonstrating little or no knowledge of the buyer to whom the program is directed. Without a thorough understanding of who buys, why they buy, when they buy, where they buy, and how they buy, the marketer is greatly increasing the likelihood of market failure and wasted resources—and is, in effect, becoming a gambler. There are many "better mousetraps" in the proverbial junkpile of discarded visions and unrealistic dreams.

This problem is especially critical for industrial companies, where technical experts and production managers are typically quite influential in organizational decision making. Moreover, the person in charge of marketing may well be a repositioned engineer, and under such circumstances, it is important that market-related decisions reflect more than just technological capabilities and product design specifications. The people making decisions regarding product development, market segmentation, pricing, distribution channels, sales management, advertising, and sales promotion should assume the conscience of the customer.

The marketer, in the final analysis, is responsible for the provision of value to customers. Value is not a tangible or absolute phenomenon; it is perceived in the mind of the buyer. For example, AT&T could sell designer telephones to offices for much more than a standard black rotary dial telephone because the customer perceived a marked difference in the value of the two products, not because the standard phone was all that much cheaper to produce. The value transmitted to customers transcends the physical product itself. Value may be enhanced through product packaging, support services, delivery reliability, warranties, customer training, special features, and even a strong vendor reputation, among others. Further, the attributes one group of customers places high value on may be of little or no importance to another group of buyers.

All of this points to a need to begin marketing efforts with the buyer, not with the product. Tucker (1974), in fact, encourages marketers to study customers the way marine biologists study fish, rather than the way fishermen study fish. Fishermen, of course, only care about catching as many fish as possible. A preoccupation with customer needs is the essence of the marketing concept. Now, one might argue that buyers are not completely aware of their needs, and must be assisted in understanding what to buy, and why. This premise is only partially true. Certainly, a customer did not invent the personal computer, nor did marketing research lead to its invention. However, for the personal computer to become a successful innovation, the entrepreneur had to be able to match technological capabilities and production requirements with marketplace needs and abilities. Ultimately, that entrepreneur had to ensure that the product represented value to the customer, and that it could be produced, promoted, and distributed at a price commensurate with that value.

Actually, it is not unusual in industrial markets for customers to be important sources of new product ideas (Von Hippel 1982). In many instances, the customer has identified a problem with his organization's product or production process, and requests help from a salesperson who is there to sell something else. Alternatively, it is the customer who may see how, with slight modifications, the marketer's product could be used in entirely new applications, opening up new market opportunities.

SELLING TO ORGANIZATIONS

Chapter 1 emphasized that the most distinctive aspect of buyer behavior in industrial markets is that the *customer* is an *organization*. It is important for marketers to recognize that an organization is both a *social* and an *economic* entity. There is a significant social dimension to all organizations, because they are made up of individuals and groups who must work together. These individuals frequently have differing backgrounds, personalities, and motivations, and rely on a variety of approaches to problem solving. At the same time, organizations ultimately exist to provide some economic functions, i.e., to provide some good or service. Whether an organization is profit-seeking, governmental, or nonprofit, survival is dependent upon successful completion of a mission. The behavior of the individuals within the organization must directly or indirectly contribute to this mission.

When organizations purchase, both the social and economic dimensions come into play. Although the marketer is selling to organizations, the customer is actually some individual or subset of individuals. These individuals are at work, reacting to some formal measurement and reward system, and are attempting to achieve both personal and professional goals. In many cases, a purchasing decision may reflect the behavioral interactions of a number of individuals working with or through one another. As such, the decision might be characterized by conflict, compromise, and coalitions.

From an economic standpoint, the goods and services an organization purchases are likely to directly affect the day-to-day operations and economic health of the enterprise. As was discussed in the preceding chapter, industrial products are either used to make other products (foundation goods), or become part of other goods (entering goods), or are used to enable the operation of an enterprise (facilitating goods). Given this diversity and the fact that all organizations have limited resources, a bad purchasing decision can lead to interruptions or stoppages in production, reductions in product quality, slowdowns in distribution, dissatisfied end customers, and wasted resources. As a result, costs may rise, sales and net cash flow decline, and profits suffer.

Because of the potentially critical impact of buying decisions on organizational performance, purchases are often characterized by formal contractual relationships, considerable search and negotiation, a lengthy buying process, multiple sourcing, and source loyalty. These characteristics of industrial buying enable the purchaser to reduce the risk of making an incorrect decision. In fact, both the social and economic aspects of organizational life have a bearing on how the risk inherent in a purchase is dealt with, which will be discussed later in this chapter.

Perhaps the most apparent feature of selling to organizations is the smaller absolute number of customers to be reached, compared to those found in mass consumer markets. This unbalanced customer base increases the relative dependence of the industrial marketer on each customer account. For many purchases, this dependence requires the marketer to take into account the distinctive needs of each potential customer, in a promotional process that stresses personalized communication. Moreover, a smaller potential customer base suggests the need for the marketer to foster long-term relationships with customers.

TECHNICAL, COMMERCIAL, AND BEHAVIORAL COMPLEXITIES

Because both the buyer and seller in industrial marketing transactions are organizations, it should be increasingly apparent that purchase decision making represents a behavioral process that has the potential to become very complex. If there were some way to organize these complexities, a truer picture of organizational buying would begin to emerge.

Hillier (1975) has done some important work in this regard. He explains that the industrial marketer should recognize three major types of complexities facing the industrial buyer. The first of these types is the technical complexity of many of the products being purchased—a point brought out in the discussion of categories and characteristics of industrial products in Chapter 2.

Technical product characteristics have a greater impact on buying decisions, as a rule, than does any other single factor. Unfortunately, especially given this importance, these characteristics are not always easy to assess. With rapidly changing technologies, shorter product life cycles (and hence, product obsolescence), and the myriad of buying decisions an organization must make, the effort to completely understand and evaluate the technical qualities of every vendor's product(s) is an imposing task. Moreover, frequently the design of those products involves numerous trade-off decisions by the vendor regarding technical specifications. For example, some quality or precision may be sacrificed for speed of performance, or a trade-off made among product durability, flexibility, and cost. From the buyer's perspective, these trade-offs are often difficult to discern and quantify precisely. This is why value analysis (see Chapter 2) is increasingly used as a purchasing tool. The difficulties posed by the technical nature of industrial products are further affected by the source of product specifications. Products can be buyer-specified (typically by technical personnel in the buying organization) or supplier-specified. There is some evidence that the buying process may take longer to conclude, with more people involved, when specifications are set internally (e.g., Hillier 1975).

A second major dimension of industrial buying is the commercial complexity of the negotiations. These negotiations are complicated by a number of factors, among them the increase in legal precepts in negotiating purchase contracts. The contract formalizes the responsibilities of buyer and seller, and provides a fairly precise statement of what is expected of both parties. A written contract also limits the likelihood of misrepresentation or fraud on the part of buyers or sellers. Preparing such a formal and precise statement can require extensive and complex negotiations.

Problem areas include concerns over product liability and nonperformance of contractual terms. The courts are predisposed to place complete liability on the vendor for damages incurred by the customer in the use or misuse of the vendor's product. Given dramatic changes in inflation, the cost of money, transportation costs, and the availability of key resources, vendors may find themselves worse off economically if they fulfill the terms of an earlier agreed-upon contract than if they do not.

Commercial negotiations are also greatly affected by the relative power positions of the buyer and seller—power positions that determine the types and extent of concessions made by either party. Dynamic changes in the environments of organizations can significantly alter these power positions, and make it more difficult to define power relationships. For example, a sharp increase in interest rates can make a buyer more dependent on a vendor for financing, thereby enhancing that vendor's power position. Turbulent change makes it more difficult for the industrial marketer to discern which concessions are of greater importance to the buyer, and in which areas to make compromises.

Overall, then, the complexity of commercial negotiations will vary with the characteristics and complexity of the product, the dollar value and volume of the purchase, the types of services which must accompany the product, the existence of reciprocity between buyer and seller, the number of parties involved in the commercial and contractual relationships, and the characteristics of each party. The trend is toward greater complexity, leading purchasing professionals to seek specialized training in negotiation and in the legal aspects of the sales contract.

The third type of complexity found in industrial buying involves the human behaviors which eventually result in a purchase decision. The buying process may not only involve negotiation with the seller, but also engender extensive negotiation within the buying organization. Purchasing is a problem-solving activity, and the purchase decision may actually represent a number of decisions by the buyer. Such decisions concern not only what to buy, and from whom, but also how to pay for it, what technical specifications are to be met, whether to lease instead of buy, which information sources to rely upon, when to require delivery, how much inventory to maintain, and how total requirements should be divided among the vendors selected.

The way these questions are answered impacts on a number of people in the buying organization. Each of these individuals becomes a stakeholder, and is likely to work to ensure the decision outcomes which most benefit him or her. Thus, the behavioral interactions among these stakeholders become a complicating factor in industrial buying. As with any behavioral process, the more people involved, the more complex the interactions. Moreover, the greater the technical and commercial complexities, the greater the behavioral complexities.

THE INDUSTRIAL MARKETER'S LAMENT: WHO BUYS?

Consider the plight of the marketer who sends a salesperson to call on an organizational customer, perhaps a new account. The first and foremost problem for both the marketer and the salesperson is to determine where they should target their efforts in the client organization. Who makes the buying decision? Which individual (or group of individuals) is the true customer? The marketer must figure out where to concentrate company resources to support the sales effort, while the salesperson must determine whom to call upon.

Most organizations have a person or department charged with purchasing or procurement. It might seem logical, then, for the salesperson to go first to that person or department. Unfortunately, those persons formally responsible for purchasing frequently have only limited authority to make buying decisions. Because purchases impact on many aspects of organizational performance, people in different areas of the organization are affected by purchase decisions. As a result, a number of individuals tend to get involved in buying decisions.

As a case in point, recall the importance of the technical characteristics of many industrial products. The concern for precise design specifications, and for compatibility with existing equipment and capabilities, may well lead those in R & D, quality control, product development, or production to get involved in the buying decision process. In addition, the relative cost of many purchases may encourage those in financial management to monitor or influence purchase decisions. Further, when the items an organization is purchasing directly impact on the products or services it sells, marketers or salespeople in the buying organization have a stake and may get involved in the buying process. Table 3.1 provides examples of these and other functional areas to be considered in determining the identity of the industrial buyer.

The implication is that any number of specific individuals or departments might actually make a purchase decision, and a number of individuals can be expected to play a role. While the purchasing department would seem to be the most obvious participant, it may be primarily responsible only for order processing, negotiation, value analysis, sourcing, expediting, and vendor relationships. Actual buying decisions frequently are made elsewhere. At the same time, the marketer cannot afford to ignore the purchasing department. Purchasing agents may not always be authorized to select a vendor, but they often can ensure that a particular vendor *does not* get selected. The purchasing department is also an important source of information to the marketer regarding (a) the identity of key decision makers, (b) the product and vendor attributes of greatest importance to these decision makers, (c) ways in which the salesperson can get access to the decision makers, and (d) company policies and procedures that govern purchasing.

Table 3.1 Functional Areas Frequently Involved in Purchase Decisions and their Primary Concerns in Purchasing

Examples of Functional Area	Key Concerns in Purchase Decision Making
Design and Development Engineering	Name reputation of vendor; ability of vendors to meet design specifications
Production	Delivery and reliability of purchases such that interruption of production schedules is minimized
Sales/Marketing	Impact of purchased items on marketability of the company's products
Maintenance	Degree to which purchased items are compatible with existing facilities and equipment; maintenance services offered by vendor; installation arrangements offered by vendor
Finance/Accounting	Effects of purchases on cash flow, balance sheet, and income statement positions; variances in costs of materials over estimates; feasibility of make-or-buy and lease options to purchasing
Purchasing	Obtaining lowest possible price at acceptable quality levels; maintaining good relations with vendors
Quality Control	Assurance that purchased items meet prescribed specifications and tolerances, governmental regulations, and customer requirements

INTERNAL AND EXTERNAL PUBLICS

Actually, salespeople are not just looking for one key decision maker. Their job is to sell, often on an ongoing basis, to a number of individuals in the customer organization. They must become jugglers, in some instances, balancing the different needs and interests of all those people involved in some way with the purchase of their products. That is another way of saying that they serve several publics inside the customer organization.

The marketing and sales jobs are further complicated by a number of external publics—interested groups outside the buying organization that impact directly or indirectly on the purchasing process (see Figure 3.1). For example, financial institutions may regulate the inventory policies of the customer, the number of supply sources it uses, and its make-or-buy (or lease) decisions. Similarly, government agencies can affect buyer behavior through tax policies, safety and environmental regulations, and fair trade policies, among others. The capabilities of the buyer's distributors can also influence what is bought, and in what quantities. In addition, where the customer is engaged in reciprocal trading arrangements, its trading part-

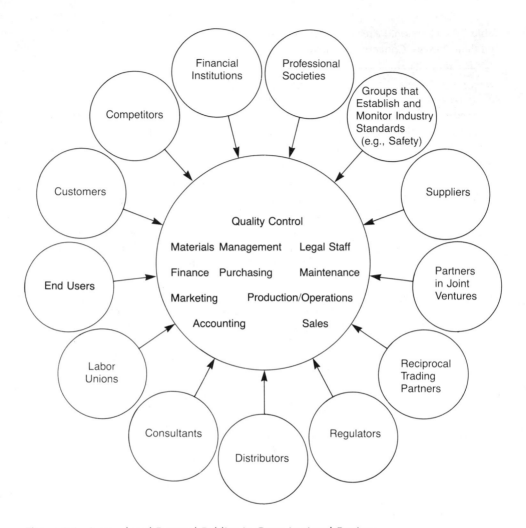

Figure 3.1   Internal and External Publics in Organizational Buying

ners can have an impact on how much of a given item is bought from each qualifying vendor. Partners in joint ventures might have a similar impact, given the mutual stake they have in good purchasing practices.

Further, in some product areas, there are formal bodies that establish standards governing technical specifications or safety requirements for purchased items (e.g., the National Electrical Manufacturers Association). A customer's buying patterns are also influenced by the purchasing practices of their competitors—especially in highly competitive industries where alertness to new product offerings can create a marketplace advantage. Additionally, some of those individuals involved in purchase decisions belong to professional societies or associations that offer guidelines for buying behavior (e.g., the National Association of Purchasing Management, or the American Institute of Electrical and Electronics Engineers).

Of course, purchasing by customers is significantly affected by their own customers. The influence of customers' customers can determine the establishment of product specifications, the selection of component parts, or even the choosing of vendors. For example, if a customer sells to the government, that customer may be required to direct some of its purchases to minority vendors.

Finally, suppliers themselves affect buying behavior. A given customer buys from a number of vendors, any one of whom can directly or indirectly affect how that customer buys a certain product. For example, if a vendor begins a value analysis or inventory management program with a customer, that customer may place demands on other vendors for similar programs.

The marketer should recognize the multiplicity of external publics confronting the organizational buyer, and attempt to discern the implications each has for the marketer's ability to establish and maintain a successful relationship with the customer. It is also important to recognize that these publics represent potential sources of valuable information. A marketer might learn a considerable amount about a customer from other (noncompeting) suppliers with whom he or she regularly interacts. In addition, other customers may provide insights regarding a particular customer account.

IS INDUSTRIAL BUYING RATIONAL?

Related to the questions of "who buys?" and "upon which of these publics should the marketer focus?" is the rationality of the buyer or group of buyers. Economists assume, in their models of marketplace behavior, perfect rationality on the part of customers; they assume that customers maximize the marginal utility gained per dollar spent on each and every purchase. This assumption is unrealistic and typically does not apply to either consumer or industrial buyer behavior.

If not perfectly rational, then how rational? One might be tempted to assume that consumers are quite frequently irrational in their purchases, or at least much less rational than industrial buyers. But is either of these conclusions accurate? First of all, consumers demonstrate a high degree of rationality in decisions regarding many types of product areas, in spite of strong social or emotional influences. Secondly, industrial buyers may, as we shall see, make decisions that are not much more rational than those made by consumers and households.

There are a number of reasons to expect greater rationality on the industrial side: the products being purchased are for use in the daily operations and functioning of the buying organization; the people doing the buying are being evaluated and rewarded based on the quality of the decisions they make; and organizational buyers are professionals. Moreover, management frequently imposes a formal structure on the buying process that might include a specific set of steps to be followed, criteria to be used in evaluating vendors, stipulations regarding the number of bids to be taken, and provisions requiring various approval signatures on the purchase requisition.

At the same time, organizational buying decisions are made by people subject to some of the same emotional and social factors that impact on them as consumers. Especially where the performances of the available products or vendors are not perceived to differ all that much, the buyer may be influenced by factors such as personal friendships with salespeople, personal dislike of certain vendors, personal favors granted by some suppliers, or the social influence of peers not involved in the transaction, but who urge that a given vendor be used or another be boycotted.

The same tactics which Strauss (see Table 3.2) found popular among purchasing agents suggest a concern on their part with personal needs and objectives that are not always directly related to, and may occasionally conflict with, organizational goals and objectives. The purchase decision maker may be tempted to favor the use of vendors or products (or decide not to purchase a product) when that action makes him or her look good, or enables him or her to achieve desired formal or informal rewards. Self-aggrandizement may come at the expense of long-term organizational welfare.

Dichter (1973), a well-known advertising and marketing consultant, calls it a common fallacy to believe that someone trying to solve a technical problem can somehow overcome ordinary emotions and act coldly and mechanistically. He explains that "although (the industrial buyer) studies specifications, prices and quality much more than the consumer, when we dig a little bit deeper, we find that he is governed by just as many emotions as the average housewife. He, too, suffers from illusions and is much more embarrassed to admit the often irrationality of his behavior." Dichter goes on to explain how, for example, engineers can be subtle, complex, sensitive, contradictory, and inconsistent, and frequently hold an exalted image of themselves and who they ought to be. He points to the engineer who has strong prejudices about the strength of aluminum when compared to steel or cast iron. Another example is the technical person who refuses to accept that a seemingly documented fact has become obsolete because of some new development. As a result, the marketer may find it effective to create an illusion of rationality, while playing on the same (sometimes subconscious) irrational and emotional factors found in consumer buying.

Moreover, up to this point the discussion has primarily focused on an individual decision maker. Because a number of people frequently become involved in the industrial buying process, it is essentially a group process, and *any* group is likely to contain some degree of potential conflict. As a case in point, consider the conflicts that typically arise among a group of students working on an industrial marketing case. In a buying context, an examination of the respective interests of the group members identified in Table 3.1 suggests a strong potential for conflict. For example, those in purchasing are concerned with cost savings, which may conflict with the design engineers' desire to establish extremely tight technical specifications, or production management's demand for rapid delivery. If, in fact, conflict is present, the rationality of organizational buying becomes dependent on the rationality of the tactics used in the conflict resolution process. As we shall see, this process has the potential to become quite political in nature.

Just as social or emotional factors can produce less than optimal purchasing behavior, so can an overly conservative orientation toward buying. Purchases that involve large sums of money, or that include critical items used in the production operations of the buying organization, represent a significant amount of risk. Those responsible for decision making may want to minimize the chance of making wrong

Table 3.2 Strauss's Tactics of Lateral Relationships

George Strauss, in a classic study of organizational behavior, interviewed a large number of purchasing agents in industrial organizations. Noting that those in purchasing frequently do not play a major role in buying decisions, he sought to determine whether or not they tried to enhance their role and, if so, the approaches they used. Not only did Strauss find concerted attempts on the part of purchasing agents to increase their influence, but also he was able to identify specific techniques which he called "tactics of lateral relationships." This label is used because such tactics were frequently directed at those in functional areas or departments at approximately the same horizontal level in the organizational hierarchy.

An excerpt from Strauss's work provides examples of the five types of gamesmanship tactics. In this scenario, the purchasing department is trying to counteract a requisition from the scheduling department for immediate delivery of some object to be purchased.

1. Rule-oriented tactics

    a. Appeal to some common authority to direct that this requisition be revised or withdrawn.
    b. Refer to some rule (assuming one exists) that provides for longer lead times.
    c. Require the scheduling department to state in writing why quick delivery is required.
    d. Require the requisitioning department to consent to having its budget charged with the extra costs (such as air freight) required to get quick delivery.

2. Rule-evading tactics

    a. Go through the motions of complying with the request, but with no expectation of getting delivery on time.
    b. Exceed formal authority and ignore the requisition altogether

3. Personal-political tactics

    a. Rely on friendships to induce the scheduling department to modify the requisition.
    b. Rely on favors, past and future, to accomplish the same result.
    c. Work through political allies in other departments.

4. Educational tactics

    a. Use direct persuasion, that is, try to persuade the scheduling department that its requisition is unreasonable.
    b. Use what might be called indirect persuasion to help the scheduling department see the problem from the purchasing department's point of view (ask the scheduler to sit in and observe the difficulty in getting the vendor to agree to quick delivery).

5. Organizational-interactional tactics

    a. Seek to change the interaction pattern; for example, have the scheduling department check with the purchasing department as to the possibility of getting quick delivery before it makes a requisition.
    b. Seek to take over other responsibilities; for example, to subordinate scheduling to purchasing in an integrated materials department.

Source: Excerpt from G. Strauss, "Tactics of Lateral Relationships: The Purchasing Agent," *Administrative Science Quarterly*, 7, (September 1962), 166. Reprinted with permission.

decisions, and thus take a more conservative approach to selecting new products and services. For example, when confronted with an excellent new product at an attractive price, but from a relatively unknown supplier, there may be a tendency to retain the status quo; i.e., existing vendors and familiar products.

It is impossible to resolve conclusively the question, "is industrial buying rational?" or even "is industrial buying more rational than consumer buying?" The formal and informal constraints placed on the buying process by the organization would seem to impose a kind of rationality not always found in consumer buying. However, it is a rationality defined by the behavior of individual employees, and subject to their own perceived self-interest.

The issue of rationality can be restated as a concern with the *quality* of purchase decision making. It is a subject which warrants further attention—specifically, what are the explanatory factors that underlie making a *good* rather than a *mediocre* buying decision? To address this issue, buying is first approached as a logical process, and then analyzed (in Chapter 4) for its behavioral dimensions.

BUYING AS A PROCESS: THE BUYSTAGES

One of the most simple, yet far-reaching, insights into buying behavior is that it is actually a *process*—much more than the physical act of exchanging goods or services for an agreement to pay for them. There is a logical sequence of stages which collectively result in product and vendor choices. And, a number of purchasing-related decisions have to be made in each stage (see Table 3.3 for examples). These stages take place over time, frequently over months or years.

Approaches to defining buying processes generally include five generic steps. First, a need is recognized. Second, information is sought out. Third, products are evaluated. Fourth, a purchase decision is made. Fifth, there is some kind of postpurchase evaluation. This general framework applies to both consumer and industrial buying.

Robinson, Faris, and Wind (1967) have taken these generic steps and tailored them to the industrial buying process, by developing a set of eight sequential steps called *buystages*. These include the following:

Stage 1. Anticipation or recognition of a problem (need) and a general solution

Stage 2. Determination of characteristics and quantity of needed item

Stage 3. Description of characteristics and quantity of needed item

Stage 4. Search for and qualification of potential sources

Stage 5. Acquisition and analysis of proposals

Stage 6. Evaluation of proposals and selection of supplier(s)

Stage 7. Selection of an order routine

Stage 8. Performance feedback and evaluation

In the first buystage, someone in the buying organization becomes aware of a need that is currently not being met in a satisfactory manner, if at all. This recognition of a need or problem can originate in any number of places. A sampling of points of initiation for industrial purchase decisions follows: a computerized inventory monitoring system automatically delivers a signal that it is time to reorder;

Table 3.3   Twenty Potential Decisions Facing the Industrial Buyer

---

1. Is the need or problem pressing enough that it must be acted upon now? If not, how long can action be deferred?
2. What types of products or services could conceivably be used to solve our need or problem?
3. Should we make the item ourselves?
4. Must a new product be designed, or has a vendor already developed an acceptable product?
5. Should a value analysis be performed?
6. What is the highest price we can afford to pay?
7. What trade-offs are we prepared to make between price and other product/vendor attributes?
8. Which information sources will we rely upon?
9. How many vendors should be considered?
10. Which attributes will be stressed in evaluating vendors?
11. Should bids be solicited?
12. Should the item be leased or purchased outright?
13. How far can a given vendor be pushed in negotiations? On what issues will that vendor bend the most?
14. How much inventory should a vendor be willing to keep on hand?
15. Should we split our order among several vendors?
16. Is a long-term contract in our interest?
17. What contractual guarantees will we require?
18. How shall we establish our order routine?
19. After the purchase, how will vendor performance be evaluated?
20. How will we deal with inadequate product or vendor performance?

---

production personnel recognize that plant machines are producing an inordinate number of defective items; R&D engineers encounter the need for a customized solution to a technical problem in developing some new product; the purchasing department determines that a particular vendor is becoming less dependable or will soon be bought out by a competitor; the sales department receives a number of customer complaints regarding some component part in the company's product; or management anticipates new government regulations which will limit the organization's ability to use certain materials.

The person who begins the buying process by identifying a need is not necessarily the one who ultimately decides what, if anything, will be purchased to satisfy that need. Nonetheless, the marketer should recognize where and why the buying process was initiated. Among other things, this knowledge will provide a more complete understanding of the context within which the customer need exists.

Further, the industrial marketer can act as the initiator by helping the customer recognize a need. Industrial marketing frequently is characterized more by marketers seeking out customers than by customers seeking out vendors. The marketer can create a demand for some products by emphasizing the generic need of any buyer for cost savings, more dependable sources of supply, or higher quality. The perception of a need can be created by raising doubts in the buyer's mind whether or not he or she is paying too much for existing products, staying current with the opportunities presented by the latest technologies, or keeping abreast of the innovations being adopted by competitors.

The second and third buystages are closely related. In the second, members of the buying organization identify potential solutions to the needs recognized in the first buystage. Thus, they establish the types of products or services which conceivably could resolve the perceived problem. They may look internally or externally for solutions, and frequently rely on alternatives which historically have been successful. Where the problem is novel, of course, the only reference point may be a competitor's experiences.

The marketer can play a key role in this stage by inducing buyers to see solutions that otherwise might not be considered. That is, the marketer can help broaden buyers' fields of vision and suggest creative approaches to problem solving.

Once a general solution has been established, the organization translates its needs into a more precise statement of the specific characteristics and quantity required of some product or service. Through this process of formally describing product characteristics, needs can be better communicated to others in the organization, as well as to potential vendors. At this stage, product specifications are established—specifications that can range from a statement of the minimum cleaning power required of an industrial detergent, or the copy quality and run-length capability of a copier, to detailed blueprints describing some key component, or exact temperature tolerances for a machine tool.

The decisions made in the second and third buystages can prejudice what happens throughout the remaining stages of the process. Product requirements or specifications can be, and frequently are, written so that only one or two particular vendors can readily satisfy them. That is, the description of needs is tailored to products which well-known and favored vendors are currently offering or easily could be offering. This preclusion creates problems for the marketer whose products would readily fulfill the buyer's needs, but do not meet the precise specifications.

The message for the marketer, to this point, is that the marketing effort must begin early in the buying process. The marketer, in some instances, can not only help the buyer recognize a need, but he or she can also work to ensure that required product characteristics and specifications are written to include, if not favor, his or her company's product(s).

Because the establishment of requirements can be instrumental in determining what is eventually purchased and from whom, a number of stakeholders within the buying organization get involved at this stage in the process. The marketer is well-advised to identify these stakeholders, their respective positions, and their objectives. In some cases, for example, tolerances are set more conservatively than necessary, primarily as a risk-avoidance strategy. The intelligent salesperson may be able to counter such a strategy by directly communicating with those who are influential during this stage.

Once the buying organization has a firm idea of what it wants, a source of supply must be located. Thus, the organization is actually making two key decisions: (a) to buy a product, and (b) to buy from a particular vendor. Unaware marketers could conceivably be in the ironic position of having convinced a buyer to purchase a product, only to have that customer select some other source of supply.

The fourth buystage involves searching for, and qualifying, acceptable vendors. Using obtainable information sources, the buyer may first identify the universe of available suppliers, and then reduce this number to some subset of vendors who can viably meet the established quality and quantity requirements. The purchasing department will often maintain a cross-referenced index of vendors, orders, prices, and contracts. Sales calls, word-of-mouth, catalogs, industrial directories, trade shows, trade journal advertising, and other key sources also will be relied upon for information. The first problem for marketers is to ensure that the buying organization is aware that their firm has a product offering in the area under consideration. Then, they must ensure that their firm satisfies the vendor evaluation criteria used by the buyer.

The vendor evaluation process typically will be directed at quality and dependability. A supplier who has an excellent product, but an unstable labor force, or unreliable delivery capabilities, or is inflexible in adapting to the buyer's needs, or constantly tries to hard-sell or over-sell the buyer, may be more trouble than the buyer cares to tolerate. The critical nature of many industrial purchases suggests that the relationship between buyer and seller is akin to a marriage. As a result, the buyer will evaluate a vendor's production facilities, quality assurance program, financial health, service and delivery record, and even the quality of its management.

In the fifth buystage, after the field of suppliers is narrowed to an acceptable group of qualifying vendors, the buying organization acquires and evaluates specific proposals. A proposal can take the form of a formal bid, a price quote from a salesperson, or a listing of sales terms in a catalog. It is in this fifth stage that the process of negotiation with vendors over price, inventory levels, contract dates, delivery requirements, warranties, trade-in policies, and so forth, receives the sharpest focus. However, for many routine purchases, or those with which the organization has past experience, buystages four and five are indistinguishable. That is, they actually occur simultaneously, and become a single stage. For these types of purchases, the information needs of the buyer are relatively low.

The buyer may still be negotiating with selected suppliers, or requesting new bids, as he evaluates proposals and makes final supplier choices (buystage six). The actual selection of the source, or more typically, sources of supply may also involve considerable negotiation within the buying organization among stakeholders with conflicting interests. The individuals involved in the decision often place different importance weights on various supplier attributes, and have differing perceptions of how well each vendor can perform on a given attribute.

The buying organization may attempt to quantify the selection process, and rely upon formal rules for making a choice. For example, decision makers may evaluate each vendor on a set of agreed-upon attributes, and then opt to select those that exceed the minimum required standards on all attributes. Or, they may choose the vendors whose performance is best on the most attributes. A number of such decision rules are possible.

A more comprehensive approach is illustrated in Table 3.4, where each vendor is evaluated on each attribute, using a rating scale. For the sake of example, a 100 percentage point scale is used to evaluate vendor X, where .00 equals very poor

Table 3.4 A Weighted-Attribute Approach to Evaluating a Vendor

Attribute	(A) Vendor Performance Evaluation	(B) Weight (Importance Rating)	Vendor Rating (A × B)
Delivery	.4	.25	.10
Product quality	.8	.30	.24
Price	.4	.15	.06
Flexibility	.2	.10	.02
Service capability	.6	.20	.12
		1.00	.54

performance, .50 equals medium performance, and 1.00 equals outstanding performance. The results are in column A. Then, the importance of each attribute is established, this time by dividing 100 percentage points across the attributes. A higher percentage is given to the most important attributes (e.g., .00, of no importance, .50, moderately important, and 1.00, extremely important). These totals are put in column B, which must add up to 100 percent. Next, the evaluation scores for each attribute (column A) are taken times the importance weights (column B), and the products are summed. The result is a score for vendor X. The process is repeated for other vendors, and those receiving the highest scores receive the organization's business.

Having decided on what to buy and from whom to buy it, the buyer then resolves how much is to be bought from each vendor and how frequently orders will be placed and should be filled. The levels of inventory to be kept are agreed upon. In addition, the parties agree on the procedures for placing orders, taking delivery, making returns, and monitoring and expediting the process. This is buy-stage seven, and it is principally concerned with working out the mechanics of the exchange. Although the relationship with a vendor usually lasts beyond the initial purchase, especially given how involved the choice process can be, loyalty is not automatic. Buystage eight involves the generation of feedback and the ongoing evaluation of each supplier. This evaluation can be formal in nature, such as the method presented in buystage 6, especially with first-time purchases and untried vendors. Poor performance by a supplier or a product is not likely to go unnoticed, as it will probably affect the job performance of someone in the buying organization. Most often this will be the product user. In addition, individuals involved with the buying decision, who held reservations concerning a vendor selected by the organization, are especially attuned to negative feedback regarding that vendor. When such feedback is not properly channeled, it may lead to frustration and harbored feelings of resentment regarding a vendor. These negative attitudes may surface much later, in the context of a completely different purchase decision.

The point for the marketer is that marketing does not end with the sale; the crucial importance of ongoing relationships with customers suggests that the marketing effort is really never over. The marketer not only must continue to promote the advantages of a product to key stakeholders in the customer organization, but also must monitor the feedback and evaluation process. Measurement by the marketer of user satisfaction levels and complaints is invaluable for ongoing success. Problems can be corrected before too much damage is done. In fact, quick response to customer problems can lead to even stronger buyer-seller ties; it also can provide an opportunity to identify new or changing customer needs.

This discussion is not meant to suggest that the process is the same for all products. Actually, with different products, the length of each stage will vary, and some stages will be omitted. For example, in repurchasing floor wax or typewriter ribbons, the organization may simply be loyal to its current supplier, automatically reordering without reevaluating needs or acquiring proposals from vendors. In a study of the purchase of intensive-care monitoring equipment by hospitals, Laczniak (1979) was able to find only four clearly identifiable stages: (a) the identification of needs, (b) the establishment of purchase objectives, (c) the identification and evaluation of buying alternatives, and (d) final deliberations and selection of supplier.

Also, some of the stages in the process may take place simultaneously, rather than sequentially. The organization may be involved in describing the characteristics of the needed item (buystage three) at the same time that it searches for vendors (buystage four). In addition, the process can be iterative, where the results of later stages lead the organization to return to and modify earlier-stage decisions. In acquiring proposals (buystage five), for example, the buyer may find that the capabilities and requirements of vendors make it necessary that specifications be rewritten (buystage three) or that the organization's needs have changed (buystage two). Or, the entire process can be terminated at any one of the stages.

To better understand the nature of the buying process for industrial products, and the potential marketing implications, it is worth considering different types of buying situations, or scenarios.

BUYING SCENARIOS

The actual stages involved in the buying process, and the kinds of activities that take place in each stage, vary with the type of product or service being purchased. More specifically, the stages depend upon the characteristics of the buying problem facing the organization. For example, the purchasing process might differ, based on the amount of money being spent, or on the perceived riskiness of the decision.

Diagnosis of the industrial buying process might be aided by identifying some of the more common types of buying situations. The problem is to determine the significant characteristics or criteria which differentiate various types of buying situations. One popular approach is to classify buying scenarios based on: (a) the newness of problems and amount of relevant past experience, (b) the amount and type of information needed by those who influence the buying decision, and (c) the number of alternatives given consideration (Robinson, Faris, and Wind 1967). Three types of buying situations, or buy classes, can be identified: straight rebuy, modified rebuy, and new task purchases.

A *straight rebuy* situation is one in which the organization has purchased an item in the past, and probably will simply reorder it from the source(s) of supply currently being used. This is a routine decision involving low levels of perceived risk, and low information needs. Decision choice criteria have previously been established and evaluated. Given this, few people tend to get involved in these decisions. Little or no search and evaluation effort takes place on the part of the buyer, generally because it was performed on some previous occasion.

The *modified rebuy* scenario tales place when the organization has some past experience purchasing the item in question, but some aspect of the buying task has changed. For example, the technical people in the buying organization may have slightly modified the required product specifications, the marketing department may be asking for some new product feature not included on the original purchased item, the purchasing department may be under pressure to find better prices, and production personnel are asking for improved service and better delivery. As a result, some new search effort for information could become necessary. Suppliers are reappraised, and some new ones could be considered. Based on past experience, the decision criteria for selecting products and vendors may also have been changed.

With a *new task purchase,* the organization is buying the item for the first time. Generally, the need to buy is initiated by the occurrence of some problem or need not previously encountered within the organization, or by a management decision to deal with a recurring problem in a markedly different way. Hence, the organization may have decided to purchase its first computer, or to hire a firm to steam-clean machines that were previously manually cleaned by company employees. Because of the relative lack of previous experience with the product area, the information needs of the organization are considerable. The vendor identification, evaluation, and selection process is more involved here than in the other buying scenarios. New task decisions, which contain more risk, are likely to take longer and involve more people.

THE BUYGRID

Combining the stages of the buying process with the types or classes of buying situations produces a matrix or grid, as shown in Table 3.5. This *buygrid* has important strategic implications for marketing.

As the buying process evolves, a number of decisions are being made (see Table 3.3), and the number of viable options open to the buying organization is effectively being reduced. In other words, the combined effect of the formal (and informal) decisions made during the buying process is to eliminate some vendors, and create a growing commitment toward others. The vendor who gets involved too late in the buying process may never really have a chance, especially in the new task situation. Alternatively, with a straight rebuy, many of the decisions have been made in the past, and are, in effect, automatically renewed.

For items purchased on a repeat basis, the goal of the marketer should be to create a straight rebuy situation where her company is the specified vendor. Once this is achieved, the marketer's focus will be on the latter stages in the buying process. Because buyers in this situation know what they want and are not typically seeking new information or proposals, the marketer concentrates on the negotiation,

Table 3.5   Buygrid Framework for Industrial Buying Situations

Buystages	Buyclasses		
	New	Modified	Straight
1. Anticipation or recognition of a problem (need) and a general solution			
2. Determination of characteristics and quantity of needed item			
3. Description of characteristics and quantity of needed item			
4. Search for and qualification of potential sources			
5. Acquisition and analysis of proposals			
6. Evaluation of proposals and selection of supplier(s)			
7. Selection of an order routine			
8. Performance feedback and evaluation			

Source: Patrick J. Robinson, Charles W. Faris, and Yoram Wind, *Industrial Buying and Creative Marketing.* Copyright © 1967 by Allyn and Bacon, Inc. Reprinted with permission.

order routine, and evaluation stages. On the other hand, where a straight rebuy exists, but the marketer is currently not the vendor (an out-supplier), the goal is to identify potential areas of buyer dissatisfaction, possibly creating dissonance. In this manner, the marleter is attempting to change the buying situation into a modified rebuy.

Because of the concern by marketers with the identity of the key decision maker(s) in the buying organization, the buygrid framework is helpful for understanding the number and types of individuals involved at various points in the buying decisions. For example, more people should be involved in the early stages of the process, especially for a new task purchase. Similarly, engineers and production/operations managers might play the major role in the early stages of the new task and modified rebuy scenarios, while the purchasing department may be less a factor. Giunipero (1984), for example, found that purchasing personnel exerted less influence in the early stages of purchases involving more technical products with which the organization had little past experience. Conversely, the purchasing department may be of key importance throughout the stages of a straight rebuy decision. Others have found, more generally, a dominant role by engineers in product selection, and by purchasing agents in vendor selection (Cooley, Jackson, and Ostrom 1977).

The manner in which purchasing decisions are made will vary as changes occur in the number of people involved, and in the functional areas having the strongest influence. Different product and vendor attributes will be stressed, the amount of conflict will vary, and the ways in which trade-off decisions are made will change, depending on the stage and class in the buygrid.

The marketer, in turn, must tailor the product, price, distribution, and promotional programs to the requirements of the different cells in the buygrid. As a result, the relative emphasis on price versus delivery reliability, on trade journal advertising versus direct mail, or on an in-house sales force versus manufacturer's representatives, will depend on who is involved in the purchasing process. This can be expected to change with the stage and class in the buygrid. For example, the use of middlemen, such as industrial distributors, may be less effective in the early stages of a new task purchase than in a straight rebuy scenario. The marketing message in a modified rebuy situation may focus more on comparisons of product and company performance relative to that of the competition. Personal selling can become more important than other forms of communication as the buyer moves closer to making an actual purchase decision for both new task and modified rebuy purchases. Direct mail might be quite effective in reinforcing buyers during the evaluation stage of a straight rebuy decision. Such suggestions are only hypothetical, and care is essential in generalizing across products and customer organizations of all types (Bellizi and McVey 1983). Nonetheless, the buygrid remains an important foundation around which marketers can begin to organize their efforts.

PURCHASING AS MUTUAL PROBLEM SOLVING

The buygrid framework is a very rational, task-oriented approach to understanding industrial buying. The task of buying goods and services is undertaken to resolve some organizational problem. In other words, the buying task is problem-solving behavior. From the buyer's perspective, a product or service consists of a set of benefits or attributes. The industrial customer does not buy a product per se, but purchases those benefits the product is capable of delivering. Although it may seem a matter of semantics, this distinction is very important. When a transportation company buys trucks, then, it is actually buying hauling capacity, durability, weight, or fuel efficiency. Similarly, the demand for quarter-inch drill bits is, in reality, a demand for quarter-inch holes (Levitt 1983). Depending on the type of problem(s) facing the organization, different attributes are sought (Lehman and O'Shaughnessy 1982).

The importance of product and vendor attributes has been stressed throughout this chapter. However, the actual attributes upon which industrial buyers base their decisions may not be apparent. These attributes tend to be much more functional than those which are emphasized in consumer buying. Some of the key product-related attributes include technical specifications, performance reliability, newness of technology, supply availability, ease of installation, training time required, ease of operation or use, maintenance requirements, compatibility with existing equipment, and necessary support services. Important vendor attributes include reputation, delivery reliability, financing terms, price structure, technical service offered, inventory policies, training provided, confidence in salespeople, and flexibility in adapting to buyer needs, among others (see also Table 3.6).

Table 3.6 Vendor-Related Attributes Used in Evaluating Potential
Sources of Supply.

I. Convenience-Related Attributes

1. Advises of potential trouble
2. Can deliver quickly
3. Delivers without constant followup
4. Answers all communications promptly
5. Handles rejections promptly and efficiently
6. Adapts to specific needs
7. Accepts small order quantities
8. Offers broad product line
9. Is located in close proximity
10. Anticipates our requirements
11. Allows credit for scrap or salvage
12. Is direct source of supply

II. Economic-Financial Attributes

1. Has competitive prices
2. Sells at a lower price
3. Guarantees price protection
4. Offers volume discounts
5. Offers higher cash discounts
6. Has favorable financial position
7. Offers extended payment terms

III. Caliber-Capability Attributes

1. Regularly meets quality specifications
2. Has knowledgeable salespeople
3. Maintains up-to-date stock
4. Has technical ability and knowledge
5. Has good packaging, including packing slips
6. Has high caliber management
7. Has potential to expand capacity
8. Has research and development facilities

IV. Image-Dependabilty Attributes

1. Reliable in quality
2. Reliable in delivery
3. Is fair and honest in dealings
4. Keeps promises
5. Has favorable attitude
6. Has favorable reputation
7. Is a progressive firm

8. Offers well-known brands and/or products
9. Exhibits desire for business
10. Maintains favorable labor-management relations
11. Utilizes effective selling methods
12. Is a well-known firm
13. Is a large firm

V. Intercorporate Relations Attributes

1. Source has been used before
2. Is known to our firm
3. Is a current supplier
4. Is recommended by our other departments
5. Is accepted by our other departments
6. Is a customer of ours
7. Is affiliated with our firm

VI. Service-Related Attributes

1. Helps in emergency situations
2. Provides needed information
3. Willing to cooperate in the face of unforeseen difficulties
4. Makes salespeople available as needed
5. Offers frequent delivery service
6. Helpful in overcoming our occasional errors
7. Maintains technical service in the field
8. Supplies parts lists and operating manuals
9. Offers better warranties
10. Makes available test or demonstration models
11. Maintains consignment stocks at vendor plant
12. Maintains repair service
13. Invoices correctly
14. Supplies special reports
15. Maintains frequent sales calls
16. Provides information through advertising
17. Helpful in providing special handling equipment
18. Provides information through promotional activities

Source: Reprinted by permission of the publisher from "Vendor Attribute Evaluations of Buying Center Members Other than Purchasing Executives," by G.E. Kiser, C.P. Rao, and S.R.G. Rao, *Industrial Marketing Management,* 4, 45–54. Copyright 1975 by Elsevier Science Publishing Co., Inc.

Where the product in question is standardized, with little product differentiation among competitors, the buyer can be expected to place more emphasis on economic or cost-related attributes (sales price, discounts, delivery and installation expenses, usage costs) and vendor-related attributes. A company buying wood pulp or polypropylene might be expected to weigh price and vendor relations much more heavily than it would when buying a sophisticated microprocessor to run its assembly line. In the case of complex or highly differentiated products, products incorporating sophisticated technologies, or products being applied to a problem for the first time, performance attributes become paramount.

The perceptions of those in the buying organization regarding their own problems and vendor attributes are critical factors in determining the direction the buying process will take. The marketer can find it useful to adopt the role of a problem solver, trying to match the customer's problems to a set of product and vendor attributes.

Both parties to the marketing exchange relationship are seeking certain attributes. The seller is trying to satisfy specific objectives through the buyer, while the buyer is doing the same with regard to the seller. Only if each party is satisfied with the performance of the other on the attributes of greatest concern will a long-term relationship ensue. Long-term relationships are vital in many industrial product areas, especially where the absolute number of users is comparatively small or market growth is slow. With time, exchange becomes routine and the expectations of the buyer and seller toward one another become quite clear. This is not the case, however, at the outset of the relationship.

The parties to a marketing exchange are not just exchanging products or services for money; they also are exchanging information about one another and their respective requirements. Moreover, human interaction between buyer and seller represents a type of social exchange through which mutual trust is established (Hakansson 1982).

The two-way nature of the industrial marketing relationship can be appreciated by considering the perspectives of two of the frontline players in this process: the salesperson and the purchasing agent. Webster (1984) calls both of these boundary role functions, in that each operates at the boundary between its own organization and the external environment (in this case, other organizations). Table 3.7 summarizes research in which salespeople and buyers have evaluated one another. It is interesting to note that each is concerned with the professionalism, cooperativeness, and human relations skills of the other. Each wants the other to be well-acquainted with her own product lines, and each is concerned that the other has sufficient authority and influence within the respective organizations.

THE DYADIC APPROACH

The traditional approach to marketing is to examine the customer as an object responding to a set of stimuli controlled by the marketer. This exchange relationship is approached as a one-way or unidirectional flow from seller to buyer. This concept is hardly descriptive of reality—especially with industrial transactions. Here, the focus should be on the buyer-seller dyad. A dyad is a unit consisting of two members,

Table 3.7 Salespeople and Purchasing Professionals Look at One
Another

Salespeople Evaluate Buyers	Buyers Evaluate Salespeople
TRAITS OF A GOOD BUYER:	TRAITS OF A GOOD SALESPERSON
a. Does not act aloof toward seller or products	a. Offers thorough presentation and good follow through
b. Does not try to get a lower price to use as leverage against current supplier	b. Has a good working knowledge of his or her product line
c. Assists in contacting appropriate people in his or her firm when he or she lacks knowledge or authority; explains buying process in his or her firm	c. Is willing to go to bat for the buyer within the supplier firm
d. Allows adequate time for sales presentation	d. Shows knowledge of the market and willingness to keep the buyer informed
e. Has a working knowledge of his or her company's products	e. Has a good working knowledge of the buyer's product line
f. Maintains good credit standing and pays invoices promptly	f. Uses imagination in applying his or her products to the buyer's needs
g. Has good relations with his or her company's top management	g. Uses diplomacy in dealing with operating departments
h. Follows ethical sales purchasing practices	h. Prepares for sales calls

Source: A.J. Dubinsky and T.N. Ingram, "Salespeople View Buyer Behavior," *Journal of Purchasing and Materials Management,* (Fall 1982), 6–11.

Source: S. Dowst, "Supersellers Get Green Light to Go Extra Mile," *Purchasing,* (August 1983). 39–50.

or, in this case, two organizations. Each member affects and is affected by the other, and a complete appreciation for what is taking place requires that both be considered.

To better understand the dyad which exists between an industrial marketer and an organizational buyer, it is helpful to examine the major components or variables operating within any dyadic relationship. There are four sets of variables which determine the workings and results of any buyer-seller dyad: relational variables, social structural variables, social actor variables, and normative variables (Bonoma, Bagozzi, and Zaltman 1978).

Relational variables are concerned with the power/dependence relationship between buying and selling organizations. Both parties need each other, or are dependent upon one another. The question concerns who needs whom the most. In times of critical shortages of a key raw material or component part, the buyer may be more dependent; when demand is down and the economy is recessionary, the seller may be more dependent. Examining the relative power positions can suggest insights into the negotiating tactics and flexibility of each party.

Social structural variables focus upon the positions, in their respective organizations, of the actors involved in the industrial transaction. For example, a newly hired and inexperienced salesperson calling on a vice-president for purchasing represents a buying situation in which a sizable social structural gap exists between the parties. Similarly, a salesperson with little or no technical background who calls on an R&D engineer will encounter a similar social structural gap. There can be both horizontal or vertical differentiation of the social positions of the actors in the dyad. This is one reason that salespeople are sometimes given titles such as "senior account executive."

Social actor variables relate to the traits of the individuals themselves—age, sex, educational background, charisma, expertise, personality, communication style, and other characteristics. Some companies attempt to hire salespeople with characteristics that are similar to those of their customers. Others might work on the theory that opposites attract, and hire salespeople with distinctive traits that make them more interesting to individuals making buying decisions.

Finally, *normative variables* include the rules of the game, the norms, the accepted practices, and the role expectations of those involved in the buyer-seller dyad. Representatives of both the buyer and seller organizations typically will have specific expectations concerning how the other party is expected to behave throughout the buying process. Unofficial rules exist that are understood by each party. For example, purchasing agents may feel it is highly inappropriate to attempt to play vendors off on one another in price negotiations. Thus, they may expect the vendors to offer their best feasible price—not cut their bid only after finding what the competition is charging. There may also be norms for conducting negotiations, deciding when price is to be mentioned, setting protocol to follow in calling on various individuals in the buyer (or seller) organization, determining how frequently to call on an account, and so forth.

All of these variables in the dyad combine to determine the results of marketing exchange. The implication is that every dyadic relationship is likely to have its own distinct nature. Importantly, in industrial markets, dyadic relationships evolve and become more personal over time. That is, they move beyond the formal discussions regarding task-related product and vendor performance criteria, to informal social interaction and personal friendships. In the process, long-term buyer-seller arrangements are established.

SUMMARY

The marketer faces a distinct challenge when selling to organizations, because industrial customers frequently have complex needs and a relatively complex buying decision process. The marketer must not only determine what to sell, and how it can best be sold, but also must determine to whom it should be sold within the customer organization.

Any number of individuals, representing a variety of functions in the firm, can get involved in organizational buying decisions. These individuals are motivated by needs and goals that are both personal and organizational. And, since some degree of conflict may exist among these needs and goals, industrial buying decisions have a social or behavioral dimension, and can be less than perfectly rational.

The industrial purchasing process evolves through a series of stages that begins with the recognition of a need, and ends with a postpurchase evaluation process that impacts on subsequent buying decisions. Along the way, a number of key decisions are made regarding product and vendor choices. The nature of this process will vary, depending on the type of product or service being purchased, and on the buyer's past experiences in this product or service area.

The effectiveness of various marketing approaches is dependent upon the stage of the buying process and the type of product in question. The marketer is a problem solver, tailoring product and vendor attribute bundles to the perceived requirements of organizational customers. Marketing efforts should begin early in the buying process, and endure well beyond the close of the sale. In fact, the job of the marketer continues as long as a customer relationship is desired. This relationship, by definition not a one-way street, is a two-way dyadic interaction process that develops over time.

QUESTIONS

1. Industrial customers are often good sources of new product and service ideas. Why is this the case? What are some ways in which the marketer can systematically tap customer ideas for new products and services?

2. "Customer perceptions are all that matters. What they perceive is the only reality that counts." What does this statement mean? Do you agree or disagree?

3. Pick an industrial product and identify examples of technical, commercial, and behavioral complexities that are likely to come into play when marketing that product.

4. Assume you are selling valves for use in heating, ventilating, and air conditioning (hvac) systems. Your primary market consists of older buildings in which your valves could be installed (retrofitted) into the existing hvac system. If you are thinking about focusing your efforts on public school systems, how will you go about determining the key decision maker?

5. Cite five reasons why you might expect industrial buying to be more rational than consumer buying. What are some reasons industrial buying might not be all that rational?

6. Let's say you were the marketer of a new industrial product that was clearly superior in quality to the products of all the existing competitors, and was priced slightly under their prices. Further, you offered better delivery terms, a better warranty, and could produce as many units as a customer desired. Why might a company never buy your product? Assume that they have a need for the product, and currently purchase from one of your competitors.

7. How are the stages of the buying process likely to differ when selecting an advertising agency for the first time, compared to rehiring or replacing the advertising agency a company has been using for three years? Which stage is likely to last the longest in each of these two buying situations?

8. If you were developing a model, based on the eight buystages, of the way a customer or group of customers purchases your product, what specific questions would you attempt to answer about each stage?

9. What are the limitations of the weighted attribute model from the buyer's perspective? What are the implications of this model for the development of industrial marketing strategy?

10. The dyadic perspective is based on the assumption that industrial transactions represent a two-way process, and that both parties seek attributes and both impact on one another. What does this mean? Provide some specific examples of ways in which the vendor affects the customer, and ways in which the customer affects the vendor.

CHAPTER 4

CONCEPTS AND MODELS OF ORGANIZATIONAL BUYING BEHAVIOR

Key Concepts

Bases of power

Buying center/decision-making unit

Buying center roles

Coalition formation

Conflict resolution

Decentralized buying

Lateral involvement

Measurement/reward systems

Models of buyer behavior

Nontask factors

Source loyalty

Task factors

Types of buying risk

Vertical involvement

Learning Objectives

1. Provide deeper insights into the complexities of organizational buying behavior.
2. Introduce the buying center as a concept for explaining the group nature of industrial buying decisions.
3. Develop a number of different perspectives for understanding behavior within the buying center.
4. Describe simplified versions of the Webster-Wind and Sheth general models of organizational buying behavior.
5. Discuss source loyalty as one of the most important outcomes of buying decisions, and identify various types of loyalties.

*Organizational buying is a negotiated social process
whereby people interact, explore their thoughts and
feelings, exchange information, and perhaps evolve to
new or novel positions and relationships.*

T. Bonoma, R. Bagozzi, and G. Zaltman

Chapter 3 discussed the distinct challenges encountered when marketing to an organizational customer. Buying was approached as a fairly rational and logical process, but one that is compounded by a number of complexities. The focus was on the many dimensions of the buying task, and ways in which the marketer could benefit from an understanding of the problems facing the buyer in completing that task.

This chapter will pursue the complexities which characterize the buying decision process within the customer organization, presenting a number of different perspectives. Buying behavior can be defined as:

> "the decision-making process by which formal organizations establish the need for purchased products and services, and identify, evaluate, and choose among alternative brands and suppliers. 'Decision making' is used here to include information-acquisition and -processing activities, as well as choice processes and the development of goals and other criteria to be used in choosing among alternatives" (Webster and Wind 1972)".

The chapter will introduce key concepts, tools, and models which are helpful in making sense of this process. The major variables which explain who is involved in the buying process, how and when decisions are made, why individuals behave in certain ways, and which alternatives are pursued, among others, are evaluated.

THE BUYING CENTER

One approach to understanding buying in organizations is to view the decision process as involving a set of roles, rather than simply a set of individuals or departments. Webster (1984), for instance, explains that buying activities within the customer organization can be understood as a form of role-playing, as can interaction between buyers and sellers.

The *buying center* is a valuable tool developed by those who study industrial buying and selling (Robinson, Faris, and Wind 1967; Webster and Wind 1972; Wind 1978; Bonoma 1982). It is defined as all the individuals and groups participating in the buying decision process who have interdependent goals and share common risks. The buying center concept assigns these individuals to six primary roles that collectively enable the organization to accomplish the buying task. (Note: the buying center is sometimes referred to as the buying group or the decision-making unit [DMU]).

The six roles are: initiator, buyer, user, influencer, decider, and gatekeeper. They are defined as follows:

initiator—first recognizes a need or identifies a problem which could potentially be resolved with a purchase. This person effectively defines the buying situation

buyer—has formal, though often constrained, authority for selecting vendors and consummating the purchase. Responsibilities may include vendor evaluation, solicitation of bids, negotiation, preparation of requisitions and contracts, order processing, and expediting

user—will be making on-the-job use of the product or service to be purchased. Users usually have little formal authority to make purchase decisions. They frequently also play the role of initiator

influencer—does not make specific product or vendor choices, but significantly impacts on the type of decision made. A person who, in effect, places constraints on the decision process by establishing quality, delivery, design specification, or need description requirements which limit the number of acceptable alternatives

decider—is the actual maker of the buying decision. This person may not have the formal charge to make the decision in question, but does so as a function of his or her power and influence in the particular decision area under question. As a result, this can be the most critical, and yet most difficult to identify, member of the buying center

gatekeeper—controls the types and flows of information regarding products and suppliers received by other members of the buying center when making a particular buying decision. The gatekeeper can determine which promotional materials and internal vendor information reaches key influencers, and whether salespeople are given access to the appropriate buying center members

For some decisions, most or all of the roles in the buying center could be filled by one or two individuals. This is the case with many straight rebuy and routine purchases. Alternatively, six or more different people could fill the roles, each representing a different functional area in the firm. For example, if a company was purchasing simple mechanical pencils, the purchasing agent might play most or all of the roles. If the same firm was purchasing a packaging design for a temperature-sensitive product line, the initiator could be a R&D engineer, the user a production manager, the buyer a purchasing agent, the influencer a quality control inspector, the decider a project manager, and the gatekeeper a sales manager. Further, more than one person could fill any of the roles. There might be three or four influencers, and the decider role could actually be the majority vote of a committee.

In addition, the composition of the buying center can be expected to vary over the stages of the buying process. Sources of influence can vary depending on whether the organization is trying to specify its needs or, alternatively, trying to evaluate different vendors. Because numerous decisions are made during the buying process (see Table 3.3), the actual decider could change. Different types of information requirements over the buying stages suggest that the gatekeeper role could also change hands.

Unfortunately, it is difficult to stereotype the buying center roles in terms of functional areas in the firm or organization. One might expect to typically find the user in the operations or production department, and the gatekeeper in the purchasing department. But even these generalizations do not hold up across all types of buying decisions. Buying center membership tends to be product- and company-specific. In general, the dynamics of industrial buying resist such attempts at simplification.

Whenever two or more individuals fulfill the roles in the buying center, purchasing becomes, in effect, a group decision process. This is frequently the case. In studies of industrial buying behavior, estimates of the average size of the buying center have ranged from 1.5 (Patchen 1974) and 3.5 (Buskirk 1970) to 5.5 (Laczniak 1979) and between 8.9 and 11.9 (Weigand 1966). In an examination of twenty-one different industries, Spekman and Stern (1979) found buying centers averaging anywhere between 3.0 and 8.0 members.

When the buying center is a group, decisions represent group behavior. In some cases, this is a formal buying group that regularly meets to make decisions. More often, however, it is an ad hoc or informal group that does not actually convene. Instead, the members communicate with one another directly and indirectly, formally and informally. Each role member has certain goals and objectives which are shared with others in the buying center, but he or she can also have goals that conflict with the needs of the others. Each is attempting to perform a task within the confines of departmental and organizational policies, procedures, and employee evaluation systems.

Two central problems arise concerning the members of the buying center. The first has to do with identifying exactly who is filling each role—which can be a fairly challenging feat in some purchase decisions. The most common approach is to utilize some variation of the snowball sampling technique (Moriarty and Bateson 1982). This technique involves contacting someone in the customer organization (usually a purchasing agent) and asking for the names of the three or four key people impacting on a buying decision. Each of these people is, in turn, contacted and asked for a list of names. The process is continued until a list is generated on which the names are fairly consistent among respondents.

Keep in mind that identifying buying center members is not the same thing as determining the identity of the key decision maker. Johnston and Bonoma (1981 p.144) suggest that "finding the key buying influence may be a highly complex, if not impossible, process. It may be much more important to examine who influences which tasks and act accordingly."

The second, and more difficult, problem is to develop an understanding of the behavioral interrelationships which take place among buying center participants over the stages of the process, or from decision to decision. Product and vendor choices are heavily dependent upon the expectations, power positions, coalitions or alliances, and approaches to conflict resolution relied upon by those in the buying center. The remainder of this chapter delineates some of the major conceptual approaches available to the marketer for understanding these behavioral interactions.

A Communications Perspective

One approach to explaining what takes place among participants in the purchasing decision process is to focus on the structural dimensions of the buying center. Since the buying center is not usually a formal group, its structure is not formally established by the organization. Instead, the structure of the buying center is determined by communication linkages among the members. If we examine all of the communications that take place within an organization regarding a particular purchase decision, then we could identify who was involved in the buying process (the identities of those in the buying center), as well as the relative importance of some of these individuals. Those who were communicated with most frequently regarding the decision are likely to play fairly critical roles.

By tracing the communication linkages within a number of organizations making purchasing decisions, Johnston and Bonoma (1981) were able to identify five key structural dimensions to the buying center. These are:

(a) vertical involvement—the number of managerial levels in the organization hierarchy that get involved in the purchase decision. Different decisions will involve individuals as high up as the president or CEO, or as low as clerical workers;

(b) lateral involvement—the number of departments, functional areas, or divisions within the organization that play a part in the buying decision. Examples include the purchasing, design engineering, production, marketing, and finance departments or areas;

(c) extensivity—the total number of people involved. More than one person can get involved from a given hierarchical level or functional area in the organization, and so this number can be different than the total for vertical and lateral involvement;

(d) connectedness—the extent to which the members of the buying center directly communicate with one another regarding the purchase decision. Some members will receive extensive communication from others in the buying center, while others are fairly isolated, receiving infrequent communication;

(e) centrality of the purchasing manager—the extent to which much of the communication within the organization regarding a purchase decision flows through the purchasing department.

Each of these dimensions has important implications for the marketer. If more vertical levels are involved, those at the higher levels are likely to exert a disproportionate influence on final purchase decisions, whether they intend to or not. Greater lateral involvement suggests that the buying process will be less formal, and probably involve more conflict. This is especially the case where departments have differing goals in purchase decisions. Extensivity is of concern because the buying process becomes more complex, and lasts longer, as more people get involved. It becomes more difficult for the marketer to reach all those involved in the decision process, or to tailor the marketing program to each member of the buying center. The evidence suggests, for example, that the industrial salesperson frequently does not contact more than half of those involved (Manville 1978). Connectedness is also of importance, in that a lack of much direct communication among decision participants means the marketer's message may have to be communicated separately to each individual and some people are just not reached. In addition, connectedness provides insights into the identity of the central players. Finally, the centrality of the purchasing department is especially relevant because the marketer's initial customer contact is often made through the purchasing department. Purchasing can help (or hinder) the ability of the marketer to understand the buying process in an organization, and to know where to concentrate his or her efforts.

A Power Perspective

Another approach to the organizational buying decision process is to examine the different sources or bases of power in the buying center. Knowing the members of the buying center is not enough. The marketer must determine the identity of the key influencers and the decider. A person's ability to influence or make buying decisions is a reflection of that person's power in the organization. In many cases, however, power is situation-specific. That is, a given person can have more or less power to influence things depending on the situation. In the case of organizational buying, it may depend on the type of purchase, the time pressure involved, the perceived risk of making a wrong decision, the number of alternatives to be considered, and a variety of other factors.

Where do members of the buying center get their power? French and Ravens (1959) have identified a number of power bases which apply whenever people interact in a social context, including any sort of group or organization setting. These bases include:

Reward Power—Ability to influence others because you control monetary, social, political, or psychological rewards that they desire

Coercive Power—Influence comes from the ability to provide monetary or other punishments to those who do not cooperate

Referent Power—Others comply with your wishes because they like you. This attraction is based on personality, charisma, and persuasive ability

Expert Power—Influence is rooted in one's expertise regarding the issue under question. A person achieves power because others perceive that he knows more than anyone else about the problem at hand

Legitimate Power—Influence is based on one's formal position or title. The group or organization has formally granted the individual authority in some decision area

These can be readily applied to the buying center (Thomas 1984). *Legitimate* power and *reward* power bases become especially relevant when higher level managers are members of the buying center (i.e., more hierarchical involvement). Such managers may have formal power to determine buying decision outcomes. The managers may also control the rewards and evaluations of others in the buying center, leading to compliant behavior on the part of the others when it comes to evaluating a product or vendor. Some members may achieve reward power (e.g., the purchasing department) because of their ability to perform favors for members of the buying center. *Coercive* power might be displayed when a buying center member, seeking the compliance of others regarding a buying decision, makes life more difficult for those who choose to disagree with that member. For example, the purchasing department could exert some coercive influence by making others follow rigorous requisition procedures, including a detailed written justification of each and every item requested. *Referent* power can be held by any potential member of the buying center, so long as that person has the personal following, attractiveness, or persuasiveness when it comes to managerial decision making. *Expert* power can be especially important in new task purchases, as well as some modified rebuy situations. Engineers can achieve influence in the buying center because of their technical expertise regarding product specifications and performance capabilities. Production managers often have expertise regarding product applications in the production process. Purchasing agents provide expertise concerning vendors and their performance capabilities.

These bases of power suggest that things may not be as they appear in the organizational buying decision process. A given individual may have the formal authority for purchase decisions (i.e., legitimate power), but the actual decider is some other person who holds expert or reward power. Also, the bases of power are not mutually exclusive. A buying center member may have legitimate power, and have achieved this position due to his or her expertise. This legitimate power base may also provide the ability to reward others.

Bonoma (1982) has drawn some important implications for the marketer when analyzing power in the buying center. Some of his conclusions include the following:

1. Those with less power must frequently rely on persuasion and argument to influence the more powerful regarding company needs, product attributes, vendor capabilities, or some other purchasing-related issue;

2. When a buying center member raises questions about the opinions or abilities of another member, it is frequently an indication that the person being criticized is an important source of power in the buying center;

3. Those who hold the greatest power will tend to be the members who receive the bulk of information and communications which are exchanged concerning a buying decision;

4. The most powerful buying center members are not the most easily identified or most talkative member of their groups. Powerful individuals often send others to meetings in their place, knowing that no final decision will be made without their approval;

5. No correlation exists between the functional area of a manager and power in the buying center. The power of a functional area varies depending on the organization and the product being purchased;

Table 4.1 Matrix for Gathering Psychological Information

Who's in the buying center, and what is the base of their power?	Who are the more powerful buyers, and what are their priorities?	What specific benefits does each important buyer want?	How do the important buyers see us?	Selling Strategy
_____	_____	_____	_____	_____
_____	_____	_____	_____	_____
_____	_____	_____	_____	_____
_____	_____	_____	_____	_____

Source: Reprinted by permission of the *Harvard Business Review*. An exhibit from "Major Sales: Who Really Does the Buying" by Thomas V. Bonoma (May/June 1982). Copyright © 1982 by the President and Fellows of Harvard College; all rights reserved.

6. Power and formal authority in buying decisions are not necessarily the same thing.

Bonoma proposes that the marketer prepare a matrix such as that in Table 4.1 to assess power in the buying center. The first step is to identify the members of the buying center, and attempt to identify the base of power each is likely to rely upon. Then, the strength of each of the power positions is evaluated, as well as the primary motives each of the more influential members has in making the buying decision. Next, the specific product and vendor attributes of greatest importance to each of the important buying center members are established. The perceptions of each of the key influentials regarding the marketer's product, company, and personnel (e.g., salespeople, technical support staff) are then determined. Once all of this data has been placed into the matrix, the marketer is in a stronger position to design a set of marketing and communication approaches tailored to the key influencers in the buying process.

A Risk Perspective

Buying can be viewed as an activity filled with risks and uncertainties, and purchase decision processes as risk-reducing behavior. Using this perspective, the person or department best able to cope with relevant risks should have greater influence in deciding what is bought, in what quantity, from whom, and based on what criteria.

There are actually two major dimensions or components that combine to determine the overall amount of risk in a buying decision (Peter and Ryan 1976). The first is the probability of loss due to a bad decision. How likely is it that the organization will experience some economic loss if the wrong choices are made? The second is the amount of loss that could result from an incorrect decision. If the organization were purchasing ink pens from a disreputable source, the probability of receiving faulty pens might be high, but the potential loss is fairly insignificant. Conversely, an expensive and very sophisticated piece of machinery purchased from a well-established vendor may represent low probability of loss, but in the event of failure, the amount of loss could be considerable. When the probability of loss is taken times the magnitude of loss, the result is a potential measure of the total purchasing risk.

Purchasing situations vary, however, in the problems they pose for the buying organization. Upah (1980) has identified seven major types of purchasing problem areas: supplier-related, product-related, customer-related, price-related, financially related, legally related, and regulatory-related. These problem areas can be related to the two major dimensions of risk. That is, within each of these problem areas one can talk about the likelihood of loss and the magnitude of loss. Table 4.2 is an

Table 4.2 Classification Scheme for Purchasing-related Categories of Risk

Purchasing Problems:	Risk Dimensions: Likelihood of:	Magnitude of Loss From:
Supplier-related	Problems due to supplier failure in meeting product specifications, delivery requirements, service needs, etc.	
Product-related	Problems due to the failure of the purchased items to satisfy company needs, to be compatible with other components and/or equipment, or to require unexpected capital expenditures	
Customer-related	Problems due to adverse reactions from customers of the purchasing organization to the use of the item in production	
Price-related	Problems due to paying too high a price given the product's value to the organization, the price of competitors' products or substitutes, or the cost in making or leasing the item instead of buying it	
Financially related	Problems due to difficulty in arranging financing or leasing arrangements	
Legally related	Problems due to legal aspects of the purchase agreement or contract	
Regulatory-related	Problems due to governmental regulations regarding use of the purchase, such as with employee safety, antitrust, or environmental damage	

Source: Adapted from G.D. Upah, "Applying the Concept of Perceived Risk to Buying Influence in Industrial Firms," *Advances in Consumer Research,* 7, edited by Jerry C. Olson (Ann Arbor: Association for Consumer Research, 1980), 382.

illustration of this relationship. As can be seen, one type of risk concerns price. How likely is it that the organization is paying too high a price, and what is the potential loss the organization will suffer from paying too high a price? Total risk, then, would involve the combination of all of these problem areas.

Influence within the buying center may stem from a person's ability to cope with (lessen) the types of risks involved in the buying task. When the risk of each of the problem areas in Table 4.2 is low, the purchasing department may be the primary source of influence. Correspondingly, senior management may play the major role when the risk of each type of problem is high. In this case, the question becomes, what happens between these two extremes? We might expect production or engineering personnel to be more influential when the buying decision is characterized by problems concerning technical aspects of the product. The same may be the case when the principal area of concern is the compatibility of the product with existing equipment. If the possibility of adverse reaction by customers to the use of some purchased component most characterizes the buying decision, the sales or marketing department becomes a key source of influence. Where there are legal or regulatory problems, the legal staff should play a larger role. Influence may rest with finance or accounting personnel in purchases presenting problems with payment arrangements, make-or-buy decisions, leasing questions, or additional capital needs. The ability of purchasing managers to impact favorably on problems of delivery or supplier reliability may enhance their influence when the firm is threatened with potential loss due to such problems. Lastly, purchasing situations involving risk due to problems related to employee safety or environmental damage should engender greater involvement and influence on the part of senior management.

Risk can also be related to the purchasing tactics used by the buying organization (Webster 1984). When members of the buying center are uncertain about product or vendor performance, more suppliers will be contacted, multiple sources and shorter-term contracts will be used, and ability to meet specifications becomes a critical buying attribute. When buying center members are uncertain about the organization's needs, or anticipate adverse reactions from others to a given buying decision, more people will probably be involved in the buying decision. Consequently, the process will take longer, more information will be sought, the quality attribute will be stressed, and source loyalty will be relied upon.

Buying risk is also related to the structure of the buying center. There are a number of structural dimensions to the buying group, including how centralized or decentralized it is, how much division of labor there is, the extent to which formal rules and procedures guide its deliberations, and the amount of participation permitted in actual decision making. Spekman and Stern (1979) suggest that buying centers that are more rigid and bureaucratic are less effective in dealing with uncertainties in the buying process, but more effective when uncertainties are minimal. A more flexible structure enables the buying center members to better cope with and reduce uncertainties. When the risk or uncertainty in a buying decision is great, the buying center might be expected to be more decentralized, to involve less formal assignment of specific individuals to roles or tasks, to be less reliant on rules and procedures, and to encourage greater participation in decision making.

Risk is something the marketer may try to influence. For example, when the marketer is the in-supplier, his or her efforts will focus on reducing perceived uncertainties. The out-supplier, alternatively, will try to heighten the perceived uncertainty to the point where personnel in the buying center are willing to consider new alternatives (Webster 1984).

A Problem-Solving Perspective

What types of product and vendor attributes will be emphasized in a given purchasing situation? The risk perspective concluded that reducing uncertainty is a major motivation in organizational buying. Thus, one might logically expect decision makers to stress those attributes that most directly address the type of purchasing problem at hand.

In a study of attribute importance, Lehmann and O'Shaughnessy (1974) developed an approach to classifying products based on the problems inherent in their adoption. According to these authors, most industrial products will fall into four categories on the basis of problems likely to be encountered should the product be purchased. These are:

Routine Order Products—Items ordered and used on a regular basis. These products present no anticipated problems regarding usage or performance, and contain little risk (e.g., office supplies).

Procedural Problem Products—The overriding concern with these items is in how to use the product. To successfully adopt the product, some amount of learning must take place, perhaps through formal training (e.g., a word processor to replace typewriters).

Performance Problem Products—Items where there is serious concern about whether the product can successfully meet the user's needs. Questions are raised whether the product can perform at the level required and if it will be compatible with existing equipment and resources (e.g., machinery using new technology).

Political Problem Products—Internal political problems arise when the purchase of an item will take resources away from other areas in the organization (e.g., high-priced items), or when the product being purchased will be used by different departments, or individuals, with conflicting needs (e.g., a computer software package).

In considering product and vendor attributes, it appears that reliability of supply and price become the important attributes when purchasing *routine order products*. In addition, current suppliers (source loyalty) are favored in this situation. When purchasing *procedural problem products*, attributes which ease the learning problem become salient, such as technical service provided, ease of product operation or use, and training offered by the supplier. With *performance problem products*, the key attributes are those that facilitate judgments on how well the product and vendor will be able to do the job. Examples include product reliability data, technical service offered, and the flexibility of the supplier in meeting the specific needs of the customer. Finally, if a purchase decision poses serious *political problems* for an organization, the buying center will stress performance on those attributes that must be accomplished regardless of who in the organization will be using the item. By favoring attributes which are commonly recognized as important by all departments or functional areas involved, conflicts within the buying center are minimized.

Depending on the product under consideration, then, different attributes will be stressed (Kiser, Rao, and Rao 1975). More importantly, a useful approach for understanding the decision-making process regarding these attributes is to determine what type of buying problem the product represents.

A Reward Perspective

It has been emphasized that the members of a buying center often demonstrate considerable differences in terms of the product or vendor attributes they feel should be emphasized in a given purchase decision. These potential conflicts can be explained, in part, by differences in the individual motivation of each person in the buying center (Anderson and Chambers 1985). Because organizational buying behavior is work behavior, it is motivated by the pursuit of various rewards by those involved in the buying process.

Individuals in the buying center are pursuing their self-interest within the constraints of the organizational control system. While organizations have numerous devices to influence and control the behaviors of their employees, the employee evaluation (or measurement) system and the formal rewards available are of principal concern to the employee. Those involved in purchasing "will naturally behave in a way that maximizes their records of achievement in accordance with the ways they are measured" (Corey 1978).

When individuals join the buying center, they bring to it the values and objectives incorporated into the measures and rewards applied to them by the organization. Different departments or functional areas in the firm will frequently develop their own evaluation and reward systems. As a result, purchasing agents may be rewarded for saving the organization money, while production managers are evaluated on how well they achieve output quotas and reduce the incidence of rejects. Those in finance might be evaluated on the basis of the company's leverage and cash flow positions, and the marketing manager is measured based on whether sales and market share objectives are met. Although there are other sources of rewards for a member of the buying center, those found in their primary work group or functional department will typically have the most pervasive impact on their behavior.

The purchasing-related actions of any member of the buying center not only impact on the rewards received by that person, but also can affect the evaluation and rewards received by other members. For example, while purchasing agents may be rewarded for saving the firm money, their ability to do so may be severely limited by the manner in which engineers set technical product specifications, or by demands from finance that the company lease instead of buy. Similarly, rewards to production personnel for meeting certain production quotas may be reduced because the purchasing department saved money by using a less than dependable source of supply. It follows, then, that the members of the buying center must rely upon one another to achieve the purchasing task itself, and to receive personal or departmental rewards.

Why do purchasing agents (or engineers or product managers) push for certain product attributes, or argue for particular products or vendors when faced with a purchase decision? What determines how strongly they emphasize a given position? With whom will they form alliances or coalitions to influence the decision outcome? The reward perspective suggests that the answer to all of these questions is rooted in the evaluation and reward systems each of these individuals must face. A hypothetical purchase might find purchasing agents pushing for products and vendors with lower prices, while R&D engineers stress brand name and quality attributes, and the production manager emphasizes the vendor's delivery and inventory capabilities. In each case, the attribute being stressed relates to the ability of the individual to perform successfully in the eyes of those who evaluate and reward that person. Members of the buying center bring to it their respective department's view of reality. Overall, the system of measurements and rewards becomes a major source of potential conflict in buying decisions, as illustrated in Figure 4.1.

Bonoma (1982) gives us the example of the marketer who established list prices well under those of the competitors, but gave small quantity discounts. Although all of the competitors charged higher prices, they provided substantial discounts. Customers tended to favor the competitors, despite the price disadvantage. As it turns out, the purchasing agents were being evaluated and rewarded based more on the price concessions they obtained during negotiations than on the actual price paid.

TWO GENERAL FRAMEWORKS

While each of these perspectives provides a different insight into the workings of the buying center, there are two more general frameworks available. Both represent attempts to provide a comprehensive and integrated picture of the major factors that combine to explain organizational buying behavior.

The Webster-Wind Framework

A wide range of different factors impact on an industrial purchase decision. Webster and Wind (1972) have developed a logical approach for organizing these factors. Their framework is a useful tool for identifying and assessing key variables which might explain how decisions are made, and what the likely outcomes will be. It consists of four categories of variables: environmental, organizational, interpersonal, and individual. Each category, in turn, includes two subcategories of variables—task-related and nontask-related. Task-related factors directly relate to the buying problem at hand; nontask factors, then, have little or nothing directly to do with the buying problem itself, but affect the decisions made concerning the buying problem.

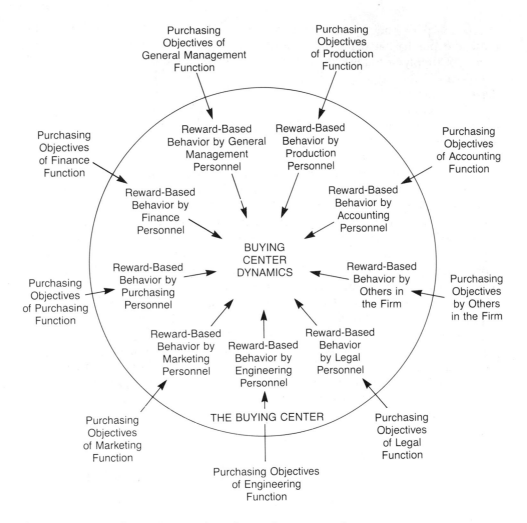

Figure 4.1   Rewards as a Source of Conflict in Organizational
Purchasing Processes

The framework appears in Figure 4.2, with examples of task and nontask items
shown in Table 4.3.

The Environment

The first category, environmental variables, includes virtually everything outside the
organization. The framework identifies six environmental forces which impact on
buying behavior: physical, technological, economic, political, legal, and cultural. To
these forces must be added the marketing programs of vendors (as well as other
information sources); they comprise an important external factor that influences the
buying process.

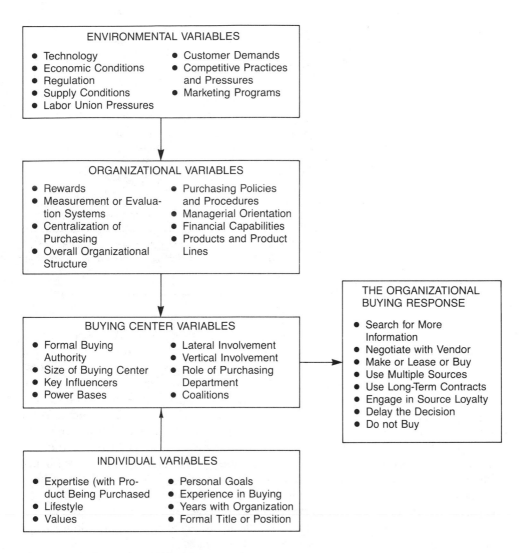

Figure 4.2 The Webster-Wind Framework
(Source: Adapted from F.E. Webster, and Y. Wind, "A General Model of Organizational Buying Behavior," *Journal of Marketing,* 36, (April 1972), 12–17. Copyright American Marketing Association. Reprinted with permission.)

The *physical* environment includes any geographic, climatic, and ecological constraints placed on the organization. For example, geographic proximity of a source of supply can improve the likelihood of selecting that source. The extent to which critical raw materials, labor, or other resources are in short supply is another characteristic of the physical environment that clearly affects the buying process.

Table 4.3 Task and Nontask Influences on Organizational Buying
Decisions

	Task	Nontask
Individual	Desire to obtain lowest price	Personal values and needs
Interpersonal	Meetings to set specifications	Informal, off-the-job interactions
Organizational	Policy regarding local supplier preference	Methods of personnel evaluation
Environmental	Anticipated changes in prices	Political climate in an elected year

Source: F.E. Webster. and Y. Wind, "A General Model for Understanding Organizational Buying Behavior," *Journal of Marketing,* 36, (April 1972), 13. Copyright American Marketing Association. Reprinted with permission.

Technology can produce changes—both in the products an organization buys and in the processes it relies upon to get things done. A new technology could result in a better component part than the buying organization is currently using. Alternatively, a technological development could change the production or assembly process the buying organization uses in making its own product. Computers, for example, have made just-in-time inventory (see Chapter 2) much more feasible in organizational procurement. The current pace of technological change found in many industrial markets creates rapid product obsolescence that increases the risk in purchasing decisions. Technology also can affect the influences within the buying center. For example, a major technological improvement in some purchased item can enable the buying organization to provide more value to its own customers. Its marketing managers may have a correspondingly larger role in the buying decision. Fast-paced technological changes may also dictate an enhanced buying role for technically qualified engineers who understand these changes.

Economic conditions can also be characterized as rapidly changing and often threatening to the organizational buyer. Double-digit inflation, unemployment, and volatile interest rates have each been in evidence at times in recent years. Business cycles recur in more frequent, and less predictable, intervals. These factors affect the stability of prices, the cost and availability of financial resources (e.g., credit), and the inventory needs confronting the industrial buyer (especially given the derived nature of demand). Buying strategies may reflect this turbulence in the economic environment. The quality of buyer-seller relationships takes on greater importance, as the buyer looks for dependable sources, predictable prices, and vendor flexibility in financing and inventory policies. The purchasing department can play a major role in establishing and maintaining these relationships. Financial personnel may also become influential when the organization is confronted by economic threats, especially in assessing alternative financing, leasing, or make-or-buy options.

The *political* and *legal* environments of an organization affect (a) what is purchased, and (b) the nature of the buyer-seller interaction process. Laws and regulations concerning pollution, energy conservation, health and safety, manufacturer liability, raw material consumption, import quotas, tariffs, and the tax treatment of a purchase, among other legal constraints, place limitations on how the buying organization designs its products or services, and thus how it specifies its purchasing needs. The buyer-seller interaction process is affected by restrictions on unfair competitive practices, such as tying arrangements, dumping, and price discrimination. Certain questionable ethical practices that affect the buyer-seller relationship, such as bribes or gifts to members of the buying center, are also restricted in many societies. In the presence of serious legal or regulatory questions regarding a purchase, both the legal staff and senior management are likely to fill important buying center roles.

Cultural factors tend to impact indirectly on organizational buying. Culture is the whole set of beliefs, attitudes, social forms, and activity patterns of a reasonably homogeneous set of people. The culture of a given society adapts or changes over time. In the context of the purchasing process, culture can affect the values and norms that are emphasized, such as efficiency or simplicity. If the culture places a high value on competition, buyers may expect and emphasize the need for vendors to compete for their business. This emphasis may affect subsequent negotiation tactics. And, social attitudes conceivably could lead firms to favor or oppose minority vendors when selecting sources.

The marketer is also part of the buying organization's external environment, representing a source of information as well as supply. As an information source, the marketer can affect the buyer's perceptions regarding the environment. For instance, he or she can influence buying center members' interpretation of the economic or regulatory environment. The marketer must also identify the environmental areas of greatest significance to those in the buying center, and ensure that the marketing program considers the buyer's concerns in those areas.

The Organization

Some of these environmental variables impact directly on the buying center, while others are filtered by a number of organizational variables. The organizational factors of importance in purchasing decisions include (a) goals and objectives, (b) structure, (c) policies and procedures, and (d) resources.

An organization can have overall *goals and objectives* as well as specific purchasing objectives. Overall goals include targets for sales, profits, market share, inventory turnover, costs, market penetration, new product development, and image, among others. Purchasing goals include negotiating acceptable prices for the required product quality, achieving on-time deliveries, and facilitating the mission of users (Corey 1978). Goals at these two different levels in the organization are, of course, interrelated. As a case in point, senior management in many companies has realized that a 1 percent reduction in materials costs can have the same effect on profits as a 20 percent increase in sales (Kiser and Rink 1980). Objectives will determine, to a significant degree, the attributes stressed in buying decisions and, more indirectly, the composition of the buying center. In total, objectives are a reflection of the value system adopted by senior management.

Structure refers to the design of the organization and its procurement function. It consists of systems of communication, authority, status, rewards, and work flow. Structure determines the extent to which people from different areas in the organization communicate about a buying problem, and the tactics they rely upon to influence and persuade one another. It affects the flow of information regarding products and vendors. The overriding structural issue in explaining organizational buying behavior is the degree to which the purchasing function is centralized or decentralized.

A centralized structure concentrates all the major purchasing decisions and activities at one location, typically the organization's headquarters or main facility. A completely decentralized structure would permit complete autonomy in terms of purchasing authority and responsibility at each facility or location. The highly centralized procurement operation will often be more formally structured, with the purchasing department playing a major role in the buying process. Centralization results in greater specialization in purchasing, and places emphasis on long-term purchasing strategy. The purchasing agent will tend to identify more with the sentiments and values of purchasing department members than with those in other areas of the buying organization. As purchasing activities become more decentralized, more individuals tend to get involved in buying decisions from other (nonpurchasing) functional areas in the organization. Social influence and informal interdepartmental relationships play a bigger part in buying decisions at each location.

The tendency toward centralization of the purchasing function, especially in larger companies, develops for a number of reasons—among them the need to better cope with supply shortages and changes in the environment, to reduce costs, and to achieve more professionalism in purchasing. Concurrently, some of the new purchasing and production technologies (see Chapter 2), such as just-in-time ordering and electronic data interchange, have permitted greater decentralization.

According to Webster (1984), centralization in the buying center affects the buyer's job in five important ways:

(a) it defines his or her geographic location;

(b) it establishes the authority relationships between buyers and users;

(c) it establishes the authority relationships between buyers and higher level purchasing executives;

(d) it influences the formal nature of communication between buyers and users;

(e) it influences the informal relationships between buyers and users.

Depending on the degree of centralization, marketers may find themselves selling at a number of different levels and locations in the same customer organization. In this situation, the use of national account management programs is a common approach to achieving coordination and consistency. National accounts, also called house accounts, are usually customer organizations that operate on a national or international scale, with operations in a number of the vendor's territories. Examples might include selling aluminum to Anheuser-Busch, paper cups to Burger

King Corporation, and motors to Otis Elevator. The major distinguishing character-istic of national accounts is large size, but house account customers can be regional, or even local. Companies will give these accounts special sales and service attention, with strategies such as establishing a separate division to deal with national accounts, setting up a separate sales force for these accounts, or using company executives to sell to these customers.

Structure is often related to the *policies and procedures* established for making purchasing decisions. These policies and procedures lend structure to the buying task itself, by governing the work flow. *Policies* can include requirements for the number of bids solicited, mandates for multiple sourcing, preferences for using local sources of supply when possible, a list of unacceptable vendors, sample sizes that must be obtained from each source, guidelines for selecting products or vendors, and rules against receiving gifts, favors or meals from salespeople. *Procedures* in-volve following the specific steps required to accomplish a purchase, completing the requisitions and other forms to initiate and fulfill a purchase request, establishing managerial levels that must sign off on a purchase (depending on its value or in-tended use), and others. Such policies and procedures can determine who must be included in the buying center, and can set the priorities regarding the relative im-portance of various product attributes. They can also represent a framework within which the conflicts that develop in buying can be formally resolved.

The *resources* of an organization provide the ultimate basis for its buying needs and capabilities. Resources include the size of the organization, its net assets, technologies, product lines, inventories, markets, and cash flow. They also include the technical and managerial capabilities of the organization's personnel. Significant resource constraints force a company to be much more conservative in what it buys and from whom, and put it in a less powerful negotiating position. A resource-poor company is unable to maintain sizable stocks in inventory, must look for external financing of large purchases, and usually does not have the option to make, rather than buy, a product or service. It may not have the ability to implement some of the newer purchasing technologies. To the extent that buying risks are greater for such organizations, resource-constrained firms might opt for more interfunctional in-volvement in the buying process.

Interpersonal Relationships

Environmental and organizational factors create the setting within which the buying center operates. Inside the buying center, there are also a number of interpersonal determinants of buying behavior. The strategies and tactics individuals use to accom-plish their personal objectives during the stages of the buying process represent the most complex aspect of organizational buying behavior. Roles, structural dimen-sions, and bases of power within the buying center were discussed earlier in this chapter. Whenever more than one person is involved, decisions are accomplished through group interaction, where members must reach some sort of consensus. It is unlikely that such a consensus will evolve automatically, because those in the buying center usually come from different functional areas within the organization, and face differing measurement and reward systems (Anderson and Chambers

1985). They speak different languages, as illustrated in Table 4.4. In addition, buying center members do not have equal power positions. Engineering and production/operations functions frequently have a disproportionate amount of influence when compared to purchasing, marketing, finance, and others. Further, those involved can have quite different perceptions of the role each is supposed to fill. Structural constraints also create problems for the efficient flow of information within the buying center.

Each person involved in the buying process is a member of two groups—a department or functional area, and the buying center. Both of these groups exert some influence on individual behavior. Because buying centers tend to be relatively small, informal, and temporary groups, the individual is likely to demonstrate strong loyalty to department values and norms.

The individual, in pursuing self-interest, may be confronted with a mixed-motive bargaining situation. There is an incentive to be competitive, fostered by the conflicting needs and objectives of the various functional areas. There is also an incentive to cooperate, in that the members of the buying center are mutually dependent upon one another to successfully complete the buying task.

Examples of the resulting behavioral strategies among decision participants include social influence, coalition formation, negotiation, bargaining, and politicking. Strauss's tactics of lateral relationships (discussed in Table 3.2, Chapter 3) provide an excellent example of purchasing agents attempting to influence decision outcomes.

Coalitions are an especially important behavioral response within the buying center; some have suggested that coalitions are responsible for most of the decisions (Bonoma and Zaltman 1978; Bagozzi 1978, and Anderson and Chambers 1985). The

Table 4.4   How Customers Refer to Your Products

Communication among departments within a firm is an important aspect of organizational buying. Individuals from different departments often develop their own languages and slang terms to describe products and their applications. This jargon affects the way in which products are specified by those requesting them, and, in turn, the ability of the purchasing department to satisfy user needs. A purchasing manager at Industrial and Textile Piping, Inc. provides examples of differences between what was requisitioned by users, and the technical product name that was actually ordered:

Product Requested by User	Actual Product Ordered by Purchasing
Chicago Air Coupler	Dixon Mfg. Co. AM-7¾″ King Air Nipple
BIP	A106, A53 or A120 Grade Black Iron Pipe, Cast or Ductile Iron Pipe
Light Bulbs	24 Each F96T12/cw fluorescent lamp
Pipe Hoist	Chisholm-Moore Model B 1½-ton capacity with 26′ lift chain and safety hook

Source: Industrial and Textile Piping, Inc.

Table 4.5   Who Will Form Coalitions in the Buying Center?

In a majority of organizational buying decisions, the key source of influence, and even decision making, is not a particular individual. Instead, it is a coalition, defined as a temporary, means-oriented alliance among individuals who differ in goals (Gamson 1964). When this is the case, the marketer is faced with the problem of identifying key coalitions and addressing the diverse interests of coalition members.

In selecting coalition partners, a member of the buying center will examine the following in evaluating specific others (Morris and Freedman 1984):

1. The size of the payoff or total benefits achievable with each coalition alternative

2. Power positions of others

3. Bargaining experience

4. How much one has to give up in forming a given coalition

The evidence suggests a decision participant is also more likely to form alliances with those buying center members with whom he has:

1. More direct communication

2. Shared attitudes and motivation

3. Compatible objectives

4. Past or anticipated future experiences

---

marketer's task becomes more complicated if the roles in the buying center are filled by coalitions rather than individuals. Two departments which ordinarily play only a minimal role may achieve the status of *influencer* or *decider* by coalescing. Collectively, they may have the power to initiate the purchasing process. Alternatively, they may be able to determine the nature and type of information sought, as well as the flow of that information through the organization (i.e., the *gatekeeper* role). In addition, coalitions from past purchasing decisions can influence present and future decisions. Table 4.5 provides some of the criteria used by decision participants in selecting coalition partners.

Individual Characteristics

The individual factors that affect the buying process refer to the set of needs, goals, habits, past experiences, information, and attitudes that each person brings to the buying center. The individual applies these factors to a given purchasing situation. Webster and Wind (1972) explain "the individual is at the center of the buying process, operating within the buying center that is in turn bounded by the formal organization, which is likewise embedded in the influences of the broader environment. It is the specific individual who is the target for marketing effort, not the abstract organization."

Specific characteristics that determine how personal goals are achieved within the context of a buying decision include risk-orientation, competitiveness, locus of control, creativity, approach to problem solving (e.g., structured or methodical versus unstructured), aggressiveness, age, years with the company, educational and professional background, and experience in purchase decision making.

Because industrial buying is work behavior, the motivation of each decision participant becomes an important variable for explaining behavior. One approach to explaining the motivation underlying individual behavior is expectancy theory (Vroom 1964; Anderson and Chambers 1985). Here, the effort an individual exerts toward some task is a function of his or her perception of the probability that the effort will result in successful performance on the task, the belief that successful performance will result in desired outcomes (e.g., rewards), and the importance or attractiveness of those outcomes to the individual. To demonstrate, let us examine the motivation a particular buying center member has to push for a change to a new source of supply. The amount of effort or support this individual puts forth is dependent upon (a) his or her perceptions regarding the likelihood of being successful in getting the organization to switch; (b) his or her belief that, if successful, the change in vendors will result in certain desired benefits, and (c) the relative importance of these benefits to that individual. Any one of these three elements could undermine the person's motivation, leading him or her to provide little or no support for the outside vendor.

To capitalize on individual characteristics, the marketer may try to ensure that key influencers see his or her product as instrumental in ensuring their own successful task performance. Toward this end, the marketer can help the buyer fulfill a particular image or role, such as that of hero, problem solver, tough negotiator, or shrewd decision maker. For example, in convincing a maintenance engineer to support the adoption of a climate control system which will save thousands of dollars in energy costs over the next ten years, the marketer is helping this individual become a hero of sorts by making him or her look good within his or her own organization.

The Sheth Framework

The second major framework within which to conceptualize organizational buying behavior was developed by Sheth (1973). Although it has some elements in common with the Webster-Wind framework, the emphasis is more on the psychology and decision-making processes found in organizational buying.

Figure 4.3 is an illustration of the Sheth framework. There are three principal components that combine to explain a purchasing decision outcome: expectations of the individual decision participants, determinants of joint versus autonomous decisions (the size of the buying center), and approaches to conflict resolution. Let us examine each of these.

Expectations

People involved in the buying process typically do not make decisions with a completely open mind. Rather, each decision participant develops expectations about the ability of suppliers and brands to meet the objectives. Differences in the expectations held by the members of the buying center are due to a variety of factors.

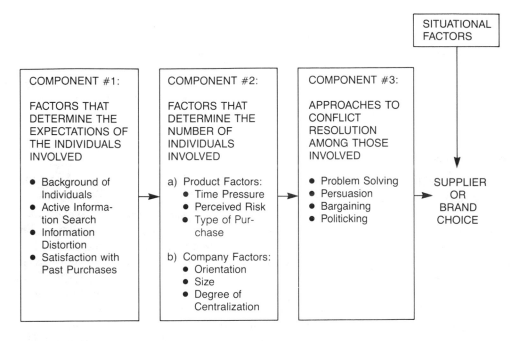

Figure 4.3 The Sheth Framework
(Source: Adapted from J.N. Sheth (1973), "A Model of Industrial Buyer
Behavior," *Journal of Marketing,* 37 (October): American Marketing
Association, 50–56.)

The most important determinant of individual expectations is a person's background. Background variables include some of the personal influences found in the Webster-Wind framework. Sheth emphasizes the educational background, the job or task orientation, and the personal lifestyles of buying center members as fundamental in explaining their perceptions and expectations.

In addition, the sources and amount of information available, and the extent of information search engaged in by an individual also affect expectations. This is where marketers come into play, as their sales force, trade journal advertising, trade shows, catalogs, and so forth, represent information sources that influence buyers' expectations. Marketers must be careful, however, that their efforts do not lead buyers to set their expectations too high. If the vendor subsequently fails to meet buyer expectations, this may have a negative impact on future sales.

At the same time, information from the marketer is not taken at face value. Individual buying center members will interpret the same information in very different ways, hearing what they want to hear, and retaining only parts of a given message. They will not be able to efficiently process all the information that is available. Their goals, values and previous experiences lead to information distortion— something the marketer has little ability to control. Also, dependent on their level of involvement with the item being purchased, they may not pursue the available information sources.

Lastly, different expectations among decision participants are based on their level of satisfaction with past purchases. A given vendor will not satisfy all buying center members equally, because the vendor will not perform equally well on every possible attribute. Buying center members may also be dissatisfied with a product or vendor because of the method of selection. Unresolved conflict from past decisions, or the simple fact that a given person's opinion was not solicited or given much credence, may lead that person to harbor negative feelings.

Joint versus Autonomous Decisions

While any number of individuals will have a stake in buying decisions, each with his or her own expectations, not all of them will actually get involved in a particular decision. Many minor or straight rebuy purchases are made by a single person (autonomously). Others can involve buying centers of twenty or thirty individuals. In the second component of his framework, Sheth attempts to address the size of the decision-making group, suggesting that group size is dependent upon a set of product-specific and company-specific factors.

For example, the greater the perceived risk in making a particular product choice, and the longer the time before the choice must be made, the more people can be expected to fill a role. For a first-time purchase, a major capital expenditure, or a once-in-a-lifetime purchase, the buying center should be larger. More people tend to get involved in larger organizations than in smaller ones, and in more decentralized organizations. The orientation of the buying organization is also important. Depending upon whether the organization is technology-oriented, risk-oriented, customer-oriented or demonstrates some other type of orientation, responsibility for buying decisions may be concentrated in specific functional areas. The technology-oriented firm may allow R&D or technical personnel to make decisions autonomously, and the production-oriented firm may give complete authority to operations personnel.

Such product and organizational characteristics provide the marketer with clues regarding the resources that must be allocated for a given account. The sales effort, the time invested, the orientation of the promotional effort, and the appropriateness of different distribution alternatives are related to these characteristics.

Conflict Resolution

Autonomous decisions lead directly to a supplier or brand choice. However, when two or more individuals are involved in buying decisions, some degree of conflict is likely. A certain amount of conflict encourages those holding different positions to be more thorough in supporting their positions, and often leads to greater creativity in generating mutually acceptable solutions. However, too much conflict encourages greater emotionalism, defensiveness, and political game-playing by participants. Indeed, conflict can be dysfunctional, when winning becomes everything.

The third component of the Sheth framework is concerned with the actual group decision process of conflict resolution in the buying center. The approaches to conflict resolution can result in rational or irrational decisions. Rational approaches include problem solving and persuasion; bargaining and politicking represent more irrational approaches. A problem-solving approach seeks more information, more supply sources, or more deliberation time to minimize conflict. Persuasion involves logically convincing dissenters to weigh overall company needs and objectives more, and personal objectives less. A bargaining mode might be characterized as "you give a little bit and I'll give a little bit." The parties are engaging in a kind of reciprocity within the buying center, and each member is making concessions. The problem here is that the negotiated position may keep everyone satisfied, but is neither optimal nor in the organization's best interest. Politicking includes the exchange of favors, the use of personal friendships, backstabbing, and other nontask-related attempts to coerce others in the buying center and generate a majority position. Some of Strauss's (1962) tactics of lateral relationship are typical of politicking.

The marketer can easily get caught between the conflicting positions in the buying center. Especially in the bargaining or politicking modes of conflict resolution, vendors who are less offensive or who are personal favorites may be selected, unless the marketer presents his or her products in such a way as to bridge conflict gaps, or appeal to the more powerful position-holders.

Within the third component of the framework, the behavioral dynamics of organizational buying take place. Sheth singles out conflict resolution as the principal focus of interpersonal behavior, but others have emphasized the manner in which a consensus is achieved within the buying center. Focusing on the differing perceptions and evaluation criteria among buying center members when selecting brands or sources of supply, Choffray and Lilien (1978) have identified four models to describe the process of final decision making: the weighted probability, the proportionality, the unanimity, and the acceptability models. With the *weighted probability* model, a weight is assigned to decision participants based on their relative power to influence the decision. The *proportionality* model assumes all roles have equivalent amounts of influence, and thus a majority vote is sufficient. The *unanimity* model, alternatively, applies where deliberations are permitted to continue until all members of the buying center are in agreement. The *acceptability* model is appropriate for decisions where extensive compromise takes place and the least controversial alternatives are selected.

The Sheth framework also allows for the fact that ad hoc situational factors sometimes determine the nature of purchasing decision outcomes. An unexpected strike among the production workers of a key source of supply, a merger with a former trading partner, or a sudden glut in the world supply of a critical resource material can redirect a purchase decision. These events occur apart from the three components of Sheth's decision-making framework.

Limitations of the Frameworks

The two general frameworks, or models, can be helpful in providing a broad, somewhat all-inclusive picture of the many factors that come into play as customer organizations attempt to make buying decisions. The frameworks suffer, however, from a number of limitations. First, it is difficult to develop a framework that applies to all types of organizations and buying situations. Moreover, the more universal a framework becomes, the less it describes what takes place in a particular customer organization. Second, the models tend to do a good job of identifying key variables, but provide little guidance to how these variables interact. Sheth does a better job at this than Webster-Wind, but still leaves room for improvement. Third, the arrows in the models which link variables all tend to go in one direction. This orientation ignores the likelihood that the direction of causation goes both ways. For example, in the Webster-Wind framework, individual characteristics are affected by, and can affect, organizational characteristics. Similarly, in the Sheth framework, individual expectations and product-specific factors both impact on one another. Also, expectations may differ as a function of the number of people involved. Finally, the models place little emphasis on the marketer, and tend to ignore the possibility that marketers can affect buying decisions. This was stressed in the discussion of the dyadic perspective in Chapter 3.

Source Loyalty as an Outcome of Buyer Behavior

Because buying decisions frequently are negotiated compromises, once a vendor is selected, there is a fairly strong tendency to be loyal to that vendor. This loyalty is particularly evident where the customer must make many buying decisions, and where considering a new vendor will only reawaken or heighten previous conflicts. Loyalty is also a risk-avoidance strategy, in that some will feel safer going with an established source of supply.

The establishment of a source-loyal relationship is equivalent to converting the buying situation into a straight rebuy, where the marketer is the in-supplier. On the other hand, the marketer who is an out-supplier faces a major obstacle when source loyalty exists. For these reasons, loyalty is a buying outcome that warrants considerable attention.

Source loyalty is more than repeat-buying behavior. There is an attitudinal component to loyalty as well as a behavioral component, which means that the buyer tends to repurchase from the same vendor, not because of need, but by choice. The buyer is, in effect, biased in favor of a particular vendor.

In trying to understand source loyalty, it is important to determine loyalty to what? Buyer commitment can be to a technology, a product category, a particular product, a vendor, or a person.

Figure 4.4 illustrates possible buyer loyalties in the telecommunications industry, which has moved from an analog to a digital technology in manufacturing communications switches for the telephone systems used by organizations. Switches are the systems which control the ways in which telephones within an office, building, or set of buildings are linked together. They provide for such features as intercom, multibutton telephones, speed dialing, call forwarding, and hold capabilities. One of the major benefits of the digital technology is the ability to transmit both voice and data over the same line. Of course, this is not a benefit that all customers require.

A customer could remain loyal to the old technology, be an advocate for the new, or be indifferent. The customer could also be loyal to a particular product

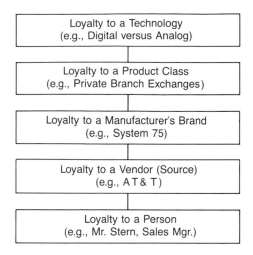

Figure 4.4   A Typology of Loyalties

category. For example, the telephone system in an office building can be designed around a private branch exchange (PBX), an electronic key system, or a central-office switch based at the local telephone company. Alternatively, the customer could be a strong proponent of a particular brand of PBX, such as the System 75, manufactured by AT&T. Or, the loyalty may be to AT&T itself, perhaps due to the company's reputation or service policies. Another possibility is that loyalty is not to the product or vendor, but instead to a salesperson, such as Mr. Stern. If Stern went to work for another company, the customer may then switch to the products of the new company.

Loyalty, where it exists, will tend to be divided, because of the concern with sole-source dependency in industrial markets. For many goods, the buying organization cannot afford the risk of relying on one vendor for all its needs. However, as firms adopt new purchasing and manufacturing technologies, such as just-in-time inventory, materials requirement planning, and electronic data interchange, they have a rationale for undivided loyalty.

Not much is known about loyalty in industrial markets, as little research has been done in this area. Wind (1970) performed a landmark study of the electronics industry and identified a number of significant determinants of loyalty. He found the most significant factor in deciding whether or not to be source-loyal was pressure for cost savings within the buyer organization. These findings are summarized in Table 4.6. Others (e.g., Morris and Holman 1987) have proposed that industrial loyalty generally takes longer to establish, lasts longer, and is more difficult to dissolve than consumer brand loyalty. Also, loyalty is more likely when the seller gets involved with the buyer in the early stages of product development.

In the coming years, marketers are likely to witness changes in the amount of loyalty and the reasons for loyalty. Strategies should be developed that attempt explicitly to manage loyalty. As an in-supplier, the marketer must be wary of becoming

Table 4.6   What Are the Determinants of Source Loyalty?

Wind (1970), in a study of the purchasing practices of electronics firms, found four key determinants of source loyalty among organizational buyers:

(a) Task concerns—tendency to use same source because it clearly is superior on traditional task variables such as quality, delivery, service, or price

(b) Organizational concerns—tendency to use same source because there have been few complaints from user departments, because an alternative source would save the organization only a small amount of money, or because the value of the order is very small

(c) Work simplification concerns—tendency to use same source because it makes things easier and involves less effort, especially when the buying center is faced with time constraints

(d) Attitudes toward source—tendency to use same source because of favorable personal attitudes and interrelationships with that vendor

Source: Y. Wind, "Industrial Source Loyalty," *Journal of Marketing Research*, 7 (November 1970), 450–457.

complacent or of taking advantage of his or her company's position in the source-loyal relationship. Even the marketer who consciously manages customer relationships can lose part or all of an account if the wrong variables are emphasized when dealing with the account. For an out-supplier, the ultimate objective is to change customer behavior. However, the real problem concerns the attitudinal component of loyalty. Marketers must focus on the reasons for the buyer's favorable attitudes toward existing sources; providing the buyer with reasons not to be loyal is insufficient.

SUMMARY

In this chapter, we have investigated organizational buying as a behavioral process. To simplify the complexities of this process, industrial buying was described in terms of a set of critical roles which collectively make up the buying center or decision-making unit. Five different perspectives were presented for approaching or understanding the functioning of a buying center: a communications perspective, a power perspective, a risk perspective, a problem-solving perspective, and a reward perspective.

These different views are effectively combined in the general frameworks of organizational buying behavior. Two such frameworks, the Webster-Wind and Sheth models, were described in detail. Marketing implications were drawn from each perspective, as well as from the components of the general framework.

Chapter 4 concludes the discussion of buying activities within customer organizations. The concepts that have been established will be used throughout the remainder of the text to develop industrial marketing strategy. An understanding of the industrial customer is also invaluable in conducting marketing research, estimating sales potential, and segmenting the marketplace—topics which are addressed in the next three chapters.

QUESTIONS

1. What are the differences between the buying center concept and a formal committee that has been assigned the task of selecting a vendor?

2. Consider the different power bases operating within the buying center. Under what circumstances would you think coercive power might be relied upon? When would expert power be most important?

3. Assume you were the purchasing manager for the Brunswick Corporation, Bowling Division, and were involved in purchasing plastics, castings, wood and rubber for pins and balls, electronic instrumentation for pin setters, and related items. What are some of the risks involved in your firm's purchasing decisions? What are some possible implications for buying center behavior?

4. Consider the purchasing operations of a middle-sized furniture manufacturer based in North Carolina. Under what conditions, and for what kinds of purchases, is there likely to be more vertical involvement in the buying decision process? When would there be more lateral involvement?

5. Develop an actual example of how the different measurement and reward systems of members of the buying center can create extensive conflict regarding what to buy or from whom.

6. Explain the differences between the task and nontask variables which influence purchase decision making. Describe a task and a nontask variable existing with each of the levels of the Webster-Wind framework. How is each likely to impact on the purchasing outcomes for a particular product or need?

7. Explain the following statement: "To capitalize on individual characteristics, the marketer may try to ensure that key influencers see his or her product as ensuring their own successful task performance." Provide an example of how this might be done.

8. How does the presence of coalitions within the buying center affect the job of the marketer? How do coalitions affect the industrial salesperson's task?

9. If you were selling the same product to two companies, one of which had a centralized purchasing operation, and the other had a decentralized purchasing operation at each of five plant locations, would you approach each in the same way? Discuss.

10. The Sheth framework indicates that one determinant of expectations concerning a purchase decision is perceptual distortion by individual decision makers. How are purchasing agents and design engineers likely to interpret the same advertising or personal selling message in different ways? What can the marketer do to address this problem?

11. If you were an outside vendor attempting to win a new account, do you think it would be more difficult to overcome loyalty to a technology, a product class, a manufacturer's brand, a vendor, or a person? Why?

CHAPTER 5

INDUSTRIAL MARKETING RESEARCH AND INTELLIGENCE

Key Concepts

Data base

Decision-making uncertainty

Decision support system (DSS)

Experimentation

External secondary data

Hypothesis

Internal secondary data

Marketing intelligence system (MIS)

Marketing research process

Model

Observation

Primary data

Reliability

Research design

Sampling strategy

SIC system

Survey method

Unit of analysis

Validity

Value of information

Learning Objectives

1. Explain marketing information as a tool for reducing uncertainty in decision making.
2. Define marketing research and identify the major responsibilities of marketing research.
3. Describe a process approach to industrial marketing research, and identify distinctive challenges in performing research on organizations.
4. Discuss the evolution from marketing research to marketing intelligence to decision-support systems.
5. Identify sources and limitations to the use of secondary information sources, including the SIC system.

A decision is the action an executive must take when he has information so incomplete that the answer does not suggest itself.

ADMIRAL A.W. RADFORD

THE ROLE OF INFORMATION IN MARKETING DECISIONS

The preceding chapters examined the complexities involved in selling to organizational customers. Added to the difficulties of understanding buyers and their changing needs is the unpredictability of competitor actions and reactions, as well as rapidly changing technologies, and turbulent economic developments. The industrial marketer attempts to make strategic decisions and tactical moves in an environment filled with uncertainties.

The best means for reducing uncertainty is to develop better information. In other words, without quality informational inputs, the marketing decision process becomes little more than guesswork. The formalized activities for generating this information constitute industrial marketing research, the objective of which is to obtain an "optimum combination of useful information within accessible time and cost limits" (Lee 1984, 3). Essentially, industrial marketing research has the responsibility of supplying facts, estimates, expert opinions, interpretations, and/or recommendations needed by industrial marketing managers to understand the marketing environment and to make intelligent decisions.

As products and services move through their life cycles, a multitude of decisions must be made, modified, abandoned, or otherwise reconsidered across all elements of marketing strategy. These elements include market segmentation, target group selection, product attribute engineering, product differentiation, price structure, advertising, promotion and sales aids, sales management, distribution policies, marketing organization, budgets, and contingency plans. Unfortunately, marketing managers never have all the relevant facts for making these decisions. They must deal with continuous change and complex interrelationships among the components of their environments. At the same time, marketing decisions cannot be delayed long enough to conduct exhaustive information searches. Even if they could, the cost of this information collection can be prohibitive. Consequently, the industrial marketing research function inevitably operates under budget constraints and time pressures.

To demonstrate the role of marketing research, consider the following example. A distributor of business supplies is considering expanding its warehouse facilities by 30 percent. The impetus for the decision has come from a series of stockouts that the company experienced in the last year. Given only this piece of information, the company might rush headlong into capital outlays to expand its warehouse and to purchase additional materials handling equipment. However, the decision would be made under a great deal of uncertainty. There is uncertainty regarding the actions of competitors, uncertainty regarding the business activity level of customers, uncertainty regarding the effect of stockouts on current customers, and uncertainty regarding the ultimate result of the capital outlay on the company's financial position.

In a relatively short period of time, marketing research could provide information that would help to clarify some of these questions. For example, the future business activity level of the target market can be judged by looking at the predictions of business analysts who have studied the industry over the past several years. The actions of competitors can be predicted by looking at their annual reports to determine financial reserves and current warehouse capacity. The reactions of key customers can be evaluated by making telephone calls to purchasing agents, asking about the importance of meeting shipping deadlines. In short, industrial marketing research activities can provide data inputs on a number of questions in the marketing manager's mind, and help reduce the uncertainty in the decision-making process. Then, the marketing manager will feel more comfortable with his or her assessment of what will happen if the expansion decision is implemented. Alternatively, he or she will gain insight into eventualities should the expansion be delayed or not implemented.

However, even with the aid of good industrial marketing research, the manager is always faced with imperfect information for decision making. Good as it is, the research function invariably represents a certain degree of error. Part of the error is due to the time pressures placed on the research function; part is due to the unpredictability of the industrial marketing environment; and part is due to the less-than-perfect tools that the marketing researcher uses. In addition, inadequately trained research personnel can contribute to this error. Fortunately, a judicious marketing researcher can minimize the amount of error which is introduced into the decision-making process. The true value of marketing research information involves a trade-off between the amount of uncertainty it eliminates from the marketing manager's decision making and the amount of erroneous new information it introduces into the process.

WHEN NOT TO DO RESEARCH

In the final analysis, the value of the information expected to be gained must always exceed the cost of obtaining that information. This rule is elementary in deciding whether or not to undertake marketing research in the first place. There are at least five situations under which research will make little or no contribution to the decision-making process. In these situations, the cost will exceed the benefits, and so the research should not be done. First, when the marketing decision has already been made, research has no effect other than to slow down implementation or otherwise add costs without gains. Unfortunately, some managers request research as a means of stroking their egos, or as artificial reinforcement after they have made decisions, rather than as a means of resolving uncertainty in the decisions themselves. Alternatively, some managers solicit research to prove their points or support their positions. The net result of this attempt will be a clash of manager subjectivity with research objectivity. If the research supports the manager's position, it will have little net benefit since no decision change would occur, and if the research conflicted with the manager's position, it would probably be ignored or discounted.

Another case of questionable research is when the manager fails to understand the scope of the research task and is unwilling to expend sufficient capital to obtain the necessary information. Here, shortcuts and financial limitations will place restrictions on the generalization of the results and probably preclude the research from assisting in the decision process. If the manager is unwilling to pay for what is needed to properly address the problem at hand, it may be better to spend no money on research, rather than do a mediocre job on a shoestring budget. Slightly different in situation, but equally adverse, is the instance where a manager experiences a great deal of uncertainty regarding the resolution of a decision, but is unwilling to enlist the aid of marketing research specialists. Usually, this reluctance is due either to false pride or a failure to judge the value of the information to be gained relative to its cost. That is, a manager may undertake the research personally as a means of hiding incompetence, or lack of understanding, from superiors or subordinates. Since there is minimal comprehension of the decision problem, there will be high likelihood of wasted research effort.

Finally, in all research undertakings, the manager must be firmly convinced that the expected results will reduce the uncertainty enough to warrant the cost of doing the research. No marketing decisions are made with complete certainty as to all eventualities, but all intelligent marketing decision makers weigh the cost of doing research against the value of reducing the uncertainty by some expected amount. The decision maker combines the known costs of research activities, including time and energies, and compares these costs to the expected gains from having a better understanding of marketplace dynamics and reactions to the manager's various decision alternatives.

MAJOR RESPONSIBILITY AREAS OF MARKETING RESEARCH

What is the focus of industrial marketing research? Virtually any decision area in which the marketing manager requires more or better informational inputs is a likely candidate for a marketing research project; the list of potential projects is endless. To bring some order to this state of affairs, let us examine the major areas where research is conducted. Most projects fall within one of the following categories:

Development of Market Potential

One of the most critical decision inputs needed by industrial marketing managers is the determination of sales and profit potential of various product-market opportunities. The marketing research function is responsible for clarifying the magnitude and future growth prospects of specific markets. This information is crucial in assisting marketing managers wishing to determine which markets to enter and exit, and how much in resources should be allocated to a given market.

Market Share Analysis

Because marketing exists in a world of dynamic competition, marketing research is assigned the responsibility of determining the relative proportion of the total market that a firm can hope to attain. Historical market share distributions are balanced against anticipated future competitive actions. The entrance and exit of competitors, the market's reactions to changes in marketing strategies and tactics, and the persistence of loyalty to industrial suppliers all go into estimating the share of the market for any product in a firm's line. Actual market share, once determined, provides a benchmark against which to compare current objectives and future performance.

Determination of Market Characteristics and Attitudes

Industrial marketing research must supply data on the salient characteristics of each market. Identification of the purchase decision-making process, the various roles played by individuals in the process, the importance of product and company attributes, the size of purchases, and the various specifications which must be matched in price bids are all part of the market characteristics which the industrial marketing manager must understand in order to compete effectively. Market characteristics would also be the area for studies designed to measure the firm's image in certain markets, and satisfaction levels among various segments of the market.

Sales Analysis

Breakdowns of sales, cost and profit figures by product line, individual products, territory, customer segments, salesperson, and distributor type are all necessary for the industrial marketing manager to have a complete picture of the sales performance of his or her responsibility areas. These microanalyses are helpful in spotting profit contribution differences, isolating high and low producers, and otherwise alerting the manager to emerging problems.

Forecasting

Predictions must be made of the velocity of the economy, the future actions of competitors, the anticipated purchasing level of customers, and conditions of supply and demand. Short-term forecasts (six to twelve months) are vital inputs to the annual marketing plan and serve to update the planning process to allow continual, appropriate revisions. These forecasts are also inputs to production planning, and to intermediate-range forecasts (one to three years) that define potential opportunities or threats. Long-range strategic planning in the industrial marketing company is facilitated by forecasts of market conditions and the business environment over periods of three to five or more years. Trends in the economy, shifts in the business cycle, changes in the international environment, the pattern of growth in markets, and the possible impacts of technological change are all inputs to the long-term forecasts used in strategic planning. Industrial firms cannot set goals or define their missions without expectations concerning the future business environment. Similarly, long-term forecasts are critical for decisions regarding product line changes, distribution channel changes, plant expansion, or capital requirements.

Studies of Business Trends

The dependence of industrial marketing firms on derived demand necessitates special-purpose studies of industries, technologies, and demographic shifts. For instance, computer components producers must have an understanding of the degree of pervasiveness of computer workstation adoption; building supply companies must have an appreciation of shifting population patterns and their consequences on business and household construction; financial institutions must anticipate the rise and fall of certain industries to plan to meet their short- and long-term financing needs. Not only must the industrial market be studied, but also the ultimate market's dynamics must be understood.

New Product Acceptance and Potential

The identification of new product concepts and their development into tangible products or services incur substantial resource commitment and financial risk. Industrial marketing researchers are invariably assigned the responsibility of assessing the substitution factor for the proposed new product. For instance, how quickly will companies adopt the new product and to what extent will they replace the old? Industrial marketing research must assess the size of the new product's market when the new product exists only in prototype form.

Competitor Analysis

Industrial marketing strategy planning relies heavily on a knowledge of the strengths and weaknesses of competitors and their products. Marketing research is often called upon to investigate customer reactions to competitors' products, to uncover those strengths and weaknesses. Alternatively, the opinions of the sales force or of distributors are often obtained to identify weaknesses in competitors' marketing programs. Further, it is important that the marketer attempt to anticipate how competitors will respond to various moves on his or her part.

Determination of Sales Quotas and Territories

Vital to the assignment and control of the sales force or the identification and assessment of distributors is information which breaks down market potential and expected market share into geographic designations and, further, specifies the level of sales which can be expected under certain market conditions. Territories must be examined to design equitable workloads for salespeople; quotas must be established to communicate performance expectations; and actual sales levels must be compared with quotas and potential to evaluate performance.

As can be seen from the brief descriptions accompanying each of these responsibility areas for industrial marketing research, the gathering and interpreting of information on the market environment is a primary function of industrial marketing research. At least from this perspective, industrial marketing research is not much different from consumer marketing research. In other words, marketing managers—whether they are targeting individuals, households, companies, nonprofit organizations, or any other entity with which their organization seeks to engage in an exchange process—must have timely and accurate information to make intelligent decisions. The marketing research process in any of these situations draws from a common body of technical know-how.

MARKETING RESEARCH AS A PROCESS

Now that some of the basic functions of marketing research have been described, let us turn to the issue of how marketing research is conducted. To appreciate the complexities of research, and the many decisions required in designing and implementing a research project, it should be approached as a *process*. Accordingly, this section will describe marketing research as a logical process that provides a means for deriving reliable and valid data useful to the manager in solving marketing problems. The focus will be on the survey technique, as opposed to some of the other methods of collecting data which will be described later. Surveys display the specialization and expertise of the marketing researchers most vividly, and are relied upon extensively in industrial marketing research. Figure 5.1 presents a series of interrelated steps which comprise a flow diagram for a survey. To appreciate this process, some important introductory comments may be helpful.

First, marketing research is an interactive system of events. Each step in the process depicted in Figure 5.1 is dependent upon previous steps and has implications for subsequent steps. This point can be illustrated easily. Take the example of a major medical insurance provider such as Blue Cross-Blue Shield that perceives a trend among its corporate accounts to drop their medical coverage and turn to self-insurance, where the medical insurance premiums are put into a company-controlled fund rather than paid to Blue Cross-Blue Shield or one of its competitors. To gain a better understanding of the gravity of this trend, marketing research could be applied in a number of ways. Let's examine two approaches, comparing how the problem is defined, and the objectives set for the study. One approach would be to interview former customers, to determine the sources of their dissatisfaction with the Blue Cross-Blue Shield corporate medical insurance plans. Here, research would be concentrated on plan administration—claims processing, payment options, plan supplements, and specific coverage provisions. Telephone calls could be made to a few former key accounts in the search for some common dissatisfaction theme. The sample size would be small, and the questions would be quite general to permit the respondents to elaborate on their frustrations and reasons for dropping the coverage.

A different approach might involve applying marketing research to determine whether the medical insurance industry as a whole was experiencing the problem. In this instance, a much broader research plan would be implemented, with information collected from several different types of companies, in surveys of current customers as well as customers of competitors. Information would also be gathered

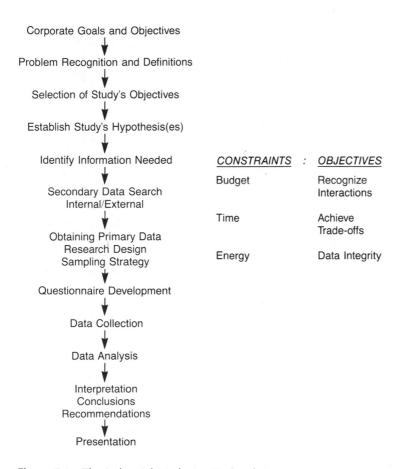

Figure 5.1   The Industrial Marketing Research Process

on medical costs to gain a feel for upward or downward trends in the prices of medical services providers. Consequently, the sample would be much larger, and the questions more precise, to facilitate tabulation and comparisons among various company types. With this alternative, the findings might determine an industry-wide phenomenon rather than a company-specific shortcoming. In short, all subsequent steps in the research process are molded by decisions in earlier steps.

The second introductory point to be made is that the special constraints of time, budget, and energy placed on the marketing research process often foster trade-offs between certain activities. For example, the ideal survey would include information from every possible respondent, that is, a census. However, the time and monetary costs for a census normally place it out of practical reach. Similarly, it is desirable to let respondents elaborate on their answers to the various questions, but practical limitations to data analysis preclude this luxury and force the use of a standardized questionnaire. Also, personal interviews are frequently the most desirable form of data collection, but the necessities of travel and appointment-setting sometimes make this method infeasible, leading the marketing researcher to use a mail questionnaire or telephone interview. In other words, more substantive information would be gained from fewer respondents through personal interviews, and less elaborate information would be gained from more respondents in a telephone survey. Marketing survey designers often find that they must make similar trade-off decisions between the amount of information, the quality of the information, the sample size, the time horizon, analysis techniques, and other factors in such a way as to generate relevant information subject to reasonable and manageable error.

Finally, the marketing research function has the responsibility for ensuring the reliability and validity of the information that is gathered and interpreted for marketing managers. There are a variety of concerns which can be raised about the integrity of the results from any research study. One concern is the reliability, or consistency, of the results. This is the degree to which the measures (i.e., questions) used in the research generate similar results over time, and across situations. If they are inconsistent, the information pertaining to any one question is unreliable: some respondents may be confused about the question; they may be ambivalent or uncertain about their answers; or they may be unintentionally giving different answers because of low motivation to help the marketing researcher. Reliability, then, is a concern with random error.

In contrast, the validity objective pertains to the extent to which the research measures what it purports to measure, and so, is free of systematic error. Respondents may have intentionally misrepresented their opinions; the sample may not have been representative; interviewers may have been biased in recording answers; data analyses may have been inappropriate; or the interpretations of the results may have been systematically erroneous. Regardless of the origin of the invalidity or unreliability, either one destroys the integrity of the finding; marketing researchers must constantly scrutinize their survey designs with reliability and validity as necessary criteria.

DESCRIBING THE STEPS IN THE PROCESS

To demonstrate in more detail what takes place in the steps or stages in the research process presented in Figure 5.1, it may help to go through each stage as it might apply to a research project for a firm attempting to make an expansion decision.

Problem Recognition and Definition

An environmental services company that specialized in the disposal of industrial wastes was quite aware of the increasing scrutiny the government was giving local chemical and other plants regarding the disposal of their by-products and other residual wastes. More and more stringent regulations were being instituted at the national, state, and local municipality levels. Consequently, the waste disposal industry had grown rapidly in terms of total volume as well as in the number of competitors. Normally, the environmental services company has contracted with production facilities to carry away solid and liquid waste products that had been sealed in large metal drums. Occasionally, however, the client plants experienced spillages, pipe ruptures, or containment tank failures that resulted in large pools of dangerous liquid waste that needed to be cleaned up with special equipment. Consequently, the environmental services company was considering the purchase of one or more vacuum trucks that would clean up caustic liquids quickly and efficiently. The approximate cost of a single truck was $100,000. Would the market support this investment?

This example illustrates how the recognition and definition stage involves the sensing of changes in the environment (government regulation, competitive intensity, and market demand), and translating them into possible marketing actions to capitalize on opportunities or avoid threats. It also points out the uncertainty factor involved with solving the problem.

Specify the Study Objectives

The study objectives were clarified using the foregoing problem definition. These objectives included determining: (1) the incidence of liquid waste spillage in target market plants; (2) whether prospective customers were inclined to attempt to clean the spill themselves or call in an outside service; and (3) what industrial waste disposal companies they might call in. Also, it was decided that the information should be gathered within 60 days so that any decision to purchase equipment could be funded in the budget for the next year.

This step should result in a crystallization of the problem into specific information needs and a time frame. Usually, the allowable budget is specified here as well. The interactive nature of the marketing research process can be seen in this example, for if the time frame had been longer, activities such as intensive study of the competitors, in-depth interviews of several prospective customers, or more expensive steps might have been considered.

Establish the Study Hypothesis

By definition, a hypothesis is the statement of what a study is expected to reveal. The hypothesis of this study was that firms in the target market area who experienced liquid waste spillage would be inclined to call in outside specialists who were familiar with the legal and other regulatory factors and who could clean up the liquid waste and dispose of it efficiently. In short, if the environmental services company bought the vacuum truck, its use by the target market would be sufficient to justify the investment. That is, based on observations of the market, the company managers anticipated some level of demand for the vacuum truck, but the uncertainty concerned how much. Other, more specific, hypotheses might be developed regarding the specific characteristics of companies that would most want such a service.

Identify Information Needed

The information sought was articulated as follows. For the incidence of spillage, it was necessary to determine the historical frequency and the amount, as well as obtain estimates of future spillage amounts. For internal versus external cleanup, it was important to determine what equipment each target company owned or expected to purchase in the next few years to facilitate internal cleanup. For rival companies, the information needed was the perceived level of satisfaction with their current industrial waste transport services across the various evaluative dimensions. It should be noted that the information sought comprised a small and concise set. This example points out the effects of the three constraints of budget, time, and resources placed on the research process. The marketing research project director, and the marketing decision makers, engaged in lengthy discussions to agree on the precise set of questions to address in the study.

Secondary Data Search

Secondary data is information that has already been collected, such as that available in government reports, trade association studies, past marketing research studies, or internal company reports. Primary data, then, is information actually generated by the marketing researcher to address a particular problem. In the case of the environmental services company, secondary sources were appraised to determine whether the required information was already in existence in some form, or could be estimated from existing data. It was concluded that this was not the case; thus, primary data had to be collected.

Develop the Research Design, Including Sampling Strategy

With these information requirements, and the operating constraints, it was determined that a cross-sectional survey involving personal interviews was the appropriate research design. The environmental services company's familiarity with prospective clients suggested that approximately sixty different chemical plants and other waste-producing facilities were located in the target area. Purchasing agents were defined to be the relevant contact point for each plant, since arrangements for the transport service companies were generally made through these agents. Because of the urgency of spill cleanup needs, the purchase decision process was often concentrated on one person; it was assumed that the purchasing agent would have the primary decision-making responsibility. Interactions and trade-offs are illustrated well in this stage. The target area was constrained to include companies familiar to the industrial waste disposal company. Similarly, only purchasing agents were to be interviewed despite the knowledge that other managers would have some input in the decision to use or not use the vacuum truck service.

Determine the Method of Data Collection

Again, time and budget constraints posed problems for determining the best way to gather information from a sufficiently large and representative sample. Ultimately, a telephone survey was selected as the appropriate mode of data collection. Purchasing agents have busy schedules and it might be difficult to schedule an appointment for an on-site interview. In addition, the purchasing agents do a great deal of their business over the telephone, and would be very comfortable with this mode of questioning. Finally, the telephone interview approach was selected because a single interview might require several callbacks to find the purchasing agent in the office and with sufficient time to answer the questions without interruption. Of course, the vacuum truck service would have to be described verbally to the respondent—an important trade-off necessitated by using the telephone as the data collection method. Personal interviewers would have carried pictures (perhaps even video tapes) of the service. Supporting the decision to rely on a telephone approach was the belief that the respondents would be familiar with the nature of the service in question, and could envision it sufficiently to guarantee the integrity of their reactions over the telephone.

Develop the Questionnaire

A telephone survey questionnaire was devised, with much consultation between the environmental services company managers and the marketing research team that was assigned the task of executing the survey. The environmental services managers reviewed the questions for proper terminology and appropriate response categories, while the marketing research team guarded against the use of leading questions and maintained proper disguise of the sponsor of the survey. This stage further illustrates an interaction between the steps in the survey and underlines the concern for integrity, in that the industry's jargon was inserted in certain questions to enhance respondents' understanding. Further, telephone interviewing limited the complexity and variety of response scales the interviewer could use off each question on the survey.

Data Collection

A local telephone interview service was used to gather the data. This service was selected because of the expertise of its professional interviewers who had gained the reputation of being persistent yet polite in securing executive interviews. From the target sixty companies in the market area, a total of forty-nine completed interviews were collected in a two-week period. The interviewers were instructed to contact the purchasing agent at the respondent plant, identify themselves as professional interviewers working on a marketing research project for an industrial waste company, and identify the general purposes of the survey. At no time during the survey was the client environmental services company identified to the purchasing agent. Similarly, agents were assured of confidentiality of their responses and anonymity with regard to their opinions. The interviewers were instructed to call back as many times as necessary to obtain a completed interview—or a refusal.

Employment of a professional interview service incurred expense, but the objectives of reliability and validity were paramount in this decision. The interviewers administered the questions identically among respondents. Moreover, they were trained to sense when the respondent was interrupted by important business, to temporarily suspend the interview and to set an appointment to call back and complete it. Also justifying the additional cost were the benefits of a higher response rate, confidentiality assurances to encourage truthful responses, and the overall professionalism of this important step.

Data Analysis

The completed questionnaires were turned over to the marketing research department, and tabulation of the data was performed through a series of steps which transformed (coded) the raw responses into computer input, scrutinized the accuracy of this transformation, and computed means, percentages and other descriptive statistics in order to gain a picture of the respondents' opinions. Computer analysis was performed quickly and efficiently, and at a minimum cost, since the computer hardware and software were owned by the environmental services company.

Interpretation and Presentation

Approximately one-half of the respondents indicated a present or possible future need for a wet materials cleanup and transport service. Of these, the most commonly estimated volume was in the 100-barrel-per-month range. The results further indicated that the company was the most preferred waste transport service among 30 percent of the companies surveyed, and it was mentioned as the second choice by an additional 25 percent of the companies. Thus, the environmental services company could anticipate being called in as their first choice by approximately 15 percent of the companies in this market and by approximately 12 percent as their second choice. Further analysis revealed that the respondent purchasing agents indicated a high level of general satisfaction with their current supplier of industrial waste transport service, but were least satisfied with their supplier's rates and personnel. The purchasing agents indicated that they would evaluate supplier attributes in this order of priority: competitive rates, technical expertise, dependable and reliable service, and the ability to meet legal requirements.

The information was then compared against the total cost of purchasing and operating a vacuum truck in the target market area. Comparisons of the estimated revenues under various scenarios (best case, worst case, most likely case) revealed that the environmental services company would at least break even on the venture in the worst case and could realize a return of investment of over 20 percent in the best case. Given these findings, the decision was made to purchase a truck and begin marketing the company's new service. In the marketing program, the environmental services company endeavored to price at or just below the rates of its competitors, and to emphasize the technical expertise of its personnel as well as the company's long history of successful industrial waste disposal in compliance with legal restraints.

This description of an industrial marketing survey demonstrates the several steps and safeguards which should be followed to derive valid information on the industrial marketplace from primary data sources. Keep in mind that, throughout the research process, the overriding objective is to execute the survey to gain the most accurate information possible within the established budget and time constraints. Information which distorts the truth can be very costly in the long run.

ARE THERE DIFFERENCES BETWEEN INDUSTRIAL AND CONSUMER MARKETING RESEARCH?

Previous chapters pointed out the major differences between industrial and consumer marketing, but is there a difference between consumer and industrial marketing research? To answer this question, one can look at the types of marketing research studies conducted, and compare the types of research techniques used by consumer companies with those used by industrial marketers. Table 5.1 presents a summary of one such comparison.

The results of the study summarized in Table 5.1 reveal some important commonalities, as well as significant differences, in the types of marketing research activities in consumer companies and industrial companies. The similarities can be attributed to the fact that all firms, regardless of market orientation, must engage in the design and execution of marketing planning. Consequently, forecasts and other special-purpose studies devoted to sensing opportunities in the marketplace, as well as assessments of the company performance, are relied upon equally by both types of companies. Moreover, corporate responsibility concerns affect both types of firms.

It should be recognized that major differences in the types of studies conducted are attributable to differences in the strategic importance of certain marketing variables. For instance, industrial companies tend to make less use of advertising research than do consumer companies. This difference is largely a function of the fact that industrial companies rely more on the sales force element of the promotional blend than do consumer companies. By the same token, consumer companies place relatively more emphasis on research activities that tap the consumer psyche and life style.

The first chapter of this book designated three critical distinguishing characteristics of industrial markets. These same considerations help to further explain some of the ways in which industrial marketing research is different. The first of the three stressed the technical nature of many industrial products. In the industrial market, there is substantial need for an understanding of production technology, service support, and the special technical background of prospective buyers. For example, a chemicals company might be interested in learning why sales for an industrial catalytic agent have declined. Proper research requires an understanding of the chemical compounds involved and the conditions, such as temperature, pressure, and time of the chemical reactions where the catalyst is used. It would necessitate an understanding of the degree of volatility of chemicals and the by-products of chemical reactions. Transportation and storage aspects would need to be studied. Conditions of supply and demand for raw material ingredients would be examined along with the buying process for the catalyst. In short, several highly technical factors would be studied by the marketing researcher to guarantee that the survey was custom-tailored to the problem.

The second point of difference between industrial goods and consumer goods noted earlier in this book stressed that industrial products directly affect the operations and economic health of buyers/users. For example, a cleaning service company may not realize that its clients value scrupulously clean customer-contact areas as an important company image component. Research might reveal that clients would pay

Table 5.1 Marketing Research Activities: Industrial vs. Consumer
Goods Companies

Research Activity	Industrial Companies	Consumer Companies	Absolute Difference
ADVERTISING RESEARCH			
Motivation Research	29	61	32
Copy Research	55	78	23
Media Research	57	72	15
Studies of Ad Effectiveness	67	86	19
Studies of Competitive Advertising	54	73	19
BUSINESS ECONOMICS AND CORPORATE RESEARCH			
Short-Range Forecasting (Up to 1 Year)	98	97	1
Long-Range Forecasting (Over 1 Year)	94	96	2
Studies of Business Trends	99	90	9
Pricing Studies	90	91	1
Plant and Warehouse Location Studies	78	71	7
Acquisition Studies	89	81	8
Export and International Studies	82	69	13
MIS	90	89	1
Operations Research	68	71	3
Internal Company Employees	80	73	7
CORPORATE RESPONSIBILITY RESEARCH			
Consumers' "Right to Know" Studies	12	21	9
Ecological Impact Studies	35	37	5
Studies of Legal Constraints on Advertising and Promotion	46	58	12
Social Values and Policies Studies	29	47	18
PRODUCT RESEARCH			
New Product Acceptance and Potential	73	89	16
Competitive Product Studies	92	97	5
Testing of Existing Products	86	11	75
Packaging Research: Design or Physical Characteristics	61	16	45
SALES AND MARKET RESEARCH			
Measurement of Market Potentials	99	99	0
Market Share Analysis	98	99	1
Determination of Market Characteristics	99	99	0
Sales Analysis	99	98	1
Establishment of Sales Quotas, Territories	95	93	2
Distribution Channel Studies	83	89	6
Test Markets, Store Audits	36	88	52
Consumer Panel Operations	31	87	56
Sales Compensation Studies	73	83	10
Promotional Studies of Premiums	36	82	46

Source: Adapted from Dik W. Twedt ed., *1983* Source Survey of Marketing Research. (Chicago: American Marketing Association, 1984), 41, 43.

a little more for meticulous cleaning of these areas. In other words, clients would see the cleaning service as an investment in image enhancement, not as a low-bid commodity purchase. Another example might involve a financial institution that buys an automatic teller machine network. If the machines are unfriendly, slow, or subject to downtime, the bank's customers quickly think about changing to a more responsive system at another bank. So research done for Diebold Corporation, which manufactures ATMs, must take into consideration the end users of the systems which prospective customers will buy.

Thirdly, it was pointed out that, typically, organizational rather than individual buying decisions are involved. More decision makers, with more varied concerns, are thrown into the purchase decision-making process. Major purchase decisions are the result of a much more formalized and complicated process than is found in consumer purchasing. That is, the deliberation process and formality of buying and service arrangements as well as product performance to expected standards is paramount. This characteristic complicates the survey process in the sense that the several members of the buying center in any one company must be considered, and perhaps all must be questioned. Preliminary research must be invested in the identification of purchasing criteria, review and retention standards, and of the source loyalties involved. Research has identified no less than six different roles played by different organization members in the buying center (see Chapter 4). Clearly, the marketing research function is confronted with special circumstances, both when deciding which organizational members should be included in the research sample, and when conducting research aimed at determining how buying decisions are made.

An alternative means of comparing industrial with consumer marketing research is to break down the various aspects of the survey process. Table 5.2 reveals some basic mechanical differences in the actual conduct of research. For example, instead of markets with hundreds of thousands (or more) consumers, industrial markets tend to be characterized by hundreds (or fewer) target companies. Often, extensive secondary data exists on these companies. Also, personal interviews with managers often must be performed, as opposed to random household telephone surveys or large mailings of questionnaires. Subjects are people at work who may be inaccessible, or may not have time to participate in elaborate research projects. As a result, samples may be biased in favor of the opinions of purchasing agents, who are more frequent participants.

The complexity of the buying process sometimes requires information from two or three respondents in a single target company. The inputs from these respondents may have to be weighted in some fashion to reflect the different level of influence each has in the buying decision process. Keep in mind that the organization, and not the individual, usually is the desired unit of analysis. Interviewers must be trained in the technical terminology and the proper approach to conducting personal interviews, often with managers from different backgrounds. Also, the sales force is sometimes used to collect data in industrial marketing research projects. Further, even though sample sizes tend to be smaller in industrial marketing research studies, surveys may take a longer time to complete and cost more in total. Finally, small sample sizes and sizable differences between and among organizations

Table 5.2 How Aspects of the Survey Process Can Differ in Consumer vs. Industrial Marketing Research

Marketing Research Decision Area	Consumer Research	Industrial Research
Universe/ Population	Large—dependent on category under investigation	Small—limited in total population
Respondent Accessibility	Fairly easy—interviews at home, mail or by phone	Difficult—usually only during working time
Respondent Cooperation	Becoming more difficult, but possible samples are large	Of major concern—sample is small
Sample Size	Can be as large as is required	Usually very small
Respondent Definitions	Fairly simple—users are usually purchasers	More difficult—purchasers not always users
Unit of Analysis	The individual or household	The organization
Interviewers	Easily trained—are also consumers	Difficult to train; must have expertise; the sales force can sometimes be used
Study Costs	Key dictators are sample and incidence of target group members in the population.	Critical elements time and sample size

Adapted from Katz, "Use Same Theory, Skills for Consumer, Industrial Marketing Research," *Marketing News* 12, (January 1979), 16. Copyright American Marketing Association. Reprinted with permission.

place severe limitations on the generalizability of study results to other organizations.

The answer to the question posed at the beginning of this section is, therefore, "yes." Yes, industrial and consumer marketing research are different, because the sources of information and the techniques applied to tap those sources vary considerably. They also differ due to variances in the strategic importance of marketing variables, and because the underlying dynamics of industrial markets are driven by factors separate from those driving consumer markets. But both types are identical in their roles of providing accurate information to help reduce the uncertainty in the marketing manager's daily decision deliberations. In spite of this, managers of industrial products companies tend to perform less marketing research than do their consumer product counterparts.

FROM MARKETING RESEARCH TO MARKETING INTELLIGENCE

Up to this point, research has been considered an isolated activity undertaken to address a specific problem. Unfortunately, managers often feel that an occasional marketing research project is sufficient to take care of all the firm's marketing information needs. A more comprehensive perspective on these needs is achieved by moving to the concept of marketing intelligence, of which marketing research is one part. For purposes of comparison, consider research to be a single activity in the marketing decision-making process, with marketing intelligence operating throughout the marketing decision-making process. Figure 5.2 illustrates steps in marketing decision making together with two quite different views of the role of information gathering.

As Figure 5.2 demonstrates, the narrow view relegates marketing research to a periodic data-gathering and analysis role. For instance, if a company is considering a change in its service policies, the alternatives might be: (1) increase the amount of service; (2) decrease the amount of service; or (3) maintain service at its current level. If a primary objective of the company is to maintain customer loyalty, a marketing research study would be undertaken to determine the impact of each of these alternatives on customer propensity to shift to other suppliers. If the information gained revealed that increased service levels would increase the loyalty factor, and, further, that the increased service level would be cost justifiable, the decision would favor that alternative. It would be implemented and the results monitored by the marketing manager.

Industrial marketing intelligence, alternatively, is an enlightened view of the role of information-providing activities in the industrial management process. *Intel-*

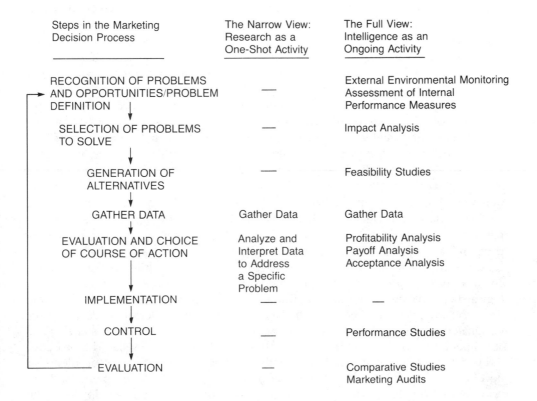

Steps in the Marketing Decision Process	The Narrow View: Research as a One-Shot Activity	The Full View: Intelligence as an Ongoing Activity
RECOGNITION OF PROBLEMS AND OPPORTUNITIES/PROBLEM DEFINITION	—	External Environmental Monitoring Assessment of Internal Performance Measures
SELECTION OF PROBLEMS TO SOLVE	—	Impact Analysis
GENERATION OF ALTERNATIVES	—	Feasibility Studies
GATHER DATA	Gather Data	Gather Data
EVALUATION AND CHOICE OF COURSE OF ACTION	Analyze and Interpret Data to Address a Specific Problem	Profitability Analysis Payoff Analysis Acceptance Analysis
IMPLEMENTATION	—	—
CONTROL	—	Performance Studies
EVALUATION	—	Comparative Studies Marketing Audits

Figure 5.2   Research Versus Intelligence

ligence is a term that has its roots in the military, and it may be helpful to recast some of the characteristics of the industrial market in a military context, as some writers have proposed (Kotler and Singh 1981).

First, just as in warfare situations, there often are a few relatively large, well-identified competitors vying to win the marketing battle. This condition means that the focus of intelligence can be isolated on a few of the competitors. Second, there is a limited number of customers, analogous to the finite number of suitable battle-grounds on which wars are fought. Third, the value of each customer is a function of the demand which it derives from its own business. That is, the customer is sought because of the size of its business, just as a port city is battled over for the strategic value of its location, or a country is fought over because of the value of its raw materials and natural resources. Third, price bidding or promotional campaigns often take place just as offenses and counterattacks occur on a battleground. Finally, the cost of failure in the industrial marketplace is very high, and the loss of a single account or a small set of accounts may prove fatal to the industrial marketing firm just as the loss of a significant battle may prove fatal for a combatant.

The role of intelligence activities in a military context is to provide a continuous flow of information for use in developing strategies and tactics—both for winning the war and keeping the peace. These activities can be defensive or offensive in nature, focusing on information relevant for maintaining current position, or for making inroads into an adversary's position. A wide variety of information is collected, covering everything from identifying strengths and weaknesses of the opposition to uncovering untapped strategic opportunities. The information must be constantly updated, with regular reports provided to the senior military staff.

The parallel with a firm's marketing information needs is unmistakable. Marketers require the same continuous flow of information. Although some of this data can be obtained with periodic marketing research studies, a more systematic and ongoing information gathering process is needed.

A marketing intelligence system can be defined as an interrelated set of specialists, procedures, hardware, and software which accumulates, stores, interprets, and disseminates (usually in report form) raw data on the external and internal marketing environments. Its purpose is to provide relevant, accurate, and otherwise valuable information to marketing decision makers on a timely and ongoing basis.

As indicated in Figure 5.2, the marketing intelligence system (MIS) serves as a partner to the industrial marketing manager. For instance, in the recognition of problems and opportunities, the MIS provides information by monitoring the environment and providing the marketer with information on shifts in the economy, changes in the regulatory system, competitors' actions and policy changes, technological breakthroughs, or the identification of new market segments. At the same time, the MIS maintains constant vigilance on the critical performance measures designated by the industrial marketing manager such as sales, market share, quota attainment, distributor accounts retained, stock levels, or service visits. The proactive industrial marketing manager is constantly informed of symptoms of problems or developing opportunities. He or she periodically prioritizes the problems and opportunities. The MIS serves a vital role by providing information to help assess the probable impact of possible problems on future business activities, as well as evaluating the scope and attractiveness of opportunities which may come on stream in the near or distant future.

The industrial marketing manager is also concerned with generating alternative courses of action that he or she might implement in order to capitalize on opportunities or to solve problems. Here, the MIS can perform feasibility studies which assess the appropriateness, cost, and viability of each alternative. The evaluation and choice stage of the industrial marketing management process is assisted through profitability analysis, payoff analysis and other studies which help to evaluate the attractiveness of various alternatives to prospective buyers or distributors. Once the course of action is selected, the implementation stage takes place. This stage is the only one where the MIS has no active role—since it is a staff function. However, once implementation is effected, the MIS provides constant vigilance of the actual performance measures used to gauge whether the course of action selected is eliciting sufficient sales or market share. Finally, an overall evaluation of the decision-making process is assisted through the MIS, which performs comparative studies such as *what if?* scenarios and integrated marketing audits.

STEPS IN ESTABLISHING AND OPERATING AN MIS

A marketing intelligence system must be planned and custom-tailored to the unique information needs of every industrial marketing firm. The steps involved in the development and fine-tuning of an MIS are illustrated in Figure 5.3, which shows that the beginning point of the marketing intelligence system design is the identification of the marketing decision makers in the company. Product managers, sales managers, advertising managers, strategic planners, in fact, all members of the organization who have marketing decision responsibilities are identified. Next, the information needs of these individuals are specified with special concern for the quality, scope, frequency, and timing of information required for them to operate effectively and efficiently. Then, the available sources of information must be determined, and methods of obtaining the information from these sources must be identified and/or designed. The storage place(s) for information that flows into the company must be identified and maintained. The raw data inputs must be translated or grouped into categories that are meaningful in marketing analysis, such as expenses that are described as *variable* or *fixed*, or as *direct* or *indirect*. Methods of reporting information to executives must be established, and the format and routing system designed. Special-purpose access and retrieval methods must be provided. Finally, there is the evaluation and fine-tuning of the marketing intelligence system.

The actual component parts in a marketing intelligence system can be seen in Figure 5.4 . The heart of an MIS is a centralized data base—raw information that has been gathered, processed, recorded, and summarized. The data base is usually organized into separate files, such as a customer file, a competitor file, a territory file, a product performance file, and a marketing activity file. Dedicated files could be set up for each marketing research project undertaken. The design of the data base constitutes the basic structure of the MIS; it can range from very crude to elegant. Data in these areas, and others, is gathered from internal (e.g., the sales force, ac-

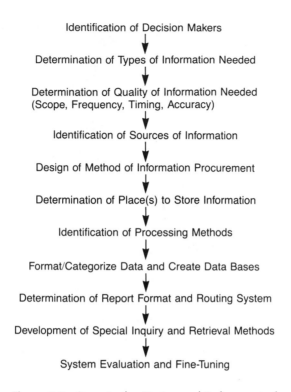

Identification of Decision Makers

↓

Determination of Types of Information Needed

↓

Determination of Quality of Information Needed
(Scope, Frequency, Timing, Accuracy)

↓

Identification of Sources of Information

↓

Design of Method of Information Procurement

↓

Determination of Place(s) to Store Information

↓

Identification of Processing Methods

↓

Format/Categorize Data and Create Data Bases

↓

Determination of Report Format and Routing System

↓

Development of Special Inquiry and Retrieval Methods

↓

System Evaluation and Fine-Tuning

Figure 5.3   Steps in the Design and Refinement of an MIS

counting records) and external (e.g., government publications, competitor catalogs) sources. These sources are labeled *data providers* in Figure 5.4.

The raw information is edited into usable form, and then entered into a storage device—at the simplest level, on file cards kept in a cabinet. A sophisticated system might involve storage on a central mainframe computer that can be accessed from a series of remote terminals. Between these two is the more common system, where data is stored on floppy disks for use on a personal computer, or on a hard disk drive PC. The method used to input the data will vary depending upon the amount and complexity of the information, and the type of storage device. The input mechanism could range from a member of the marketing department simply keying in data, to the marketing analyst downloading data files stored in the company's central mainframe. The input process is continual, as files are constantly updated.

Once in place, the MIS can be accessed to provide assistance in marketing analysis and planning. Basically, data users generate an information request. The desired information is then retrieved from the storage device, often simply by calling up a file on the computer terminal, and having it printed out. Prior to retrieving the data, however, it may first be necessary to perform some manipulations or tabulations on the stored data. This is the *data processing* component. Tabulations may involve constructing averages or dividing one column of numbers by another.

A standard feature of an MIS is a set of reports that are generated for management at periodic intervals. These might include a weekly sales activity report, a

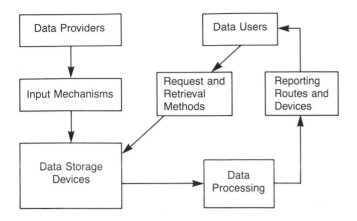

Figure 5.4   Components of a Simple Marketing Intelligence System

monthly report of profitability by product line, or a quarterly advertising effectiveness report, among others. The MIS exists to satisfy both irregular information requests when particular problems or issues arise, and regular information needs for ongoing decisions.

Take for instance the MIS which operates inside Acme Business Machines Company. This company manufactures and sells business machines such as duplicating equipment, copy machines, and dictaphones to a wide variety of companies. The decision makers who have constant need for marketing intelligence information are: (1) the president, (2) the vice-president of marketing, and (3) the sales manager. Obviously, there are similarities and differences in the information needs of these managers. The sales manager requires specific breakdowns on salespeople, territories, and products. The marketing vice-president is more concerned with market share statistics, competitors' strategies, and the performance of product lines. The president tends to look long term, and identify economic, political, and technological opportunity and threat areas.

Over time, the MIS at Acme has evolved to become an integral part of the daily operations of the company. Both formal and informal company policy support its use as follows. Salesmen are required to submit monthly reports which detail their activities: calls, expenses, sales invoices, account prospects, and observations of market conditions. Service representatives submit reports of service calls, types of problems solved, ages and configurations of machines repaired. Trade association reports, business periodicals, and financial analysts' observations are scrutinized. Periodic telephone calls are made to major customers to gain insight into their expected business activity changes and intentions to purchase equipment. Business trends and population shifts to warmbelt areas are abstracted; market share studies are executed; literature from competitors collected; and trade shows attended to research new products and technology.

All of this data is systematized into reports, which are issued at regular intervals and in the form required by the manager involved. For instance, the sales managers are given trend-line analyses of individual salesperson performance, along with comparisons to their past performance. The marketing vice-president receives a summary of product line performance with detailed breakdowns appended for inspection. In addition, a newsletter is issued to highlight national trends, competitors' product introductions, and other observations of the industry. The system will also satisfy occasional data requests, such as an inquiry from the marketing vice-president regarding the number of new accounts generated in the past six months, compared to the preceding six-month period.

FROM INTELLIGENCE TO DECISION SUPPORT

Although an MIS provides a systematic approach for collecting, storing, and disseminating marketing information, its end product is primarily reports. In practice, the MIS is designed and used only for routine marketing decisions. As marketing managers develop their skills and knowledge base, and as marketing decisions grow in complexity, information needs exceed the capabilities of an MIS. It becomes appropriate, then, to move to a decision support system (DSS), which is the next logical extension of an MIS. Again, just as periodic marketing research was part of the MIS, the MIS is part of a DSS. Decision support systems will play a growing role in marketing decision making in the years to come, especially on the creative side of marketing strategy formulation.

An MIS is used in a regular, planned, and anticipated manner, often to generate standardized reports, but DSS is concerned with unstructured problem solving and decision making. In other words, an MIS is purposely designed to complement the step-by-step nature of the formal decision-making process; a DSS is designed to be available to the manager who breaks out of the routine and casts imagination and personal creativity into the formula. Thus, the DSS must be broader in content and more accommodating of *what if?* inquiries. It must have the flexibility to respond to unusual requests as well as provide the structure for the routine inquiries and reports relied upon by the bulk of the company's managers.

Users of an MIS are primarily concerned with retrieval questions. They want a system that is capable of quickly retrieving a piece of information, such as quarterly revenue in territory A, or average gross margin on sales of product X. But the manager who asks questions which require (often nonroutine) performing analysis on stored data may be better served with a DSS. Such nonroutine questions might include How much did the competition's 10 percent price cut affect our sales of product X? or How will the replacement of distributors with our own direct sales force affect profitability?

A decision support system comprises data, statistics, models, and optimization, as illustrated in Figure 5.5. The *data base* is the same as that provided through the MIS. *Statistics* are simple tools for manipulating the data. There are a number of complex multivariate statistical tools, but managers more often are concerned with simple ratios, frequency distributions, and basic descriptive *statistics* such as averages, ranges, and standard deviations. *Models* are attempts to examine relationships between or among variables; they could be based on the marketer's own hypothesis regarding how these variables are related. For example, models might be developed concerning the relationship between price charged and product sales (i.e., elasticity), or between advertising expenditures and the cost of a sales call. *Optimization*

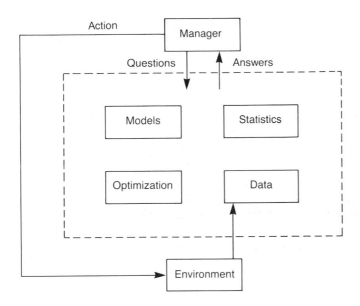

Figure 5.5 Elements of a Decision Support System
(Source: J.D.C. Little, "Decision Support Systems for Marketing Managers," *Journal of Marketing,* 43 (Chicago: American Marketing Association, Summer 1979, 10. Reprinted with permission.)

refers to the development of a set of decision rules for determining the best alternative using the available data base. So, the DSS may rank order sales territories based on the total contribution as a percentage of sales. Linear programming models might be used to determine the optimal level of sales support required.

THE USE OF SECONDARY DATA SOURCES IN INDUSTRIAL MARKETING INTELLIGENCE

Marketing intelligence, when organized around an MIS or DSS, provides a living information system which operates within the industrial firm and facilitates the marketing decision-making process. If designed, implemented, and maintained properly, the intelligence system can become a significant competitive advantage for the company itself. Other companies might not have as up-to-date knowledge of marketplace events and trends, or profiles of the history of the marketplace and the performance of competitors under various marketplace conditions. In short, the system will provide ongoing information which will serve to reduce the uncertainty level of marketing managers as they wrestle with marketing decisions.

A well-designed intelligence system is likely to rely heavily on secondary data sources. Industrial marketing situations are especially amenable to the use of secondary data because of its availability, and the earlier mentioned problems in collecting primary data. Normally, for example, it is possible to quickly identify any number of government reports, industry association studies, business periodical articles, or company publications that might provide timely information useful in any one of a number of marketing intelligence functions. Typically, secondary data sources are divided into two basic types: internal and external.

Internal Secondary Data Sources

Internal sources of secondary data are those reports and reservoirs of information which the company maintains as a normal part of its operations. For instance, sales records, salesperson's reports, annual reports, technical analyses, notes and memos from new product evaluation teams, past marketing research reports, financial records, and all of the documentation maintained in the company's files constitute the internal secondary information pool. A wealth of internal secondary information exists in raw form. The difficulty arises in finding specific pieces of information, for they are invariably mixed in among a wide array of data. The value of a good marketing intelligence system is readily apparent in this case. If the MIS can accommodate inquiries and conduct searches of key words or other identifiers, the retrieval process will be much faster and more complete.

External Secondary Data Sources

Data sources that are considered external are those which originate outside the company. The list of possible sources is almost limitless, as the following brief descriptions will indicate.

General Business Indices

A number of business source books which cross-reference the locations of publications on various business topics. The most popular ones include:

Business Periodicals Index

Public Affairs Information Service Bulletin

Readers Guide to Periodical Literature

Social Sources Citation Index

Wall Street Journal Index

Government Sources

The U.S. Government publishes a number of census and other documents which are used extensively by industrial marketing researchers. Examples include:

Census of Agriculture

Census of Business

Census of Housing

Census of Manufactures

Census of Population

Census of Retail Trade

Census of Selected Services

Census of Transportation

Census of Wholesale Trade

In addition, the U.S. Government publishes a number of general information secondary sources, including:

County and City Data Book

Historical Statistics of the United States

Statistical Abstract of the United States

Monthly Catalogue of United States Government Publications

Congressional District Data Book

Finally, the various departments in the U.S. Government publish their own business data sources, including:

Business Conditions Digest

County Business Patterns

Economic Indicators

Economic Report of the President

Federal Reserve Bulletin

Handbook of Basic Economic Statistics

Monthly Labor Review

Standard Industrial Classification Manual

Statistics of Income

Survey of Current Business

United Nations Statistical Year Book

U.S. Industrial Outlook

Commercial Sources

Numerous publications are distributed by members of the private sector. These include:

Annual Survey of U.S. Business Plans for New Plants and Equipment

Funk and Scott Index of Corporations and Industries

Guide to Consumer Markets

Market Guide

Sales and Marketing Management "Annual Survey of U.S. Industrial and Commercial Buying Power"

Standard Corporation Descriptions

Survey of Buying Power

Thomas Register of American Manufacturers

Also, there are over 2,000 on-line data bases that the marketer can access, and the list is rapidly growing. Many of these are of high quality, and a number are quite specialized. On-line data bases allow the marketer to perform rapid searches to identify the available information in virtually any area. For instance, these searches can produce bibliographies on specific business topics (e.g., current uses of robotics in industry, techniques for evaluating trade show effectiveness, or uses of discounts when setting industrial prices). They can also provide actual data on employment or shipments in a particular industry, financial information on specific companies, or current economic statistics, among many others. To use these services, the marketer generally pays an hourly computer access charge for the amount of connect time required to complete the information search. The end result is a printed report of the information requested. Some of the major data base producers and distributors are:

Dow Jones News Retrieval: (Dow Jones, Inc.)	provides a wealth of financial information; data bases include daily summaries of *The Wall Street Journal*, *Barron's*, and a variety of financial services from diverse sources.
The Source: *(Reader's Digest)*	contains over 45 data bases, including UNISTOX (timely information on stocks and bonds), UPI news service, flight schedules, and employment data bases.
Disclosure II: (Disclosure, Inc.)	extracts of reports filed by 8,500 companies to the U.S. Securities and Exchange Commission.
PTS-Series: (Predicasts, Inc.)	statistical information, forecasts, and time series for 50 major countries, and historical time series on 500 key variables in the U.S.
ABI/INFORM: (Data Courier, Inc.)	designed to meet the information needs of executives, covering all phases of business management and administration; stresses decision sciences information.
NEXIS: (Mead Data Central)	provides current and recent news articles relevant to business from a large number of newspapers, magazines, and wire services.
FIND/SVP Reports and Studies Index: (FIND/SVP Co.)	indexes and describes all industry and market research reports, studies, and surveys from over 300 U.S. and international publishers; also includes reports from investment research firms.
HARFAX Industry Data Sources: (Harper and Row Publishers, Inc.)	includes bibliographic sources (both primary and secondary) of financial and marketing data for 60 major industries.

ORBIT: (Systems Development Corp.)	contains over 80 data bases on such subjects as energy, business, agriculture, government publications, law and patents, among others.
DIALOG: Information Services Division, Lockheed Corp.)	offers access to more than 150 data bases (Dialog containing over 55 million records); perhaps the most powerful on-line system with particular relevance to business research.

Secondary Data and the SIC System

The ability of industrial firms to conduct marketing research and gather intelligence has been greatly enhanced by the development of the Standard Industrial Classification (SIC) system. This system was alluded to in prior chapters. SIC codes are numbers, consisting of up to seven digits, that represent different types of economic activity. Establishments are assigned to an SIC code based on the major type of economic activity in which they are involved. Note that because one company might operate a number of different establishments, it would receive a code number for each of its establishments based on the primary product of that location.

The numbering system is hierarchical in nature. The more digits included in a particular SIC code, the more descriptive that code becomes. Each of the digits has a meaning. In a given seven-digit code, the first two digits refer to the *major category* of economic activity. There are ten major categories, as illustrated in column 1 of Figure 5.6. For example, all mining activity falls between SIC 10 and SIC 14. Therefore, the first two digits of the SIC code for any establishment primarily engaged in mining will be a number between 10 and 14. Each of these two-digit numbers is a *major group* within the mining area. SIC 10 is the major group that consists of companies which mine metals (see column 2, Figure 5.6).

If a third digit is added, the code refers to a *group*. SIC 104 is the group representing those who mine gold and silver ores (see column 3). With the addition of a fourth digit, the code now represents a *specific industry*. Much of the available secondary data is organized by four-digit SIC code. Using our same example, SIC 1044 includes those establishments involved in mining silver ores (see column 4). The inclusion of a fifth digit allows for *product categories,* while the sixth and seventh digits represent *specific products*.

Figure 5.7 offers another example of the organization of the SIC system. The marketer confronted with a research question regarding the nature and size of opportunities in the electronic components market can find a wealth of information regarding the number, location, size of shipments, number of employees, and number of large establishments for organizations involved in producing electronic components. Some of the major sources of this information include the *Census of Manufactures, The U.S. Industrial Outlook, The Survey of Current Business*, and the "Survey of Industrial and Commercial Buying Power," published by *Sales and Marketing Management.*

At the highest level of the SIC systems, the marketer would select the manufacturing sector from among the several possible major categories. Within manufactur-

Figure 5.6   Standard Industrial Classification (SIC) as a Segmentation
Basis: Overview of the Digit System

(1) Major Categories in SIC	(2) Major Groups of Mining Industries 2-Digit SIC	(3) Groups of Metal Mining Industries 3-Digit SIC	(4) Specific Gold and Silver Mining Industries 4-Digit SIC
01–09 Agriculture, forestry, fishing	10 Metal mining	101 Iron ores	1042 Lode gold
10–14 Mining	11 Anthracite mining	102 Copper ores	1043 Placer gold
15–17 Contract construction	12 Bituminous coal	103 Lead and zinc ores	1044 Silver ores
20–39 Manufacturing	13 Crude petroleum and natural gas	104 Gold and silver ores	
40–49 Transportation, communications, electric, gas	14 Nonmetallic minerals	105 Bauxite	
50–59 Wholesale and retail trade		106 Ferroalloy ores	
60–67 Finance, insurance, and real estate		108 Metal mining services	
70–89 Services		109 Miscellaneous metal ores	
90–93 Government			
99 Others			

ing there are 84 major groups. Because the market of interest is electronic components, the marketer would focus on SIC 36, which consists of manufacturers of electrical and electronic machinery. Within this group there are 596 subgroups. The marketer decides to pursue electronic transmission equipment (SIC 361) in which there are 976 industry categories. Finally, the makers of switchgear and switchboard apparatus (SIC 3613) are identified as the prime target. Data is then gathered on the number of establishments in SIC 3613, their geographic concentration, and their size. With this data, the marketer can begin to estimate market potential, and to make targeting decisions. Marketing programs can be developed, and resources allocated, based on the needs and potential of this market.

Two helpful statistics are available for use with SIC data—the primary product specialization ratio and the coverage ratio. The first ratio expresses the percentage of total shipments by a given four-digit SIC industry that is accounted for by its primary product. This percentage represents, for the industry as a whole, how much of its output is just the primary product produced by that industry, and how much is other products. This is important to the industrial marketer, because he or she is usually interested in the companies within a given SIC category only because of their principal product. The second ratio indicates how much of a particular product is made by establishments within the SIC code primarily associated with that product,

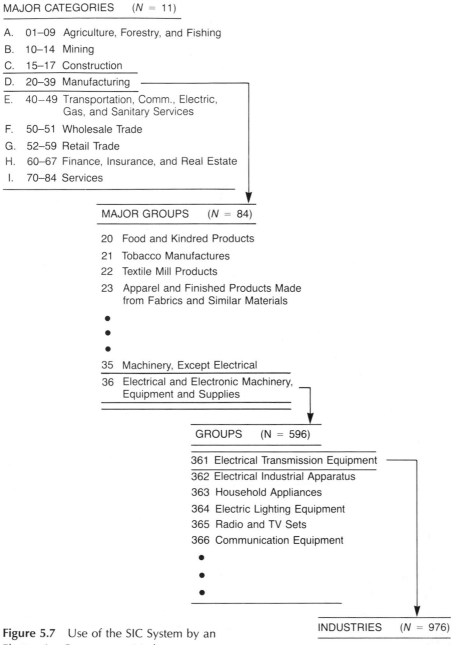

MAJOR CATEGORIES   (N = 11)

A.   01–09 Agriculture, Forestry, and Fishing
B.   10–14 Mining
C.   15–17 Construction
D.   20–39 Manufacturing
E.   40–49 Transportation, Comm., Electric,
            Gas, and Sanitary Services
F.   50–51 Wholesale Trade
G.   52–59 Retail Trade
H.   60–67 Finance, Insurance, and Real Estate
I.   70–84 Services

MAJOR GROUPS   (N = 84)

20   Food and Kindred Products
21   Tobacco Manufactures
22   Textile Mill Products
23   Apparel and Finished Products Made
     from Fabrics and Similar Materials
•
•
•
35   Machinery, Except Electrical
36   Electrical and Electronic Machinery,
     Equipment and Supplies

GROUPS   (N = 596)

361 Electrical Transmission Equipment
362 Electrical Industrial Apparatus
363 Household Appliances
364 Electric Lighting Equipment
365 Radio and TV Sets
366 Communication Equipment
•
•
•

INDUSTRIES   (N = 976)

3611 Electric Measuring Equipment
3612 Power Distribution and
     Specialty Transformers
**3613 Switchgear and Switchboard
     Apparatus**

Figure 5.7   Use of the SIC System by an
Electronics Components Marketer
(Source: Adapted from P. Robinson, C. Hinkle, and
E. Bloom (1967), "Standard Industrial Classification for
Effective Marketing Analysis," Working Paper,
Marketing Science Inst., Cambridge, Mass., 4 - 6.
Reprinted with permission.)

compared to how much of that product is made by establishments whose principal line of business is classified in a different SIC code. Therefore, it is the ratio of shipments of a primary product by producers in one SIC code to shipments of that product by producers in all SIC codes. The marketer, in attempting to focus on makers of a particular product, wants to know how much of the product is made by establishments outside the basic SIC code to which it is assigned.

Problems with Secondary Data

Unfortunately, external secondary data poses a basic dilemma for the marketing intelligence system manager: although this secondary data is readily available, extensive, and often contains information in encapsulated form, it must always be scrutinized for applicability and accuracy. Figure 5.8 illustrates the series of steps which a MIS manager must follow to examine these secondary data sources, to determine whether or not the information is useful for the marketing decision-making problem at hand. This figure reveals that two levels of scrutiny take place. First, the fundamental purpose of the secondary data is inspected to determine whether it varies from the basic objectives of the problem under consideration. For instance, there may be a mismatch in the comparison of populations under study, timeliness of the data, or units and classifications used in measurement.

On the other hand, if there is a consistent fit between the secondary data objectives and the problem being investigated, there may be reservations regarding the accuracy of the data reported in the secondary data source. For example, in Level II, the original sources of information may have been misquoted or misrepresented. It is possible that the methods of data collection or reporting have distorted the information as it was reported. Or, the reservations regarding the accuracy of the data may be sufficiently strong to disallow its use, regardless of how inexpensive the secondary data is.

The detailed process for scrutinizing secondary data is another example of the constant balancing act between the value of information and its inherent error. Here, because the data was collected by a third party for a purpose other than the current research project, steps must be taken to ensure that the information fits the circumstances. If the fit is poor, the error factor will outweigh the accessibility and low cost of the data.

Trends in Industrial Marketing and Intelligence Systems

What lies in the future for industrial marketing research and marketing intelligence systems? This question can be answered from two perspectives. The first involves an observation of trends in the information management capabilities of businesses, including their abilities to collect, store, and manipulate data in an efficient manner. The second offers a synopsis of the trends in industrial marketing research.

With respect to information management capabilities, the most profound change in corporate marketing departments is the move to computer-driven operations; with every passing day, personal and other workstation computers penetrate deeper into marketing analysis and decision making. And, since these computers are

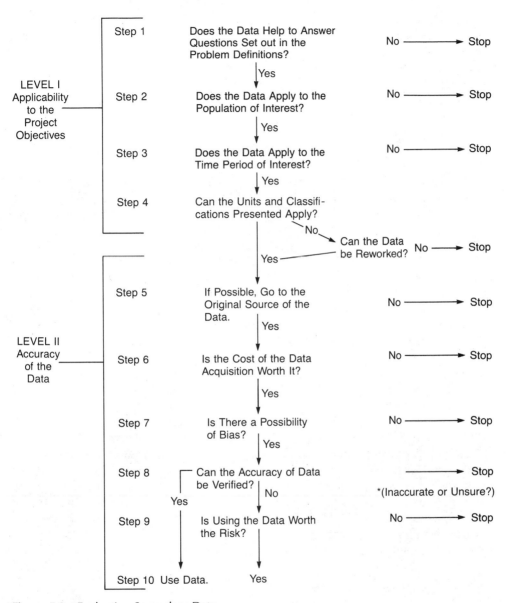

Figure 5.8 Evaluating Secondary Data
(Source: Robert W. Joselyn, *Designing the Marketing Research Project*
(New York: Van Nostrand Rheinhold, 1977). Reprinted by permission of
Van Nostrand Rheinhold Company.)

the hardware of decision support systems, increasingly more marketing management decisions are made with more and better information than ever before. Software packages and internally programmed data analysis packages are well along in terms of adoption by industrial marketing firms. Similarly, more and better dial-up data bases are appearing every year, offering a wide array of information in various forms. Many of these data bases are becoming very specialized in terms of SIC codes. Finally, the training and mindsets of marketing managers have shifted to computer-maintained and computer-manipulated data as well as information inquiries and retrieval. Given these developments, one can only expect that marketing research, and especially marketing intelligence systems, will necessarily become integral to marketing decision making in the coming years.

Continuing developments in research tools and methods hold promise for the conduct of industrial marketing research. Some of these developments are in areas where breakthroughs in industrial marketing research can have a significant effect on marketing strategy (Cox and Dominguez 1979). Examples include: (1) the continued development of sophisticated yet economical-to-apply models and measures of market potential; (2) development of comprehensive methodologies for surveys of those in the buying center, such as sociograms, key informant studies or delphi techniques; (3) development of simulation-based procedures for allocating expenses to segments and territories; (4) development of commonly agreed-upon performance measures for marketing investment and productivity; (5) application of special-purpose measuring devices and analysis to study of consumer preferences; (6) continued studies of product portfolio strategy for product/market strategy formulation; (7) industry-wide and interindustry studies of the sales, cost, and profit impact of marketing strategy, market and industry structure, and product and product life-cycle characteristics; (8) systematic research into organizational buying behavior, with special emphasis on: (a) coping with and anticipating environmental discontinuities; (b) research on the buying decision center; (c) information processing of organizational buyers; and (d) the buyer/seller interface; and (9) developments in market segment identification and assessment.

In sum, the area of industrial marketing intelligence will fill a bigger role in the planning and implementation of industrial marketing strategy than in past years. While the acceptance level among managers of the importance of marketing research and intelligence activities has risen considerably, the years to come will witness rapidly growing expectations of what these activities ought to be contributing. Managers will not only grow in their dependency on marketing intelligence, they will demand more sophistication in the timeliness, modeling capability, analytical power, flexibility, and comprehensiveness of both the people and support systems involved in marketing research and intelligence.

SUMMARY

This chapter has emphasized the need for quality information when making marketing decisions. Information represents a means for reducing the uncertainty that surrounds most of the decision alternatives confronting industrial marketers. For this reason, information has value. Marketers, when considering whether or not to spend resources on information gathering, need to compare this value to the costs.

One of the most important sources of information is marketing research, and a wide variety of subject areas fall within its domain. Nine of these were summarized in this chapter: developing market potentials, market share analysis, determining market characteristics and attitudes, sales analysis, forecasting, business trend studies, estimating new product acceptance and potential, competitor analysis, and determining sales quotas for salespeople and territories.

A systematic process was introduced for conducting marketing research. Such a process provides direction for the research effort and helps to ensure that research dollars are spent in the most effective manner. In the absence of a systematic approach, the marketer often ends up performing research which is unnecessary, incomplete, or inconclusive.

The distinctive challenges in conducting industrial marketing research were discussed as they relate to the stages of the research process. Most of the difficulties have to do with the problem of conducting research when the subject, or unit of analysis, is an organization rather than an individual consumer. The individual stages of the research process were further demonstrated with an actual example.

Companies tend to approach the marketing research process as an activity they rely on only when a significant problem or opportunity arises. Yet, managers require a broad spectrum of information on a continuous basis. To fill this need, the concept of marketing intelligence was introduced. A marketing intelligence system (MIS) is an ongoing mechanism for gathering, recording, storing, and analyzing all forms of marketing-related information. Marketing research is one component of the MIS. The output of an MIS is usually a series of weekly, monthly, quarterly, and/or annual reports to management. The reports include information in areas such as product and territory profitability, sales force performance, advertising effectiveness, customer satisfaction, and competitor activities.

One step above the MIS is the decision support system. The DSS allows the manager to ask nonroutine, *what if?* kinds of questions. The focus is on building marketing models, statistically manipulating the data in an MIS, and developing marketing decision rules.

As industrial firms grow in their appreciation for the importance of marketing, and invest more heavily in the marketing function, their expectations for marketing intelligence will also grow. Decision support is increasingly prevalent in nonmarketing areas, such as finance and production. The implication is that those in marketing must be conversant in designing and working with data bases, model building, statistical analysis, and a variety of computer software packages.

Finally, the chapter expanded on the use of secondary data when gathering marketing intelligence. A few of the more commonly used secondary sources were identified, including on-line data base services. Limitations of secondary data were highlighted through the use of a step-by-step procedure for evaluating the data sources.

QUESTIONS

1. Discuss some of the uncertainties surrounding the decision to enter a new geographic market with an established product. How can marketing research help to reduce these uncertainties? How would you use cost-benefit analysis to determine whether the value of the marketing research information exceeded its costs?

2. Industrial firms have relatively few buyers, so it is easier for those buyers to know the problems and needs of the market accurately and early than it is for buyers in consumer product firms. Do you agree or disagree?

3. Identify examples of situations in which you would argue that industrial marketing research should not be performed, using the reasons provided in the chapter.

4. How does the statement of research objective influence decisions made at subsequent stages in the research process?

5. Provide examples of some of the trade-off decisions made during the marketing research process. How do decisions made at one stage influence decisions made in subsequent stages?

6. What are the limitations of mail surveys in industrial marketing research? Describe an industrial marketing research problem that would lend itself to a mail survey.

7. What are the pros and cons of establishing your own marketing research department or team, rather than hiring an outside firm to perform your research?

8. As a marketer, what skills do you need to effectively develop and use a decision support system? Assume that you have a computer expert to take care of any computer software or hardware you might require.

9. Identify a number of possible *what if?* type questions the industrial marketer might attempt to address using a decision support system. Then, using one of these questions, identify the data requirements, and cite an example of a model that might be helpful.

10. Which of the nine responsibility areas identified in the chapter would tend to require primary data collection, and which could be accomplished principally with secondary data? In which areas might SIC data be useful?

CHAPTER **6**

ASSESSING MARKETS: DEMAND MEASUREMENT AND SALES FORECASTING

Key Concepts

Absolute market potential
Assumptions
Breakdown method
Build-up method
Business cycle
Chain-ratio method
Combination approach
Company composite approach
Complex model building
Demand analysis
External data source
Extrapolation
Industrial demand characteristics
Intermediate-term forecast

Internal data source
Long-term forecast
Market response curve
Regression analysis
Relative market potential
Rolling planning
Sales forecast
Seasonality
Short-term forecast
Statistical series method
Substitution factor
Time series decomposition
Trend line

Learning Objectives

1. Define key terms and concepts in the area of demand analysis.
2. Identify characteristics of industrial demand that have implications for estimating market potential and forecasting sales.
3. Determine the major uses of demand analysis.
4. Explain key decisions made in selecting demand analysis techniques.
5. Summarize some of the major techniques used to estimate market potential and to make sales forecasts.

Differentiate between errors of commission and those of omission. The latter can be more costly than the former. If you're not making many errors, you might ask yourself, How many opportunities am I missing by not being more aggressive?

ROGER VON OECH

The preceding chapter stressed the critical need for quality market intelligence. Two of the most important questions to be addressed through the marketer's research efforts involve estimating the size of current and prospective markets, and forecasting the company's expected sales in those markets. Both of these are forms of market assessment, or demand analysis. The success of the industrial firm is directly tied to the size, growth rate, and competitive circumstances of the marketplace in which it operates. Daily operations and strategic decision making are both dependent upon accurate measures of market potential and projected sales activity for each of the company's products and markets.

This chapter is devoted to these topics. Initially, some of the basic concepts integral to understanding demand potential are presented. Then, these concepts will be related to the special characteristics of demand in industrial markets. Next, we will examine the roles played by demand estimation in three different areas: (1) marketing planning; (2) control of marketing activities; and (3) new product assessment. Finally, the chapter describes some of the market measurement and sales forecasting techniques used by industrial firms—qualitative methods as well as quantitative methods.

BASIC CONCEPTS IN EXAMINING INDUSTRIAL DEMAND

Before investigating how markets are actually measured, it may be helpful to examine a few key concepts and definitions in the area of market assessment. Included among these are various types of market potential, the company sales forecast, customer budgets, the importance of underlying assumptions, and the development of market response curves.

Types of Market Potential

An industrial market can be defined as the set of organizations with plans and budget capacity to purchase goods and services that satisfy a particular need. Market potential is either the total number of goods (or services) which could be purchased, or the total dollar value of these purchases. It is based both on the number of potential users in a market, and the rate of purchase by each user. To be included in the market, a customer must potentially have both the willingness and ability to purchase the product or service in question.

Demand potential exists on three levels: total or absolute market potential, relative market potential, and individual company potential (see Figure 6.1). *Absolute* market potential is equal to the total purchases of all prospective buyers who could potentially use a particular good or service, and have the accompanying budget capacity, under specific environmental conditions (e.g., recession versus prosperity), during a specified time frame. Absolute potential represents the upper limit on demand for the entire market. If the actual level of industry sales is subtracted from the estimate of absolute potential, the difference is called a demand gap.

Relative potential, on the other hand, is the upper limit on demand within any portion or segment of the market, such as an SIC category or a geographic region. Relative potential can be expressed as a percentage of the entire market (i.e., of the absolute potential).

The companion to these two measures of market size is the sales potential for any single firm competing within that market. This is called *company* potential, and refers to the maximum amount of sales that any one company could reasonably expect to obtain from the market during a specified time period.

In Figure 6.1, absolute potential is equal to 100 percent of the potential sales in the entire market. The amount of actual industry sales has been established at 40 percent of the absolute potential, indicating that the combined sales of all the companies within the industry represent a 40 percent penetration of the total market. Thus, the demand gap is 60 percent of the absolute potential. Company A competes primarily in the midwestern part of the United States. Relative market potential in the Midwest is equal to 20 percent of the total market (i.e., of absolute potential). Management at company A believes that the firm could conceivably capture 10 percent of the absolute market potential. This sales volume is the company potential. If all these sales were in the Midwest, company A would be capturing 50 percent of the relative market. However, the company's sales forecast estimates it will actually capture 3 percent of the absolute market this year.

The estimates of absolute, relative, and company potential are affected by a number of factors. In Figure 6.1, these factors have been divided into those related to prospective customers, and those related to the competitive marketplace. Key characteristics of prospects include their absolute number, their intentions to buy, their budget capacity, and the environmental conditions they currently face. Market/industry considerations include the number of competitors and their respective market shares, company A's marketing strategy, the amount of marketing effort put forth by competitors, and the environmental conditions faced by company A and its competitors.

The Company Sales Forecast

A sales forecast is defined as the expected level of sales for a company in a specified time period under certain conditions. With estimates of total market potential and company sales potential in hand, it is much easier to develop a forecast of company

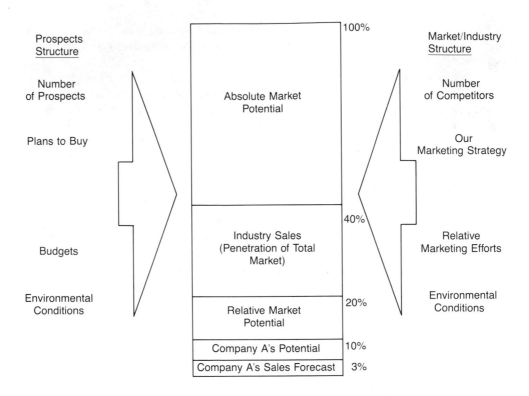

Figure 6.1   Basic Concepts in Industrial Demand Potential

sales within a given market. If it were known how much of the market potential would be captured by the industry, the sales forecast would be equivalent to the percentage the company expects to get (i.e., its market share).

The company may actually develop a set of sales forecasts covering different time periods. These can include immediate-term (daily, weekly, or monthly), short-term (from one to six months), intermediate-term (6 months to two years), and long-term (beyond two years). These particular time distinctions are arbitrary, as companies will vary in their definitions of the short run versus the long run. The different forecasts are used in a variety of ways. For instance, short-term forecasts are helpful in establishing promotional tactics, intermediate-term forecasts can be valuable in assessing sales personnel needs and setting promotional budgets, and long-term forecasts are used in evaluating product line changes and determining capital requirements.

Sales forecasts must take into account several customer, competitor, and environmental considerations. They also must reflect the anticipated response of the marketplace to the company's marketing strategy and the aggressiveness of the company's efforts relative to those of competitors. The level of sales that can be expected in a given time period can be strongly affected by how much effort the marketer puts forth.

Customer Budgets

Customer organizations usually engage in a planning process, which is ordinarily done in one-year increments. Therefore, if a customer intends to expand production facilities, add materials handling equipment to its warehouses, build new offices for staff and executives, or add new items to its product line, these intentions are expressed in the form of a one-year business plan. Similarly, the customer's managers know from experience that certain products and services, including raw materials, office supplies, insurance, and utilities, must be routinely purchased for the company to go about its daily business. All of these factors are built into the business plan for the coming year.

Accompanying the plan is the customer's intended operating budget. In organizations without a formal plan, the budget may serve as a plan. Expenditures funded in the budget typically are divided into capital outlays and operating expenses. Capital outlays are those major investments that will benefit a number of accounting periods, such as increasing production capacity, expanding office space, or purchasing a new mainframe computer. Operating expenses are payments for the purchase of day-to-day raw material requirements, basic supplies, small equipment, and advertising services, among others.

As in all business planning, the budget is based on certain assumptions about what will happen in the industry, to the company, and in the macroenvironment for the coming year. For an organization to purchase the products and services of vendors, they must have the budget capacity. Major purchases typically are budgeted well in advance. Minor items are built into the general expense categories in the customer's operating budget. Many items are not specifically budgeted, but are purchased if and when funds permit. In attempting to estimate both market potential and company sales, marketers should be cognizant of the budget capacity and budgeting process for the types of organizations in their target markets.

Assumptions

Demand projections are always based on assumptions. The ability of marketers to accurately assess demand is entirely dependent upon their ability to make correct assumptions. The marketer might assume that the industry will grow at a rate of 1 percent per month, that two or three new competitors will enter the market, or that costs and prices can be kept below a certain level for the next twelve months. These assumptions must be fairly close to the mark in order for the predicted amount of demand to be realized.

In some cases, the marketer may not actually realize that an assumption has been made. By ignoring the possibility of a certain development taking place (e.g., a drop in interest rates), the marketer is implicitly assuming that the development will not take place. As a result, the answer to the question. What have we assumed in making this sales projection? may require considerable thought. This is a question worth asking frequently.

Assumptions usually contain a degree of error, and occasionally they are completely wrong. The sensitivity of demand projections to violations of assumptions depends upon how critical the assumption is. Being wrong in assuming that the competition will maintain the same level of promotional expenditures as last year may be less critical than being wrong about how much inventory customers will be willing to hold.

During an unanticipated oil glut, such as the one in the early 1980s, companies (including the vendor's customers) suddenly find that their energy costs, as well as the costs of petroleum-based materials, have declined. Some of these companies may decide to add the savings to their profits, but others will accelerate capital expansion plans, stockpile lower-cost resources, and increase their finished goods inventories. Any of these decisions can have an impact on the demand for the vendor's goods or services.

Once projections of market potential and company sales have been developed, then, management must be ready to adjust these estimates to reflect assumptions that do not hold. This may lead to changes in marketing strategy, to be discussed later in this chapter. What should be most apparent is the need to closely monitor assumptions once they are made.

Market Response Curves

It is generally believed that markets respond positively to the marketing efforts made by a company. However, determining the actual shape of the response curve is critical for understanding the ultimate effect of these efforts on a company's sales. Figure 6.2 offers some illustrative examples of response curve shapes.

The basic characteristics of market response curves are twofold: (1) they are usually nonlinear; and (2) they are sometimes discontinuous. For instance, the market response curve for sales force size in Part A of Figure 6.2 increases slowly, then rises rapidly, and finally reaches a plateau as more salespeople are added. This behavior suggests that a point of saturation is reached where further increases in sales force size do not affect demand significantly. On the other hand, the sales response function is negatively related to the price level, and either elastic or inelastic demand curves can result. The figure also illustrates that trade show exhibitions may not affect market response until a certain critical mass has been reached in terms of sales, at which point there is a very positive effect on demand. Alternatively, product quality may have an impact on demand, but due to the specification requirements of many industrial customers, the effect may be discontinuous. For example, there may be no demand until product quality passes a certain minimum level. Demand may then be stable until product quality passes another somewhat higher level, opening up the market to companies which have more stringent product specifications.

Part B of Figure 6.2 demonstrates the possible effects of relative competitive effort on a company's demand. Relative competitive effort is defined as the ratio of a company's marketing expenditures to the total marketing expenditures of all of its competitors—or to a small group of relevant competitors. Sales response curves are entirely different when the company's relative efforts are low, than when they are high, but if a company's marketing effort increases relative to total marketing effort, it can anticipate a greater proportion of the total market demand.

A. RESPONSE CURVES FOR VARIOUS TYPES OF MARKETING EFFORT

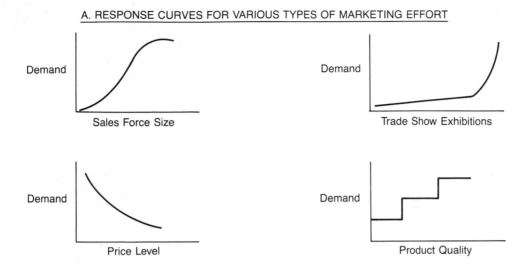

B. RESPONSE CURVES FOR RELATIVE COMPETITIVE EFFORT

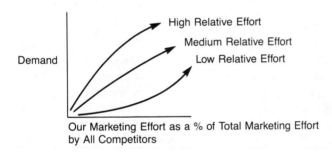

C. RESPONSE CURVES BASED ON QUALITY OF MARKETING EFFORT

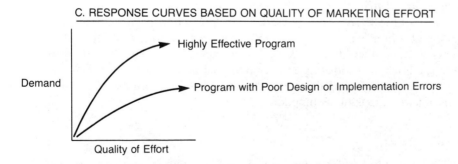

Figure 6.2 Using Market Response Curves in Sales Forecast Determination

Finally, the quality of the firm's marketing is important. The basic marketing strategy can have such uniqueness and appeal in the marketplace that, regardless of the amount of effort, the quality of that effort influences buyers positively. Conversely, the strategy may be hampered by poor design, implementation errors, or other factors which render it unappealing to the marketplace. In this case, there will be a low demand response, as illustrated in Figure 6.2, part C.

SPECIAL CHARACTERISTICS OF INDUSTRIAL DEMAND

When making demand projections, the marketer should keep in mind the special characteristics of the industrial market that complicate the tasks of estimating market potential and forecasting sales. Essentially, four characteristics are relevant for understanding the nuances of industrial demand analysis.

The Derived Nature of Demand

The purchasing plans of an industrial marketer's customers are dependent upon what they expect to happen to their own sales. These expectations are affected by the sales of the customer's customer, and, in turn, by the sales of that customer's customer.

To achieve accuracy in sales estimates, the marketer may need to monitor the inventory and purchasing patterns of organizations at different levels in the production chain. Further, a variety of economic, political, and social factors contribute to the level of demand at the most basic or generic level. For example, the total demand for earth-moving equipment depends on the amount of planned highway construction, the number of homes being built, and economic development activities in other countries. To estimate highway construction activity, the marketer would need to understand how the political process works. Also, new home construction is strongly affected by the level of, and expected changes in, interest rates. International construction is linked to exchange rates, global politics, regional economic trends, and world competition (Hughes 1978). By studying and understanding the dynamics of the markets served by prospective buyers, the marketer can better appreciate the motivation and circumstances of the target customers.

Keep in mind that personal expectations play a major role in market projections. Because of the derived nature of demand, projections may depend upon the expectations of a number of people in different organizations regarding likely developments in their respective markets. These expectations introduce a significant possibility for error in estimating market potential and forecasting sales. Assumptions must be made regarding these expectations. This again points out the need for skillful insight when making assumptions.

Concentrated Demand

Industrial markets tend to be composed of relatively few prospective buyers, concentrated in terms of both geographic location and the percentage of market potential accounted for by any one buyer. The concentration has mixed implications when projecting demand. On the one hand, the ability to estimate demand within an industrial market is enhanced because there are relatively few prospects to examine. On the other hand, the loss or addition of a single buyer representing a relatively large proportion of total sales potential may cause wide fluctuations in the total sales picture.

Source Loyalty

A sizable component of an industrial company's demand frequently comprises an established set of source-loyal customers. Some companies find it much more expedient and efficient to depend on a single source of supply and to issue routine reorders to that supplier. Buyers who use a just-in-time inventory system are good examples. With this type of relationship, the buyer is much more likely to share information regarding growth plans, budgets, and expectations with the vendor. Loyalty is even more firmly established by the linking of vendors and buyers through computer-driven automatic reorder systems. The presence of single-source or few-sources loyalty implies that the industrial demand for any one customer will be more easily and reliably predicted, because competitors will have a difficult time breaking into the relationship.

Price Bidding for Capital Equipment

Demand analysis is complicated by the fact that a substantial proportion of a company's sales in a given year might come from projects involving competitive bidding. Winning or losing a bid can significantly alter the sales picture, making it difficult to estimate sales. The probability of winning specific bids should be factored into these sales projections. But, since the marketer may not know which projects are going to come up for bid during a given fiscal period, the uncertainty in market assessment increases.

The marketer's intelligence system should continually scan the environment to identify timely information on the number, size, and nature of bid invitations to be offered in a given product area. Because major capital expenditures are usually budgeted at the beginning of a fiscal period, research efforts can be devoted to determining which companies are considering capital expansion, and what types of expansion they are considering.

THE USES OF DEMAND ANALYSIS

Market size projections and sales forecasts are used by both marketing and nonmarketing managers. Marketing applications are our primary concern, but there is also heavy reliance on these estimates by personnel in production, purchasing, and finance. For example, in the production area, production schedules, output quotas, and inventories of materials and component parts are all directly dependent on sales projections. If sales or market size are over-estimated, the company is left with large inventories of finished products, and may have to lay off employees. If they are under-estimated, the company may alienate distributors and lose potential customers who are unwilling to wait for production to gear up.

Estimates of market potential and sales forecasting play a vital role in three important marketing functions. Two of these uses pertain to the marketing planning process. Industrial demand analysis is used at both the beginning and the end of the process. In the beginning, it is used in setting objectives, and at the end, it helps determine whether implemented marketing programs are meeting these objectives. The third use of demand analysis involves determining the marketability of new product ideas and product line expansion. Estimates of market potential are vital in making go/no-go decisions about new products or entrance into new markets.

Demand Estimation and Marketing Planning

Figure 6.3 depicts the roles of market potential estimates and the sales forecast in the industrial marketing planning process. As can be seen, estimates of market potential serve a primary role in the identification of opportunities, and sales forecasts are a key input when setting marketing objectives, developing strategies, and establishing budgets. Let us consider a detailed example.

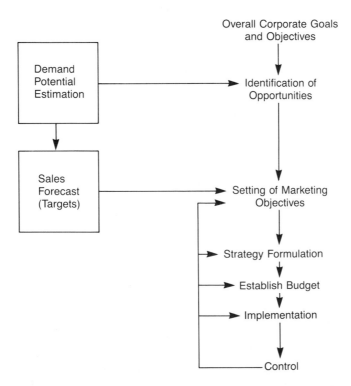

Figure 6.3   Demand Estimation and Industrial Marketing Planning

A company that makes pipe from polyvinyl chloride (PVC) was considering expansion of its market territory into the states of Louisiana, Texas, Arkansas, Mississippi, and Alabama. This expansion could best be accomplished by building and operating a plant somewhere near the geographic center of these five states. Preliminary studies revealed that a location somewhere along the Mississippi River, most likely in central Louisiana, would be acceptable. Further study determined that tracts of land were available with reasonable access to roads, railways, and airports, and that major metropolitan areas such as New Orleans, Jackson, Mobile, Houston, Memphis, Little Rock, and Dallas were within 500 miles. The company was already producing PVC water pipe and PVC sewer pipe in 20-foot lengths in diameters of 4, 6, 8, 10, and 12 inches. The demand potential for these products in this new market area became the major issue.

A study team was formed in the marketing department to determine the feasibility of the project. The objectives of the team were as follows: (1) to determine the nature of PVC demand nationally and regionally; (2) to determine any significant trends in PVC demand; (3) to identify and assess the relative presence of PVC producers in the five-state proposed market area; (4) to investigate the market conditions affecting PVC demand, including the competitive atmosphere, distribution system relationships, the relative importance of marketing variables, and the factors affecting demand for a particular producer. These inputs would enable the company to perform a break-even analysis for the proposed facility under differing scenarios, or sets of assumptions.

The investigation involved scrutinizing secondary data in sources such as the U.S. Census, industry trade association literature, publications of industry members, promotional literature, and computer library search services. In addition, primary data was acquired informally from representatives of the PVC industry at the producer level as well as the distributor level. Similarly, information was obtained from chemical engineers, construction engineers, and knowledgeable persons in state and city planning offices.

Unfortunately, data on pipe consumption was available only in aggregate form, and for the United States as a whole; no data existed on consumption of PVC pipe. As a result, demand potential could be estimated only by working backwards, starting with the market for PVC itself.

The study team ascertained that the total U.S. consumption of PVC resin had been increasing at a rate of approximately 3 percent per year. In 1985, consumption was estimated to be 7,138 million pounds, of which approximately 95 percent had been produced by domestic PVC resin production facilities. The remaining 5 percent had been supplied by foreign PVC resin producers, particularly those in Mexico, Canada, and Brazil. Further investigation determined that foreign production had been increasing at approximately 50 percent per year.

This PVC resin is converted into two different types of pipe. One type, known as pip, typically is sold to contractors for household and light commercial construction, or through retailers such as hardware stores for homeowner use. The other type is water and sewer pipe such as that currently produced by the company at its existing production facilities. These products are sold through distributors to contractors bidding for major municipality projects. The number of such projects is dependent upon population growth, metropolitan commercial growth, climate, and competitive factors. It was determined that population for the five-state area had increased at a rate of 1.5 percent over the last 10 years and was anticipated to increase at a rate of 0.6 percent for the next 15 years. Metropolitan growth in the Sunbelt states was estimated to exceed the U.S. average by one to 5 percent for the next 15 years. In addition, the mild climate found in the Sunbelt plus the imposition of federal regulations discouraging the use of asbestos pipe were highly favorable. Finally, PVC-type pipe is competitively advantageous compared to its primary competitors, such as concrete and other nonplastic products, with regard to weight, cost, installation, and longevity.

The marketing team concluded that PVC pipe demand would grow in the range of 3.5 percent to 4.3 percent annually for the next 10 years. The demand for PVC pipe in the targeted five-state region was believed to be moderately higher than the national average due to the several regional factors just cited. Thus, a conservative annual growth estimate for the market area was pegged at 4.0 percent and an optimistic estimate set at 5.0 percent. In terms of total demand potential, the industry was found to be viable and attractive to new entrants.

Investigation of industry characteristics revealed that there were twelve separate companies selling PVC products in the area. Nine of these companies operated one or more facilities in the five-state area, while three located outside of the area had ventured into the market through their distribution systems. Knowledge of competitors' production facility sizes and other primary data suggested that market shares were highly concentrated. In particular, three companies dominated both the sewer and the water pipe markets with 20 to 30 percent of the market each. The remaining market was divided fairly evenly among the smaller competitors. Estimates were made of sales levels per company by type of product. It was determined that the industry was operating at 70 to 80 percent capacity in meeting the demand of the target market area. This finding was verified by interviewing distributors, who indicated that they had no difficulty in obtaining a supply of the various types of PVC pipe, nor did they have any problem in meeting delivery deadlines. The research team estimated total industry production capacity for PVC water pipe to be between 128 million and 146 million pounds, while total capacity for sewer pipe was estimated to be somewhere between 75 million and 86 million pounds.

The final consideration involved examining demand potential for the company itself. Here, the research team focused on the structure of the distribution system. The industry competitors were known to rely heavily on marketing intermediaries who interface with local users of PVC-type products. Industrial supply firms located in the metropolitan areas monitored local construction, municipal expansion, refittings, and other sources of PVC pipe demand. In general, upon notification of an invitation to bid, industrial supply firms would contact PVC pipe producers and obtain price quotes from them. The industrial supply companies then bid on the local construction jobs, and, if granted the contract, placed the order with the PVC producer. Experience, and some direct questioning, suggested that most distribution system members tended to concentrate their relationships on two or three producers. Also, long-term relationships were typical, and price quotes were compared across these few producers-suppliers on large bid orders. Decision criteria used by the industrial supply firms placed heavy emphasis on price sensitivity, availability of inventory, and quick delivery. Although source loyalty was common, buyers would switch sources if significant differences existed among competitors in terms of these criteria. Further, it was determined that most of the industrial supply firms' purchasing agents had knowledge of virtually all of the PVC producers operating in the region, even though they had not bought PVC pipe from most of them.

The end users of PVC pipe often had no knowledge of the producers of the pipe itself. Instead, they tended to select industrial distributors who conducted business in proximity to construction sites, and their primary decision criteria were weighted heavily toward low bid considerations. In addition, delivery was often a critical element in continuing relationships between the end users and distributors. In short, PVC sewer and water pipe was considered a commodity purchase by end users.

The research team arrived at the following conclusions regarding market potential in the five-state area. The industry was dominated in terms of market share by three producers. The basis of this dominance was primarily production capacity, with distribution system contacts being secondary. Since the industry was found to be operating at between 70 percent and 80 percent of capacity, rapid expansion capability existed with little fixed cost requirements. The industry relied heavily on derived demand, translated to the producers by industrial supply companies in contact with local contractors, municipality departments, and other end users. The industrial supply houses tended to solidify relationships with a very small number of producers, but appeared willing to consider products from other low bidders. Thus, the market was judged to be clearly price-driven, with buyers prone to shop for bids with each major project. Distribution members typically did not stockpile PVC pipe in sufficient quantity to respond to large local construction projects; consequently, current prices were the primary decision factor. In addition, intermediary buyers were generally aware and knowledgeable of most producers. Thus, the industry appeared to have most of the earmarks of a perfectly competitive environment. The opportunity for a new competitor was clearly dependent on its ability to set up a highly efficient production facility and pass cost savings on to its buyers in the form of low prices.

Bearing these findings in mind, the company next investigated two areas where cost efficiencies could be realized. First, its representatives negotiated with the state commercial development department for a tax-free bond and other special tax considerations that would lower its fixed costs. At the same time, a team searched for and ultimately found high-technology PVC pipe extrusion equipment that could operate much faster and at a lower cost per pound than the major competitors in the area. In short, the company was able to increase the effectiveness of its marketing strategy relative to the known competitors.

Demand Estimation and Control of Industrial Marketing Efforts

Demand estimation also plays a role in controlling or monitoring marketing strategies after they have been implemented, as illustrated in the lower part of Figure 6.3. This role is accomplished through sales forecasts, which determine targets for marketing efforts. Once the firm identifies opportunities and sets objectives to expand, maintain, or even decrease its presence in certain territories or product lines, specific sales targets must be identified, to determine how well customers are reacting to strategy changes or how effectively specific marketing tactics are performing in the marketplace. Actual performance is compared to these targets.

The complementary roles of sales forecasting and control are often seen in the sales force management area. Here, salespeople are given sales quotas based on several considerations, including past sales records, forecasts of changes in the marketplace, anticipated loyalty of current customers, the degree of aggressiveness inspired by the company's compensation package, sales force motivation techniques, and planned levels of advertising and sales support.

Table 6.1 gives an example of how a sales quota system might be set up on a product-by-product basis, to create a baseline for comparison of each salesperson on each product. In this case, the salesperson, John Brown, is responsible for five items in the product line. The quota established for Brown is based on a consideration of all the elements that affect company demand—but narrowed to a territory level. That is, if Brown has responsibility for the state of New Jersey, the quotas set for him are a reflection of the demand potential for customers in that territory, the environmental forces operating in the territory, the degree of aggressiveness of competitors in his territory, estimates of the market's response to Brown's company's marketing strategies implemented in that territory, and the ability of John Brown himself. Scrutiny of the percentage of quota realized indicates that Brown has exceeded his quota in three of the five product item categories (C, D, and E) while he is close to making his quota in sales of product A. However, for item B, he has attained only 75 percent of his specified quota. If 75 percent of quota is considered lower than an acceptable level of performance, certain control factors should be implemented. For instance, the sales force manager who supervises Brown may suggest a counseling session to determine why his performance in product B sales is lower than the quota. The session may determine that Brown has been working to push products C, D, and E because their commission rates are higher. Or, he may have lost a key account which had a great negative impact on sales of product B. In

Table 6.1 Sales Quotas as a Control Device

SALESPERSON: *John Brown*

	Product Line				
	A	B	C	D	E
Quota	150	400	200	100	75
Actual	140	300	250	120	80
% Quota	93%	75%	125%	120%	107%

either case, the company can make modifications to bring Brown's actual sales performance into line. For example, if other salespeople also are not aggressively pushing sales of product B, the commission system can be adjusted to encourage more sales emphasis on product B. With the lost account, Mr. Brown can be directed by his manager to concentrate more effort on servicing existing accounts by calling more frequently or maintaining more written and telephone contact.

The control aspect of sales forecasts can be applied at any level of performance evaluation. Industrial demand potential can be converted into sales forecasts that are useful in evaluating the success of the total marketing effort or of individual elements in the marketing program such as salesperson Brown. At the aggregate level, where the complete marketing program is evaluated, the sales forecasts are converted into financial ratios or other indicators of total company success, such as return on investment, relative market share, or total sales volume. On the micro level, sales forecasts can be modified to pertain to individual members of the sales force (e.g., John Brown), specific territories, certain items in the product line, and even to the retention of old accounts or the addition of new accounts.

Demand Estimation and New Product Development

The third critical role played by estimates of demand potential involves their use in determining the attractiveness and marketability of new product ideas. Chapter 9 will examine the specific steps in developing and evaluating new product concepts. At this point, our concern is with the importance of market projections during those steps.

The essential difference between the previous roles of market potential analysis and its role in new product assessment is that, in the case of new products, the company has no history in the market. With truly innovative new products, the market itself may have no history. New products are developed to supersede old products, to fill out a product line, or to meet needs that, until now, have been ignored by the firm. Consequently, the assessment of the market potential for innovations requires different methodologies and involves substantially more uncertainty than does the analysis of demand potential for products which are already marketed and have complete market structures (PVC pipe).

Consider for example, the Macintosh computer which was developed to replace the IBM standard work station computer used by many businesses. Those who are familiar with the Macintosh may have noted that the human-computer interface is completely different and requires the learning of totally new behaviors. For instance, instead of using cursor keys, one moves a *mouse* across a pad. The cursor on the monitor moves in parallel with the movement of the mouse on the pad. A pressure-sensitive area on the mouse causes lines to appear on the screen, and a complete array of tools such as scissors, erasers, and coloring devices are available to the user at the touch of a finger. In short, acceptance of the Macintosh computer concept required learning of completely new behaviors in interfacing or interaction with computer machines.

Imagine the difficulty in determining whether or not companies would be willing to invest thousands of dollars into machinery which has great intuitive appeal from a customer's perspective, but would require massive education of users, and further, run the risk of being incompatible with all other computer products on the market.

The determination of demand potential for new products, therefore, requires judgment of a substitution factor. This factor pertains to the degree of compatibility and obvious advantage represented by the new product concept over old ways of doing things. In the case of the Macintosh computer, historical analysis could determine the degree of acceptance of conventional computer products by businesses, but some assessment must be made of the degree to which the new product would supersede the old ones. Complicating the picture is the natural hesitancy of humans to change their ways and reluctance of businesses to invest in capital equipment that may prove less than satisfactory. Also, many new products require the customer to spend additional sums for plant or office modifications, for related or complementary products (e.g., software in the example above), and for training.

This example portrays the fundamental dilemma of demand estimation for innovations in the industrial market: the initial investments of dollars, time, and energy, and the need to change established patterns deter the adoption of all but the least disruptive new products. Stated differently, the more revolutionary a new product concept, the more uncertainty is involved in estimating the market's reaction to it.

BASIC OPTIONS WHEN SELECTING DEMAND ANALYSIS TECHNIQUES

It should now be apparent that demand estimation and sales forecasting require the careful inspection of several factors and the application of judgment regarding the possible impacts of these factors on the market and a company's share of that market. Because of the complexity of this task, industrial marketing managers and their research specialists have come to rely on several different types of analytical techniques. The remainder of this chapter describes some of the most common. When selecting among these methods, the marketer must first make decisions about four parameters. These decisions pertain to: (1) the degree of judgment used; (2) the starting and ending points; (3) the sources of estimates; and (4) the sophistication of assumptions used. It is helpful to think of each of these options as a continuum. Our discussion will focus on the ends of each continuum. That is, industrial marketers can opt for either end of the continuum, or someplace along the middle, depending upon their circumstances and preferences.

Qualitative versus Quantitative Techniques: How Much Judgment?

Demand analysis tools are most commonly characterized as either qualitative or quantitative. The distinction concerns the amount of subjective judgment involved. Qualitative techniques are highly judgmental; reliance is placed exclusively on the estimates of knowledgeable individuals. The basic risk is that individuals are not completely objective in their evaluations and assessments of marketplace phenomena. Consequently, it is often advantageous to compare the judgments of a number of individuals and seek common perceptions. There is also the question of which individuals should be asked to make the judgments. Nonetheless, qualitative techniques are quite popular in industrial marketing, especially due to the close relationships that often exist between marketers and their customers.

Quantitative techniques, at the other end of the continuum, involve statistical and/or mathematical manipulations of numbers that represent current and past marketplace developments. For instance, a company's sales pattern over the past five years is assessed to determine the average increase, which is then used to estimate next year's sales level. Like qualitative approaches, quantitative approaches pose serious questions—precisely which numbers to use and how much to rely on them.

Breakdown versus Build-up Methods: Where to Begin?

A second distinction in demand analysis concerns breakdown versus build-up approaches. This is a decision of whether to start at a very macro level and work down, or at a very micro level and work up. In breakdown approaches, information is gathered to initially estimate patterns and trends at the highest levels of aggregation—tax law changes, environmental regulations, prime interest rates, energy prices, and the economy as a whole. Next, judgments are made on how these trends would impact the relevant market sectors from which demand for industrial goods is derived. Then, that information is used to determine assessments of the impacts on the particular industrial goods industry. This process is continued until the analyst reaches the individual firm level.

With build-up approaches, the reverse pattern is used. For example, market potential and sales forecasts could be determined at the individual product item level, the territory level, or the salesperson level. In estimating market potential, the marketer conducts a thorough and separate appraisal of the requirements of each account in the market, and adds them together. Or, a representative sample of accounts is surveyed, and the results projected for the entire marketplace. In forecasting sales, each salesperson estimates how much he or she expects to sell in a given time period. These estimates are added together to get a total for the entire sales force. Adjustments are made in either approach, to reflect competitors' activities, specific regional considerations, and changes in the the company's marketing strategy. The result would be a total sales forecast for the company.

Internal Versus External Sources: Where to Get the Data?

A third dimension of choice concerns the use of company sources of information versus the use of outside sources of information. Company (or internal) sources include corporate records, sales force reports, inventory policies, and a host of other types of proprietary information that are used in the sales forecast. On the other hand, outside sources of secondary information such as census data, government reports, trade association statistics, and even business periodical articles are valuable in assessing markets. In addition, the opinions of knowledgeable individuals who watch and analyze industries and companies might be sought.

Assumptions: Simple versus Complex?

Earlier, this chapter emphasized that all estimates of market potential and company sales are based upon assumptions about environmental conditions. These assumptions can be extremely naive or they can be highly complicated. For instance, it may be assumed that the average percentage change in sales levels over the last three years can be used to estimate next year's sales levels. The basic assumption here is that the last three years are good indicators of what will happen next year. In other words, all conditions will remain at status quo, or any changed conditions will be cancelled out by changes in other conditions to maintain a status quo appearance.

At the other end of the assumptions continuum are complicated mathematical and computer simulation models of the economy, of the industry, and of the effects of changes in marketing tactics on customer response in various markets. These simulation techniques can rely on a large number of complex and interrelated assumptions. The marketing analyst should endeavor to become well-acquainted with the assumptions underlying any technique, with an eye towards (a) ensuring that these assumptions hold true, and (b) determining how critical these assumptions are, for the reliability of the final demand projections.

Let us review some of the frequently used tools for assessing market potential, and for projecting actual sales.

COMMONLY USED TECHNIQUES IN ESTIMATING MARKET POTENTIAL

Market measurement treats the entirety of the market and serves as a beginning point for most marketing planning. There are some standardized methods for estimating total market size; they are fundamentally quantitative in nature and embody a number of assumptions about the market. The methods are based on external data sources, usually in the form of secondary information, and they generally pertain to the highest levels of demand rather than to individual product lines. Two of these methods of market measurement are: (1) the chain-ratio method; and (2) the statistical series method.

Chain-Ratio Method of Market Measurement

Just as market demand was defined as a composite of several different factors, so the chain-ratio method embodies systematic consideration of each relevant factor. Estimation is accomplished through the stringing together or chaining of simple assumptions about these factors. The following example illustrates this approach.

A plant maintenance company wishes to determine the market potential for its plant rental service, which provides live green foliage to businesses for aesthetic display. Targeting malls, shopping centers, and large retail stores, the company places, maintains, and guarantees the health of live plants in high-traffic areas. The chain-ratio approach might take this form:

	1,000	Total number of malls, shopping centers and retail stores in the market area
×	.75	Percent that would use plant rental services
=	750	
×	200	Average number of plants rented per month
=	150,000	Total estimated demand (in units)
×	$.25	Rental cost per plant per month
=	$37,500	
×	12	Months in a year
=	$450,000	Total demand estimated (in dollars)

Thus, based on the assumptions and information on the total number of candidate retail establishments, the total market size is estimated to be close to one-half million dollars.

Statistical Series Method of Market Measurement

This statistical approach, sometimes termed the *SIC Method* because SIC data is among the most popular, also places heavy reliance on secondary data in making estimates. These statistics can be found in such sources as the *Census of Manufactures,* the *U.S. Industrial Outlook, County Business Patterns,* and *Sales and Marketing Management.* The Standard Industrial Classification (SIC) system was described in Chapter 5. To appreciate the mechanics of this method of market measurement, it may be useful for the reader to review that discussion.

The use of a statistical series can be seen in two examples, one fairly simple, and the other a bit more complex. Consider the Cleanchem Company, which has developed a water treatment chemical for paper manufacturers. Paper mills use large quantities of water in their production processes (usually about one gallon for every $100 in shipments), and this water cannot be returned directly into rivers or ponds without proper treatment to eliminate waste and by-products accumulated during production. The problem is to estimate total market potential for the chemical additive among paper mills (SIC 2621) in the Northeast, where Cleanchem currently operates.

The Census of Manufactures provides information on a number of establishments, employees, payroll, production workers, value added, cost of materials, value of shipments, and new capital expenditures for each SIC industry, by state. New Hampshire, for instance, had 13 paper mills, which employed a total of 26,000 workers and produced $281.5 million worth of paper shipments in 1982. Total paper shipments in the Northeast would be determined by adding together the dollar values for the several states. Let's assume the total is $700 million.

Projecting its knowledge of the industry, data found in paper industry trade reports, and information received from local water utilities, Cleanchem estimates that paper mills use 0.01 gallons of water per dollar of shipment value. Further, Cleanchem engineers recommend 0.25 ounces of the water treatment chemical per gallon of water to be minimally effective, and 0.30 ounces per gallon of water to be optimal.

Using these inputs, market potential is estimated to range between 1,750,000 ounces ($700,000,000 times .01 times .25) and 2,100,000 ounces ($700,000,000 times .01 times .30). The marketer may want to adjust the estimates, however, based on some relevant assumptions. For instance, the activity level of paper mills may have been dropping by about 3 percent annually for the past five years. If the marketer assumes this trend will continue, the projection of market potential must be adjusted downward. Importantly, if no such adjustment is made, the marketer is also making an assumption.

Another assumption is that water usage varies with the dollar value of shipments produced by a paper mill. This can create a problem if the average price of paper moves up or down (e.g., if the price level fell, more water would be used per dollar of shipment).

To further understand how SIC data can be applied to estimating demand potential in organizational markets, consider a second example. The Tober Corporation, a maker of industrial lubricants located in St. Louis, Missouri, was contemplating expansion of its operations into three new metropolitan markets. The leading candidates were Chicago, Minneapolis, and Detroit. One of the primary criteria in selecting new markets was the potential of each, which had to be estimated.

The company first determined that a disproportionate amount of the sales of industrial lubricants tended to be made to apparel manufacturers (SIC 23), chemical producers (SIC 28), and those in the fabricated metals industry (SIC 34). Based on this premise, both primary and secondary data were collected, and then combined. First, a random telephone survey of purchasing agents from each of the SIC groups was conducted by the marketing department at Tober. The agents were asked to estimate their company's annual purchases of lubricants, and to determine total employment in their production plants. Purchasing agents were used because of their familiarity and involvement with buying decisions for standard products (such as lubricants), and because of their accessibility.

The figures for lubricant purchases per company (in pounds) were divided by the estimated number of employees per company, to arrive at pounds per employee. This figure was then averaged across all the companies surveyed in the SIC category. The result for Wayne County, Michigan (which includes Detroit) can be found in column three of Table 6.2.

Next, secondary data for employment in each of the metropolitan areas was obtained from *County Business Patterns*. This employment data was broken down by SIC code and by county. Column four of Table 6.4 lists these figures for Wayne County.

Finally, average pounds per employee (the primary data) were multiplied by the number of employees in the SIC category (the secondary data). These totals are summed across the SIC categories to arrive at the potential for lubricants in the Detroit area (column five of Table 6.2).

The process is repeated for the other prospective markets. Additional information would be collected on the competitors in each market, and projections made about market growth rates and differences in the costs of serving each market.

The markets can then be ranked on their attractiveness, and resources can be allocated according to the relative strength of each of the selected markets.

Table 6.2 Estimating Market Potential for Industrial Lubricants in
Wayne County, Michigan (Hypothetical Data)

SIC Code	Industry	Pounds per Employee	Number of Employees	Estimated Potential
23	Apparel	25	9,045	226,125
28	Chemicals	40	49,111	196,440
34	Fabricated Metals	71	75,620	5,369,020
			TOTAL POTENTIAL	5,791,585 lbs.

Source: Adapted from *Measuring Markets: A Guide to the Use of Federal and State Statistical Data,* U.S.
Department of Commerce, (August 1974), 51.

Underlying this method of estimation are the assumptions that companies
within an SIC are fairly similar in terms of their usage of lubricants, that differences
among SIC categories are meaningful, and that usage of lubricants varies fairly consistently with number of employees. The marketer may want to investigate the extent
to which companies are labor-intensive, and to see if companies within an SIC code
are fairly similar in this aspect. In addition, other correlates of lubricant usage, such
as sales, might be evaluated. Another assumption is that the estimates of lubricant
purchases for each firm are based on a representative period, and do not reflect an
exceptionally good or bad year. The marketer is also assuming that the companies
surveyed were using as much of the lubricant as can reasonably be expected, and
that their usage could not be increased.

COMMONLY USED TECHNIQUES IN FORECASTING SALES

Whereas market measurement is vital for setting the goals and objectives that guide
the marketing plan, sales forecasts are crucial for the specific design of marketing
programs. Sales forecasts are either implicitly or explicitly derived from market potential estimates, and should be consistent with expectations regarding the size of
the total market. However, because of the day-to-day needs of marketing managers
preparing forecasts, sales forecasting has its own set of techniques, each of which
embodies unique advantages and disadvantages. The most common approach to
classifying these techniques is along the qualitative/quantitative distinction introduced earlier.

Qualitative Approaches

Qualitative methods require the application of personal or subjective judgment, and
we typically distinguish between the judgment of people inside the corporation and
the opinions of outsiders. An example of the use of the former is the *company
sources composite,* while the latter is illustrated with the *Delphi technique* and the
survey of buying intentions.

Company Sources Composite Approach

A popular method of sales forecasting involves the exclusive use of company sources. This technique frequently takes the form of either the *composite of sales force opinion* or the *jury of executive opinion* approaches. However, there is no reason to exclude other members of the organization from providing input as well. A brief description of the two techniques follows.

One method for implementing the composite of sales force opinion technique might involve inviting members of the sales force to an annual sales meeting which has numerous purposes, one of which is to obtain salespeople's estimates of the sales levels of various products in their territory for the coming year. The meeting agenda might include marketing strategy changes, timetables for marketing action implementation, new product introductions, product line prunings, and assessments of competitors' actions expected in the coming year. At the same time, the salespeople are given information concerning the nature of demand for consumer goods or other industrial goods that will affect their customers' purchasing behavior. They are briefed on national economic conditions as well as specific regional factors. They are appraised of any changes in production facilities, production scheduling, raw materials procurement, and conditions of supply and demand in the industry.

At some point in the process, the salespeople are required to present estimates of what they believe to be the most likely sales levels for their customers in the coming year. Embellishments of this technique may require salespeople to give not only most likely, but also pessimistic and optimistic levels. The composite nature of this technique is effected through the accumulation of all salespersons' estimates to determine a final sales forecast, by product in the product line, across the entire target market area. One of the major benefits of this process is that the salespeople are more committed to sales goals if they were involved in setting those goals.

This technique has several pitfalls. Salespeople are often reluctant to provide true estimates of what their customers will buy, especially if they believe these estimates will affect the quotas established for the coming year. Also, this technique is very judgmental. In other words, the salespeople must judge for themselves how the conditions in the marketplace will affect their customers; plus, the salespeople must make assessments of the impact of their own effectiveness under these market conditions. Finally, the approach may fail to include elements of the big picture to which individual salespeople may not be exposed.

The jury of executive opinion technique is also subjective, but is relied upon heavily by industrial firms. The marketing manager, or other senior executive, requests independent forecasts from a number of executives. These executives can be expected to consider a number of factors in developing their individual forecasts, such as previous sales, proposed marketing programs, competitive actions, and economic conditions.

Because the executives are likely to differ in their respective outlooks, the company may want to bring these managers together to reconcile their differences. Such a meeting can bring out key issues or points that not everyone considered in formulating the individual forecasts. Out of this discussion should come a final forecast to which managers are willing to commit.

The jury of executive opinion technique offers the additional benefits of being relatively quick and easy to implement. In addition, the forecasts that result from this approach are frequently very accurate, when it is used in an organized and systematic manner.

Delphi Approach

Juxtaposed to the company sources composite approach is the use of external experts, sometimes called the *Delphi* method. Just as the Greek oracle of Delphi was believed to have the ability to see into the future, certain experts who watch the industry and its many environmental factors may have a clearer picture of trends and their impacts on various companies in the industry. Consequently, it is advantageous to attempt to identify these individuals. They may be trade association economists, investment company analysts, business periodical staff members, former chief executives, major suppliers of raw materials, or even major customers. The use of these experts requires a much more informal means of access and information gathering than was the case in the company sources method. Personal visits, telephone calls, and other correspondence may suffice as data collection methods.

Often, the Delphi method will involve surveying a group or panel of experts more than once. After getting an initial estimate from a number of experts, these results may be tabulated and sent back to the group members to determine if they want to revise their projections in light of the opinions of others. By taking repeated measures, the variability in the estimates should be reduced.

With this approach, the assessments are judgmental, but the judges are knowledgeable of many factors impinging on the company and its competitors. The basic problem in the Delphi method is breaking down information to a specific product or territory level, to be useful as a planning or control mechanism.

Survey of Buying Intentions Approach

In those industrial markets with a fairly limited number of firms with specific needs, an effective method for forecasting is the *survey of buying intentions.* In the survey, a sample of customers is asked how much of a particular product or service they anticipate needing in a specified time period. Customers (usually purchasing agents) are surveyed by telephone, mail, or personal interview. These estimates are then added together for all the customers surveyed, and projections are made for the entire market. The sales forecast for the firm is then prepared by multiplying its current or expected market share times the total market demand estimate.

These surveys can be costly and time-consuming, and their accuracy is dependent upon companies actually purchasing as much as respondents claim they will. However, for many products, respondents can be expected to have a fairly precise knowledge of company needs, especially if the company has already prepared its own sales forecast. Further, the fact that customer organizations typically budget in advance for purchases suggests that these estimates can be quite accurate.

Difficulties with Judgmental Methods

The industrial firm will invariably encounter difficulties when using qualitative methods to determine market potential and develop sales forecasts. Regardless of the approach adopted, three basic difficulties will arise: (1) the existence of vested interests; (2) the resolution of discrepancies in estimates; and (3) the imprecision of information obtained.

The vested interest problem is most serious when relying on internal company people for projections. As noted earlier, salespeople can exhibit reluctance to provide true estimates if they believe that the company will use them when setting quotas. Outside sources, on the other hand, are not influenced by such concerns, but are probably less reflective of the local conditions faced in each of the company's territories. The issue becomes one of balancing self-serving estimates which are precise against objective estimates which are more general. If a company is convinced of the integrity of estimates from the sales force and from various managers, the vested interest problem can be avoided. If not, more reliance has to be placed on external sources, and the marketer must draw inferences about company territories from general market information. The most appropriate approach is to use both internal and external sources, comparing the estimates for consistency and investigating the causes of any discrepancies.

Quantitative Approaches

Five different quantitative methods will be introduced here. Each requires different assumptions and informational inputs. Some rely on statistical methods that have been developed over time, and are highly regarded by marketing researchers. Others are based on simple logic and rely on more fundamental computations. Figure 6.4 presents examples of the five basic types.

Extrapolation

Extrapolation is defined as the process of projecting to future years the pattern of change noted in past sales figures. These past sales figures are placed in chronological order, and are then referred to as a *time series.* The extrapolation example in Figure 6.4 presents the case of two products, A and B. Unit sales figures for both products are shown, and the percentage of net change from one year to the next is calculated.

In the case of product A, it is apparent that a fairly smooth pattern of increases from year to year of approximately 6 percent seems to characterize the sales growth pattern. However, for product B, the growth pattern has been much more volatile, ranging from 30 percent less than the average, to almost 60 percent more than the average.

The comparison between product A and product B illustrates the basic problem in using extrapolation. For product A, one would have much more confidence that the sales forecast of 191 units would be realized. But for product B, the sales

EXTRAPOLATION

	Product A			Product B		
	Sales	% Change		Sales	% Change	
3 Years Ago	150			200		
2 Years Ago	160	7%		250	25%	
1 Year Ago	170	6%	Average	375	50%	Average
Last Year	180	6%	6.3%	450	20%	31.7%
Forecast:						
Next Year	191			593		

TIME SERIES DECOMPOSITION

SIMPLE CHAIN RATIO

Sales = (Establishments) × (Average Number of Units) × (Market Share)

REGRESSION ANALYSIS

Sales = f(Advertising, Sales Force, Distributors,
Price, . . . , Competitors' Efforts)

COMPLEX MODEL BUILDING

Figure 6.4   Quantitative Sales Forecasting Techniques

forecast of 593 units prompts much more uncertainty because wide fluctuations are evident in the growth rate from year to year. In short, extrapolation takes the naive view that the pattern (a percentage increase in this case) exhibited in the recent past will be repeated in the coming year. This approach assumes that all circumstances surrounding sales growth in the recent past will be very nearly the same in the future. At the very least, it assumes that next year will be an average year.

Time Series Decomposition

A body of statistical forecasting techniques exists in the form of *time series decomposition* analysis. Decomposition means to break down or separate data into its subcomponents; time series data for sales can be broken down into four elements: (1) the overall trend; (2) any cyclical pattern; (3) seasonal fluctuations; and (4) any irregular movements. When projecting future sales, the forecast can be expressed as a combination of the four components (sales = T + C + S + I).

The trend pertains to the long-term persistent growth pattern exhibited in the sales of a product. It is concerned with the overall general direction of the past data. In Figure 6.4, the sales trends for product A and product B over a series of quarters are depicted as straight lines. It is obvious that the trend line for product A shows slow growth, while the trend line for product B shows very rapid growth. A trend line is essentially an extrapolation which has been calculated over a number of years.

An integral part of time series decomposition analysis is the business cycle, which connotes the upward and downward swings of the economy over periods of three to seven years. Extensive study of these swings has indicated that repetitive cycles particular to industries can be identified. Such cyclical behavior can be seen in the quarterly data for product A in Figure 6.4. It is important to realize, then, that there will be years when the entire industry benefits from upward swings in business across the nation, as there will be years where the entire industry is somewhat depressed due to external factors such as high interest rates. Knowledge of the upward or downward aspects of the coming year can be used to modify the sales force forecast accordingly.

Seasonality is the pattern of sales from month to month, or quarter to quarter, within a one-year period. Climatic factors are often the culprits in seasonality—as in the case of construction equipment, which in northern climes is purchased in anticipation of warmer months and not purchased in the colder months. Product B in Figure 6.4, demonstrates a seasonal pattern in that sales drop off every fourth quarter. Knowledge of the seasonal swings of demand is extremely valuable in the planning of production schedules and inventory control. On the other hand, in a depressed season, it may make sense to drop price or otherwise stimulate demand. Companies can use these low periods to count inventory, construct annual plans, and give vacation time to key personnel.

The pattern in sales over time is also subject to an occasional random or irregular movement—sometimes due to an isolated event, such as a temporary strike in the industry. Other times, the cause is more difficult to identify. Because this irregular data is not reflective of the more typical state of affairs, the marketer may want to place less weight on them when making forecasts.

Figure 6.5 includes a time series and overall trend extrapolation line. When the data is decomposed, a number of insights can be drawn. There is, for example, a clear positive trend, although a substantial amount of fluctuation is taking place within the trend. Assuming that the first and third years are more representative, then there is a short-term downward cyclical trend in the second year. A clear seasonal trend is also apparent, as sales increase markedly in the third quarter. Finally,

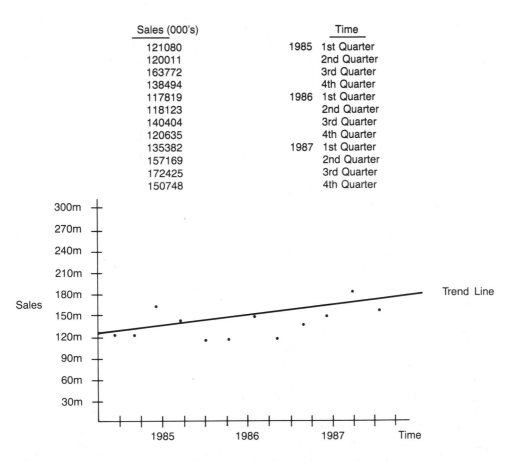

Sales (000's)	Time	
121080	1985	1st Quarter
120011		2nd Quarter
163772		3rd Quarter
138494		4th Quarter
117819	1986	1st Quarter
118123		2nd Quarter
140404		3rd Quarter
120635		4th Quarter
135382	1987	1st Quarter
157169		2nd Quarter
172425		3rd Quarter
150748		4th Quarter

Figure 6.5   Sales as a Function of Time

the second quarter of 1987 is an example of an irregular movement in the data. Sales had been almost constant in moving from the first to second quarters, but in 1987, they are increasing significantly.

Identifying these trends over time, and continually verifying them, can greatly enhance the marketer's ability to forecast with insight and accuracy.

Simple Chain Ratio

A somewhat different method of sales forecasting can be accomplished through the linking up of several factors in a *ratio equation* such as that illustrated in Figure 6.4. For example, if the number of prospective buying establishments is determined from census data or other secondary information and the average number of units purchased in a year can be ascertained, the product of these two factors plus the addition of a typical market share proportion that a firm normally experiences will effect a rough estimate of the total sales expected. Extensions of this approach may take the forms of optimistic and pessimistic estimates of the company's market share over the coming year. Alternatively, the number of establishments or average number of units purchased per establishment may be subjected to experimentation through the use of *what-if?* scenarios. Through this process it is possible to obtain ballpark estimates of sales forecasts.

Regression Analysis

One of the most powerful, and yet fairly easy to use, statistical techniques for sales forecasting is *regression analysis.* This is a causal method of forecasting, because the marketer is *implying* a causal relationship between sales and some other variable. Where time series approaches look at sales as a function of time, causal approaches look at sales as a function of some variable thought to influence (or cause) sales. Basically, regression analysis relies on past data collected on a number of variables believed to have some sort of positive or negative association with a company's sales level. A basic model is constructed with sales as the dependent variable, and these factors as independent variables. Simple regression uses only one independent variable; multiple regression uses two or more. For example, the number of dollars spent on advertising, the size of the sales force, the number of distributors, current interest rates, or the average relative price could be examined to see how these factors individually or collectively affect company or product sales.

Regression analysis procedures can be applied to these relationships (or models) through the use of a small computer or sophisticated hand calculator. The outcome of this data analysis is a single equation which relates the independent variable(s) to sales (see Figure 6.6). The equation is for the straight line which best captures the relationship between these variables and sales. In this equation, coefficients are determined for each of the variables such that if any one of them is increased or decreased by one unit, total sales will be incrementally changed by the amount of the coefficient. Some of the coefficients may turn out to have negative signs, which means that as they increase, the forecasted sales level will decrease. For instance, competitors' sales force size may be found to have a negative coefficient. This equation is then used to forecast next period sales by plugging in values for the independent variable(s). Most computer programs will also provide a goodness-of-fit statistic (R^2) for the regression equation.

Regression analysis is a well-respected statistical approach with many nuances, one of which is the ability to lag variables. Here, the researcher can examine the effect of the independent variable (e.g., advertising) on sales. Current sales can be regressed against current advertising expenditures, against advertising one period ago (say, last month or quarter), two periods ago, and so forth. In this way, the marketer can determine which model best explains how long it takes changes in advertising to affect sales. Another nuance allows for the statement of a relevant range of forecasted sales, accompanied with a level of confidence or probability that the actual sales will fall within that range. In addition, it is possible that some of the factors originally input into the regression analysis have no significant statistical association with sales, and these will be deleted from the final equation. Regression analysis does involve a number of underlying assumptions, some of which are highly technical, and its proper application requires an understanding of these assumptions and the implications of violating them.

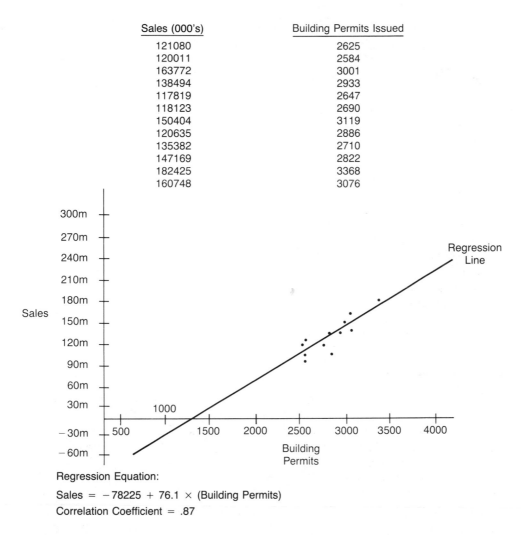

Sales (000's)	Building Permits Issued
121080	2625
120011	2584
163772	3001
138494	2933
117819	2647
118123	2690
150404	3119
120635	2886
135382	2710
147169	2822
182425	3368
160748	3076

Regression Equation:

Sales $= -78225 + 76.1 \times$ (Building Permits)

Correlation Coefficient $= .87$

Figure 6.6 Sales as a Function of Building Permits: A Simple Regression Equation

Complex Model Building

The most sophisticated approach in the quantitative realm of sales forecasts is the building of mathematical or simulation models of the relationship of sales to factors in the industrial marketing mix, competitive activities, the economy, and anything else the model builder believes should be put into the model. Complex model building is an extension of regression analysis in that, rather than involving only one regression equation, a series of equations can be formulated to describe the various relationships between company sales and numerous other factors under considera-tion. Using historical data, these equations can be modified to fit the company's unique situation. The primary value of these complex model-building approaches comes from their ability to accommodate the many curvilinear relationships believed to exist in marketing phenomena. That is, relationships between independent variables and sales may be more complex, such as where price changes have a sizable effect on sales within certain price ranges, and little effect within other ranges. Independent variables may interact with one another in the way they affect sales, such as where the effect of price on sales is greater at certain levels of advertising than at other levels. Such complications require the model builder to critically examine all of the elements in the marketing environment, and may help the marketing manager to discover relationships that had gone unnoticed. Finally, the complex mathematical models are sometimes converted into computer simulation models and run under various scenarios such as different marketing strategies, different competitive environments, conditions of tight supply, or the introduction of new technology in the marketplace.

Many large corporations also subscribe to professional forecasting services from organizations that have constructed complex models of various sectors of the U.S. economy. For a fee, subscribers can purchase the output of these models. This output is usually a set of forecasts for such variables as gross national product, interest rates, inflation, new construction activity, capital spending by businesses, and consumption of durable and nondurable goods. Examples of such services include Chase Econometrics, Data Resources, Inc. (DRI), General Electric, and The Wharton School's Economic Forecasting Unit.

Resolving the *Final* Sales Forecast

As we have seen, a wide variety of choices is available in the sales forecasting area. These choices range from techniques that are essentially simplistic, subjective, and highly intuitive to those which are complex, computer-designed, and perhaps beyond the comprehension of the average manager. The final choice is usually the result of several considerations.

One such consideration must be the level of faith that the company has in the opinions of inside executives, as opposed to the need to incorporate the views of outsiders and accommodate complex relationships which are believed to exist in the marketplace. As a general recommendation to the company seeking the *one best* sales forecasting method, it is advantageous to use a corroborative, step-by-step approach to solving the problem. That is, the ease of administration and speed of the *composite of company sources* approach should be balanced against the more rigorous design exhibited in many of the quantitative methods.

Qualitative approaches should be compared with quantitative approaches. If there are inconsistencies, the industrial marketing manager must investigate the various aspects of both approaches to determine critical flaws. For instance, the sales force members may be underemphasizing the acceptance level of new products while the chain-ratio method may be overemphasizing the substitution factor for these products. Only through cautious and critical analysis of the assumptions and the specifics of each method can the industrial marketing manager hope to discover why the discrepancies have occurred and make provisions to resolve them.

As a final recommendation on the eternal search for the one best sales forecasting technique, the marketing manager is encouraged to constantly review specific aspects of the sales forecasting process. In particular, the marketer should address a number of critical areas of investigation, in attempting to refine the sales forecast.

The first area involves insights into the nature of customers. It is vital to develop an understanding of the motivations, buying process, evaluative criteria, and individuals involved in the decision to purchase or not to purchase. Only through this understanding of the decision-making process and the stimulants of customer demand can the marketer hope to predict accurately what customers will do in the future.

Next, the marketer must develop and continually update insights into competitors. Through experience, the marketing manager becomes knowledgeable of the degree of retaliation various competitors can be expected to undertake in response to his or her marketing programs. At the same time, he or she comes to know the leaders and the followers in the industry in terms of aggressive marketing actions and must learn to anticipate the extent to which competition in the industry will be volatile or stable.

A third area concerns the environment. What changes will occur in the business environment, the political environment, the resources environment, and the regulatory environment? Further, to what extent will these changes (if they occur) affect customers and competitors?

A final area requiring review is the forecasting time horizon. Forecasts into the near future can be made with more certainty than those looking to the distant future. Many companies rely on *rolling planning* as a solution to the time problem. That is, a one-year forecast is derived from a five-year ballpark expectation. The one-year forecast is then revised on a quarterly basis, necessitating changes in budgets, marketing action timetables, and sales targets.

SUMMARY

This chapter has described the various concepts and methods involved in the assessment of industrial market demand and the forecasting of company sales. An industrial market was defined as the set of organizations with needs and budget capability to purchase a particular class of goods or services. A distinction was drawn between absolute and relative market potential, on the one hand, and between these two and company potential, on the other hand. Marketers typically are most concerned with their company's potential within its relevant markets, and with forecasting how much of that potential they can expect to capture in a given year.

Estimates of market potential and expected company sales are dependent upon developments in the external environment and on the firm's internal marketing programs. Throughout the chapter, extensive emphasis was placed on the critical role played by assumptions in market analysis. These assumptions concern external developments such as competitor actions, economic variables, or government actions, as well as the likely effect of the firm's internal marketing programs on sales. A useful tool for establishing some of these assumptions, especially those regarding the effectiveness of internal marketing programs, is a set of market response curves. These are estimated based on productivity analysis.

Some of these distinctive characteristics of industrial demand were reviewed. These included the derived and concentrated nature of demand. A sizable number of sales will frequently come from existing, loyal customers. Also, much of the available demand may come in the form of projects that require competitive bidding. Each of these phenomena poses special problems in making market projections.

Market analysis provides vital inputs into three major strategic areas. First, estimates of market potential and company sales are artificial ingredients in the establishment of sales and market share objectives for the firm. Second, these estimates provide benchmarks against which to compare actual results. This comparison is the marketing control or tracking function. Third, these estimates are the basis for evaluating new product and market opportunities, and deciding in which products and markets the firm should invest.

Given these uses, there are a number of specific tools and techniques for performing market analysis. These differ in the degree of judgment used, the starting and ending points, the sources of estimates, and the sophistication of the underlying assumptions. In estimating market potential, common techniques discussed include the chain-ratio method, the statistical series method, and a combination approach. In the sales forecasting area, four qualitative approaches were examined: the composite of sales force opinion, the jury of executive opinion, the Delphi forecast, and the survey of buying intentions. Five quantitative techniques were also reviewed: trend extrapolation, time series decomposition, the simple chain ratio, regression analysis, and complex model building.

Finally, it was argued that, no matter what technique is used, market projections almost always require a degree of informed judgment by the marketer. Minor, and occasionally major, adjustments must be made based on the marketer's insight into the underlying nature of the market. The development of such insight depends on a continual reassessment of customers and their motivations, of competitor strategies and orientations, and of the dynamics of the environment.

QUESTIONS

1. If you were estimating relative market potential for a new type of industrial trash bag that is more durable than anything currently on the market, but also more expensive, what type of data would you try to collect? In what areas might you need to make assumptions?

2. What are some of the major difficulties in estimating sales-response curves? How could a company that is considering participating in its first trade show go about estimating the sales-response function for an expenditure of $25,000 on the show?

3. Discuss the implications of derived demand for estimating market potential and forecasting sales. How would the derived demand concept be used in making specific projections of market potential or company sales?

4. When attempting to forecast company sales in each of the following situations, would you be more concerned about avoiding overestimation or underestimation?

(a) Your product has a large market share and a loyal customer base;

(b) Your product is not greatly different from those of the competition;

(c) You compete in a market where there are frequent technological advances;

(d) You are new to the market and are attempting to build market share.

5. Trumark Chemical Corporation produces various inks that are used in printing operations. The midwest sales manager at Trumark, in attempting to establish sales quotas for her district, wanted to determine market potential for the product line. The district included Ohio, Pennsylvania, Michigan, Indiana, and Illinois. Past sales data for Trumark suggested that most of its ink customers were in SIC 2711 (newspapers), SIC 2721 (periodicals), SIC 2732 (book printing), and SIC 2751 (letterpress commercial printing). The sales manager also determined, from historical experience in the industry and further analysis of company sales, that expenditures for printing ink comprised about 0.1 percent of the value of shipments for the using industries. Using *Sales and Marketing Management's* 1987 "Survey of Industrial and Commercial Buying Power," determine:

(a) The total market potential for the midwestern district.

(b) The relative market potential for each state in the district.

(c) The relative market potential for each state in the district as a percentage of total U.S. potential.

6. How could inaccurate estimates of market potential result in ineffective marketing plans and programs?

7. If sales are projected too low for a company that manufactures air conditioned truck trailers, what are the possible adverse effects this error could have on company operations and market performance?

8. Sales forecasts based on the composite or combined projections of company managers tend to be fairly accurate. Why do you think this is true, considering the qualitative nature of this method?

9. What is the underlying logic behind time series methods and causal methods of sales forecasting? What are the limitations of each?

CHAPTER 7

INDUSTRIAL MARKET SEGMENTATION

Key Concepts

Average analysis
Concentrated marketing
Contribution analysis
Cost-Benefit analysis
Coverage ratio
Homogeneity
Macro bases
Marginal analysis
Market segmentation
Micro bases

Nested approach
Primary product specialization ratio
Resource allocation
Sales response curve
Segmentation process
Segment evaluative criteria
Submarket or segment
Target marketing
Undifferentiated marketing

Learning Objectives

1. Establish the role of market segmentation in marketing planning and as a marketing strategy.
2. Describe a process approach for using market segmentation and targeting.
3. Establish useful criteria for evaluating segmentation as a practice, for evaluating specific bases of segmentation, and for allocating resources to target segments.
4. Identify bases for segmenting industrial markets.
5. Propose a cost-benefit/nested approach to market segmentation.

An organization that decides to operate in some market . . . recognizes that it normally cannot serve all the customers in that market.

P. KOTLER

This is the final chapter concerned with examining and analyzing industrial markets. Having defined the market, estimated demand potential, and assessed buyer behavior, the marketer must determine if it is realistic to attack the entire market, or whether to focus on some subset or smaller part. This chapter is concerned with market segmentation, a well-respected means of pinpointing target markets.

The definition of market segmentation begins the chapter, followed by an explanation of why it is a helpful, and sometimes vital, process for the industrial marketing manager. Several criteria for judging the usefulness of segmentation and for selecting target markets are discussed. The problem of allocating scarce resources is introduced and related to market segmentation and target market selection. Different methods of segmentation are subsequently described. A dynamic cost-benefit/nested approach to the process of market segmentation in the industrial market is proposed. Some observations on the practice and future of industrial market segmentation close the chapter.

DEFINING MARKET SEGMENTATION

A market segment is a group of existing or potential customers sharing some common characteristic which is relevant in explaining (or predicting) their response to a company's marketing programs (Wind and Cardozo 1974). The process the marketer goes through in identifying such groups is *market segmentation*. Different opinions exist regarding how a firm should view this process, and the nature of the appropriate tools for implementing segmentation. A popular approach is Kotler's (1984) three-step segmentation process, which involves: (1) using some method of dividing the total market into smaller parts which are similar within themselves but dissimilar between themselves; (2) selecting a market segment or market segments which offer attractive targets for the firm; (3) custom-tailoring the marketing mix to cater to the needs and special problems of the selected target market. In contrast, Bonoma and Shapiro (1984,1) have limited market segmentation to the process of separating a market into groups of customers, prospective customers (prospects), or buying situations, so that the members of each resulting group are more like the other members of that group than like members of other segments.

The differences between these approaches reside in the distinction between a marketing strategy orientation and a market analysis orientation. In the former, the process and outcome of market segmentation is an entire marketing program which has pinpointed the target market, identified the circumstances and competitive forces in that target, decided that the target is appropriate for the firm, and attempted to penetrate the market with a custom-tailored marketing mix. The latter orientation is geared toward the techniques and specifics of identifying firms that have similar needs and circumstances. The approach taken in this chapter is a mixture and extension of both of these views. We will explore the various bases and techniques often used to divide markets up into segments, and will relate the various considerations industrial marketers use in evaluating: (1) the worth of segmentation as a strategic tool; and (2) the attractiveness of various market segments if market segmentation is used. The extension concerns the need for a periodic evaluation of market segmentation as a general practice, of the bases used for defining market segments, and of the firm's success in penetrating specific market segments. Underlying this evaluation is the need for effective allocation of the firm's scarce marketing resources. The marketing manager must always bear in mind the costs and the benefits involved in serving diverse market segments, and must balance the costs against the benefits—with the goal of achieving long-run profitability for the company.

AN EXAMPLE OF MARKET SEGMENTATION

On an intuitive level, segmentation is easy to comprehend and usually represents clear advantages for the company using it. Figure 7.1 offers a conceptual diagram of market segmentation.

Figure 7.1 illustrates that a market can be envisioned as an accumulation of numerous submarkets. For instance, a tire manufacturer realizes that there are several different types of industrial tire buyers. These buyers vary greatly in their characteristics and needs. Some tire buyers are automobile manufacturers who wish to buy large quantities of passenger tires. Others include transportation companies who wish to buy tires for 18-wheel tractor-trailers. Yet another category of buyers would be construction companies who are seeking tires for large equipment such

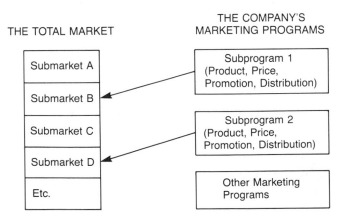

Figure 7.1 Concept, Procedure, and Benefits of Market Segmentation

as earthmovers and dump trucks. Also, discount stores, independent garages, and even some drug stores engaged in scrambled merchandising are prospective sub-segments of the total tire market. Consequently, the tire manufacturer has several alternative strategies available to segment its markets. For example, it may concentrate all of its efforts on one single submarket, such as a major domestic automobile manufacturer. In this case, the tire manufacturer must have strong conviction that it understands the purchasing decision characteristics of the automobile manufacturer and can beat the competition on most of the key attributes necessary to gain long-term contracts with the automobile company.

In contrast, an alternative strategy would be to expand the tire product line so that several segments are targeted, each with its own unique marketing mix. Now, in addition to a strategy aimed at domestic automobile manufacturers, the tire manufacturer would also have different and distinct marketing mixes aimed at construction companies, discount retail stores, and other targeted submarkets.

THE PROCESS OF SEGMENTATION

This tire manufacturer example illustrates the basics of market segmentation. Segmentation involves the identification of submarkets or segments within the total market, the decision on which one (or ones) to pursue, and the design of individualized marketing mixes for the chosen market segments. These activities can be envisioned as a six-step process, as illustrated in Figure 7.2. Let us examine each of these steps in more detail.

A PROCEDURE FOR SEGMENTING MARKETS:

Step 1   Identify Relevant Bases
↓
Step 2   Determine Homogeneous Groups
↓
Step 3   Evaluate Each Segment
↓
Step 4   Select Target Market(s)
↓
Step 5   Design Marketing Strategy
↓
Step 6   Implement and Monitor

THE BENEFITS:

• Better Understanding of Market

• Economy of Effort

• Enhanced Specialization

• Pinpointed Prospects

• Exploitation of Competition

Figure 7.2   Procedure for Segmenting Markets

Identify Relevant Market Segmentation Bases

The beginning point of market segmentation is an inspection of the total market, with an eye toward different ways in which it might conceivably be broken down. Discussions of buyer behavior and the general nature of industrial markets in previous chapters included numerous characteristics useful in grouping customers and/or prospects. A few of the possibilities include:

a. company size (e.g., under 1,000 employees)

b. company location (e.g., large urban areas)

c. type of industry (e.g., SIC code)

d. technology used (e.g., analog versus digital)

e. ordering policies (e.g., frequency or size of purchases)

f. product application (e.g., different uses of the same product)

g. buying center characteristics (e.g., background of key decision maker)

As a point of comparison, consumer goods markets are often segmented based on demographic characteristics of purchasers and/or their reasons for buying. For instance, the large number of brands and types of soft drinks can be seen as evidence of the extensive number of ways in which that consumer market has been segmented. Numerous subgroupings of consumers are identifiable in terms of age, sex, consumption capacity, levels of sweetness desired, and concerns for sugar or caffeine content. Conceptually, there are no differences between industrial and consumer market segmentation at this step, but the characteristics (or bases) used to segment the market vary greatly.

Determine Homogeneous Groupings

The second step in market segmentation, once potential bases for segmentation have been identified, is to use those bases to group members of the total market into submarkets such that there is *homogeneity* among the members of the submarket. Homogeneity refers to similarities or commonalities among the members of the subgroup setting them apart in some way from members of other subgroups. A critical point, however, is that these commonly shared characteristics must relate to the buyer's susceptibility to differing marketing programs. While this may seem somewhat confusing, it simply says that a good segment includes a group of organizations with a shared descriptive characteristic (e.g., company size measured in terms of employees), and that this characteristic (or base) must be further related to the way in which these companies purchase the product or service in question. So, companies in a given size category must be homogeneous in terms of how, when, where, what, or why they buy. If companies with over 1,000 employees tend to purchase in much larger quantities, or more frequently, or to place more emphasis on quality when making a purchase than do companies in other size categories, then size might be a good variable to use in segmenting the market. Marketing programs can be tailored to reflect such differences in buyer needs or behaviors.

Another way to think about this point is to view company size as a *descriptor* of the segments, and the tendency of organizations of a given size to purchase in a certain manner as the underlying source of marketing opportunity.

Most common among the bases used to segment industrial markets are company size, geographic location, and SIC categories. These may be popular only because they are easier to use, and data is usually readily available on markets broken down in such ways. The appropriateness of a given basis for segmentation *depends on the product or service in question*. Unless organizations of a given size, geographic locale, or SIC category have homogeneous needs or buyer behaviors with respect to the particular product or service sold by the marketer, segmentation may be a waste of time and money.

Evaluate the Attractiveness of Each Market Segment

Separating the total market into identifiable and homogeneous submarkets is a necessary step toward the company's ultimate targeting decision. An intermediate step is an evaluation process which serves to determine the attractiveness of each market segment relative to others in light of the company's objectives. For now, attractiveness will be equated with long-run profitability of the market segment (this issue will be expanded on later in the chapter). That is, through the application of marketing research and forecasting techniques, judgments can be made about the total size and probable market share to be gained in each market segment. These judgments could be translated into estimates of long-run profits, based on the marketing strategy the firm would probably adopt in each case. Segments can be ranked on their relative attractiveness, or ability to meet objectives.

Select Target Market(s)

The outcome of the evaluation process is a selection of a specific submarket or set of submarkets which are appropriate targets for the company in some relevant planning horizon. If the firm's objectives include the maximization of profit in the long run, it would be appropriate to select out those market segments that appear to embody this objective and to disregard those market segments expected to be less profitable. Once a market segment is selected for targeting, additional market research may be conducted to better understand that segment's unique characteristics. Furthermore, intensive analysis would be devoted to assessing the strengths and weaknesses of competitors in the chosen segments, so as to identify areas of competitive opportunity for the firm.

Align the Marketing Strategy to Market Segment(s)

Strategic marketing planning now focuses on designing or aligning a marketing mix geared to penetrating the chosen target market through the embodiment of customer satisfaction and the gaining of competitive advantage. It is at this stage that marketers make a clear distinction between the concept of industrywide differentiation and the application of market segmentation. Industrywide differentiation is involved when a company designs its marketing program to distinguish it in some way from the programs of competitors who are seeking to penetrate the market. The focus is on using the marketing mix to convince the entire market that the company's product or service is unique compared to those of competitors. Industrywide differentiation can be achieved through brand image, a technology, product features, quality, customer service, and so on. For example, IBM differentiates itself from other computer companies by providing superior customer service. Market segmentation and targeting, on the other hand, involve designing individualized marketing programs which cater to the distinct needs or problems of subgroups within the entire market. So, a computer company that focuses on the distinct computer needs of hospitals in its product design, price, promotional efforts, and distribution system would be pursuing a segmentation and targeting strategy.

A segmentation approach makes sense only if there are subgroups of customer organizations in the market whose distinct needs or buying behaviors can be reflected in the firm's marketing programs. Otherwise, one common approach to the market is appropriate.

Consider another example, a company that sells security alarm systems, and segments the market for these systems based on the average unit value of the products in an organization's inventory. Assume the company has divided the market into organizations with very high inventory value, those with moderately valued inventory, and those having inventory of low unit value. The company is considering focusing its efforts on the first two segments.

Further analysis suggests that firms with inventory of high unit value are much less price-conscious about security systems than the other groups, and tend to hire consultants to recommend alarm systems. Organizations in the moderate group, alternatively, appear to rely much more heavily on word-of-mouth referrals in evaluating security systems than do the other groups, and tend to be very conscious of brand names. These differences suggest a number of ways in which the marketing mix can be designed to better meet the needs of each segment. The design of the company's product line, as well as its pricing programs, advertising appeals, and personal selling efforts can be made to reflect such major differences.

Implement and Monitor

The final stage of the market segmentation process involves the actual implementation of the custom-tailored marketing program and careful monitoring of the reactions of prospective customers and competitors in that market segment. The monitoring system should not only look at market share and other competitive dynamics within the market segment, but also should periodically assess the underlying bases used to identify and uniquely characterize that market segment. Better bases may emerge over time, or become apparent after the company has had significant experience with this market segment.

The alarm system manufacturer, for instance, might find that the buyer behavior of companies with inventory of moderate unit value is becoming more and more like that of companies with high-value inventory. Or, the manufacturer may find that the physical location of a customer's facilities is becoming a more important factor than inventory value in explaining how they buy alarm systems. Further, new segments may be emerging, such as companies requiring mobile alarm systems.

DEGREES OF SEGMENTATION

One of the distinctive characteristics of segmentation in industrial markets is the greater precision that is possible in a company's segmentation efforts. At one extreme, the marketer can approach the entire market as a whole, and not use segmentation at all. This approach is equivalent to treating the entire market as one big segment, and is called *undifferentiated marketing*. At the other extreme, every customer could be treated as a distinct segment, with specific programs tailored to its needs. When one, or relatively few, organizations are given sole attention, this approach is termed *concentrated marketing*. Between these two extremes, numerous options exist in terms of the size and scope of the marketer's segmentation efforts in various product-market areas. A number of segments could be pursued with a number of marketing mixes. Figure 7.3 illustrates these possibilities.

With undifferentiated marketing, the company seeks to compete on a broad, middle-of-the-road basis. It develops a limited product line with standardized pricing, promotion, and distribution channels geared to what the company thinks are the typical or vast majority of market needs. With a concentrated marketing approach, the company channels its resources toward winning and satisfying a single company or segment. The marketing effort would be intense and the stakes obviously high, since losing a single account might result in the demise of the company itself.

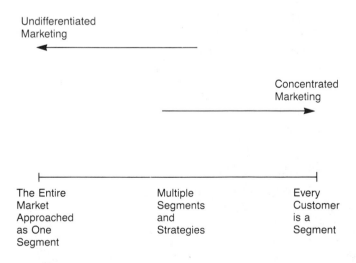

Undifferentiated
Marketing

Concentrated
Marketing

| The Entire Market Approached as One Segment | Multiple Segments and Strategies | Every Customer is a Segment |

Figure 7.3   Strategic Options Possible through Segmentation

The choice of any one of these approaches is constrained by two considerations. First, there is the question of the number of identifiable and meaningful segments. If the customer market is dominated by a variety of organizations which do not fall readily into any logical subgroupings, or if the market itself is not large, then segmentation is not feasible. Second, if the company has limited resources, it may be forced to focus on a concentrated approach. That is, it may not be able to afford the costs involved in tailoring the marketing mix to a number of different segments, or of competing head-on for the entire undifferentiated market.

WHAT SEGMENTATION DOES FOR THE INDUSTRIAL MARKETER

With conscientious application of the six-step process described earlier, segmentation can provide the marketer with a number of benefits. Perhaps the most important of these benefits is improved efficiency in the use of the firm's marketing resources. When a company identifies specific target markets, it does not waste time and resources attempting to comprehend the needs of, and compete in, market segments which are less profitable or otherwise unattractive. Also, with undifferentiated marketing, the company is reaching many customers who are not really viable prospects. It may be spreading its limited resources too thin.

Market segmentation also enables the marketer to reap the benefits of specialization. Target marketing can be seen as a form of specialization in which the company seeks to apply its special skills or capabilities and match them to the unique needs, wants, and problems of the market segments selected. Granted, specialization requires extra investment and will often result in higher unit costs; however, the result is a marketing program that is more satisfactory and therefore more highly valued by prospective buyers.

In addition, the application of market segmentation helps pinpoint specific customer prospects. This benefit is particularly relevant to the industrial market arena where market segments may, in fact, comprise only one or a very small number of potential buyers. Market segmentation in this case would help to reveal those prospects who reside in target segments, and trigger the marketing intelligence system to initiate information-gathering activities regarding those particular prospects.

Finally, the adoption of market segmentation helps the company to identify and exploit the weaknesses of its relevant competitors. By studying prospective buyers in selected segments, the company will simultaneously become aware of the competitive environment and knowledgeable of the capabilities of competitors who are also targeting that particular segment.

DECISION CRITERIA IN MARKET SEGMENTATION AND TARGETING

In evaluating the entire range of possibilities illustrated in Figure 7.3, a company must first decide whether segmentation is a useful practice that will serve company goals. In addition, if segmentation is deemed useful, the company must assess market segments with regard to relative attractiveness. Further, the company must determine precisely how much marketing effort to allocate to each of the targeted market segments. Accordingly, it is important to discuss three categories of concern:

(1) criteria for assessing the usefulness of market segmentation; (2) criteria for the selection of prospective target markets; (3) considerations and decision rules for the allocation of marketing resources to selected target markets.

Criteria for the Usefulness of Market Segmentation

The initial question the firm must ask itself is whether the practice of market segmentation is useful and will serve its needs. To make this assessment, the company must address four points.

1. Does market segmentation fit the firm's basic marketing strategy?

Some companies will not entertain the practice of market segmentation because it is inconsistent with their basic approaches to marketing. That is, a company may have employed undifferentiated marketing as its basic approach in the past and have no desire to consider changing something that has been successful. Senior management may be unreceptive to the perceived risks involved in changing the basic marketing strategy, or the resource base of the firm may be so miniscule that it cannot respond, even if it identifies attractive market segments. Another case in point may be a company which has fortuitously linked with one large buyer and has a guaranteed purchasing arrangement for the long term. Here, the company may be complacent or the single buyer may be adamant about its suppliers not selling to competitors.

2. Does homogeneity exist within the total market?

A criterion established earlier in our discussion of the concept of market segmentation was that of homogeneity. That is, for market segmentation to take place, companies grouped together must be similar in their underlying behavioral characteristics and dissimilar from the characteristics of other groups. These behavioral commonalities are often difficult to identify with market research, and sometimes are not clearly established until the marketer has gone through the process of segmentation. If a company cannot identify commonalities for subgroups of buyers, the application of market segmentation will be futile.

3. Are the segments measurable?

Even if subgroupings can be identified, there is the question of measuring the various market segments identified. Before target groups can be selected, the descriptive characteristics, sales potential, and potential profitability of each market segment must be measurable. While considerable secondary information is usually available to help in this regard, there are special cases where the measurability factor is troublesome. For instance, if prospects are privately owned companies, the amount of public information will be minimal. Decision makers within prospective companies may be reluctant to divulge information to interviewers in a marketing research study seeking to determine the size of the various segments. Certain descriptive characteristics, such as the structure or orientation (e.g., innovativeness) of buying organizations may not lend themselves to easy measurement. Alternatively, the uncertainty of future circumstances may be so great that whatever indicators of size and profitability can be derived for the present, it may be too risky to project them into the future.

4. Are the market segments accessible?

Accessibility refers to the degree to which a market segment can be reached through a unique marketing program. That is, members of a market segment must be approached, to become aware that a company has targeted them and to consider that company's offer. It may be that the company's sales force, channels of distribution, or promotional capabilities will not reach certain segments. A good example of accessibility problems involves the bid listing practices of many state and municipal governments. To gain access to the list and thereby be invited to make a bid on construction projects or capital equipment, a vendor must qualify to the satisfaction of the state or municipality. This qualification may require bonding of the company and employees; it may require submission of financial records; it may require demonstrated expertise in certain areas. Obviously, lack of accessibility to market segments precludes further consideration of market segmentation as a viable marketing tool.

Criteria for the Selection of Target Markets

Once the four questions posed above have been answered in the affirmative, the next set of criteria involves the selection of market segments as target markets. Here, five different issues must be addressed.

1. Does the target market fit the company's image?

The targeting of a market segment must be aligned with the total corporate image. Generally, companies attempt to have an integrated and consistent image across all of their activities. Therefore, a target market which is not consistent with this image will be eliminated from consideration. Take, for example, Texas Instruments' (TI) attempted move into the consumer goods market with its TI-59 microcomputer in the mid-1970s. Firmly established in the industrial market as a manufacturer and marketer of high quality business machines, for some unknown reason, TI endeavored to penetrate a market segment which was inconsistent with its previous experience and marketing know-how. Movement into this market segment with a microcomputer meant that TI had to establish new channels of distribution, think of a new frame of reference with regard to communicating to households and prospective buyers, engage in discount pricing and retail-level consumer goods pricing wars, and ensure that the product was designed so that a child, literally, could use it. The result was a failure often cited as one of the classic marketing mistakes of the time.

2. Will the segment be responsive?

Responsiveness is the extent to which companies within a segment are susceptible to the vendor's marketing programs. If prospective customer organizations are not open to considering the influence of marketing stimuli (e.g., product features, a price deal, or a promotional program), then these programs are wasted on them. This rejection can occur where managers are strongly committed to old, established ways of doing things. They are closed to considering new alternatives. It can also happen when a prospective customer has little or no leeway to consider the marketer's programs because of limited resources (including time), or because of regulations and procedures that must be observed (e.g., in government purchasing).

3. Will the segment be substantial over time?

Substantiality refers to the longevity of a target market. In other words, market segments can be seen in terms of the product life cycle where for short periods of time they exhibit rapid growth and great opportunity. However, some segments may become saturated or mature fairly quickly, after which growth will be very slow and opportunities to penetrate much fewer. Other segments may lose their attractiveness or meaningfulness as changes take place in the underlying needs or buyer behavior characteristics of the organizations in those segments. In the industrial market, substantiality is an extremely critical consideration, given the sudden demise of market segments due to technological breakthroughs. Rotary telephones, for instance, have been almost completely superseded by touch-tone models in most offices. On the horizon, however, loom voice-activated and computer-driven telephone systems which could rapidly destroy the touch-tone market.

4. Can the company be competitive in the target segment?

The key to marketing success is competitive advantage. Consequently, while a market segment may fit the company's image and seem substantial, it may be that the competitive circumstances dictate dropping it from consideration at this time. IBM and other computer companies are so dominant in the mainframe computer arena that practically no new company ventures into segments within this market despite the fact that some of these segments may be very attractive in other dimensions. Alternatively, despite NCR's dominance in selling point-of-sale cash register systems to retailers, a competitor specializing in the distinct sales transaction needs of, say, very small clothing stores may be able to establish a beachhead in the industry. The company must be able to convince itself that it has the relative strengths necessary to maintain a competitive advantage over a reasonable length of time within a particular segment.

5. Is the target market profitable?

Profitability is, of course, the bottom line in all marketing decisions. Consequently, profitability and the maintenance of profitability over time are prime considerations in the selection of a target market. The candidate market segment may fit the company's image, and it may satisfy the criterion of substantiality; however, to maintain a competitive edge, the costs (e.g., promotion, distribution, or product development) of focusing on firms in this segment may be so excessive that the hurdle rate for return on investment cannot be attained within a reasonable time period. In this instance, the market segment would be deleted from consideration as a target.

Criteria for the Allocation of Resources

The final step in the market segmentation process is the determination of the amount of marketing effort to be put into each of the target market segments. This distribution is sometimes referred to as the *allocation of resources*. There are two separate avenues for consideration which the marketer must keep in mind when making this determination. The first pertains to quantitative, and primarily financial, criteria for the allocation of resources, while the second pertains to qualitative, and primarily strategic, strength considerations.

With regard to the financial criteria used in deciding how much marketing effort to expend on each target market segment, the marketer can consider marginal analysis, average analysis, or contribution analysis. Each is a measure of return, or profitability. Since the marketer is allocating resources to segments, he or she requires some rate of return on that investment. The marketer also must examine these returns over some prespecified time frame.

Marginal analysis, which has its origins in the field of economics, is theoretically the most elegant, but also the most difficult to implement on a practical basis. Here, the mandate is to allocate resources on the basis of marginal return. In other words, the total marketing effort must be envisioned as a resource budget to be distributed in an optimal fashion across all market segments. Moreover, the distribution must consider differential response rates to marketing mix factors within segments.

Figure 7.4, part A, considers marginal analysis at the target segment level. The figure presents three target segments that have been identified for this particular planning year; each is characterized by a sales-response curve. It is important to realize that the sales-response curve is different for each market segment, and that the curves are curvilinear. In other words, there are unique growth factors and points of diminishing returns that must be understood in each case. With each additional dollar allocated to the marketing effort for any one target market, there is a movement to the right on the horizontal axis and a subsequent movement to the right on the sales-response curve. Since the response curve is nonlinear, the change in response expected from the next additional dollar will not always be the same. By comparing the expected increase in sales for each additional marketing dollar spent in each of the target segments, a decision can be made as to which one should receive the next dollar. The marketer follows the decision rule of allocating each additional dollar to that market segment which has the largest expected sales response for that additional dollar. This process is continued until he or she arrives at a one-to-one point, where an additional dollar of effort (cost) will derive, at most, one additional dollar of response (revenues). At this point, where the additional dollar of budget does not bring any profit, the budget allocation stops.

There are some basic problems with the use of margin analysis. Very few marketers have the good fortune to be able to work with sales-response curves of sufficient precision. Furthermore, the one-dollar-at-a-time approach to budget determination is impractical. One modification might be to measure the marginal returns from each additional expenditure of $100, or $1,000.

The next method of resource or budget allocation, average analysis, is a more commonly used approach which embodies some of the aspects of marginal analysis. Because of the difficulty in estimating sales-response curves and the impracticality of allocating resource dollars one at a time, marketers sometimes make assumptions about the average sales response of a market segment to a block of funds which could be expended on marketing in that market segment. For example, in Part B of Figure 7.4, market segments 1, 2, and 3 are now represented by straight-line sales-response estimates rather than curvilinear functions. These straight lines are assumed to hold over a certain range of effort. Moreover, the curves can be estimated through the use of marketing research and the application of regression techniques.

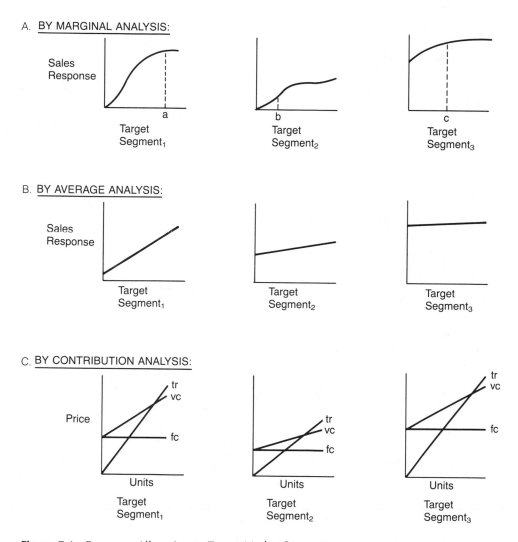

Figure 7.4   Resource Allocation to Target Market Segments

The marketing manager has the opportunity to apply marketing research methods and to include his own experience and personal knowledge of the typical response of each market segment to his marketing effort. Because judgment is applied in the averaging approach, this method of resource allocation is less appealing theoretically, but, it is much more implementable.

Contribution analysis, the final method of resource allocation to target market segments, is the method that will be proposed as the most appropriate. Contribution analysis goes one step beyond average analysis and includes the marketing manager's knowledge of the two types of costs involved with marketing effort. That is, fixed costs in the form of obligatory overhead expenses, and the mandatory costs of being in business are identified, as are variable costs, which are the costs incurred with the production or sale of each unit of a product. Variable costs include sales commissions, transportation costs incurred by the marketer, raw materials and labor invested in the product, and any other cost that can be linked directly to the average sale.

The total contribution from a particular segment is equal to revenue generated in that segment minus the variable cost associated with the sales made in that segment. Given estimates of these costs as well as the anticipated revenues from units sold at the expected price, it is possible to identify the contribution margin dollars associated with any one sale. This knowledge leads to estimates of break-even points and levels of profit (or loss) given certain anticipated unit sales targets (see Figure 7.4, part C). To go a step further, fixed costs are divided into direct and indirect, as will be discussed in Chapter 14. In this case, assignable fixed costs would be subtracted for each segment before determining segment contribution margin.

The following example will illustrate the use of contribution analysis in resource allocation to target market decisions. A desk manufacturer has identified three possible target markets. One is schools, where low bidders are awarded the contract. Another is small businesses, where moderate prices and quality are appropriate, and the third is banks, where presidents desire high quality and prestige brand names. The estimated prices, costs, and other specifics for contribution analysis are illustrated in Table 7.1.

The figures in Table 7.1 point out the desirability of targeting small businesses and the danger of seeking to market to schools. Even though the total units expected to be sold to schools (1,000) exceeds those anticipated to be sold to small businesses (750), the desk manufacturer would just meet fixed cost obligations and derive no profit, selling to schools. At the same time, the luxury desks for bankers, which have a greater contribution per unit sold, would derive less total contribution due to lower total unit sales, but this target market is still more attractive than is the school desk segment.

Table 7.1 Segment Contribution Analysis for a Desk Manufacturer

Market Segment	Schools	Small Businesses	Bankers
Price per desk	$ 1,000	$ 1,500	$ 2,000
Variable Costs per Unit			
Raw materials	500	700	1,000
Labor	300	400	500
Sales Commission	100	150	200
Total Variable Cost	900	1,250	1,700
Contribution Margin per Desk	100	250	300
Projected Unit Sales	× 1,000	× 750	× 500
Total Contribution	100,000	187,500	150,000
Fixed Costs	100,000	100,000	100,000
Expected Profit	$ —0—	$ 87,500	$ 50,000

In sum, the quantitative approach to determining the amount of marketing effort (i.e., budget) to allocate to target segments should be based on profitability assessments. The basic profitability formula which the marketer uses must consider the size of the market segment, the share or portion of the market anticipated to be claimed by the marketer, growth trends of the market segment, and any efficiencies which the marketer believes he or she can effect, given the anticipated size of the market, the velocity of growth, and company share. All of these can be translated into an estimate of the contribution margin per unit sold.

Other criteria often used in the selection of market segments are the qualitative or strategic benefits associated with successful catering to a segment. One qualitative dimension, which might compel a company to move into a certain market segment, would be the image benefits which are derived by the corporation as a whole. For example, General Motors operates a coach division which manufactures buses sold to public and private schools. In comparison with other market segments served by General Motors, the size of this market segment can be described as miniscule. In addition, there are substantial dangers of product safety criticisms from the public. Nonetheless, General Motors has decided to maintain its presence in this market, to maintain the qualitative image benefits gained by marketing in the relevant segments.

Another qualitative reason for selecting a target market is to insulate the company from competition. Very small marketers often select market segments that have been ignored or otherwise overlooked by larger competitors; they do so to minimize their presence in the eyes of their larger competitors and to survive in quieter competitive circumstances.

Finally, there is the qualitative consideration of control. All companies seek to gain control over their operations. Lack of control is apparent in the forms of volatility in demand, instability in market share, or loss of important components in their operations such as raw material sources, personnel, or distributors. Thus, while a market segment may not be the most attractive in terms of profitability and other quantitative measures, it may provide a means of gaining more certainty of control over sales and operations, and therefore be an attractive business arena.

Applying the Criteria: The Cost-Benefit Perspective

In applying these criteria to evaluate a particular segment, the marketer is basically attempting to identify what will be gained from focusing on the segment, and at what cost. Given this premise, it often is a good idea to perform a formal cost-benefit analysis on each segment, with the intention of determining the specific costs and benefits associated with tailoring the firm's marketing programs to the requirements of a particular segment. Keep in mind that a good segment is one that provides a distinct response to the firm's marketing stimuli.

Table 7.2 provides a demonstration of how the possible costs and benefits associated with a potential segment can be examined. A number of evaluative criteria, including image, accessibility, measurability, fit with resources, competitive advantage, and longevity, have been considered in identifying these costs and benefits. For example, if the segment is not easily accessible, or if competition is well-en-

Table 7.2 Analysis of a Market Segment Cost Benefit

Sample Benefits	Sample Costs
estimated revenues	product modification costs
enhanced image	transportation
volume purchases	marketing research
referrals—pass-along sales	selling effort required
access to customer's technology	discounts provided
	distribution channel costs
	promotion expenditures
	inventory costs
	small order lot size costs
	opportunity costs (e.g., tied-up production capacity)
Total Benefits	Total Costs

trenched, expenditures for selling, distribution, and promotion are likely to be exorbitant.

Not only should benefits exceed costs, but also the company should prioritize segments based on the size of their net benefits. To quantify all of the costs and benefits, the marketer may have to make some subjective estimates. As a case in point, the value to a company of receiving access to a given technology, or of benefiting from a segment's image, has to be subjectively evaluated. Where actual dollar figures cannot be determined, an alternative approach might be to develop a rating form including High (a value of 3), Medium (2), and Low (1) on each benefit or cost. Totals could then be determined, resulting in an overall score for the segment.

METHODS AND BASES FOR SEGMENTING INDUSTRIAL MARKETS

Investigators and experts on the topic of industrial market segmentation have made distinctions between different levels of segmentation bases available to the industrial marketer. A base is a characteristic of a firm that can be used to categorize it; bases are useful only to the extent that firms can be categorized along them. One classic article on the topic of market segmentation (Wind and Cardozo 1974) separates these bases into macro and micro levels. A more recent work by Bonoma and Shapiro (1984) introduces some intermediate bases between the macro and the micro levels. They call this a nested approach (see also Plank 1985).

The Macro and Micro Approach

One method for segmenting an industrial market is to first identify subgroups which share common macro characteristics, and to select target segments from among these subgroups. Rather than stopping at this point, though, the marketer then breaks down these so-called macro segments into subgroups which share common micro characteristics. In this manner, the marketer goes through a two-step process of breaking markets down.

Macro segmentation involves dividing the market into subgroups based on overall characteristics of customer organizations. Examples include their size, usage rate of the product or service being sold, the application made of the product or service, the SIC category in which they belong, company structure, geographic location, the end market they serve, and whether the marketer's product represents a new or repeat purchase to them.

Macro bases share the distinctive feature of being relatively easy to use, because data are readily available for identifying the organizations which belong to a particular macro segment. Such information can usually be obtained from secondary data sources.

Micro bases for segmentation pertain to characteristics of the decision-making process and the buying structure within customer organizations. This includes such factors as the position of the buying center in authority and communication networks, the amount of influence held by key departments, demographics and personality characteristics of key members of the buying center, the perceived importance of the purchase, the relative importance of specific attributes in the organization's buying decisions, attitudes toward vendors, and decision rules used in selecting vendors.

Micro bases can have many more direct marketing implications than do macro bases. The fact that a customer resides in a particular geographic region, or belongs to a certain four-digit SIC category, can provide some general guidance in developing the marketing mix. However, much greater insight can be obtained by knowing how buying decisions are made, or how much influence design engineers wield in comparison to production managers. These micro bases are more directly related to the purchasing decision.

At the same time, characteristics of micro segments can be more difficult to identify, because information on these characteristics usually is not readily available. This means that primary data may have to be collected, or, at the very least, extensive knowledge of the internal operations of prospective customers must be developed. Some of this knowledge can be obtained from sales representatives or others who call on the firm.

In a study of the data terminals market, Moriarty and Reibstein (1982) provide an example of the value of micro segmentation. Their focus was on the relative importance of specific attributes in the organization's buying decisions. As Figure 7.5 illustrates, the research identified fourteen different product attributes or benefits sought by buyers of these data terminals. Further analysis resulted in the discovery of four market segments. One, the hardware buyers, was concerned with delivery speed and comparative price, but unconcerned with sales competence of vendors. Another, the brand buyers segment, relied on the manufacturer's image much more than the other segments. The people buyers centered their concerns around the interpersonal aspects of the sale and of terminal operation, with more desire for competent vendor sales personnel plus ease of equipment operation. Finally, the one-stop shoppers tended to seek a complete package from a single vendor and consequently identified the breadth of the vendor's product line and

BENEFITS SOUGHT BY POTENTIAL BUYERS	HARDWARE BUYERS	BRAND BUYERS	PEOPLE BUYERS	ONE-STOP SHOPPERS
Speed of Operation	0	0	0	0
Operator Ease of Operation	0	0	+ + +	0
Aesthetic Aspects	0	0	0	0
Compatibility with Present System	0	0	0	0
Service	0	0	0	0
Delivery Speed	+ + +	0	0	0
Absolute Price	+ + +	0	0	0
Price Flexibility	+ + +	0	0	– – –
Software Support	0	0	0	+ + +
Broad Line of Equipment	0	0	0	+ + +
Manufacturer Image	0	+ + +	0	0
Manufacturer Stability	0	0	0	0
Competence of Sales Personnel	– – –	0	+ + +	0
Reliability of Operation	0	0	0	0

Key:

+ + + = Attributes significantly more important to this segment.

– – – = Attributes significantly less important to this segment.

0 = Insignificant attributes.

Figure 7.5 Micro Segmentation in the Data Terminals Market (Adapted from Moriarty and Reibstein, *Benefit Segmentation: An Industrial Application*, Report No. 82-110, (Cambridge, Mass.: Marketing Science Institute, 1982), 21.)

software support as primary benefits. Interestingly, this segment exhibited lower price sensitivity than the others.

Taking their findings one step further, we can see the marketing strategy implications of the distinctive benefit characteristics of each segment. To target the hardware buyers, a company would emphasize low price and rapid delivery and would place less emphasis on training of sales personnel as a means of reducing its costs which could be passed on in the form of lower prices. The brand buyer segment, on the other hand, would need to be approached with a complete corporate image-building strategy. Well-known and respected vendors such as IBM would be frontrunners in the minds of these prospects. A completely different strategy would be appropriate for the people buyers segment, however. For these prospective terminal purchasers, the marketer would stress the interpersonal relationship between sales personnel and decision makers in the target company. Also, product design implications are apparent in the desired benefit of ease of operation; consequently, the terminal should be engineered to be maximally friendly. Finally, the one-stop shoppers segment consists of decision makers who seek to purchase complete systems from single vendors and would respond to package proposals of hardware, software, installation, training, and other support even if they are priced somewhat high.

When macro segmentation is used with micro segmentation, the result can be improvement both in the effectiveness of marketing programs, and in the efficiency of resource usage. If the target market consists of companies in SIC 3613 (a macro base) whose key decision makers are very price-conscious (a micro base), then marketing programs can be customized accordingly. Care must be taken, however, that the costs of serving such a narrowly defined audience do not exceed the benefits.

The marketer may not always perceive that there are clear advantages to be gained from focusing on micro segments. He or she may stop after identifying macro segments, especially if this produces segments that are felt to be sufficiently well-defined in light of the company's marketing resources.

Intermediate Bases: The Nested Approach

Bonoma and Shapiro (1984) have expanded the use of macro and micro segmentation into what is called a *nested* approach. This method assumes a hierarchical structure of segmentation bases which move from very broad or general bases to very organization-specific bases. Rather than a two-step process, the nested approach allows three, four, or five steps. An illustration can be found in Figure 7.6. Here, macro bases are in the outermost squares (e.g., company size), with micro characteristics in the innermost squares (e.g., personal characteristics of members of the buying center).

The figure further suggests that a number of intermediate segmentation bases, such as situational factors or the general purchasing approach of the firm, lie between these two extremes. Intermediate bases refer to the set of segmentation possibilities that lie between broad overall organizational characteristics and very specific personal characteristics of the individuals involved in decision making. Situational factors could include the urgency of the purchase or the specific application of the purchased product. The purchasing approach might be the degree of formal structure in the customer's purchasing operations, general purchasing policies of the organization, or the decision criteria used to make a vendor or product choice. Moving from very macro through intermediate to very micro, each more specific segmentation base is contained within a broader base. That is, the more specific customer characteristics are nested inside the broader situational or orga-

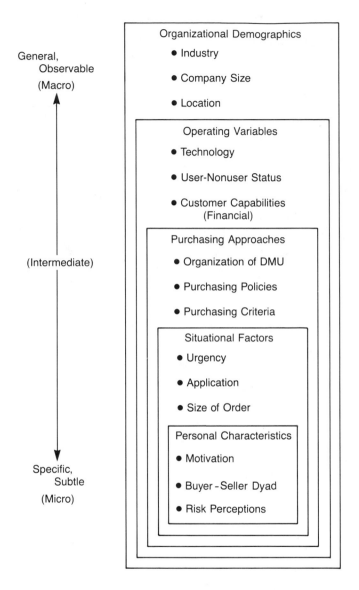

Figure 7.6 Major Potential Bases for Segmentation (Nesting)
(Source: Thomas V. Bonoma and Benson P. Shapiro, *Segmenting the
Industrial Market,* (Lexington, Mass.: Lexington Books, D. C. Heath and
Company, 1983), 10. Reprinted with permission.)

nizational bases. Consequently, the more specific customer characteristics are nested
inside the broader customer characteristics.

To implement this approach, let us look at an example. A firm selling mail
equipment (e.g., postage meters, weighing scales) to organizations may first segment
the market based on broad organizational characteristics, such as company size. It
may decide to focus only on companies with 1,000 or more employees. However,

rather than stop here and focus on all such companies, the firm then further segments the market based on operating characteristics, such as whether the company
has a mail department. Focusing only on those with a mail department, the firm
goes one step further, and pinpoints only those companies that emphasize low price
as a key attribute in the purchase decision, and so on. The marketer can move
through all five nests if he or she wants that much specialization, or can stop at any
point.

A Dynamic Cost-Benefit/Nested Approach to Industrial Market Segmentation

Now that the general concept of market segmentation has been established, and the
various segmentation approaches and bases used by industrial marketers described,
it is appropriate to present a recommendation regarding how to best pursue industrial market segmentation. This recommendation embodies the general objective of
seeking to break down, efficiently and effectively, the total market into target markets. Here, efficiency pertains to the extent to which we derive benefit greater than
the cost invested, and effectiveness pertains to achieving a superior competitive position and a satisfactory level of profitability. The recommended approach combines
nested segmentation with cost-benefit analysis.

Figure 7.7 illustrates the recommended approach. The segmentation strategy
is developed around three questions, each of which involves cost-benefit analysis.
First, the industrial marketer must pose the question of whether segment identification is worthwhile. That is, does market segmentation make sense—does the value
of the benefits of trying to identify market segments exceed the cost? The answer
requires a return to the four basic questions posed earlier in the chapter. That is,
are segments measurable, accessible, sufficiently homogeneous, and fitting to the
basic marketing approach of the firm. If the evaluation of these criteria turns out to
be negative, market segmentation at this level is not useful.

However, if the assessment of all four criteria is positive, the next question
concerns which types of segments to pursue. Again, a set of criteria is evaluated
from a cost-benefit perspective. These criteria, you will recall, are fitted to the company image, responsiveness, substantiality, competitive advantage, and profitability.
You will recall also that the cost-benefit analysis at this stage includes judgmental
considerations, (e.g., enhancement of the company's image), as well as financial considerations (e.g., contribution margin). The analysis progresses systematically from
the evaluation of macro segmentation bases through intermediate bases to the evaluation of micro segmentation bases.

The third question involves ways in which marketing resources should be allocated across the market segments that have been selected. The various segments
will require differing amounts and types of resources. The marketer determines the
investment to be made in each segment, again on a cost-benefit basis.

Figure 7.8 illustrates how a company marketing a point-of-purchase electronic
scanning system might apply the cost-benefit/nested technique. These systems use
infrared sensors to detect the product codes imprinted on merchandise and ring
them up automatically at the check-out counter. Simultaneously, the system main-

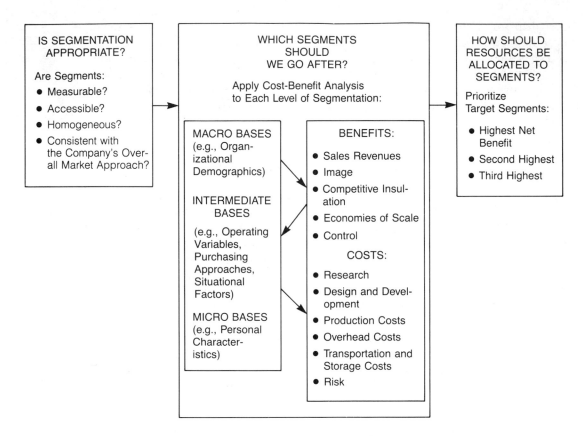

Figure 7.7   A Dynamic Cost-Benefit/Nested Approach to Industrial
Market Segmentation

tains accounting records of inventory sold, prices charged, taxes, and other details
of transactions. In this example, we will assume that the company involved is new
to the industry, it is just entering this market, and it is quite small—but it has a
dependable product.

Macro segmentation could begin with general designations such as those indicated in Figure 7.8. Actually, preliminary segmentation has already taken place,
since the company has developed a retailer software package; consequently, lack of
compatibility automatically excluded wholesalers, manufacturers, and other such
companies. Three types of retail companies are noted as candidates: independents,
catalog sales companies and discount chains. These segments have been selected for
their high volumes of business, which are consistent with needs for automatic scanning rather than manual cash register operations. Review of secondary information
reveals that there is a multitude of independent retailers, and targeting them would
take more resources than the software company has available. On the other hand,
too few catalog companies exist to warrant the cost of targeting them. The selection,
then, is to target discount retail chains.

MACRO SEGMENTATION BASES	COST-BENEFIT ANALYSIS
Type of Retailer:	
Catalog Sales	Too Few Catalog Sales Retailers
Discount Chain	Too Many Independents
Independents	Select: Discounters
Size of Company:	
Very Small	Very Small, Too Costly
Medium	Large, Too Competitive
Large	Select: Medium

INTERMEDIATE SEGMENTATION BASES

Current System:	
Manual	Manual Inconsistent
Automated	Automated, Already has system
Mixed	Select: Mixed
Capabilities:	
Programming Expertise	System is Turnkey
No Ability	Select: No Ability

MICRO SEGMENTATION BASES

System Benefits:	
Inventory Control	Limited Capacity for Inventory Control
Accounting Primarily	Select: Accounting Primarily
Decision Criteria:	
Compatibility	Company is Start-Up; Unknown
Vendor Reputation	Select Compatibility

Figure 7.8 Application of the Dynamic Cost-Benefit/Nested Segmentation Approach to a Point-of-Purchase Software Package Vendor

Next, the size of retail chain is considered. Again, secondary information might reveal three categories: very small single-city chains; medium-size regional chains; and large national chains. Cost-benefit analysis is used to resolve this stage. Because of the need to demonstrate the system, plus the installation requirements if purchased, the small chains are eliminated due to excessive cost. At the other extreme, the competitive environment for the large chains is recognized as intense, requiring extensive sales and promotion expenditures, so this segment is eliminated. The decision is to target regional discount retail chains, where the sales and competitive environment benefits exceed costs.

Intermediate segmentation bases (e.g., point-of-purchase systems already in place) might be considered next. Some prospect retailers may have resisted switching to computer-driven systems and still have manual check-outs. Others might have modern scanning systems. In the latter case, penetration will be difficult since competitors have already won the accounts; in the former case, significant resistance to new technology seems evident and marketing efforts to change old ways might be unsuccessful. The target group, then, becomes those who have mixed systems—discounters who have computerized their personnel or inventory control systems, but still have many operations that have not been converted.

Further intermediate segmentation can be accomplished by determining the internal software programming capacities of these discount retailers with mixed manual and automated systems. Past experience may have revealed that the more responsive prospects are those who wish a turnkey system, where the vendor installs the system and guarantees its satisfactory operation without requiring a programmer in the retailer's organization to serve a support function. In other words, the greater likelihood of a positive response from this group makes it a more appealing target from a cost-benefit standpoint.

Then, micro segmentation can come into play with investigation of more specific benefits sought and decision criteria used by this segment's members. For example, one subgroup may desire essentially an accounting records system because it already has a satisfactory inventory control system that is quite compatible with the marketer's current system. Another subgroup may desire a point-of-purchase system that can provide an on-line linkage to bank networks, so that checks and credit cards can be approved immediately. Attempting to provide the networking capability benefit might require extensive redesign and debugging, but the cost of that effort may not exceed the projected revenues from this segment. Finally, marketing research or informal discussions with prospects could uncover two more decision criteria: the consideration of a point-of-purchase system which fits or does not fit into the computer system already in place, and sensitivity to the vendor's reputation. Here, because the marketing company is new and relatively unknown, it should select retailers who are less concerned about company reputation. Also, if the software (IBM or otherwise) is compatible with the computer hardware already in the retailer's possession, it would be more efficient to target this segment.

SUMMARY

This chapter has introduced the concept of market segmentation as an approach to industrial markets. While segmentation is not appropriate in some cases, it is often a means to achieve efficiencies and specialization in the firm's marketing efforts. To use this strategic tool effectively, the marketer should follow a systematic process in which segments are carefully identified, evaluated, selected, targeted with marketing programs, and monitored.

When using segmentation, the marketer must evaluate three key decision areas: 1) as a general practice, is segmentation realistic for our firm?; 2) which bases of segmentation are most appropriate, given our resources?; and 3) how should the firm's marketing resources be allocated to specific segments? A set of evaluative criteria were presented for use in addressing each of these decision areas, the most basic of which is cost-benefit analysis.

Although a number of approaches for segmenting industrial markets exist, two closely related techniques were emphasized, macro/micro segmentation and nested segmentation. The chapter argued for the use of a nested approach in which cost-benefit analysis is integrated at each step in the segmentation process.

Overall, segmentation is an under-utilized practice in industrial firms. In a critical review of industrial market segmentation, Plank (1985) has made clear that research on, and the practice of, segmentation have much room for improvement. He notes that the practice of segmentation is applied unevenly and, in some cases, has been completely ignored by members of the industrial market. All too often, companies enter the market with no specific target group in mind. Then, much later, when they have determined who appears to be purchasing their product or service, they argue that this was how they segmented the market. In this sense, segmentation becomes a post hoc justification for an unplanned result.

In sum, practitioners of industrial market segmentation should observe a number of cautions as they adopt this valuable tool:

1. Market segmentation should balance the firm's total information needs with budgets and other constraints.

2. Segmentation should be considered an ongoing process and, to the extent possible, be built into a company's marketing intelligence system.

3. Industrial marketers must first decide on the appropriateness of market segmentation before attempting to implement it.

4. Micro segmentation bases should be geared towards customer needs and requirements.

5. Strategic implications of the application of market segmentation must, at a minimum, look at the economic aspects and, hopefully, embody a cost-benefit frame of reference.

QUESTIONS

1. The president of Pilgrim Manufacturing Company, a maker of refrigeration units such as those commonly found in supermarkets, firmly believes his market consists of all potential buyers of the company's product line. You are the new marketing manager at Pilgrim. Present an argument for introducing market segmentation and targeting, where Pilgrim focuses on particular market segments.

2. Segmentation is not possible without differentiation, but differentiation is possible without segmentation. Do you agree or disagree? Explain.

3. If the product being sold is virtually a commodity, such as motor oil, muriatic acid, copper wire, or computer paper, segmentation of the market really makes little sense. Agree or disagree?

4. Identify two products for which segmenting the market would be a mistake, and explain why segmentation has little to offer in those cases.

5. Gorman Machine Tool concentrates its sales and marketing efforts on large companies (over five hundred employees) with the logic that these firms represent much greater sales potential. Why might size be a poor basis for market segmentation?

6. Corwin Commercial Paints finds that its sales are growing slowly, but profits are declining. How might this problem be caused by an ineffective market segmentation program?

7. Segmentation is not only a decision regarding who to go after, but also, a decision on who not to go after. Explain. Do you agree or disagree?

8. You sell temperature control devices for use in appliances, such as refrigerators, air conditioners, and clothes dryers. Identify a market segment, and some of the potential costs and benefits that would be involved if you targeted that particular segment.

9. Evaluate the homogeneity, accessibility, sizability, responsiveness, and sustainability of banks as a market segment for a company that sells marketing research and advertising services.

10. Your firm sells to three segments, and wants to perform a contribution analysis on each segment. Assume the segments represent different SIC codes. What specific data would you need, and how would you go about performing this analysis?

11. When using the nested approach to segmenting a market, why would you not want to stop at organizational demographics? That is, why might you first select key demographic bases, such as geographic location, to focus on, but then segment further, by focusing only on companies within a geographic region that use a particular purchasing approach? Alternatively, why might you skip over organizational demographics and go directly to operating variables or situational factors?

PART III INDUSTRIAL MARKETING MANAGEMENT FUNCTIONS

Marketing management is a creative undertaking. The marketer seeks to develop strategies and tactics that provide the company with a competitive advantage in the marketplace. Initiative, judgment, and alertness are the key ingredients, but these elements must be exercised within a logical managerial framework.

Part III examines the design and implementation of marketing programs, using the marketing mix as a unifying framework. Separate chapters are devoted to product, price, promotion, and distribution. In addition, each of the chapters includes a process framework which can be used in managing one of the elements of the mix. The goal is not to place limits on the marketer's creativity, but rather to provide positive direction and ensure that all the key decision variables are being considered.

Part III builds on the analytical concepts and approaches presented in Part II. The strategies and tactics used by the industrial marketer should reflect an in-depth understanding of the forces operating within the industrial marketplace, many of which the marketer cannot control. As the development of specific marketing programs is discussed, the reader is encouraged to relate concepts from the discussions of buyer behavior, demand analysis, marketing research, competitor analysis, and market segmentation to the program decisions.

Chapter 8 introduces the concept of strategy and strategic thinking. A strategic planning process is presented, together with a number of tools that can be useful in planning. The central strategic role of the industrial product or service is emphasized.

Chapter 9 is devoted to the process of developing new products and services. The theme of this chapter is that innovation is vital to the success of industrial firms today, and marketing must play a key part in corporate innovation.

Pricing is the focus of Chapter 10. Here, we emphasize that price must be a reflection of customer value, not costs. Issues and approaches which are relevant when establishing industrial prices are discussed in four key areas: pricing objectives, cost evaluation, demand analysis, and competitor assessment. Attention is also devoted to competitive bidding, transfer pricing, and the determination of price discount structures.

Chapters 11 and 12 are concerned with the promotional mix decisions confronting the industrial marketer. Chapter 11 examines advertising and sales promotion, and Chapter 12 focuses on sales management. Although separated into two chapters, decisions in these areas must be closely coordinated to effectively meet the overall communications needs of the firm.

Part III concludes with an investigation of industrial distribution strategy. Chapter 13 looks first at channels of distribution, and then at the area of logistics. Because of the tendency to overlook distribution as a strategic marketing variable, the chapter stresses the importance of managing distribution decisions from a customer satisfaction perspective.

CHAPTER **8**

STRATEGIC MANAGEMENT OF INDUSTRIAL PRODUCTS AND SERVICES

Key Concepts

Business screen
Core, tangible, augmented product
Depth and breadth
Differentiation
Economies of scale
Experience curve
Focus strategy
Perceptual map
Primary demand strategy
Product deletion
Product items, lines and mixes

Product life cycle
Product portfolio
Product positioning
Selective Demand Strategy
Strategic business units (SBU)
Strategic marketing
Strategic orientation
Strategic planning process
Strategy
Tactic
Technology life cycle
Types of strategies

Learning Objectives

1. Explain the nature and importance of marketing strategies versus tactics, and provide examples of types of strategies.
2. Establish the meaning and importance of a strategic orientation, and differentiate strategic marketing from marketing management.
3. Describe a systematic planning process for identifying opportunities and developing marketing strategies.
4. Identify a number of conceptual tools for planning marketing strategies and tactics.
5. Discuss the central role of product-related considerations in marketing strategies.

The nature of business is to make your own product obsolete. If we don't do it ourselves, we know our competitors will do it for us.

AKIO MORITA

THE CONCEPT OF STRATEGY

A common theme throughout this book is that corporate environments are rapidly changing, and that the successful firm is the one that can most effectively anticipate and manage its environment. To do so, the firm has to be able to discern and interpret opportunities in the environment, and then capitalize on these opportunities in a timely fashion. This capability is the essence of strategic management.

Strategy has been defined in a variety of ways, all of which derive from its traditional use in a military context. Basically, a strategy is a statement regarding what the company wants to be, and how it plans to get there. Others see strategy as a way of thinking that strives to ensure the long-term prosperity of the firm. A more practical view is that strategy consists of a timed sequence of moves, which allows for contingencies. All of these perspectives are correct. Strategies are based on clearly defined objectives; they take a comprehensive approach to the organization's problems; they adopt a longer-term time horizon; and they are flexible. For the purposes of this discussion, however, strategy will be defined broadly as "the specification of an organization's objectives, and policies and plans for achieving those objectives, including allocation of resources and organization structure" (Jain 1981). It is an attempt to match the strategic advantages of the firm to its environment.

Companies can develop strategies at a number of different levels, ranging from overall corporate strategies, to strategies for individual products and markets. These may be formally planned, simply evolve over time with changing circumstances, or occur haphazardly. In any case, a strategy generally exists, whether recognized by management or not. In fact, many managers are hard put to actually describe the corporate strategy currently in use.

Our concern is with marketing strategies, which must be logically consistent with overall corporate strategies. That is, marketing strategies must fit with corporate efforts in such areas as finance, personnel, technology, and production. From a strategic standpoint, marketing focuses on questions regarding where, how, and when to compete. Marketing strategy is a specification of the organization's target markets, with a related marketing mix to satisfy each distinct market. The marketer seeks to develop a unique competitive advantage in each market served as he or she develops a marketing strategy.

A good marketing strategy has certain characteristics. First, it serves to coordinate the marketing activities of the firm. In other words, there is a sense of some overall theme that sets the tone of the strategy. This theme might be high quality, low price, or custom-tailored service. Regardless of which theme is selected, the coordination requirement means that some marketing activities will be subordinated to others to achieve synergy. Consider, for instance, an armored car service which picks up receipts and cash and delivers them to a central bank. The cars are bulky, unattractive, slow, and energy-inefficient, but they provide protection and deter wrongdoers.

Second, a marketing strategy should respond to current and anticipated future market conditions. This point alludes to the responsibility that the marketing function has to sense opportunities or threats in the environment and to plan accordingly. Marketing is the only business function that interfaces with all facets of the environment, and formal monitoring systems are often established to track technological, economic, political, or even social changes which might affect the company's operations. For instance, some companies chose to withdraw from South African markets because of the racial policies of the South African government, not because of any lack of demand for their goods or services. However, this case is unusual, and a more typical example would be the adoption by many companies of computer-controlled production and physical distribution systems that have spawned new products and even new companies.

Third, a marketing strategy must solve customers' problems. Here, the importance of buyer behavior analysis becomes evident. All marketing decisions must include an understanding of, and/or assumptions regarding, the needs of prospective customers. Consequently, industrial marketing firms take pains to study the buying decision criteria, individuals involved, and specific requirements of representative members of their target markets.

Fourth, the strategy should serve to better the competition. Marketing strategy is invariably pitted against the marketing strategy of competitors, and current, as well as prospective, customers are usually well aware of the alternative sources of supply. In some instances, such as price bidding, the choice of one vendor over another is based on a single criterion, and the most efficient bidder is rewarded with the contract. However, in many other cases, a number of considerations is involved, and the competitors are compared on quality, delivery, reputation, service, and other marketing characteristics as well as price. Consequently, a marketing strategy must begin with the target customer's needs and then assess how well the competitors' marketing efforts suit these needs. If there are areas where a company can achieve a unique competitive advantage in the eyes of prospective customers, this advantage increases the number of reasons for customers to select that company over its rivals.

Finally, there is the need for strategy to contribute to the company's financial success. Here, the overall financial picture of the company across a relevant planning horizon is emphasized. Rather than including profit maximization in the definition of strategy, the focus is on contribution to a number of financial objectives. Companies frequently have minimum required rates of return on investment (or hurdle rates) which are expected from different products and services in the product lines. At the same time, management will establish certain cash flow stipulations. To be of use, the marketing strategy must reflect individual product goals as well as the company's overall financial objectives.

STRATEGIES VERSUS TACTICS

Companies frequently fail to adopt a strategic perspective at either the corporate or marketing level. Rather, they rely entirely on a tactical approach, and often do not see the difference between a strategy and a tactic. Tactics are short-term, action-oriented moves that seek to achieve a fairly narrow, immediate goal. They are sometimes called action plans. Generally, a series of tactics coordinated over time is required to constitute a strategy, and so, to accomplish overall objectives.

To use a football analogy, a strategy is an overall scheme for winning the game. A tactic is a specific approach to getting a first down, when the team is facing a third down with twenty yards to go. The team not only has to achieve a number of first downs, they must also outscore the opposition before game time runs out. In football, as in business, there are always going to be future games to play, and new sets of strategies and tactics to develop.

A sharper distinction between strategies and tactics can be drawn by considering an example. A company that sells process control instruments is deciding how best to market one of its products. Under consideration is an expenditure of $12,000 for advertising in a trade journal, or a 5 percent price reduction. Note that both of these are tactics. Assuming there is no strategy currently in place, management has little guidance as to which tactic to pursue, except past experience. Perhaps neither tactic is appropriate. Further, the effectiveness of either of these tactics may be limited, if it is not part of an overall plan. Conflicts and/or duplication of effort may exist between these tactics and other actions of the firm. Also, once in place, these tactics limit the options available to the marketer in future months. Such obstacles are overcome when the tactics are part of a coherent strategy.

The real question to be addressed by the manager who is considering these tactics should be, What exactly is the firm trying to accomplish? Four different possibilities come to mind, although others do exist (see Guiltinan and Paul 1985):

a. attract new users to the marketplace;

b. increase usage rates among current customers;

c. take customers away from competitors;

d. prevent competitors from taking our customers.

The first two could be referred to as primary demand strategies, since both focus on untapped market potential. The other two are called selective demand strategies, because they focus on redistributing existing market share. These two strategies shall be revisited in the next section.

The important conclusion here, however, is that the price cut and the advertising expenditure might be pursued as part of any number of strategies. That is, the firm could be using them to accomplish any one of the four goal possibilities. The reasons for choosing a particular tactic can vary widely, then, depending upon the strategy in question. If managers fail to step back from the situation long enough to develop and update strategies, they are destined to jump from tactic to tactic with little sense of whether the organization's best interests are being served.

TYPES OF MARKETING STRATEGIES

A single marketing strategy is usually not developed for the entire company, especially in a fairly large organization. Similarly, separate strategies are not developed for each and every product—but, it makes sense to design strategies around strategic business units (SBUs). An SBU consists of a product or product line which is fairly unrelated to other lines or products in terms of customers, competitors, prices, cross-elasticities, or other market-related characteristics. Products with shared technologies, production processes, or costs could also constitute an SBU, because such commonalities can have implications for marketing strategy. A single SBU could be a particular division or product line, but could also cross over divisions or lines. A company, or one of its divisions, can have any number of SBUs. Correspondingly, the company needs to develop strategies for each one.

There is, however, no one right strategy for a particular SBU. From the long list of possible strategies, any number of quite different approaches could be effective at a particular point in time. The challenge is to find a strategy which profitably matches company strengths to environmental conditions. The major limitations are the marketer's creativity and resources. Exhibit 8.1 provides a set of characteristics which are useful in evaluating the merits of any one strategy.

There are some major categories of strategies which are helpful to the marketer in trying to sort out the many possibilities. Let us examine three ways in which marketing strategies can be classified.

A very general approach is to distinguish between an emphasis on new versus existing products, and new versus existing markets. This distinction produces four categories of strategies, as illustrated in the top portion of Figure 8.1. Where the firm goes after existing or current markets with existing products, a *market penetration* strategy is being used. Basically, the firm is trying to continue doing what it has been doing, only better. *Market development* is taking current product programs into new markets, and centers around market selection and targeting. When new product programs (such as new versions of a product, line extensions, or flanker products) are introduced into existing markets, the strategy is termed *product development*. Finally, a company going after new markets with new product programs is *diversifying*.

Another way to classify strategies is based on the distinction (mentioned earlier) between primary and selective demand. These types of demand are illustrated in the diagram in the middle of Figure 8.1. When the strategy seeks to close the gap between estimated market potential and current industry sales (called a primary gap), this is a primary demand strategy. Primary demand has two components: the number of users, and the usage rate per customer. These components can be increased by focusing on either the willingness or the ability of customers to buy, as circumstances dictate. Selective demand involves the gap between current industry sales and current company sales. Strategies aimed at closing this gap, or at least keeping the gap constant, are selective demand strategies. These strategies can be offensive (taking market share from competitors), or defensive (maintaining current customers).

Exhibit 8.1   Characteristics of Good Strategies

Although it is not possible to know whether a particular strategy is the best one available, or even if it will be successful, a good strategy should have certain characteristics. Once a strategy is on the drawing boards, the marketer can look systematically for flaws or areas for improvement, using the following six criteria provided by George S. Day:

Suitability. Is the proposed strategy consistent with the foreseeable environmental threats and opportunities? Does the strategy exploit or enhance a current competitive advantage, or create a new source of advantage?

Validity. Are the key assumptions about environmental trends and the outcomes of the strategy realistic? Are the assumptions based on reliable and valid information?

Consistency. Are the basic elements of the strategy consistent with each other and with the objectives being pursued?

Feasibility. Is the strategy appropriate to the available resources? Are the basic elements and premises of the strategy understandable and acceptable to the operating managers who will have the responsibility for implementation?

Vulnerability. To what extent are projected outcomes dependent on data or assumptions of dubious quality and origin? Are the risks of failure acceptable? Are there adequate contingency plans for coping with these risks? Can the decision be reversed in the future? How long will it take? What are the consequences?

Potential rewards. Are the projected outcomes satisfactory in light of the provisional objectives for the business? Are the adjustments to the objectives acceptable to the stakeholders?

Source: G.S. Day, *Strategic Market Planning: The Pursuit of Competitive Advantage,* (St. Paul, Minn.: West Publishing Co., 1984), 152. Reprinted with permission.

A third set of strategies is based on the work of Michael Porter (1980). He claims that virtually all strategies fall within one of three generic categories: overall cost leadership, differentiation, and focus (see Figure 8.1, bottom). Cost leadership is an attempt by the company to have the lowest cost position in the industry. By doing so, the company also hopes to be the price leader, setting the trend for other firms to follow. *Cost leadership* is often achieved by taking advantage of economies of scale and the experience curve, strategic concepts to be discussed later in this chapter. Cost reductions come from high volume production, and so the firm pursues strategic actions to maximize market size and share.

Differentiation also finds the company going after the entire marketplace, but now the goal is to be perceived as somehow different, or unique, compared to firms producing the same product(s). Companies differentiate themselves based on quality, service, features, distribution, warranties, and any number of other factors. The key to this strategy is that customers must perceive significant differences among

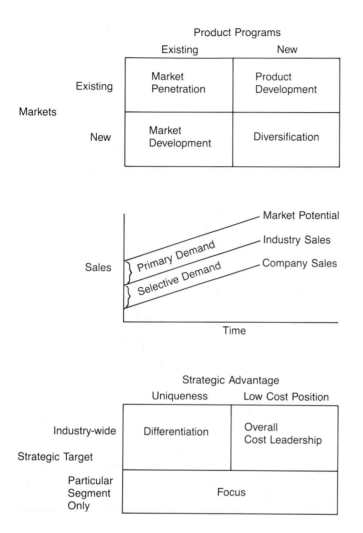

Figure 8.1 Three Approaches to Classifying Strategies

competitors on a particular factor, and the factor must be meaningful to customers. Note that differentiation requires an investment of resources, and so may come at the expense of the firm's cost position.

Unlike cost leadership and differentiation, a *focus* strategy does not seek to capture as much of the entire market as possible. Instead, this is a segmentation and targeting strategy, where the firm specializes in meeting the needs of a particular niche of customers. Through specialization, the company is able to tailor products or services to the exact requirements of a group of customers, and can completely penetrate that segment. A focus strategy may be achieved either through differentiation or the low cost position, but only within the segment(s) in question.

These three general classification schemes are not independent. For example, a firm could pursue market penetration, primary demand, and differentiation at the same time. The marketer may find it helpful to consider all three when beginning to shape ultimate strategy.

STRATEGIC MARKETING MANAGEMENT

More important than the development of individual strategies is the need for industrial marketers to adopt a strategic orientation in approaching the marketing challenges confronting the firm (Day 1984). A strategic orientation emphasizes the continuous search for competitive advantage. Management's attention is focused on identifying and understanding changes in key success factors, the requirements of market segments, and the nature of competitor strategies. There is also a recognition that the company's marketing interests can best be served by working closely with personnel in the operations and finance departments. For example, by working with operations, the marketer can influence the inventory and servicing policies of the firm. By working with finance, the likelihood is greater that the marketer can get funding for strategies, as opposed to individual tactics.

Those who adopt a strategic orientation understand that goals for all products and markets are not the same. Rather than attempt to maximize profit from each product or service area in which the firm is involved, the strategic view is that different products serve varying roles. Some products are in dynamic growth markets requiring greater investment, and warranting higher sales and profit expectations. Others are new and need time to get established. Still others have been around some time, producing very stable returns, but with slow growth. And there are products generating meager financial results, but which serve an important role in filling out the product line, or in helping to support sales of other products in the line.

Strategic marketing, because of its concern with the longer-term considerations, with the bigger picture, and with interfunctional cooperation, is quite different from traditional marketing management. Marketing management centers around day-to-day decisions regarding the elements of the marketing mix, and is a reactive approach to problems as they arise. Table 8.1 provides a more complete summary of these two kinds of marketing. At issue, however, is not whether one is better than the other. Rather, marketing management activities must be accomplished within the strategic marketing framework. Once the core strategy is in place, marketing management becomes appropriate.

THE STRATEGIC PLANNING PROCESS

An ability to plan effectively is a vital ingredient for adopting a strategic marketing orientation. Regardless of a company's size, or whether selling a product or service, there is a prevailing emphasis on planning as an ongoing activity. Short-term (quarterly, annual) and longer-term market plans are increasingly seen as a necessity. Strategic planning can be defined as a "line management activity centered on getting

Table 8.1 Salient Differences between Strategic Marketing and Marketing Management

Point of Difference	Strategic Marketing	Marketing Management
Time Frame	Long range, i.e., decisions have long-term implications	Day-to-day, i.e., decisions have relevance in a given financial year
Orientation	Deductive	Inductive
Decision Process	Primarily bottom-up	Mainly top-down
Relationship with Environment	Environment considered ever-changing and dynamic	Environment considered constant with occasional disturbances
Opportunity Sensitivity	Ongoing to seek new opportunities	Ad hoc search for a new opportunity
Organizational Behavior	Achieve synergy between different components of the organization, both horizontally and vertically	Pursue interests of the decentralized unit
Nature of Job	Requires high degree of creativity and originality	Requires maturity, experience, and control orientation
Leadership Style	Requires proactive perspective	Requires reactive perspective
Mission	Deals with what business to emphasize	Concerns running a delineated business

Source: Reprinted by permission of the publisher from "The Evolution of Strategic Marketing," by S.C. Jain, *Journal of Business Research*, 11, 419. Copyright 1983 by Elsevier Science Publishing Co., Inc.

the right people, agenda, and information together on a timely schedule in order to make decisions that commit cash and people to market positioning assignments extending beyond the current operating cycle" (Brandt 1986, 15).

Marketing strategies follow from a logical, step-by-step planning process. This process is illustrated in Figure 8.2, although there are alternative versions. The beginning point is a company mission statement, which seeks to answer the question, What business are we in? This mission statement is a long-run vision of what the organization intends to be. The statement should be reflective of the organization's past accomplishments and current distinctive competencies, and should focus on generic marketplace needs. That is, the company should define itself not in terms of products or technologies, but in terms of needs. This definition serves to provide direction to all areas of the company, while leaving room for managers to capitalize on new opportunities. The mission statement for an office equipment manufacturer

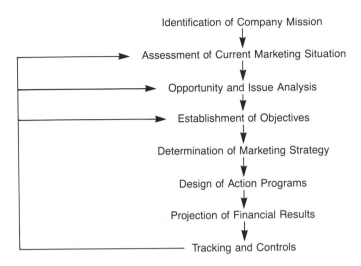

Figure 8.2   The Strategic Marketing Planning Process
(Source: Adapted from P. Kotler, *Marketing Management: Analysis, Planning and Control,* (Englewood Cliffs, N.J.: Prentice-Hall, 1984), 281.)

might be as follows: "We are in the business of problem solving. Our business is to help solve administrative, scientific, and human problems" (Peter and Donnelly 1986).

The core of the planning process is a detailed situation analysis that seeks to generate a data base of relevant background information on the industry, company, product, market, competition, distribution system, and macro environment. Information is not just collected, though. The data must be interpreted using insight, and managerial implications must be drawn. This planning activity can be divided into internal and external analyses. The internal section examines key aspects of the company and its products, including benefits offered, available resources, distinctive competencies, cross-product elasticities, current marketing mix programs, and financial performance. The external section looks at everything outside the company. This overview would include an examination of industry trends, estimations of market size and growth rates, an assessment of customer needs and buying processes, a critique of market segments, a determination of competitor strengths and weaknesses and apparent strategies, an evaluation of suppliers and distributors, and characteristics of the economic, technological, regulatory, and social environments.

With a good situation analysis in hand, the marketing planner performs an opportunity and issue analysis. This involves attempting to identify (a) company strengths and weaknesses, (b) major opportunities and threats facing the firm in a particular product/market area, and (c) notable issues that must be addressed. In a sense, the planner is drawing summary conclusions from the information uncovered in the situation analysis. The ability to do this effectively is dependent upon a marketer's analytical skills, insightfulness, and most importantly, objectivity.

The determination of objectives comes next. Both objectives and strategies should follow from a matching of strengths and weaknesses to opportunities and threats, as illustrated in Figure 8.3. Some call this SWOT analysis. Objectives are established for overall financial performance as well as marketing performance. Financial objectives are set in such areas as cash flow and profitability. Marketing objectives can include sales levels, market share, penetration levels for various mar-

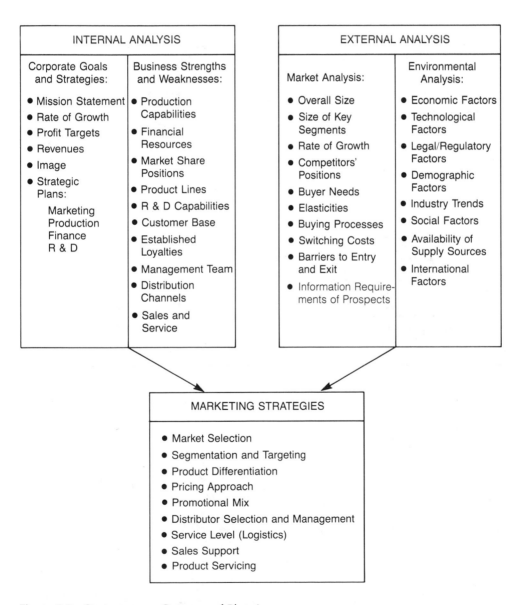

Figure 8.3 Strategy as an Outcome of Planning

ket segments, customer awareness or attitude levels, growth in distribution, and average price charged. Objectives should be challenging, but achievable. They must be measurable and consistent with one another.

Strategy follows from objectives, and tactics from strategy. A good idea is to formulate an overall strategy statement, and then break it down into statements regarding the target market, positioning, marketing research, and the elements of the marketing mix. Tactics are the set of strategy implementation moves the marketer will make over the planning period. The discussion of tactics should include an explanation of dollar expenditures and the proposed timing of each action.

Strategic planning allows the marketer to judge systematically the relative merits of the various options open to him or her at a given point in time. This evaluation is illustrated in Table 8.2. A company that sells air filtration systems is considering changing its price, reengineering its current product/process, or developing an entirely new product/process. The planning framework used by this firm stresses the comparative assessment of each alternative, using six measures. Table 8.2 summarizes the conclusions drawn by management after a detailed situation analysis.

Strategies and tactics are likely to affect both revenues and expenses. It is appropriate, then, to perform a break-even analysis to determine the required level of sales needed to cover any expenditures and to reach goals. Also, a projection of the income statement for the end of the planning period, should the strategies and tactics be implemented, is worth constructing.

The marketer then needs to establish benchmarks to compare actual performance against planned performance over the course of the planning period. This activity is called tracking or control. Benchmarks are set for key operating and performance variables at a number of stopping points (e.g., quarterly, monthly) over

Table 8.2 Application of Planning Criteria to the Evolution of Decision Alternatives

Planning Factors	Price Change	Reengineering of Existing Product or Processes	New Product Development or Major Process Change
Longer-term market impact	low	moderate	high
Investment necessary	low	moderate	high
Risk	low	moderate	moderate–high
Ability to implement on timely basis	high	moderate	low
Ease of competitive response	high	moderate	low
Likelihood of similar competitive response	high	high	low

the planning horizon. Where there are positive or negative performance discrepancies, this data can be used as inputs to modify objectives, strategies, or tactics.

A Case Example of the Need for Strategic Planning

As a means of further describing the strategic marketing planning process, consider an example involving business insurance. Insurance Associates (IA), located in the capital city of a Sunbelt state, marketed specialized policies to professionals. These insurance policies covered office equipment and provided liability coverage, except for malpractice. IA, an agent for a number of national insurance suppliers, employed about fifteen people, including the president, sales manager, and a product specialist. For the past several years, IA had prospered by targeting two "affinity groups,"— members of the state's medical association and dental association. The company had the formal endorsement of both associations.

The president of IA, a dedicated student of the industry, perceived important changes in the competition and an upward drift in the rate structures of insurance suppliers. In particular, many companies and associations had changed agencies, and some had turned to self-insurance, dropping insurance policies and funding their own insurance internally to avoid rising insurance premium costs.

Membership of the state dental association's insurance committee changed recently, and now had a majority in favor of IA's major competitor—Gilsman, Incorporated. Anticipating this change in circumstances, IA had commissioned a marketing research study to determine the importance of the association's endorsement in the insurance decision process of dentists. Simultaneously, IA undertook a search for other professional associations in the state that were rethinking their insurance endorsements. This situation analysis revealed that most dentists were concerned about insurance rates but unaffected by the association endorsement. Insurance industry analysis revealed that the major provider companies, including those represented by IA and Gilsman, were contemplating substantial premium increases in the coming year.

The strategic planning scene was apparent. Threats were evident in the loss of the association endorsement and the encroachment of Gilsman on IA's territory. In fact, Gilsman was lobbying intensely with the dental association's insurance committee to persuade the members to drop IA and endorse Gilsman. Part of Gilsman's strategy included offering rates lower than IA's current rates. A further threat was the probable premium hikes by insurance providers, which both IA and Gilsman would be forced to pass on to the dentists. Unusual as this seemed, Gilsman was apparently unaware of the rate hikes planned by its insurance suppliers. In the meantime, two important opportunities were identified. Both the attorneys' and CPAs' state associations were shopping for office insurance providers.

To fight Gilsman for the dental association endorsement seemed ill-advised, but IA did offer token resistance by making presentations to the insurance committee and protesting its lack of consideration of IA's long service to the association in favor of Gilsman's price advantage. Part of this resistance was to divert Gilsman from the realization that rates were going up, given the firm's apparent ignorance of the industry's plans.

Both long-run and short-run objectives were designed by IA's management team in light of the opportunities and threats analysis. For the long run, IA's success would depend on its ability to spread itself across more target markets and thus minimize the negative impact of adverse circumstances such as those which had come about in the dental association. In fact, a five-year goal of entering new markets was agreed upon, so that no one customer group would represent more than twenty percent of the company's profit stream. Ideally, IA would add a new target market customer group each year. For the short-run planning horizon of one year, IA sought to shift its emphasis away from the dental association and toward the more attractive of its two possible targets, the attorneys' group. At a minimum, IA needed to add new business from the attorneys equal to its anticipated losses of dentists, or roughly seventy-five clients, based on survey estimates. The sales manager took on the responsibility of reporting monthly losses and gains in business from each target market and making updated projections for the end of the year as a means of monitoring the progress toward this objective. The management team agreed to watch the monthly figures carefully and to adjust plans and tactics accordingly, if the projections suggested that this objective would not be achieved.

At the same time, plans were laid to "open up the bar." An advertising agency was employed to design a campaign for lawyer-oriented periodicals. Negotiations were begun with insurance company suppliers to allow IA to represent them to attorney client prospects. A portable sales presentation booth was purchased for IA to set up at the bar association's next annual meeting.

Ultimately, the dental association's insurance committee dropped IA's endorsement in favor of Gilsman. About one-fifth of IA's dentist accounts gravitated to Gilsman in the first six months. When Gilsman announced the rate increases, the flow of lost accounts stopped. The attorneys' association opted to not endorse any company, but IA's promotional efforts proved successful in attracting a number of lawyer's offices to their services. In the meantime, CPAs were being targeted as the next year's step in IA's diversification program.

Pitfalls of Strategic Planning

Despite the many advantages of the strategic planning process, planning can actually inhibit successful marketing performance. The reasons are threefold: poor planning motivation, poor planning ability, and unanticipated environmental change.

The first issue has to do with the purpose or goals of planning. Marketing plans are sometimes done for all the wrong reasons and, correspondingly, in all the wrong ways. For example, the plan is being done to prove a point, or to support a decision which already has been made. In reality, a plan is meant to be a comprehensive assimilation and interpretation of the available information, followed by an objective determination of the goals, strategies and action programs which represent the most opportune path for the organization to follow.

In other cases, a plan is prepared as defensive strategy. If things do not work out as the manager expected, the plan is pulled out to serve as a rationalization. Otherwise, the document is never really used. Many companies have volumes of planning documents that do little more than collect dust on shelves. Plans are also sometimes prepared simply to impress others, such as senior management, creditors, or suppliers. There is no real intent to live by the plan, or to use the plan as an actual blueprint.

The second issue concerns inept planners, who generally produce inadequate marketing plans. Planning is both art and science. Those involved must have a detailed knowledge of analytical concepts, tools and techniques, and a large measure of creativity and insight is required. This insight includes an ability to see products and markets in ways that others do not. Another critical skill is the ability to estimate reliable figures in key decision areas based on data sources that are diverse, incomplete, and often inconsistent.

The underlying logic of market planning is lost on many decision makers. This logic, though, can produce the margin of difference between market failure and success. Gen. Dwight D. Eisenhower once said that plans are nothing, planning is everything. The focus, then, is as much on the process as on the end result.

A marketing plan is a road map. The planner is building a case, the outcome of which is a set of strategies and a program for implementation and control. As a logical argument, the plan requires the same kinds of structure a good manager applies to rational decision making.

Many planners begin with a set of judgments regarding product positioning, segmentation, pricing, promotional programs and so on. This approach is the biggest mistake the planner can make; it is putting the cart before the horse. The backbone of a good marketing plan is a detailed analysis of an organization's current situation, on which logical marketing mix decisions can be based. Inadequate analysis has an important link with product failure. Some of the leading causes of weak market performance involve problem areas that should be addressed in a good situation analysis.

The final issue involves the rate of change in the environment. Of course, change is what creates the need for strategic planning. A plan is an attempt to see the future and to incorporate it into current thinking. An important requirement then, is that a plan be flexible and allow for contingencies. One approach is to include opportunistic, expected, and pessimistic views.

The importance of marketing plans in operational decision making will only continue to grow, especially as firms' abilities in data collection and data management improve. To be effective, though, putting together a plan must become more than a once-a-year activity. Planning is a continual process involving constant updating, modification of figures, changes in assumptions, and forecast revisions.

CONCEPTUAL PLANNING TOOLS

In planning, marketers increasingly rely on a variety of conceptual tools. Included among these are the product life cycle, product portfolios, experience curves/economies of scale, and technology life cycles.

Product Life Cycle

The product life cycle (PLC) is perhaps the most widely known of marketing concepts, and is a focal point of marketing planning. While there are drawbacks, the PLC is popular because of its intuitive appeal, and its direct implications for marketing strategy. Put simply, the PLC plots the sales volume and profit curves for an industry (or company) over the history of a product. The sales volume trend is generally shown as an S-shaped curve, as found in Table 8.3, which contributes to its intuitive appeal.

Take, as an example, the market experience of pocket pagers. These pagers are the small beeper and voice communication devices carried by many professionals and salespeople who are in the field but who must be available to a central office or message center. Prior to the advent of pocket pagers, these people had to call in frequently to find out who had called them or what tasks needed to be performed immediately. Alternatively, doctors' telephone exchanges tracked down physicians through the many telephone number locations where they might be found, to update them on emergencies or other events requiring their attention. In the mid-1970s, the first pocket pagers appeared on the scene. They were bulky, could only beep, had short range, and were subject to interference and other problems; they were also expensive. Initial adoption of these units was slow, but their relative advantage over the old system was appealing. Gradually, sales grew from this foothold.

Technical advances such as miniaturization and two-way voice communication rendered the pagers more attractive, and prices fell with volume production. As sales spurted, more companies entered the market, further stimulating demand with increased promotion, availability, and price competition. Eventually, however, the sales velocity began to slow as the market approached saturation. With more penetration, fewer potential new adopters remained; furthermore, these prospects were more resistant to change than earlier adopters. The sales slowdown led some companies to exit the industry, and squeezed the profits of those who remained. Ultimately, the market will reach the point at which most sales will be replacement of older models of pagers, with a small proportion of first-time buyers.

The PLC is divided into five stages; market development, rapid growth, competitive turbulence, maturity, and decline. Other versions use different names and/ or a different number of stages, but these five are fairly descriptive of industrial products.

Market development is a period of slow growth during which the marketer is attempting to encourage trial of a new product by customers. Unanticipated product problems are being worked out, and the company may be adding distributors. Profits and cashflow are usually negative. This stage can be lengthy for new products that involve considerable learning on the part of users. Conversely, market development will normally be short for low learning products which have a clear advantage over existing alternatives. Because many new industrial products are fairly complex, this stage will tend to be longer than that for consumer products.

The rapid growth stage finds sales growing at an increasing rate from period to period. The marketer is attempting to establish and solidify a loyal customer base and strong brand preference. The product is expanded into a product line. Production may be approaching capacity with accumulating back orders. Competitors are showing up with new features and improved versions of the original product which appeal to certain benefit and user segments. Profits are now being realized and are growing.

In the competitive turbulence stage, sales continue to increase, but at a decreasing rate. Competitors have established a firm foothold in the market, and mar-

Table 8.3 Dynamic Competitive Strategy and the Life Cycle

	MARKET DEVELOPMENT (Introductory period for high learning products only)	RAPID GROWTH (Normal introductory pattern for a very low learning product)	COMPETITIVE TURBULENCE	SATURATION (MATURITY)	DECLINE
STRATEGY OBJECTIVE	Minimize learning requirements, locate and remedy offering defects quickly, develop widespread awareness of benefits, and gain trial by early adopters	To establish a strong brand market and distribution niche as quickly as possible	To maintain and strengthen the market niche achieved through dealer and consumer loyalty	To defend brand position against competing brands and product category against other potential products, through constant attention to product improvement opportunities and fresh promotional and distribution approaches	To milk the offering dry of all possible profit
OUTLOOK FOR COMPETITION	None is likely to be attracted in the early, unprofitable stages	Early entrance of numerous aggressive emulators	Price and distribution squeeze on the industry, shaking out the weaker entrants	Competition stabilized, with few or no new entrants and market shares not subject to substantial change in the absence of a substantial perceived improvement in some brand	Similar competition declining and dropping out because of decrease in consumer interest
PRODUCT DESIGN OBJECTIVE	Limited number of models with physical product and offering designs both focused on minimizing learning requirements. Designs cost- and use-engineered to appeal to most receptive segment. Utmost attention to quality control and quick elimination of market-revealed defects in design	Modular design to facilitate flexible addition of variants to appeal to every new segment and new use-system as fast as discovered	Intensified attention to product improvement, tightening up of line to eliminate unnecessary specialties with little market appeal	A constant alert for market pyramiding opportunities through either bold cost- and price-penetration of new markets or major product changes. Introduction of flanker products. Constant attention to possibilities for product improvement and cost cutting. Reexamination of necessity of design compromises	Constant pruning of line to eliminate any items not returning a direct profit
PRICING OBJECTIVE	To impose the minimum of value: perception learning and to match the value reference perception of the most receptive segments. High trade discounts and sampling advisable	A price line for every taste, from low-end to premium models. Customary trade discounts. Aggressive promotional pricing, with prices cut as fast as costs decline due to accumulated production experience. Intensification of sampling	Increased attention to market-broadening and promotional pricing opportunities	Defensive pricing to preserve product category franchise. Search for incremental pricing opportunities, including private label contracts, to boost volume and gain an experience advantage	Maintenance of profit level pricing with complete disregard of any effect on market share
PROMOTIONAL GUIDELINES Communications objectives	a) Create widespread awareness and understanding of offering benefits b) Gain trial by early adopters	Create and strengthen brand preference among trade and final users Stimulate general trial	Maintain consumer franchise and strengthen dealer ties	Maintain consumer and trade loyalty, with strong emphasis on dealers and distributors. Promotion of greater use frequency.	Phase out, keeping just enough to maintain profitable distribution
Most valuable media mix	In order of value Publicity Personal sales Mass communications	Mass media Personal sales Sales promotion, including sampling Publicity	Mass media Dealer promotions Personal selling to dealers Sales promotions Publicity	Mass media Dealer-oriented promotions	Cut down all media to the bone—use no sales promotions of any kind
DISTRIBUTION POLICY	Exclusive or selective, with distributor margins high enough to justify heavy promotional spending	Intensive and extensive, with dealer margins just high enough to keep them interested. Close attention to rapid resupply of distributor stocks and heavy inventories at all levels	Intensive and extensive, and a strong emphasis on keeping dealer well supplied, but with minimum inventory cost to him	Intensive and extensive, with strong emphasis on keeping dealer well supplied, but at minimum inventory cost to him	Phase out outlets as they become marginal
INTELLIGENCE FOCUS	To identify actual developing use-systems and to uncover any product weakness	Detailed attention to brand position, to gaps in model and market coverage, and to opportunities for market segmentation	Close attention to product improvement needs, to market-broadening chances, and to possible fresh promotion themes	Intensified attention to possible product improvements. Sharp alert for potential new inter-product competition and for signs of beginning product decline	Information helping to identify the point at which the product should be phased out

Source: C.R. Wasson, *Dynamic Competitive Strategy and Product Life Cycles,* 3d ed. (Austin Press, 1978), 256–57. Reprinted with permission.

ket leadership may be up for grabs. At the same time, this tends to be a shake-out period for many of the marginal competitors. The marketer is attempting to differentiate his or her product(s), while uncovering untapped market segments. Attention is being focused on keeping the established customer base satisfied, giving them little reason to switch suppliers. Unit profits begin to decline, and total profits generally peak out.

At the maturity, or saturation stage, sales begin to level off, and the strategic posture becomes more defensive. The competitive environment stabilizes, and is usually characterized as oligopolistic. As new prospects become fewer and fewer, marketers may attempt to stimulate existing customers to increase product usage and find new applications. Even so, the opportunities on the revenue side are limited, especially given the downward pressure on prices. The pressure is due to the slowdown in sales, and the fact that customers may increasingly see little difference between the offerings of the various vendors. This reaction is especially pertinent when selling component parts and materials to customers whose own products are becoming mature; often, these are customers with whom a long-term relationship has been established. Limited revenue possibilities lead to a focus on the cost side of the equation. Management looks for efficiencies in production and distribution. Profits are stable or falling, and net cash flow peaks out.

Decline tends to proceed fairly rapidly for industrial products, as new technologies or technological applications make an established product obsolete. Competitors are dropping out. Customers have little choice but to abandon such a product in order to maintain their own competitiveness. There are generally a few customers who continue to depend on the product, though, and their demand may be relatively inelastic. The marketer has a number of options. An obvious choice is elimination, but even that choice presents a timing question. Alternatively, promotion and sales support could be cut, while price is maintained to get whatever profit can be milked from the market. Or, the price could be cut and the product could be used to support sales of other products of the company.

While the S-shaped product life-cycle curve is straightforward, in reality the curve is not smooth, and is different for virtually every product. Models are available of standard curves for products having certain basic characteristics, but research in this area has not progressed to any degree. Another major problem involves determining current position in the life cycle. Where an industry or company is (in terms of the stages of sales growth) may be difficult to determine until that industry or company has been there for a while. A slowdown in sales may not mean maturity has arrived. Instead, this trend may be caused by a relatively temporary fluctuation in the environment.

Generally, product life cycles are shorter for industrial products than for consumer products. Further, industrial product life cycles are getting shorter because of rapid changes in technology and the information systems that are available to companies and customers. It was not many years ago that a life cycle of forty years for some capital goods, such as huge machine presses, was not unusual. Now, even these major items are maturing much more rapidly, sometimes in only a few years.

The message of the product life cycle is that products do not last forever. Sales potential and profitability change over time; strategies for product, price, promotion, and distribution must be modified to reflect these changing conditions. To be useful, however, the life cycle must be more than a plot of sales over time. The marketer needs to track changes in costs, cash flow, unit profitability, market structure, competitor activities, and customer needs in each major stage of product evolution.

Also, the life cycle is not a deterministic function. That is, the marketer is in a position to affect the shape and duration of the PLC through the marketing strategies and tactics pursued by the firm. Just as a company needs to incorporate the impact of company actions and expenditures into its own sales forecast, these activities should influence how the PLC is interpreted by the marketer.

Product Portfolios

The product lines of industrial companies will include products at various stages of their life cycles. This diversity is logical, and can be quite effective if strategically managed. Earlier, this chapter introduced the SBU concept, a way in which products can be grouped for strategy development purposes. Each SBU, and each product, has a role in contributing to overall objectives. Each may have different prospects for growth and profitability. Therefore, it is useful to consider the set of products, or SBUs, as a *portfolio*.

Portfolio thinking is prevalent in the field of finance, where a portfolio is defined as a combination of assets. Financial managers attempt to select an optimal set of financial assets (e.g., stocks and bonds) that will produce the highest rate of return at an acceptable level of risk. Some assets will be more risky, others less so. Some will generate immediate or steady growth, while others will provide long-term returns. As funds are generated from a given asset, they can be reinvested to support other parts of the portfolio.

The decision to develop a particular product or business area represents a type of investment for a company. It makes sense, then, to examine the firm's portfolio of products. To design a portfolio, management must have criteria by which products can be classified. As mentioned above, the financial world uses risk and rate of return. These attributes probably will not suffice, as marketers need criteria that reflect the competitive marketplace.

Some years ago, the Boston Consulting Group developed a type of product portfolio called the *growth-share matrix*. Products or businesses are classified according to the industry growth rate (a proxy for the PLC) and a product's relative market share. Figure 8.4 is a demonstration of the growth-share matrix. Products or businesses are classified within one of the four cells, based on management's assessment of their growth prospects and market performance to date. Depending on where products fit in the portfolio, management can determine which are the best investments, which provide the best cash flow potential, and which might be candidates for elimination. For simplicity, the cells have been given easily remembered descriptive names.

A *cash cow* is a product with high relative market share (compared to the leading competitor) in a slow-growth industry. The name is appropriate, because these products generate considerable positive net cashflows for the SBU or company. These are generally well-established products in the competitive turbulence

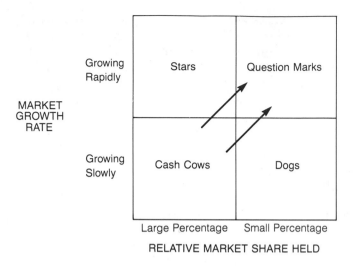

Figure 8.4   Product Portfolio Grid

or maturity stages of the PLC. Strategies tend to emphasize defending market share while maintaining a market leadership position. Because of their advantageous market positions, cash cows do not require heavy investments in R & D, market research, and promotion. Excess cash can be redistributed to support other products in the portfolio, especially question marks. This is a point of some controversy, however, as cash cows often have considerable remaining profit opportunity and market staying power. In such cases, they may warrant heavier investment.

Stars are potential cash cows, but have yet to achieve a healthy net cashflow. These products have a strong market position in a dynamic growth market. Although profitable, they require substantial investment, because the competition is intense. Many firms are attracted by rapid growth prospects, and the battle is typically over new customers and new product applications.

A product is classified as a *question mark* if it is doing poorly in a rapidly growing industry. Profit margins are anemic, but the investment required to remain competitive is sizable. If management is not willing to invest either the excess cash from other products, or borrowed money, these products become candidates for elimination. Another growth possibility is to increase market share by acquiring competitors and/or distributors. An alternative option would be a segmentation and niching strategy, where the firm concentrates on a specific customer group.

A large percentage of the products on the market qualify as *dogs*. They have relatively small market share, and their industry is growing at a slow rate, if at all. The company may be breaking even or losing money. The obvious conclusion would be to get rid of such apparent losers, either through sale or licensing (both of which provide additional sources of cash), or by outright abandonment. However, there are other roles for dog products. They can be used to support complementary products that fit in other cells, or costs can be cut back while management harvests the remaining profit potential.

The major benefit of portfolio thinking is that management is encouraged to move away from a narrow product mentality and toward considering the roles of products within a larger strategic framework. Also, effective utilization of resources across products is emphasized. On the other hand, it is not clear that growth rate and market share are the most appropriate criteria. An alternative version of the portfolio which addresses this concern is called the *business screen*.

Business Screens

The screen is a more elaborate portfolio developed by General Electric. The concept replaces industry growth with industry attractiveness, and market share with business strengths. The underlying logic is to match attractive opportunities to current strengths. Also, the classification grid uses a three-by-three matrix, permitting an *average* category. Figure 8.5 provides an example of the business screen, with sample industry attractiveness factors and business strengths. Each circle is a distinct product, or business; the size of the circle represents market size. The pie-shaped area within each circle identifies the firm's market share.

The three cells in the upper left hand corner of Figure 8.5 contain opportunities in which the firm should invest resources with an eye toward long-term growth. The diagonal cells, moving from top right to bottom left, are equivalent to question-mark products in the growth-share matrix. These receive a medium priority in terms of investment. The strategy is to maintain position and selectively focus the firm's profit-seeking efforts. The remaining cells in the lower right hand corner contain products that are equivalent to dogs, where the industry is not all that attractive, and the company has few real strengths with which to capitalize on the market.

The firm first determines importance weights for each of the factors on the industry attractiveness dimension of the screen. These weights should add up to 1.0. Then products are evaluated on each factor possible, using a five-point rating scale. The importance weights are taken times the evaluation scores. The results are then added together across the factors, and an overall score can be determined for the industry attractiveness dimension. This process is then repeated for the company strengths dimension. In this manner, the marketer arrives at a product's position within the screen.

Alternative Portfolio Approaches

It should be increasingly apparent that a planning matrix could be developed with any number of cells, using a wide range of evaluative criteria. This concept is not only feasible, but also is a positive feature of portfolio thinking. The particular approach used depends on a firm's resources, market, competitive position, and goals. At the same time, the usefulness of a portfolio depends upon its relative simplicity. As more variables and dimensions are added, collecting and organizing the necessary data for properly classifying types of products becomes significantly more difficult.

A sample alternative portfolio approach is provided in Figure 8.6. Here, strategies are developed around a firm's competitive position in a given product area,

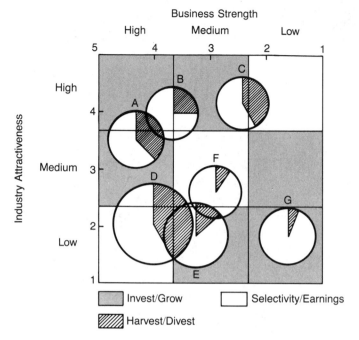

INDUSTRY ATTRACTIVENESS:

- OVERALL MARKET SIZE
- MARKET GROWTH RATE
- HISTORIC PROFIT MARGINS
- COMPETITIVE INTENSITY
- TECHNOLOGICAL INTENSITY
- INFLATION VULNERABILITY
- ENERGY REQUIREMENTS
- ENVIRONMENTAL IMPACT
- SOCIAL/POLITICAL/LEGAL

COMPANY STRENGTHS:

- MARKET SHARE
- SHARE GROWTH
- PRODUCT QUALITY
- BRAND REPUTATION
- DISTRIBUTION NETWORK
- PROMOTIONAL EFFECTIVENESS
- PRODUCTIVE CAPACITY
- PRODUCTIVE EFFICIENCY
- UNIT COSTS
- MATERIALS
- R&D PERFORMANCE
- MANAGERIAL PERSONNEL

Figure 8.5   The GE Business Screen
(Source: Adapted from W. F. Glueck, *Business Policy and Strategic Management*, (New York: McGraw-Hill, 1980), 166. Reprinted with permission.)

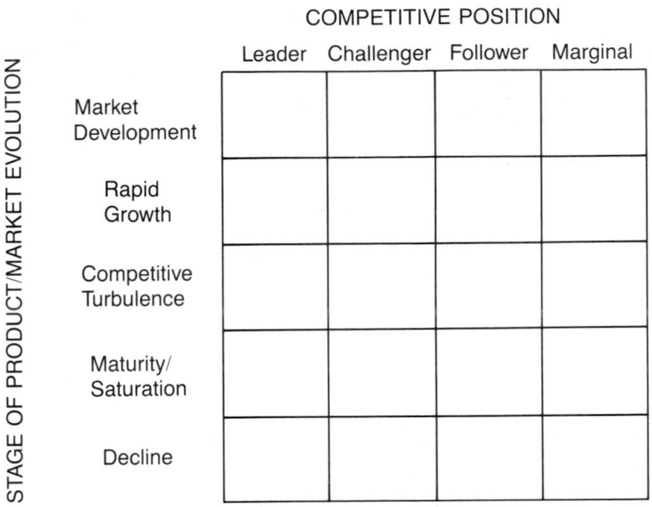

COMPETITIVE POSITION

	Leader	Challenger	Follower	Marginal
Market Development				
Rapid Growth				
Competitive Turbulence				
Maturity/ Saturation				
Decline				

(Left axis label: STAGE OF PRODUCT/MARKET EVOLUTION)

Figure 8.6   Example of Alternative Portfolio Approach

and that product's position in the life cycle. The *market leader* generally is the firm that either is largest, has the biggest market share, or has the most favorable cost position. *Challengers* and *followers* are runners-up in terms of market share. However, the challenger is aggressively attempting to overtake the leader, while the follower is satisfied with the status quo. Followers may achieve satisfactory returns by imitating the successful programs of leaders and challengers. *Marginal competitors* are barely holding on to a piece of the market. A policy of specializing on a segment or niche may prove profitable for marginal types of firms.

The portfolio in Figure 8.5 encourages management to objectively determine what its competitive position has been, as well as the competitive posture it is capable of assuming. Different objectives, strategies, and resource allocations are appropriate, depending on this competitive posture. But subsequent modifications must be made in these areas as a product moves through the life cycle.

Experience Curves/Economies of Scale

The next planning tool, the *experience curve*, attempts to find strategic marketing advantages in a company's production and cost control systems. The basic idea is that the more times a person performs an activity, the better the performance. As more efficient ways are learned to get the job done (i.e., through division of the job into particular tasks, and learning over time of better techniques and short cuts in terms of those tasks), unit production costs fall. Workers can produce more in less time, and material usage declines as waste and mistakes are eliminated. All the while, quality is improving. This notion of producing better quality products at lower costs is the strategic basis for many of the industrial inroads made by the Japanese into world markets.

An experience curve is a plot of the relationship between unit costs and cumulative volume (as opposed to absolute volume in a given time period, which would produce an *average* cost curve). Numerous studies have shown that unit costs fall a fixed percentage each time cumulative volume doubles. This fixed percentage ranges as high as 20 to 35 percent for many industrial products. The cost savings come primarily from lower variable production costs (e.g., direct labor and materials), but can also take the form of lower selling and distribution costs. Purchasing and inventory costs can also be reduced, especially if just-in-time systems are adopted. Figure 8.7 contains a cost curve with a 75 percent learning effect.

One means to take advantage of the experience curve is through product standardization. By reducing the number of options available with a product, and modularizing components, a company can more quickly move out to the right on the experience curve.

The experience concept applies especially to continuous process-manufacturing situations and to capital-intensive heavy industries; its application to service industries and products with short life cycles is unclear. To benefit from the concept, the experience curve must be managed over a product's life cycle. Strategies must be designed that will allow for large volume production of fairly standard units of a product. Penetration strategies which emphasize capturing market share can be effective, if competitive conditions permit. One lesson of the experience curve is that industry price tends to follow costs down. As this price drop occurs, new applications of the product become economically feasible, leading to even greater proliferation. The integrated circuit, an industrial product whose costs dropped about 28 percent with each doubling of volume, is a good example.

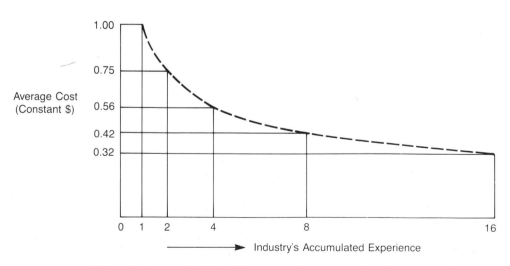

(Note: Cost per unit is falling 25 percent with each doubling of accumulated output.)

Figure 8.7   A 75 Percent Experience Curve

Economies of scale is a related concept sometimes confused with the experience curve. For discussion purposes, economies of scale will be approached as a fixed cost phenomenon. By investing in the capital equipment necessary to operate on a larger scale of operation (e.g., 5,000 units per day versus 50), unit costs can be reduced. This point may seem confusing, because costs are increasing due to the capital investment (i.e., depreciation). However, this is a fixed total. As more and more units can now be produced, the fixed total is spread over this output. The net result can be a reduction in unit costs as all fixed costs are spread or allocated.

Consider a firm which sold marketing research services, and performed a lot of mass mailings. A mailing can be broken down into a number of tasks—including letter signing, folding, stuffing into envelopes, sealing, stamping, affixing an address label, and bundling. Assume management employs three laborers, each performing all these tasks. Output is initially 300 letters per hour. At an hourly wage rate of $5, the labor cost per letter is $.05. With time, however, workers become more dextrous, and develop systems and techniques for breaking the task down and getting tasks done more efficiently. Output per worker increases appreciably. The experience effect finds unit costs falling with each doubling of accumulated output, as labor time per letter is reduced. Wastage of materials (letters, envelopes, and stamps) is also reduced. Both labor and materials are variable costs. At the same time, finished letter quality goes up. This scenario happens, of course, only in a work environment that encourages and rewards learning.

Staying with the same example, assume management purchases machines to perform all of these tasks. One employee is paid $10 an hour to run the equipment and move materials from machine to machine. The total investment is $20,000, depreciated over five years. Machines are operated about 1,600 hours per year. There is also a cost of about $2 per hour to run the machines (i.e., for electricity, lubricants, maintenance). However, output per hour is now 9,000 letters. Unit costs per letter (excluding materials) drop all the way to $.0016, due to the economies brought on by large-scale production. The fixed costs are higher, but are being spread over many more units.

Technology Life Cycles

Just as products evolve through some sort of a life cycle, so do the technologies that generate these products (Ford and Ryan 1981). When a new technology is first discovered, it represents a scientific breakthrough. At this point, the technology generally has several potential applications, some of which are as yet unclear. Some technologies never result in practical commercial applications, if the cost projections prove to be enormous. If the investment is made, and the technology is successfully embodied in a new product, then the PLC concept comes into play. Next, design engineers come up with product modifications and possible applications of the technology to other product areas. Licensing the technologies to other manufacturers is considered. Then, there may be a kind of take-off, where significant growth comes in the number of applications. The technology eventually matures, although modifications and improvements are being made. At this point, the firm might consider selling the technology. The application opportunities are becoming limited and it may make sense to focus on transferring the technology to lesser-developed countries. Finally, the technology becomes degraded, having been fully exploited, and new technologies have been developed.

The suggestion is that technologies evolve through the same type of S-curve as that for products (see Figure 8.8). Here, technology A is developed and eventually begins to mature. By the time it does, technology B has begun to generate product applications superior to those from technology A.

Industrial marketing managers would be wise to monitor technology life cycles. They drive product life cycles, and can influence the rate at which a product moves through the PLC. Customers of the industrial marketer who benefit from consciously seeking ways to achieve and maintain an advantage over their competitors, are more likely to consider novel solutions to their needs that have been developed from new technologies. As a result, the technology life cycle can serve as an early warning system for marketing managers, forecasting the impending maturity and decline of their own products (Shanklin and Ryans 1987). On the other hand, sales volume, which is the focus of the PLC, tends to be a lagging indicator of a product's maturation.

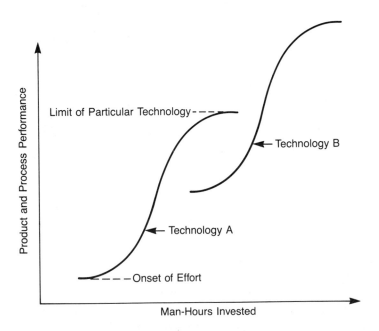

Figure 8.8   Two Technology Life Cycles
(Source: Richard N. Foster, "A Call for Vision in Managing Technology,"
McKinsey Quarterly Summer 1982, McKinsey and Company, Inc.
Originally appeared in *Business Week*, May 24, 1982. Reprinted by
permission.)

THE ROLE OF THE PRODUCT IN INDUSTRIAL MARKETING STRATEGY

The planning process, as well as the conceptual planning tools that have been discussed, focuses on the design of well-fitting strategies for a set of products being developed and marketed by an industrial firm. Products are at the heart of the firm's marketing strategy. They are the primary vehicle for delivering the benefits sought by a target market. The product is the lead element in the marketing mix.

As a result, and as will be shown in the next chapter, the product area requires the greatest amount of effort in planning, development, and execution. For instance, a medical technology firm may spend years in the development of a machine that will deliver high resolution photographs of internal organs. The machine would enhance the ability of physicians to diagnose patients' symptoms without performing exploratory surgery or exposing them to potentially harmful drugs. On the other hand, in only a matter of months or weeks, the price, promotion, and the distribution strategies designed to support this product can be decided upon and implemented. The machine itself is the most tangible and permanent aspect of the marketing mix. It remains with the customer for a longer period of time, and ultimately determines whether or not the user is satisfied. The vital strategic role of products and product management will be examined in the remainder of this chapter.

What is a product? This might seem like an obvious question. A design engineer or production manager might say that a product is a set of physical characteristics, ingredients, components, dimensions, design tolerances, and technical features produced by a formal design and development process (see Chapter 9 for a description of this process). But from a marketing manager's standpoint, this answer is not at all how a product should be defined.

The marketing concept requires that the customer's perspective on products be adopted. Customers do not really purchase physical characteristics, ingredients, or components; they buy need-satisfying benefits. They are trying to solve problems, and so a product is a set of problem-solving attributes.

Approached in this manner, the product that a customer buys can consist of much more than the physical item itself. If company A and company B are selling identical versions of the same product, but company B provides superior after-sale service, or a warranty agreement not provided by company A, then B is really selling a different product. This has led Levitt (1980) to suggest that even the most standard or commodity-like products (copper wire, grains, primary metals, screwdrivers) can be differentiated in the marketplace.

As illustrated in Figure 8.9, products exist at three levels: the core product, the tangible product, and the augmented product (Levitt 1980; Kotler 1984). At the core level, the focus is on the key problem the customer is trying to solve. For the purchase of oil filters for use in plant equipment, the core benefit might be fewer machine breakdowns.

The core benefit is then transformed into a tangible product. At this level, products are distinguished by quality levels, features, styles, brand names, and packaging. A distinctive feature or brand name can produce, in the customer's view, an entirely different oil filter product.

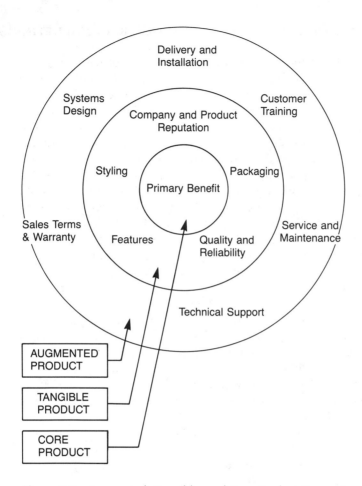

Figure 8.9 Augmented, Tangible, and Core Product Concepts
(Source: P. Kotler, *Marketing Management: Analysis, Planning, and Control,* (Englewood Cliffs, N.J.: Prentice-Hall, 1984), 463. Reprinted with permission.)

The tangible offering can then be augmented by a variety of services, including installation, delivery, credit, warranties, advice, and post-sale servicing. While a warranty, for example, is not part of the physical oil filter product, the customer does not see the warranty as distinctively separate. Such services or benefits are an integral part of the total value the customer is receiving.

Post-purchase support is an excellent example of a product dimension frequently ignored by product developers. Even marketers can be guilty of addressing this area only as an afterthought. Product support covers anything that contributes to maximizing a customer's satisfaction after the sale (Lele and Karmarkar 1983). These services include parts availability, equipment loans during downtimes, operator and maintenance training, serviceability engineering, and warranty performance.

Support programs should be flexible, since they require frequent modification. Flexibility is important because customer needs for product support usually become more sophisticated as the product moves through the life cycle. Also, expectations regarding support will frequently vary by market segment. For example, the tolerable amount of downtime for a malfunctioning machine will differ depending on type of customer, and also by time of year (e.g., peak order time versus a period of slack demand). The same premise is true for the tolerable number of breakdowns.

A good product support program is built around an accurate measurement system. Timely measures of customer support expectations and current levels of customer satisfaction are needed. These criteria are difficult to gauge because the marketer is measuring intangible attributes, such as reliability or availability. The easiest measures are often the least accurate. For example, the volume of customer complaints can be a poor measure of customer satisfaction, because complaints occur after a problem has surfaced, rather than before the problem can be prevented. Also, many customers voice their complaints simply by switching suppliers, in which case the marketer may never recognize what the problem was.

PRODUCTS: ITEMS, LINES, AND MIXES

To better understand the task of product management, a distinction should be made between individual items, product lines, and product mixes. An item (or product) is any clearly identifiable offering sold to customers on a regular basis. This definition includes all the dimensions found in Figure 8.9. Although individual items often have distinct requirements demanding special attention from the marketer, managing them in isolation is a mistake. This potential error was emphasized in the discussion of strategic business units and portfolio approaches.

Items can stand alone, but more typically are part of a line. For example, companies carry low-, medium-, and high-quality versions of the same item. And, they sell products which are complementary to one another, or are used in basically the same application (e.g., different kinds of building materials). A product line can be defined as a set of items related to one another by technology, production processes, distribution requirements, or customer applications. Companies, including those in the same industry, will not necessarily use the same definition, with a given line consisting of completely different items. Precise definitions depend on the organization's purpose in grouping products. The general aim is to simplify product planning, analysis, and control.

Companies do not, as a rule, seek to maximize profits on individual products. Instead, they attempt to achieve desired profit, market share, sales, and cash flow objectives for the entire product mix. This mix is the total set of items and lines offered by the firm. As we have seen, some products may be used to support sales of others. A computer company may find overall profitability enhanced if computers are sold at a price barely above their cost, but then a premium price is charged for accessories or software. A copier company may attempt to establish a solid base of customers with aggressive selling and discounting of copier equipment, but with the real goal of tapping the very profitable market for service after the sale.

If this same copier company sold a line of four copiers that vary in terms of features and quality, actions which maximize revenues on one of the copiers may actually take sales away from the others. Further, if some of the other copiers generate a higher gross margin per unit sold, then overall corporate profitability may be harmed by this approach. Also, let's say that one of the copiers is only marginally profitable, or causes significant cannibalism of the markets for the other three. These drawbacks may be worth enduring, because of the overall benefits gained from being perceived as a full-line supplier or from limiting competitive inroads.

In fact, marketers should regularly attempt to formally assess the relationships among the various items in the product mix. When sales of one item affect those of others, the products are linked by cross-elasticity. Positive cross-elasticities occur when products are viewed by customers as substitutes for one another. Negative cross-elasticities suggest that the market sees the products as complements. Cross-elasticities can be identified by monitoring sales, prices, and marketing support for each item over a period of time.

DEPTH AND BREADTH

After a new product is introduced to a company's portfolio, improvements are made and features are added. As the product moves through its life cycle, a normal strategy is to introduce alternative versions of the same item. And, complementary items are frequently added. Management's focus is now on the breadth and depth of the product mix.

Breadth is measured by the number of different lines carried by a firm. General Electric and 3M are examples of firms with extensive breadth. Managing this issue requires that attention be given to line consistency—the degree to which product lines are related in terms of technology, production or distribution requirements, and customers. Industrial organizations should be wary of spreading themselves too thin, or getting into product areas that do not emphasize their distinctive competencies.

Depth is the number of items in a given line. Lines can be too shallow and too deep. A shallow line will appeal to fewer segments. Unit costs may be relatively higher. A direct sales force may not be affordable. As the line proliferates (gets deeper), cannibalism becomes a bigger problem. Although economies of scale can be realized with a deeper line, there is also a point of diseconomy. Also, individual items not receiving sufficient attention fall though the cracks. Customers find that staying aware of all the items in a vendor's line is difficult.

Product strategy includes long-term considerations of depth and breadth. The strategies of most industrial firms can be characterized as one of the following: full-line/all market, market specialist, product-line specialist, limited product-line specialist, and special-situation company. General Electric has traditionally been a full-line provider, attempting to compete in virtually every market for their products. Aerospace firms such as McDonnell Douglas specialize in particular markets. A company that markets a full line of valves for all heating, ventilating, and air conditioning applications is a product-line specialist. One that sells only diaphragm metering pumps is a limited-line specialist. Lastly, a job shop that produces custom-designed metal window frames is a special-situation company.

POSITIONING THE LINE

Product strategy also includes decisions regarding how the firm wants products or lines to be perceived by customers. This is called positioning. Products are positioned with respect to (a) perceptions regarding their underlying benefits, and (b) perceptions regarding the performance of competitors. The marketer seeks to "select those associations which are to be built upon and emphasized and those associations which are to be removed or de-emphasized" (Aaker and Shansby 1982, 56).

Customer perception is the key. The marketer must find out not only how the company is perceived by customers in a given product area, but also how competitors are perceived. Market research studies in this area often give managers a rude awakening regarding their own assumptions. These perceptions are influenced by consistent behavior. Once in place, considerable effort is required to change them.

There are many ways to position a product, most of which involve the establishment of an explicit segmentation and targeting strategy. Some of the more popular methods include positioning by attribute (e.g., the most durable tractor), by price/quality (e.g., a low budget manufacturer of pay telephones), by competitor (e.g., a new market entry compares itself to the market leader), by product application (e.g., a synthetic fiber for parachutes), by product user (e.g., computer software for hospitals), and by product class (e.g., door locks positioned as security devices).

There is an errant tendency to approach positioning as a promotional strategy. Certainly, promotional efforts can go a long way toward establishing, reinforcing, or changing a product's position—especially for consumer products. With industrial goods, product performance features, pricing arrangements, service policies, and the efforts of distributors can have a bigger impact on how products are perceived than does promotion. Remember that the product evaluation process used by industrial customers is much more detailed, and the buyer-seller relationship is often long-term.

Positioning can be illustrated with the use of a perceptual map (see Figure 8.10). This is a pictorial representation of how a vendor or product is perceived by customers in comparison to other products or vendors. Although these maps can consist of any number of dimensions, a two-dimensional approach is easiest to work with. Each dimension represents a product or vendor attribute. Perceptual maps can be generated by statistical tools available with a number of computer programs, and are usually based on customer data. Customers rank products or vendors on certain attributes, or evaluate how similar or dissimilar products or vendors are.

Three significant pieces of information result from perceptual mapping. First, the marketer identifies the key attributes used by customers to distinguish among products or vendors. Second, the marketer determines how his or her product or firm is perceived with respect to these attributes. Third, the marketer is able to see the position of his or her product or firm relative to the competition. Note that maps can be used to demonstrate how the products in one company's product line are

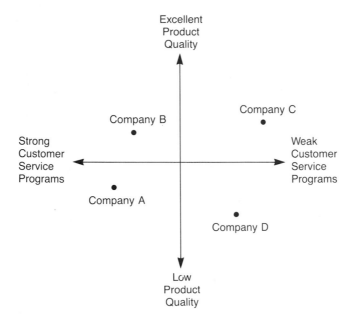

Figure 8.10   Two-dimensional Perceptual Map of Vendors and
Attributes in the Postal Equipment Industry

perceived relative to one another, and to compare the perceptions of different types
of purchase decision makers, such as engineers and purchasing agents.

The perceptual map presented in Figure 8.10 illustrates the positions of four
manufacturers of postal equipment (e.g., postage meters, labeling equipment). Product
quality and customer service are the most salient attributes in this market. Customers
perceive vendor A as having superior service, in absolute terms, and better
service than any of the competitors. However, vendor A's quality is mediocre. Vendor
C has the best quality, but the worst service. Vendor B has the strongest combined
performance on both attributes. Vendor D is perceived as a low quality, low
service competitor. This image may be intentional, because vendor D may also be
the low price vendor. The point is to purposefully manage one's position, rather
than assume that customers will perceive products or vendors correctly.

INDUSTRIAL PRODUCT ELIMINATION

Discussion of the strategic management of industrial products should not end without
examining one of a marketer's most controversial decisions: when to drop a
product or product line. This area is controversial because of the many stakeholders
in a company who are threatened by product elimination. Either their jobs may be
on the line, or they are concerned about the effect of elimination on other products,
or they simply do not wish to be associated with the stigma of failure. In terms of
this last point, dropping a product need not be construed as failure. The product

may simply have run its course in the life cycle. Better opportunities may have come to the fore.

Little is known at present regarding the best time to delete an item. Avlonitis, who has done extensive work in the area of product elimination, finds that industrial firms generally do not have a formalized procedure for making a deletion/retention decision. They do, however, tend to rely upon a systematic set of considerations (Table 8.4) which they evaluate.

These considerations can be grouped into financial issues, marketing issues, released resource issues, and alternative opportunity issues. The preoccupation is with financial issues, where management is mostly worried about how elimination will affect the allocation of existing overhead and the profitability of other items. Also included here is an evaluation of the fixed and working capital invested in the product. Marketing issues are concerned with the effect on customers of dropping a product. Sales of other products may be hurt, or may be expected to pick up the lost revenues resulting from deletion. Further, the corporate image may suffer, and the overall product line strategy may be undermined. Released resources involve a concern with how the human, physical, and financial resources assigned to a product will be affected by deletion. Management is further influenced by alternative opportunities that can be capitalized upon, should a product be dropped. Executive time, production capacity, distribution channels, and cash flow are freed up. These last considerations tend to come into play when management is faced with strong pressures from competitors.

The nature of these issues suggests that deletion decisions should involve representatives from the major organizational specialties—finance, production, marketing, and engineering. Purchasing is also a desirable participant. Remember that

Table 8.4 Ten Leading Considerations in the Product Deletion Decision

1. How will elimination affect the company's full-line policy?
2. Will the sales of other products be affected?
3. Are customer relationships going to be harmed?
4. Are substitute products available to satisfy customers?
5. Will the profitability of other items be affected by changes in production overhead allocation? Selling overhead allocation?
6. How will fixed and working capital be affected?
7. Is a new product available to replace the deletion candidate, and how much in the way of resources will be freed up to support the new product?
8. What are the likely competitive moves if the product is eliminated?
9. How will corporate image be affected by the elimination?
10. How will employees respond to the elimination?

Source: Reprinted by permission of the publisher from "Industrial Product Elimination: Major Factors to Consider," by G. Avlonitis, *Industrial Market Management*, 13, 81. Copyright 1984 by Elsevier Science Publishing Co., Inc.

product deletion/retention is a strategic decision area, meaning that deletion decisions must be consistent with the overall objectives and strategies of the firm.

SUMMARY

This chapter began by introducing the concept of strategy, with a specific focus on marketing strategy. Marketing strategy is a specification of the target markets a company is after, and the related marketing mix to satisfy each distinct market. The next few chapters will elaborate on each of the elements in the marketing mix. A marketing strategy serves to coordinate marketing activities in a manner that reflects current and anticipated future market conditions, and addresses customer problems to provide a distinctive competitive advantage—all done in a manner that contributes to the organization's financial objectives. A distinction is drawn between strategy and marketing tactics, the actions and expenditures used to implement a strategy.

Industrial firms not only need to build their marketing efforts around coherent strategies, but they also need to adopt a strategic marketing perspective. Here, the managerial orientation is on environmental analysis, a longer-term time frame, and cooperation among the major strategic areas of the firm in designing marketing strategies. Products are seen as playing different roles, making different contributions to the overall performance of a company.

Recognizing the large variety of potential strategies open to the industrial marketer, methods of grouping or classifying strategies were presented—these included strategies aimed at new/existing products and new/existing markets, primary versus selective demand strategies, and Porter's three generic strategies. While such classification schemes provide direction, it is important to keep in mind that strategy development is a creative process on which few limits should be placed.

The chapter next provided a planning framework within which industrial marketing strategies can be developed. Marketing planning involves projecting the future and determining the courses of action which will best achieve marketing objectives. Toward this end, strategic planning should not be a once-a-year activity. Rather, planning should be an interactive, continuous process in which assumptions are tested, performance deviations are analyzed, and strategies are modified. Strategic planning is a philosophy as much as an activity. Viewed in this way, proper motivation and skills are prerequisites.

A number of conceptual tools can be useful in successful planning. Among these tools are the product life cycle, product portfolios, the experience curve, and technology life cycles. Each of these were explained, with implications drawn for the determination of strategy. The remainder of the chapter examined the central role played by the organization's product offering in marketing strategy. Products were defined as bundles of attributes existing on three levels: core, tangible, and augmented. They combine to form product lines, which are part of the firm's overall product mix. Strategic decisions reflect items, lines, and mixes, as well as the depth and breadth of a firm's product mix.

Another dimension of marketing strategy concerns the manner in which the organization wishes to position its product offerings relative to those of competitors. A firm's position in a particular product market exists, ultimately, in the minds of those in customer organizations. Positioning strategy should direct all of the elements of the marketing mix toward influencing customer perceptions.

A final strategic product management issue is the decision on when to delete a product or product line. This controversial question raises a number of internal political problems. For a number of reasons, determining the optimal point in time to drop a product, if that point even exists, is quite difficult. A set of diagnostic questions were presented to guide managers in addressing this problem. The nature of these questions suggests the need for interfunctional involvement in deletion decisions.

QUESTIONS

1. A medium-sized firm that provides temporary employees to companies on an as-needed basis has traditionally relied on a short-term, reactive approach in managing its marketing-related activities. Why is it important for this company to adopt a strategic orientation? How would such a strategic orientation affect the way in which the firm approaches and carries out the marketing function?

2. Identify an example of a marketing tactic. Demonstrate how that same tactic could be part of two different types of marketing strategies. Explain the different purposes the tactic might be serving in each of the strategies.

3. How might a firm be pursuing primary and selective demand strategies at the same time and for the same product? Assume the company is NCR and the product is electronic cash registers.

4. In examining the strategic marketing planning model presented in the chapter, why are objectives established in the middle of the process, instead of at the beginning?

5. What are some potential dangers in placing too much emphasis on market share gains as the objective when designing and implementing marketing programs?

6. What kinds of information would you need to estimate the experience curve for a new product? Can you have economies of scale without the experience curve effect?

7. How would you expect your sales, costs, cash flow, unit profits, customer demand, and competition to change in moving from the growth stage to the maturity stage if you were a manufacturer of automated teller machines sold to financial institutions?

8. Walker Wire Corporation manufactures copper wire for use in electrical cords. A number of companies compete with Walker, and each produces an almost identical product line. Given this apparent homogeneity in what is being sold, what are some ways in which Walker might differentiate its product offerings?

9. Would portfolio thinking be useful in developing marketing strategies for a small company which sells video production services (e.g., for television commercials, training films, industrial films, convention support), but also sells and leases video equipment (e.g., monitors, cameras, recorders), as well as video accessories (e.g., cables, switchers, tripods, carts, tapes, jacks, and plugs)?

10. AT&T manufactures pay telephones traditionally sold to local phone companies. The market for such telephones is relatively mature, with sales continuing to rise at a slow but steady rate. The ongoing deregulation of the telecommunications industry has attracted many new competitors, providing lower quality phones at a price well under that of AT&T. In addition, these pay telephones can now be purchased outright by customers, where before they were always owned and maintained by the local phone company. Discuss the alternatives that AT&T should consider if it were contemplating the deletion of pay telephones from its product line.

CHAPTER 9

MARKETING AND PRODUCT INNOVATION

Key Concepts

Barriers to product success
Brainstorming
Cannibalism
Categories of adopters
Concept testing
Continuous innovation
Discontinuous innovation
Dynamically continuous innovation
Embodiment merit
Imitation strategy
Innovation diffusion process
Intrapreneurship
Inventive merit
Market launch

Market merit
Operational merit
Proactiveness
Product innovation charter
Product failure categories
Product testing
Profitability analysis
Screening criteria
Strategic window
Structures for innovation
Synergy
Technical feasibility analysis
Test marketing
Venture team

Learning Objectives

1. Establish the importance of innovative activities in industrial firms, and identify major types of innovation.
2. Determine major reasons for new product success and failure.
3. Explain the concept of a product innovation charter, and the need for a strategy in the new products area.
4. Describe a process for developing new products, and outline the role of marketing during the stages of the process.
5. Identify ways to structure organizations to encourage innovation, and emphasize the need for marketing departments to be a source of corporate entrepreneurship.

The essence of business is to deliver a product which satisfies a need and whose market value exceeds its costs.

R.C. BENNETT and R.G. COOPER

THE IMPORTANCE OF NEW PRODUCTS

The marketing concept (Chapter 1) dictates that consistent financial success over time can only be achieved if a company identifies and stays in touch with the needs, wants, and problems of the market. Further, the company must develop products and/or services that address these needs, wants, and problems better than competitor offerings. Maintaining this competitive advantage involves fighting a never-ending war. Battles may be won or lost, but the war continues—because needs, wants, and problems change, and so do the competitors. As a result, product and service innovation should be a normal, ongoing activity within the industrial firm.

The primary markets of customers may expand or contract. Their raw material sources may become scarce or more expensive. Financial conditions may change, forcing customers to restructure their purchasing criteria. New technologies may be adopted which render their production operations more efficient. Such developments might force customers to gravitate toward, or away from, the vendors they currently rely upon. Even where customer conditions remain unchanged, competitors introduce advances that make a company's products obsolete. Table 9.1 provides a summary of factors initiating the need for new product development. Without a steady flow of new products and services, industrial companies invite their own demise. In fact, new products are accounting for a larger percentage of company profits than they have historically contributed.

This is not to say that any given company must always be the leader in new product introduction. In some cases, it may be profitable to adopt an imitation strategy, following the lead of others into a new product or technology. Whatever the approach, the firm must keep abreast of innovative opportunities, or the capacity to adapt to changing market conditions is lost.

This chapter examines various types of new product activity and the several types of risks involved with new product development. Reasons for new product success and failure are discussed, together with ways in which marketers can reduce high product failure rate. Approaches to organizing the company for innovative activity are assessed, and recommendations made. Sources of conflict between those responsible for marketing and those in R&D are identified. A step-by-step process model for developing and launching a new product is presented, and the role of marketing throughout this process is emphasized. The position is taken that market-

Table 9.1   Factors that Initiate the Need for New Product
Development

Companies are generally motivated to develop new products by one or more of the
following interrelated factors:

1. the perceived inability to achieve final goals of profit and earnings per share with the
   existing product line;
2. the desire to maintain an established rate of sales growth;
3. moves by competitors to develop new products or reposition existing products;
4. management recognition that the product life cycle of an existing product is reaching
   maturity;
5. rapid changes in technology, placing pressure on management to innovate as
   competitors develop the new technology;
6. major inventions that open entirely new markets, and create opportunities for a
   number of new products;
7. government regulation or deregulation, forcing firms to consider new products or
   product changes in compliance with the current regulatory environment;
8. major changes in the cost or availability of key raw materials;
9. changes in customer demographics which cause changes in their wants or needs;
10. requests from customers who have encountered a particular problem or need;
11. identification of a new product opportunity by a supplier, who then induces the
    manufacturer to pursue the opportunity.

Source: Adapted from G.L. Urban, J.R. Hauser, and N. Dholakia, *Essentials of New Product Management,*
(Englewood Cliffs, N.J.: Prentice-Hall, 1987), 5–10.

ing, both as a philosophy and as an organizational activity, is an important vehicle
for achieving an entrepreneurial orientation in industrial companies of all sizes.

TYPES OF INNOVATIVE PRODUCT ACTIVITY

Discussions of new products bring to mind major innovations that create whole new
markets and change the way customers satisfy their needs. While a sudden breakthrough is sometimes the case, most new product activity takes the form of improvements to existing products or extensions of the current product line. Robertson
(1967), for instance, has identified different degrees of innovation. He draws distinctions between a discontinuous innovation, a dynamically continuous innovation, and
a continuous innovation.

A *discontinuous* innovation is fairly revolutionary, and has a disruptive impact
on established buyer behavior patterns. These types of products address needs that
have previously gone unmet (e.g., the first airplane or the integrated circuit) or
change the way in which customers satisfy a need (e.g., facsimile machines). *Dynamically continuous* innovations, alternatively, generally do not alter established ways

of satisfying a need, but do have some disrupting effects. Examples include the electric stapler, or the cellular telephone, when each was introduced. *Continuous* innovations are the most common type, and they have little or no disruptive effect. Existing products are incrementally improved. New features (bells and whistles) may be added, or quality may be increased. Obviously, the risk to the buyer, as well as the marketer, is lowest for these types of products. Consequently, the long-term profit potential is generally lower.

Figure 9.1 provides a more complete breakdown of new product opportunities. A continuum of product-related activity ranges from whole new-to-the-world products, on the one end, to significant cost reductions that affect existing products, on the other. What becomes apparent is the amount of room for innovation beyond that involved in major technological breakthroughs. Different kinds of innovation are appropriate, depending on the company in question and its current circumstances. Also, a firm may be pursuing efforts in a number of the areas along this continuum at the same time.

The resources necessary to engage in the different types of innovation will vary widely. Clearly, while an adept value analysis team with a modest budget may be able to effect cost savings in production or distribution, much more funding would be needed to develop a new product line for the company. In the same vein, companies often will find that they must create different organizational structures to match the type of innovation they are encouraging. This point will be elaborated on later in the chapter. Finally, the role of marketing varies along the innovation continuum. This changing role is another area to be expanded upon later.

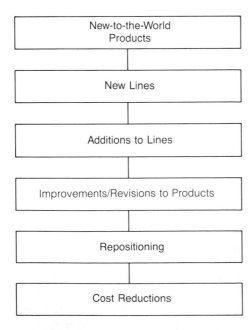

Figure 9.1   Continuum of New Product Opportunities

RISKS AND DANGERS IN PRODUCT INNOVATION

Despite what has been said up to this point, there is a tendency in industrial firms to actually resist, or even fight against, innovation. There is a natural desire to resist any kind of change, especially if the change means learning new ways of doing things, or if it might take resources away from existing product programs. Also, new product failure rates are quite high, and substantial funds can be spent on products that never get past design, development, and test marketing. As a result, product and service innovation sometimes seem to represent a kind of catch-22—innovation is vital to the survival of the modern industrial firm, yet the high costs and uncertain market reaction associated with an innovation can cause the same failure the company was attempting to avoid.

What are the effects of new product failure on a company? First, the obvious danger of negative financial and economic effects on the company exists. New product innovation requires the application of cash, fixed assets, people, and other scarce resources. If the effort fails, the overall profit performance of the firm is affected. A string of product failures could cause a company to become insolvent. Further, any product failure only serves to increase the required returns from the next innovation.

A more subtle type of danger is the effect of failure on company image. Current and prospective customers who see new products fail generalize these observations onto their image of the company. A succession of new product failures will have a negative impact on customer assessments of the ability of the company to deliver satisfactory products. At the same time, stockholders and other investors may begin to lose faith in the ability of senior management and specialists in the firm to perform their jobs adequately.

Another area of concern could be described as the psychological well-being of the company. Just as a series of product successes builds pride among company personnel, a string of failures tears down their faith in the organization. Salespeople, for instance, might become reluctant to push new products on trusted customers, or they may begin to doubt their company's claims of product superiority over the products of leading competitors. Also, personnel retention becomes an issue where product failures are not managed and held to a reasonably low level. Loss of personnel, particularly salespeople and senior management personnel, results in more than the loss of bodies. Training investment, product and market knowledge, and perhaps even company secrets may be lost.

Even where innovation produces market success, there are potential dangers. A new product, once introduced, can absorb substantial amounts of company resources, leaving fewer dollars to support research, or the promotion and distribution of existing products. The sales force and/or distributors have less time to support those products.

Management's time is also diluted, especially given the high visibility of new product efforts. Distraction of managerial time is especially serious where new products are either very successful or unsuccessful. With very successful products, the company usually has not established new organizational structures to accommodate the growth of these products, which results in greater demands on management.

With unsuccessful new products, a hesitancy to admit failure finds management preoccupied with correcting problems and improving results. Meanwhile, internal pressures to perform continue to mount.

A new product that represents a significant technological improvement can speed the decline of the existing product line. Cannibalism, where new products take sales away from existing ones, becomes a problem. More discussion on cannibalism is provided later in this chapter. Also, new products significantly different from those traditionally sold by the company, can dilute or alter the company's image or position in the marketplace. Successful new products may also absorb a sizable portion of the firm's production capacity, resulting in more stock-outs and longer delivery lead times for existing products.

Beyond putting pressure on existing products, innovations that really take off in the marketplace cause significant cash flow problems in their own right. The escalating costs of inventory and receivables can produce a negative cash flow, in spite of impressive sales growth. Although there is likely to be a payoff down the road, severe financial pressures develop in the interim.

WHY DO NEW INDUSTRIAL PRODUCTS FAIL?

A surprisingly high number of new products do not achieve management's minimum performance objectives in the marketplace, and are deemed failures. Some years ago (1968), a Booz, Allen and Hamilton study found that less than 15 percent of all products introduced became commercial successes. More recently, Crawford (1979) concluded that 20 to 25 percent of new industrial products fail, while the rate for consumer products is between 30 and 35 percent. Cooper (1983) claims that the overall success rate is only about 59 percent. Further, even where new industrial products initially succeed, rapid technological change shortens their life cycles. Success can frequently be short-lived.

How can the probability of success be improved? A first step is to identify the underlying causes of failure. In a landmark attempt to address this issue, Calantone and Cooper (1977) examined a wide variety of industrial product winners and losers. They found that the product failures could be grouped into six basic categories.

1. *The better mousetrap no one wanted* (28 percent of failures). These products, despite being unique in certain ways, did not satisfy the needs of many potential customers, and were ignored by the bulk of the market. Typically, the company overestimated market penetration. There were usually no other obstacles to the product. Technical problems were minimal, the competitive environment was not intense, the selling effort usually was adequate, and there were no problems in the timing of the product introduction. This type of failure often results from technical R&D efforts that are not guided by marketing research or other inputs from sales and marketing personnel.

2. *The me-too product meeting a competitive brick wall* (24 percent of failures). In these failures, the product was very similar to products already on the market. The imitative product met customers' needs, but faced intense competition from entrenched firms with established market shares and a loyal customer base. In

essence, these imitations lacked a significant differential advantage, and were not welcomed by the marketplace. Such noninnovative new products are commonplace, however, because management sees them as low risk.

3. *Competitive one-upsmanship* (13 percent of failures). New products falling into this category might be described as orphans of the new product development process. They often received insufficient market analysis, internal development, or market launch support. Consequently, once in the market, they were one-upped or copied by competitors who had done their marketing homework. While the market clearly appreciated the products, their producers were beaten to the marketing punch by competitors.

4. *Environmental ignorance* (7 percent of failures). Products in this category were plagued by a variety of deficiencies, beginning with the planning process and carrying through to the implementation and launch. Product development and/or introduction did not reflect the requirements of the technical, regulatory, competitive, economic, or customer environments.

5. *The technological dog product* (15 percent of failures). These products simply did not do the job; they did not perform in the manner expected by the marketplace. Interestingly, the companies marketing these products often clearly understood what their customers wanted in product design, but were unable to deliver. As a consequence, the product was labeled a dog.

6. *The price crunch* (13 percent of failures). With this group of products, the market price was not commensurate with the value that customers felt the product contained. Price must be a reflection of value, and value is perceived in the minds of the customers. Too often, when new products are introduced, management expects to recover the costs of design, development, and introduction too quickly. These costs should be recovered over the life cycle. Also, companies preoccupied with costs often will expect new products to immediately cover a sizable amount of corporate overhead.

Usually, there are a number of specific underlying reasons for any product failure. The company may not possess, or may not allocate, resources sufficient to ensure product success. These resources include financial support, engineering skills, R&D expertise, marketing research efforts, production capabilities, and selling activities. But, even if the company possesses and spends the resources, product development may be performed in an inept or deficient manner. Internal incompetence can produce poor technical assessment, loose screening criteria, inflated estimates of market potential, inaccurate financial analysis, and weak production quality control standards. Failure can also be traced to a host of marketing-related errors. Marketers often show bias in their marketing research efforts, by underestimating customer loyalties to current vendors and customer switching costs, or inaccurately assessing products already on the market. It is easy to misinterpret the reasons for a competitor's success. The timing of new product introduction can be early or late, or may not be coordinated with the timing of marketing efforts such as promotional programs or distribution channels. Also, the elements of the marketing mix can be inconsistent with one another. In short, then, new product failure is a multidimensional problem facing most industrial organizations.

DIMENSIONS OF SUCCESS

Success in the industrial marketplace appears to be contingent on a few key conditions (see Figure 9.2). Research by Cooper (1979), which compared 102 new product successes with 93 failures, determined that the most important success factors are product uniqueness and superiority in the market. This finding underlines the need for companies to identify a truly unique product and a meaningful differential competitive advantage. Success also appears to be directly linked to the company's knowledge of the marketplace and its proficiency in marketing activities (i.e., selling, distribution, and promotion). In other words, companies that have a firm under-

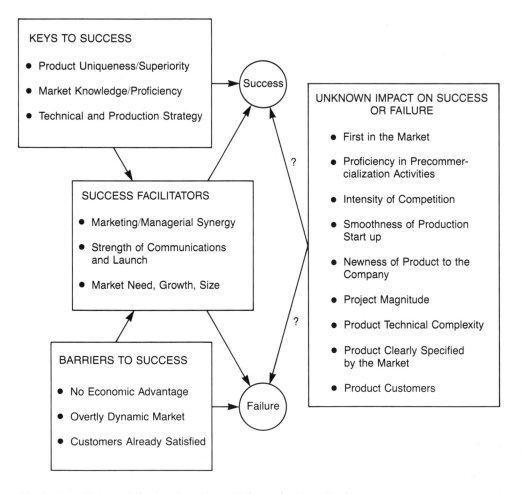

Figure 9.2 Factors Affecting Success or Failure of a New Product (Source: Adapted from R. G. Cooper, "The Dimensions of Industrial New Product Success and Failure", *Journal of Marketing*, 43 (Summer), (Chicago: American Marketing Association, 1979), 100-102. Reprinted with permission.)

standing of the needs, wants, and characteristics of target customers, and are able to translate this knowledge into appropriate marketing actions, tend to achieve market-place results. One implication is that, when developing new products, it may be more appropriate to emphasize existing markets and avoid new markets. Success also requires certain technical capabilities. Specifically, the company must be proficient both in technical engineering and production, and should be able to achieve synergy between the two.

In addition to these keys to successful new products, Figure 9.2 identifies certain facilitators of success. Among them are the availability of sufficient marketing resources (money, people) and the managerial skills to manage those resources, a strong marketing communications and launch effort, and a large, growing market with a clear need.

On the other side of the coin, some significant barriers to success should be taken into consideration. The most important barrier involves the need for a vendor's product to be perceived as offering an economic advantage to the customer, and to be priced competitively. Problems in this area often occur due to a high cost structure on the part of the manufacturer. Success is also more difficult in markets characterized by numerous product introductions in short periods of time. Under such circumstances, the level of uncertainty and the aggressiveness of competitor actions suggest that any new product is in jeopardy. Another barrier to success is the attitude of potential customers who are already well-satisfied with entrenched competitors, and where source loyalty is fairly well established. In such cases, even products that are better quality and lower in price can be resisted or ignored in the marketplace.

In Figure 9.2, the box to the far right includes a number of factors whose impact on product success or failure remains unclear, and continues to be debated For example, being the first company to introduce a new product, having a smooth production start-up, or pushing products that are more technically simple, does not necessarily increase or decrease the chances for success.

THE PRODUCT INNOVATION CHARTER

Recognizing the opportunities and dangers in new product activity, management must take positive steps to improve the probability that innovative efforts will be successful. Toward this end, there is a need for industrial companies to develop a specific new products strategy. This strategy can be expressed in terms of the firm's product innovation charter (Crawford 1987). By formulating such a charter, management is forced to think through, and make cognitive decisions regarding, a number of new product strategies (see Table 9.2).

Major decision areas include the characteristics of new products to be focused upon, the types of technologies to be developed, the nature of the markets for which new products are to be developed, and the kind of product development program to be relied upon. In making decisions in these areas, the company must decide how conservative or innovative new product efforts will be, how offensive (proactive) or defensive (reactive) they will be, and how much these efforts will be synergistic or diversified. Innovativeness concerns the degree to which a new product

Table 9.2   Major Decision Areas to be Addressed in Product Innovation Charter

A. Nature of new products developed
   1. Degree and nature of the product differential advantage sought
   2. Product innovativeness
   3. Product quality level
   4. Product concentration versus diversification
   5. Product type, e.g., customization

B. Nature of technology (production and development) used
   1. Concentrated versus diversified technology
   2. Technology fit or synergy with the firm
   3. Maturity of technology, e.g., state of the art versus old technology

C. Types of new product markets sought
   1. Market size, growth, and potential
   2. Competitive situation
   3. Stage of the product life cycle
   4. Marketing synergy with the firm
   5. Market newness to the firm

D. Orientation and nature of the new product program
   1. Whether the program is defensive or offensive
   2. Internal versus external sources of new product ideas
   3. Technical versus market orientation of the program
   4. Whether the R&D effort is true or applied
   5. Risk level of projects
   6. Magnitude of spending

Source: Adapted from R.G. Cooper, "The Dimensions of Industrial New Product Success and Failure," *Journal of Marketing,* (Summer, 1979), 100–102. Copyright American Marketing Association. Reprinted with permission.

is a complete departure from existing products, relies on state-of-the-art technologies, or is a high-risk venture. Offensiveness (proactiveness) concerns the extent to which a company takes the aggressive lead in developing new products or markets. Synergy is the consistency or compatibility of new products with the company's resources, especially marketing resources such as promotion, distribution, selling, and market research.

The product innovation charter will determine the amount of emphasis placed on the development of new products in the company's total marketing effort. At one extreme, a company may opt for no innovation whatsoever. Management may simply emphasize existing products, and devote no resources to sensing marketplace changes or meeting competitors' new product introductions. The focus would be on tapping the full profit potential of existing products. At the opposite extreme, a company may seek to be the innovation leader in an industry, with a steady and continuous flow of major product improvements and entirely new innovations. Such major breakthroughs hold the lure of sizable, untapped profit opportunities. Between these two endpoints is an intermediate position where new products are balanced against existing ones, and product development activity emphasizes product modifications, revisions, line extensions, and occasionally a new item or line.

Figure 9.3 illustrates these different orientations as they relate to the amount of risk the company assumes. As can be seen, risk is high when the company ignores new product opportunities, and when it pursues truly innovative opportunities. Those companies that do not innovate are faced with higher risk of market shifts which go unperceived and are capitalized on by competitors. Unless a company has a strong customer franchise, and enjoys stable market demand assumed to last for long periods of time, market share will be lost to proactive competitors. Those firms which engage in extensive innovation are often moving into uncharted waters where no one has been before. Consequently, there is high risk of market failure through improper market analysis, mismatch of technology to market needs, or inadequate design of marketing programs. Also, these companies may find themselves inundated with product launches, and in real danger of being unable to devote sufficient time, energy, and other resources to all of these projects. In the middle of the continuum, risks are moderate to low, and product success rates are the highest.

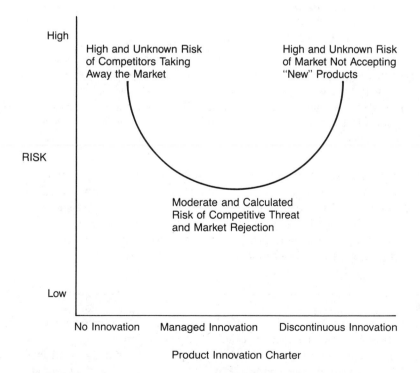

Figure 9.3 To Innovate or Not: The Curvilinear Risk Function

Exhibit 9.1   Six Keys to Making Innovation Work

Rothwell (1980) has identified six traits which characterize innovative companies. These are firms which have developed a business environment that fosters the entrepreneurial tendencies of their managers, and where these creative energies are translated into commercially successful new products or services.

1. COMMITMENT TO INNOVATION—Innovative capacity is associated with an active policy of finding and developing new products. Successful innovators undertake a deliberate search for innovation. Successful projects are initiated by the firm's top management. Success is promoted by enthusiastic and committed top management. The executive in charge has more involvement with, and enthusiasm for the project; he or she has more status, power, and authority. The clear will of management to innovate is essential to achieve successful innovation.

2. INNOVATION AS A CORPORATE-WIDE TASK—Innovation is a corporate task, not an R&D activity in isolation; it cannot be left to one functional department. The balance of functions of production, marketing, and R&D is important to success, and is a question of qualitative as well as quantitative balance. Successful firms, on average, out-perform failures in all the areas of competence encompassed by the innovation process. Harmonious cooperation among research, development, production, and financial departments contributed to the project's success and was an important characteristic of the technically progressive firm. Successful firms take steps to coordinate the efforts of the various functional departments.

3. ATTENTION TO MARKETING, USER NEEDS AND AFTER-SALES SERVICING—Successful innovators understand user needs better and pay more attention to marketing and sales; successful innovations arise in response to a market need. Technically progressive firms also adopt an effective selling policy. Knowledge of demand is an important factor in success. Successful firms have a formal marketing policy, and offer good technical service to customers. These firms provide an efficient and reliable after-sales maintenance and spares supply service. They pay more attention to user education and to adequate preparation of customers.

4. EFFECTIVE DESIGN AND DEVELOPMENT WORK—Successful innovators perform their development work more efficiently than failures. They eliminate technical defects before commercial launch. A characteristic of technically progressive firms is conscientiousness in R&D. Success is considerably facilitated if the enterprise overcomes operational problems before commercial launch, and adequately prepares facilities for solving emergencies during the course of pilot production. These innovations suffer from fewer after-sales problems.

This position is, however, not necessarily the one that generates the best-performing new products—as measured by profit, sales, cost, or other objectives.

This discussion makes clear that innovative activity must be managed. In fact, the most successful innovators do not spend the most on R&D and product launch. Instead, they are the companies that manage innovation as an integral aspect of the

Exhibit 9.1   Continued

5. GOOD INTERNAL AND EXTERNAL COMMUNICATION—Good internal communication is associated with success, as is good intrafirm cooperation. Successful innovators have better contacts with the scientific and technical community in the specific area associated with the innovation. Technically progressive firms enjoy better contacts with outside technical establishments and a higher quality of incoming information. They collaborate with potential suppliers and customers during development, and maintain frequent contact with customers thereafter. Technically progressive firms show a willingness to share knowledge and to cooperate with outside agencies.

6. MANAGEMENT SKILLS AND PROFESSIONALISM—A characteristic of technically progressive firms is the good use of management techniques. In the case of successful innovations, planning is more highly structured and sophisticated. These firms formulate explicit innovation policies. Their other characteristics include: good recruitment and training policies and good quality—and enough—intermediate managers. Technically progressive firms possess an open-minded, high-quality chief executive. Senior staff are often engineers, but other graduates are included. They have an ability to attract talented and qualified people and provide ample scope for management training.

Source: R. Rothwell, "Policies in Industry" in Pavitt, D. (ed.), *Technical Innovation and British Economic Performance* (London: Macmillan, 1980), 300–1, Copyright 1980, Science Policy Research Unit.

strategy and structure of the organization (see Exhibit 9.1). The beginning point is to recognize that innovation consists of a variety of activities that must be integrated into a logical process. Let us now examine the stages of this process and the control of marketing over these stages.

PRODUCT INNOVATION AS A PROCESS

Management implies planned, controlled, and predictable activities, while innovation is often unplanned, uncontrollable, and unpredictable. However, the terms *management* and *innovation* are not necessarily contradictory. As a creative process, innovation requires direction and a certain amount of control. Otherwise, money is wasted, projects are not coordinated and often not completed, and efforts are duplicated. The end result can be a variety of impressive technical innovations for which there is no market.

The product development process usually does not evolve in a neat, orderly fashion. Its complexity is demonstrated in Figure 9.4. As Pinchot (1985) explains, "despite the apparent rationality of later recountings, innovations never happen as planned because no one can accurately plan something that is really new!" Others have referred to the management of innovation as controlled chaos. Nonetheless, there are some key steps that generally must be accomplished to produce a commercially successful new product.

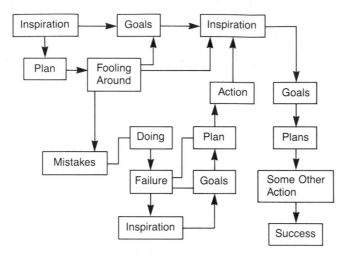

Figure 9.4 How Innovation Actually Works
(Source: Figure 1-3 on page 18 of *Intrapreneuring* by Gifford Pinchot III.
Copyright © 1985 by Gifford Pinchot III. Reprinted by permission of
Harper & Row Publishers, Inc.)

These are outlined in Figure 9.5. Let us briefly examine what takes place in each step, keeping in mind that ideas are being discarded all along the way. Each stage from idea generation through market testing represents a go/no-go decision. As a result, only one of every 100 new product ideas might actually get to the market.

Idea Generation and Screening

The ideas for new products come from a variety of sources. R&D engineers often discover the potential for a new product by exploring new and existing technologies, or by examining new patents. Production managers identify opportunities for product improvement, modifications, or cost reductions based on their understanding of current and alternative production techniques. Those in marketing and sales generate new product ideas through their formal and informal marketing research efforts. These efforts can focus both on competitors and customers. To the extent possible, competitors' R&D strategies (including expenditures) and market testing efforts should be monitored. Similarly, many new product ideas come from customers. In industrial markets, customers are likely to do extensive analysis of their own problems and needs, often coming up with ideas for technical solutions. However, they are not in a position to actually develop the products to meet those needs.

Managers and employees not involved with new products are also a vital source of creative thinking. Companies will institute suggestion boxes, contests, and other formal programs to reward employees who present viable ideas for new innovations. For such programs to work, however, careful attention must be given to submitted suggestions. Employees become skeptical of these programs if the focus

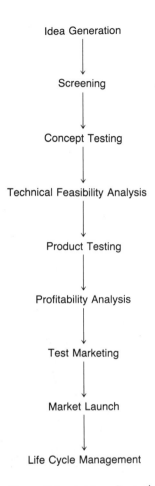

Idea Generation

Screening

Concept Testing

Technical Feasibility Analysis

Product Testing

Profitability Analysis

Test Marketing

Market Launch

Life Cycle Management

Figure 9.5   A More Formal New Product Development Process

is simply to ignore or find out what is wrong with an idea, rather than what is right with the idea.

Brainstorming sessions involving key new product personnel can also be useful. People with different backgrounds are assembled after having a few days to think about a particular customer problem or market opportunity. They try to generate as many ideas as possible, worrying more about quantity than quality. Criticism of ideas is not permitted; the group tries to build on ideas, rather than attack them. Often, trying to address a problem using a frame of reference that no one has thought of before, or which initially seems a bit outlandish, can produce innovative solutions. Once the session is over, raw ideas are categorized, evaluated, and tested.

The largest number of new ideas are discarded during the screening stage. The company applies a set of evaluative criteria to the ideas and rates each one. This evaluation concerns how well the idea fits with the company and how well it fits with the market. Specifically, does the firm have the internal resources to turn the

Table 9.3   Checklist for Selecting New Product Ideas

Fit With the Company

   —equipment necessary
   —production knowledge and personnel necessary
   —raw materials availability
   —relation to present product lines
   —effects on sales of present products
   —relation to present distribution channels
   —quality/price relationship
   —salability, promotability
   —fit with company culture and image
   —impact on development of other projects

Fit With the Market

   —number of potential users, uses
   —extent to which customers would be new or current
   —growth rate of users, usage
   —breadth of market
   —extent to which customers currently perceive a need
   —learning required of new users
   —similarity/dissimilarity to current products on market
   —number and aggressiveness of direct and indirect competitors
   —barriers to market entry
   —seasonal and cyclical nature of demand
   —time before product becomes obsolete

idea into a commercially successful product, will the product be consistent with the current strengths and strategies of the firm, and what is the growth potential of the market? Examples of screening criteria are listed in Table 9.3.

The more radical a technical innovation seems, the more difficult the evaluation process becomes. In such cases, it is useful to investigate four considerations regarding the product concept: (1) inventive merit, (2) embodiment merit, (3) operational merit, and (4) market merit (White and Graham 1978).

Inventive merit is the degree to which the innovative concept relieves or avoids major constraints in the existing way of solving a problem or need, and so, advances the scientific state of the art. *Embodiment merit* is the assessed value of the physical form given to an inventive concept. Having come up with a technological advance, the concern now becomes design engineering expertise application, so the form the product takes offers as many enhancements as possible. *Operational merit* pertains to the effect of an innovation on a company's existing business practices. This merit is derived from eliminating or superseding certain business opera-

Table 9.4   Assessment of Boeing 707 and the McDonnell Douglas DC-8
Jet Aircraft Compared to Piston and Turboprop Aircraft

Inventive merit	Pratt & Whitney J57 jet engine provides major power and fuel economy advances over previous jet engines, dramatic speed advantage over propeller engines.
Embodiment merit	Big aircraft with sharply swept wings exploits jet advantages to provide high capacity, long range, and maximum subsonic speeds.
Operational merit	Design and manufacturing simplified by B52 and KC135 similarities; long-range flights and high reliability simplify maintenance support.
Market merit	Speed and comfort preference of passengers curtails piston and turboprop usage, brings increased demand for long-range travel.

Source: Reprinted by permission of the *Harvard Business Review*. An exhibit from "How to Spot a Technological Winner" by George R. White and Margaret B.W. Graham (March/April 1978). Copyright © 1978 by the President and Fellows of Harvard College; all rights reserved.

tions, such as eliminating required service support, or reducing required inventory levels. *Market merit* refers to the revenue opportunities provided by the innovation. Revenue opportunities can be substantial where innovations are clearly more attractive to customers, than existing competitive offerings. There are, of course, trade-offs among these four sources of merit; for example, the form of the product may dilute the value of the inventive concept. Table 9.4 illustrates the four forms of merit. Note that the first two forms are primarily related to the technical potency of the innovation; and the second two are more concerned with the business advantage provided by the new product.

Concept Testing

Those few remaining ideas that are consistent with company objectives and resources, and with market conditions, must then undergo further scrutiny through concept testing. At this point, the company is working only with a hypothetical product, and is often considering a number of different versions. A concept test provides initial reaction from customers regarding their intentions and probabilities of purchasing the different versions of a product, should it be developed. This test usually is carried out through individual interviews with key decision makers and users in prospective customer organizations, and occasionally with focus groups. When test results are combined with estimations of awareness and distribution coverage, management has a tool for generating an initial sales forecast. A determination can also be made of the benefit segments most likely to buy the product. In addition to soliciting customers' basic responses to the product concept, usually they are asked which aspects they like and dislike, how the product is similar or different to products currently in use, if they see any potential usage problems, and for suggested improvements.

Technical Feasibility Analysis and Product Testing

The surviving product concepts, now fairly well-defined around some core benefit, must be transformed into a physical product and undergo performance testing. Technical feasibility analysis involves identifying the technical requirements for designing and producing the product. Despite an enthusiastic response by the market, the company may be unable to translate the product concept into a finished product at a reasonable cost. Management must determine if this can be done, and estimate the R&D spending necessary to overcome all the technical constraints. The required investment in plant and equipment is also estimated, together with the unit cost of production. The more specific the data generated from concept testing, the more precise these estimates can be.

Assuming the technical obstacles can be surmounted at reasonable cost, a physical product is engineered. This may be a prototype, although prototypes are sometimes developed for use in concept testing. Design engineers conceive different versions of the product, based on the many trade-off decisions that must be made among product attributes. For example, there may be a trade-off between speed of performance and product safety, or between heat resistance and ease of use. Whatever trade-offs are ultimately made, the core benefit is critical, and must not be sacrificed.

Technical product testing subjects the product to a thorough examination of tolerances and performance capabilities. Close scrutiny is given to differences in product reliability or performance under differing conditions, such as light/heavy or frequent/infrequent usage, extremely cold temperatures, or unusual power surges and outages. Companies may be asked to use the product in their businesses and to draw comparisons with competing products. Such tests will enable management to establish maintenance schedules and service requirements, and to determine the set of improper applications of the product to be avoided.

For those products that survive technical feasibility analysis and product testing, the product tests also become a valuable source of information for establishing the initial pricing, promotion, and distribution strategies. Estimates of production and user costs will influence price. Technical reports can be included with promotional materials. Personal sales calls and advertising should be built around the attribute bundle included in the final product. Sales training will emphasize technical product considerations, as will the design of the initial distribution channel.

Profitability Analysis

Products that successfully pass a detailed technical examination are not necessarily going to be profitable products. To determine profit potential, projected net cash flows (net revenues minus actual expenditures) must be estimated for the company's planning time horizon and compared to the initial investment in the product. Industrial firms tend to evaluate new products over some predetermined time period, e.g., three to five years.

Because of the time value of money (i.e., the many other things the firm could be doing with its resources if this new product were not developed), companies will generally expect that the sum of the projected net cash flows for the time period will exceed the initial investment and provide some minimum rate of return. This rate of return should reflect a number of factors, including the opportunity cost of the project, the riskiness of the project, company objectives, and expected inflation. Firms will sometimes use their current cost of capital as a minimum rate of return.

Two logical questions result from this analysis. First, how long will each project take to repay its initial investment? Second, which project(s) will exceed the minimum required rate of return over the planning horizon? Given the limited resources of most organizations, not all of the projects expected to be profitable can be pursued. Projects have to be prioritized based on their payback period and overall rate of return.

Cannibalism, a concept discussed earlier in this chapter, is a related issue that should be incorporated into this financial analysis. New product sales come from new customers attracted to the market, from competitors' customers, and from the firm's existing customer base. If the new product is taking sales away from other products in the firm's product line, this generally means customers see the new product as a substitute for something they already purchase from the same firm. The key point here is that failure to take cannibalism into account means the revenues from the new product are being overstated. Subtracting the cannibalism effect from new product revenues results in a more accurate measure of the product's financial performance.

Test Marketing

The company now has an innovation that management believes will meet or exceed objectives, and which is consistent with resources. However, rather than introduce the product to the entire market simultaneously, initial sales may be limited to a smaller geographic area. This is called a test market, and should be similar to the entire market in terms of the types of customers, their buying processes, and their needs in this product area.

Test marketing is a means of limiting risk, especially when product acceptance is uncertain, sales projections are difficult to estimate, or the costs of a full-scale launch are quite high. Through test markets, the firm is also able to better match prices, promotional efforts, and other marketing decision variables with marketplace requirements.

Conversely, test markets are expensive and can take a long time to evaluate. They are unrealistic for products with long buying cycles, those with short life cycles, and those with a relatively small customer base. In addition, a test market can tip the company's hand to competitors, and should be avoided when it is crucial to beat the competition to the market. This caution is especially appropriate for easily imitated innovations. Also, competitors are often able to distort test results, by accelerating or decelerating their programs within the test market. Because of this possibility, results must be very carefully scrutinized, with an allowance for any unusual or atypical developments during the time period of the test.

Market Launch and Life Cycle Management

The full-scale introduction of a new product is truly a team effort. Marketing, production, distribution, selling, and service must be closely coordinated. Timing is critical for each of these activities, and should be well-synchronized. The acquisition and start-up of the production process, including purchases of machinery and components, has to be accomplished early enough to ensure that bugs can be worked out of the system, and that costs can be controlled within acceptable variances. Yet, starting too early can produce costly inventories with the related carrying costs. Starting too late is even more troublesome, because customer back orders accumulate, goodwill is lost, and competitors are given an opportunity to respond. Carefully managing the start-up and growth to capacity of production will maximize benefits subsequently derived from the experience curve and economies of scale.

Not only must production be synchronized with sales efforts, but also distribution channels must be in place to capitalize on the market opportunity. Resources are being wasted if promotional efforts have been effective in creating awareness among target customers, but trained distributors are not in place, or there is no follow-up sales call. In some instances, initial promotional efforts may be moderate, to ensure that demand can be well-served as it materializes.

Timing of the launch itself is another critical decision area. Marketers refer to the concept of the *strategic window* to describe an optimal time period within which a product or market opportunity can be taken advantage of. Premature introduction (before the window is open) usually fails because the market does not yet perceive a need. Late introduction generally takes place after the window is closed, when competitors are well-entrenched, loyalties are established, or distribution channels are saturated. Determining the window of opportunity early in the product development process is important.

The considerable uncertainty surrounding a new product launch suggests the need for a preestablished tracking program. Specific market performance milestones should be in place to identify troublespots early. Assumptions regarding market price sensitivity, customer purchase intentions, and competitor response have to be monitored. The key elements are feedback and flexibility. An immense amount can be learned in the early days of market launch. Effective feedback can result in alterations or fine-tuning of product features, distribution strategy, prices, or the design of the selling effort—but only if the company is receptive to learning, and flexible in responding to change. Often, whole new opportunities are uncovered which were not envisioned during product development.

For those products that subsequently achieve commercial success, the managerial focus becomes life-cycle management. The product life-cycle concept, introduced in the preceding chapter, is directly related to the innovation diffusion process. Diffusion refers to the pattern innovations follow as they are adopted by customers in the marketplace. Keep in mind that different customers adopt an innovation at different times. Marketers want to manage, or at least influence, the diffusion of a new product to the extent possible.

The innovation diffusion process is illustrated in Figure 9.6, which plots a distribution of the number of customers adopting a new product over time, expressed as a percentage of all potential adopters of the product. Studies of the diffusion process suggest that adoption demonstrates a fairly normal distribution over time. As a result, adopters can be placed into categories based on how long they wait to try a new product, relative to other customers. These categories are innovators, early adopters, early majority, late majority, and laggards.

Rather than go after all potential adopters of an innovation, marketers are better served to first focus on innovators and early adopters. These are the organizations that tend to be more innovative, and more willing to try something new. Once these organizations experience success with an innovation, they influence the other categories of adopters through word-of-mouth and example. The task, then, is to identify the characteristics of organizations more likely to be innovators and early adopters. Unfortunately, this group varies depending on the type of new product in

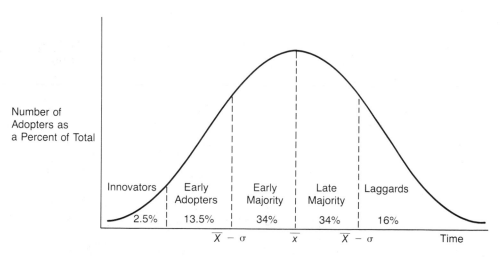

Figure 9.6 The Innovation Diffusion Curve
(Source: Reprinted with permission of the Free Press, a Division of Macmillan, Inc. from *Diffusion of Innovations* by Everett M. Rogers. Copyright 1962 by The Free Press, 162.)

question, and a number of situational factors. In one study, adoption of a new computer was more likely among companies that were larger, that had more experience with computers—and where decision makers had more education, had held more jobs, and had higher levels of specific self-confidence (Peters and Venkatesan 1973). Others have found that later adopters, although slower to consider a new innovation, moved more rapidly through the buying decision process.

Although the adoption curve is bell-shaped, or fairly normal, the length of time a new product takes to diffuse from the first adopter through complete market penetration will vary. This time period could be a matter of months (e.g., for a new airplane safety device that the Federal Aviation Authority has mandated for inclusion in all new aircraft), or a number of years (e.g., for a highly effective chemical additive for use in textiles and industrial detergents, that is potentially toxic under certain circumstances).

The speed at which an innovation will move through the diffusion process is strongly affected by its relative advantage, compatibility, complexity, divisibility, and communicability. *Relative advantage* is the degree to which customers perceive a new product to be superior to those currently in use. *Compatibility* refers to how consistent a new product is with existing customer attitudes and behavior. *Complexity* is the degree of difficulty customers will have in understanding or using the innovation. *Divisibility* concerns whether the product can be tried on a limited basis. *Communicability* is the ease with which information regarding an innovation can be communicated to users. The greater the relative advantage, compatibility, divisibility, and communicability—and the less the complexity—the more rapidly a new product will diffuse into the marketplace.

ORGANIZING FOR NEW PRODUCTS

Managing the innovation process requires appropriate organizational structure. Structure refers to the way in which a company divides its work into distinct tasks (i.e., marketing, finance) and achieves coordination among those tasks. It includes such issues as the number of levels in an organization's hierarchy, the span of control of managers, the amount of autonomy given to individuals, and decisions regarding who reports to whom. In terms of innovation, structure includes the assignment of responsibility and authority for new products to specific departments and personnel.

There is no one best way to organize for innovation. However, it appears that the effectiveness of different structural approaches depends on the type of innovative activity undertaken. Table 9.5 summarizes a number of the approaches which have been tried by firms. Each organizational structure has unique advantages and potential problems.

Many large, divisionalized firms have consolidated new product activities in a *new product division*. Such a division tends to be large and self-sufficient, serving all the new product needs of other divisions. This form seems best suited to large firms with continuing new product demand and similar products across divisions. There are a number of advantages. Coordination and control of new product activities is centralized. Top management attention and resource allocation appropriate to a long-term commitment are more likely. The division serves as a base of operations and rewards for creative and entrepreneurial personalities. As for disadvantages, a division may encounter problems of coordination with other divisions at points of contact such as the transfer of new products to ongoing operations. Because of the scale and permanence of such a division, the firm risks the perennial problems of inflexibility, vested interests, and resistance to shifts of resources.

A more common form is the *new product department*. This structure appears well-suited to any firm with continuing demand for new products. A divisionalized firm may have a number of such departments reporting to appropriate divisions. There may instead be a single department which reports either to senior management or to one of the functional areas (typically marketing or R&D). A department can be staffed with functional specialists or entirely with new product specialists, who draw on functional areas for expertise as needed. Generalizing about the departmental form is difficult because of the diversity of personnel included, functions served, and reporting relationships. A department is likely to have some benefits of specialization in common with a division, but typically with fewer resources and less power. Innovative efforts may be undermined, if the department's primary role is to integrate efforts of functional departments, unless it has full power to control those functions. If the department is attached to, or identifies with, a particular function, resistance may be encountered from others.

Some firms vest responsibility in a *new or special products manager* (in essence a one-person new products department) who reports to a corporate, divisional, or functional executive and coordinates all new products activities. A divisionalized firm may have one such position for each division. This one-person department appears to be a rather rare approach, because it is an awesome task for one manager to integrate disparate functions and activities in a firm of any size, particularly when cooperation must be engendered by personal influence rather than formal authority.

Product or brand managers in many firms are given some new product development responsibilities, in addition to responsibility for existing products. This approach appears to be effective when new products are line extensions or minor modifications of existing products for familiar markets. This form generally presupposes that the product or brand manager will be directly involved only in selected phases of the developmental process. There appear to be two major drawbacks to this approach. First, product managers are rarely suitable for the development of truly innovative products which are beyond the product and market expertise of the particular manager. Second, given the short-term orientation and time pressures characteristic of this position, combining current and new product responsibility in a single position may result in the neglect of even minor innovations whenever day-to-day operations make demands on the manager's attention. On strictly theoretical ground, such a combination of disparate responsibilities would appear to be sharply at odds with principles of specialization.

Standing *new product committees* have been used as essentially part-time new product departments. These committees are typically staffed with representatives of functional departments, and coordinate all phases of the development process (in contrast to senior-management review committees, which typically only authorize and oversee projects). This form may be effective for a smaller firm lacking the resources to support a full-time new product unit (especially when demand for new products is sporadic), and may also be used by a large firm concerned about avoiding the potential duplication when full-time functional specialists are housed in both functional and new product departments. The main weakness in the committee approach is that no single individual has full-time responsibility for new products. As a result, commitment can become diluted, and problems which do not fit neatly into any member's area of responsibility can be neglected.

Firms whose new product needs are sporadic and tend to involve significant departures from existing products may develop a *task force*, essentially a temporary new product department, to coordinate particular projects. These units draw specialized personnel from functional departments on a full-time basis for the duration of the project, after which the members return to their home departments. The task force is likely to be unpopular with heads of functional departments who are asked to sacrifice key personnel needed to support current operations.

A related alternative is the *ad hoc committee*, which has the temporary nature of a task force and the part-time nature of the standing new product committee. Functional specialists assigned to an ad hoc committee on a part-time basis for the duration of a project are often supervised on a *matrix* basis, in that they report simultaneously to a functional manager and project director. While this structure may be suited to the needs and resources of a small firm, it has the major disadvantage of placing multiple demands on committee personnel.

In some cases, a *venture team* will be formed to develop a product which is beyond the product/market expertise of the existing organization. This form is similar to a task force in that some personnel will be drawn from existing departments and the team will operate only during the particular project. However, a venture team often recruits personnel from outside the firm, and if the project is successful the team typically forms the nucleus of a division or spin-off business. Crawford (1983) explains that the venture concept is an extreme form of matrix structure, where full authority is given to the team leader. The teams typically are full-time during their period of operation, independent from the rest of the firm, able to circumvent existing policy, and concerned with a single project. Such projects focus on high-risk, highly uncertain, and highly important products which are disruptive to regular company operations. This form is most common in large industrial firms, although the burgeoning literature on venture teams appears out of proportion to the actual extent of their use.

Some small firms which lack formal new product units nevertheless succeed in developing new products by making use of *outside suppliers*. These suppliers have proliferated to the point where every phase of product development can now be contracted out for specialized attention. This approach can be costly and difficult to coordinate and control; however, it is a relatively cost-effective way for a firm of any size to take short-term advantage of external expertise until internal resources can be developed.

Multiple organizational forms for new product development are used by a large and increasing number of firms. It would seem sensible for a firm not to become wedded to a single organizational form, but rather to develop a hybrid or

Table 9.5 New Product Development Organizational Structure
Alternatives: Advantages and Disadvantages

Type of Organizational Structure	Description	Advantage(s)	Disadvantage(s)
New Product Division	Large and self-sufficient division	Centralized coordination and control Top management attention assured Resources adequate Long-term commitment	Coordination with other divisions Inflexibility due to size Opportunity for vested interests
New Product Department	Department within division	Specialization Integration of efforts	Fewer resources Less authority
New Product Manager	One manager who is responsible for a new product	Simplicity	Can overwhelm one manager Cooperation from others difficult
Product or Brand Manager	New product responsibility added to normal duties	Best for line extensions or modifications	Not suited to truly innovative products Manager torn between regular and new product duties
New Product Committee	Standing committee with diverse representation	Several functional areas involved	Dilutes responsibility across members
Task Forces	New product department set up on a temporary basis	Tap specialized managers on full-time basis	Unpopular with heads of departments who lose the managers
Ad Hoc Committee	Temporary matrix task force	Tap specialized managers on part-time basis	Multiple demands placed on group members
Venture Team	Internal as well as external personnel used	Brings in outsiders' expertise	May garner resources greater than the worth of project
Outside Suppliers	Contract with another company to develop product	Utilizes specialists for independent work	Can be costly Coordination and control problems
Multiple Organization Forms	Use of hybrid forms depending on nature of project	Form designed to fit needs of the project	No theoretical basis available for form determination

Adapted from R.C. Bennett, R.J. Calantone, and M.H. Morris, "The Implications of Structure for New Product Success," *Proceedings,* Southern Marketing Association (1985), 235–239.

combination of forms appropriate to its own circumstances and the types of products being developed. Large firms frequently have brand managers working on line extensions, while one or more task forces simultaneously coordinate radical innovations, and outside suppliers are used for specialized development services. Reliable estimates of the proportions of firms using various combinations would be difficult to obtain because of methodological limitations of previous research, wide variations in particular applications and terminologies, continuous structural change in dynamic firms, and the temporary nature of some of the forms in question.

Companies have experimented with these approaches essentially on a trial-and-error basis. There is still much to be learned about what works and why, and only a few concrete conclusions have been drawn. It appears, for instance, that new product development efforts either headed by marketing personnel, or including strong marketing representation from start to finish, achieve higher success rates (Souder 1978). Also, team efforts tend to outperform one- or two-person shows and more cumbersome organizational structures.

THE MARKETING–R&D INTERFACE

The critical element in any new product development project is the dialogue between marketing personnel and R&D personnel. Innovation requires proper direction, or little is accomplished. R&D managers are often unacquainted with basic management principles. They frequently are not delegated sufficient authority, but are overstretched in terms of accountability. Marketers can play a major role in providing direction. It has been suggested that the probability of commercial success with an innovation is inversely proportional to the square of the distance between marketing and technical people (Bogaty 1974). R&D needs marketing to decipher increasing complex customer demands. Marketing depends on R&D for a flow of genuinely new products, especially given the dynamics of competition, and the pressures of inflation, resource shortages, and government regulation. Yet, there is evidence that the relationship between these two functional areas in today's corporations has substantially deteriorated in recent years (Warren 1983).

Marketers and R&D people have completely different orientations, at least partially due to the ways they are evaluated and rewarded. Marketers may see company actions in terms of specific products, sales quotas, competitive position, or, ideally, long-term customer satisfaction. Alternatively, the frame of reference for researchers might be a specific project, the development of a particular technology, the quest for the perfect product, or the need to exhaust but not exceed a research budget. R&D personnel reason from vision and scientific judgement, often putting forth plans which are enveloped in technical jargon, hope, and uncertainty (Rousel 1983). Theirs is an orientation shared by few others in the firm.

The implication of these differing orientations for the marketer is that he or she must have a solid grasp on the technologies, perspectives, and limitations of other functional areas in the firm, particularly R&D. He or she must develop an understanding of the unique orientations and decision-making techniques used by research personnel.

Cooperation between marketing and R&D is vital throughout the stages of the product development process. Table 9.6 outlines some of the areas where the efforts

Table 9.6   Areas Requiring R&D/Marketing Integration

A. Marketing is involved with R&D in . . .

    1. Setting new product goals and priorities
    2. Preparing R&D's budget proposals
    3. Establishing product development schedules
    4. Generating new product ideas
    6. Finding commercial applications of R&D's new product ideas/technologies

B. Marketing provides information to R&D on . . .

    7. Customer requirements of new products
    8. Regulatory and legal restrictions on product performance and design
    9. Test-marketing results
  10. Feedback from customers regarding product performance on a regular basis
  11. Competitor strategies

C. R&D is involved with marketing in . . .

  12. Preparing marketing's budget proposal
  13. Screening new product ideas
  14. Modifying products according to marketing's recommendations
  15. Developing new products according to the market need
  16. Designing communication strategies for the customers of new products
  17. Designing user and service manuals
  18. Training users of new products
  19. Analyzing customer needs

Reprinted by permission of the publisher from "R&D and Marketing Dialogue in High-Tech Firms," by A. K. Guptka, S. P. Raj, and D. L. Wilemon, *Industrial Marketing Management,* 14, 293. Copyright 1985 by Elsevier Science Publishing Co., Inc.

of these two groups should be integrated, and Figure 9.7 demonstrates this integration over the stages of the product development process. Note in this figure that the stages of the process have been grouped into three major phases. Commitment to this integration by *both* parties tends to distinguish successful from unsuccessful new product programs. Senior management must promote this integration, perhaps by establishing joint reward systems for R&D and marketing personnel.

The importance of the R&D and marketing departments sharing the blame for product failures should be emphasized. Companies—particularly the marketers within them—often use the lack of innovation as a scapegoat for their own poor performance, but are not supportive of technologically new products when they do arrive. Even where the innovative resources of the firm have been directed toward a legitimate market need, marketers may become a barrier to new product success.

They sometimes worry excessively about protecting current products, distribution channels, sales territories, and customer relationships from the unsettling threat of change. Despite verbal support for innovation, marketers may find security in the status quo. The result is an antagonistic, mutually suspicious relationship which involves confrontation rather than cooperation, with each party blaming the other for failure.

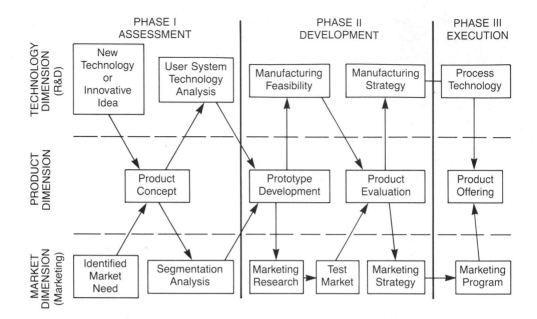

Figure 9.7 Interaction Between Marketing and R&D in the New Product Development Process
(Source: Adapted by permission of the publisher from "A Systems Approach for Developing High Technology Products," by G. Miaoulis and P.J. LaPlaca, *Industrial Marketing Management,* (November, 1982). Copyright 1982 by Elsevier Science Publishing Co., Inc.

CORPORATE ENTREPRENEURSHIP

Innovation in industrial companies gets stifled for a variety of reasons. Over time, this restraint has led to a loss of competitive position in the marketplace on the part of many firms. The severity of this problem in recent years has produced a call for *corporate entrepreneurship,* which refers to a "revolutionary system for speeding up innovation within established firms by making better use of their entrepreneurial talent" (Pinchot 1985). This concept is also called "intrapreneurship," to distinguish it from the new start-up venture pursued by the individual entrepreneur. Corporate entrepreneurship has three major dimensions—proactiveness, risk-taking, and innovativeness. Proactiveness is the opposite of reactiveness. An emphasis is placed on trying bold new ideas and ways of doing things, seizing growth opportunities, and aggressiveness in dealing with competitors. Risk-taking in this context is a willingness to pursue ideas now, despite inherent uncertainties. This risk is calculated, and represents a moderate amount of chance. Innovativeness is an emphasis on a continuous flow of new products/services, changes in methods of production and/or delivery, and a search for unusual and novel solutions to problems.

A growing set of concepts and tools is available for encouraging corporate entrepreneurship in industrial firms. A complete discussion of these is beyond the scope of this book, but some of the major ones tend to focus on organization structure, resource allocation, reward systems, and value systems. In general, more decentralized and flatter (fewer hierarchical levels) structures are encouraged to allow for greater flexibility in responding to the environment. These structures also permit more interfunctional communication. Planning and staff functions should be made as lean as possible. Specific resources should be made available to those who develop innovative ideas and are willing to see them through to commercialization, regardless of the obstacles that must be overcome. Reward systems must be designed to encourage people to develop and try new ideas, to foster cooperation among functional areas, and to emphasize long-term results. While success should be rewarded, failure should not be punished severely. Otherwise, the fear of failure will be much stronger than the lure of success. Virtually all major successes come only after a string of failed efforts.

MARKETING AS THE HOME FOR THE ENTREPRENEURIAL PROCESS

Those in marketing within a corporation often work within a set of well-established (by experience) rules of thumb. These helpful guidelines cover decisions regarding how to price, what to spend on advertising, ways to motivate distributors, and so on. Examples include "maintain advertising at 4 percent of sales" or "cut prices if the proposed-to-order ratio goes above four." These rules can become misleading, however, if market conditions change, or if the company changes its overall strategic direction.

Thomas Bonoma, of the Harvard Business School, argues that when conditions are changing, companies need *marketing subversives*—managers who challenge old practices and bend company rules. Such improvisation might include circumventing normal communications channels to ensure customers are talking to production people, or ignoring the official budget by bootlegging resources to support products and markets ignored by senior management. Subversives, finding the formal corporate reporting process too general and slow, tend to uncover ways to obtain their own profit and performance measures for products, segments, salespeople, or distributors. They form networks to generate support for issues in which they believe. Bonoma (1986, 115) summarizes one marketer's philosophy as follows: "Look, if I followed the rules around here, my brand would fail. I do what it takes, which is usually a little bit of creative rule breaking followed by begging for forgiveness when I get caught. As long as I've got the numbers, the boss will be pretty flexible."

This book has repeatedly stressed marketing's role as the keeper of the organization's customer orientation. Marketing can also take the lead in fostering an organization's entrepreneurial orientation. Murray (1981, 96) explains:

> "of all the areas of technical and professional expertise within the firm, marketing is uniquely equipped and indeed should feel uniquely responsible for analyzing environmental evolution and translating its observations into recommendations for the redesign of the corporate resource base and its product-market portfolio."

Companies today must learn new and different ways to compete. Creativity and innovativeness are necessary not only in promotional activities, but also in finding profit opportunities through new products, lines, features, distribution arrangements, services, and customer segments. As environmental change has become a way of life, marketers can provide direction in managing that change, redefining the product and market context within which the organization operates. In fact, there is some evidence that marketing departments in entrepreneurial firms tend to be key sources of direction in terms of innovation, and tend to significantly affect the strategic direction of such firms (Morris and Paul 1987).

The skills of those in marketing need to reflect the entrepreneurial dimensions of proactiveness, innovation, and risk-taking. Marketers must have the insights necessary not only to find and understand customers, but also to further translate developments in the technological, economic, social, regulatory, and competitive environments into commercially viable products and service concepts. One possible approach is to make the marketing department a profit center, with specific objectives for new products and markets.

SUMMARY

This chapter has focused on innovation as a marketing-oriented activity within industrial companies. New products and services are the lifeblood of the organization, especially in today's competitive environment. Yet, a sizable percentage of new product efforts fail. These failures create a dilemma for the managers of industrial firms. They cannot afford the loss in competitive position that results from not innovating, but they also are not anxious to risk the losses that come with product failure.

To better understand this dilemma, six major categories of new product failures were examined. Underlying most of these would seem to be the lack of a marketing orientation among those responsible for new product innovation. Common causes of failure include developing technically advanced products for which there is little perceived need, underestimating current customer loyalties, underestimating the strength of competitor response to new products, pricing at a level inconsistent with perceived value, and misinterpreting environmental change. Each of these is traceable to an underemphasis on marketing activities, and a tendency to give those with marketing responsibility an insignificant role in new product decision making.

Product success appears to be directly associated with a firm's ability to link superior technical capabilities to in-depth understanding of the marketplace. Successful innovations are those which achieve a differential competitive advantage based on their uniqueness and superiority. Doing so implies a thorough understanding of the needs, wants, and problems of target customers, and an ability to translate these into marketing actions.

Innovation is an activity that does not lend itself to tight managerial control, bureaucratic structures, or overly constraining policies and procedures. It often occurs in a haphazard fashion, and requires an environment that encourages risk-taking and creativity. At the same time, projects cannot be pursued blindly, without managerial direction or financial control.

Overall direction can be achieved by developing a product innovation charter, which is an explicit corporate strategy for new products. Specific project direction can be accomplished by identifying the major stages or steps involved in the product development process, and establishing goals and performance criteria for each stage. Eight major stages were presented, although alternative versions of the process exist. The stages will generally overlap, with those individuals involved sometimes going back and forth among them.

Perhaps the most important responsibility of senior management during this innovation process involves facilitating interfunctional cooperation among R&D, production, marketing, finance, and other specialties. The chapter placed special emphasis on the interface between marketing and R&D. Areas where cooperation is critical were identified, as were reasons for the inherent conflict between these two areas.

Management must also ensure that the company is properly organized for innovation. A variety of different structural approaches exists, ten of which were evaluated. The most appropriate structure appears to depend upon the type of innovative activity the company is trying to pursue. As a result, structure should follow from the product innovation charter.

For their part, marketing personnel often resist innovation, focusing their creative energies on support activities for existing products, and emphasizing minor product improvements or line extensions. These are types of innovative activity, but they have a more short-term payoff, and leave the firm vulnerable over time.

This book urges marketing departments in industrial firms to adopt an entrepreneurial perspective. This perspective is a proactive, innovative, and calculated risk-taking approach to translating environmental developments into profitable new product and market opportunities. Marketers need to adopt a longer-term perspective on both customer satisfaction and profitability. New approaches to deciphering present and future needs must be adopted, matching them to technological possibilities. Marketers must, in short, redefine the rules regarding how, where, and when to compete.

QUESTIONS

1. Assume that your company manufactures and sells cardboard boxes in a variety of sizes and designs. What might be some of the specific factors that create the need for innovation in your firm?

2. Why must firms selling industrial services innovate as much or more than those selling industrial products?

3. Provide examples of continuous, dynamically continuous, and discontinuous innovations in the industrial market. What are some process innovations within a firm that might have marketing implications?

4. The most common type of product failure in industrial markets is the better mousetrap nobody wanted. Explain what is meant by this type of failure. Why do you think it is so prevalent in industrial firms? How can this problem area be avoided?

5. Identify possible roles for the marketing department of an industrial firm at each stage in the new product development process.

6. What is the purpose of a product innovation charter? What would be the key issues or areas addressed in a product innovation charter for a company that develops and markets computer accounting software to small and medium-sized businesses?

7. There appears to be no relationship between being first to the market with a new product innovation, and the likelihood of product success or the likelihood of failure. What are some possible reasons?

8. Consider a company that makes hand-held portable radios and is working to develop a new mobile radio (e.g., for use in utility trucks, police cars, corporate vehicles). Identify some of the major areas in which marketing, R&D, and manufacturing might have conflicts with one another during the new product development process.

9. Why are different types of organizational structures required for major new product innovation, compared to minor product improvements or cost reductions?

10. Marketing is the home for the entrepreneurial process in industrial organizations. Do you agree or disagree? Why?

CHAPTER 10

INDUSTRIAL PRICING

Key Concepts

Base-point pricing
Bid rigging
Cash discount
Closed bid
Collusion
Competitive bidding
Contribution analysis
Cost-plus pricing
Cross-elasticity
Demand elasticity
Economic value to the customer (EVC)
Financial lease
Gold-standard pricing
Hard benefit
Life-cycle costing
Margin distribution index
Negotiated pricing
Oligopoly
Open bid
Operating lease
Opportunistic pricing

Parallel pricing
Parity pricing
Penetration pricing
Pressure pricing
Predatory pricing
Price discrimination
Price fixing
Price leadership
Probabilistic bidding
Profit-payoff matrix
Quantity discount
Reference product
Skimming pricing
Soft benefit
Standard cost analysis
Start-up cost
Target-return pricing
Trade discount
Transfer pricing
Value

Learning Objectives

1. Identify factors that complicate setting prices for industrial products and services, and reasons marketers often fail to take full advantage of the price variable.
2. Define price as a measure of value, and determine key sources of value.
3. Describe a four-part framework for determining the price of an industrial product or service.
4. Explain how to establish competitive bids using probabilistic bidding.

5. Discuss a number of special topics in industrial pricing, including discounts, leases, and transfer prices, and summarize key legal issues in pricing.

A man indicates by the price he offers for a good, the importance he attaches to another unit of the good.

G. STIGLER

The second element of the marketing mix to be addressed is the price variable. Industrial pricing represents a challenging task that can be characterized as both an art and a science, and which requires both creativity and flexibility. Pricing is a complex decision area that management too often tries to oversimplify. The price of a product is a valuable marketing tool that can be used in a number of ways to accomplish a variety of objectives.

This chapter examines a number of the major concepts and tools available for managing prices, and presents a practical framework for making pricing decisions. In addition, a number of specialized pricing topics are discussed, including price discrimination, discounts, bidding, leasing, and transfer pricing.

COMPLICATIONS AND THE UTILIZATION OF PRICE

Industrial pricing is complicated by a number of factors. First, the true price an industrial customer pays is more than just the list price quoted by a salesperson or printed in a catalog. The actual price which must be paid includes delivery and installation costs, discounts, training costs, trade-in allowances, two-for-one price deals, and financing costs, among others. Importantly, because the customer is likely to see a product's price in terms of the total cost to his organization, the marketer must also take such a comprehensive view.

Second, price is not an independent variable. Pricing interacts with product, promotion, and distribution strategies to achieve the firm's overall marketing objectives. For example, a high price can help convey a quality product image. A special price deal can be an integral part of the firm's promotional program. A trade discount can be an incentive for distributors to provide stronger support in pushing the company's products.

Third, prices for industrial goods cannot be set without considering other products which are complements or substitutes sold by the company. Cross-elasticities often exist, where the price of one item affects sales of other items. For example, the price a firm charges for its computer terminals may affect sales of its computer printers. The same dependency exists between products sold by other companies, but which are used in conjunction with the firm's products.

Fourth, prices can be changed in numerous ways. Some of these include: (a) changing the quantity of money or goods given up by a buyer; (b) changing the quantity of goods and services provided by the seller; (c) changing the premiums or discounts which are offered; (d) changing the time and place of payment; and (e) changing the time and place of transfer of ownership (Monroe 1979). As a result, pricing is often a more flexible decision area than, say, product or distribution. When the industrial firm decides upon a price, it is in effect making a whole set of decisions regarding the time, form, quantity, and place of payment. Unfortunately, because price is relatively easy to change, managers may make hasty decisions for short-run reasons that are harmful in the long run.

Fifth, industrial prices are frequently established through a process of competitive bidding, on a project-by-project basis. As a result, the marketer may have to determine a price without knowing exactly what competitors are charging. Alternatively, where bidding is not used, prices are often resolved through a process of negotiation. The demands of the marketplace suggest that considerable flexibility is required in managing the price variable, and that the firm may need to delegate some pricing authority to the sales representative.

Sixth, industrial pricing is often characterized by an emphasis on fairness (Corey 1976). When attempting to raise a price, the industrial marketer will often encounter experienced and fairly sophisticated buyers who are able to estimate the vendor's approximate production costs. These buyers expect price increases to be justifiable on the basis of either cost increases or product improvements, and not on the basis of whatever the traffic will bear.

Seventh, industrial prices are dramatically affected by a host of economic factors beyond the control of the firm. For example, if prices are not adjusted to reflect inflation rates, they are understated in real terms. This problem is especially critical for the marketer locked into a long-term contract with no escalation clause. Interest rate fluctuations affect the cost of money, which is an important component of price when goods are purchased on credit. Ups and downs in international rates of currency exchange undermine the effectiveness of a firm's pricing strategy, in terms of both its costs and prices. Costs of key entering goods purchased from foreign suppliers can change significantly due to currency fluctuations. For goods sold abroad, a change in the exchange rate determines whether the marketer's price is competitive (high or low). The currency exchange problem is even more complex for companies selling goods in a number of different countries.

In part because of these complications, the potential of the price variable is not fully realized in many industrial firms. However, there are some additional reasons for the underutilization of price as an industrial marketing tool. It is not unusual in industrial companies for price decisions to be made by finance or production personnel. People in these functional areas are oriented more toward achieving rates of return and covering costs than toward customer value or competitor actions. In fact, cost considerations tend to play the predominant role in industrial pricing. Creative pricing is also neglected because of the relative importance of other (non-price-related) product attributes. For example, a customer may be so concerned with product quality or delivery reliability that pricing issues become secondary. The marketer, correspondingly, focuses on these other attributes.

PRICE AS A MEASURE OF VALUE

The ultimate task of the industrial marketer is to convey value to a customer. The price that customer is charged is both a determinant of, and a reflection of, the amount of value being received. A company can easily fail in the marketplace by charging an initial price that exceeds the value customers perceive in the product or service. This overcharging often happens when the firm tries to recover its investment in R&D and related product development costs too rapidly, or too early in the life cycle. Similarly, a price can be set so low that management is not taking full advantage of the profit potential of the item. The price is below the value customers associate with the good or service. Customers may, in fact, perceive the product to be somehow inferior because of its low price.

Value can be defined as the customer's *subjective* estimate of a product's capacity to satisfy a set of goals (Kotler 1984). It is perceived, then, in the minds of buyers. Different customers are not likely to perceive the value of a good in the same way. For example, consider the purchase of a small electric generator. The importance of such a purchase can lead the buyer with little generator experience to place more value on the product made by a vendor with a well-established reputation, than the product made by a lesser-known supplier. This reputation is a product attribute that he or she may be willing to pay a higher price to get. Another, more experienced, buyer may see these two alternatives as roughly equivalent and place equal values on each. The attribute called *quality reputation* adds little value to the product in the case of the second buyer. In a similar vein, the value of a product that provides energy savings to a company will vary depending upon a number of company-specific factors. Some of these include the firm's total energy consumption, its current cash flow, and its relative concern with cost control.

Values for goods are determined *objectively* in the competitive marketplace. Based on the freely interacting forces of supply and demand, a market price is established. That is, the value of a product at any point in time is determined by the willingness and ability of a set of customers to buy and the willingness and ability of a set of suppliers to sell. From a marketing standpoint, value-based pricing is a means of allocating available supplies to customer groups. This value can be distorted, however, when the market operates inefficiently. In the absence of sufficient competition, or where regulatory constraints exist, the company may be charging a price which is not reflective of its true value.

Economic Value to the Customer (EVC)

Because value is perceived in the mind of the buyer, it is likely to reflect psychological, social, and economic factors. Of these, economic factors are more easily measured, and are especially relevant in industrial markets. These economic factors are based on the estimated costs of a product over its useful life, or life-cycle costs, compared to what those costs would be using the best available substitute (also called a reference product). The life-cycle-cost concept was explained in Chapter 2. The reader may want to refer to that discussion.

Let's consider two products, A and B. Product A is currently sold for $100, has estimated start-up costs of $50, and postpurchase costs of $80 over its useful life of six years. For simplicity, assume there is no salvage value, although this is rarely the case. Total life-cycle costs are $230. Product B is a new competitor going after the same market as Product A, and is also good for six years. A successful product development effort has resulted in start-up costs for B of only $30, while its postpurchase costs are estimated at $60. The price of B has yet to be determined.

Taking the life-cycle costs for the product currently being sold (A) and subtracting the start-up and postpurchase costs of the new product (B), the result is the economic value to the customer (EVC) of product B. In this case, EVC is $140. Another way to arrive at this figure is to take the price of the existing product and add the savings in start-up and postpurchase costs provided by the new product. Also, if product B had any features not found in product A, these would raise EVC for product B even higher, for the features are a source of incremental value.

EVC provides a justification for charging a higher price than that currently charged for available substitutes. This can be seen in Figure 10.1, which presents an illustration of the EVC for product B. Subtracting the competitor's price ($100) from this EVC figure ($140) gives us $40, which is product B's competitive advantage. However, let's say the price for B is set at $120. The difference between EVC and the actual price charged can be thought of as an inducement to the customer ($20, in this case).

Of course, getting the customer to see the advantages to be found in buying the higher-priced product requires a convincing sales effort. Many customers may not take such a long-term viewpoint. Life-cycle costs are estimates, based on an evaluation by the firm's technical product experts. Further, because start-up and

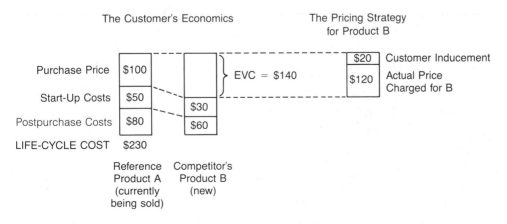

(Note: If Product B is sold for $120, then life-cycle costs for Product B would equal $210).

Figure 10.1 Calculation of Economic Value to the Customer

postpurchase costs are incurred over time, they must be discounted and expressed in present-value terms. Nonetheless, unlike other sources of value, estimates of economic value should be somewhat similar across companies using the product for the same purpose or application.

A FRAMEWORK FOR SETTING INDUSTRIAL PRICES

A number of factors are important in setting an industrial price; examples can be found in Table 10.1. To apply these factors effectively, a comprehensive framework is needed for managers to use in arriving at a price. The framework proposed in this chapter involves the systematic examination of four decision inputs: objectives, costs, demand, and competition. A fifth consideration, legal restrictions, will be discussed toward the end of the chapter. While each of these factors is critical, its relative importance will vary depending on the circumstances which surround the pricing of particular products or services. As a generalization, however, the objectives to be achieved represent the most important element in price setting.

Setting Pricing Objectives

There is no one best price to charge for a given product. Economists would suggest, for example, that profits are maximized if the firm sets price where marginal revenues equal marginal costs. Not only is this conclusion based on a set of impractical assumptions, but also it suggests that the *only* goal in establishing a product's price is profit maximization. In fact, companies can have a number of different pricing objectives.

Table 10.1 Factors in Setting Industrial Prices

market conditions

excess productive capacity

competitive prices

what substitutes are available, at what price

product differentiation

phase of the product's life cycle

growth rate of the market

whether other prices are rising, stable, or falling

your market share

the market's ability to buy

the market's expectations about prices

competitors' typical responses to price changes in your industry

Source: Seymour E. Heymann "Consider Other Factors and Cost When Pricing Industrial Products." *Marketing News,* (April 4, 1980), 11. Copyright American Marketing Association, Reprinted with permission.

Once the need to set or change a price has been recognized, the marketer should address the question, What are we trying to accomplish with the price for this product? The answer might seem obvious: to sell more of the firm's output. But this response is too general, and may not even be the case. For example, a cartel may restrict output and drive up prices on the assumption that the overall effect will be bigger profits.

Table 10.2 provides a partial listing of possible pricing objectives. At the top of list is the profit objective. Even here, however, the marketer must distinguish between long-term and short-term profit goals; one may come at the expense of the other. Also, profit can be defined in a number of ways, including return on investment, return on sales, net income, and earnings per share. At the same time, firms

Table 10.2 Possible Objectives in Setting a Price

1. Target return on investment
2. Target market share
3. Maximum long-run profits
4. Maximum short-run profits
5. Growth
6. Stabilize market
7. Desensitize customers to price
8. Maintain price-leadership arrangement
9. Discourage entrants
10. Speed exit of marginal firms
11. Avoid government investigation and control
12. Maintain loyalty of middlemen and get their sales support
13. Avoid demands for more from suppliers—labor in particular
14. Enhance image of firm and its offerings
15. Be regarded as fair by customers
16. Create interest and excitement about the item
17. Be considered trustworthy and reliable by rivals
18. Help in the sale of weak or other items in the line
19. Discourage others from cutting prices
20. Make a product visible
21. Spoil market to obtain high price for sale of business
22. Build traffic
23. Maximum profits on product line
24. Recover investment quickly

Source: P.J. Peter, J. Donnelly, and L. Tarpey, *A Preface to Marketing Management* 3rd Ed., (Plano, Texas: Business Publications, Inc., 1985), 192. Adapted from Alfred J. Oxenfeldt "A Decision-Making Structure for Price Decisions," *Journal of Marketing,* (January 1973), 50. Reprinted with permission.

rarely maximize profits. Rather, they pursue multiple objectives, and accept trade-offs among these goals. This is a phenomenon termed *satisficing*.

Market share is another common objective in pricing. Conventional wisdom has been that firms that achieve leading market share positions will achieve the volume necessary to take advantage of the experience curve and economies of scale (see Chapter 8 for a discussion of these concepts). The result will be a cost-leadership position that enables the firm to be a price leader. Further, there is some evidence of a direct positive relationship between market share and profitability, where profitability is measured using ROI (Buzzell, Gale, and Sultan 1975). Where high market share is the objective, the pricing approach is generally some variant of a penetration strategy. Here, a price which is low, relative both to perceived customer value and to competitor prices, is charged. The emphasis is on low margins and high volume, with the expectation that those margins will improve somewhat as costs begin to come down. Some other objectives of this low pricing scheme could include creating product visibility, discouraging new market entrants, and speeding the exit of marginal firms.

If a penetration strategy is placed at one end of a continuum of pricing alternatives, a skimming strategy would be found at the other end. Skimming is charging a premium, or relatively high, price for the product or service. The price is set high, relative to what customers are used to paying, or to competitor prices. A number of possible objectives might lie behind such a strategy. The firm may be trying to establish an image as the superior-quality producer of the industry, since buyers often associate higher prices with higher quality (Monroe 1979). Alternatively, the objective may be to capitalize on a market segment whose demand is relatively inelastic. Or, the firm may be trying to allocate its output during a period of supply shortages or scarcity.

Between these two extremes is an intermediate range of moderate pricing alternatives. Since the options are closer to competitor's prices, this approach is called parity pricing. An intermediate-level price might be used when the marketer is trying to stabilize the market, avoid government intervention, be regarded as fair by customers, or maintain a price leadership agreement, among other goals.

At the same time, establishing the prices of products or services in a vacuum should be avoided. Companies are not so much concerned with maximizing returns from individual products as from the overall product mix. Objectives must reflect product line considerations. This kind of product line objective could be found in the firm that sells farm tractors as well as attachments and implements which expand the capability of the basic tractor. The tractors themselves may be priced relatively low, but popular attachments may carry a high price tag to help support overall revenue objectives.

The most commonly used method for setting prices is termed cost-plus pricing—a product's unit costs are estimated, and then some predetermined margin or markup is added to arrive at a list price. Here, the only objective is profit, narrowly defined. This approach is relied upon because of its relative simplicity (especially when the manager is responsible for a large number of products), and because it makes intuitive sense to charge a price that covers product costs and delivers some acceptable rate of return. Cost-plus approaches permit ignoring the complexities of determining demand function, or of anticipating competitor behaviors. This type of

Exhibit 10.1   Managing the Pricing Function: Two Case Studies

In a detailed study comparing how companies within the chemical and construction industries in South Africa set their prices, Abratt and Pitt (1985) developed some interesting insights. Their investigation covered pricing responsibility, factors considered when setting prices, pricing objectives, approach to cost analysis, specific price policies, and pricing strategy used with new products. The following is a summary of their major findings:

(a) In both industries, a high percentage of the people responsible for pricing decisions come from the marketing/sales department, although in the construction industry, senior management tends to get more involved.

(b) In both industries, the most important factors influencing price-setting are costs and the competition; however, the construction industry also regards the economic climate as important. Cost-plus pricing is prevalent in construction and chemicals.

(c) When setting objectives, the construction industry places heavy emphasis on target return on investment followed by market share target. Chemical companies emphasize market share target most frequently, followed by target markup on cost.

(d) One-third of construction companies use full-cost pricing, 17 percent use contribution pricing, and 50 percent use both. In the chemical industry, one-third use full-cost pricing, one-third use a contribution approach, and one-third use both.

(e) When setting pricing policies, the construction industry tends to emphasize uniform prices to different customers, and does not rely heavily on discounts. Chemical companies are more apt to vary price to match the competition, and place slightly more importance on discounts; in general, pricing policies are not well-defined.

(f) When a new product is launched, both industries initially use a price-skimming strategy.

Source: R. Abratt and L.F. Pitt, "Pricing Practices in Two Industries," *Industrial Marketing Management* 14 (New York: Elsevier Science, 1985), 301–306.

pricing might seem a risk-aversive strategy on the surface, but in fact places real limits on the manager's flexibility in responding to marketplace conditions (Guiltinan 1976).

Examining Costs

When a company's pricing objectives have been determined, the second element in the pricing framework is *costs*. They indicate what must be charged for a product to break even, or to achieve a certain rate of return. Even here, however, there are instances where a firm will set price below the full cost of a product. Possible reasons for this include: (a) maintaining the work force and keeping facilities running during temporary periods of slack demand, (b) helping sales of other products in the line, (c) bidding low on an individual contract to establish a relation with a certain customer or a position in a particular market, (d) gaining experience, or (e) to acquire some new skill (Corey 1983).

In this section, two approaches to cost analysis for pricing are presented: standard cost analysis and contribution analysis.

Standard Cost Analysis

A popular approach to assessing costs for the purpose of price setting is *target-return pricing*—a type of cost-plus pricing (discussed earlier), where the manager attempts to establish a price for a product which will generate a predetermined rate of return on capital.

To set a price, the manager first must estimate the quantity or volume of the product to be produced during the next year, or the average annual volume over a number of years. This forecast becomes the cornerstone of the firm's pricing strategy, so its accuracy is critical. The estimate is called *standard volume*.

For a given standard volume, the manager determines what unit labor and material costs will be, then adds any other variable costs (e.g., sales commissions), to arrive at variable cost per unit. In addition, the total fixed costs are estimated for this range of production, and then divided by standard volume to get fixed costs per unit. Fixed costs are allocated evenly across units of production for a given product. These variable cost and fixed cost estimates are called *standard costs*.

The desired level of profit per unit is added to these standard costs. This desired level of return is determined by taking the required rate of return times the amount of capital, or operating assets, employed in producing and distributing the product, and then dividing that total by standard volume. In summary, the price to be changed is equal to:

$$P = DVC + \frac{FC}{Q} + \frac{rK}{Q}$$

Where P = price
    DVC = direct variable cost per unit
      FC = fixed cost
       r = desired rate of return
      K = capital employed
      Q = estimate of standard unit volume

So, assume that direct variable costs per unit are $8, and total fixed costs are $400,000. The company projects standard volume at 200,000 units. The product will require $1 million in capital. Further assuming a required rate of return of 20 percent, the formula will produce a price of $11 per unit.

In practice, industrial firms often use much more elaborate versions of the formula. Other factors built into the equation might include debt interest rates, tax rates, or an inflation factor. Further complicating the calculation, costs frequently are not so easily placed into fixed and variable categories; they may be broken out and allocated in any number of ways for the purpose of a target-return formula.

The target-return approach to pricing has a number of limitations. If actual sales fall short of the standard volume estimate, then the only way to achieve the desired rate of return is to raise prices, which seems counter-intuitive. This approach also can lead to what has been called the doom loop. Prices are raised, volume subsequently falls, causing unit costs to rise as scale economies are lost—whereupon the formula will force the marketer to raise price further, and so on.

In addition, wide fluctuations in demand create problems for firms using target-return pricing, as it becomes difficult to determine reliable standard volume estimates. These fluctuations may be due, in part, to competitor actions, and may warrant a pricing response. AT&T provides an example. Prior to deregulation in the telecommunications industry, and the company's forced divestiture of the local telephone operating companies, demand for many of its products was fairly predictable. Most of this demand came from the operating companies, so it was captive. Target-return pricing worked fairly well in such a constrained and stable environment. In a less regulated and more competitive market, demand is more volatile, and the inflexibility of target-return pricing results in prices that are too high for some products, and too low for others.

Target-return prices are arrived at by fully allocating fixed costs to units of a product. The method used to allocate is arbitrary, regardless of how logical it may seem. In fact, alternative methods for allocating overhead can produce quite different prices. This allocation problem is especially apparent where a company produces a number of products with shared fixed costs, and these products vary in terms of how labor- or capital-intensive each is. Full-cost pricing also ignores the idea that products in different stages of their life cycles will not be equally profitable, or that companies may initially price low to generate volume which will, in turn, bring unit costs down (Monroe 1979).

Contribution Analysis

When setting the price of a new product, the marketer often will find it useful to estimate the volume of sales necessary to either break even or achieve some level of profitability at different prices. The marketer who is considering a price cut wants to know how many more units must be sold, to at least maintain the current level of revenue. If a price increase is under consideration, then the concern becomes the number of unit sales which can be lost before the firm is any worse off than its current position.

What must happen? questions can be answered through contribution analysis. This analysis is based on the logic that a product first should be held accountable for those costs which are directly attributable to its production and distribution (i.e., direct costs). Then, assuming it generates enough revenue to cover these costs, any remaining revenue would be applied to indirect costs (i.e., costs which are not directly attributable to the product) and profits. To perform contribution analysis, the total variable costs for a product are subtracted from its total revenue. The difference is called the variable contribution margin. This margin can be expressed on a per unit basis by taking the product's price and subtracting unit variable costs. Dividing contribution per unit into fixed costs, the result is the number of units which must be sold to break even. If a profit of, say, $10,000 was desired, then this figure would be added to fixed costs before dividing by contribution per unit. (A more detailed discussion of costs can be found in Chapter 14).

As a hypothetical example, consider Everlight Corporation, a manufacturer who develops a standard 72-inch-long fluorescent lamp that burns 50 usage hours longer, and uses 10 percent less energy, than available lamps. Primary customers would be factories, packing houses, assembly operations, and similar types of production facilities. The variable manufacturing costs incurred in producing the new lamp are estimated to average six dollars per unit. A plant to manufacture the lamp would have to be built and equipped for, let's say, $7,000,000 and depreciated over seven years. Administrative overhead is projected to be $200,000 annually, while sales and distribution expenses are estimated at $300,000 per year. Therefore, annual fixed costs will be $1,500,000.

Assume that annual sales of fluorescent lamps of this particular type are 5 million units. Further, assume that these sales are primarily accounted for by ten major manufacturers, the three largest having 70 percent market share among them. The market leader currently charges its distributors eight dollars for lamps of this standard variety.

The manufacturer of the new lamp wants to evaluate the viability of various prices, initially assessing the feasibility of charging $9.00, $8.00, $7.50, or $7.00. These prices have been selected because of their proximity to competitor prices, and to provide management with a starting point from which to assess costs using a contribution approach. If the contribution margin is calculated for each of the pricing alternatives, the result is:

$$
\begin{array}{cccc}
\$9.00 & \$8.00 & \$7.50 & \$7.00 \\
\underline{6.00} & \underline{6.00} & \underline{6.00} & \underline{6.00} \\
\$3.00 & \$2.00 & \$1.50 & \$1.00
\end{array}
$$

The units and market share required to break even at each price can now be calculated:

Price	Breakeven Units		Breakeven Market Share	
$9.00	$\dfrac{\$1,500,000}{\$3.00}$	$= 500,000$ units	$\dfrac{500,000}{5,000,000}$	$= 10\%$
$8.00	$\dfrac{\$1,500,000}{\$2.00}$	$= 750,000$ units	$\dfrac{750,000}{5,000,000}$	$= 15\%$
$7.50	$\dfrac{\$1,500,000}{\$1.50}$	$= 1,000,000$ units	$\dfrac{1,000,000}{5,000,000}$	$= 20\%$
$7.00	$\dfrac{\$1,500,000}{\$1.00}$	$= 1,500,000$ units	$\dfrac{1,500,000}{5,000,000}$	$= 30\%$

As can be seen, the new manufacturer will need to capture 15 percent of this market, if the competitor's price is matched, just to break even. If a penetration pricing strategy is attempted, where the manufacturer attempts to attract attention and market share by going in below the current market price, a price cut of only $.50 would require 20 percent share, and a cut of $1.00 would require 30 percent share. Given the competitive structure of this market, this goal might seem overly ambitious, especially if the competition is able to duplicate this innovation. Now, it might be argued that the 30 percent is achievable given how superior the new lamp is and, at such a relatively low price, that customers would be lining up to purchase it. However, if the lamp is that much better, then it is providing the customer with more value. A higher price may be in order to convey this superior value.

At a price of nine dollars, only 10 percent of the market must be captured to break even. Such an approach is closer to a skimming strategy. The marketer may be trying to achieve a quality image then, or to go after a particular segment that is less price-sensitive. Or, the marketer may use the EVC concept to argue that he or she is actually saving money for the customer over the product's useful life.

The point is that cost analysis does provide some important insight into what price should be charged. This analysis must be considered, however, within the context of the objectives management is trying to achieve (e.g., market share, image, and profit). The final pricing decision depends further, however, on a detailed analysis of demand and competitive reaction.

Assessing Demand

Cost/Benefit Analysis

Earlier, this chapter stressed that price should be a reflection of the value a customer is receiving from a product. Accordingly, the marketer must have a thorough understanding of the customer's usage of the item and the utility it provides. When assessing demand, it is helpful to perform an analysis of the benefits received, and the costs incurred, by the customer in purchasing and using the product.

In examining benefits, a distinction can be drawn between hard and soft benefits. *Hard* benefits refer to the physical attributes of the product, while *soft* benefits include service, training, warranties, delivery, company reputation, and other supporting elements which were referred to in Chapter 7 as the augmented product. It is generally easier to evaluate the customer's utility for hard benefits. A given customer will have specific requirements regarding such physical product characteristics as horsepower, production rate, durability, error rate, or performance tolerances. The marketer can calculate price-performance ratios if he or she divides the price in dollars by the benefit measured in units. For a copying machine, then, the price-performance ratio might be dollars divided by copies produced per minute. Comparisons can then be drawn between the price-performance ratios of various competitors.

Soft benefits are more difficult to assess. The relative importance of a warranty, for example, will vary widely from customer to customer, and even among those within the buying center in a given organization. At a minimum, the marketer should attempt to estimate the utility of the benefit by market segment.

In examining the cost side of the equation, the marketer wants to consider the complete range of expenses a customer will incur in purchasing and using the product in question. The marketer may need to go further, however, because the customer may be concerned about costs which would be incurred only if something went wrong. For example, in purchasing a piece of machinery, the customer may be concerned about what it would cost if the machinery became defective and the production process had to be shut down. The risk of such a development represents a real cost.

Having identified the important benefits and costs to the customer, the next step is to evaluate possible cost-benefit trade-off decisions. Customers who are willing to hold more inventory in return for slower delivery by a less expensive mode of transportation are trading off costs and benefits. A quantity discount may also provide the incentive to purchase larger stocks, if the amount of the discount exceeds the costs of maintaining the inventory. Similarly, the decision to purchase an optional feature on some product should reflect the perception that the benefit received exceeds the price paid (including life-cycle costs).

Elasticity of Demand

Cost-benefit trade-offs that an industrial customer is willing and able to make will be reflected in that customer's price elasticity. Demand elasticity is a measure of the sensitivity of the customer's quantity demanded to changes in price; it is an important indicator to the marketer of the feasibility of various pricing alternatives.

The demand curve for most products is normally negative in slope, indicating that customers buy more at lower prices. This is illustrated in Figure 10.2. To prop-

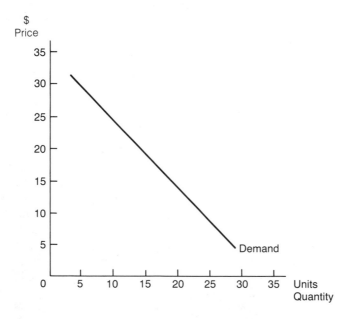

Figure 10.2   Illustration of a Demand Curve

erly gauge this price-quantity relationship, the analyst must control any other variables which impact upon customer demand, such as the customer's sales volume, customer preferences, the price of substitute goods, customer expectations regarding inflation or product availability, and others. Only by factoring out these variables, or holding them constant, can the marketer begin to accurately describe the nature of the demand curve for his or her products. Usually, a different demand curve exists for each market segment. These curves can be combined into an aggregate demand function for the product in question.

Elasticity is measured over some range of a demand curve, and in fact, changes along the demand curve. To determine elasticity, divide the percentage change in quantity (which results from a price increase or decrease) by the percentage change in price (which caused that increase or decrease in quantity demanded). If the percentage change in quantity exceeds the percentage change in price, demand is said to be *elastic,* or sensitive. If the percentage change in price exceeds the percentage change in quantity, demand is said to be *inelastic,* or insensitive. Similarly, the flatter (more horizontal) the demand curve, the more elastic is demand. As the curve becomes steeper (more vertical), demand is becoming more inelastic.

Elasticity is an indicator of how price changes can be expected to affect total company revenues. Cutting prices will lead to a loss of revenue if demand is inelastic, and an increase in revenue if demand is elastic. Conversely, raising prices will result in higher revenues if demand is inelastic, but lower revenues where demand is elastic.

Keep in mind that an increase in revenue does not necessarily translate into an increase in profits. The behavior of costs must be examined. For example, the marketer may cut price because demand appears quite elastic. The increased demand, induced by the price cut, results in increased production volume and higher revenues. However, because of capacity limitations, raw material shortages, or labor constraints, unit costs of producing and distributing this extra volume are higher. Consequently, overall profit may actually be lower.

Four major factors determine how elastic a customer's demand will be: the availability of substitutes, the extent to which the product in question is a necessity, the relative dollar size of the purchase, and time. Demand for a product will tend to be more elastic in a situation where there are many substitutes, the item is not a necessity, or the item represents a sizable percentage of the customer's budget or spendable income. Demand also tends to become more elastic over time. The most important factor—and fundamental to all of them—is the availability of substitutes, or the number of alternatives available to the customer for satisfying a given need.

As a generalization, the demand for industrial products tends to be relatively inelastic, or price-insensitive. This is because many industrial products are technically sophisticated, customized, or critical to the customer's operations. That is, they are necessity items with few available substitutes.

However, there are many exceptions. Industrial customers may demonstrate elastic demand for many routine-order products that are fairly undifferentiated in terms of performance or delivery characteristics, and for which there is considerable competition. Demand elasticity tends to be situational, dependent upon customer and marketplace circumstances at a given point in time.

For a given customer group and product type, elasticity will also change over the range of the demand curve. Thus, demand may be fairly inelastic for a product within a given range of prices, but may become elastic once price exceeds some threshold level. Importantly, substitutes which would not have been considered in the lower price range become viable alternatives once price exceeds that threshold.

The marketer is in a position to affect a customer's elasticity of demand. Ideally, it may be beneficial to the marketer for customers to be relatively inelastic in their demand for his or her product. This inelastic demand can be achieved by convincing customers that there are few *acceptable* substitutes, and that the product is a "must" item that they really should not be without (i.e., that they require to achieve a competitive advantage). Companies such as 3M, IBM, Sperry, and Xerox have successfully achieved this image in establishing loyal customer franchises for their brand name products.

Marketers often will find that demand elasticities vary across market segments. Where variation exists among segments, there may be an economic justification for price discrimination. That is, two different segments might be charged different prices, dependent upon how elastic their respective demand functions are. The price variable may be more important to purchasers in one segment than those in another. If large users are given a price break, for example, such a tactic would suggest not only that it is more economical to sell to large users, but also that such customers are sensitive (elastic) to such price breaks.

Before leaving the concept of elasticity, it is worth noting that products also can have *cross-elasticities,* where the price of one product affects the demand for another product. The coefficient of cross-elasticity is defined as the percentage change in quantity demanded for product A divided by the percentage change in price for product B. This coefficient can vary from minus infinity to plus infinity. Where products are complements (e.g., electrical drills and drill bits) they will have negative cross-elasticities. Substitute commodities (e.g., delivery by truck rather than by train) have positive cross-elasticities. In making pricing decisions, then, it is worth evaluating other products in the line to determine positive or negative cross-elasticities (see Exhibit 10.2). The marketer also wants to be wary of the effect which the prices charged by other companies have on his or her sales. Again, such cross-elasticities can be positive or negative.

Cross-elasticity analysis can be accomplished to some extent with informal observation, and its application to pricing is common for companies with large product lines. An office supply company provides an example. The typical office supply company has a set of clients who have a standard reorder pattern for supplies. It also has another set that reorders more sporadically, and may even shop among the various local office supply companies for better prices on specific items. Periodically, an aggressive supply house will run price specials on items in its line. If a 20 percent price saving was offered on printers, computer paper, and printer ribbons, the saving would probably elicit a good response in terms of total unit sales. However, reflection on the cross-elasticities of demand would reveal that these are complementary products (paper and ribbons are normally bought along with printers), so it would actually be better to offer a special on printers and to hold paper and ribbon prices at their normal levels, since the price incentive would not be as im-

Exhibit 10.2   How Cross-Elasticities Can Cause Problems

When products have positive cross-elasticities within a product line, customers see them as effective substitutes. Products are sometimes perceived as substitutes against the wishes of management. Often this is due to errors in pricing strategy. AT&T provides us with an example in the computer business.

In the second quarter of 1986, IBM announced a list price decrease for their PC-XT/AT product line. In response, AT&T dropped the list price on the PC 6300 PLUS, a top-of-the-line product which competed directly with IBM. At about the same, product management for the PC 6300 line introduced product improvements and updates for some of the products in the line (increased RAM from 256K to 640K and new ROM B105 revision 1.43) with an *increase* in the list price on the affected product.

The company used value-added resellers (VARs: middlemen who combine the separate products of different manufacturers within the computer industry into a tailored operating system for specialty markets, such as banks, retailers, law firms, or hotels). The VAR channel viewed the new price differentials within AT&T's personal computer line as being too close together. They concluded that the PC 3600 PLUS must not be as good a top-line product as previously thought. Further, the VARs were upset with the increased prices on some of the products in the line at a time when competitors were slashing prices on MS-DOS, 8086 processor machines (especially when the price increases were for memory increases, the VARs could add value at a greatly reduced cost themselves).

portant to the buyer of printers. In fact, it would be more advantageous to offer a discount based on repurchases of printer paper and ribbons over time and thereby convert the price-sensitive supplies buyers into more loyal customers.

Analyzing the Competition

Industrial pricing policies that reflect company objectives, costs, and demand considerations can still be ineffective unless they also address the competitive environment. Given the complexity of the price variable, the importance of life-cycle costs, the role of discounts, and the many ways in which prices can be varied, it becomes crucial that competitor actions and reactions regarding pricing decisions be anticipated and continually monitored.

The purpose in examining competitor prices is not simply to ensure the marketer is charging the same amount or less, although this goal tends to be emphasized in competitive bidding. Rather, the marketer is attempting to examine the value his or her product delivers to different customer groups in comparison to that provided by the competition. However, he or she must go one step further, and anticipate ways in which a competitor will alter its pricing policies once the price is established.

Industrial markets tend to have an oligopolistic structure. That is, a relatively small number of firms have a disproportionate share of the market. Fewness is the name of the game; four or five companies may account for 80 to 90 percent of a given market. This economic concentration has a major impact on the pricing practices within the industry. Where markets are oligopolistic, the strategies pursued by companies are heavily interdependent. That is, whatever one firm does, say with its price, is dependent upon what other firms do, and its actions also affect the decisions of those other firms. This has led to the development of profit-payoff tables, such as the one illustrated in Figure 10.3.

The profitability of both the Abel Company and the Baker Company in Figure 10.3 is determined by the price each charges; four possible prices are considered. Thus, if Abel charges $7 for its product, and Baker charges $8 for a competitive product, it is estimated that Abel will make $12.8 million in profits, while Baker makes $13.8 million.

Pricing Strategies for Baker Company

Pricing Strategies for Abel Company

Baker's Price / Abel's Price	$10	$ 9	$ 8	$ 7
$10	$13.5 / $20.1	$10.3 / $17.9	$16.9 / $17.8	$14.0 / $15.3
$ 9	$12.4 / $15.5	$ 5.6 / $13.4	$13.0 / $13.4	$ 8.5 / $11.0
$ 8	$14.4 / $16.2	$10.8 / $14.2	$17.3 / $14.2	$14.6 / $11.5
$ 7	$11.7 / $15.0	$ 7.8 / $12.8	$13.8 / $12.8	$10.6 / $10.7

Key:

Baker's Profit Before Taxes (Millions) / Abel's Profit Before Taxes (Millions)

Figure 10.3 A Profit-Payoff Matrix

However, assume Abel charged $7 and Baker matched that by also charging $7. Note that there is still a difference in the profits earned by each firm, despite their similar prices. This difference is due to a disparity in their underlying cost structures. Abel would appear to be operating more efficiently at this level of price and corresponding volume. After further study, Baker may see that its profits would be improved if it raised its price to $8. If Baker does so, however, Abel may then conclude that its profits would improve if it now charges $10. Prices may well stabilize at this level, for neither party can gain from a change to another price within this range.

It has been suggested that the industrial firm in an oligopolistic market will pursue one of four strategic pricing options: pressure pricing, opportunistic pricing, gold-standard pricing, and negotiated pricing (Sultan 1974; Webster 1984). The first two represent longer-term strategies over time, while the latter two are appropriate for short-term individual transactions. *Pressure pricing* involves a market leader maintaining price at a fairly stable level regardless of fluctuations in demand, and managing price increases in a controlled manner. Competitors, facing prices kept stable during periods of demand upswing, are discouraged from entering the market. *Opportunistic pricing,* on the other hand, involves raising a price as high as customer elasticity and goodwill permit, and similarly lowering it in accord with market forces. *Gold-standard pricing* is the short-run policy of quoting all customers the same price, regardless of specific circumstances. Alternatively, *negotiated pricing* involves tailoring the price charged to the individual customer or customer segment based on the demand elasticity of, and the nature of competitive alternatives available to, that particular type of customer. The marketer may find it effective to combine an overall longer-term strategy with a more specific short-term strategy. For example, the firm that relies upon opportunistic pricing over time is likely to use negotiated pricing in dealing with a specific account.

Putting the Four Together

With the completion of a detailed analysis of the competitive situation, the marketer has now moved through all four components of the pricing framework, and is now in a position to establish pricing positions. Note that the sequence started with objectives, then considered costs, demand, and finally, competition. However, they do not have to be approached in this particular order. Also, once objectives are established, the relative emphasis placed on cost, competition, or demand considerations will differ, depending on the pricing problem. Exhibit 10.3 shows how these four components come together for the example of a price change.

In many instances, a company's price takes the form of a competitive bid. In these cases, competitive considerations become paramount. Let us turn to a more detailed examination of this type of pricing.

Competitive Bidding

Formal bidding is encountered most frequently when selling to the government and other public agencies, as discussed in Chapter 2, and when selling nonstandard

Exhibit 10.3   Analysis of a Price Change

Jefferson Chemical Company produces a variety of specialty and commodity chemicals, including muriatic acid, for industrial use. Based on a decline in market share over the past year, the product line manager has proposed that the firm either cut price by 10 percent or increase sales and promotional support by $50,000. How would a marketer go about evaluating the price component of this manager's suggestions?

The first step would concern product and company objectives. What are the implications of the price cut for the image of our product? How will the price cut affect other products in the line? What is the profit goal associated with such a price cut? Much of the remaining analysis follows from objectives in these areas. Assume the goal to be a 5 percent increase in profit, and that this increase is the sole objective of concern.

The next step would involve examining costs. A logical approach would be to determine the increase in sales needed to cover the lost unit revenue from the price cut (i.e., to break even on the price cut) plus the sales necessary to increase total contribution by 5 percent. This could be accomplished by determining the total amount of contribution dollars currently being generated by the product (before the price cut), and adding to this a 10 percent increase in contribution. This total figure would then be divided by the new contribution margin (P–VC) which would result from the price cut. The result would be a required sales figure. Current sales would be subtracted from this figure, leaving the required sales increase.

The required increase would next be expressed as a percentage of current sales. Assume it to be 20 percent. This brings us to demand analysis. The company requires a 20 percent increase in sales in response to a 10 percent price reduction, which suggests demand must be fairly elastic. Is this likely to happen? Based on experience and knowledge of the market, management must determine if customers are that price-sensitive. This analysis raises questions about the importance of price compared to other product attributes, the strength of existing customer loyalties, and the extent to which market potential (both users and usage rates) has already been reached.

Finally, even if the analysis up to this point indicates that the price cut makes sense, management must anticipate competitor reactions. How does our cost structure compare to theirs? How dependent on cash flows from this product are they? How well-established are their customer ties in this product area? Do they view this market as growing, mature, or declining? The answers to these questions will provide insight into whether or not competitors will match the price cut.

materials or complex products made to buyer specification (usually at prices which exceed $300) to commercial enterprises. Job-shop companies, and those making products with a long manufacturing cycle, often will rely on a bidding process to secure business. Although government bidding generally awards the contract to the lowest bidder, this outcome is much less frequently the case for commercial bidding. Commercial enterprises will generally solicit fewer bids, and often temper a given company's bid by an evaluation of that bidder's ability to meet quality, design, and delivery requirements. Alternatively, the invitation to submit bids (i.e., request for proposal) will have very precise quality and service specifications, and bidders may be asked to provide a performance bond with their bids.

In addition, bidding can be either sealed or open. Sealed (or closed) bidding requires each potential vendor to submit a sealed written proposal, and typically all bids are opened, evaluated, and a decision rendered at a prespecified point in time. The lowest bid will usually win. With open (or negotiated) bidding, offers are formally made, sometimes verbally, after which the buyer may provide feedback that prompts a vendor to adjust its bid. This method is, in a sense, a combination of bidding and negotiation.

The industrial marketer should consider a number of key criteria in determining whether or not to bid on a project (Dobler, Lee, and Burt 1984). Some of these include:

(a) Is the dollar value of the purchase large enough to warrant the expense involved in making a bid?

(b) Are the specifications of the product or service precise, and can the cost of producing the product or service be accurately estimated?

(c) How will getting the bid affect capacity utilization and our ability to serve other customers? Will it affect other products in our line?

(d) How many potential bidders are there likely to be, and how anxious are they to get this business?

(e) How much time is available to put together an adequate bid and to have it considered by the customer?

Once the decision has been made to make a bid, a bidding strategy must be developed. One of the more popular approaches to competitive bidding, and one with a proven record of success, is probabilistic bidding. This technique assumes the pricing objective to be profit maximization. Also, the assumption is made that customers will select the lowest bid submitted. Three variables are focused upon: the size of the bid, the expected profit if the bid wins, and the probability that the bid will win. A trade-off exists between bid amount or profit, on the one hand, and the probability of winning, on the other. With probabilistic bidding, the marketer is objectively trying to identify the optimal trade-off.

The optimum bid, then, seeks to maximize the basic equation provided below (Morse 1975):

$$E(X) = P(X)Z(X)$$

Where X = dollar amount of the bid
$Z(X)$ = profit if the bid is accepted
$P(X)$ = probability of acceptance at this bid price
$E(X)$ = expected profit at this bid price

The most difficult task facing the marketer when using this formula is estimating the probability of a given bid being the lowest one submitted (the probability of winning). This factor is P(X) in the equation above. The ability to make that estimate is dependent upon the marketer's experience in this market and with these competitors.

The marketer can use such experience to estimate data similar to that in Table 10.3. Determining actual probabilities would involve the following step-by-step process. For simplicity, assume the marketer is only bidding against a single competitor. First, determine how much the competitor bid in the past on projects similar to the one being bid on (Column 1, Table 10.3). Second, determine how much the mar-

Table 10.3 Estimating Probabilities for Use by the Marketer in
Competitive Bidding

	Competitor's Bid ($)	Marketer's Estimated Direct Costs ($)	Competitor's Bid as a Percentage of the Marketer's Direct Costs	Number of Times Competitor Submitted a Bid Higher Than This % of Direct Costs	Percent Higher (Probability of Underbidding if Marketer's Bid is Less Than This % of Direct Costs)
Project 1	39,600	30,000	132	16	0.80
Project 2	176,800	130,000	136	12	0.60
Project 3	125,600	80,000	157	02	0.10
Project 4	67,500	50,000	135	13	0.65
Project 5	145,000	100,000	145	07	0.35
Project 6	22,200	20,000	111	19	0.95
Project 7	129,720	94,000	138	11	0.55
Project 8	24,160	16,000	151	04	0.20
Project 9	107,520	64,000	168	00	0.00
Project 10	198,800	140,000	142	10	0.50
Project 11	59,400	44,000	135	13	0.65
Project 12	121,800	84,000	145	07	0.35
Project 13	79,800	60,000	133	15	0.75
Project 14	59,600	40,000	149	05	0.25
Project 15	46,500	30,000	155	03	0.15
Project 16	68,880	42,000	164	01	0.05
Project 17	95,040	72,000	132	16	0.80
Project 18	86,400	60,000	144	08	0.40
Project 19	82,320	56,000	147	06	0.30
Project 20	147,500	118,000	125	18	0.90

Source: Adapted from W.J. Morse, (1975), "Probabilistic Bidding Models: A Synthesis," *Business Horizons,* 18 (April), 79–80.

keter's own direct costs would have been to complete each of those projects (Column 2). Third, express the competitor's bid on each of those projects as a percentage of the marketer's direct costs (Column 3). Fourth, for each of the bids submitted by the competitor, count the number of times the bid was higher than this percentage of the marketer's estimated direct costs on a project (Column 4). Looking at Project 14, the competitor's bid was 149 percent of the marketer's direct cost on that job. Only five times did the competitor submit bids that were a higher percentage of the marketer's direct costs. Finally, express this number as a proportion of all twenty bids (Column 5). This proportion represents the probability of the marketer winning the bid if he or she bids less than a given percentage of his or her own direct costs.

So, let's say the marketer submitted a bid on Project X (a new product) that was equal to 149 percent of his or her company's estimated direct costs on the project. If, in total, the competitor had submitted bids on similar projects twenty times in the past, and five of those were at a price exceeding 149 percent of the marketer's estimated direct costs on the project, then the marketer has a 25 percent probability of winning bids on projects similar to Project X at this bid.

Unfortunately, the marketer frequently either has no experience in a particular product market area, or is unable to obtain reasonably accurate data concerning the previous bids of competitors, or their costs. As a result, probabilities are estimated in a subjective manner, based on bidding and pricing experience, competitor analysis, market intelligence, management intuition, and related factors. Whether it is

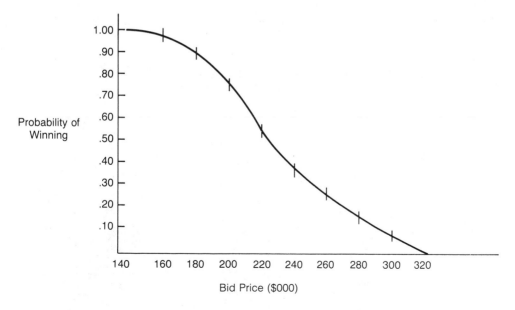

Figure 10.4 Thompson Corporation's Estimated Probability of Underbidding the Competition
(Source: Adapted from W.J. Morse, (1975), "Probabilistic Bidding Models: A Synthesis," *Business Horizons*, 18, (April), 69.)

based on hard data regarding previous bids or upon more subjective estimates, the objective is to detail the relationships between winning the bid and the range of possible bid prices.

Take the example of a computer manufacturer, Thompson Corporation, bidding on a job to provide computers to a chemical company for training new plant operations personnel. At least three other firms are expected to submit bids. All are qualified sources of supply, so the lowest bid should be the one selected. Thompson's costs to produce the computers have been estimated at $180,000. The marketing department, based on an evaluation of competitor positions and an assessment of historical bidding processes on similar jobs, has constructed a diagram relating the range of possible bid prices to the estimated probabilities of winning the bid. This is illustrated in Figure 10.4, which suggests that a bid of $140,000 has 100 percent chance of winning, while a bid of $320,000 has zero chance of winning.

With these probabilities in hand, the marketer can now determine expected profit at each price using the basic equation described earlier. Table 10.4 illustrates the profit at each bid price. These profit figures are then taken times the probability of being selected at that bid price, resulting in the expected profit figures. The analysis indicates that $220,000 is the optimum bid price, for this is where expected profit is highest. To corroborate this optimum bid, calculate expected profit for intermediate bids of $215,000 and $225,000.

The approach described here represents a more basic bidding model. While this model and more complex ones do produce an *ideal* bid price, the decision maker must recognize that these are only tools to aid in the price decision. In practice, such bids are often further modified by managerial judgment. The models may be used to simply provide direction in bidding strategy.

Table 10.4 An Application of the Probability Bidding Model to Thompson Corporation

Bid Price	Cost	Cumulative Probability of Winning at this Bid	Profit	Expected Profit
$320,000	$180,000	.00	$140,000	$ 0
300,000	180,000	.05	120,000	6,000
280,000	180,000	.15	100,000	15,000
260,000	180,000	.25	80,000	20,000
240,000	180,000	.35	60,000	21,000
220,000	180,000	.55	40,000	22,000
200,000	180,000	.76	20,000	15,000
180,000	180,000	.90	0	0
160,000	180,000	.97	(20,000)	(19,400)
140,000	180,000	1.00	(40,000)	(40,000)

Source: Adapted from R. Haas, *Industrial Marketing Management,* (Boston: Kent Publishing, 1982), 335.

Bids, once made, are also not always at a fixed price. When the supplier's costs are unstable and inflationary, a common approach to hedging risk is the use of escalator clauses. Here a fixed price bid is agreed upon, but the agreement allows for price increases if certain of the supplier's costs rise during the period of the contract. Such costs may be linked to economic indices, such as the wholesale price index. Changes in the index permit adjustments in certain cost estimates and the price charged.

PRICING OVER THE LIFE CYCLE

The concept of the industrial product life cycle was introduced in Chapter 8. The marketer will rely on varying strategies as a product moves through the stages of its economic life; pricing strategy provides an example. Price is a key factor in each stage, but particularly in the introductory stage.

For example, earlier in this chapter, a range of options was presented, with penetration (low) pricing at one end, parity (matching competition) pricing in the middle, and premium or skimming (high) on the other end. The question of which to use must be addressed in the introductory stage of the life cycle.

This initial strategy places constraints on any subsequent pricing decisions. As a case in point, consider the marketer who uses a penetration strategy in anticipation of significant cost savings with large volume production—then does not achieve such economies. Although a price increase may be desirable, the market may strongly resist such a change, for it has come to equate a certain amount of value with a given price. It is almost always easier to lower price than to raise price.

Also, the marketer does not necessarily set a single price for a product in each stage of its life. Different segments come into play in each stage, perhaps with differing demand elasticities. Charging a relatively high price initially may be related to an initial target segment that views the product as a necessity with few or no substitutes. As other segments enter the market, different pricing strategies can be tailored to their differing needs.

One danger in introductory stage pricing is attempting to recoup too quickly any R&D expenditures incurred prior to introduction. These expenditures can be significant, and place an undue burden on the new product. Their recovery, together with an acceptable rate of return, should be achieved over a product's life cycle.

A product in the growth stage typically is facing new competitive entries and the development of more specialized need segments. The benefits of scale economies and the experience curve, if any, are beginning to surface. A common market price begins to emerge in this stage, with the range of acceptable prices narrowing. The marketer is encountering downward pressure on prices, although this depends upon the extent of product differentiation among competitors, and the rate at which technological improvements are being made to the product. Exhibit 10.4 provides a graphic example, using the computer chip. Also, in the growth stage, individual benefit segments may surface, varying in their willingness to pay for specific attribute bundles (e.g., faster delivery, smaller inventories, better service). There may still be a substantial primary demand gap (see Chapter 8), meaning the marketer need not focus solely on price-based competition.

Exhibit 10.4   Life Cycle Evolution for the Computer Chip

The pricing implications of a product racing through its product life cycle and experiencing dramatic improvements in production efficiencies are vividly seen in the microcomputer chip industry. The first chips, introduced in the early 1970s, necessarily carried the burdens of heavy R&D costs. In addition, they were produced with new plants and production processes, which added to these cost burdens. The graph provides a simplified comparison of the capacity and cost aspects of microcomputer chips over several years. Whereas a 64K chip may have been priced at close to $500 in the early 1970s, it was priced close to $10 in 1987. Both demand and the supply sides of the product life cycle are responsible for this sharp decrease in price. In the instance of demand, the workstation computer has been transformed from a luxury to a near-necessity for most companies today. That is, the number of buyers has increased thousands-fold, to the point that almost every business has come to depend greatly on some type of computer. The knowledge that the market has grown to such a huge size allowed companies to expand their plants and production capacities with more confidence and to effect lower average costs per unit. At the same time, technological advances, some incorporating the same microchips produced in previous generations, allowed for greater quality control and more memory capacity on each chip. The industry has moved from slow hand assembly to fast robotic and computer-controlled assembly. Once research and investment costs were paid back, or alternatively, spread over thousands of units rather than hundreds, and as more competitors rushed into the industry, wholesale prices dropped dramatically.

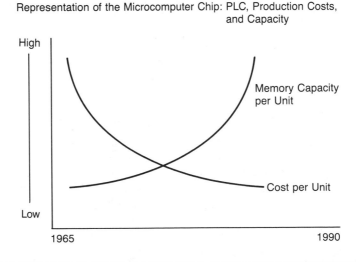

Representation of the Microcomputer Chip: PLC, Production Costs, and Capacity

With maturity comes an increasingly saturated market, and fairly well-entrenched and aggressive competition. At the same time, competitors may see the product area as a cash generator, which they use to support newer, growth stage products and services. The marketer focuses largely on repeat sales to established customers, and on internal cost efficiencies. Competition is more heavily price-based, although head-to-head price wars are likely to be dysfunctional. Under such circumstances, the marketer should probably attempt to maximize short-term direct product contribution to profit.

Market decline presents a number of pricing opportunities. For example, the marketer may raise price, to take advantage of any remaining segments with inelastic demand. The spare parts business represents an example. Alternatively, the strategy might be to cut expenditures and leave the price alone, letting the product die a natural death. Another strategy might be to cut the price perhaps to break-even or lower, and use the product as a loss leader to help sell other complementary products in the line.

SPECIAL TOPICS IN INDUSTRIAL PRICING

The Role of Discounts and Incentives

The industrial marketing organization has at its disposal a variety of price concessions that it can offer a customer. These include prepaid freight, drop-shipping privileges, installment financing, postdating, liberal returns allowances, rebate programs, and others. Chief among these, at least in terms of use, is the structure of discounts provided to customers.

Three types of discounts are provided to industrial customers or to middlemen: cash, quantity, and trade. Cash discounts are given to encourage speedy payment of invoices. A cash discount might be quoted as 3/10, n 30, indicating the buyer will receive a 3 percent discount if the invoice is paid within ten days. Otherwise, the credit period until full payment is due extends for thirty days. Additional price incentives may be given for payment prior to receipt of goods or upon delivery.

Quantity discounts are also quite common in industrial markets, providing an incentive to buy in large dollar amounts or large unit amounts. The discount can also be cumulative or noncumulative. Cumulative quantity discounts allow the buyer to include a series of purchases over some prespecified time period in determining the size of the discount for which he or she qualifies. Noncumulative discounts apply only to a single purchase. These discounts frequently are applied not just to a single item, but also to a set of products within the marketer's line.

Trade (or functional) discounts are provided to middlemen such as industrial distributors, to encourage distributor support for the marketer's products. Discounts frequently are used to encourage the performance of specific functions, such as storage or warehousing, selling activities, transportation, and promotional efforts.

Discounts can result in significant saving off the list price. Consider the case of a manufacturer selling fire extinguishers to commercial firms and institutions through industrial distributors. Assume the discount structure includes terms of

Table 10.5 Application of Manufacturer's Discount Structure to the
Hospital Distributor Company

The Hospital Distributor Company order:	
10 extinguishers at $45.00 each	$ 450.00
15 extinguishers at $24.00 each	360.00
10 extinguishers at $60.00 each	600.00
5 extinguishers at $90.00 each	450.00
Total	$1860.00

Step 1:	Apply quantity discount	
	Total order amount	$1860.00
	Discount ($1860.00 × .10)	186.00
	Net order amount	$1674.00
Step 2	Apply trade discount	
	Net order amount	$1674.00
	Discount (1674.00 × .30)	502.20
	Amount due manufacturer	$1171.80
Step 3	Apply cash discount	
	Amount due manufacturer	$1171.80
	Discount ($1171.80 × .02)	23.44
	Actual (net) remittance	$1148.36

Source: Adapted from K. Monroe, *Pricing: Making Profitable Decisions,* (New York: McGraw-Hill Book Co., 1979), 171.

2/10, n 30, plus a 10 percent incentive for orders of $500 or more, and a trade discount of 30 percent. One of the manufacturer's middlemen, Hospital Distributors, Inc., has placed an order for four different types of extinguishers. The distributor will, in turn, sell them to hospitals and health care facilities. The list price for the total order comes to $1,860, as illustrated in Table 10.5. If the customer qualifies for all three discounts, the actual remittance comes to $1,148.36. This represents a 38 percent saving off the list price. Table 10.5 also illustrates the logical order in which the discounts would be taken. Those charged with setting prices should recognize, then, the potential price flexibility which a competitive discount structure provides to both the marketer and the purchase decision maker.

Leasing

A sizable volume of industrial transactions involve a customer leasing a product rather than purchasing it outright. A lease is defined as "a contract by which the owner of an asset (the lessor) grants the right to use the asset for a given term to another party (the lessee) in return for a periodic payment of rent" (Anderson and Lazer 1978). Leasing might be considered a form of product differentiation, a way to broaden a firm's product offering, or a means of product augmentation. It can be a means to attract customers that otherwise might find a product unaffordable. To a customer, a leasing arrangement means avoiding the need to pay the cash purchase cost of the product or service, as well as avoiding any maintenance and operating expenses paid by the lessor. A lease also offers the buyer certain tax advantages, and preserves the buyer's debt capacity. And, a lease is a hedge against rapid product obsolescence, such as with electronic data processing equipment.

There are two major types of leases: financial or full-payment leases, and operating or service leases. A *financial lease* is a longer-term arrangement that is fully amortized over the term of the contract. Because the lease may cover the economic life of the product, the sum of the lease payments should exceed the price paid for the asset by the marketer (lessor). With such longer-term commitments, the buyer (lessee) is usually responsible for all operating expenses and any liabilities associated with product use. The buyer also may be given the option of purchasing the asset upon fulfilling the terms of the lease, and applying a portion of the lease payments to the purchase. This type of lease might be used for a manufacturing facility, a major piece of operating equipment, or company trucks. An *operating lease* is for a shorter time period, is cancellable, and is not completely amortized. The marketer (lessor) assumes liability and responsibility for ownership expenses. Typically, there is no purchase option, and the lease price is higher than that of a financial lease for a comparable period of time. These leases are desirable for equipment or space that is needed only for a relatively short period of time—such as special plant cleaning equipment, temporary storage space, or an outdoor billboard.

A lease price will reflect a variety of factors, somewhat different from those used to price a product to be sold. In addition to the original cost of purchasing an item or its manufacturing cost, the marketer may want to consider the projected product life, the expected salvage or scrap value, investment tax credits and tax rates, inflation rates over the term of the lease, debt interest rates, servicing costs, and maintenance costs. Careful evaluation of these and other factors is necessary to establish a lease price that provides a reasonable rate of return over the product's useful economic life.

The marketer faces a problem in that not only must a price be determined for the lease, but also, a price must be set for outright sale of the product. The lease-to-purchase price ratio becomes a strategic variable in that it indicates whether management wishes to encourage lease arrangements or outright sales. While leasing may be attractive to customers, it places financial strains on the supplier. Cash flow is tied up and inventories must be financed. As a result, higher lease prices relative to purchase prices may be established.

Lower relative lease prices might be offered, however, to encourage lease renewals or sales of other products in the line. The lessee may be encouraged to trade up to higher quality products in the marketer's line by granting lease credits that can be applied to these other products. The marketer must consider implications of the lease price for the entire product mix.

Transfer Pricing

While price decisions are generally made for products to be sold to customer organizations, industrial companies also manufacture products that are used internally. In many cases, one division of a company will supply components and materials to another division. An internal price, called a transfer price, may be established for these items. This transfer price is the amount one division charges another division of the same company.

The division attempting to establish a transfer price is influenced by two key considerations. The first is a desire to ensure that the price covers manufacturing and delivery costs. The second is a desire for the transfer price to reflect the going market price for similar goods. In fact, the real problem often is that of determining whether to set the price based on production costs plus some markup, or to base it on going market prices. Market price is the average amount which other companies charge for the product. The transfer price should fall somewhere between production cost and market price. The issue becomes how much of the difference between cost and market price is credited to the supplying division, and how much to the buying division. This allocation can create internal political problems, for the selling division would like as high a markup over cost as feasible, and the buying division would prefer as big a discount off the market price as possible. Some important strategic issues are involved, for the approach used to set transfer prices determines how profitable both the selling and the buying divisions will be. Transfer prices influence the selling division's amount of incentive to control or reduce cost; however, they also affect the ability of the buying division to price finished goods competitively in the marketplace. When transfer pricing is used, both divisions can be profit centers; if so, the transfer price will determine, in part, how profitable each division is.

One suggested approach to resolving the potential dilemmas is for the two divisions to engage in an annual (or periodic) negotiation process, the purpose of which is to agree upon a *margin distribution index* (Maitlandt 1976). This index serves to allocate the margin between the supplying and buying division. For example, assume the parties agree on an index of two, indicating that for every two dollars of profit made by the supplying division, the buying division will receive a one-dollar discount from the market price. So, if the total cost to the supplying division is seven dollars, and the comparable market price is ten dollars, the transfer price will be nine dollars. The index itself remains constant, even if production costs or market prices change. The result is that the supplying division is given a financial incentive to be cost-efficient, as the index permits a profit performance measure. The buying division is given the incentive to purchase internally, which also saves them purchasing and inventory costs.

Transfer pricing is important to the industrial marketer because of its effect on some of the major costs of the final product the company is attempting to market. Marketers in the buying division have a large stake in the transfer price, and are likely to get involved in the negotiations with the supplying division. The marketer is also in a key position to provide information regarding market prices charged for products which are manufactured internally.

The ability of the marketer to establish an effective industrial pricing strategy is heavily influenced by a host of legal issues. Some of the practices which raise legal questions include price-fixing, the sharing of price information with competitors, parallel pricing, delivered pricing, price discrimination, and predatory pricing (see Stern and Eovaldi 1984). Let us briefly examine each of these.

Price fixing involves competitors getting together (colluding) to set industry prices at a level above the competitive equilibrium which an open market would establish. It is an illegal practice under any circumstances. Regardless of whether or not price-fixing actually has an adverse effect, or whether it leads to higher or lower prices, it is an unacceptable practice in a free market economy.

Price-fixing can also take the form of bid-rigging in industrial markets. Here, competitors will agree on a minimum bid, and all but one will bid higher. This minimum bid is higher than would otherwise be the case in the absence of rigging. As they bid on subsequent jobs, competitors will rotate on who gets to submit the low bid. In another approach, all competitors submit the same bid.

Related to price-fixing is the *exchange of information* among competitors regarding prices, shipments, inventories, and similar data. This information exchange occurs in a number of ways, such as through trade associations. It becomes a questionable practice, however, when it leads to price agreements or related forms of anticompetitive behavior.

A common phenomenon in oligopolistic industrial markets is *parallel pricing,* where all competitors charge fairly uniform prices based on their analysis of one another's likely actions and reactions, but do not collude. That is, they do not have a formal agreement to collectively charge higher prices. The question concerns whether the independent behavior of competitors can in any way be interpreted as a conspiracy in restraint of trade. Price leadership, discussed earlier in this chapter, is an example of parallel pricing which is generally seen as acceptable. Here, competitors find it in their best competitive interest to follow the price set by the market leader.

Related to parallel pricing is the use of *delivered pricing* systems. Also called base-point pricing, selling prices are quoted from a base-point location such that all customers within a certain locale or geographic region are charged the same price, regardless of differences in actual shipping costs. Where competitors charge the same delivered price (i.e., use the same base-point system), the behavior may be viewed as collusive and in restraint of trade.

Price discrimination is the practice of selling the same commodity to different customers at price differentials not based on differences in costs. This is common in industrial markets, where different prices are used for different market segments. The legal ramifications of price discrimination are especially relevant to the marketer, for there is a strong economic rationale for the practice. If two customers (or segments) differ in their elasticity of demand toward a particular product, the most profitable strategy would be to charge each a price reflecting these different elasticities. This tactic assumes that neither of these two customers (or segments) can resell the item to the other, which is one reason why this practice is often applied to services.

Concerns about price discrimination include the possibility that a supplier will set prices artificially low in particular markets (compared to what it charges in other markets) for the express purpose of harming the competition in that market. In addition, the potential exists for less powerful buyers to be placed at a disadvantage. Certain discounts can be construed as having this effect.

At the same time, the use of price differentials is generally acceptable if it does not, or is not likely to, substantially lessen competition. Further, price differentials are justified if it costs the marketer more to sell and distribute to one type of customer than another.

Predatory pricing involves cutting prices to a level at or below cost for the express purpose of eliminating competitors. While the initial result is lower profits, the opposite occurs once competitors are removed. The marketer is attempting to monopolize the market. It is often unclear, however, whether a price cut which adversely affects competitors is unlawfully predatory, or simply a legitimate response to competitive pressures within the marketplace. It is generally inadvisable, however, to drop prices below the product's average variable or marginal cost.

SUMMARY

Price is one of the more visible of marketing management decisions. It is also one of the most flexible. Traditional approaches have ignored the marketing potential of the price variable, however, and emphasized more simple cost-plus formulas.

Price of a product or service is a statement of how much value has been provided to the customer. Value is a subjective commodity, existing in the mind of the buyer. The task of the marketer, then, is to weigh the costs and benefits a customer receives from a product, and compare them to available alternatives.

The chapter has presented a framework for establishing and managing industrial prices, consisting of objectives, costs, demand, and competition. Each of the inputs is likely to change over a product's life cycle, with the price reflecting such changes. Of these inputs, the most important is objectives—what is the company attempting to accomplish with the price of a particular item, within the context of its overall set of product and market strategies?

A number of special pricing topics of relevance for industrial markets were addressed, including discounts, leasing, and transfer pricing. Each has important implications for the actual price a customer is charged for a commodity. In addition, the legal implications of a number of pricing practices were raised. Unfortunately, legal restrictions often make it unclear what is, and what is not, an acceptable pricing tactic.

Industrial pricing is likely to become only more complex in the years to come. New forms and sources of competition, shorter life cycles, widely fluctuating inflation, volatile interest and exchange rates, and the availability of alternative purchasing and payment schemes affect both the industrial buyer and seller. Decision makers must become more sophisticated, not only to ensure they are charging an appropriate price, but also (and increasingly) to recognize the potential of the price variable as a tool for product differentiation.

1. What does it mean to say that price is a measure of value? What different sources of value might a customer perceive in purchasing a Caterpillar tractor?

2. Trane Corporation manufactures and sells central air conditioning units to a wide variety of customers, including building contractors and owners. Discuss some of the ways in which Trane can vary the prices actually paid by customers, without changing list prices.

3. What information would you need to calculate the economic value to the customer for a new type of blood pressure machine that also measures a patient's pulse and temperature, assuming these functions traditionally had to be accomplished separately?

4. Why do you think cost-plus pricing approaches are so prevalent in industrial markets? How does this approach limit the marketer's flexibility? How is it possible that this approach could be costing the firm some potential profits?

5. Omega Tool produces a line of power tools, including sanders, saws, and electric impact wrenches. Cite examples of ten different pricing objectives that might be relevant when establishing pricing strategy for Omega's line of portable hand drills, comprising three different models.

6. How does the presence or absence of a significant experience or learning effect (see Chapter 8 on experience curves) relate to industrial pricing programs? Specifically, how might it relate to the establishment of pricing objectives, and to reliance on a penetration, parity, or premium pricing strategy?

7. What are the determinants of demand elasticity? Using these determinants, evaluate the elasticity of demand for:

   a major canning company purchasing aluminum for its cans;

   a small regional airline purchasing aircraft maintenance services;

   a restaurant chain purchasing uniforms for its employees.

8. To increase your probabilities of winning bids, you should bid on as many projects as possible. Agree or disagree? Describe how you would estimate your probabilities of winning bids at various price levels, if you were an architectural firm bidding on a local hospital construction project.

9. Your company manufactures keyboards for computer terminals. What are the arguments for and against offering quantity discounts to your customers?

10. Why is it easier to use price differentials (charging different customers different prices) when selling industrial services than when selling industrial products?

CHAPTER **11**

INTRODUCTION TO INDUSTRIAL COMMUNICATION: ADVERTISING AND SALES PROMOTION

Key Concepts

Advertising
ADVISOR studies
Budgeting methods
Buying process models
Catalog
Communications objectives
Direct marketing
Eight-M formula
General business publications
Hierarchy of effects models

Horizontal publications
Industrial directories
Personal selling
Promotional mix
Publicity
Sales promotion
Technical reports
Telemarketing
Trade shows
Vertical publications

Learning Objectives

1. Explain the need for a strategy that integrates the promotional mix variables to accomplish communication objectives of the industrial firm.
2. Relate promotional strategy to different models of the ways customers make buying decisions.
3. Discuss the role of advertising in selling industrial products and services.
4. Describe a process for formulating industrial advertising programs.
5. Establish the importance of sales promotion in industrial marketing strategy, and identify major sales promotion tools.

(Those in the advertising industry) have a vested interest in prolonging the myth that all *advertising increases sales. It doesn't.*

DAVID OGILVY

WHAT IS INDUSTRIAL PROMOTION?

Industrial promotion consists of a mix of personal and impersonal communications directed toward various audiences, including direct customers, indirect users further down the channel, industrial middlemen, and the general public. Promotion serves a number of functions, but its ultimate purpose is to stimulate and maintain demand for the company's products, product lines, and services. The major components of industrial promotion are personal selling, advertising, sales promotion, and publicity. These combine to form the *promotional mix*.

As a mix, the individual forms of promotion combine to accomplish the organization's communication goals during the stages of the organizational buying process. *Personal selling*, usually the cornerstone of the promotional effort, involves direct contact with potential and present customers, either in person or by telephone. *Advertising*—an impersonal method of communication that utilizes a variety of different media for a fee—has the capability to reach a much larger number of potential buyers, users, influencers, deciders, and gatekeepers than does personal selling. *Sales promotion* is a catchall category of personal and impersonal communication tactics usually directed toward specific purchases. Trade shows, samples, premiums, rebates, trade-in allowances, calendars, and customer entertainment are familiar tactics. They are generally short-term in nature. *Publicity* attempts to influence target groups without actually paying to do so. It involves the release of company or product information to print or broadcast media with the hope that it will be disseminated. Impersonal in nature, publicity is perceived by the target audience as objective information.

INDUSTRIAL PROMOTION IS DIFFERENT

A promotional mix that works effectively with industrial products and services is likely to be quite different from the appropriate mix for most consumer goods. This is due to the technical nature of industrial products, the smaller relative number of potential buyers, and the complex nature and length of the organizational buying process. A strong personal sales effort is a vital ingredient in successfully communicating the technical merits of the vendor's product or service. The salesperson plays a key role in the negotiation process with key members of the buying center. Further, the ongoing relationship between the salesperson and representatives of the buying firm can help engender long-term source loyalty. Because of its importance, the next chapter will examine personal selling in detail.

Advertising, sales promotion, and publicity generally fill supporting roles in the industrial promotional mix. On its own, none of these promotional areas usually is sufficient to actually accomplish a sale. Rather, they support the general sales effort by generating customer interest, influencing customer attitudes, and reinforcing the customer after the sale.

Advertising, when used in industrial marketing, relies very little on mass media vehicles such as television and radio. Mass media is not only expensive, but also it does not permit the marketer much opportunity to specifically target his efforts to different types of industrial customers. In addition, use of the mass media results in extensive wasted exposure, since many of the individuals reached are not part of the marketer's target market. This waste drives up the cost per targeted exposure. As a result, the primary vehicle used in industrial advertising is print media, with trade journals, general business publications, direct mail, industrial directories, and technical literature the most heavily used advertising outlets. The advertising message will tend to emphasize factual information and functional product benefits. Examples of key industrial promotional tools are described in Table 11.1.

The various promotional alternatives can be distinguished in terms of what each is capable of accomplishing, and how effectively. Figure 11.1 presents a partial illustration. The extensiveness of the message and personal involvement possible with personal selling can be contrasted with the high cost per customer contact. On the other hand, print advertising offers only a brief message and less involvement, but the cost per contact can be quite low, given the number of people reached.

Industrial buying poses a number of specific complications for the promotional effort. Differences between individual customers and their needs can be great enough to warrant a separate promotional effort tailored to each organization. Further, because there are a number of potential decision participants from various functional areas within a given buying organization, each with a different background, a promotional effort that effectively communicates with one person may be ineffective with another. Even if two members of a buying center receive the identical message, they are likely to selectively distort or modify the message to make it consistent with their own goals, values, and expectations. This phenomenon is called *perceptual distortion*. In addition, many decision participants are not reachable through promotion, except perhaps at exorbitant cost.

To better understand the role of promotion in communicating with organizational customers, it is helpful to consider two perspectives on the buyer: a *micro* approach, and a *macro* approach.

PROMOTION AND THE BUYER: A MICRO APPROACH

An individual involved in organizational buying goes through a mental process in selecting a particular vendor or product. An examination of the steps which take place inside the mind of a decision maker can shed some light on promotional strategy.

The buyer first must be made aware of the vendor and what is being sold. Next, the buyer develops a knowledge and understanding of the vendor or product,

Table 11.1 Types of Promotional Alternatives Available to the Industrial Marketer

General Business Publications

General business publications are aimed at a wide variety of markets and buying influences. (e.g. *Fortune, Business Week, Forbes*)

Trade Publications

● Vertical publications are directed towards a specific industry and its members. (e.g. *Modern Plastics, Iron Age*)

● Horizontal publications are directed towards a specific task, function, or area of concentration across multiple industries. (e.g. *Purchasing, Modern Materials Handling, Production Engineering, Electronic Design*)

Industrial Directories

A compiled list of known suppliers within a large variety of product areas that is intended for use as a reference group for industrial buyers. There are general directories covering most industries, directories for individual states, and private directories. (e.g. *Thomas Register*)

Trade shows

A formal exhibition at which a supplier rents space to introduce and display its products and make sales. Competitors' products are also demonstrated at these exhibitions. Personal contacts with a large number of prospective and present customers in the industry can be established in a short period of time and in one location.

Catalogs

Printed material containing information describing a supplier's products, their applications, and other product specifications (e.g., price) which is distributed among organizational buying influences for use as a reference and buying guide. Catalogs often contain enough information so the buyer can purchase products direct from them.

Direct Mail

Letters or brochures sent to selected buying influences to provide information on a supplier and its products or services. This type of media allows a marketer to relay personalized messages to these influences.

Technical Reports

Written, detailed descriptions of product design specifications and performance capabilities. Results of product testing are summarized, including data on quality and reliability.

Samples

Products given to certain customers on a trial basis for the purpose of promoting and demonstrating a supplier's product.

Publicity

A presentation of company and product information for which the marketer does not pay and does not control. These presentations appear in media forms (e.g., newspapers, trade journals) that can increase public awareness and can develop a favorable image for an organization.

Novelties

Free gifts such as calendars, pens, and paperweights that are imprinted with a company's name and possibly an advertising message. These small, useful items are given to customers as a reminder of a supplier and its products or services.

Telemarketing

Using the telephone to find out about a prospect's interest in the company's products, to create an awareness or understanding of those products, and even to make a sales presentation or take an order.

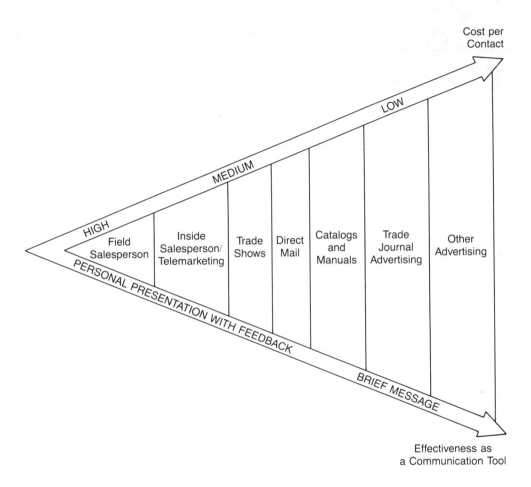

Figure 11.1   Comparing Components of the Industrial Promotion Mix on
Cost and Performance
(Adapted and modified from R. Haas, *Industrial Marketing Management*,
(New York: Van Nostrand Reinhold Co., 1976), 222.)

including technical characteristics, performance capabilities, and selling requirements. Following this, if the buyer is sufficiently interested in the vendor or product,
favorable or disfavorable attitudes are developed. Favorable attitudes can then create
a predisposition to buy from the vendor; such conviction or intention to buy may
translate into an actual purchase if conditions are right.

This process is called a *hierarchy of effects*. There are alternative versions of
the hierarchy, but the basic idea is that the customer moves from cognition (or
awareness) to affect (or attitude) to behavior. This sequence is especially the case
for high-involvement purchases, including many industrial products and services.
The marketer, through effective promotional programs, can affect the buyer's progress through the hierarchy. This guidance can be accomplished by directing pro-

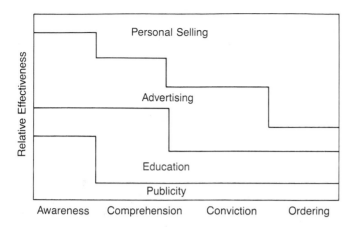

Figure 11.2   Relative Effectiveness of Four Promotional Tools at Different Stages of the Customer Buying Process
(Source: Adapted from P. Kotler, *Marketing Management: Analysis, Planning and Control,* 5th ed. (Englewood Cliffs, N.J.: Prentice-Hall, 1984), 631. Reprinted by permission of Prentice-Hall, Inc.)

motional efforts at specific stages, such as creating awareness, educating the buyer, or changing attitudes.

A common error in promotion management is for the marketer to expect a direct relationship between expenditures for advertising or sales promotion, and product sales. It may be more appropriate to examine the impact of such expenditures on customer awareness levels, or on customer attitudes. Further, a strategy that does a good job of creating awareness may have no effect on the customer's understanding of the product, or on the level of the customer's interest. The hierarchy of effects model, correspondingly, provides the marketer with some direction in the establishment of promotional objectives. Each stage in the hierarchy presents a distinct potential objective, but the ultimate concern may be generating sales.

As demonstrated in Figure 11.2, the relative importance of the elements contained in a company's promotional mix change, over the hierarchy of effects. Advertising and other impersonal forms of communication, especially effective in creating awareness, have a smaller impact as the buyer moves towards conviction and actual purchase behavior. At the same time, the role of personal selling increases in importance, and is paramount in achieving conviction and getting the customer to place an order.

PROMOTION AND THE BUYER: A MACRO APPROACH

Not only should the marketer consider the mental processes that take place within individual decision makers, he or she will also find it useful to take a more macro approach, and examine the overall buying process of the customer organization. The buying process for a product or service is evolutionary, involving a series of deci-

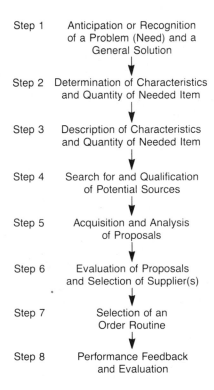

Step 1   Anticipation or Recognition
          of a Problem (Need) and a
          General Solution

Step 2   Determination of Characteristics
          and Quantity of Needed Item

Step 3   Description of Characteristics
          and Quantity of Needed Item

Step 4   Search for and Qualification
          of Potential Sources

Step 5   Acquisition and Analysis
          of Proposals

Step 6   Evaluation of Proposals
          and Selection of Supplier(s)

Step 7   Selection of an
          Order Routine

Step 8   Performance Feedback
          and Evaluation

Figure 11.3   Stages of the Organizational Buying Process

sions. As explained in Chapter 3, eight potential buystages collectively result in product and vendor choices (see Figure 11.3).

Customers have particular information requirements in each of these stages, and the promotional mix should reflect these needs. Customer reliance on internal versus external information sources, on objective versus subjective sources, and on personal versus impersonal sources will vary with the stages of the process. Table 11.2 provides examples of each of these types of information. Also, the key role-players in the buying decision change during these stages, suggesting that promotion directed at a particular stage should reflect the characteristics and goals of the relevant individuals.

Consider, for example, the need recognition or arousal stage for a product with which the customer has little or no purchasing experience. The task of the promotional effort might be to help the buying organization members see that they have an unmet need, and isolate that need. The target group might be senior management or current product users. Trade shows and advertisements in trade publications can be effective and efficient tools in accomplishing this task.

The same organization, once a need is clearly established, must express that need in the form of a specific product or service. The characteristics of acceptable products or services have to be determined and described. The marketer's communication task is to demonstrate how a particular product class meets a need and

Table 11.2 Types of Industrial Communications

Internal	*External*
Information provided by sources within the buying organization (e.g., company vendor files, using departments)	Information obtained from a source outside the organization (e.g., trade shows, advertisements, colleagues in other companies)
Objective	*Subjective*
Information from a source not controlled or strongly influenced by the vendor (e.g., publicity, consultant's report, word-of-mouth, a technical report)	Messages paid for and controlled by a vendor attempting to influence buying decisions (e.g., sales calls, direct mail, advertisements)
Personal	*Impersonal*
Information directly communicated between two or more individuals (e.g., sales calls, word-of-mouth from colleague, trade show, personal letter)	Information communicated through some formal medium (e.g., trade journal or radio advertising, catalogues, rating services, technical report)

satisfies technical requirements; the focus is on the buying organization's technical experts in the specific area of need. Catalogs, samples, and trade journal advertising may be appropriate, but the sales force must get involved where those in the buying organization tend to tailor the description of product requirements to the characteristics of a competitor's product.

When vendor evaluation is the concern, buying organization members are more susceptible to communications that demonstrate an established record of vendor and product performance. The marketer might be tempted to use comparative advertising (i.e., advertisements that draw comparisons with, and suggest superiority to, competitors), or even testimonials from other customers. The evaluation process may be fairly formal, however, suggesting the need for a more persuasive, direct approach. Personal sales calls by the field sales force, technical reports, and favorable publicity are likely to be more effective. The relevant target group may now be purchasing managers or whoever is playing the role of buyer. The target selection depends, of course, on the product and buyer in question.

There is, in general, heavy concentration on personal selling in the middle and later stages of the buying process. In these stages, it is necessary to provide specific, detailed communications concerning the product and the vendor that usually cannot be conveyed through impersonal forms of communication. These buystages may involve an extensive negotiation process over the terms of the transaction, the adaptation of a given product or service to the needs of a particular organization, or a discussion of the decision criteria used in evaluating proposals and making a final decision. All of these situations usually require direct personal contact between the potential supplier and the buying organization.

In the postpurchase stage, the communication task is to reassure customers, encouraging source loyalty and positive word-of-mouth publicity. The perception of negative discrepancies between customer expectations and actual experiences must be minimized. Inside salespeople and direct mail can be helpful in keeping the customer sold.

Implicit in this discussion is the assumption that marketers can affect the industrial buyer's decision through the source, time, and quality of information they provide. Moriarty and Spekman (1984) have provided evidence of this. In addition to the relationships just discussed, and summarized in Figure 11.2, they found buyer reliance on inputs from personal noncommercial information sources earlier in the buying process, on impersonal commercial sources during the search for alternative vendors stage, and on impersonal noncommercial sources in both the recognition and search stages.

Keep in mind, however, that there is no one right way to design promotion strategy. The overriding requirement of the marketer is to determine (a) which stages of the buying process are the *most* critical for the particular type of product and market segment in question; and (b) which promotional tools can best communicate with the appropriate individuals in those stages. Not all purchases involve all eight stages, and the length of the stages will depend on what is being sold and to whom. Also, the amount of information sought by the buyer will tend to be directly related to the amount of risk and conflict in the purchase decision. The challenge is to allocate promotional expenditures to the key decision points in the buying process, within the budget constraints placed on these expenditures.

WHY ADVERTISE?

Our discussion of promotional strategy up to this point has made frequent mention of advertising as a promotional tool. And yet, industrial advertising (also called business-to-business advertising) has generated considerable controversy over the years. Some argue that advertising is a waste of money because it is such a limited form of communication. As has been indicated, industrial advertising relies heavily on the print media because of the need to target specific industries, organizations, and individuals within those organizations. There are occasional uses of television or radio, but these media tend to be for products and services with broadbased markets and universal applications—such as copying machines, small computers, and business insurance.

Print media is limited in its ability to convey technical product information to the appropriate members of the decision-making unit in sufficient quantity and detail and at the right time. An industrial advertisement cannot hope to address the multiplicity of questions and concerns that ultimately determine what is bought and from whom. And, the length of the buying process makes it difficult to ascertain whether or not advertising is effective. As a result, companies question the advisability of spending money on advertising, and may do so only because their competitors advertise.

There are a number of valid reasons to advertise, especially if the functions of advertising are considered within the context of the overall promotional mix. Let us examine some of the major functions industrial advertising is capable of serving (see also Table 11.3).

First, advertising has the ability to extend beyond the salesperson and reach inaccessible or unknown members of the buying center who exert considerable influence on an organization's purchases. It has been estimated that, on average, salespeople do not reach two-thirds of those who fill an influential role in buying decisions (Manville 1978). Some are never identified, some will not or cannot talk with the salesperson, and the salesperson may not have the resources to spend time with others. In addition, the salesperson may violate protocol and offend certain members of the buying center by meeting with others. But a message placed in a trade journal read specifically by electrical engineers, or in a publication that deals solely with school supply products, may be read by otherwise unreached decision participants. Table 11.4 provides additional examples. The importance of advertising's ability to reach inside the buying center is further emphasized in recent research by Cahners Publishing. In a survey of industrial advertising managers, 55.9 percent indicated they need to reach two or more primary buying influences with their advertising message to get products specified and purchased (Cahners Advertising Research Report #551.9).

Advertising is also a tool for customer prospecting. Customer response can be encouraged by including a reply card, a toll-free telephone number, or simply an information-request address as part of an advertisement in a trade journal or busi-

Table 11.3 Some Findings from 1100 Research Studies on the Effectiveness of Industrial Advertising

---

In a review of a large number of studies that dealt in some way with industrial advertising, Arthur D. Little, Inc. drew the following conclusions:

(a) The number of buying influences in companies has grown;

(b) It is difficult for the salesperson first to *find,* and second to *cover* all buying influences;

(c) Cost per sales dollar can be reduced by proper allocation of funds between direct sales effort and industrial advertising;

(d) Companies which maintain their advertising in recession years have better sales and profits in those and later years;

(e) Companies with product entries in categories which are not directly associated with the companies' past history need to advertise the particular product to be considered in that category by potential buyers;

(f) The effect of industrial advertising can be tracked through intermediate variables, and its quantitative impact on sales can be measured;

(g) There is no overall formula that managers can apply to determine when to increase, and when not to increase, the advertising budget or what return to expect on their advertising investment.

Source: Arthur D. Little, Inc., *An Evaluation of 1100 Research Studies on the Effectiveness of Industrial Advertising,* report to American Business Press, Inc. #C-73383, May 1971. Reprinted with permission.

Table 11.4 How Trade Journals Can Be Used to Reach Target Groups

If you're looking for engineers and professionals in . . .	Look for them in these magazines . . .
CONSTRUCTION	
Civil engineers	*ENR*
Architects	*Architectural Record*
Electrical engineers	*Electrical Construction & Maintenance*
HIGH TECH	
Aeorospace/avionic mechanical engineers	*Aviation Week & Space Technology*
Computer scientists, engineers	*Byte*
Data systems, telecommunications	*Data Communications*
Electrical, electronic	*Electronics*
CHEMICAL	
Chemical engineers	*Chemical Engineering*
Management	*Chemical Week*
Plastics engineers	*Modern Plastics*
ENERGY	
Electrical/nuclear utility engineers	*Electrical World*
Electrical/power nuclear/mechanical	*Power*
MINING	
Coal mining; geological engineers	*Coal Age*
Mineral, Mining, Metallurgical	*Engineering & Mining Journal*
METALWORKING	
Manufacturing engineers	*American Machinist & Automated Manufacturing*
Metallurgical engineers	*33 Metal Producing*
ENTRY LEVEL	
All engineering disciplines	*Graduating Engineer*

Note: All above magazines are published by McGraw-Hill.

ness publication. The marketer can generate a list of new sales prospects by carefully scrutinizing the names of those who request product information.

In addition to prospecting, advertising can provide the foundation for a salesperson's call by creating an awareness of vendor capabilities and providing general information about products and services. This approach is especially valid when selling products which are in categories that customers do not associate with the company's past history. Some of the preliminary questions of the buyer can be ad-

"I don't know who you are.

I don't know your company.

I don't know your company's product.

I don't know what your company stands for.

I don't know your company's customers.

I don't know your company's record.

I don't know your company's reputation.

Now—what was it you wanted to sell me?"

MORAL: Sales start **before** your salesman calls—with business publication advertising.

McGRAW-HILL MAGAZINES
BUSINESS • PROFESSIONAL • TECHNICAL

Figure 11.4 McGraw-Hill's "Man-in-the-Chair" advertisement.
(Source: McGraw-Hill Publishing Company. Reprinted with permission.)

dressed. This is cogently demonstrated in the well-known McGraw-Hill man-in-the-chair advertisement, shown in Figure 11.4. McGraw-Hill is a leading publisher of trade magazines such as *Modern Plastics, Textile World, Aviation Week and Space Technology, Byte,* and *Chemical Engineering.* This message is directed toward sales and marketing managers, encouraging them to do more industrial advertising. It emphasizes how an advertisement can lay the groundwork for the salesperson by addressing the kinds of questions being raised by the gentleman in the chair.

Properly directed advertising can work to bring down the average cost of sales calls. More specifically, advertising designed to support the sales effort can bring down the selling cost per sales dollar generated (Morrill 1970). The significance of this finding cannot be understated. It suggests that advertising should be examined not only on its own merits, but also within the context of the promotional mix. The cautious marketer will recognize, however, that the effect of advertising is dependent upon the frequency with which one advertises. It is possible to advertise too little as well as too much—a point to be discussed later in this chapter.

Industrial advertising also represents a means for motivating and supporting sales intermediaries, such as industrial distributors. Most intermediaries sell many products, produced by a number of firms. Their loyalties are correspondingly mixed, and their strongest efforts are likely to be devoted to the manufacturer whose products are easiest to sell, have the highest commission or margin, or with whom the intermediary has the closest working relationship. Advertisements which directly or indirectly support a middleman's sales can contribute to the strength of the on-going manufacturer-intermediary relationship.

In addition, derived demand can be stimulated through industrial advertising, by extending the firm's promotional focus to the customer's customer. Exhibit 11.1 provides an example. More often than not, the target is the ultimate user in the consumer market. For example, G.D. Searle and Co. advertises its NutraSweet sugar substitute to consumers. Occasionally, however, ads are aimed at business end users. The Ventron Division of Morton Thiokol, Inc. makes an antibacterial product called Bio-Pruf, which can be used as a germ-killer when applied to floor mops. Ventron promotes the product directly to hospitals, recognizing their acute concern with sterile facilities. The hope is that hospitals will pressure mop manufacturers to add Bio-Pruf to their products (Milsap 1986). When targeted to consumer markets, such pull-through strategies become quite expensive, and results are very difficult to measure.

Another role for industrial advertising involves conveying a desired corporate image to target audiences. A firm might run ads featuring the company name or logo, emphasizing an image it wishes to portray, rather than advertising specific products or services. For example, such ads might stress the firm's position as an innovation leader, that it is socially responsible, that the firm stands behind its products, or that it is especially customer-oriented. Image and credibility of the firm are quite important with industrial goods, for the customer is buying the company and its reputation as much as it is buying products and services. Image advertising is also a way to keep the company's name before the public.

Advertising can play a significant role in the industrial marketer's overall communication program. Unfortunately, many industrial advertising programs generate unclear or even dismal results, because those responsible do not really understand

Exhibit 11.1 Who is DuPont Trying to Reach with This Ad? (An Example of Derived Demand)

Times like this call for ultra-tough luggage of Cordura.

It stands up to the rigors of travel without losing its good looks.

You get there with style and aplomb when you travel with luggage made of Du Pont CORDURA® nylon. It stays serviceable and good-looking, no matter what tortures it has to take. Here are some good reasons why.

Tests show CORDURA resists abrasion 3 times better than standard nylon, 2 times better than ballistic nylon, and 1½ to 3 times better than vinyl. And it resists punctures and tears 5 times better than standard nylon, 3 times better than vinyl, and 2 times better than leather.

Lightweight luggage made of CORDURA comes in a wide variety of colors and styles—plain weaves, fancy weaves, and tweeds. It won't rot or mildew. And it's easy to clean and quick to dry.

Luggage made of CORDURA stands up to the rigors of travel like nothing else. Ask for it at leading department stores and luggage shops.

*DuPont's registered trademark for its high-tenacity air-textured nylon fiber. DuPont makes the fiber, not fabric or bags.

Reprinted with permission.

why or how to use advertising. To be consistently effective, advertising programs must be well-planned, carefully executed, and regularly monitored.

MANAGING THE INDUSTRIAL ADVERTISING EFFORT

The marketer should resist the temptation to manage advertising on a piecemeal basis, such as where each message and each media alternative is evaluated and decided upon individually, or advertising budgets are set in a vacuum. A strategic approach is needed, where individual decisions are coordinated as part of a larger plan to achieve specific communication objectives. A process model for planning, executing, and controlling advertising strategy is provided in Figure 11.5; principal decision areas are highlighted in Table 11.5.

Advertising should be positioned as an integral part of overall marketing strategy. The company might be pursuing any number of possible strategies, such as product differentiation, niching, or market development. With a strategy in hand, the marketer then determines the communications necessary to implement that strategy. For example, if the firm were attempting to differentiate itself on the basis of service or product quality, then the communication requirement may be to change the be-

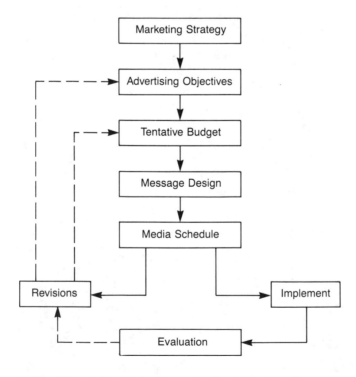

Figure 11.5 A Model for Managing the Advertising Program
(Source: J.P. Guiltinan, and G. Paul, *Marketing Management: Strategies and Programs,* (New York: McGraw-Hill Book Co., 1985), 240.
Reprinted with permission.

Table 11.5   Preparing the Advertising Campaign: The Eight-M Formula

Effective advertising should follow a plan. There is no one best way to go about planning an advertising campaign, but, in general, marketers should have good answers to the following eight questions:

1. The Management Question:	Who will manage the advertising program?
2. The Money Question:	How much should be spent on advertising as opposed to other forms of selling?
3. The Market Question:	To whom should the advertising be directed?
4. The Message Question:	What should the ads say about the product?
5. The Media Question:	What types and combinations of media should be used?
6. The Macro-scheduling Question:	How long should the advertising campaign be in effect before changing ads or themes?
7. The Micro-scheduling Question:	At what times and dates would it be best for ads to appear during the course of the campaign?
8. The Measurement Question:	How will the effectiveness of the advertising campaign be measured and how will the campaign be evaluated and controlled?

Source: J.P. Peter, J. Donnelly, and L. Tarpey *A Preface to Marketing Management,* 3rd Ed., (Plano, Texas: Business Publications, 1985), 192. Adapted from Alfred R. Oxenfeldt "A Decision-Making Structure for Price Decisions," *Journal of Marketing,* (January 1973), 50. Reprinted with permission.

liefs of target groups about the capabilities of various vendors and their offerings. The next step is to determine the role which advertising can play most effectively in meeting these communication needs.

Objectives

Having established the role of advertising, specific advertising objectives should be determined. Setting objectives is critical, both for directing the program and for providing standards against which to gauge its effectiveness. For these reasons, it is important to state objectives in specific terms, and, where possible, quantify them. Advertising objectives can be stated in terms of sales or market share, and these measures are certainly quantifiable. However, as the discussions of the hierarchy of effects and the stages of the buying process suggested, making a sale is not the goal of each and every advertisement. It is helpful, then, to emphasize intermediate communication objectives. Some of these include creating specific awareness levels (e.g., increase awareness of our new self-cleaning feature from 5 percent to 50 percent among metallurgical engineers), changing attitudes about the application of the product form (e.g., a synthetic material used in producing tires can also be used in carpeting), changing beliefs about vendors and their products (e.g., repositioning ourselves as the premier service provider), or changing perceptions about the importance of product attributes (e.g., stressing life-cycle costs to the buyer who focuses only on initial cost). The goal of advertising also might be simply to remind the buyer to use a product or service, or to reassure the buyer after the purchase (Boyd, Ray, and Strong 1972). Moreover, each of these objectives should be stated in terms of specific target audiences.

Budgets

The next step is to determine how much to spend. A number of methods exist for establishing an advertising budget, including percentage of sales, competitive parity, product profitability, productivity judgments, and product objectives. *Percentage of sales* involves setting the budget as a straight proportion of projected sales for the coming year. For most industrial companies, advertising expense is a relatively small percentage of sales, often less than 1 percent, and of the total promotion budget, often about 10 percent. Figures for a select group of industries can be found in Table 11.6.

Some companies will, alternatively, take the previous year's advertising expenditures and add a percentage increase based on the projected growth rate for sales in the coming year. These sales-based approaches tend to limit the marketer's flexibility in responding to marketplace demands, especially during periods of recession

Table 11.6 Estimated Advertising Percentages in Selected Industries

	Estimated Advertising and Promotion Budget As % of Net Sales	
	1986	*1987*
Metalworking equipment	4.3%	4.5%
Petroleum refining	0.3	0.3
Textile products	2.1	2.1
Paper and allied products	1.4	1.4
Chemicals	2.0	2.1
Industrial inorganic chemicals	17.3	17.8
Plastics materials and synthetic resins	0.7	0.7
Rubber products	2.1	2.2
Fabricated metals	2.6	2.7
Office computing and accounting machines	1.0	1.0
Food and kindred products	5.1	5.0
Glass products	2.2	2.2

Source: Reprinted by permission of *Sales and Marketing Management,* "1987 Survey of Selling Costs" (February 17, 1987), 98.

or aggressive competitor action. More fundamentally, the advertising budget is being set as a result of the organization's sales volume, rather than the sales volume being approached as a direct result of advertising efforts. These sales-based methods are popular, however, because they are easy to use and understand.

Competitive parity involves matching the budget to the expenditures of your competitors. It assumes, unwisely, that the competitor is spending the correct amount. Budgets set on the basis of *product* or *service profitability* reward financial performance, but result in underinvestment in low profit areas which could be made more profitable. *Productivity judgments* evaluate how effective expenditures will be in accomplishing objectives; budgets are established, then, based on a cost-benefit analysis. The *product objectives* approach sets budgets in accordance with the specific goals established by management for individual products or lines. This method is the most advantageous, because it has the capability to reflect the criteria (sales growth, competitor actions, profitability, and advertising effectiveness) emphasized by each of the other methods.

One of the dangers in determining budgets is to "spend what we can afford." While it is logical to ensure the company or division does not spend money it does not have, what the company can afford in no way reflects the demands of competitive strategy. Ineffective advertising often can be blamed on the failure to spend enough money. For this reason, spending what one can afford may produce results that are little different from those produced by spending nothing at all.

Some of the more interesting research on advertising expenditures can be found in the ADVISOR studies sponsored by the Massachusetts Institute of Technology and the Association of National Advertisers (Lilien and Little 1976; Lilien 1978). In two separate studies, the relationship between the marketing communications budget and various product and market characteristics were examined for 34 companies and 191 products. The analysis focused on three ratios: marketing budget to sales (M/S), advertising expenditures to the total marketing budget (A/M), and advertising expenditures to sales (A/S). The results of both studies were quite similar; the M/S ratio averaged close to 7 percent, A/M was about 10 percent, and A/S approximated 0.7 percent.

It appears that industrial companies change their advertising and marketing budgets in response to a number of influences. One of these is the stage of the life cycle in which a product currently resides. Both the M/S and A/S ratios tend to decrease over a product's life. And, both ratios tend to be lower for products with larger market shares, suggesting economies of scale in the level of a company's marketing expenditures. These two ratios are positively related to growth in sales volume and growth in number of users. Products purchased more frequently apparently justify a higher A/M ratio. Alternatively, when a company relies on a relatively small number of customers for a disproportionate amount of its sales, the M/S and A/S ratios are lower, but A/M is unaffected or increases.

In terms of product characteristics, A/S rises with a product's uniqueness, quality, and identification with the company. Each of these is a means for differentiating products from those of competitors, and such differentiation is, in part, accomplished through strong advertising efforts. Also, companies that concentrate on customized products will spend less on marketing overall, and on advertising in particular. Marketing expenditures appear to be higher, as a percentage of sales, for more complex products, and products whose characteristics and benefits are harder to communicate.

The CARR Reports, prepared by Cahners Publishing Co., provide additional insight into industrial advertising spending. Figure 11.6 illustrates the relationships between advertising efforts and product standardization, product line breadth, quality, price, plant utilization, and purchase amounts.

The Message

Although the actual message communicated through industrial advertising is limited only by the advertiser's creativity and budget, there are sound principles in developing good advertising. Ten rules have been proposed by the Copy Chasers, a group of anonymous advertising professionals who regularly critique industrial advertisements in *Business Marketing*. These rules are summarized in Table 11.7.

A common theme in the rules is the importance of taking the customer into account. Advertisements that do not capture the reader's attention, involve the reader, reward the reader, or logically approach the reader on a personal basis, are likely to be ineffective. And yet, the failure to understand customers and their buying criteria has been identified as a common malady afflicting industrial advertisers when designing appeals (McAleer 1974). It is easy to assume that customers think and act just like the marketer. They rarely do.

The message communicated through industrial advertising should reflect two points concerning the customer: the typical buyer is fairly well-informed and learned; the customer seeks benefits and examines advertisements for information regarding those benefits.

Because the audience is knowledgeable, the advertiser has to be especially wary of talking down to customers in the advertising message. In addition, puffery and exaggerated claims will detract from advertisements directed at an industrial audience. The effectiveness of emotional claims is also subject to question under such circumstances.

Emotional appeals, which are directed toward a person's feelings, values, and beliefs, can play a useful role in industrial advertising only if carefully and professionally managed. Especially in copy written to influence technical people in the buying firm, creative appeals to their prejudices, ego, need for reinforcement, pride, and self-image help get through the psychological barriers the marketer faces in motivating these individuals to consider new alternatives. Dichter (1973) has provided examples of situations in which flattery (e.g., "you have a flexible mind"), imagery (e.g., a picture with a house inside a vat to demonstrate the vat's size), and even humorous methods of conveying a rational or technical fact have been successful. Positive emotional appeals stress the benefits and rewards to be gained from a product or service; negative appeals emphasize the undesirable consequence that might result from *not* using the item. In terms of the latter, companies might attempt to capitalize on the buyer's fears of failure, disapproval, competition, or economic loss. Exxon, for example, has attempted to build on buyer's fears by depicting the office automation systems market as exploding and revolutionary, with rapidly

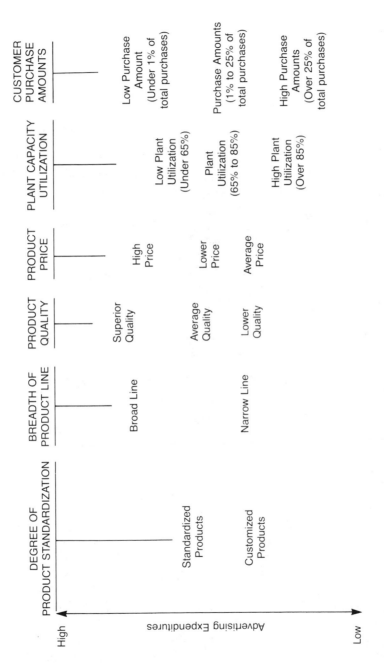

Figure 11.6 How Much Do Companies Spend on Media Advertising?
(Source: Developed from Cahners Advertising Research Reports
#2100.01, 2100.04, 2100.06, 2100.07, 2100.08, 2100.09, 2100.10.)

Table 11.7 What Makes Good Business/Industrial Advertising

1. ***The successful ad has a high degree of visual magnetism.***
   A good industrial advertisement should capture the reader's attention so that a single component—either the picture, the headline, or the text—will dominate the area.

2. ***The successful ad selects the right audience.***
   The reader's first glance at a picture or headline should let him know that the advertisement contains information that is related to his job interests.

3. ***The successful ad invites the reader into the scene.***
   The advertisement should visualize, illuminate, and dramatize the selling proposition that will appeal to the reader's job type.

4. ***The successful ad promises a reward.***
   A good advertisement should give the reader specific promises of benefits whether explicit or implicit, positive or negative.

5. ***The successful ad backs up the promise.***
   An advertisement must provide evidence to support the validity of the promise through a description of the product's characteristics, a competitive comparison, case histories, or testimonials.

6. ***The successful ad presents the selling proposition in logical sequence.***
   The advertisement should be organized so that the reader is guided through the material in a sequence consistent with the logical development of the selling proposition.

7. ***The successful ad talks "person-to-person".***
   The advertisement's copy should speak to the reader as an individual, in a friendly tone, and in terms of the reader's business. The writing style should be simple using short words, short sentences, short paragraphs, active rather than passive voice, and no advertising cliches.

8. ***Successful advertising is easy to read.***
   The advertisement's type should appear black on white, stand clear of interference from other parts of the ad, and should not be more than half the width of the ad.

9. ***Successful advertising emphasizes the service, not the source.***
   A good advertisement should make the reader want to buy or consider buying before telling him where to buy it.

10. ***Successful advertising reflects the company's character.***
    The advertisement should favorably portray the company's personality and remain consistent over time and across the spectrum of corporate structure and product lines.

Source: "The Copy Chasers Rules: What Makes Good Business/Industrial Advertising," *Industrial Marketing*, (Chicago: Crain Communications, Inc., December 1982), 51–2.

changing technologies and costs. However, an overemphasis on fear can backfire, for the anxiety it creates may be manifested in more negative feelings towards the advertiser.

In practice, rational messages are much more common than emotional appeals. Rational messages present a factual and informative perspective on companies and their products or services. Emphasis is placed on logically conveying information regarding dependability, quality, durability, cost savings, and meeting technical requirements, among others. Even here, though, it is important to have creative, interesting copy and a vivid presentation of the main theme. Some researchers have suggested that those in the buying center look for technical information in copy, but others claim that engineers, managers, and purchasing agents differ in their relative concern with purely technical information (Bellizzi and Hite 1986). Advertisers err frequently with messages that discuss product features, and give little attention to actual customer benefits. The advertiser who highlights the physical characteristics and makeup of the product is forgetting that the customer is trying to solve a problem, and is concerned primarily with how purchases from this vendor will benefit his or her organization.

A fundamental question in advertising copy preparation concerns whether to place emphasis on the company name, or to stress individual products and product lines. Appeals that emphasize the company are commonly referred to as *institutional advertising*. Exhibit 11.2 depicts a good example. The underlying rationale is that the customer is buying the company, not just a product. Company reputation, delivery reliability, service levels, and returns policies are often as important to the buyer as specific product characteristics. There is a distinction between corporate image advertising and business-to-business advertising which emphasizes the corporate name. The former is directed at the financial markets, the overall business community, the government, employees, and the general public. The latter is targeted at customers. William Marsteller (1984), of the public relations firm Burson-Marsteller, claims that "most (corporate advertising) is still vague and vacant, a teetering assemblage of platitudes resting on a meaningless slogan. Few people seem to be able to do it well." And yet, companies are spending more on this type of advertising than ever before.

The argument for an emphasis on products and their trademarks has a number of legitimate bases as well. Copy that stresses the company, its logo, and perhaps a motto can be generalized and taken for granted by the reader, so that individual products receive little benefit. Also, when the product is pushed with institutional advertising, poor product performance or failure is likely to reflect more negatively on the company and its reputation. On the other hand, featuring a product that performs well and becomes recognized can help build the company reputation.

Beyond the written copy, the physical characteristics of advertisements can be manipulated to accomplish communication objectives. McGraw-Hill has conducted research evaluating the relative impact of advertisements with different characteristics during the stages of the buying process (Donath 1982). A large number of ads were rated to determine their respective abilities to establish contact, create awareness, arouse interest, build preference, or keep the customer sold. In *establishing contact*, for example, four-color ads with illustrations tended to be important, as did the use of bleed (running an illustration off one or more edges of the printed page). *Awareness* is created by showing the product by itself, and by including long copy (300 words or more), and tables or charts. Techniques for *arousing interest* include featuring the product by itself, using toll-free telephone response numbers, including three to five illustrations, as well as tables/charts. Four or more copy blocks help *build preference*. Long copy is good for *keeping customers sold*. Adopting these find-

Exhibit 11.2   Example of Institutional Advertising

Digital has it now.

Computing solutions you can count on to keep you in the game.

Digital: The Official Computer Vendor to the NBA

It all comes down to extra effort. Working harder individually and as a team. That's why the ability to communicate is built deeply into every Digital computer. Every system we sell responds smoothly – whether it's one-on-one or in response to the needs of your entire organization.

Teamwork. It's the stuff productivity is made of. And it's what distinguishes Digital's computing solutions from the rest of the pack. For ways to give your company a competitive advantage now, write: Digital Equipment Corporation, 200 Baker Avenue, West Concord, MA 01742. Or call your local sales office.

digital™

© Digital Equipment Corporation 1987. The Digital logo is a trademark of Digital Equipment Corporation. The NBA logo is a registered trademark exclusively licensed by NBA Properties, Inc.

Reprinted with permission from Digital Equipment Corporation.

ings should be done with care, but they do suggest that, all other things being equal, certain physical characteristics can make a difference.

The Media Decision: Some Industrial Alternatives

Numerous media outlets are available to the industrial advertiser. Major alternatives were identified in Table 11.1. The decision to rely on a particular form of media should reflect the goals which the marketer seeks to accomplish. These can include credibility, timing, motivating the audience, imparting information, audience control, audience reach, and cost expended per contact. Let's compare different media alternatives in terms of such tasks.

General business publications, such as *Forbes, Fortune, Business Week* and in-flight magazines, cover a broad range of subject areas and reach a wide variety of people in business. They tend to have a superior editorial quality. This is a good type of media for advertising products and services with wide appeal to a large and geographically disperse customer base. For example, office automation products such as personal computers, telecommunications equipment, and office equipment have become the most advertised items in general business publications in recent years. Also, a company such as an office supply distributor that is based and operates in a given geographic area, will advertise in regional editions of these publications. General business publications are also a medium for institutional advertising, as they represent an effective vehicle for projecting a favorable corporate image to a broad-based audience, and for keeping the business community aware of changes or new developments in the organization.

Advertisements are run in this medium to supplement other forms of more specific trade publication advertisements. General business publications may be read by upper levels of management who may not read specialized types of trade journals in their industry. This is a good medium for marketers to reach senior-level buying influences with messages of overall benefits for the organization (e.g., increased productivity or cost savings)—information that otherwise may not be conveyed through a sales call, advertisements in industry journals, or other types of promotional efforts.

On the other hand, certain disadvantages exist with this type of publication. Advertising pages in the general business magazines cost up to ten times the amount charged by an equivalent trade journal. Since they are read by individuals representing a multitude of occupations and industries, it is difficult for a marketer to define, and try to reach, a specific target market with these publications. Significant waste exposure generally results from exposing a large number of people in a variety of organizations to advertisements when only a portion of these people are potential customers. The marketer also might have difficulty in developing a message that will communicate effectively with a wide variety of markets and individuals, and yet contain enough information to effectively stimulate interest in the product or service. Advertisements may not be detailed enough for potential customers to realize what a particular product or service can offer them.

Trade journals, or business papers, are more specific in nature, and are directed towards a distinct industry, technology, organizational function, occupation, or other area of specialization. The readers of these publications have a special interest in the topics that pertain to their field. Since trade journals are read by individuals knowledgeable in their specialized areas, the advertisements contain more exact, detailed information that would help these individuals learn more about the product and its application and recognize a need for the product in their operations.

A marketer can acquire extensive data on trade publications from professional rating services, and from some of the publications themselves, to determine which trade publications are read by those buying influences the marketer is targeting the advertising toward (See Table 11.4). Using data compiled by rating services such as the Audit Bureau of Circulation, a marketer can learn how the readership for various publications is broken down into industries classified by SIC code. The marketer can then match the target audience with the appropriate trade publications read by those individuals, selecting publications that will most effectively and efficiently accomplish the organization's promotional goals. A common error is to spread the company's advertising dollars over a wide variety of media, rather than concentrate on publications that best reach likely buyers.

Trade publications are of two basic types: vertical and horizontal. Vertical publications contain articles and advertisements of interest to individuals in a specific industry. *Iron Age, Modern Plastics,* and *Chemical Week* are good examples. *Modern Plastics* covers the subjects of management, engineering, machinery, and new materials within the plastics industry; *Chemical Week* discusses subjects such as the markets, technology, management, and research in the chemical industry.

Research (Cahners Research Report #411.2) indicates that 95.7 percent of purchasing influences read the specialized business magazines serving their industry. Many company personnel, from the top executives to the people on the shop floor, are likely to read these publications. It follows, then, that a marketer can reach a variety of key buying influences in a specific industry by advertising in one or two of the publications serving that industry. For example, Bethlehem Steel advertises in automotive publications to reach purchasing agents and designers in the automobile industry with the description of Bethlehem's low-cost steel for car bumpers.

Horizontal publications are directed to individuals working in a particular technology, occupation, organizational function, or other area of specialization. Advertising in these publications does not limit a marketer to a particular industry, but instead enables him or her to reach interested buying influences in a specialized area, across industries. *Electronic Design, Modern Materials Handling, Robotics Age,* and *Assembly Engineering* are a few examples of horizontal publications. *Electronic Design* contains articles and advertisements that appeal to engineers and engineering managers in electronics worldwide. *Modern Materials Handling* examines the equipment, systems, trends, and the management of the functions that relate to handling of inventories.

Trade publications are useful for directing specific, technical advertising messages about specialized products and services to buying influences in publications they are most likely to read and refer to for information. Marketers do not have to waste space providing general information, since they can use more technical information that the readers of specific trade journals will comprehend and find useful in their decision making. Through advertising in these publications, marketers can often reach inaccessible and unknown buying influences who do not have direct personal contact with the salesperson—but do read journals. This advertising is also a less costly form of promotion, since it reaches many prospective and present customers (both known and unknown, accessible and inaccessible) at a low cost per thousand members of the target market reached (i.e., CPM).

Industrial directories, or buyer's guides, are comprehensive listings of the current suppliers of a wide array of product types. Vendors can advertise in these publications in addition to their company listing—just as in the business-to-business Yellow Pages. General directories cover most industries, regional directories compile data for individual states or groups of states, and private directories limit their coverage to specific industries.

The *Thomas Register of American Manufacturers*, one of the most widely known general directories, covers most industries and product areas, listed under more than 40,000 headings. Suppliers are grouped by products or services and then broken down by state and city. A company's name, address, phone number, and value of its tangible assets are included in this directory. An extension of *The Thomas Register* is the *Thomas Register Catalog File*, also called the *Thomcat*, which contains the catalogs of various suppliers, lists them in alphabetical order as opposed to product area. These catalogs describe and often illustrate the products and their applications.

State and county industrial directories provide information on the industries in their areas, classified by SIC codes. For example, some state directories contain an economic overview of the state and list suppliers alphabetically, geographically by county and/or city, by SIC codes, and by product group. These directories are usually published every one or two years.

Private directories, such as *Chemical Week Buyer's Guide*, are published annually and list suppliers in a specific area or industry. The *Chemical Week* directory is divided into two sections: 1—Chemicals, Raw Materials, and Specialties, and 2—Packaging, Shipping, and Bulk Containers. Suppliers are listed by product; they can submit technical data such as product line descriptions, formulas, and product applications, using advertisements or inserts in the directory.

Directories serve as references for industrial buyers. Industrial buyers looking for a particular product refer to their directories to determine the number of suppliers of that product and which suppliers to contact. In some instances, industrial buyers may learn about the existence of suppliers that would otherwise never have been considered. When referring to directories, it has been estimated that 83 percent of users consult the manufacturer listings, 72 percent examine the advertisements, 53 percent take action by phoning or writing the manufacturer, and 50 percent send in a reader service card (Cahners Research Report #450.4). Most users keep the directory for over one year, so advertisements in directories serve as continuous reminders of suppliers and products, for long periods of time. Also, advertisements may supplement the listings, increasing the exposure of suppliers to potential buyers. Furthermore, advertisements contain more information regarding the supplier and its product than does the listing.

Some industrial marketers see certain disadvantages to advertising in industrial directories. They argue that both an advertisement and a listing by product group is duplication and unnecessary exposure. Since the various suppliers of that product are listed together, there is considerable competition within each product group. Directories are expensive, so certain industrial organizations may not purchase them or may depend on older editions. Another disadvantage is that a marketer cannot develop a specific message targeted at a defined audience, since the buying influences referring to these publications represent a broad range of industries—and interests.

Telemarketing utilizes the telephone in performing certain marketing functions, including both advertising and personal selling. This often involves the use of a toll-free telephone number and/or a WATS (Wide Area Telephone Service) line. This type of marketing communication is a personal way to handle customer complaints and inquiries, take orders, receive requests for customer service, and maintain personal contact with customers.

Telemarketing provides the opportunity for an immediate response to a customer inquiry for additional information in catalogs or other literature, or a request for a salesperson to call. Instead of reader response cards found in advertisements in publications, an advertisement can contain a toll-free telephone number the customer can call.

Due to the high cost of a sales call, some organizations have replaced personal selling with telemarketing, supplemented with catalogs and other types of direct mail literature. Customers who purchase directly from catalogs can phone in their orders. If an organization uses personal selling, telemarketing can be used to identify prospects, answer questions, maintain contact between sales calls, and get feedback from customers. Customers can be informed immediately of any situations that require their attention such as partial shipments, out-of-stock problems, or product performance problems.

For a company using the WATS line, a three-minute call used for tasks such as receiving customer inquiries or handling customer complaints costs as little as three dollars. This amount is acceptable to many industrial organizations, whose orders are usually for large volumes and large dollar amounts.

Bigger organizations may want to use an inquiry-handling company whose only job is to respond to calls on a toll-free line. The companies can take requests for literature and provide information such as names, phone numbers, and locations of dealers and representatives.

Direct mail consists of letters, brochures, and other correspondence, delivering a personalized message direct to selected individuals. Catalog and other forms of sales promotion are often included. Mail is a flexible type of industrial promotion, since marketers can control the content, the timing, and the target audience.

Prior to a salesperson's call, a letter can introduce and answer general questions concerning the salesperson, the company, and the product or service. Direct mail can serve as a way of personally maintaining continuous communication with industrial buying influences between sales calls or after the sale has been made. Remaining in contact with a buying organization acts to remind customers about the supplier and also can work to establish a favorable buyer-seller relationship. Letters and brochures can be sent to key individuals, some of whom a salesperson may be unable to call on, in order to introduce and promote products or services. In addition, direct mail can elicit customer feedback, serving as a form of market research.

The industrial marketer faces several problems using direct mail. Establishing and maintaining a mailing list of prospects may be a lengthy, complex task. In fact, the cost effectiveness of direct mail is directly related to the quality of the mailing list. Prospects need to be identified by their organization, position, and name. Lists can be rented or purchased from commercial list houses or publishers of trade publications. Lists can be compiled from within the organization if a concerted effort is made to collect and update data files on past and current customers, customer inquiries, and contacts made at trade shows or through referrals. Often, salespeople are aware of present and prospective customers to which direct mail should be addressed. In some cases, the mailing list may be too general or may not reach the potentials the organization needs to reach. In addition, a marketer must know the customer's location, organization, and other customer characteristics to design and individualize a message that directly addresses that customer's needs. This is complicated further if a supplier has multiple, diverse types of products or a long product line. Problems exist for the marketer if the selected individuals who receive the mail disregard its content. Organizational buying influences receive many pieces of mail a day, and may be too busy to read or refer them to others. Mailing product literature that is not read can be wasteful and expensive for the marketer.

Evaluating Advertising

Management is sometimes skeptical about allocating sizable amounts for advertising industrial products and services due to the difficulty in determining whether or not those expenditures were well-spent. Many a manager can be heard to say "I know that half of my advertising is wasted, but I don't know which half" (Belizzi and Hite 1986). This problem has a number of causes.

First, managers often fail to set specific advertising objectives, so they have no standard or guideline against which to compare the results of an advertising campaign. Whether they focus on sales, reach, customer awareness levels, attitude change, or some other indicator, objectives provide a basis for resource allocation, and a means for control over those resources once they are allocated. In the absence of objectives, the industrial advertiser is virtually shooting in the dark.

Second, in the absence of other goals, managers look for bottom-line results in terms of sales. However, sales are affected by a variety of factors, including pricing policies, sales force efforts, competitor actions, and economic developments. It is difficult to control for these other factors and isolate the impact of advertising on sales. In addition, although managers frequently will look for a direct linear relationship between advertising and sales, the relationship is generally nonlinear, because diminishing returns set in at some point.

A third issue which poses difficulties for evaluation lies in estimating the time it takes for the advertising to have its impact. Almost never can an instantaneous impact be expected. Further, for advertising to achieve results, the target audience usually must be exposed to the message more than once. The time lag between instituting an advertising program and realizing results can extend to a number of months, and occasionally longer.

Sales tend to be emphasized in the evaluation not only because of a concern with the bottom line, but also because sales data is readily obtainable. The same reasoning lies behind the frequent reliance on circulation data for print media, and attendance figures for trade shows as performance indicators.

If not just sales, and in addition to overall objectives, what should an evaluation focus upon? Key areas for investigation include determining if the right audience was reached, which media most effectively reached that audience, if the message registered, and if the message had a favorable/unfavorable/neutral bearing on the customer's predispositions toward the vendor and/or product.

If the firm emphasizes communication objectives, such as influencing customer awareness levels, comprehension, or perceptions, the evaluation process often requires the collection of data before and after an advertising program has been implemented. Surveys after the campaign, directed at a representative sample of those in the target audience, can be used to identify changes in audience predispositions relative to some benchmark. As valuable as this approach appears to be, it presents a number of measurement problems and can be expensive. Awareness, recall, attitude, and behavioral intention are difficult concepts to measure reliably. They are unobservable phenomena, subject to a variety of influences beyond the marketer's advertising effort.

In addition to communication effect, the marketer is concerned with measuring efficiency of the firm's advertising expenditures. Toward this end, it is useful to develop and monitor efficiency indicators such as advertising expense per sale, inquiries generated per advertisement (and how this varies by size), or advertising cost per person reached in the target audience. Also, to measure any impact on sales force productivity, advertising effectiveness can be monitored by tracking the cost per sales call, for example. In this way, the focus is placed on advertising's role in the communication mix.

At the same time, performance evaluation should not focus just on the effectiveness of the organization's media or message choices. Frequency of exposure is also an important area of concern, because it can be a major source of waste expenditures. As indicated earlier, advertising run too few times can be as ineffective as advertising run too many times. Even if a single advertisement reaches all the members of its target audience (a highly improbable outcome), it does not cognitively register with many of these individuals on the first exposure. They block it out, or are distracted by other stimuli. As a result, it often takes multiple exposures to be noticed and absorbed. At some number of exposures, however, the advertising objective is accomplished and further exposures serve little purpose.

Evaluation should be an integral and ongoing component of the strategic approach to advertising management. The ability to evaluate can be greatly enhanced through the development of a strong data base to assist in decision making. This was referred to as a marketing information system. As a case in point, Rank Xerox, the European subsidiary of Xerox Corporation, developed a computerized, data base marketing system that enables it to target promotional efforts directly to specific companies. This system contains such information as the machines a company is currently using, the products that will best satisfy that particular company's needs, inquiries received per product, and the medium used when making inquiries (response card or telephone call), to name a few (Milmo 1984).

THE ROLE OF SALES PROMOTION

While our focus has been on industrial advertising strategy, sales promotion also performs an essential function in the total communications mix. As with advertising, it typically fills a supplemental and complementary role with the personal sales effort. Occasionally, though, sales promotion actually incorporates or replaces personal selling. Of the many sales promotion tools available to the industrial marketer, we will examine three in this section: trade shows, catalogs, and technical reports.

Trade shows permit the formal exhibition of a supplier's products for the purpose of demonstrating, promoting, and ultimately selling these products. A show is an excellent forum for delivering a message to, and making personal contacts with, a large number of present and prospective customers at one location. The show-and-tell format is especially useful for customers in the information search and alternative evaluation stages of the buying process. For the exhibitor, the average cost per visitor contacted at trade shows is estimated at $67.88. When exhibitors reach 70 percent or more of their potential audience, the average cost per visitor is reduced to $36.27 (Cox 1985). Either of these costs is appreciably less than the cost of a cold sales call.

Trade shows can be used by a supplier to:

1. Introduce and demonstrate product improvements, product applications, and new technological developments. Salespeople have the opportunity to demonstrate products that are too bulky or complex to demonstrate during a sales visit. Also demonstrations can be made to a number of people at one time.

2. Build awareness of the supplier and its products among organizational buying influences previously inaccessible or unknown to the salespeople.

3. Make personal contacts with present and prospective (often unknown) customers, answer questions, provide company and product information, obtain feedback, discuss problems, generate leads, produce sales, and promote goodwill. Keep in mind that prospects come actively seeking information, and have specifically set aside their own time to do so. Trade shows provide a medium for satisfying customer information needs more completely and immediately.

4. Remain competitive by participating in trade shows attended by the supplier's top competitors. This participation allows customers to compare products, and suppliers to evaluate developments and trends in their industry.

5. Hire personnel and establish relations with new representatives and distributors. A successful appearance at a trade show can, for some products, make enough contacts, generate enough leads, and produce enough sales to make trade shows the focal point of an organization's promotional efforts (Green 1985). Some firms report that as much as 25 percent of annual sales are generated from a single show (Mee 1979).

To help ensure that a show appearance is successful, the marketer should begin by establishing clearcut objectives for using a trade show. Many exhibitors do not, and the frequent result is an unsuccessful show (Donath 1980). Cavanaugh (1976) suggests six considerations in setting trade show objectives: (a) the company's overall reason for exhibiting (e.g., establish contacts, make sales, project an image); (b) the target audience to be reached; (c) the relative advantages of national, regional, and local exhibiting; (d) the balance between efficiency (e.g., cost per person contacted) versus effectiveness (e.g., contacts made or sales gained at shows versus through other channels); (e) competitors' trade show strategies; and (f) the budget and projected cost ratio per sales lead obtained.

Proper selection of the trade show(s) in which the company will participate is also critical for success. Those shows that attract the target audience the organization is trying to reach are the ones for consideration. There are national, regional, and local trade shows to choose from. Data is available in the form of surveys and audits on the attendance level of various shows, audience quality, and certain demographic characteristics of individuals who attend these shows. These reports are done by organizations such as Exhibit Survey, Inc., and the Trade Show Bureau.

After selecting the show, the displays and literature to be used at the show must be developed. The display should be unique and interesting, to selectively attract the attention of those with a real interest in the products on display. On the average, 67 percent of those who visit an exhibit are actually interested in that company's type of product, 31 percent plan to buy that type of product, and 74 percent have some influence in the buying decision for it (Cox 1985).

Four major types of exhibit techniques include static displays, attention-getters, audiovisual presentations, and live product demonstrations. A *static display* features display areas for products, but no demonstration. The emphasis is on salespeople working individually with prospects. *Attention-getters* include special performances (e.g., magic acts, celebrities) and contests meant to attract large crowds. *Audiovisual presentations* might include films, tapes, or computer screen displays, and can involve multimedia presentations. Product applications can be demonstrated, detailed product information can be conveyed, and both product and company can be dramatized. *Live product demonstrations* are quite effective, and should be used where possible. Some suggest that these demonstrations last no longer than 10 to 12 minutes.

The single most important aspect of the show is the selection and training of booth personnel. Failure to make one-on-one contact with over one-half of the potential audience is generally attributable to the people working the booth (Cox 1985). The sales task is different from a personal sales call, because the salesperson has much less time to establish the relationship and work the sale, and frequently knows little or nothing about a particular prospect.

Advertising efforts should be coordinated with shows to enhance their effectiveness. Trade show visitors often have limited time, and are confronted with a sizable number of exhibits, not all of which they expect to see. Marketers want to ensure that their exhibit is on the customer's must-see list. It is also important to advertise the occurrence of trade show exhibits for products which cannot be demonstrated during routine sales calls. Also, giveaways that visitors carry around the show after leaving an exhibit can be helpful. Direct mail or advertisements in trade publications can be used to contact key buying influences about a supplier's planned participation in a show and possibly of the products to be displayed or the theme of the display. During the show, advertisements sometimes will be taken by exhibitors in local media, including billboards. Following the trade show, the supplier will follow up on contacts with prospective customers through letters, phone calls, or sales calls.

The effectiveness of the trade show can be determined by measuring the number of those who visited the supplier's display, the number of inquiries received at the show for more information or a sales call, and/or the amount of sales generated by the show. Also, a survey can be conducted of the show's visitors to determine the percentage that visited the exhibit, talked to a salesperson, and/or received literature. Such data should be examined in relation to the total potential audience at a show. These results can help the industrial marketer determine the effectiveness of the display in creating interest, making contacts, and generating sales. In addition, the marketer can use these results for planning which trade shows he or she will continue to participate in.

Many managers still fail to appreciate the utility of trade shows, so trade show budgets tend to be cut before advertising budgets or other marketing expenses. Companies fail to realize that their own poor management of this valuable resource diminishes the potentially sizable benefits of shows.

Printed *catalogs* contain information that describes the supplier's line of products, their applications, and other important product information, including price lists, warranties, and service requirements. Industrial buyers can use catalogs as reference guides in selecting potential suppliers and products and in comparing a supplier's products against those of its competitors. Further, catalogs can help user companies keep up with a supplier's new product introductions, improvements, and modifications. Companies with extensive product lines design their catalogs to contain just a brief summary of the most important information to be relayed to industrial buyers. An alternative to this would be to print a number of smaller catalogs for specific products or product groups and distribute them to individuals interested in those specific areas.

Catalogs can be distributed in a number of ways. They can be distributed by mail to a selected list of organizational buying influences or to those individuals who request more information on a supplier's products. Many industrial advertisements will contain an address or toll-free telephone number that can be used to request a catalog. Salespeople can distribute them to buying influences during sales calls or at trade shows. In addition, a supplier's catalog can be combined with the catalogs of other suppliers, in industrial directories.

Other than salespeople themselves, catalogs are one of the few promotional alternatives that provide buyer company members with specific, detailed information concerning a supplier's product line and prices. A catalog received prior to a salesperson's call can prestructure the visit by allowing the buyer to become familiar with the products and certain specifications and applications. After the sales call, it can be referred to for answers to questions the buying center member might have. Those influential members of the buying center who do not have direct contact with the salesperson may have access to catalogs. Often, catalogs contain enough information (especially on standardized products that require little explanation) that an industrial buyer can purchase from them directly. For companies with extensive lines, the catalog may be the only way to keep customers informed of all the items the firm sells.

Catalogs can be an invaluable form of promotion, if they are distributed to significant buying influences who can effectively utilize them. They can generate sales calls or even sales themselves; consequently, poor distribution can result in lost sales opportunities. Buyers may rely heavily on catalogs for some purchasing decisions, ignoring suppliers whose catalogs are not available. At the same time, the considerable costs of planning, designing, printing, and dispersing the catalogs suggest that mailing lists be updated and maintained to ensure catalog delivery to the appropriate buying influences. Catalogs themselves must be frequently updated to reflect changes in the vendor's products or services.

Technical reports are distributed by the supplier of a product, to disseminate specific, detailed product information. These reports describe the product, its applications, and its specifications in technical terms, to provide information necessary for technically qualified buying influences to see how the product can be used in their organization. The reports contain illustrations and diagrams that provide a detailed analysis of the product's composition and its functions. Technical reports usually detail results from product testing—including product performance and data such as product quality and reliability. Exhibit 11.3 typifies the use of such technical test results in a direct mail piece. These types of literature can be used in training people for production and maintenance work, since the reports describe the installation, use, repair, and servicing of the product.

These reports can be distributed through direct mail, during a salesperson's call, and at trade shows. Organizations often keep these reports to refer to when making buying decisions, comparing a product against that of its competitors, and when repairing the product. Technical reports are useful to supplement the supplier's catalog. Catalogs usually provide general product information, but buyers more familiar with the complex nature of the product may find in technical reports the information they require to make buying decisions. Reports can also alert them to any possible problems in the installation, use, or maintenance of the product.

SUMMARY

This chapter has focused on the advertising and sales promotion components of the industrial promotional mix, approaching them primarily as support activities supplementing the personal selling effort. It was argued that the role of promotion will vary depending upon the steps in the hierarchy of effects (a micro perspective) as well as the stages of the organizational buying process (a macro approach). Further, differences between individual customers, their needs, and their buying decision processes can be so great as to warrant separate promotional efforts tailored to each organization or each market segment.

The controversy over the merits of advertising to industrial customers was examined, and some of the major reasons for advertising were established. These included reaching unknown or inaccessible buying decision makers, identifying new prospects, laying the groundwork for the sales call, supporting intermediaries, stimulating derived demand, and projecting a favorable corporate image to customers and other publics.

Exhibit 11.3   Technical Test Results Used in a Direct Mail Program

CONNECTOR SPECIALISTS OF FLORIDA

5880 Macy Avenue   •   Jacksonville, Florida 32211
904-744-3567   904-744-3563

IMPORTANT NOTICE...IMPORTANT NOTICE...IMPORTANT NOTICE
****
****
BI-LOK TUBE FITTINGS MEETS RIGID TESTING OF INDEPENDENT LAB

"This major breakthrough can lead to
substantial cost savings for your
company in tube fitting purchases."

SWAGELOK VS BI-LOK

A test performed by Newport News Shipbuilding and Dry Dock
to answer concerns of Virginia Electric & Power Co. determined that there were no significant differences which would
adversely effect the Safety, Performance and Remake
Capability between Swagelok/Bi-lok fittings and "INTERMIXED"
assemblies of both.

The test encompassed over 300 man hours to conduct all the
test phases which addressed the major concerns of tube
fittings related to Industrial applications.

On the heaviest wall thickness recommended for 1/4" (.065)
3/8" (.065) and 1/2" (.083) stainless steel tubing, Swagelok,
Bi-lok, and two lots of "intermixed" fittings all passed the
following pressure test with no significant differences in
performance.

A. A MAKE-BREAK TEST (25 CYCLES)
   Connected adaptors, unions and caps to tubing. Assembled
   fittings according to manufacturers instructions, dis-
   assembled and reassembled. After 5 cycles, pressurized
   the assembly to 2 times working pressure. This procedure
   was repeated until 25 cycles were completed and then the
   system was pressurized to 3 times the working pressure
   for 15 minutes.

B. A BURST TEST
   Test used assembly identical to the make-break test
   and pressurized system to tube burst.

C. A TENSILE PULL TEST
   Connected two 6" pieces of stainless steel tubing with
   a union; inserted assembly into test machine and increased load until union broke or tubing pulled out of
   union.

CONNECTOR SPECIALISTS OF FLORIDA

5880 Macy Avenue   •   Jacksonville, Florida 32211
904-744-3567   904-744-3563

page 2

D. HELIUM TEST
   Test used assembly identical to the make-break test; installed
   fittings to a helium leak detector and recorded leakage when a
   vacuum was pulled off the system

All fittings passed the Helium leak test to a rate of 1 x 10-5 cc/sec.
Forty-seven (47) of the forty eight (48) fittings used in this test
passed a rate of greater than 1 x 10-9 cc/sec.

The fittings which were tested consisted of complete Swagelok and
Bi-Lok assemblies (with spare ferrules) and two lots of "intermixed"
Bi-Lok/Swagelok fitting assemblies as follows:

LOT I		LOT II	
Nut	Swagelok	Nut	Bi-Lok
Rear Ferrule	Bi-Lok	Rear Ferrule	Swagelok
Front Ferrule	Swagelok	Front Ferrule	Bi-Lok
Body	Bi-Lok	Body	Swagelok

The test results proved "all assemblies (48) showed their capability
to work properly in pressure systems." With this new breakthrough in
reference to our products performance capability, we would like to
discuss your tube fitting requirements for your facility. We have a
HIGH PERFORMANCE TUBE FITTING that can take the punishment in your plant......

AND

********** WE HAVE THE PRICE!!!! **********

Sincerely,

Rumsey Huston

encl: Newport News Shipbuilding and Dry Dock Company
      Newport News, Virginia
      Report No. Y-5963
      Author D.G. Paxton
      Title: "Tube Fittings Performance Test"

To properly manage an industrial advertising program, it should be approached as an integral part of the firm's marketing strategy, with its own strategic framework. Starting with marketing strategy, the suggested approach included setting measurable objectives, establishing operational budgets, designing effective messages, selecting appropriate media, and evaluating performance. Issues, approaches, and findings in each of these decision areas were assessed. Emphasis was placed on the importance of reflecting the nature of the market and the needs of the customer throughout the process of conceptualizing and implementing the advertising program. The temptation to get so caught up in the appeal of various promotion techniques and alternatives often overshadows the basic need to provide product education to target groups.

The major media alternatives available to the industrial advertiser were described. These included general business publications, vertical and horizontal trade publications, industrial directories, telemarketing, and direct mail. Advantages and disadvantages of each were identified in areas such as audience reach, ability to impart information, timing, flexibility, and cost per contact.

Finally, the chapter examined sales promotion, highlighting the uses of trade shows, technical reports, and catalogs. These tools serve to complement the personal sales effort, and must be coordinated with advertising strategy. In some cases, they can be used to accomplish sales.

As technology progresses, as product life cycles grow shorter, and as industrial buyers become more sophisticated and demanding, promotion and advertising take on new dimensions. Advertising budgets are likely to grow, and advertising programs will become more aggressive. Companies will increasingly rely on an array of media to build recognition and position products. Increased emphasis placed on evaluating promotion results will lead to the development of sound data bases and up-to-date marketing information systems.

QUESTIONS

1. What is the industrial promotional mix? Why are personal selling, advertising, sales promotion, and publicity grouped together? How do these four areas affect one another?

2. Explain the hierarchy of effects. How might an understanding of this model be useful in designing the communications strategy for a company that manufactures paper shredding machines?

3. Marketing does not end with the sale, especially in industrial markets. Explain this statement. What kinds of activities might the marketer pursue in the post-purchase evaluation stage when selling business forms to corporations?

4. Unlike in consumer markets, the industrial customer does not come to the vendor, or "shop." Given this, what role does advertising fill in industrial markets?

5. Although setting communication objectives (as opposed to sales or profit objectives) would seem to make sense, such objectives are not very practical, because they cannot be quantified or measured. Do you agree or disagree? Why?

6. Freightway Transportation Company, a freight hauler serving most of the United States, sets its advertising budget for the coming year as a percentage of the projected sales for the year. Explain the advantages and disadvantages of this approach. How would you suggest Freightway determine the budget?

7. Why would you emphasize the company instead of its specific products in your trade journal advertising? Why would you stress a number of product lines instead of individual products? When might you place the emphasis on individual products instead of broader product lines, or instead of the company itself?

8. It is generally a mistake to use emotional appeals (i.e., humor, fear, sex) in industrial advertisements. Do you agree or disagree? Why?

9. Six months ago, Fendt Engineering Corporation spent $40,000 to participate in its first major trade show. At the show, heavily attended by buyers and managers from the retailing industry, Fendt featured its new electronic cash register. Hardly anyone visited the company's exhibit at the show, and it does not appear that any orders were subsequently received as a direct result of the show. Identify ten possible reasons for this apparent failure. Assume the product itself is a significant improvement over existing products, and is priced competitively.

10. How might direct mail be used as a promotional tool during the stages of the buying process? Explain the different uses of direct mail at each stage.

CHAPTER 12

PERSONAL SELLING AND SALES MANAGEMENT

Key Concepts

Activity points
Buyer-Seller dyad
Call planning
Customer servicing
Draw
Expectancy model
Incentive pay
Missionary selling
National account
Negotiation process
New prospect selling
Order taker
PAIRS model
Postsale stage
Preparation

Presentation
Prospecting
Psychological testing
Relational characteristics
Roles and norms
Sales force structure
Sales management
Sales quota
Selling aids
Sliding scale commission
Social actor characteristics
Structural characteristics
Technical selling
Trade selling
Workload method

Learning Objectives

1. Establish the central role of personal selling in the promotional mix for industrial firms.
2. Identify distinctive characteristics of personal selling in industrial markets.
3. Advocate the need for adopting a dyadic perspective when selling to organizations, and draw sales implications from each dimension of the dyad.
4. Describe a process for managing the industrial sales effort.
5. Discuss a number of analytical tools and concepts which are useful in evaluating decision alternatives at each stage in the sales management process.

PERSONAL SELLING IS THE CENTERPIECE

The preceding chapter pointed out that few sales are closed solely as a result of advertising or sales promotion. Unlike many consumer decisions, the complexities of organizational needs often demand personal forms of communication before, during, and after a purchase decision. Where the customer may seek out the supplier's product by going to a particular store, the vendor often has to seek out the organizational customer. The vendor's own sales force, and/or the selling efforts of intermediaries, play the central role, while other forms of promotion fill a supporting or supplemental role.

The sales force is the physical link between the selling and buying organizations. Not only are salespeople communicating information regarding the attributes of the vendor and its products or services to customers, they are also communicating information regarding customer problems or changing needs back to the vendor organization. In this manner, at least ideally, those in R&D, production, quality control, shipping, order processing, collections, and other key areas can adapt their operations to better serve the customer. Sales force inputs are also valuable in sales forecasting. In addition, the salesperson frequently serves to negotiate price and delivery terms, including discounts, returns policies, shipment quantities and supplies, and transportation forms. Further, the sales force will often service customer accounts, as well as provide demonstrations and training in the use of the vendor's products. In sum, then, an industrial salesperson might be characterized as playing at least four roles: crusader for the company's cause, market researcher, negotiator, and consultant or problem solver.

Personal selling has been defined as "personal interaction for the purpose of facilitating exchange to mutual advantage" (Enis 1979). Selling is not manipulation, for the salesperson cannot *make* people buy. A salesperson can persuade, cajole, stimulate, encourage, and entice, but cannot force customers to buy. Selling is simply a more direct, immediate, and personalized form of communication, but one which requires an immediate response of some kind from the buyer. In industrial markets, personal selling is also a more expensive but more effective form of communication.

Industrial personal sales expenditures can be as much as two to three times as high as those for consumer sales (see Table 12.1). These costs can be attributed to

Table 12.1 Sales Force Selling Expenses as a Percentage of Sales in Major Industries

Industry	Compensation		Travel and Entertainment Expenses		Total	
	1985	1984	1985	1984	1985	1984
CONSUMER GOODS						
Durable goods	1.8	2.1	0.7	1.3	2.5	3.4
Food	1.4	1.9	0.5	0.5	1.9	2.4
Major household items	1.8	3.3	0.6	0.7	2.4	4.0
INDUSTRIAL GOODS						
Automotive parts & accessories	2.2	2.6	0.7	1.0	2.9	3.6
Building materials	1.2	1.2	0.3	0.5	1.5	1.7
Chemicals and petroleum	1.6	2.4	0.5	0.4	2.1	2.8
Computers	1.5	4.2	0.4	1.7	1.9	5.9
Containers, packaging materials, & paper	0.4	1.0	0.2	0.2	0.6	1.2
Electrical equipment	1.5	1.6	0.5	0.6	2.0	2.2
Electronics	2.2	3.4	1.6	1.3	3.8	4.7
Fabricated metals (heavy)	1.5	1.0	0.5	0.4	2.0	1.4
Fabricated metals (light)	2.0	2.5	0.7	1.4	2.7	3.9
Fabrics & apparel	2.1	2.2	0.7	0.5	2.8	2.7
Iron & steel	0.8	1.4	0.3	0.6	1.1	2.0
Machinery (heavy)	2.1	2.0	0.8	0.7	2.9	2.7
Machinery (light)	1.3	3.3	1.2	1.3	2.5	4.6
Office & educational equipment	8.2	2.1	1.2	1.2	9.4	3.3
Printing & publishing	5.5	5.2	1.1	1.3	6.6	6.5
Rubber, plastics & leather	1.6	1.9	0.8	1.0	2.8	2.9

Note: percentages in this table are percentages of sales by the sales force.

Source: Reprinted by permission of *Sales and Marketing Management.* "1986 Survey of Selling Costs," 17, 56.

the technical nature of industrial products, the longer buying process, and the larger size of the buying center. In industrial markets, there are fewer organizational customers, and they place large dollar orders for large volumes of products. Industrial customers are more involved with their purchases than the average consumer, as the purchased items will affect the organization's operations, end products, and profits. Moreover, industrial buyers spend more time, effort, and money making purchasing decisions than those in the consumer segment, and are, themselves, technically qualified. Industrial markets also tend to be characterized by more direct, shorter channels, which places more responsibility on a vendor's own sales force.

The average cost of a business-to-business sales call has risen from about $71 in 1975 to over $230 in 1986—a rate of increase that has easily outpaced inflation (McGraw-Hill 1986). The rate of increase has dropped in recent years; however, as companies have introduced efficiency measures into the sales management process, computer technology has been a major factor in cost control. It also appears that the cost per call is higher for companies with ten or fewer salespeople and for those that sell direct rather than through distributors.

THE DISTINCTIVE REQUIREMENTS OF INDUSTRIAL SELLING

Personal selling is usually the cornerstone of the industrial firm's communications strategy. And, the nature of industrial selling is, in itself, unique. Let us examine the distinguishing characteristics of industrial selling in five areas: the salesperson, selling aids, the sales process, negotiation, and sales management.

The Salesperson

Are industrial salespeople different from those who sell consumer goods and services? Keep in mind that there are a number of different types of salespeople, some of which are discussed below. As a general statement, however, the training and skills required to successfully sell many industrial goods and services are distinctly different from those necessary for the consumer goods salesperson. Industrial selling requires more technical background, usually obtained through college education, corporate training, or practical experience. Many sales representatives today also hold advanced degrees. Salespeople must be able to communicate with a variety of people, many with different backgrounds and orientations. They must be able to *speak the language* used in various functional areas (e.g., engineering, production, finance) within the customer organization, and to service their accounts. They often require the skills to build and harvest a long-term customer relationship. In addition, they typically must be able to effectively negotiate terms favorable to the supplier in a variety of areas.

There are five basic types of sales positions (based on the activities performed), any combination of which a given salesperson might fill. That is, they are not mutually exclusive. The five types are trade selling, missionary selling, technical selling, new prospect selling, and customer servicing. Other categories have been identified, such as order takers and trade servicers, but this chapter will focus on these five (see, for example, Moncrief 1986). Table 12.2 provides some cost data on types of sales positions.

Trade selling is used when the vendor is using intermediaries such as industrial distributors. The sales force attempts to ensure that distributors are supporting the company's marketing strategy and working to achieve the organization's sales goals. Toward this end, salespeople will call on distributors to explain how both they and the manufacturer will benefit from specific advertising, sales promotion,

Table 12.2   Cost Per Call by Type of Salesperson

	Median 1985 Cost Per Call
Account representative (calls on existing accounts)	$108.45
Missionary salesperson	46.50
Sales engineer (technical selling)	145.75
Nontechnical industrial products salesperson	75.55
Service salesperson	56.70

Source: Reprinted by permission of *Sales and Marketing Management.* "1986 Survey of Selling Costs," 12.

inventory, pricing, or product-assortment policies. The sales force will also provide service to the distributor, helping in such areas as product training, information requests, expediting delivery, handling complaints, and processing goods the distributor wishes to return to the manufacturer.

A *missionary salesperson* does not actually attempt to close the sale. Rather, customers are called upon and encouraged to purchase the vendor's products or services, but the purchases are actually made from a distributor, or ordered direct from the company. Missionary salespeople are concerned, then, with providing information and promoting goodwill.

Technical selling is one of the most common types of selling in industrial markets. This type of salesperson has technical expertise, and often holds a degree in the sciences or engineering. Frequently, however, such technical sales personnel have limited formal business training. Their focus is on providing customers with extensive technical information and advice, helping with product applications, and solving problems in the use or adaptation of the vendor's product to customer needs. Such technically qualified salespeople are often paid as much as 15 percent more than nontechnical salespeople, and are more apt to receive a larger portion of their earnings in the form of salary (Bellizzi and Cline 1985). One approach to technical selling is to put together a sales team, which might consist of a nontechnical salesperson who makes the formal sales presentation, a financial expert, a production specialist, and the technical sales expert. This team approach allows the technical sales expert to concentrate on the product and its complex specifications and applications.

New prospect selling focuses on the generation of new accounts, as opposed to increasing sales to existing accounts, or to supporting distributor sales. In new prospect selling, the salesperson makes cold calls on potential buyers, or follows up on unsolicited inquiries and inquiries generated through other promotional efforts.

The final type of selling position, *customer servicing,* involves activities that facilitate and complement the selling process. Here, the salesperson works directly with the end user to ensure effective and satisfactory usage of the vendor's product.

Not unlike the service function provided in trade selling to distributors, customer servicing includes handling complaints, assisting in training, installation, repair and maintenance, and developing positive personal relationships.

Selling Aids

When building a relationship with a particular customer, the industrial salesperson supplements regular calls with selling aids. These include small gifts, plant tours, business lunches, and other entertainment activities which help to support sales and maintain good standing with buyers.

Small gifts (such as paperweights, lighters, memo pads, rulers, inexpensive calculators, or business card holders) will usually have the vendor's name on them, and serve as a constant reminder to the prospect. Characteristics of effective gifts include usefulness, generality, permanence, conspicuousness, quality, tastefulness, and some apparent relationship between the gift and the vendor's product (Zinkhan and Vachris 1984). Such small gifts are generally accepted, although a measure of tact is called for in their distribution. Many companies have policies that employees cannot accept substantial gifts from vendors. Suppliers of these (mostly inexpensive) items have combined to register over $4 billion in annual sales in recent years.

A buyer tour of the supplier's plant is another effective selling aid. This activity allows the buyer to enter the selling organization's territory, as opposed to the norm in which the salesperson calls at the customer's location. A tour has the additional advantage of limiting the factors that distract the prospect during a normal sales call, such as telephone calls or interruptions by other employees. This environment enhances the salesperson's ability to establish a personal rapport. And, a tour educates the buyer about the vendor's plant facilities and quality control.

Entertainment activities also represent valuable tools for use by the industrial salesperson. Finn and Moncrief (1985) have identified five of the many types of such activities: taking clients out to lunch, for an evening meal, for a drink, for leisure activities (e.g., professional sporting events, fishing), and parties for clients. These activities provide a neutral ground where the buyer and salesperson can discuss transactions or terms and get more personally acquainted. The business lunch is especially important. Compared to other entertainment options, a business lunch can be inexpensive (usually under $20). As illustrated in Table 12.3, taking clients to lunch is the most frequently used of entertainment activities, and is a fairly common practice. This data is based on surveys of a cross section of 1,350 salespeople from 51 industrial companies. In a separate study of sales records for a single industry, business forms, Zinkhan and Vachris (1984) found a positive relationship between first purchase and whether the new buyer had been taken to lunch. Even so, companies have reduced entertainment expense budgets, in an attempt to control costs.

Additionally, many sales organizations have policies about the use of selling aids, or what they will allow as a reimbursable salesperson expense. Meals appear to be the most widely accepted expense; drinks, sporting events, and cocktail parties are less frequently allowable, and at-home entertainment or hunting/fishing trips are rarely acceptable.

Table 12.3   Various Entertainment Activities Performed by Industrial
Salespeople (N = 1350)

	Frequently Done (%)	Occasionally Done (%)	Infrequently Done (%)	Never Done (%)	Average Time Spent (Minutes)
Taking clients to lunch	37.7	50.0	11.9	2.4	72.8
Taking clients to dinner	7.7	30.0	42.9	19.4	107.9
Taking clients out for a drink	7.0	31.8	32.5	28.7	70.7
Leisure activities with clients (e.g., golf or fishing)	3.7	21.3	29.2	45.8	142.4
Giving parties for clients	1.2	6.3	17.0	75.5	128.9

Source: Reprinted by permission of the publisher from "Salesforce Entertainment Activities," by D.W. Finn and W.C. Moncrief, *Industrial Marketing Management* 14, 230. Copyright 1985 by Elsevier Science Publishing Co., Inc.

The Selling Process

The industrial sales process also has distinctive characteristics. This process has four major steps: prospecting, preparation, presentation, and postsale. *Prospecting,* or identifying potential new accounts, involves more than finding organizations that can use the vendor's product. The cost of a personal sales call is such that the sales manager wants to ensure that a given organization is a viable prospect. High customer-switching costs, deep-seated loyalties to other vendors, small potential orders, excessive service level demands, and an inefficient location are but a few of the many reasons to avoid particular potential customers. Prospecting is often done through telemarketing, referrals from current customers, inquiries generated through information request cards or toll-free telephone numbers included in print media advertisements, and through trade shows. Cold calls are also used, but are an inefficient means for finding customers, given the type of product that is usually being sold and the manner in which it is purchased.

One of the more recent advancements in the management of sales leads is specialized software developed to qualify, or classify, prospective customers. Leads are considered worthless to salespeople unless qualified. The goal is to determine if the prospective buyer is a key decision maker and when he is ready to make a purchase.

Whether the inquiry comes over the phone, via modem, or by mail (typically reader response cards), sophisticated lead-processing systems are capable of significantly reducing qualifying time, sometimes to as little as twenty-four hours. These systems range in price from $89 for a basic personal computer version up to $240,000 for a complex, marketing-oriented mainframe system. These top-notch systems are capable of identifying market trends, locating and developing profitable markets, enhancing sales forecast accuracy, and measuring media effectiveness (Kent 1986).

Preparation for the sales call can involve extensive research. The salesperson wants to develop a feel for the nature of a customer organization's needs in a particular product or service area, and the way in which that customer would apply the vendor's product. Research on an organization's buying process is equally important. The salesperson is attempting to determine which members of a prospective customer organization are influential in his or her product area, as well as which ones are accessible. Further, an effort should be made to determine which individuals cannot be ignored, and which ones require spending the most time with. Personal information on these individuals is often helpful. In addition to identifying key personnel, the salesperson wants to become acquainted with the policies and procedures used by the prospective customer organization in purchase decision making, such as those governing the setting of specifications, bid solicitation, supplier selection, and rules governing the behavior of purchasing agents (e.g., free lunches, gifts). Preparation for a sales call may be further enhanced by learning as much as possible about the organization, including the organization's history, which competitors it has purchased from previously, and the current trends and common trade practices of the industry in which the customer operates.

Major differences in the *presentation* itself include the likelihood that one presentation will not be sufficient. This need for repetition is due to the lengthy buying decision process, and because the content will have to be tailored to different members of the customer organization, given their differing backgrounds and needs. It is important to remember that the buyer in an industrial transaction is a professional, and is likely to be wary of the salesperson who is too anxious to close the sale, who tries to oversell the prospect, or who is unlikely to be around if problems develop in using the purchased item.

The *postsale* stage of the process is of special consequence for the industrial marketer. Once a sale is closed, the salesperson continues to work with the customer in areas such as installation, training, servicing, maintenance, and returns— attempting to establish and solidify a source-loyal relationship. He or she is now better informed regarding the purchasing decision process in the customer organization, and is in a position to reinforce key buying influences while establishing more personal relationships with them.

Negotiation

Although industrial goods and services are sometimes purchased at a standard or list price, the more typical scenario involves negotiation between buyer and seller. These negotiations can include any number of individuals and issues. They can be formal or informal, and last hours, weeks, or months. Howard Raiffa, a leading authority in the field, explains (1982) that negotiation is both art and science. The scientific aspect involves systematic approaches for resolving conflicts between two parties. The artistic side concerns interpersonal skills, the ability to convince and be convinced, and judgment regarding which ploys to use and when.

Both parties gain from a transaction. The customer acquires a need-solving product or service, and the vendor makes a sale. The possibility of mutual gain is what brings the buyer and seller together. The amount of gain realized by either party creates conflicts that must be negotiated. This conflict occurs because the two parties find themselves competing for some of the same gains.

There is a tendency to approach the negotiation process as a *zero sum* game, in which one party's gains come completely at the expense of the other, in exact proportion. For example, if the seller gains revenue by negotiating 5 percent more in terms of the price charged, then the buyer experiences an expense to his or her organization's budget in the same amount.

It is frequently possible to turn the negotiations into a *positive sum* game. Creative thinking is the key. The seller focuses on finding options that hold merit for both parties. An example might be standing firm on the price increase, but giving the customer a favorable cash and quantity discount structure, or adding to the provisions of the warranty. Another possibility is a longer-term contract with the customer, guaranteeing that the price will not be raised during the period of the contract. The goal, then, is to increase the size of the pie, rather than merely competing for existing pieces of a fixed pie.

The best negotiation strategies are tailored to the particular buying situation at hand. Underlying any negotiation is the set of risks and rewards confronting both buyer and seller representatives and their respective organizations. Before establishing a bargaining position, the risks and rewards faced by those on the other side should be calculated. These estimations require the seller to determine the best alternative available to the buying organization should no agreement be reached with the seller's firm (Fisher and Ury 1981); they also require an evaluation of a buying organization's resources, and the motivations of its negotiating representative(s).

Buyers can be assumed to establish threshold values for the key variables under negotiation, based on the best alternative available to them. These are the absolute cutoff values they will accept before walking away, such as the maximum price they will pay, or the minimum service level they will tolerate. The vendor also establishes threshold values (e.g., minimum price, maximum service level). The amount of difference between the two positions is called the *zone of agreement* and the negotiation process seeks to produce a resolution that falls within this zone. As a result, marketers must develop a fairly good understanding of the buyer's threshold values in the early stages of negotiation.

Negotiation strategy should also reflect the structural characteristics of the relationship between the vendor and the buying organization. Let us briefly outline some of these characteristics, keeping in mind that each can have a direct impact on the ultimate outcome.

The extent to which the representatives of buyer and seller organizations are actually speaking for their respective organizations is a primary consideration. How much clout do these representatives have in terms of the issues under negotiation? Are there conflicts within the organizations on some of these issues? The degree of interdependence between the organizations is another consideration. How much does each need the other? The final agreement, if one is reached, is likely to be closer to the more dependent party's threshold level.

It should also be determined if the negotiation will be repetitive. That is, is it a one-time sale, or will there be frequent negotiations in the future? Repetitive bargaining usually finds the parties adopting a more cooperative stance. Separately, the marketer should evaluate the presence of any linkage effects—where a particular negotiation, and its outcome, are linked to other negotiations. Obstacles can sometimes be overcome by using linkages creatively.

Bargaining can be further characterized by the number of issues involved. Price is not always the central thrust; delivery guarantees, returns policies, the volume of goods purchased, quality standards, financing, and servicing arrangements are examples of items that may be on the agenda of the vendor or the customer. When multiple terms are involved, it is a real challenge to determine which trade-offs the other party will be inclined to make.

Next, the existence of time constraints should be noted. By optimally using the time frame available, the disadvantages of hasty negotiation by one party can be averted. In addition, marketers need to assess how public the negotiation will be. In industrial markets, different terms are often worked out with various customer accounts. The ability to negotiate flexibly with any one account is affected by how much other customers will learn of the tactics used and final terms agreed upon. Competitors are also in a position to benefit from learning a firm's negotiation strategy. Lastly, as will be discussed later in this chapter, it is critical to determine if any norms exist that govern the kinds of negotiation tactics used by either party.

Sales Management

Sales management, defined as "the planning, implementation, and control of personal contact programs designed to achieve the sales objectives of the firm" (Dalrymple 1982), has distinctive characteristics in the industrial environment. Industrial sales managers are concerned with recruiting, training, organizing, motivating, evaluating, and compensating the sales force.

These activities must reflect a number of characteristics of the industrial marketplace. For example, recruiting and training efforts must stress the ability of an individual to communicate and negotiate over complex product benefits with different individuals, of diverse backgrounds, in a given organization. This diversity takes the form of a wide range of social and intellectual sophistication among the people involved. The organization of the sales force should reflect the fewer absolute number of customers, the time required to close a sale, and the specific activities each salesperson is required to perform, in addition to more traditional considerations. Motivation, evaluation, and compensation must reflect the dollar value of purchases, the longer process, and the desirability of establishing long-term buyer-seller relations, among other factors.

Sales management will be investigated in further detail later in this chapter. Before doing so, however, a more general framework within which to examine industrial selling must be established.

A DYADIC PERSPECTIVE ON INDUSTRIAL SELLING

Marketing transactions involve, by definition, at least two parties. Industrial transactions include at least two organizations, both of which seek benefits, and both of which determine the outcome of the transaction. To properly understand and manage exchanges of industrial goods and services, the seller and the buyer should be examined together, as they affect one other. This is called the dyadic approach, where a dyad is a unit of two. It is in contrast to traditional approaches, which examine buyer or seller activities in isolation.

Among all the elements contained in the marketing mix, the dyadic approach has its greatest usefulness when applied to industrial selling—where the two-person or two-party interaction is most conspicuous. There are four key dimensions to a dyadic relationship: relational characteristics, social structural characteristics, social actor characteristics, and normative characteristics. These four interact to determine the outcomes of the industrial marketing exchange process. Table 12.4 provides examples of questions a sales manager might raise, based on the dimensions of the dyad. Let us look at each of these dimensions in further detail.

Relational Characteristics

As with any two-party relationship, the buyer-seller dyad can be characterized by the relative power positions of each party. Power is a function of dependency. The power that organization A has over organization B is a function of how dependent B is upon A. Organization B's dependency is determined by how much it needs those resources controlled by organization A, and how available such resources are from alternative sources. For example, if organization A manufactures a critical component part needed by organization B, and has an exclusive patent preventing anyone else from making a similar component, then A's power (or B's dependency) is high. However, power is always a two-way street. Both parties involved in an industrial transaction need, or are dependent upon, each other. The buyer needs a source of supply, the seller needs a profitable sale. The real concern is with the power balance: which party needs the other more?

Some of the other factors that determine power positions include reciprocity relationships between buyer and seller, supply shortages in a particular market, purchasing a disproportionate amount of one's total needs from a single supplier, selling a disproportionate amount of one's total output to a single customer, the service level requirements of a just-in-time inventory arrangement, proximity to a particular supplier or buyer, and financial or physical plant constraints.

Power positions of buyer and seller are likely to evolve and change over time. For example, a supply shortage may be a temporary phenomenon that enhances the position of the seller. Entry of a new competitor or changes in technology, however, may reduce the seller's bargaining position. A serious mistake can result from efforts

Table 12.4 Applying the Dyadic Perspective to Sales Management

Characteristics of the Seller-Buyer Dyad	Relevant Sales Management Questions
Relational	a. How dependent are we on this customer? b. How dependent are they on us? c. What are the sources of our respective dependencies? d. What are the implications of the power balance (or imbalance) for negotiation strategies? e. Where are the major sources of conflict between us?
Structural	a. How centralized and formalized is the buying process? Does our sales approach reflect this degree of centralization and formalization? b. At what level in the organizational hierarchy are key buying decision makers? c. What functional areas play a key role in buying decisions? d. What is the level, title, and functional background of our sales representative? e. Are differences in the structural or status positions of buyer and seller representatives significant enough to affect decision outcomes?
Social Actor	a. What are the demographic and personality characteristics of key members of the decision-making process in the buying organization? What is their experience level? What is their history of rewards? b. What are the demographic and personality characteristics of our sales representative? What is his or her experience level? c. To what extent are seller and buyer representatives similar or dissimilar? d. In what areas are they similar or dissimilar, and how might this relationship affect their interactions?
Roles and Norms	a. Are there certain rules of the game or unwritten norms that determine acceptable and unacceptable tactics on the part of the seller and buyer? b. What are our expectations of the roles which representatives of the buying organization are to fill in their dealings with us? c. What are their expectations of our sales representative both in terms of his or her actions and authority? d. Are there differences between our perceptions and their perceptions of roles and norms?

to pursue sales tactics that reflect a current power advantage, but do not consider potential future changes in relative power positions.

Relational characteristics also include any conflicts between the organizational capabilities or requirements of the two parties in the dyad. If the seller must have minimum orders of a certain amount, or the buyer requires a two-year fixed price agreement, and these restrictions are at odds with the interests of the other party, the outcome of the exchange relationship is in serious question. It must be recognized that such conflicts affect the costs and benefits of each of the two organizations doing business with one another. The sales manager can best manage these conflicts by identifying costs and benefits to each party of various conflict resolution approaches, and by working toward those solutions which best serve the objective of establishing and maintaining a profitable dyadic relationship.

Social Structural Characteristics

The salesperson is not selling to an organization, but rather to specific representatives of an organization. The representatives hold formal positions in their organization, as well as both formal and informal positions in the purchasing decision process. A significant determinant of the nature and outcome of seller-buyer interaction is the relative horizontal and vertical differentiation of the positions of seller and buyer representatives in their respective organizations. That is, is the salesperson primarily dealing with a purchasing agent, or with an engineer or financial expert? These different groups have distinct languages, goals, and values. A nontechnical salesperson giving a presentation to the chief of R & D is a type of horizontal or functional differentiation, and represents a significant structural gap.

Similarly, do the representatives of the seller and buyer organizations carry the same stature in the respective organizations, or do we have a rookie salesperson calling on the vice-president for materials management? This is a second type of structural gap, and might be one reason for designating your sales representative a senior account executive, or something equivalent. Status differences can undermine credibility and affect the nature of the interaction. The perception that the salesperson is able to simplify the buying task and save the buyer's time and effort is directly a function of respective social structural positions.

The salesperson must, further, determine the interdependencies among various representatives of the buying organization. How, for example, does the purchasing department interact with personnel in production, design engineering, and finance in arriving at a purchase decision? On the other side of the relationship, the buyer is looking beyond the salesperson at the set of interdependencies within the seller firm. How does the salesperson interact with personnel in production, design engineering, or finance in satisfying the buyer's requirements? A buyer is often looking for a salesperson who has influence within the vendor organization, and who will be an advocate within the vendor firm for the buying organization's needs.

Another social structural variable is the extent of formalization, centralization, standardization, and complexity in the customer's purchasing operation. More formalized or standardized or centralized processes may limit the salesperson's flexibility. At the same time, these characteristics can simplify the salesperson's job of identifying decision makers and decision criteria.

The salesperson should, in addition, attempt to identify any differences between the customer's formal policies and structure, and the manner in which things are done in practice. For example, when selling the plastic connectors used in splicing telephone lines, 3M found that the telephone companies often have formal policies of standardizing vendors to be used at the division level. It would seem that the sales effort should, correspondingly, focus on the decision makers in the central office. Yet, 3M effectively penetrated this market by sending salespeople out to work with repairmen who were actually doing the splicing in the manholes. These users would routinely specify 3M in their requisitions.

The dyadic perspective also suggests considering the design and structure of the marketing and sales effort in relation to the buyer's requirements. The decisions to organize the sales force around products rather than markets, to employ team selling, to use sales engineers, or to have centralized or decentralized distribution points, among many others, can be as important in determining the outcome of the dyadic relationship as are the policies and structure of the purchasing organization.

Characteristics of the Players

An examination of the personal characteristics of the members of the dyad can also be helpful in interpreting interaction between seller and buyer. Here, the focus is on the personalities, physical resources, personal goals and standards, and history of rewards of the seller and buyer representatives involved in the transaction. As Evans (1964) explains, "the result of the (face-to-face) contact depends not on the characteristics of either party alone but how the two parties view and react to each other."

Interpersonal attraction between salesperson and prospect can be an important ingredient in building relationships and making sales. One stream of thought is that people are attracted to those who are like themselves, and so similarity between the sales force and prospects should be emphasized. Unfortunately, this is often impractical, and can be costly. The problem lies in determining a) the types of buying situations in which similarity is important, and b) the dimension(s) on which the two parties should be similar. Certainly there are buying situations where the other dimensions of the dyad play an overriding role, and social actor characteristics are less important. In terms of the second problem, the ways in which buyer and seller might be similar are virtually limitless. A few examples include age, experience, educational background, lifestyle, race, gender, and personal goals. Also, there may be situations where the sales manager wants to emphasize differences between salesperson and prospect, based on the idea that opposites attract.

One implication is that the sales approach should be tailored to the audience, not limited to the canned presentations used by some companies. Ability to recognize the salient characteristics and personal needs of a prospect, and to empathize in terms of his or her own behavior, become important characteristics of the salesperson. Also, from a sales management vantage point, the industrial firm might attempt to hire salespeople with characteristics similar to those of major customer segments (e.g., a person with an agricultural background to sell farm machinery to farmer cooperatives). This becomes untenable, though, where a company is selling to a widely diverse audience.

Gender is a personal characteristic of the dyad which has received considerable attention. Women have encountered difficulties attempting to gain sales positions for certain industrial products because of traditional biases that selling is a man's game, or that male buyers prefer to deal with male salespeople. In fact, about 80 percent of industrial buyers are male, and they do not always accept female salespeople as openly as they accept males. Exhibit 12.1 highlights some of the areas in which women are perceived differently from men by industrial buyers. Such out-moded stereotypes ignore the growing pool of women with technical qualifications and selling skills equal or superior to those of their male counterparts, and do not make economic sense. But women continue to be heavily underrepresented in the industrial sales force, comprising less than 16 percent of the total count in the 1980 census of population. However, they have made important inroads in recent years.

Roles and Rules of the Game

The fourth dimension of dyadic relationships, the normative dimension, is con-cerned with any norms, laws, rules, or guidelines which govern the manner in which the sales force and representatives of the buying organization interact.

Many of these so-called rules are not formal or written, but are simply under-stood. As a case in point, some purchasing agents may feel that attempts to play vendors off one another to get better terms are inappropriate. If this perception is correct, the vendor who encourages such behavior may be committing a faux pas. Another possible rule violation might involve the salesperson who circumvents the purchasing agent and attempts to sell directly to a production manager, or who is too quick to try and close a sale. Giving gifts, taking a prospect to lunch or for a drink, and giving parties for purchase decision makers represent other actions for which the buying and/or selling organizations may have stated or unstated policies.

The normative dimension is also concerned with what might be called role prescriptions. People are filling a role when they act as buyers or sellers for their organization. Each party has certain expectations regarding the behavior of the other. The consumer who is purchasing a new car is likely to open the hood and examine the motor, in spite of knowing absolutely nothing about automobile en-gines. Consumers engage in this behavior because they perceive it to be part of their role as a buyer. More than likely, they think the salesperson expects them to act in this way.

In the same vein, the industrial buyer may feel compelled to negotiate a slightly lower price, even if the quoted price is actually acceptable. The salesperson may feel he or she has to be aggressive, or has to compliment the buyer, also because it is expected. Some relevant questions, then, include the following: What does the other party expect of me? What do I expect of myself? What do I expect of them? How might their own self-expectations differ from mine? By recognizing such dyadic complexities, the salesperson can better understand his or her role in the exchange process.

Three role concepts are relevant here: role ambiguity, role consensus, and role fulfillment. *Role ambiguity* results from an unclear understanding of the specific responsibilities that constitute the role. This uncertainty can result when it is unclear how much authority an individual has in making a company's buying decision, or how much authority an individual has in negotiating the selling company's price or delivery terms. *Role consensus* refers to the degree to which buyer and seller rep-

Exhibit 12.1   Differences in Industrial Buyers' Ratings of Salesmen and Saleswomen

Do women who pursue industrial selling careers confront sex role stereotyping both within their own companies, and in their dealings with customers? In a study of two separate samples of purchasing agents, Swan, et al. (1984) examined how male and female salespeople were perceived on twenty-three attributes. The purchasing agents saw little difference between men and women on most of the attributes. However, there were a few exceptions. Men were seen more favorably than women in terms of their product knowledge, and in providing technical assistance to the buyer. Women were seen as having more drive, knowing how to listen better, following up on deliveries better, being more willing to handle rush orders, and as having less of a tendency to engage in back-door selling (bypassing the purchasing department) than their male counterparts.

Attributes of Salespeople

1. Understanding of other people
2. Friendly
3. Regarded by the buyer as a person
4. Willingness to go to bat for the buyer within the supplier firm
5. Vigorous, has a lot of drive
6. Knows how to listen
7. Stability of judgments
8. Inquisitiveness
9. Knowledge of firms selling to
10. Knowledge of buyer's product line
11. Imagination in applying supplier products to buyer's product line
12. Confidence
13. Self-reliance
14. Product knowledge
15. Preparation for sales presentations
16. Understanding of buyer's problems
17. Follow-through on deliveries
18. Regularity of sales calls
19. Has a personalized presentation for each buyer
20. Providing technical assistance
21. Presents many new ideas to the buyer
22. Willingness to handle rush orders
23. Does not bypass purchasing with back-door selling

The researcher also found that these attitudes were consistent regardless of a respondent's age, education, years of experience with industrial saleswomen, or professional certification. Of course, the purchasing agents may have tended to give socially acceptable answers rather than express their true opinions. Nonetheless, the results suggest that opportunities exist today for women in industrial sales.

Source: Adapted from J.E. Swan, et al. (1984), "Industrial Buyer Image of the Saleswoman," *Journal of Marketing,* 48 (Winter), 110–116.

resentatives agree on their respective roles. *Role fulfillment* concerns how satisfied the buyer or seller representatives are with the way the other fulfilled his or her role. Inadequate role consensus or role fulfillment can undermine the dyad, perhaps resulting in an end to the buyer-seller relationship.

A Negotiated Social Process

The relative importance of each of the dimensions will vary depending on the buying situation. Buyer and seller personal characteristics may be irrelevant, because of their power relationship, or their respective social structural positions. Or, in a given power-dependency situation, buyer-seller similarity may take on greater importance.

Putting these four dimensions together provides a more complete picture of the dynamic and intricate nature of the relationship between industrial buyer and seller. Examining the customer organization in isolation is a mistake. A real understanding of what happens when the sales force works with buyer representatives over the stages of the buying process requires that we consider both parties as they see and impact upon one another. The sales transaction involves a "negotiated social process whereby people interact, explore their thoughts and feelings, exchange information, and perhaps evolve to new or novel positions and relationships" (Bonoma, et al. 1978, 62).

MANAGING THE INDUSTRIAL SALES FORCE

Keeping the dyadic perspective in mind, let us now turn to a more detailed discussion of sales management. The role of the sales manager varies from company to company. It is not unusual for them to get involved with product innovation, research, strategic planning, budgeting, pricing, channel management, advertising and sales promotion decisions, production, and plant location. Some have responsibility for all marketing activities. However, the more traditional aspects of this position, and the focus here, concern organizing, staffing, training, motivating, supporting, and evaluating the sales force.

Figure 12.1 illustrates the sales management process, which begins with determining the role of personal selling. As discussed in Chapter 11, personal selling is part of the promotional mix, which is in turn a component of the marketing mix. The sales program, then, must fit within the firm's overall marketing plan. Sales objectives are supplemental to, and should be compatible with, the organization's marketing objectives. The marketing plan will provide the sales manager with some direction in attempting to define what we want to accomplish with the sales force. Does the purpose lie in establishing new accounts, servicing current accounts, supporting distributors, or some other area? Are sales made apart from the sales force, or is that group the centerpiece of the promotional mix? To what extent should we rely on intermediaries, rather than our own sales force? With the answers to these questions in hand, the sales manager must then determine how many salespeople to employ, and how they should be organized.

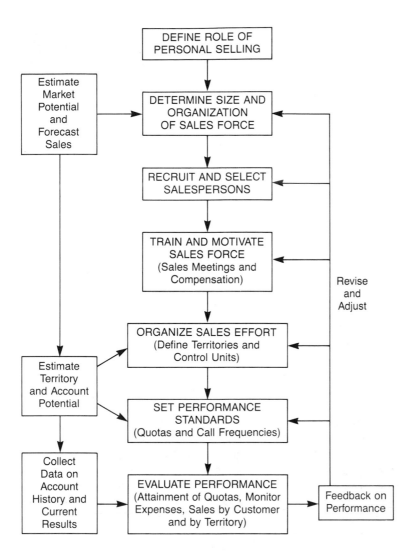

Figure 12.1   The Sales Management Process
(Source: D.J. Dalrymple, and L. Parsons, *Marketing Management,* 4th
ed., (New York: John Wiley and Sons, 1986), 663. Reprinted with
permission.

Sales Force Size and Organization

The number of people that should constitute a company's sales force is affected by
a number of issues, including the work load to be accomplished, the marginal productivity of one more salesperson, and the rate of turnover among the sales force.
Let us examine how this decision area might be approached by using a hypothetical
example.

Consider the development of a new piece of computer equipment to monitor patients' vital signs and medical treatments during a hospital stay. The initial plan is to market the product to hospitals within the state of Florida. Assume that there are 300 hospitals within the state, of which 50 are large (400 or more beds). To effectively sell to large hospitals, it has been estimated that they must be called on at least once a month. The smaller facilities can be called on every two months. The average call takes two hours, including travel and waiting time. The company estimates that the typical salesperson has about 1,300 hours available per year to make sales calls. This total is based on 190 days and 7 hours per day. Using these data estimates, the requisite size of the sales force is 4.15 (or about 5) people. The calculation is based on the following formula:

$$\frac{\substack{\text{Number of Accounts} \\ \text{(Current and Potential)}} \times \substack{\text{Ideal Call} \\ \text{Frequency Per Account}} \times \substack{\text{Average} \\ \text{Call Length}}}{\text{Selling Time Available Per Salesperson}} = \substack{\text{Required Number} \\ \text{of Salespeople}}$$

This method, which is called the workload method, ignores the costs and profits involved, and assumes a standard level of customer service for each category of customer (e.g., large and small hospitals). The sales manager can vary service level by changing call frequency or call length for different types of customers.

From a cost and profit perspective, the sales manager may want to examine the marginal productivity of additions to the sales force. That is, in determining the size of the sales force, the manager attempts to estimate a response function for additional expenditures or personnel. As more salespeople are assigned to a territory, do sales increase by more than the cost? Are sales increasing at an increasing or decreasing rate with each additional salesperson? Historical data for company sales, sales per representative, and number of representatives can provide insights regarding the marginal productivity of each additional person.

In addition, the sales manager may want to factor in the sales force turnover rate in determining the number of salespeople needed. Turnover results in lost sales, disaffected customers, termination costs, and additional expenditures to hire and train new people. The turnover rate is equal to the number of separations per year divided by the average size of the total sales force.

Hand-in-hand with the question of how many people to hire is the problem of organizing the sales force. Common approaches include organizing by function, product, customer type, geographic area, or by some combination of these.

If the sales manager wishes to ensure that critical marketing functions are being accomplished effectively, he or she may find it worthwhile to have different salespeople specialize in certain tasks. For example, individuals might be assigned to outside sales, inside sales, new account development, account maintenance, or distributor support. This allocation would constitute a functional structure. It is appropriate when there is little diversity in the company's products or markets.

When the firm sells a mix of products with distinctive characteristics, user applications, and selling requirements (i.e., products with little in common), it may make sense to assign salespeople to individual products or product groupings. Here, products receive individual attention, and those which are harder to sell or which have lower margins are not ignored by the sales force. A problem arises, though, in that product-oriented structures tend to produce duplication of effort. If a customer is a potential user of a number of products, then several salespeople might call on this organization and/or send key decision makers overlapping sales promotion materials.

The sales manager often finds that the market includes customer groups with quite divergent needs. For example, the manner in which the marketer's product is used, the nature of the purchasing decision process, or the service level requirements of various customer groups may be sufficiently different as to warrant assigning a number of salespeople to each customer category. The sales force might be divided, then, based on large versus small accounts, or based on governmental, institutional, and commercial accounts, or based on SIC categories of customers, among many other possibilities. In this manner, the sales manager can better react to the needs and requirements of a particular type of customer, and can provide more timely service to these accounts. These capabilities are especially relevant when selling in dynamic competitive and customer environments.

Assignment of specific salespeople to national accounts is also not unusual. National accounts are both large and complex, frequently involving geographically dispersed buying points, dispersion of buying influences among various functional areas, and dispersion of these influences across operating units within the company. The selling effort must, correspondingly, cut across multiple levels, functions, and operating units. Formal national account programs are often developed to support this part of the sales force.

Perhaps the most popular approach to organizing the sales force is the use of geographic territories. Salespeople will be assigned to regions, trading areas, states, MSAs (metropolitan statistical areas), municipalities, or some other logical geographical breakdown. This method generates more intense coverage of a territory, and engenders more efficiency in travel expenditures and time. Geographic structures can, at the same time, require more spending on overhead, including the cost of branch, district, and region managers. They are useful, then, when selling to large national and international markets.

A combination structure can involve any or all of the above. The company may have salespeople assigned to specific products or customer types within a given geographic locale. The combination approach allows the sales manager to realize the attributes of more than a single structural approach at one time. In this example, the benefits of both a product structure (i.e., emphasis on the unique characteristics of individual product groups) and a geographic structure (i.e., thorough market coverage) can be achieved.

Recruiting and Selecting Salespeople

Sales force selection is both difficult and risky. Hiring salespeople is perhaps the most critical decision area facing the sales manager, and usually involves a multistage screening process. The first step is to develop a job description and job qualifications, based on a detailed analysis of what constitutes a given job. This description will vary considerably among different types of positions, e.g., order taker compared to technical sales representative. Establishing the job qualifications, or the determinants of personal selling performance, can be extremely difficult—further suggesting a need to develop a firm definition of successful personal selling performance.

Managers, like many of us, when confronted with a difficult and recurring problem, look for simple decision rules to aid in decision making. The job of selecting individuals as company salespeople is just such a problem. As a result, companies have tried to identify the characteristics of a successful salesperson, and then look for potential employees among people with those characteristics. Psychological tests and other rating devices that attempt to measure and weight such factors as age, education, interests, longevity in other jobs, personality traits, past performance, and personal goals are often used to identify desirable prospects, or to eliminate candidates who do not fit a minimum profile.

Such hiring tools have produced questionable results, because of the difficulties in identifying and measuring the set of factors that will indicate whether a person will be successful in a particular type of selling job. The complexities of human nature, combined with the considerable diversity among industrial products and buying organizations, raise serious question about the ability of a single test to determine the characteristics of the best person for a job.

Where companies have been successful in this area, it is usually because they have tailored the tests or rating method to their industry, customer needs and expectations, and products or services (i.e., to the specific selling job with which the candidate for employment will be confronted). This tailoring requires the development of a fairly extensive data base which includes information on a large number of variables—for both successful and unsuccessful salespeople. Even after developing a good tool or methodology, there must be some flexibility in interpreting how an individual is rated, or qualified candidates will slip through the cracks because they fail to meet a specific criterion.

Effective hiring practices can also be aided by the creation of a data base which monitors employment referrals. The sales manager will want to track sources of leads regarding potential employees (e.g., recruiting at colleges and other schools, employment agencies, newspaper ads, recommendations from present employees, referrals from suppliers or customers). Data is kept, in addition, on which leads resulted in new hires, and the performance of these employees. In this fashion, the manager develops intuition concerning where to concentrate recruiting efforts.

Training and Motivating the Sales Force

Once an individual has been selected to join the company's sales force, he or she must be assimilated into the organization through appropriate training methods. Loss of a new sales representative following a detailed selection process and extensive training is wasteful and often preventable. Turnover rates vary widely among industries, but retaining between 50 percent and 70 percent of new recruits beyond two years is considered good performance.

Lack of formal training results in underachievement. New recruits, experienced or not, require training to become socialized into the organization's way of doing things, as well as to be effective at selling. The salesperson must develop a knowledge of company operations and policies, products and product lines, the market, the competition, the customer organization, and the customer's product(s). The five major areas most frequently found in effective training programs will include an orientation, product or service education (including demonstrations if necessary), procedures for booking and servicing orders, time management (including call frequency, duration, and scheduling), and sales techniques (prospecting, presentation methods, countering objections, closing the sale).

Training can take place in a classroom atmosphere or in the field. The actual instruction will generally be handled by the sales manager, a training manager and staff, current or former sales representatives, or outside consultants. In the classroom setting, the program might include lectures, role-playing, demonstrations, and group discussion. Field training, alternatively, provides the recruit with hands-on experience, where learning is achieved through observation and participation in actual selling situations. Table 12.5 identifies the most frequently used sites for industrial sales force training, while Table 12.6 examines the average length of the training period. The median time period is close to four months. Continuous refresher training may also be necessary to keep the sales force abreast of new products and applications, policy changes, or to improve on existing selling skills.

Training represents one of the more expensive outlays in operating a company sales force. Depending on the type of sales position in question, the training cost per recruit can range from $15,000 to $50,000, with average costs around $25,000.

Table 12.5 Sites Most Frequently Used for Sales Training

Location	% Of Companies Conducting Training At This Location			Median Length of Training Time At This Location		
	Industrial Products	Consumer Products	Services*	Industrial Products	Consumer Products	Services*
Home office	67%	58%	58%	5 wk.	2 wk.	5 wk.
Field office	67	83	50	4	9	8
Regional office	58	42	42	6	2	4
Plant locations	33	17	0	2	1	0
Central training facility (away from home office)	42	17	17	2	2	1
Noncompany site (hotel, restaurant, club)	0	8	25	0	1	1

*Includes insurance, financial, utilities, transportation, retail stores, etc.

Note: Length of time should not necessarily be considered cumulative because not all training programs include all locations.

Source: Reprinted by permission of *Sales and Management*. "1987 Survey of Selling Costs," 62.

Table 12.6 Length of Training Period for New Salespeople (Type of Company: Industrial Products)

Time Period	1986	1985
0 to 6 weeks	25%	27%
Over 6 weeks to 3 months	8	18
Over 3 months to 6 months	42	37
Over 6 months to 12 months	17	9
Over 12 months	8	9
TOTAL	100%	100%
Median Training period (weeks)	17	17

Source: Reprinted by permission of *Sales and Marketing Management.* "1987 Survey of Selling Costs," 62.

In 1986, for example, the average training cost, inclusive of salary paid to the salesperson during the training period, was $27,525 (*Sales and Marketing Management,* 1987).

A well-trained salesperson is not necessarily a highly motivated salesperson. Motivation, from a sales management perspective, represents an individual's desire or drive to perform the specific selling-related tasks that the manager deems necessary to accomplish the organization's sales objectives. So our interest in motivation is better stated as a concern with a salesperson's drive to call on new versus existing accounts, to call more frequently, to perform customer service activities, or to provide managers with detailed customer feedback in the form of sales reports, among others. A poorly motivated member of the sales force is costly to the firm in terms of unsatisfactory performance, excessive turnover, increased expenses, increased use of the sales manager's time, and negative impact on the morale of fellow employees.

One of the more practical approaches to explaining a salesperson's motivation is called the expectancy model (Vroom 1964; Porter and Lawler 1968). Simply stated, this model posits that motivation is determined by (a) how much a person perceives a direct relationship between the effort he or she puts forth and successful performance on the organization's measurement or evaluation system; (b) how much that person perceives a direct relationship between good performance and rewards; and (c) whether or not the organization is offering the correct rewards. The expectancy model is illustrated in Figure 12.2.

In a real selling situation, the specific tasks toward which the manager desires the salesperson to expend effort could include any of those mentioned above, and others. The performance measurement system refers to management's formal method of evaluating a salesperson's work output. This might be something as simple as a sales goal or quota, or as involved as a multiple-item rating scale subjectively

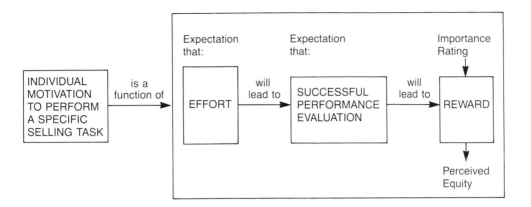

Figure 12.2   Expectancy Framework for Explaining Salesperson
Motivation

filled out by the manager. Rewards refer to the benefit or gain the employee receives in return for his work efforts. Rewards can be extrinsic or intrinsic, but the
principal concern is with those rewards that managers control or can affect. Examples include regular pay, bonuses, job security, an expense account, a company car,
a promotion, a particular territory, recognition (plaque, pat on the back), or even
an office with a window.

The flow diagram presented in Figure 12.2 can help identify some reasons a
salesperson might *not* be motivated. The first linkage in the model is between effort
and management's evaluation of performance. If the salesperson feels that the sales
quota has been set unrealistically high, and cannot be achieved, then he or she may
be unmotivated. Or, the salesperson working on a straight commission may be unmotivated to spend a lot of time on account servicing, as the performance evaluation
system is stressing sales, not servicing. Alternatively, if the salesperson feels the evaluation system is biased, providing the same evaluation regardless of the effort expended toward a particular task, then motivation concerning that task is unlikely.
Also, the task or the evaluation system may simply be too vague or ambiguous.

The second linkage in Figure 12.2 involves identifying reasons salespeople
might not see a relationship between doing well on the performance evaluation
system and receiving a reward. Managers often ask for one behavior, but actually
reward some quite different behavior. One possibility is the situation where the
reward (perhaps a sales salary) will be earned whether or not effort is put forth
toward a particular task (say, calling on new accounts). The salesperson facing this
circumstance has little motivation to spend a lot of time on new accounts. Another
possibility would be the salesperson who perceives other ways to earn the reward
(perhaps a bonus) than putting effort towards the task in question (again, calling on
new accounts). Maybe he or she feels that the bonus can be achieved by currying
favor with the boss. So, effort is expended toward this activity rather than toward
new account development.

Finally, even if the salesperson sees a link between effort and performance, and between performance and reward, he or she may be unmotivated because management is offering the wrong rewards. They could be wrong in the sense that the salesperson does not attach much importance to them, or because they are considered inequitable or unfair. The sales manager may be offering money in the form of a commission, when the salesperson would much prefer to receive a better territory or a promotion. Or, the manager may be offering a bonus, but the salesperson feels the amount of the bonus is not commensurate with the effort required, or with bonuses received by others for simpler tasks. Keep in mind that salespeople have economic needs, but they also have social and self-actualization needs (Demirdjian 1984).

These instances are but a few of the many ways that sales force motivation can become a problem. The sales manager has to ensure that the salesperson sees the desired linkages, and ensure that the proper rewards are being offered. The expectancy model suggests that considering the perceptions and needs of individual salespeople is a necessity. Ford, Walker, and Churchill (1985) have demonstrated, for instance, how the attractiveness of different rewards will vary significantly as a function of such demographic characteristics of the sales force as sex, family structure, financial situation, and educational level, as well as a variety of personality traits. Also, the needs of individuals change, so a reward that worked last year may be unsuccessful this year.

Management cannot develop distinctive reward and measurement systems for each employee, but they can attempt to include enough flexibility in these systems to at least partially accommodate individual requirements. The assumption that all salespeople will be motivated by the same reward is likely to cost the sales manager a high turnover rate. The manager who relies on this assumption must determine whether this cost can be justified.

Motivation does not, however, always translate into performance. On the one hand, a motivated salesperson may lack the real abilities to successfully do what is being asked. This limitation further emphasizes the importance of the screening and selection process. On the other hand, salespeople are sometimes unable to perform well because they do not understand the role management expects them to fill. Role conflict and role ambiguity are two possible reasons. Role conflict might occur because the territory sales manager directs the salesperson to concentrate on selling more, while the sales vice-president tells the individual to spend more time working with current customers to uncover problems or untapped needs. Role ambiguity might occur because management fails to provide the salesperson with clear job responsibilities, specific goals, or proper training. As a result, the salesperson is unclear as to exactly what is, or is not, supposed to be done.

A distinction should be made between worker performance and worker satisfaction. One of the more controversial issues in employee management is whether satisfaction leads to good performance, or if good performance leads to worker satisfaction. This issue is important, for the answer indicates whether management should place more emphasis on making the employee happy or enhancing the employee's ability to be productive. Performance and satisfaction actually both impact upon each other, but it appears that performance is the antecedent condition. That is, the emphasis should not be on satisfying the sales force and then hoping for performance. Rather, the sales manager should focus on providing the support activities, goals, and structure that will better enable salespeople to do the job.

Clearly, one of the most potent tools the sales manager has to affect both motivation and performance is the organizational compensation system. A variety of reward alternatives are available; Table 12.7 summarizes some of the key options. Let us assess the relative effectiveness of these alternatives.

A straight-commission system is especially effective at generating sales. If the salesperson does not sell, he or she does not get paid. This system is advantageous for a company with small resources, or a company experiencing a widespread downswing in sales, such as during a recession. However, selling activity is all that is being encouraged, leaving the manager with little control over other sales force activities. A straight-commission system can also cause sales force stress and burnout, encouraging turnover. Although this system requires little supervision, it can be complex to administer. Complexities come into play when the company has a variety of commission rates on different products or customer types, or when a sliding scale is used, where the amount of commission on a particular sale depends on how

Table 12.7 Types of Compensation for Industrial Salespeople

Straight Salary

Salespeople are paid a fixed income regardless of performance. Emphasis is placed on the quality of the sales transaction (e.g. customer service) rather than the quantity of transactions. This type of compensation is good for low volume products or ones that involve a long buying process. Disadvantages to straight salary include a lack of incentives to generate new sales, the need for close managerial supervision, and high selling costs when business is down.

Straight Commission

The salesperson is paid only a percentage of whatever he or she sells. This method provides a great incentive for salespeople to generate high sales although nonselling tasks tend to be neglected. Salespeople have control over their income, do not require close supervision, and are weeded out if they are poor producers. Straight commission is good for homogeneous, undifferentiated products.

Salary Plus Commission

Salespeople are paid a base income and are given a percentage of their sales in addition. This method provides more of a balance between the security of a salary and the incentive to earn additional income through high sales. Salespeople can perform nonselling as well as selling tasks.

Salary Plus Bonus

Salespeople are paid a fixed income but are given a bonus periodically for their level of performance. The bonus may be based on the individual salesperson's performance, on the performance of the sales force as a whole, or on the performance of a group of salespeople in a specific territory.

---

much the salesperson has sold to date during the current operating period. Commissions, further, can be set as a percentage of sales or as a percentage of gross margin. Compensation based on gross margin encourages the salesperson to focus on the profitability of a sale. However, salespeople sometimes find these plans confusing.

A straight-salary compensation plan provides the sales manager with the ability to exert more control over non-selling activities such as paperwork, customer feedback, customer servicing, and call planning. The salary plan involves more initial investment when the salesperson first begins with the company, but can result in greater profits once the person is established and has become a high producer. This plan gives the inexperienced salesperson time to establish contacts and a client base; it also gives the sales manager more freedom in changing the customers or territories to which a salesperson is assigned. Salary is generally easier to administer, and results in longer retention of employees.

A mixed-compensation program, which contains elements of both salary and commission, represents the most popular reward system among industrial companies. This system combines the benefits of both forms of compensation, and provides the sales manager with more flexibility in reflecting the needs of individual salespeople. The sales force has the security of a salary, and is encouraged to put effort towards nonselling activities, but also is given incentive to achieve high levels of sales. The system can be quite expensive, because the company is guaranteeing a base for little or no sales, while also paying out potentially substantial commissions to the high achievers. The trade-off may be higher levels of motivation.

Providing salespeople with an advance (draw) is another approach to reducing the pressure of a straight-commission program. This draw is generally deducted from future commissions. Draws are sometimes guaranteed, however, so that the salesperson keeps the advance whether or not his commissions exceed that amount. Of course, failure to exceed the draw is inviting dismissal.

Incentive compensation is used by many companies as a supplement to the regular salary and/or commission system. Incentives take the form of cash bonuses, vacation trips, tickets and travel to major sporting events, home computers, stereo equipment, cellular phones, and even furs and jewelry. Table 12.8 presents some guidelines for their selection. Incentives are generally given based on a point system, a sales contest, or simply for exceeding quota. Point systems give the sales manager more flexibility to weight different factors, such as the rate of increase in a given person's sales, the type of customer to whom sales were made, or the percentage amount by which a person exceeded quota. Contests can be effective motivators and generators of sales. However, contests that are held too frequently, have unattainable goals, or do not clearly specify terms for participating or winning will have little appeal, and may demoralize salespeople. Also, since contests often require direct competition among salespeople, the rivalry this competition engenders can be a plus, but can also become dysfunctional and create added managerial problems. See Exhibit 12.2 for an illustration of a company that successfully uses incentive programs.

Comparative data on the use of different compensation systems by sellers of industrial and consumer products is provided in Table 12.9. As can be seen, salary

Table 12.8 What Constitutes a Good Incentive?

A good incentive is something the salesperson wants, but normally wouldn't buy personally.

A good incentive is something that hasn't saturated the market, and therefore hasn't been discounted to death.

A good incentive has a recognized brand name.

A good incentive fits the sales force's demographics.

A good incentive is self-contained.

A good incentive ties into a larger company theme when possible.

A good incentive should be part of a short-term program.

Source: D. Kent, "Seven Tips to Build 'Premium' Incentive Programs", *Business Marketing,* (April), (Chicago: Crain Communications, Inc., 1985), 60. Reprinted with permission.

tends to be involved to some degree in the systems used in most industrial goods companies, while some sort of incentive (commission or bonus) for individual sales performance is also found in over 85 percent of industrial companies.

Territory Management and Allocation Decisions

In addition to these issues of training and motivating the sales force, the sales manager must design efficient and profitable territories, and then allocate the sales force within those territories. This managerial task includes, further, decisions regarding call frequency as well as salesperson authority and responsibility. Note that these decisions are interdependent with the determination of sales force size and organization, discussed earlier.

When designing sales territories, the sales manager generally has a number of criteria in mind. He or she seeks territories for which it will be easy to estimate sales potential and which are simpler to administer. But the sales manager also seeks territories which minimize travel time and expense while providing equal sales potential and workload. Accomplishing all of these goals is a tall order.

An initial step is to estimate market potential for current and prospective accounts in each product category, and the projected market share the company expects to achieve (see Chapter 6). This projection is sometimes done by county, state, or MSA, if not for individual accounts. Accounts (or small geographic units) are then assigned to territories so that each has approximately equal potential. A problem arises, though, in that one territory may be much more geographically dispersed than another. The potentials of each territory are equal, but the workloads are not. One may require more travel time or call frequency than another. One may have more key accounts than another. Hence, an alternative approach might be to construct territories based on the number of sales calls required, but equalizing workload can create discrepancies in sales potential.

The likelihood is that territories will not be equal on all criteria; some will be more desirable, and others less desirable. This disparity causes difficulties in assign-

Exhibit 12.2   How One Company Uses Incentives to Encourage
Industrial Sales

Burroughs Corp., the large computer systems and services company based in Detroit, Michigan, positions incentive programs as an integral part of its overall sales and marketing strategies. An in-house staff of incentive planners, as well as a marketing manager of incentive programs, is maintained for each of its five major corporate groups. The company has programs geared to motivating all salespeople within a district or branch, as well as programs that focus on individual top performers. A distinction is also made between company-wide programs, and those which are exclusive to a particular business group. Most incentives are nonmonetary, based on the belief that money does not have the keepsake quality of plaques, pins, merchandise, or trips.

The Worldwide Legion of Honor is an eleven-month program (January to November), which recognizes sales and marketing people throughout the company. Membership is competitive, and is based on accumulated points received for the percentage of orders and revenues generated over a minimum of quota. The point system doubly rewards sales to new accounts. Progress reports, including names of leaders and contenders, are updated and published internally every month. Some 400 winners receive a five-day trip to a vacation spot such as the Bahamas, Hawaii, or Palm Springs, California, accompanied by an adult guest of their choosing. An awards conference enables attendees to participate in a question-and-answer session with the CEO and president.

The Marketing Excellence Award, on the other hand, is exclusive to the business machines group. It is a plaque that recognizes the sales and managerial skills of outstanding branches, districts, or regions every quarter. Marketing and sales offices are evaluated on orders, revenue, cash collections, expenses, expense-to-revenue ratio, and overall performance as a unit.

Other Burroughs incentive management efforts include the U.S. Tennis Open program, the Super Bowl program, and the group-level Legion of Honor. Both the sales force and managers at a number of levels are offered a mix of incentive opportunities that serve both personal and corporate needs. The result tends to be high levels of enthusiasm, teamwork, and sales performance.

Source: From C.R. Milsap, "How Burroughs Gains an Edge in Sales Force Motivation," *Business Marketing* (April), (Chicago: Crain Communications, Inc., 1985), 50. Reprinted with permission.

ing salespeople to territories. Are the better territories given to the top performers, or to the more senior representatives? Are rookie salespeople assigned to weaker territories, where their mistakes will not be as costly? Should the compensation packages be adjusted to reflect differences in territory potential? These approaches to handling inequities among territories are but a few of the alternatives available.

Table 12.9 Alternative Sales Compensation and Incentive Plans

| | % Of Companies Using Plans | | | | |
| | All Industries | | Consumer Products | Industrial Products | Other Commerce/ Industry |
Method	1985	1984	1985	1985	1985
Straight salary	17.4%	17.1%	9.3%	14.1%	30.4%
Draw against commission	6.5%	6.8%	7.5%	6.0%	7.0%
Salary plus commission	30.7%	29.0%	22.4%	35.8%	23.4%
Salary plus individual bonus	33.7%	33.6%	45.8%	32.5%	29.3%
Salary plus group bonus	2.7%	2.3%	4.7%	2.1%	2.9%
Salary plus commission plus bonus	9.0%	11.2%	10.3%	9.5%	7.0%
TOTAL	100.0%	100.0%	100.0%	100.0%	100.0%

Note: Some year-to-year differences reflect changes in the organizations reporting data.

Source: Executive Compensation Service, Inc., a subsidiary of Wyatt Co., reproduced in *Sales and Marketing Management* "*1986.* Survey of Selling Costs," 57.

Establishment of equitable sales territories is directly related to, and must be coordinated with, the allocation of sales force resources to accounts. Thus, the amount of sales effort warranted by different customers must be determined. Various computer models are available for this task, one of which is the PAIRS (Purchase Attitudes and Interactive Response to Salesmen) model (Parasuraman and Day 1977). This method allocates sales effort based on an analysis of customer and salesperson characteristics in a specific sales territory. The analysis is performed by sales managers together with members of the sales force. The PAIRS model consists of the following components:

1. Customer organizations found in a specific sales territory are classified into groups. These customers are grouped according to the similarities that exist in the type of industry, potential dollar volume of purchases, combination of different products purchased, and key buying influences.

2. Management defines a set of salesperson characteristics found to be relevant to the nature of their organization's type of selling. These characteristics may include experience, education, knowledge of the company's product, and personal traits. Different customer groups will respond differently to variations in these characteristics. Since the degree of sales success depends on appealing to different customer groups, the PAIRS model allows for variations in the set of characteristics. Each salesperson is evaluated on these characteristics, resulting in an effectiveness index.

3. The effect that the salesperson's effort will have on a customer group depends on the selling ability of that salesperson, as well as the number of sales calls that will be made on that customer group during a given time period. Salespeople project what sales would be at four different levels of call frequency. Both salesperson ability (i.e., the effectiveness index) and sales call effort are weighted to reflect their relative importance in generating sales.

4. The model examines a multitude of time periods, since the impact of the sales effort in one period might carry over into following time periods.

5. For each time period, a maximum and minimum limit is put on the number of calls a salesperson can make on each customer group.

6. The anticipated total sales volume is estimated, based on the potential sales volume that exists for each customer group.

The model depends, then, on the subjective estimates of salesperson ability, customer response to different levels of call frequency, and potential sales for customer groups. A major benefit is that it gets managers and salespeople to discuss customers in sufficient depth to make these estimates. The output of the model is an actual sales revenue projection for each customer group (groups might include only one firm). Management can see how the sales response projected by the model varies from actual sales, and make corrective modifications—in the assignment of salespeople to customer groups (matching customer characteristics to salesperson abilities), in territory design (assigning customer groups to territories), or in call frequency.

Whether or not such formal models are used, sales call frequency is a valuable resource which must be carefully managed. Table 12.10 presents an approach where estimates of total calls are based on account size, specific sales objectives, and unplanned calls. As with the PAIRS model, this approach requires estimating the differential effects of call frequency on account response. Table 12.11 illustrates actual call patterns for different types of salespeople.

It should be apparent that extensive planning and analysis are vital ingredients in territory and account management. A major objective should be to maximize the

Table 12.10   Estimating Total Required Calls

Account Group	Number of Accounts	Regular Call Frequency	Additional Calls to Meet Program Objectives	Unplanned Calls	Total Calls
A	100	22/yr	4/yr	4/yr	3,000
B	300	10/yr	2/yr	2yr	4,200
C	600	6/yr	0/yr	0/yr	3,600
New	50	0/yr	2/yr	0/yr	100
					10,900

Source: J. Guiltinan, and G. Paul, *Marketing Management,* (New York: McGraw-Hill Book Co., 1985), 329. Reprinted with permission.

Table 12.11 Call Patterns by Type of Salesperson

		Average Number of Calls per Day		Estimated Days in Field Per Year	Average Number of Calls Per Year	
		A	B		A	B
Account Representative (Calls on large, already established accounts)	Range	4 – 6	2 – 3	190	760 – 1140	380 – 570
	Mean	5	2.5		950	475
Detail Salesperson (Concentrates on introducing products & promotional activities)	Range	6 – 10	4 – 6	190	1140 – 1900	760 – 1140
	Mean	8	5		1520	950
Sales Engineer (Sells products that require technical knowledge)	Range	4 – 7	3 – 4	141	564 – 987	423 – 564
	Mean	5.5	3.5		775.5	493.5
Industrial Products Salesperson (Sells tangible products that require little technical knowledge to industrial or commercial organization)	Range	6 – 8	3 – 5	190	1140 – 1520	570 – 950
	Mean	7	4		1330	760
Service Salesperson (Sells intangible services such as advertising, insurance, or consulting)	Range	8 – 10	4 – 6	190	1520 – 1900	760 – 1140
	Mean	9	5		1710	950

Territory A: Usually a metro area where customers are concentrated, the salesperson can make several calls at one location, or the sales manager's philosophy emphasizes maximum calls per day.

Territory B: Customers are dispersed and longer sales calls are required to sell a product or service.

Source: Reprinted by permission of *Sales and Marketing Management.* "1986 Survey of Selling Costs," 12.

time and effort spent in face-to-face interaction with customers, and minimize the time and effort spent in activities such as traveling, waiting, and paperwork. Salespeople need a systematic plan for complete and efficient coverage of their territory. The computer can be a major asset in this area. As a case in point, Ori-Dri Corporation of America uses a microcomputer-based system known as Sales Track. This system helps salespeople plan their work by organizing the many facets of the customer/prospect base: account number, name, address, zip code, telephone number, contacts, products, prices, and status of account. Sales Track allows the sales manager to accurately analyze buyers' needs, target marketing programs, and direct salespeople's efforts with a sales call analysis by category (Johnson 1985). Exhibit 12.3 de-

Exhibit 12.3 Using the Computer to Improve Sales Force Productivity

The difference between superior performance and average performance by salespeople is often a question of how well they organize themselves. A salesperson frequently has extensive demands on his or her time, and must perform a variety of nonselling activities. The computer can be an invaluable tool for better organizing the salesperson's efforts, and increasing productivity.

Westinghouse Electric Corporation, with their WesMark office automation system, provides an example of how the computer can be used as an effective competitive tool. WesMark consists of three subsystems: order processing, electronic communications, and advanced negotiation. These subsystems can be accessed using a desktop terminal or laptop computer.

The order-processing system permits salespeople to enter new orders, check on the status of existing orders, or determine whether or not an item is in stock. With the electronic communications system, the salesperson finds it possible to perform a variety of communications-related activities, including word processing for sending letters, an electronic filing system for information on customer accounts, the ability to work up spreadsheets, and an electronic mail system for sending or receiving information from the home office. Advanced negotiation is a system for developing price quotations for customers. For products which are built to customer specifications, the salesperson enters any special product features into the terminal, and is provided with a quote.

WesMark's strongest attribute, however, is that a salesperson can immediately switch from one subsystem to another. Using a laptop computer while out in the field, for example, the salesperson dials into the office, and gets tied into the main computer system. He or she can check the mail, write a letter—and in the middle of composing the letter, check the status of an order. While sitting in a customer's office, he or she can place an order, and quotations can be worked up. Important customer information can be recorded, such as a reminder to send a particular piece of literature, or to check on a particular problem the customer is encountering.

Westinghouse expects to get a payoff of at least two-and-one-half times its investment in the WesMark system. More importantly, the sales force has enthusiastically embraced the system. The actual rate of usage is triple that expected by the company in earlier studies.

Source: D.L. Kastiel, "New Tools for Enhanced Sales Force Productivity," *Business Marketing* (March) (Chicago: Crain Communications, Inc., 1986), 86–88.

scribes a different but related computer-based system used by Westinghouse Electric Corporation.

Organizing the sales effort also involves questions of authority and responsibility. How much of each should the sales manager delegate to individual salespeople? Call planning (i.e., research, account selection, scheduling, preparation of presentation) is an example. This activity is normally delegated to the salesperson, but sales managers want to have an impact on what is done in the field, and representatives often are not well-versed in structured, formal approaches to planning. These dilemmas also arise in other areas—pricing authority, negotiation, sales forecasting, and customer feedback.

Determining Performance Standards and Evaluating Salespeople

The final step in the sales management process involves sales force evaluation. The manager must ensure that sales goals and objectives are being met, or that proper progress is being made toward their accomplishment. Standards are developed in the sales plan when setting objectives, so that the salesperson's actual performance can be compared to planned performance. Planned performance is often stated in terms of sales quotas.

Quotas provide the salesperson with a target to shoot for, and management with a source of control. They should be challenging, reflecting realistic market potential, but not unachievable. Set too conservatively, they will not be a successful motivator, and may lead to game-playing and sandbagging. Quotas can be based on dollar sales volume, unit sales, sales by type of account, gross margin, net profit, or activity points. Activity points are given to salespeople for certain tasks, such as number of calls made, new accounts generated, missionary service provided, and so on. Involving the sales representative in the quota-setting process is a good idea, as this helps in providing timely feedback on reasons for falling short of quota, and in rewarding quota achievement meaningfully (Weaver 1985).

Performance evaluation focuses not just on the salesperson, but also on territories, segments, individual customers, products, and average order size. Territories may need to be modified, customers may be dropped, or some segments may warrant heavier investment of sales resources. Table 12.12 provides evidence regarding the use of various performance control practices.

An important feedback loop between performance evaluation and motivation was illustrated in the discussion of the expectancy model. An unfair, inconsistent, or ambiguous evaluation system is frequently the reason for a poorly motivated salesperson.

Table 12.12 Percentage of Small and Large Firms that *Extensively Use* Various Sales Force Performance Control Measures

Sales Force Performance Control Measures	Percentage of Small Firms	Percentage of Large Firms
Sales-and-cost analysis by sales territory	46	62
Sales-and-cost analysis by product	45	51
Sales-and-cost analysis by customer	28	53
Return-on-investment analysis of market segments	23	34
Sales-and-cost analysis by order size	12	21

Source: Reprinted by permission of the publisher from "A Survey of Sales Management Practices," by A. Dubinsky and T. Barry, *Industrial Marketing Management* Vol. II, No. 2, 138. Copyright 1982 by Elsevier Science Publishing Co., Inc.

SUMMARY

This chapter has examined the characteristics of the industrial salesperson, the sales task, and the sales management process. Personal selling plays the central role in the industrial promotion mix, and represents the front line of the vendor's interaction with customers. There are similarities with consumer or retail selling, but the industrial sales task has its distinctive challenges. Unlike consumer marketing, the industrial sales effort must reflect the technical nature of products or services and their applications, the conflicting needs of different members of the buying center, the lengthy buying process, and the low absolute number of customers. The result can be seen in a more technically qualified sales force, different types of sales positions, heavier reliance on a variety of sales aids, more thorough research on a given account, more extensive negotiation, and stronger postsale account servicing, among other differences.

The chapter introduced a general framework within which to approach the industrial selling task. This framework is built on the idea that the outcome of exchange relationships is determined by the needs, expectations and behaviors of representatives from buying *and* selling organizations. Implications of four dimensions of any dyadic relationship (relational, social structural, social actor, and normative) were drawn for selling strategy in such areas as negotiation, sales force design, and sales approaches.

Fairly detailed attention was devoted to the industrial sales management process. This process began with a determination of the role of personal selling, which follows from organizational objectives and the company's overall marketing plan. The sales force size and organization is then determined, salespeople are recruited and trained, motivational problems are addressed, territories are established, and salespeople and sales responsibilities are assigned. Finally, an ongoing evaluation process is applied to salespeople, products, customers, segments, and territories.

The importance of formal planning and analysis in modern industrial selling is an underlying theme of this chapter. One reason why highly successful salespeople do not always become successful sales managers rests with their inability to systematically assess customer and market requirements and match them with a properly recruited, trained, motivated, and organized sales force. Further, as the role of marketing takes on greater weight in industrial organizations, the need to integrate sales efforts with ongoing marketing strategies becomes paramount.

QUESTIONS

1. Why is personal selling usually the central ingredient in the industrial promotional mix? What are some specific ways in which the personal selling effort can be coordinated with the other elements of the promotional mix?

2. Identify a product or service situation in which it would be more appropriate to use:
   —technical selling
   —missionary selling
   —trade selling
   —new prospect selling

3. What information would you attempt to gather prior to going into a negotiating session over prices and related terms with a new prospective customer? The customer is a regional cable television company, and you are attempting to sell them technical engineering services. Your services involve grounding all their installed cable lines in the local area.

4. The similarity hypothesis suggests that the sales manager might want to hire salespeople who are similar to, or share characteristics with, the customer. What are some of the difficulties encountered in attempting to implement this idea? Assume the sales manager is working for a company selling fiberglass to companies that manufacture boats.

5. What might be some of the differences in the four stages of the personal selling process (prospecting, preparation, presentation, and postsale) when selling various types of springs to manufacturers, compared to selling stocks and bonds to consumers? Assume the springs are a component part in the manufacturer's final product.

6. A company that sells credit report services to financial institutions in the eastern part of the United States is expanding its markets to include California. Describe the step-by-step approach you would use to determine how large a sales force the company will require in California.

7. You are attempting to design sales territories on a geographic basis. Your customers are schools of all types within the New England States and New York. Discuss some of the major difficulties you are likely to encounter, and some of the conflicts which your decisions, whatever they are, are likely to create among the sales force.

8. Discuss the pros and cons of a compensation program that emphasizes salary compared to one emphasizing commission, if the company in question is selling (a) glass bottles and jars to current customers in the food industry; (b) laundry equipment (washers, dryers) to laundromats; (c) large computer mainframes to businesses and government organizations; (d) audiovisual equipment to hotels, schools, and other businesses.

9. Your sales force is putting forth only nominal effort in support of a product which has only recently been added to your product line. Using the expectancy theory of motivation, identify a number of reasons for their apparent lack of willingness to push the new product.

10. Which do you think is a more serious problem: setting sales quotas too low, or setting them too high? Explain your reasoning.

11. One of the controversial issues in sales management concerns the relationship between the performance of the salesperson and his or her job satisfaction. Specifically, some feel that high performance leads to satisfaction, while others argue that a satisfied worker will be a better performer. With which position do you agree? Why? What are the managerial implications?

CHAPTER **13**

INDUSTRIAL CHANNEL STRATEGY

Key Concepts

Captive distribution
Channel evaluation
Contribution analysis
Direct distribution
Distribution channel
Distribution strategy
Distributor value
Hidden costs
Indirect distribution
Industrial distributors
   (Full-line and specialty)

Logistics
Maldistribution
Manufacturer's agent
Middleman conflict
Middleman motivation
Service level
Total cost concept
Vertical marketing system (VMS)
Weighted factor approach

Learning Objectives

1. Present the industrial distribution channel as a source of value within the overall marketing mix.
2. Explain the major distribution alternatives available to the industrial firm, including characteristics of the leading types of middlemen.
3. Discuss the major sources of conflict in industrial channels, and the need to manage the distribution function.
4. Describe a process for developing and managing distribution strategy over time.
5. Emphasize the marketing implications of the logistical decisions made by the firm, and introduce key concepts for managing the logistics function from a marketing perspective.

A distribution system is a key external resource. Normally it takes years to build, and is not easily changed.

E. RAYMOND COREY

WHAT IS A CHANNEL OF DISTRIBUTION?

A distribution channel can be defined as the set of interdependent organizations that create value through the physical flow of goods and services and the transfer of ownership. Let's examine the components of this definition.

A channel includes organizations which provide specific functions necessary to bridge the gap between the efficient production orientation of a manufacturer and the efficient consumption orientation of a buyer. These functions include transportation, storage, inventory, breaking bulk, sorting, creating assortments, financing, selling, promoting market feedback, training, service, and others. Such functions are of importance to both the manufacturer and the buyer. Members of the channel become dependent upon one another for the successful accomplishment of such functions. For example, a manufacturer with limited financial resources may depend upon an industrial distributor to hold large inventories, or a manufacturer's representative to do the sales job. These intermediaries, in turn, depend on the manufacturer for adequate supplies of a quality product.

The definition also emphasizes the flows of goods and services. *Flow* implies movement between and among members of a channel. Such flows involve not only the physical movement of products, but also the movement or assignment of risk, the transfer of title, financial flows, and the transfer of information through the channel. These flows are not in one direction, but rather, involve movement up and down the channel. Information regarding product performance characteristics flows down the channel, as information regarding order quantities (demand) and market feedback flows up the channel.

Because of the interdependence among channel members and the critical importance of a well-managed set of flows, the marketer may want to view a channel of distribution as an operating system. Like any other system, the channel is composed of a set of subcomponents that combine to accomplish a mission. The mission in distribution involves providing a certain level of value to an end user. More specifically, the goal is to provide goods to the right customers, at the right quantity, quality, time, and place.

The value of a product when manufactured is not necessarily the same as its value when placed in the hands of a customer. Channel members effectively add value to the product when they perform functions such as sorting, financing, storing, and servicing. Peterson (1976) explains, "Just as manufacturing adds value to raw

401

materials, distribution adds value to finished products." Value regarding vendors and products is defined by the perceptions of customer groups (see Chapter 10). A machine awaiting pickup 1,000 miles away, or a chemical available only in truckload quantities when just a few hundred gallons are needed, is worth less to the buyer in such form. Value is enhanced in these cases by having a local machinery distribution center, and by repackaging the chemical in smaller quantities.

WHAT'S AN INTERMEDIARY WORTH?

The notion that intermediaries contribute value to a product may run counter to the sometimes popular view that middlemen are almost parasitic institutions who do little more than drive up the cost of a product. However, when an advertiser claims to eliminate the middleman and pass the savings on to the customer, what is not made clear is that the middleman's functions are being passed on to the customer. That is, to realize the promised savings, the customer may have to travel further, buy in larger quantities, take responsibility for product assembly, or finance the purchase.

A common truism among those who study distribution is that you can eliminate the middleman, but you cannot eliminate the middleman's functions. So, if a manufacturer decides not to use a distributor, but deal directly with customers, functions such as personal selling, carrying inventory, and aftersale service still must be provided. If the manufacturer assumes these functions, then their costs will be inflated. In fact, an intermediary who specializes in certain functions may well provide those functions at lower costs than could the manufacturer, improving the efficiency of the channel in the process. Intermediaries may actually bring costs down.

The margin that a middleman adds to a product should be commensurate with the value added by that middleman. Consider the middleman who, by keeping larger inventories, enables a customer to obtain a product at a more convenient time and place than would be the case when purchasing directly from the manufacturer. The middleman will charge a markup that reflects the added costs and customer benefits resulting from larger inventories. In a competitive marketplace, a distributor who establishes excessive margins is likely to be underpriced by competitors and be replaced. Alternatively, higher margins only encourage the manufacturer to assume the middleman's functions and profits.

DISTINCTIVE ASPECTS OF INDUSTRIAL CHANNELS

Industrial channels are quite different from those for consumer goods and services, due to many characteristics of industrial exchanges. There is a smaller absolute number of customers for a given industrial product than for most consumer products. Organizational buyers tend to purchase large quantities and are very particular in their delivery and product availability requirements. Frequently, they also require a high level of technical expertise and servicing capabilities from distributors. As a result, industrial channels tend to be short, and often direct. Intermediaries, when used, tend to be technically qualified, and tend to have a fairly close relationship with the manufacturer. The types of intermediaries used with industrial goods and services also tend to differ. Where consumer goods manufacturers will rely upon a wide variety of wholesalers and retailers, the industrial manufacturer may use industrial distributors, manufacturers' agents, jobbers, or brokers to reach the customer. At the same time, fewer channel alternatives are available to a given industrial marketer. For a particular product, there may only be one type of intermediary available in a given market area with the technical, financial, and physical capabilities necessary to achieve the manufacturer's distribution objectives. Further, there may only be two or three of that type of intermediary to select from in a particular market.

Four basic approaches are used in the distribution of industrial goods: selling direct through the company's own sales force, selling through independent distributors or agents, selling through captive distributors, or selling through some combination of these three (Corey 1983).

A number of circumstances support the use of a direct sales force. When products generate sizable sales volume, are part of a broad product line, require a concentrated technical selling effort, involve a lengthy buying process, are relatively early in their life cycles, require extensive servicing, or are subject to occasional supply shortages, selling direct is more justifiable. Similarly, a geographically concentrated customer base can justify direct selling.

Using independent manufacturers' agents and industrial distributors is more prevalent when customers are geographically disperse, are very loyal to local distributors, require rapid delivery from a local source, want to avoid maintaining large inventories, or desire one-stop shopping for a variety of items beyond those sold by one manufacturer. Also, when the manufacturer has limited resources, intermediaries can assume inventory, selling, service, credit, and transportation expenses. Of course, the ability to spread these costs depends upon the type of intermediary.

A critical issue in using intermediaries concerns the marketer's ability to control their activities. The desire for greater control sometimes leads industrial marketers to develop a captive distribution system—actually acquiring independent distributors to make them directly accountable to the manufacturer. Another approach is to establish an exclusive arrangement with distributors. Such distributors will carry only one manufacturer's line in a particular product area, plus complementary or compatible (noncompeting) goods produced by other suppliers.

Mixed systems are effective when the company is selling to customers or market segments that differ in their requirements or buying behavior, and again, when the company has resource constraints. The firm may use independent intermediaries to cover territories which the direct sales force cannot reach. Alternatively, the sales force might be used just for larger accounts. In some cases, the sales force may act in a missionary capacity, or provide service and technical assistance, with the customer actually purchasing from a distributor. Figure 13.1 illustrates a mixture of distribution channels for an industrial company.

MAJOR TYPES OF INDUSTRIAL MIDDLEMEN

Channels for industrial goods and services can include manufacturers' representatives, industrial distributors, dealers, brokers, jobbers, and commission merchants. Each is characterized in Table 13.1. Of these, the most prevalent are manufacturers' representatives and industrial distributors. Let us elaborate on each.

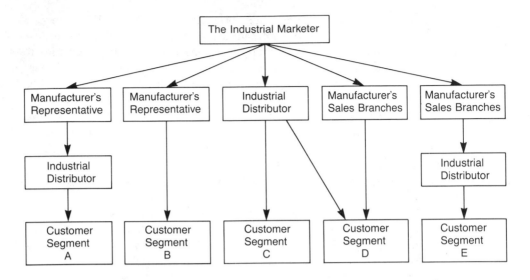

Figure 13.1   Distribution Channels for an Industrial Product

Manufacturers' Representatives

The typical manufacturers' representative, or agent, operates an independently owned business. The organization usually has fewer than ten employees, and represents from five to fifteen clients (manufacturers). These manufacturers are not direct competitors with one another, but instead, tend to sell related kinds of products. The association is often long-term, lasting as many as ten or more years. Each representative will tend to cover a large territory extending over three or four states, and including over one hundred industrial customers (Sibley and Teas 1979).

The principal function of manufacturers' representatives is selling. They do not take title to the product, and do not maintain inventories. Representatives are professional salespeople, often with technical training, who have established contractual (agency) relationships with various manufacturers. Most of the terms of sale are established by the manufacturer, although representatives may have limited authority to negotiate. Compensation comes in the form of straight commissions, which average about 6 percent. There is no fixed financial burden to the manufacturer, as the representative is paid only when a sale is made. As a result, representatives are especially appropriate for small and medium-sized companies that do not have the resources to develop and maintain a direct sales force. Keep in mind the significant overhead costs (e.g., training costs, fringe benefits) involved with a sales force. Of course, as sales volume increases, the cost advantage of straight commissions begins to disappear.

Representatives provide the manufacturer with a means of entering untapped markets, and with market coverage in geographic areas where the manufacturer does not deploy a sales force (e.g., territories with low market potential). Because of their extensive knowledge of customer needs and buying behavior in the geographic region they cover, the representative offers the manufacturer immediate

Table 13.1   Types of Industrial Middlemen

Manufacturers' representatives

Independent salespeople who represent, on a long-term basis, a number of manufacturers whose products complement one another but are not competitive. The manufacturers' agent does not take title or possession of the products. These agents have expert knowledge on technical products and the markets for those products. They are paid on a commission basis.

Industrial distributors

Local, independent sales organizations that take title and maintain inventories of specialized or diversified product lines, and resell these products at a margin above their cost. Distributors have long-term relationships with the manufacturers whose products they sell. In addition to selling, they also solicit new accounts, deliver products, offer credit terms, and sometimes provide assembly and repair services.

Jobbers

Jobbers represent manufacturers of products sold in bulk (such as raw materials) for which they take title but do not take possession. The relationship between jobbers and manufacturers is usually short-term.

Brokers

Brokers bring together the buyer and seller to complete transactions involving large quantities of products that are usually highly standardized or seasonal. The broker may represent either the buyer or the seller, but the relationship is short-term and sometimes only a one-time arrangement. Brokers do not take title or possession of the goods and are paid on a commission basis.

Commission merchants

Commission merchants deal on a short-term basis with manufacturers of products sold in bulk (such as raw materials). They do not take possession of the materials. Commission merchants represent the manufacturer; they can negotiate prices and complete sales.

access to key customers and decision makers in the region. Establishing a sales force in a new market is time-consuming and expensive, and rarely will an unfamiliar sales force gain such acceptance. Representatives often have, and work closely with, an established customer base. Their contacts may have been established years earlier, perhaps when the representative was employed as a salesperson for a particular manufacturer.

A key concern of the manufacturer is the extensive control that is sacrificed when opting for representatives instead of a direct sales force. Because they represent a number of companies, the representatives' time is a scarce commodity for which each manufacturer is competing. The manufacturer who provides higher commissions, better quality products, a more personalized relationship, or stronger sales promotional support is encouraging a more concerted effort from the representative. (See Exhibit 13.1). Motivation of representatives can also be affected by the kind of year they are having, or whether they believe the manufacturer plans to replace them with a direct sales force, once the market is developed.

Exhibit 13.1   How One Company Motivates Its Agents

A creative approach to ensuring reps are knowledgeable about the manufacturer, his products, and their potential applications is used by RHG Electronic Laboratories, of Deer Park, New York. The company holds an annual contest which consists of an examination administered to all company reps. The test consists of questions such as:

Question: If a log amp with a power connector is desired, which of the following series is not suitable?

Answer: (a) ICLP; (b) ICLWP; (c) LST; (d) ICLT; (e) LLT

Question: Monopulse receivers:

Answer: (a) always use phase comparison.
           (b) always use amplitude comparison.
           (c) use neither (a) nor (b).
           (d) may use either phase or amplitude comparison.

Other questions involve matching the names of individuals in the company with their titles (i.e., to ensure the rep knows which engineer to contact with a given customer problem), as well as questions on where company ads are featured, what literature is available, company testing capabilities, and when the rep last visited the plant.

Points are given for each question, with top scorers winning prizes. All reps are required to participate. Those that do not are reprimanded, and could be terminated. Those rep organizations that score poorly on the examination are sent letters from the president with messages such as "A disappointing score, but I guess that's because you don't have much going for RHG these days," or "You're sort of at the bottom of the barrel; I still have doubts about our successful relationship." The contest acts as a measuring device on the effectiveness of the reps, for their scores tend to correlate with their sales performance. Knowledge appears to be a valuable sales tool.

Source: Adapted from D. Weaver, "Keeping Manufacturers' Reps Motivated," *Business Marketing,* (Chicago: Crain Communications, Inc., November, 1985), 130. Reprinted with permission.

Manufacturers may also want representatives to increase the extent to which they specialize in a particular product area. Additional concerns include the tendency for representatives to provide poor market feedback and aftersale servicing. As an independent salesperson, the representative may not spend extensive time surveying problems that customers have with the manufacturer's product(s), or in identifying new applications or unmet needs the product(s) could fulfill. Similarly, the representative is paid to make sales, and so is not especially motivated to provide a quality service function after the sale, unless this action directly leads to further sales. Qualified representatives do tend, however, to provide good technical advice to customer organizations.

The key concerns of the representative in deciding upon principals (manufacturers) to work with include product quality and reliability, support from the principal, sufficiently high commission rates, reputation and image of the principal, and product training provided by the principal (Bobrow 1976). Of these, income-related concerns are paramount. The representative is concerned not just with the amount of income received, but also with the likelihood that the manufacturer will be a stable source of income over time. He seeks an ongoing relationship with the principal, and is anxious that the products being sold will not soon become obsolete. The enthusiasm a representative demonstrates toward a particular product or product line is also greatly affected by the quality of his or her relationship with the manufacturer. Table 13.2 illustrates factors that representatives use to identify the most desirable manufacturers.

Industrial Distributors

The second major type of intermediary is the industrial distributor, defined as "a wholesaler who sells the majority of its goods and services to industrial, commercial, and institutional customers, the government, builders, and farmers" (Narus, Reddy, and Pinchak 1984). A distributor is an independently owned and operated merchant intermediary who takes title to products, keeps them in inventory, provides for delivery and frequently for credit, and may service products after the sale. Occasionally a distributor will also become involved in manufacturing or product assembly.

There are two main categories of industrial distributors: general line and specialized. A *general line* distributor is much like an industrial supermarket store, carrying a wide array of differing products. As a rule, no one product category generates over 49 percent of the organization's sales. In fact, the general line distributor may carry literally thousands of products either in inventory or available through catalog sales. *Specialized distributors,* as the name implies, focus on a narrower range of related products, such as cutting tools. A trend toward specialization in recent years has found this type of distributor growing in size and numbers, while general line distributors have introduced specialized departments. A third type of distributor, the combination house, sells in both consumer and industrial markets.

A sizable portion of the assets of industrial distributors (as much as 90 percent) is accounted for by inventory and accounts receivable. Inventory averages about 15 percent of sales for both general line and specialty distributors. Correspondingly, there is a heavy reliance on short-term debt and retained earnings to meet these asset requirements (Narus, Reddy, and Pinchak 1984). The firms themselves tend to be small, privately held organizations employing between 15 and 20 people. Many have a single warehouse. Sales average just over $2 million for both types of distributors, although some larger organizations annually exceed sales of $100 million. About 45 percent of the employees are salespeople, both outside and inside. An outside salesperson calls directly on customer accounts in person, while an inside salesperson sells via the telephone (i.e., telemarketing) or to customers who come

Table 13.2   Factors that Manufacturers' Agents Use to Rate Principals

Statement	Relative Importance Ranking
The quality of this principal's performance in supporting my firm's selling efforts is above average.	1
This principal is interested in what I say.	2
This principal is well organized.	3
When selling this principal's products, I work under incompatible policies and guidelines.	4
When selling this principal's products, I feel certain about how much authority I have.	5
This principal's operations are efficient.	6
This principal does not know my territory situation.	7
When selling the principal's products, I have to work under conflicting directives or orders.	8
This principal is loyal.	9
I have sufficient influence on decisions about the granting of credit to my customers.	10
I have sufficient influence on decisions concerning delivery time of products.	11
I often try out my own selling ideas without obtaining advanced authorization from this principal.	12
This principal sends me all pertinent product information.	13
I have sufficient influence on decisions concerning prices to charge customers.	14
This principal allows me to set my own goals and objectives for selling his products.	15
I make price quotes on my own without first checking with this principal.	16
This principal aggressively promotes his products.	17
This principal respects my judgment.	18
This principal keeps me informed of the communications between my principal and my customers.	19
I make delivery promises on my own without first checking with the principal.	20
This principal is unaccessible.	21

Source: Reprinted by permission of the publisher from "The Manufacturer's Agent in Industrial Distribution," by S.D. Sibley and K.R. Teas, *Industrial Marketing Management* November, 289. Copyright 1979 by Elsevier Science Publishing Co., Inc.

Exhibit 13.2 Strategic Attempts of an Industrial Distributor to Gain
Market Share

The competitive pressures facing industrial distributors are exemplified by
Hughes Supply, Inc., a regional distributor of construction supplies based in
Orlando, Florida. Over the past few years, two of the largest national distributors of construction supplies, Noland Company and Ferguson Enterprises,
opened thirty new branch outlets in Florida. Meanwhile, a number of statewide
and regional distributors have also branched into Hughes's stronghold markets. The result has been flat earnings and shrinking profit margins for the
company.

To maintain market share and revive stagnant profits, Hughes has moved
aggressively to acquire a number of medium-sized building supply companies,
while also diversifying into manufacturing and retail sales. Distributors acquired have included Carolina Pump and Supply (water and sewer systems),
Tri State Supply (electrical fixtures, lighting fixtures, and industrial tools), Mar-
but Company (heating and air conditioning equipment), Peninsular Supply
(plumbing supplies), Paine Supply (plumbing and refrigeration supplies), and
USCO, Inc. (plumbing supplies and water systems). These acquisitions enabled
Hughes to double its number of distribution outlets to seventy-five in just two
years, and to increase the product line to more than 60,000 different items.
The firm now has a foothold in Georgia, North and South Carolina, Mississippi,
and Alabama, together with its traditional base in Florida. The acquisition
moves have been concentrated on distributors of fairly complementary building supply products located in areas where Hughes Supply did not have a
presence.

To offset the cyclical swings of the construction industry, the company has
also established a manufacturing division that produces PVC pipe, concrete
power-transmission poles, and prewired control devices such as traffic-light
boxes. In addition, four retail lighting showrooms and nine plumbing showrooms for building contractors have been opened.

While it is not clear how profitable these moves will be, they should provide a more solid base for future growth, a stronger position from which to
counter the moves of competitors, and enhanced bargaining power with manufacturers.

Source: A. Yeomans, "Hughes Uses Purchases to Expand," *Orlando Sentinel,* (April 23, 1987), C-1, C-7.

to the distributor (i.e., counter sales) (Webster 1984). The outside sales force tends
to generate the bulk of company sales.

Many of these organizations are growing rapidly, and mergers among them are
increasingly commonplace (see Exhibit 13.2). Recent years have also witnessed a
growth in distributor chains, some of which are regional or national in scope. Such
chains have the advantage of deeper inventories, centralized warehousing, volume

discount purchasing, multiple-brand coverage (providing the customer with greater choice), and even private labeling (*Marketing News* 1976).

About 75 percent of the unit sales of industrial goods move through distributors, but this activity represents only 15 to 20 percent of the total dollar sales. In other words, distributors tend to stock smaller-ticket items, such as machine parts, lubricants, fasteners, bearings, hand and power tools, small machinery and equipment, and even nuts and bolts. The average order size is under $300. The small percentage of dollar volume through distributors is also due to the tendency of manufacturers to make direct sales to large customers, using distributors for small customers.

The principal functions provided by industrial distributors include selling, local market coverage, holding inventory, and providing credit. The inventory function is important because it represents a means for the manufacturer to spread risks. Distributors can also provide the manufacturer with valuable information regarding local market trends. Because of their proximity to customers, industrial distributors are relied on to sell products for which rapid delivery and servicing is critical. Distributors are used most frequently for stockable, standardized items that appeal to a large potential customer base, and that can be sold in small quantity lots (Hlavacek and McCuistion 1983). Many of these products are routine-order or straight rebuy items requiring the approval of a junior decision maker in the buying organization.

Manufacturers can bring down sales and distribution costs through the use of industrial distributors. Consider the case of AT&T, a major supplier of copper wire and cable for use in telephone systems. Serving the needs of small customers who purchase limited amounts of such commodity-like products may not be economical for the company sales organization. Rather than ignore such potential users, the company was able to reach large numbers of them efficiently, through distributors. In this manner, distributors are supporting a market segmentation strategy. The sales force is free to concentrate on larger accounts.

The key concern of the manufacturer in using industrial distributors is control, as was the case in using manufacturers' representatives. However, the problem is more marked with distributors, because they also carry competitor's product lines, and because of the sheer number of products they carry. And, some distributors are sufficiently large, especially compared to the size of the manufacturer, to create control problems. The manufacturer may well need the distributor more than the distributor needs the manufacturer, especially where dealing directly with the end user is uneconomical for the manufacturer.

The manufacturer loses some or all control over variables such as sales effort, generation of new accounts, delivery reliability, service quality, returns policies, pricing, and customer feedback. Some of these variables, such as sales effort and service, require technical capabilities which the distributor may not have, and may resist developing or updating.

And yet, distributor responsibilities are, if anything, growing. Their willingness to be cooperative depends on how easy they find the manufacturer to deal with, as well as the support and incentives the manufacturer provides. Also, some distributors are simply satisfied with the status quo. They have an established customer base, are achieving stable sales and profit levels, and are not especially motivated to develop new accounts.

Industrial marketers face a number of decisions in managing relationships with distributors; many of these involve trade-offs. For example, if the manufacturer pushes the distributor to carry larger inventories of a given item, this probably means the distributor is less able or willing to carry or support all of the items in the manufacturer's line. Another trade-off comes in the form of exclusivity agreements—a tactic used to motivate distributors. It involves offering the distributor an exclusive arrangement where no other intermediary is allowed to sell the manufacturer's line within the distributor's market area. The marketer is betting the arrangement will lead to more aggressive support from this exclusive distributor, in exchange for the lost potential sales from other intermediaries in the region.

These examples are but two of the many trade-off situations in dealing with distributors. Working with distributors, the marketer should attempt to strike a balance between what is being given up and what is being gained. When manufacturers provide technical training programs, discounts, free merchandise, exclusive arrangements, or other incentives to the distributor, they should carefully evaluate what they are getting in return. Is training resulting in better service and more complete market penetration? Do exclusive arrangements result in distributors carrying and supporting only the manufacturer's brand? It is not unusual for manufacturers to provide a missionary sales effort for distributors. In such circumstances, are distributors maintaining adequate stocks and providing timely delivery in support of these sales? Distributors should be managed much the same as a direct sales force. All too often, manufacturers establish a relationship, and then provide costly incentives from which they receive little benefit.

Motivation of distributors is the key. A popular approach is to provide direct incentives to the distributor's sales force, such as contests offering prizes or bonuses. Many of these are ineffective, however, because they are not well-publicized, they're too complicated, too many occur at once, they do not meet distributor's goals, they last too long or not long enough, and they fail to reward the right people (Milsap 1985). Often these problems arise because the manufacturer designs the incentive program without any input from the distributor. Distributors handle thousands of products, and so many incentives are available that salespeople can literally win prizes for contests they did not know about.

In addition to confusion over incentive programs, industrial distributors have a number of other concerns in their dealings with manufacturers. Complex ordering procedures, late deliveries, unwillingness to expedite orders, and unsatisfactory returns policies on unsold, defective, or discontinued products are some of the more common complaints (Narus, Reddy, and Pinchak 1984). These and other problems confronting the modern industrial distributor are summarized in Table 13.3.

The problems perceived by both the manufacturer and the distributor point up the need for effective communication between them. The relationship is multifaceted, for the distributor is a customer, a partner, and a hired hand (*Marketing News* 1985). The success of either organization very much depends on the actions of the other.

Table 13.3   Twenty Pressing Problems Facing Industrial Distributors

Problems
 1. Customer purchases are off
 2. Intense price competition
 3. High interest rates
 4. Late payment by customers
 5. Customers switch distributors for slightly lower prices
 6. High cost of outside sales force
 7. High labor costs
 8. Finding new employees
 9. Manufacturer returns policies
10. Training new employees
11. Motivating inside sales force
12. Manufacturer discounts too low
13. Dumping by distributors
14. Keeping track of inventory
15. Keeping catalogs up-to-date
16. Setting prices
17. Slow delivery by suppliers
18. Data processing
19. Dumping by manufacturers
20. Competition from manufacturer-owned distributors

Source: Reprinted by permission of the publisher from "Key Problems Facing Industrial Distributors," by J.A. Narus, N.M. Reddy, and G.S. Pinchak, *Industrial Marketing Management* 13, 143. Copyright 1984 by Elsevier Science Publishing Co., Inc.

CONFLICT IN INDUSTRIAL CHANNELS: THE NEED FOR A SYSTEMS VIEW

The importance of managing channels is rooted in differences in the objectives and needs of the different organizations within the channel. Such differences can lead to conflict among individual channel members, a fairly common occurrence. Conflict itself is not necessarily a bad thing, unless it escalates to a dysfunctional level. At this point, the involved parties refuse to recognize their mutual objectives. Alternatively, low levels of conflict can encourage competitiveness and creativity on the part of those in the channel.

The manufacturer and intermediary can find themselves at odds with one another in a number of areas. Table 13.4 demonstrates some of these. For example, manufacturers may complain about an intermediary who rarely calls on new accounts, carries the lines of competitors, is concerned only about making the sale,

Table 13.4 Possible Conflicts Between the Interests of Manufacturers
and Industrial Intermediaries

The Manufacturer May Prefer:	The Intermediary May Prefer:
lower manufacturer inventories	higher manufacturer inventories
high distributor inventories	lower distributor inventories
lower distributor margins	higher margins
limited discounts to distributors	generous manufacturer discounts
lower promotional expenditures	strong manufacturer promotional support
well-trained field representatives	salespeople in field, not in training
accepting few returns	liberal returns policies
timely customer feedback from distributors	salespeople who sell, not market researchers
continuous product improvements	products that do not continually become obsolete
product line extension	a limited assortment of the manufacturer's products
sales to new accounts	sales to existing accounts
delivery by most cost-efficient means	timely delivery
sales support for its products over others	sales of those products with highest margins and/or commissions

and returns a disproportionate amount of merchandise. The intermediary may be frustrated with low-quality products, continual new product introductions, slow deliveries, manufacturers who keep the big accounts for themselves, and manufacturers who seem distant and unconcerned about the intermediary's problems. In either case, the result can be arbitrary actions intended as retribution against the other party. The manufacturer may lessen support, or terminate the relationship; the intermediary may push the goods of other manufacturers.

Industrial marketers not only must be cognizant of existing and potential conflicts experienced by intermediaries, but also must continually monitor such conflicts. They should seek to insure that conflict has an outlet or a means to constructively express itself. Otherwise, conflict will only tend to escalate. This control can be achieved through an open and effective communication network between manufacturer and intermediary. Regular meetings, site visits, a complaint telephone line, distributor councils, and surveys of intermediaries are some possible steps to enhance communication.

It is also important that channel members collectively look beyond their own parochial interests, and recognize that the channel itself is a system. As a system, the channel consists of a set of interdependent components which combine to produce values. The success of the overall channel, and so of the individual members, is dependent upon how much perceived value the members combine to deliver to end users. Like parts of an engine, channel members are mutually interdependent, and the system falters if any component fails to perform its mission adequately.

Because the members of the channel are usually independent organizations, the systems perspective becomes meaningful only when purposefully adopted by managers. One approach is to develop the channel as a *vertical marketing system* (VMS). With a VMS, the marketer attempts to achieve "technological, managerial, and promotional economies through the integration, coordination, and synchronization of marketing flows from points of production to points of ultimate use" (Stern and El-Ansary 1982).

The coordination and control necessary to realize such economies in a VMS can be achieved either through ownership, legal contract, or economic power. When the coordination and control is achieved by buying out intermediaries (i.e., making them captive), a corporate VMS is established. If formal legal contracts are used to specify the roles and responsibilities of channel members, coordination and control are being achieved through a contractual VMS. Alternatively, channel members sometimes co-operate with one another because of their economic dependency on one of the members, often the manufacturer. For example, intermediaries may find a disproportionate amount of their sales are of one manufacturer's products. Or, they may find that customers are more receptive to them and the various products they sell because they carry a particular manufacturer's line. In such cases, the manufacturer is using economic power to achieve coordination and control in an administered VMS.

DESIGNING AND MANAGING INDUSTRIAL CHANNEL STRATEGY

The design and implementation of channel strategy, like pricing or promotional strategy, is an ongoing process. A common mistake made by marketers is to decide on a type of intermediary, select a number of specific intermediaries, and conclude that distribution strategy is set. Recognition that the environment is not static is critical to any type of strategy. Things change, and so too must the strategy (see Chapter 8). The *Marketing News* (1985, 24) has concluded: "Distribution is one area where change is being thrust upon U.S. corporations. Business as usual will not suffice, and no corporation is above the need for change."

Figure 13.2 attempts to illustrate distribution strategy as a continuous process. This process consists of three sets of forces or factors. First, an initial distribution strategy must be formulated, based on a variety of considerations. As changes occur in the product and market environment, changes are needed in the original distribution strategy. Change is often difficult to bring about, however, for a number of forces resist such change. New strategies reflect compromises based upon these forces.

Considerations in Formulating Initial Distribution Strategy

Designing a distribution channel involves decisions concerning whether to use intermediaries or to sell direct, which intermediaries to use, whether to use multiple channels, whether to supplement intermediaries with a direct sales force, how long

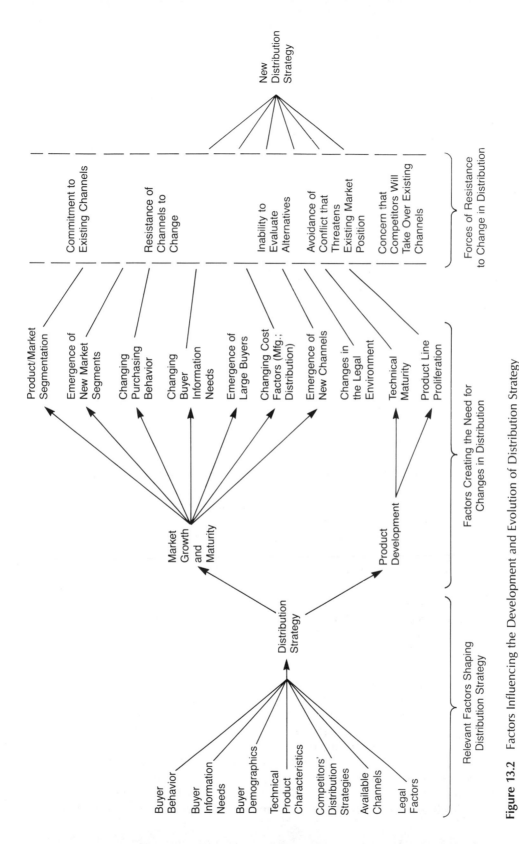

Figure 13.2 Factors Influencing the Development and Evolution of Distribution Strategy

(Source: E. R. Corey, *Industrial Marketing: Cases and Concepts*, (Englewood Cliffs, N.J.: Prentice Hall, 1983), 459. Reprinted with permission.)

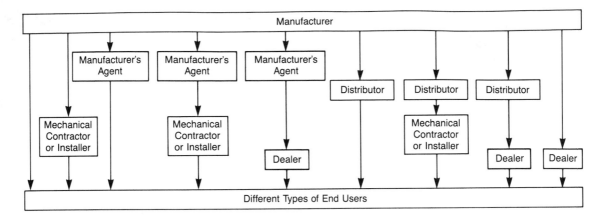

Figure 13.3 Marketing Channels for Air Conditioning Equipment
(Source: L. Stern, and A. El-Ansary, *Marketing Channels,* (Englewood
Cliffs, N.J.: Prentice-Hall, 1982), 12. Reprinted with permission.)

(number of levels) the channel should be, and where to concentrate the company's efforts in the channel. Figure 13.3 provides a series of design options that might be considered by a marketer of air-conditioning equipment. The selected options will reflect the manufacturer's needs in such areas as inventory, credit, customer service, and transportation.

The beginning point, as with all marketing decisions, is the determination of distribution objectives. These objectives will include not only sales, profits, and market share, but also market coverage, channel control, channel costs, sales effort, service level, and company image. An objective might be to reach plant engineers within certain industries and within a specified geographical area at least five times per year. Objectives will help to guide decisions regarding intermediaries. For example, manufacturers desiring extensive market coverage may not want to establish exclusive arrangements with distributors. An image-conscious firm known for high quality and customer service may consider a direct sales force the only way to maintain control over that image. A company concerned with cost reduction might find it necessary to supplement its sales force with manufacturers' representatives.

The distribution objectives a company establishes, together with the eventual distribution strategy selected, should be based on a careful analysis of the current situation. Key considerations here include characteristics of the buyer, the product, the competition, the available channels, and the legal environment.

The buyer has a major effect on distribution strategy. Where there are few buyers, and they are geographically concentrated, direct distribution makes sense. Other buyer-related concerns, which often vary by market segment, include how frequently they buy, and in what quantities. In addition, buyer information requirements are relevant. These needs will be a function of their past experience with this product category. Organizational demographics, such as whether purchasing is centralized or decentralized, also have implications for the selection of intermediaries.

Product characteristics that influence distribution include technical complexity, unit value in relation to bulk, stage in the life cycle, and perishability. Complex products that require a technically qualified salesperson may eliminate industrial distributors as a viable option. Alternatively, very bulky products, which do not require sorting, can be efficiently handled through jobbers. Beyond the product itself, the depth and breadth of the product line influence distribution choices. A broad line can be an argument for selling direct. In this case, the company salesperson is able to provide for a number of a customer's needs—justifying the cost of using a sales force. With a deeper line, exclusive arrangements with distributors are more likely to pay off.

The marketer cannot afford to ignore the distribution strategy employed by competitors, even if they differ in their objectives. Distribution can be a source of competitive advantage. For example, distribution strategy can produce economies which result in a cost advantage. Another potential result is more immediate delivery, which leads to a service advantage. Or, a customer may be loyal to a competitor only because that competitor has more complete market coverage. An analysis of the competitor's distribution strategy is also useful in identifying weaknesses (e.g., slow delivery, or distributors with mixed loyalties that the marketer is able to exploit).

A major constraining factor in industrial distribution is the number of channels available, and the functions which available intermediaries are willing and able to provide. Often, not only are few alternatives available for a particular product and market, but also those channels can be saturated. Consider the case of the Japanese personal computer manufacturers attempting to enter the U.S. business computer market. Existing channels were sufficiently swamped with competitors, significantly raising the costs of market entry. In assessing available channels, the marketer is trying to match the functions required with the functions provided by the various intermediaries. If financial and physical constraints require that the burden of inventory be shared with intermediaries, then manufacturers' representatives become untenable. In the same vein, if intermediaries provide a host of functions which the manufacturer does not require, then the manufacturer may be needlessly paying for those functions through margins or commissions.

Finally, legal considerations play a major role in distribution. In an effort to exert control over various intermediaries, or to take advantage of the different levels of distributor dependency on the manufacturer, tactics are sometimes used which raise legal questions.

Exclusive arrangements, for example, are a means of granting a territorial monopoly to the distributor—a situation that other distributors may have a problem with. Alternatively, the distributor with an exclusive sales arrangement in one geographic region may attempt to extend the arrangement by selling the product through branches in other territories. Manufacturers are apt to respond by dropping the distributor, prompting a legal suit. Another debated practice is dual distribution, where the manufacturer uses an intermediary in a given territory, but also sells direct in that territory. This approach can give manufacturers more leverage when dealing with the intermediary in that territory. Price administration is also a questionable tactic, where manufacturers try to force distributors (who take title and possession) to change a particular price, or face adverse consequences (e.g., slow delivery). Tying arrangements have been used by industrial firms, but raise particularly sensitive legal questions. Tying occurs when the manufacturer attempts to link his willingness to supply the product, or to charge a particular price, or meet a particular delivery target, to some condition the distributor must fulfill (e.g., providing free warehouse space to the supplier). In another tactic, full-line forcing, the manufacturer requires the distributor to carry a complete line of products, when the distributor only wishes to carry part of the line. Distributors may agree to do so, if the manufacturer has a particular product which they very much want or need.

The point here is not to establish the legal or ethical ramifications of such tactics. Rather, the ability to use a given tactic will have important implications for the selection of intermediaries and the overall design of a distribution strategy. Like so many marketing decision areas, it is increasingly difficult to make major creative distribution decisions without running any proposals past a lawyer.

Forces Necessitating a Change in Distribution Strategy

Once in place, distribution strategy has to be adapted to changes in the environment, in the market, and in the firm's overall marketing strategy. As the product moves through its life cycle, the market grows and then matures. The number of buyers changes, and specialized need segments develop. Existing channels may not reach, or adequately serve, new customer groups and their distinctive requirements.

The purchasing behavior of existing customers is also subject to change as these companies grow, adopt new technologies, and develop new products. They may demand larger quantities, more favorable discounts, and more rapid response to their pressing needs. The current set of intermediaries cannot be expected to automatically grow and adapt with the manufacturer's customers. For example, the end user who decides to adopt a just-in-time inventory system is unlikely to find distributors that have developed the capability to work with such a system, and so the manufacturer must be dealt with directly. If the manufacturer wants to keep this customer, distribution strategy and tactics will have to be modified.

As a market grows and matures, another common development is a change in the economics of various distribution alternatives. On the one hand, a direct sales force can become affordable once market penetration reaches a critical level. On the other, a technically mature product may be sold more efficiently through distributors, freeing up the sales force to concentrate on new or growth-stage products. New channel alternatives also become available over time, perhaps reducing the attractiveness of existing intermediaries. Companies also tend to expand the product line through time, adding alternative versions of an original item, together with product add-ons and complementary products. Proliferation of the product line makes it more difficult for the seller to concentrate on any one product without ignoring others. Customers have a more difficult time staying abreast of exactly which products are available. The manufacturer has an increasingly difficult job of motivating intermediaries, and may be well served to alter the channel design.

Forces of Resistance to Strategy Changes

Manufacturers demonstrate a strong tendency to resist changes, despite an acknowledged need to adapt to changing conditions. Channel arrangements represent a long-term commitment to a partnership in many cases. This commitment may be more moral or social than legal, but decision makers are reluctant to simply walk away from an established working relationship. In some cases, they are constrained by a formal legal commitment and their reluctance is more rational.

Changes in distribution arrangements take time to significantly affect a customer base, because of the time-consuming efforts required to identify intermediaries, evaluate them, establish formal relationships, train the personnel, and work out arrangements for product delivery, service, and returns. Even more time is consumed as these intermediaries identify appropriate decision makers in customer firms, and establish credibility with them in terms of the manufacturer's product. Because manufacturers do not always take such a long-term perspective on achieving marketplace objectives, they are less apt to view distribution changes as a viable strategic option.

Managers resist change also because they fear that an abandoned channel will be taken over by competitors. That is, even though the channel is not economical or does not serve organizational objectives, it is kept more to hurt the competition than to help the manufacturer. Such concerns are often misplaced, for the channel may be unattractive to a competitor for the same reasons the manufacturer is considering giving it up.

The decision to modify a distribution strategy can be made, at least in an ideal sense, only when sufficient data exists to justify such a decision. The necessary data is not always available. For example, in switching to a different type of intermediary, or to a direct sales force, not only must costs be estimated for inventory, accounts receivable, training, service, commissions, and transportation, but accurate assumptions also must be made concerning sales volume and revenues under the new arrangement. Loss of both revenue and goodwill during the time period of the change must be factored into the calculations.

Resistance to change can also come from those in the channel. Intermediaries may refuse to adopt new technologies, such as on-line cataloging and ordering, despite incentives from the manufacturer. They may resist new training programs, or the use of manufacturer-provided sales aids. Dropping these unwilling intermediaries may not be possible, for either legal or practical reasons, especially where the distribution alternatives are few. The marketer may feel that he or she is stuck with the current distribution strategy, and focus more on the other elements of the marketing mix.

A final reason for resistance is that all change creates some amount of disruption. Disruption causes conflict among those who must manage change; a manager's natural tendency is to avoid or minimize conflict. Conservative managers adopt a philosophy of management by exception, where new solutions are not investigated until the current system goes awry. The result can be major missed distribution opportunities.

A new strategy appears only after the filtering effect of these forces of resistance has taken place. The result may be no change, or alterations that fall far short of optimal decision making. The marketer who is cognizant of these resistance forces is in a better position to address politically the need for change.

THE NEED TO EVALUATE MIDDLEMEN

Once a relationship is established with a given type of middleman, it is good policy to formally evaluate each channel member at periodic intervals. Evaluation gives the marketer guidance in determining whether or not objectives are being met. In fact, in the absence of clear, measurable objectives, middleman evaluation loses much of its value.

Evaluation provides the manufacturer with a reading on which intermediaries are generating favorable results, and which are not. In allocating distribution resources, better performers warrant recognition and reinforcement in the form of incentives, promotion, and training support, or an extra effort to address their special concerns. With poor performers, management has a dilemma. Will extra incentives serve to motivate them, or simply be a waste of resources? Similarly, will punitive measures provide motivation, or contribute to a further reduction in their efforts?

Evaluation is also useful in the ongoing process of formulating distribution strategy. Evaluation can, for example, aid in determining whether individual intermediaries should be kept or dropped. In addition, the evaluation process is a source of data for use in analyzing the changing economics of using one type of intermediary versus another type versus a direct sales force.

The evaluation process plays a further role in terms of control. If an intermediary is aware that a formal evaluation is being conducted, and knows the criteria the marketer is using as the underlying basis of the evaluation, then he or she is more likely to strive to perform better on those criteria. This assumes that the intermediary believes the evaluation is reasonably fair, and sees a link between performing well on the evaluation and his or her own rewards.

Factors examined in an evaluation of performance can include productivity, profitability, and effectiveness measures. An assessment of productivity seeks to determine the efficiency of middlemen in the use of resources. Examples include sales per employee, asset turnover, or contribution per square foot of warehouse space. Profitability is a measure of financial performance of the intermediary, and includes indicators such as return on sales and growth pattern of revenues. Effectiveness is concerned with how well channel members are achieving channel objectives and taking advantage of channel opportunities. Here, the marketer is concerned with such issues as the number of new accounts versus existing accounts, unmet customer demand, errors in order filling, and number of customer complaints.

There are a variety of ways in which middlemen evaluation can be conducted; this chapter will focus on two. The first is contribution analysis, which represents a more objective technique, and the second is the weighted-factor method, which is more subjective in nature.

Exhibit 13.3   Distribution Strategies—Push Versus Pull

In addition to concerns regarding the types and number of intermediaries to use, and the length of the channel, the marketer must determine at what level in the channel to focus the company's effort. If we assume that the marketer has a limited set of resources at his or her disposal for use in achieving channel objectives, the question is where in the channel these resources should be directed. Should they be focused on the intermediary, on the industrial customer, or even further down, at the consumer level? When the manufacturer employs a middleman that sells to another middleman (e.g., a manufacturer's rep selling to industrial distributors) which should receive the bulk of the manufacturer's attention? The resources here include incentives such as bonuses and prizes, promotional efforts, training programs, and the company's own sales force, among others.

Two possible approaches to this problem are a *push* strategy and a *pull* strategy. With a push strategy, the marketer's efforts are concentrated directly on the next, or most immediate, member of the channel. With a pull strategy, the marketer does an end-run, circumventing the more direct channel member, concentrating on those further down the channel. The hope is that, if demand is stimulated down the channel, it will pull sales through the intervening levels in the channel.

Take the case of Cyro Industries of Woodcliff Lake, N.J., a maker of acrylic products. One of these products, Exolite, is used in building greenhouses, among other applications. The company sells Exolite to industrial distributors, who use it to build greenhouses for growers, the end users.

To stimulate weak sales, Cyro decided to promote the benefits of Exolite directly to greenhouse owners. The strategy was to get growers to specify Exolite to distributors when contracting with them to build a greenhouse. The strategy appears to have worked. Sales have boomed, and distributors who rarely used Exolite now build as much as 30 percent of their greenhouses with the product. Cyro successfully used a pull strategy, rather than rely solely on incentives to motivate distributors to push Exolite to customers in need of a greenhouse.

Source: S. Kapp, "Finding—and Making the Best of—the Right Market," *Business Marketing,* (Chicago: Crain Communications, Inc., February 1986) 90–93.

Evaluating Middlemen—The Contribution Approach

Contribution analysis was introduced in Chapter 10, in the discussion on pricing. This analysis is an approach to evaluating marketing programs based on how much a product is able to contribute to indirect (nonassignable) fixed costs and profitability once the product's own variable and direct (assignable) costs have been covered. Determining how much intermediaries contribute to company profitability is also possible when using the contribution approach.

Table 13.5 presents a hypothetical example of a manufacturer that sells all of its output through three industrial distributors. The critical piece of data is the middleman-controllable margin. This figure is obtained by first subtracting the cost of goods sold by each middleman from the sales revenue (for the manufacturer's product line) generated by that middleman. Next, variable manufacturing and physical distribution costs are subtracted. Then, any fixed costs directly traceable (assignable) to the middleman are removed. The logic, then, is that a middleman should be held accountable for generating enough revenue to at least cover the cost of producing the goods he or she is selling, plus any other costs directly incurred by the manufacturer as a result of doing business with the distributor.

Table 13.5 Channel Performance Measurement—Contribution Analysis

	($000)			
	Middleman A	Middleman B	Middleman C	Total Company
Net sales	$12,000	$10,000	$18,000	$40,000
Cost of goods sold (variable manufacturing cost)	6,000	5,000	9,000	20,000
Manufacturing contribution	$ 6,000	$ 5,000	$ 9,000	$20,000
Marketing and physical distribution costs:				
Variable:				
Sales margins	600	400	2,500	3,500
Transportation	300	70	800	1,170
Warehousing (handling in and out)	12	10	65	87
Order processing	50	10	75	135
Inventory carrying cost	38	10	60	108
Annual middleman contribution	$5,000	$4,500	$5,500	$15,000
Assignable nonvariable (Incurred specifically for the middleman during the period):				
Salaries	100	50	900	1,500
Middleman-related advertising	150	100	500	750
Bad debts	25	10	10	45
Other	25	40	90	155
Annual middleman-controllable contribution	$4,700	$4,300	$4,000	$13,000
Nonassignable costs:				9,000
Net profit				$ 4,000
Middleman-controllable margin-to-sales ratio	39.2%	43.0%	22.2%	32.5%

Source: Adapted from D.J. Bowersox, et al. *Management in Marketing Channels,* (New York: McGraw-Hill Book Co., 1980), 305. Reprinted with permission.

If the middleman-controllable contribution is divided by the sales generated by that middleman, the result is a *profitability index*. This index is a good indicator for comparing the performance of various distributors with company objectives. In the example in Table 13.5, middleman C is clearly outperforming the others in sales of the manufacturer's product line. However, after removing the costs incurred by the manufacturer because of middleman C, including production costs, middleman C is contributing less than the others to common nonassignable costs and profitability. In expressing the controllable contribution as a percent of sales, the picture becomes even clearer. The profitability index of middleman B is almost double that of middleman C. Not only is B a better performer than one might initially conclude, but also there may be inefficiencies in C's operations that are worth investigating.

Evaluating Middlemen—The Weighted-Factor Approach

A second, more subjective, approach to evaluation is the weighted-factor method. Where the contribution approach focused on a single criteria, profitability, the weighted-factor approach lends itself to a large number of different possible criteria.

Implementation of the weighted-factor approach consists of five steps. The marketer must first identify which criteria (or factors) will be used in evaluating the intermediary. In Table 13.6, five criteria have been selected. Others could include: new accounts generated, willingness to provide customer feedback, support for new products, technical service, and many more. In addition, an overall category such as sales performance can be broken down further into gross sales, sales growth, sales made vs. sales quota, and market share.

With these criteria in hand, the next step is to apply importance weights to each factor. One method is to divide these weights across the criteria so they add up to 1.0. This step forces the marketer to prioritize the factors by specifying how

Table 13.6   Channel Performance Measurement—Weighted Factor Approach

Criteria	(A) Importance Weight	(B) Middleman Evaluation	(A × B) Middleman Score
Sales Performance	.50	7	3.5
Inventory Maintenance	.20	5	1.0
Selling Capabilities	.15	6	0.9
Attitudes	.10	4	0.4
Growth Prospects	.05	3	0.15
		OVERALL PERFORMANCE RATING	5.95

Source: B. Rosenbloom, *Marketing Channels: A Management View,* 2nd ed. Hinsdale, IL: Dryden Press, Division of Holt, Rinehart and Winston, Inc. 1983. p. 353. Reprinted by permission of Holt, Rinehart and Winston, Inc.

much more important one is versus another. Thus, in Table 13.6, sales performance is not only the most important factor, it is more than twice as important as any other factor.

The third step is to evaluate each middleman on each factor. In the example, a 10-point scale was used, with 1 representing very poor performance and 10 signifying excellent performance. The analysis can become quite subjective at this point, unless the marketer has established clear standards for performance in each category. For example, sales increases in excess of 15 percent receive a rating of 10 on the sales performance criterion, increases of 13 to 15 percent receive a rating of 9, increases of 10 to 12 percent receive an 8, and so on.

Step four involves taking the importance weights for each factor times the middleman rating on that factor, and summing these products. The result is a total score representing the middleman's performance.

The final step is to compare these overall performance ratings for each middleman. The marketer cannot assume, however, that low or high relative scores mean poor or good performance. Rather, he or she must develop some standard of performance against which to compare these scores. The intermediary evaluated in Table 13.6 could have a higher score than all other intermediaries, but may be falling short of management's goal that all middlemen receive a score of at least 6.0.

Also worth noting is the usefulness of the weighted-factor approach in selecting a middleman. Trying to determine whether to use a particular type of intermediary, or a specific middleman organization, a marketer would go through the same process of selecting criteria, weighting, and then evaluating the intermediary's potential on each criterion.

IMPLEMENTATION OF DISTRIBUTION STRATEGY: THE ROLE OF LOGISTICS

In addition to tackling the problems of design, evaluation, and motivation in distribution channels, the industrial marketer also must monitor the physical movement and storage of goods. Customers are concerned that products are received in the right quantity, at the required time, using the desired mode of transportation, and in undamaged condition. The managerial decision area that deals with such concerns is *physical distribution,* or *logistics.*

Physical distribution is of strategic importance, regardless of whether the manufacturer uses an intermediary, because it is a key variable used by customers in vendor selection. In one study, industrial buyers placed physical distribution as the second most important factor, behind product quality, in deciding among alternative sources of supply (Perreault and Russ 1976). Problems in this area will undermine source loyalty with a customer who is basically satisfied with a product. Further, the importance of physical distribution increases with the frequency that a customer organization purchases an item. It should not be surprising, then, that in industrial markets, customer service is often defined in terms of physical distribution (Webster 1984).

The functions or tasks which make up physical distribution are many. They include warehousing, transportation, inventory control, materials handling, receiv-

Table 13.7 Controllable Elements in a Logistics System

Elements	Key Aspects
Transportation	Represents the single most important activity in the creation of place-values and time-values; is the means of moving goods from the end of the production line to customers in the marketplace.
Warehousing	Creates place-values and time-values by making goods available in the marketplace when needed.
Inventory management	Insures that the right mix of products is available at the right place, and at the right time, in sufficient quantity to meet demands; balances the risks of stockouts and lost sales against the risks of overstocks and obsolescence; facilitates production planning.
Protective packaging	Insures good condition of products when they arrive in the marketplace, and maximizes use of warehouse space and transport equipment cube.
Materials handling	Maximizes speed and minimizes cost of: order-picking, moving to and from storage, loading of transportation equipment, and unloading at destination; relates to product protection.
Order processing	Assists in creation of place-time values by communicating requirements to appropriate locations. Relates to inventory management by reflecting demands on current stocks and changes in inventory position.
Production planning	Insures realization of place-time values by making goods available for inventory. Permits planning of warehouse facility utilization, transportation requirements.
Customer service	Relates place-time values as seen by the company to place-time values as seen by its customers. Establishes levels of customer service consistent with marketing objectives as well as with cost limitations.
Plant location: Warehouse location, Facilities planning	Maximizes place-time values by relating plant and warehouse location to transportation services and costs in terms of markets to be served. Facilities planning insures that capacity, configuration, and throughput of warehouse and shipping facilities are compatible with product flow.

Source: M.D. Hutt, and T.W. Speh, *Industrial Marketing Management,* second edition, Hinsdale, Illinois: Dryden Press, Division of Holt, Rinehart and Winston, Inc., 1985 p. 338. Adapted from "The Many Faces of PDM," (*Japan Airlines,* 1969), p. 10. Reprinted by permission of Holt, Rinehart and Winston, Inc.

ing, protective packaging, and order processing. Each task has important marketing implications, because of the way it affects the value or utility a customer receives. This relationship is illustrated in Table 13.7, which presents the tasks of physical distribution as controllable marketing variables.

The relationship among the elements of a company's logistical system can be quite complex. On the surface level, there is an apparent trade-off between the cost of distribution and the quality of customer service. At a more operative level, numerous trade-offs are involved among all of the tasks of physical distribution. To properly manage these complexities, it is helpful to consider the total distribution cost concept.

Rather than deal with each element of physical distribution (and its cost) individually, the total distribution cost concept encourages management to consider all cost elements simultaneously, when attempting to achieve desired customer service standards. Reducing any single cost component (e.g., a cheaper but slower form of transportation) to the lowest possible level is likely to drive up other costs (e.g., the need to keep larger inventories or establish more warehouse locations). Also, reductions in certain distribution costs are made possible by spending more on others. An improved order-processing system can enable the vendor to lower the transportation costs because of a reduction in rush orders and fewer partial truckload shipments. The marketer must carefully analyze such trade-offs, and make compromise decisions with the end user's requirements in mind. When an intermediary is involved, the marketer has to look beyond the logistical relationship with that channel member, and evaluate the entire channel.

In balancing costs, one must not ignore so-called hidden costs. These lost sales and profits are due to late shipments, backorders, and customers who switch to alternative suppliers.

Failure to properly coordinate the physical distribution mix leads to inefficiencies that distort the relationship between cost and customer service. Companies end up not getting full value (in terms of customer service) for their dollars spent on distribution. This problem is *maldistribution* (Oresman and Scudder 1974). Four signs indicate the likely presence of maldistribution: relatively slow-turning inventories, low levels of customer service relative to the company's inventory investment, a high number of shipments among warehouse locations, and frequent payments of premium freight charges. Maldistribution is an invitation to competitors selling identical products in the same market to achieve a cost and price advantage.

What is an effective logistics system? A number of different combinations of physical distribution variables would seem possible, but many may be inconsistent with the level of service that management seeks to provide. Determining the appropriate service level, and then managing distribution variables efficiently to achieve that level, is the most fundamental issue in managing physical distribution. Unfortunately, customer service means different things to different customers. Some define it in terms of a specific order cycle time—the elapsed time between the initial effort to place an order and the customer's receipt of the order in acceptable condition. Other customers focus on percentage fill rate—the proportion of orders filled at the time of placement. Still others are concerned with a combination of factors—ease of ordering, billing accuracy, and percent of stockouts.

In addition, producers and customers may view service from quite different perspectives. Buyer surveys often show that customers define customer service differently than do manufacturers, and actually prefer a lower but more reliable service level than that being provided (Sabath 1978). The opportunity exists, then, for the manufacturer to improve service (as defined by the customer) while cutting costs.

One reason for misdefining customer service is the tendency for producers to place responsibility for logistics in the manufacturing or operations areas, rather than in marketing. Physical distribution is a frequent source of conflicts in industrial organizations, often between marketing and manufacturing. Manufacturing is attempting to be cost-effective and manage distribution in a manner that serves production goals; marketing is more concerned with satisfying the customer. An optimum distribution program balances these cost and service demands.

Regardless of where responsibility is placed, marketers must work with manufacturing personnel to achieve distribution objectives. This cooperation requires an ability to reconcile the company's scheduling, capacity, and inventory constraints with the service level needs of customers. Physical distribution is a valuable tool for use by the industrial marketer who can successfully manage it. Some have argued that effective management of distribution is "frequently only second in importance to the personal contact of the sales force in building a working relationship between supplier and customer" (Oresman and Scudder 1974).

SUMMARY

Distribution, possibly the most inflexible of the elements within the marketing mix, is, nonetheless, an important strategic variable which must be managed and continually reappraised. This chapter has examined the nature and scope of distribution strategy in an industrial context.

A central focus of the approach has been the role of channels in creating value. Intermediaries add value to the products of manufacturers by providing time, place, form, and possession utilities. This is accomplished through such functions as transportation, storage, credit, customer service, and marketing research. A central tenet in channel management is that marketers can eliminate the middleman, but not the middleman's function.

Industrial channels have a number of features that distinguish them from consumer channels. Industrial channels generally are shorter, place higher sales and service expectations on the middleman, and involve different types of intermediaries. The two most prevalent types of intermediaries are manufacturers' representatives and industrial distributors. Characteristics of each were examined within the chapter.

Distribution strategy is concerned with the determination of channel objectives, channel length, channel members, market coverage, and resource allocation within the channel. A number of tactical questions, such as the appropriateness of exclusive arrangements, the design of incentive systems, and the establishment of returns policies are also pertinent. The chapter presented a continuous process model for use in managing distribution strategy. This model consisted of the factors that affect initial distribution strategy, factors that necessitate change in strategy, and forces of resistance to change.

Channels exist in increasingly dynamic environments, and, the internal capabilities and requirements of the industrial firm are continually changing. To meet these challenges, channel members must be continually evaluated. Two approaches to intermediary evaluation were presented—the contribution approach, and the weighted-factor approach.

Finally, the other side of channel management, logistics, or physical distribution, was shown to be a vital part of industrial marketing strategy. Organizational buyers are especially attuned to the logistical capabilities and performance of their vendors. At the same time, supplier firms tend to place responsibility for physical distribution with personnel in production or operations. This tendency poses difficulties for the marketer, who must bridge the gap between the firm's manufacturing constraints and the customer's logistical demands.

QUESTIONS

1. How is an industrial distributor a source of value within the distribution channel?

2. You've done extensive analysis on your distribution channels, which currently include a number of industrial distributors throughout the country. It appears that you could save money by eliminating the distributors and selling direct to your end users. In spite of this incentive, why might you argue to retain the distributors?

3. Discuss the pros and cons of using manufacturers' representatives versus industrial distributors if you sold:
   — conveyors and conveyor belts
   — janitorial supplies
   — computer terminals
   — lathes

4. Why might manufacturers' representatives be considered the elite among industrial salespersons? What are some limitations in using manufacturers' representatives?

5. What does it mean to manage your intermediaries, especially if they are independent companies? What are some tools for managing these intermediaries?

6. What are some likely sources of conflict between a company that manufactures standard medical equipment (stethoscopes, thermometers, medicine carts, examining tables, x-ray machines, etc.) and its industrial distributors? Discuss methods for dealing with such conflict.

7. Discuss the factors that might necessitate a change in the distribution channel strategy once it is in place. Pick a specific industrial product.

8. Evaluate the pros and cons of the weighted-factor approach to evaluating distributors. Why might you use different factors and importance weights for two different distributors?

9. How might you define and measure customer service level if you were a manufacturer of gasoline pumps sold to oil companies and convenience store chains?

10. What are some of the trade-offs a company makes in determining inventory levels, the number and locations of warehouses, transportation methods, and customer service level?

PART **IV** CONTROL OF INDUSTRIAL MARKETING PROGRAMS

Previous chapters have emphasized the need to base the development of marketing strategies and tactics on a clear set of overall marketing objectives. Specific objectives are important in guiding the firm's efforts in new product development, ongoing product management, pricing, advertising, sales management, and distribution. One of the most critical responsibilities of the marketing manager involves determining how well these objectives are being accomplished. Performance must be continuously monitored, so that programs can be modified or updated as conditions require. This monitoring activity is called the marketing control process.

Coordination and control of marketing programs and activities is the control focus of Part IV, which consists of Chapter 14. This section defines different levels of control, and discusses some of the conceptual issues that impact upon any control system. Specific tools and approaches useful at each of the control levels are presented. Selected inputs into the control process are discussed, such as the budget, data requirements, scenario analysis, and assumptions. Suggestions are made regarding what should be done when deviations are observed between planned performance (objectives) and actual performance (results).

The marketing manager is also responsible for the ethical implications of the firm's marketing-related activities. Ethics represents another dimension of the control process. There is a wide range of behaviors and practices found in industrial markets that raise ethical questions, and that also can affect the financial performance of the firm. Some of these questions are examined in Chapter 14.

14

CONTROL AND EVALUATION OF INDUSTRIAL MARKETING PROGRAMS

Key Concepts

Annual plan control	Performance monitoring
Consumer attitude tracking	Profitability control
Control benchmarks	Profitability index
Control process	Profit center
Control tracking system	Ratio analysis
Data base management system	Scenario analysis
Direct cost	Sensitivity analysis
Efficiency control	Spreadsheet
Ethical performance	Strategic control
Expense-to-sales analysis	Strategic environmental monitoring
Full costing	Strategic intelligence system (SIS)
Indirect cost	Strategic profit model
Marketing audit	Variable cost
Performance diagnosis	Variance analysis

Learning Objectives

1. Define the process of control, and emphasize control as an integral part of industrial strategy formulation.
2. Discuss practical problems in establishing a control system in industrial firms.
3. Identify major categories of marketing control, and some of the key concepts, tools, and approaches in each category.
4. Describe a number of inputs which aid the process of control.
5. Emphasize the need to monitor the ethical aspects of marketing performance, and outline major problems in managing company ethics.

*Many centralized companies with highly sophisticated
control systems are, in fact, out of control.*

G. PINCHOT III

This final chapter will examine ways the marketing manager can ensure that strategies and programs are being effectively implemented. Control can be defined simply as the prevention and correction of deviations from plans; a control or tracking system refers to "that combination of components which act together to maintain actual performance close to a desired set of performance specifications" (Lorange et al., 1986).

A logical question in a chapter on control is control over what? In the marketing area, concern is generally with revenues and costs, with more specific interest in key decision variables such as product profitability, sales force expenses, distributor performance, advertising effectiveness, and price variances. But the real concern of control is ensuring that the strategies and tactics developed in the marketing plan are achieving management's objectives.

Control, then, must be an integral part of the planning process. The detailed measures used in performing product and market analysis during the strategy formulation process should be consistent with the measures used after the fact to measure performance. Further, the outputs of the control system become inputs into the next planning period. Unfortunately, however, many companies approach control as a completely independent activity.

Control systems are a means to an end. The company develops specific measures (e.g., sales per square foot, territory contribution margin) which are meant to be indicators of progress towards overall marketing objectives. The danger is in letting the control measure become the goal. A salesperson who knows he or she is being evaluated based on calls made per day (a control measure) will become preoccupied with making as many calls as possible, and not with achieving the company's sales goals. Cohen and Cyert (1973) have explained this phenomenon as follows: "Once the 'rules of the game' have been laid down, the players can be expected to alter their behavior so as to 'look good' according to the 'scorecard' which is kept on them." Similarly, then, if advertising efforts are evaluated by top management based on inquiries generated, the marketing manager may spend more money in the trade journals that generate the most leads. However, the real company concern is in generating names of prospects who are also *likely* buyers.

Control, or performance monitoring, represents a measurement process. That is, the manager is attempting to measure results at key stopping points (e.g., quarterly), and compare them to some benchmark. Measures are rarely perfect, though, and so the ability to ensure that the company has measured what it actually intended to measure must always be questioned. For example, salesperson performance has many dimensions. Finding one or two control measures that comprehensively convey the effectiveness of current selling efforts is difficult. Control measures are indicators; they rarely provide the complete performance picture. This limitation is further complicated by the tendency on the part of companies to rely on control measures that are easily quantified and heavily emphasize sales.

The need to distinguish between efficiency and effectiveness in marketing activity is a key issue in designing a control system. Efficiency, on the one hand, is a concern with minimizing the amount of expenditures or resources needed to accomplish a task. Effectiveness, on the other hand, is a concern with ensuring that the correct tasks are being accomplished. Having one does not guarantee the other; a company could have a very efficient distribution system (e.g., in terms of costs) that is reaching the wrong target market. Control systems tend to place a heavy emphasis on efficiency. The marketing manager must be able to establish a clear, logical relationship, however, between an efficient performance indicator and specific marketing objectives.

Another danger in designing control systems is their ability to stifle the creative energies of marketing and sales personnel. Control systems that attempt to influence the way in which resources are being used (e.g., a salesperson's time, advertising dollars), in addition to monitoring how effectively they are being used, can sometimes undermine motivation and creativity. Control measures provide structure to a marketing task, in the sense that they represent the criteria on which task performance will be evaluated. This structure is a major attribute of control. However, the more structure provided, the less freedom an individual has to approach the task in novel or creative ways. The person's efforts will be focused on doing what is necessary to produce acceptable results in terms of the control measures.

Despite potential problems of overcontrol, an ongoing tracking system tailored to current strategies and tactics is invaluable. In the absence of an effective means of control, the marketing program can stray far off track. This diversion may become apparent only much later, after customers have moved to other suppliers, profits have taken a nose dive, or major opportunities are lost. By the time corrective action is taken, even more damage is done.

THE PROCESS OF CONTROL

There are three elements in the control function:

> establishing standards of marketing and sales performance;

> periodically measuring actual performance and comparing it against these standards;

> taking corrective action in those areas where performance does not meet standards.

Note, then, that control activity is more than developing and using performance measures. There is a formal process of control which also includes goal-setting, diagnosing reasons for performance discrepancies, and developing corrective solutions. This process is illustrated in Figure 14.1.

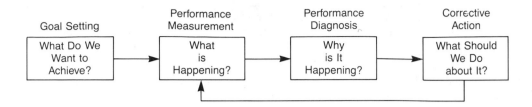

Figure 14.1   The Control Process
(Source: P. Kotler, (1984) *Marketing Management: Analysis, Planning and Control*, 5th ed., 745. Reprinted with permission of Prentice-Hall, Inc., Englewood Cliffs, N.J.)

Clearly, if the marketing manager does not have an exact idea of what he or she expects in the way of performance from products, territories, customers, distributors, advertising dollars, or other marketing resources, then control becomes a completely arbitrary activity. There is no way to objectively determine how well things are going. Measurable goals need to be established in each of the decision areas within which the manager wishes to monitor. A common problem in control is the tendency to establish goals at too general a level, such as for overall sales or market share, rather than for sales by customer type, or market share by territory.

Goals must be expressed in terms of benchmarks on key operational control measures. So, if the control measure is the contribution margin per distributor, then the benchmarks might be some specific dollar amount to be achieved at the end of each quarter. The benchmarks are based on what level of contribution the marketer sees as necessary to achieve more general profit goals. Benchmarks must also reflect reasonable, achievable performance levels that reflect historical trends, current opportunities, and available resources.

A good tracking system requires a strong data base so that historical trends in key variables can be plotted, and current performance compared against past patterns. An information base must be managed, to ensure that raw data is properly categorized (e.g., as a variable or fixed cost, as a direct or indirect expense, as revenue attributable to a certain type of customer or intermediary). Further, the figures must be expressed in the correct unit of analysis (e.g., monthly versus quarterly, net versus gross), and must be constantly updated.

Beyond performance monitoring, the control process is concerned with diagnosing reasons for discrepancies between planned and actual performance. This diagnosis further points to the need for good data. If sales were below expectations, can the problem be traced to some aspect of internal operations, or to some unanticipated external development, or to both? Were prices too high, and if so, was this because costs were higher than projected? Or, instead, is the poor sales performance due to the sales force pushing the wrong products or emphasizing the wrong customers? Perhaps the real problem lies in the commission system. In terms of external developments, the problem may actually be related to changes in competitors' prices or promotional expenditures. Alternatively, weak sales may be related to the current economic environment. Information must be collected routinely on internal, as well as external, factors, for the marketer to successfully perform this analysis and pinpoint the real causal factor.

The final step in marketing control efforts involves selecting the appropriate corrective action to deal with performance discrepancies. This action can range from doing nothing to a complete change in strategy. Between these two extremes lie several alternatives, such as a modification of marketing or sales tactics, a change in operating procedures, or an alteration of the performance benchmarks. The marketer should not be too quick to modify goals or benchmarks, because this type of inconsistency undermines the credibility of the entire control process. If performance standards were realistic, the logic of control is to find the root of the problem and make corrections. When performance discrepancies arise, the marketer may want to periodically reevaluate the underlying assumptions on which current period goals were based.

CATEGORIES OF MARKETING CONTROL

To organize the marketing control process systematically, the marketer should consider four overall areas in which control is critical. These include the overall strategic direction of the firm, the annual marketing plan, the firm's profitability, and the efficiency of marketing expenditures (Kotler 1984). Each area requires a different level of analysis.

Strategic Control

Managers can find themselves so caught up in achieving this year's goals and solving today's problems that they fail to step back occasionally from their ongoing responsibilities long enough to see if the company is missing opportunities. They should ask the question, is the organization's strategy taking complete advantage of the markets, products, and channels available to it? This assessment represents strategic control.

The turbulent and dynamic nature of the competitive, technological, regulatory, economic, and supplier environments confronting industrial firms suggests a need to continually assess the fit between company strengths and/or weaknesses and environmental opportunities and/or threats. Even with a strong fit, the manager should look for product areas, services, technologies, customer segments, distribution channels, or delivery systems that the company has not developed, but which could be synergistic with current operations and capabilities.

A tool that is helpful in strategic control is the marketing audit, defined as "a systematic and thorough self-examination of a company's market position" (Grashof 1981). Table 14.1 outlines the areas covered in a typical marketing audit. After conducting such a detailed self-appraisal, management is in a better position to see the total picture of their firm as a marketing entity. With this perspective, it is easier to identify holes or gaps in marketing efforts, and determine which resources are being underutilized.

Table 14.1 Checklist of Areas Examined in an Industrial Marketing Audit

I.   The industry
    A. Characteristics
        1. Size (in units produced, dollar sales)
        2. Number of firms
        3. Nature of competition
        4. Geographical concentration
        5. Interaction with other industries
        6. Product life cycle
        7. Government and societal constraints
        8. Barriers to entry
    B. Trends
        1. Sales volume and number of firms
        2. Geographic localization
        3. Size of firms
    C. Firm's position
        1. Size relative to industry leaders
        2. Market strength
        3. Leader or follower
II. The firm
    A. History
        1. Growth and expansion
        2. Financial history
        3. Past strengths and weaknesses
    B. Goals and Objectives
    C. Current strengths and weaknesses
        1. Market
        2. Managerial
        3. Financial
        4. Technical
        5. Market information mechanisms
III. The market
    A. General structure
        1. Number of customers
        2. Geographical spread and/or grouping
        3. Breadth of product use
        4. Switching costs
        5. Characteristics of current customers
        6. Typical buying process
        7. Nature of buying center
    B. Firm's approach to market segmentation
        1. Degree to which firm has segmented the market
        2. Degree of specification of target markets
        3. Bases of segmentation used
            a. Macro vs. micro   d. Use patterns
            b. SIC   e. Size
            c. Geographic
    C. Segments identified by the firm
        1. What are characteristics?
        2. Degree of difference among segments
        3. What segments have been selected by the firm as target markets?
    D. Has the firm considered factors which affect the market?
        1. Income effects
        2. Price and quality elasticity
        3. Responsiveness to marketing variables
        4. Seasonality
IV. The product
    A. List the company's products
        1. Strengths
        2. Weaknesses
        3. Distinctive features
        4. Economic value to the customer
        5. Stage of life cycle

Table 14.1 Continued

B. Competitive position
    1. Price and quality relative to competitors
    2. Market share
    3. Patents or trademarks
C. Product policy
    1. Written or verbal
    2. Product line width and depth
    3. New product policy
    4. Product deletion policy
V. Distribution
    A. Channels of distribution
        1. Description of channel(s) used
        2. Institutions in each channel
        3. Basis for selection of institutions used
    B. Distribution policy
        1. Extent and depth of market coverage
        2. Role of distribution in marketing mix and marketing plans
    C. Physical distribution
        1. PD organization with firm
        2. Customer service level policy
        3. Inventory
            a. Number of locations of stock
            b. Type of warehouse (i.e., public versus private)
            c. Planned and actual inventory levels
        4. Transportation
            a. Product shipment terms
            b. Mode of transportation used
            c. Type of carrier
                (1) Common
                (2) Contract
                (3) Private
VI. Promotion
    A. Goals of promotional activities
        1. Advertising
        2. Personal selling
        3. Sales promotion
    B. Promotion Blend
    C. Advertising
        1. Budget in dollars and percent of sales
        2. Tasks assigned to advertising
        3. Evaluation procedures
    D. Personal selling
        1. Organization of sales force
        2. Sales force management
        3. Tasks assigned to the sales force
VII. Pricing
    A. Goals and role of pricing in the marketing mix
    B. Approach used to set prices
        1. Basis on which prices are set
        2. Flow of pricing decisions within the firm
    C. Prices compared with competitors
    D. Trade discount and allowances
    E. Financing and credit arrangements

Source: Adapted from J.F. Grashof, "Conducting and Using a Marketing Audit," in E.J. McCarthy, et al., *Readings in Basic Marketing,* (Homewood, Ill.: Irwin, 1981), 506–7. Reprinted with permission.

Annual Plan Control

Annual plan control, the second area of control, represents an attempt to ascertain whether the objectives established in the company's annual marketing plan are actually being achieved. Some of the tools available for this type of control include variance analysis, the strategic profit model, marketing expense-to-sales analysis, and customer attitude tracking.

Variance analysis is a method for measuring the relative contribution of different factors to a gap between actual performance and marketing goals. Figure 14.2 provides a graphical illustration, and Table 14.2 presents a numerical example.

If it is assumed, for the purpose of example, that the marketing plan includes a profit objective expressed in terms of total contribution margin, the first step in the analysis is to identify the variance between actual and planned contribution (step 1, Figure 14.2). Actual quantity sold is taken times actual contribution per unit. From this total, the product of planned units sold times planned unit contribution is subtracted. Steps 2 and 3 demonstrate how this variance can be further broken down into a price/cost variance and a volume variance. This approach enables the manager

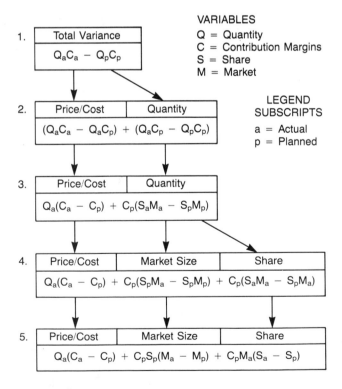

Figure 14.2 Variance Decomposition—Comparison with Plan
(Source: J.M. Hulbert and N.E. Toy, "A Strategic Framework for Marketing Control," *Journal of Marketing*, 41, 19. Copyright American Marketing Association. Reprinted with permission.)

Table 14.2 Analysis of Actual versus Planned Performance for a Hypothetical Product

Item	Planned	Actual	Variance
Revenues			
Sales (lb.)	20,000,000	22,000,000	2,000,000
Price per lb. ($)	0.50	0.4773	(0.227)
Revenues ($)	10,000,000	10,500,000	500,000
Total Market (lb.)	40,000,000	50,000,000	10,000,000
Share of Market	50%	44%	(6%)
Costs			
Variable cost per lb. ($)	0.30	0.30	—
Contribution per lb. ($)	0.20	0.1773	(0.0227)
Total ($)	4,000,000	3,900,000	(100,000)

Source: J.M. Hulbert and N.E. Toy, "A Strategic Framework for Marketing Control," *Journal of Marketing*, 41, 13. Copyright American Marketing Association. Reprinted with permission.

to determine if the overall contribution variance was due to (a) prices or costs that were higher or lower than expected; or (b) the number of units actually sold being greater than or less than expected. Steps 4 and 5 attempt to further explain the volume variance. Was the variance due to a difference between the expected market share and what was actually achieved? Alternatively, was the size of the total market larger or smaller than anticipated? The price/cost variance could, similarly, be broken down into its subcomponents to determine if the price charged was less than expected, or if production was more efficient than assumed in the plan.

Variances can be positive or negative. The marketer is concerned whether performance is consistent with the goals set out in the marketing plan, or is above or below target. This performance can be visually plotted and monitored using a product (or service) evaluation matrix (see Figure 14.3). Assume the annual marketing plan sets out specific goals for sales, profitability, market share, and industry sales for two products, A and B. The marketer uses the product evaluation matrix to track performance for each product on each of these goals, over a number of periods (e.g., quarters, years).

In Figure 14.3, the performances of products A and B have been plotted over three time periods, represented by the subscripts (1,2,3). In period 1, sales for product A increase at an accelerating rate, classifying it in the growth area. Similarly, industry sales were in a growth stage. Profits were below target, although market share achieved the target goal. In periods 2 and 3, profitability had been brought into the target range, and the same levels of performance on the other criteria were maintained. For product B, industry and company sales are initially stable, with market share and profitability below target. Market share improved in the second period, but profits remained a problem. By the third period, profits are also on target.

Company Sales → Industry Sales ↓ / Profitability → Market Share ↓	Decline			Stable			Growth		
	Below Target	Target	Above Target	Below Target	Target	Above Target	Below Target	Target	Above Target
Growth — Above Target									
Growth — Target							$A_1 \longrightarrow A_{2,3}$		
Growth — Below Target									
Stable — Above Target									
Stable — Target				$B_2 \longrightarrow B_3$					
Stable — Below Target				$\uparrow$ B_1					
Decline — Above Target									
Decline — Target									
Decline — Below Target									

Figure 14.3 Tracking Performance with the Product Evaluation Matrix (Source: Yoram Wind and Henry J. Claycamp, "Planning Product Line Strategy: A Matrix Approach," *Journal of Marketing*, 40 (January), (Chicago: American Marketing Association, 1976), 5. Reprinted with permission.)

The strategic profit model is a second tool for annual plan control. This model enables the marketer to examine how the marketing programs contained within the plan have affected key financial ratios, and ultimately how they have affected return on investment (ROI). Its use is demonstrated in Figure 14.4.

Bottom-line profit, or return on net worth, is pictured as the product of financial leverage times return on assets. Return on assets is divided into net profit margin and asset turnover components that are, in turn, further broken down. The right-hand column of Figure 14.4 presents examples of marketing actions that might be contained within a marketing plan, and shows which accounts these efforts would most directly impact on. The model shows that the effect of an increase in some marketing expense can be traced to see how profitability will ultimately be affected. Note that an action (such as a reduction in customer order cycle time) by the marketer could affect more than one financial account. Also, revenue and expense items could be both positively and negatively affected. For example, elimination of certain accounts or territories might lessen sales, but may reduce expenses even more.

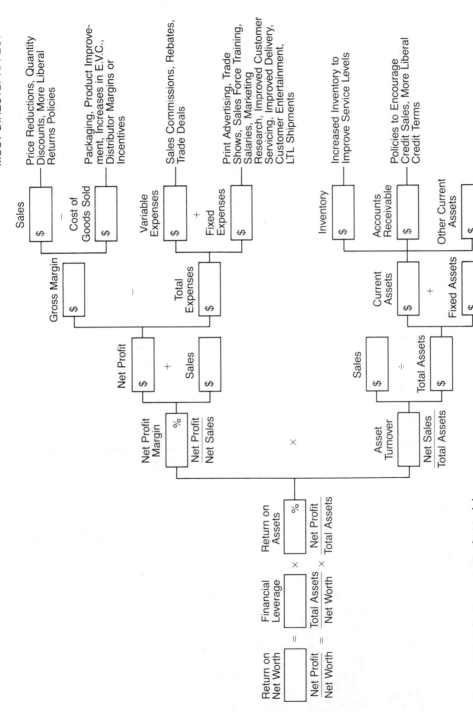

Figure 14.4 The Strategic Profit Model

(Source: Adapted from D. J. Bowersox, et al., *Management in Marketing Channels*, (New York: McGraw-Hill Book Co., 1980), 312. Reprinted with permission.)

Similarly, aggressive sales efforts might raise fixed and variable sales costs, but may produce enough volume for the firm to reduce manufacturing costs by taking advantage of economies of scale and the experience curve.

Constructing and tracking key marketing expense-to-sales ratios is still another approach to annual plan control. Here, major categories of marketing expenditures, such as trade journal advertising, trade shows, sales expense accounts, sales commissions, and marketing research, are each divided by sales and then individually tracked. Benchmarks based on marketing objectives should be set, reflecting the desired level for the ratio. Of course, the ratios will fluctuate as expenditures and sales vary over the course of the year. An acceptable range, consisting of an upper and lower threshold, should be determined. Data for the ratio is then tracked periodically (e.g., monthly, quarterly) to assure that performance is within the threshold levels. This tracking is demonstrated in Figure 14.5.

If any of the ratios deviate from the acceptable range, or demonstrate consistent patterns over a series of periods, the control process demands that the marketer attempt to ascertain the cause. Although sales are not directly controllable, they can be influenced. The real danger is in losing control over the amount spent on marketing resources, and the manner in which monies are spent.

A fourth method of annual plan control involves marketing research, in which customers are surveyed to determine the effect of the company's marketing programs. This research is especially relevant for tracking performance on communication objectives. A survey might be conducted to see if sufficient numbers of those in the target audience are being made aware of a product through either advertising or a sales call. Similarly, the marketer may wish to learn if the marketing efforts have had any significant impact on customer attitudes or perceptions.

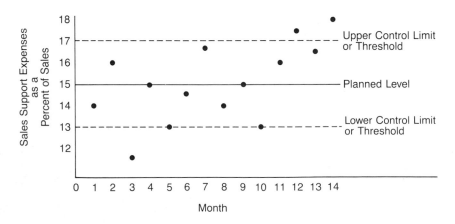

Figure 14.5   Control Chart for Monitoring Deviations from Plans (Source: Adapted from D. Dalrymple and L.J. Parsons, *Marketing Management*, 4th Ed., (New York: John Wiley, 1986), 818. Reprinted with permission.)

Effective tracking of customers often requires that the marketer perform longitudinal (over time) studies. Conducting surveys before and after a particular sales or promotional campaign will better enable the marketer to isolate whether changes in key performance variables were due to the campaign itself, or to some other factor. When developing survey instruments, it is often desirable to design questions in a way that the study can be replicated periodically. With an ongoing survey program, management can develop a data base that assesses trends over time, and that provides more opportunity to isolate the underlying causes of these trends, and the reasons for temporary fluctuations in the data.

Profitability Control

Senior management is responsible for achieving overall company profit objectives, but the marketer is, by definition, concerned for the profitability of specific products, territories, segments, customers, channels, distributors, and order sizes. Quite possibly, for example, a particular customer group, intermediary, or product could be eliminated, causing sales to be lower, but improving profitability.

Given the obvious importance of knowing where profits (or losses) are coming from, it is surprising how few managers are aware of the precise net returns the firm actually is realizing on a particular service or market segment in the current operating period. This ignorance is especially prevalent when a variety of products is being sold in a number of markets.

The ability to examine products, customers, territories, and channels as profit centers is implicit in attempts to perform profitability analysis. Therefore, the marketer must be able to assign revenues and costs to each of these areas. Of special concern is the need to assign (and hence control) marketing resources.

Perhaps the most valuable tool for use in profitability control is termed the "contribution-margin income statement" (Dunne and Wolk 1977; Beik and Buzby 1973; Mossman, et al. 1974). It is based on contribution analysis and contribution thinking, a common theme of this book introduced in Chapters 7, 10, and 13. Individual income statements can be derived for products, customers, territories, or channels, which means that each can be a unit of analysis. If the unit of analysis is products, the modularized contribution-margin income statement might resemble that demonstrated in Table 14.3, part A. A territory analysis is provided in part B of the same table.

In Table 14.3, the marketer is responsible for two products sold in two different territories. Revenues, variable costs, and direct fixed costs are attributed to products, as well as to territories. Variable costs vary directly with the number of units produced or sold. Direct fixed costs are those which exist only because the product or territory exists. Thus it can be argued that eliminating the product or territory would eliminate the expense. When the unit of analysis is products, direct fixed costs could include expenditures for promotion of individual products, as well as individual marketing research expenditures. For territories, the costs of a territorial manager and office space rental represent direct expenses.

Fixed expenses which cannot be traced to the unit of analysis are termed indirect costs. They are treated as common costs, to be subtracted only from the total

Table 14.3 Profitability Analysis of Products and Territories

Part A: Products

	Product A	Product B	Total
Net Sales	400,000	420,000	820,000
Variable Costs			
Manufacturing	200,000	189,000	389,000
Selling	20,000	31,500	51,500
Distribution	40,000	10,500	50,500
Variable Contribution	140,000	189,000	329,000
Direct Fixed Costs			
Promotion	2,000	1,500	3,500
Marketing Research	500	500	1,000
Total Product Contribution	137,500	187,000	324,500
Indirect Fixed Costs			85,400
Profit			**239,100**

Profitability index, product A: 34.4%
Profitability index, product B: 44.5%

Part B: Territories

	Territory A	Territory B	Total
Net Sales	480,000	340,000	820,000
Variable Costs			
Manufacturing	230,000	159,000	389,000
Selling	29,000	22,500	51,500
Distribution	33,000	17,500	50,500
Variable Contribution	188,000	141,000	329,000
Direct Fixed Costs			
Rent, territory office	5,000	5,400	10,400
Salary, territory manager	30,000	35,000	65,000
Total Territory Contribution	153,000	100,600	253,600
Indirect Fixed Costs			14,500
Profit			**239,100**

Profitability index, territory A: 31.8%
Profitability index, territory B: 29.6%

Source: Adapted from K. Monroe, *Pricing: Making Profitable Decisions,* (New York: McGraw-Hill, Book Co., 1979), 89. Reprinted with permission.

column. Note that a cost directly traceable to products would be indirect, when analyzing territories. The example includes $10,000 in common fixed costs, not traceable to either products or territories. So, the indirect fixed costs when analyzing products would be this $10,000, plus the $75,400 in rent and salaries which are directly traceable to territories.

Table 14.3 also includes a profitability index for each product and territory. These indexes are calculated by dividing the total contribution of each product or territory by the sales for that product or territory. The result is a performance measure, useful for control purposes. Again, the marketer may want to develop benchmarks for the profitability indexes, against which to assess the current performance of each unit of analysis.

Some suggest that this index can be taken a step further, to include the total investments tied up in a particular product, customer group, or territory (Schiff 1983). The result would be a rate-of-return index. These investments take the form of assets such as the average inventory level, or average amount of accounts receivable. A rate-of-return index for a particular territory can be determined by calculating the ratio of territory net income to territory sales, and multiplying this result times the ratio of territory sales to territory assets managed.

The logic of contribution analysis is that a unit of analysis should generate enough revenue to cover its own expenses—including controllable sales and marketing expenses. This analysis is appropriate for control purposes in the short run, such as the current operating period. Over the longer haul, the marketer may want to use a full-costing or net profit approach, where indirect fixed costs are allocated to individual products, customers, territories, or channels. Allocation of these costs might be made as a percentage of sales, a percentage of direct costs, or (among other possibilities) based on the use of some critical resource. While allocation methods are, by definition, arbitrary, expenses should be assigned based on some logical and relevant criterion. Otherwise, a profitable product or segment can be made to look only marginally profitable by holding it responsible for a disproportionate amount of overhead.

Efficiency Control

Earlier, a distinction was made between efficiency and effectiveness as a concern in marketing control. In other words, there is a difference between doing things right and doing the right things. The final, and most fundamental, level of control involves the issue of efficiency, which relates to whether the marketer is getting sufficient productivity from the company's marketing resources. More precisely, profitability control examines the profit contribution of products, markets, and channels; efficiency control focuses on the productivity of specific marketing resources, such as the sales force, trade shows, trade journal advertising, price discounts, and logistics expenditures. The obvious intent is to achieve a given level of performance with these resources, at the lowest possible cost.

The key to this form of control is the derivation of efficiency measures, many of which take the form of simple ratios or indexes. Some examples include the following:

- cost per sales call
- sales revenue per sales call
- advertising cost per inquiry generated
- advertising cost per thousand buyers reached
- sales per order size
- transportation cost per customer

- sales per inquiry per trade show
- sales per advertising dollar
- repurchase rate
- number of customers lost per period
- average number of stockouts per period
- percentage of customers taking advantage of cash, quantity, and trade discounts

- average monthly number of customer complaints
- average order cycle time per customer
- cannibalization rate
- distributor margins as a percentage of distributor sales
- product returns per distributor
- new accounts as a percentage of total accounts

Using these types of measures, the marketer can adjust or adapt the way in which resources are being applied. Efficiency measures might help determine whether sales call frequency should be increased, or whether fewer salespeople could produce the same results. Similarly, these same measures might indicate which trade journals should be dropped from the company's list of advertising outlets, or whether a particular type of appeal is working. The company's service level, which can be a common source of customer dissatisfaction and switching behavior, is also a major source of expense to the industrial marketer. Service levels are subject to considerable fluctuations and should be closely monitored. Efficiency measures can be used to determine how costs and revenues fluctuate with minor increases or decreases in service levels.

Table 14.4 summarizes a study of the control measures actually used by industrial companies. The measures listed were cited most frequently in a large survey of companies. The control efforts of many industrial marketing managers are not all that well-developed or sophisticated at present—as witnessed by the heavy reliance on very general sales and control measures. This level of control is changing as the emphasis and corresponding expectations placed on the marketing function increase.

SELECTED INPUTS TO THE CONTROL PROCESS

The Budget

The programs and plans of the marketer are usually translated into a budget. The decision to pursue an aggressive penetration strategy with increased selling and advertising efforts involves allocating specific dollar amounts for trade journal advertising, sales personnel, sales administration, trade show exhibits, and so forth. Further, because the budget is a constrained resource, this decision may mean allocating less to other areas, such as distribution or marketing research. For some companies, there is no formal marketing plan, and the budget, in effect, serves as the plan.

Table 14.4   Which Control Measures Are Used Most Frequently?

1. Products
   a. sales volume by product
   b. total contribution margin for each product
   c. sales volume as a percentage of quota or goal
   d. market share by product
   e. net profit for each product
2. Customers
   a. sales volume by customer
   b. sales volume as a percentage of quota or goal
   c. total contribution margin for each customer
3. Geographic Area
   a. sales volume by area
   b. sales volume as a percentage of quota or goal
   c. expenses incurred by area
4. Sales Force
   a. sales volume by salesperson
   b. sales volume as a percentage of quota
   c. sales expense per sale
   d. contribution margin per salesperson
5. Order Size
   a. sales volume by order size
   b. total contribution margin of each order size
   c. expenses per size of order
   d. net profit of each order size

Source: D.W. Jackson, L.L. Ostrom, and K.R. Evans (1982), "Measures Used to Evaluate Industrial Marketing Activities," *Industrial Marketing Management*, 11, 269–74.

Budgeting serves the control function in two ways. The first has to do with the usefulness of budgets in identifying problem areas in terms of projected revenues and expenditure levels. The second involves the use of these projected levels to evaluate actual performance. Because the budget contains planned or expected levels of financial performance, the marketer is forced to ensure that budgeted expenditures are sufficient to achieve forecast objectives. If an examination of the budget suggests that profit or sales goals will not be achieved at present prices or spending levels, or that required expenditures exceed available resources, action can be taken to reallocate funds. Because the budget contains projected revenue and expenditure figures, often broken down by marketing activity, the marketer is provided with a yardstick against which actual performance can be evaluated. Positive or negative performance deviations from budgeted levels help identify company strengths and weaknesses.

Consider the budgets presented in Tables 14.5 and 14.6. The company illustrated is assumed to sell only one product, at an average price of thirty dollars per unit. A monthly unit sales forecast, based on past sales patterns and sales force pro-

Table 14.5   Unit Sales Forecast and Total Budgeted Sales

Month	*Unit Sales Forecast** Existing Accounts	+ New Accounts	×	*Unit Selling Price ($)*	=	*Budgeted Sales Level ($)*
January	2,625	875		30.00		105,000
February	3,000	1,000		30.00		120,000
March	5,025	1,675		30.00		201,000
April	7,425	2,475		30.00		297,000
May	8,625	2,875		30.00		345,000
June	7,575	2,525		30.00		303,000
July	7,200	2,400		30.00		288,000
August	6,300	2,100		30.00		252,000
September	5,044	1,681		30.00		201,750
October	3,900	1,300		30.00		156,000
November	3,310	1,357		30.00		140,010
December	2,775	925		30.00		111,000
						2,519,760

*Based on a goal of 25 percent of sales from new accounts.

jections, is provided in Table 14.5. The marketing plan includes a goal of 25 percent of unit sales to new customers. Unit sales might be further broken down by type of business or territory, which would further enhance the control function provided by the budget. The unit sales are multiplied times the price to produce total forecast sales expressed in dollars.

Expenses to achieve these sales have been budgeted in Table 14.6. They also have been broken out by month, and divided into major controllable marketing expense categories. These estimates reflect managerial judgments of what it will take to achieve the sales goals incorporated in Table 14.5. As can be seen, then, the two tables are highly interrelated components of the overall budget. The sales increase in March is reflective, in part, of the participation in a trade show that month, and the expectation that some orders will be taken at the show. Similarly, the marketer has budgeted added expenditures for advertising and travel expenses to take advantage of the peak sales months of April through August.

The budget aids the control function by forcing the marketer to evaluate whether these expenditure levels are sufficient to accomplish the projected sales levels, and whether these levels are consistent with the resources available. Once the budget is in place, the marketer can use it to determine whether actual unit sales, prices charged, dollar sales, and expenditure levels are consistent with the budget—and identify any major variances. Expenditure levels as a percentage of sales can be monitored and compared to industry standards. By evaluating the productivity of these expenditures this year, the marketer is in a better position to establish the expense-to-sales ratios in future periods, and to modify these percentages as the environment changes.

Table 14.6 Sample Sales and Marketing Expense Budget ($)

Month	Trade Journal Advertising	Other Advertising	Trade Shows	Sales* Commissions	Travel Expense	Customer Servicing	Special Delivery Costs	Marketing Research	Supervision and Other Salaries	Total
January	2,000	300	0	10,500	6,000	10,000	200	1,000	12,000	42,000
February	2,000	300	0	12,000	6,500	10,000	200	1,000	12,000	44,000
March	2,000	300	13,000	20,100	6,500	10,000	200	1,000	12,000	65,100
April	8,000	600	0	29,700	12,000	10,000	200	0	12,000	72,500
May	8,000	600	0	34,500	12,500	10,000	200	0	12,000	77,800
June	8,000	600	0	30,300	12,500	10,000	200	0	12,000	73,600
July	6,000	600	0	29,800	10,000	10,000	200	0	12,000	67,600
August	6,000	600	0	25,200	10,000	10,000	200	0	12,000	64,000
September	6,000	300	0	20,175	10,500	10,000	200	0	12,000	59,175
October	4,000	300	0	15,600	6,500	10,000	200	2,000	12,000	50,600
November	4,000	300	13,000	14,001	6,500	10,000	200	2,000	12,000	62,001
December	4,000	300	0	11,100	6,000	10,000	200	0	12,000	43,600
Total	60,000	5,100	26,000	251,976	105,000	120,000	2,400	7,000	144,000	721,976
% of Sales	2.38%	0.20%	1.03%	10.00%	4.19%	4.76%	0.10%	0.28%	5.71%	28.65%

*10 Percent of monthly dollar sales

Data Requirements

The ability to implement the four types of control discussed earlier is built on a strong data base. Lack of this base is a major constraint on the control efforts of many industrial firms. Either they do not have the necessary data, or the data is not in a form that the marketer can use.

Consider the case of the marketer at an international chemical company who wishes to track something as seemingly basic as average order size in units per customer in each of five territories on a quarterly basis. Where does such information originate? Possibly data on order size and customer name can be gotten through copies of invoices available from accounting or shipping. Or, the sales manager may have field salespeople submit reports including such information. The point is that the marketing manager typically must go to other functional areas in the firm to get much of the internal data required. The data needs and uses of these other areas are likely to differ significantly from those of the marketer interested in control. As a result, the data categories, units of analysis, and timeliness of the data kept by those in other departments are probably going to differ from the inputs needed by the marketer.

Some companies have a controller on staff, and this office may be able to provide the data. However, holders of this position tend to focus on financial control, and to operate more at a strategic level. Even if the information is available through a central company data base, the marketer may need to massage the data to put it into a usable form.

Assuming that he or she has information on order size by customer, the marketer must group customers into territories (a unit of analysis that may be of no interest to the accountant or company controller), and then separate territorial orders into quarters of the year. Finally, average order sizes must be calculated for each territory in each quarter. At this point, the marketer may also want to further break down territories into companies of different sizes, or from different SIC codes, to perform a segment analysis.

Clearly, it is necessary for industrial marketing departments to adapt their own data base management systems from available information sources within and outside the firm. Such systems take random pieces of information and transform them into organized files (Cook 1984). The marketer with data base management skills is increasingly replacing one who simply made decisions based on the information and analysis provided by others. A simple example of the type of tabular data base the marketer might construct to address the problem above is presented in Table 14.7. The data base presented would allow for an assessment of average order size not only by territory, but also by salesperson, by customer, by product type, and by country. Natural extensions of this data base would include the addition of columns for customer four-digit SIC code, and for gross margin on each sale.

Construction of a data base can also involve political conflict, especially if the marketer is heavily reliant on inputs from other functional areas or departments. Information is often seen as a source of power and influence in organizations. In addition, those in one department may not see it as part of their job to prepare data inputs for the marketing department, or may see it as a low priority task. The result can be incomplete information, or untimely delivery of data.

Table 14.7   An Integrated Customer Data Base for an International Company

Product Code	Product Type	Product Name	Customer Code	Customer Name	Zone	Country	Territory	Salesperson	Date Last Order	Quantity Last Order
782	Basic	Toluene	4161	Braun Co.	Eur	Swit	4	Carpenter	10/11/81	20.9
			2396	Dagon	Asia	Thai	2	Rich	03/02/82	32.0
			7717	Jones Ltd.	Eur	UK	3	Felix	12/09/81	6.0
			4267	Pinero Co.	SA	Peru	5	Howell	03/03/82	13.0
944	Fine	Thiazide	2279	Roberts Eng.	Eur	UK	3	Felix	04/02/82	1.2
			5152	Wagner Co.	NA	USA	1	Wheeler	09/12/81	0.5
			3139	Nieuwland	Eur	NL	4	Carpenter	10/11/81	1.9

Source: Adapted from R. Cook, "Conquering Computer Clutter," *High Technology* (December 1984), 60–70. Copyright © 1984 by High Technology Publishing Corporation, 38 Commercial Wharf, Boston, MA 02110. Reprinted with permission.

Scenario Analysis

Not only should the tracking system be built on a sound data base, but also the marketer must explicitly state any assumptions being made regarding company operations and environmental developments during the control period. The reason for discrepancies between planned and actual performance may be due to goals based on assumptions that did not hold true.

In any planning process, management is forced to make numerous assumptions regarding market growth, competitor actions, costs of raw materials and components, distributor support, technological change, price stability, and government actions, among others. No matter how much careful consideration and supporting evidence went into these assumptions, the likelihood is that some of them will be violated.

Assumptions that do not hold true can undermine the company's entire marketing strategy. To deal with such uncertainties, it will be advantageous to engage in scenario planning (also called contingency planning). Here, the marketer pinpoints those key assumptions which are most uncertain, then develops scenarios representing a best-case, most-probable, and worst-case picture of the future in terms of these assumptions. For example, the best-case, or opportunistic, view might include an expectation that the rate of market penetration will accelerate by 10 percent over the rate assumed in the most-probable, or plan, view. The worst-case, or risk, view could include an estimate that the company will achieve only a 90 percent experience curve instead of the 80 percent curve projected in the plan view (i.e., costs per unit will drop to only 90 percent of their original level with every doubling of accumulated output).

Putting together alternative scenarios, the marketer can develop contingency strategies to implement, should assumptions prove to be wrong. The control or tracking system comes into play here in two ways. First, the control system must not only monitor marketing performance, but also must provide timely feedback regard-

ing the extent to which the assumptions made regarding the current operating period are not holding true. Second, the marketer may need to modify the benchmarks
used to monitor sales and marketing performance as assumptions are violated. Acceptable performance levels on the control measures may need to be raised or
lowered.

An example of scenario analysis can be found in Table 14.8. In part A, the
projected annual contribution margins are estimated for each of three territories.
The company has found that sales of its products tend to be affected by overall
developments in the economy, which is often the case for industrial firms. Different
contribution margin estimates are developed, depending on the state of the economy: recession, average growth, or above-average growth. Each of these conditions
represents a different scenario. As can be seen, the territories differ in their sensitivity to economic developments. Territory A is hardly affected, while the impact on
Territory C is dramatic. In addition, a subjective estimate of the probability of each
of these three scenarios occurring is included. If these probabilities were taken
times each contribution margin figure, the result would be expected contribution
margins.

In part B of Table 14.8, control benchmarks are established for Territory A on
a quarter-by-quarter basis under each of the scenarios. Actual performance would
be compared to these benchmarks to determine whether sufficient progress is being
made toward annual objectives. These benchmarks are based on historical data concerning the seasonal trends in company sales over the course of a year. Note that
the benchmarks used for control purposes are modified depending on the economic scenario, and that in this case, the benchmarks add up to the annual projected
contribution margin. In reality, management may want to set benchmarks at lower
levels to allow for some flexibility in quarterly performance figures. The control

Table 14.8 Scenario Analysis

A Annual Contribution Margin

State of the Economy	Territory A	Territory B	Territory C	Probability
Recession	$3,500	$ 2,000	$ (500)	.30
Average Growth	$3,800	$ 4,000	$10,000	.60
Above-Average Growth	$4,000	$10,000	$60,000	.10
				1.00

B Contribution Margin Benchmarks: Territory A

State of the Economy	1st qtr.	2nd qtr.	3rd qtr.	4th qtr.
Recession	$300	$1,000	$1,500	$700
Average Growth	$326	1,085	1,629	$760
Above-Average Growth	$343	$1,143	$1,714	$800

measures should call management's attention to significant variations in performance, not to minor fluctuations.

Productivity Judgments and Sensitivity Analysis

Another technique helpful in generating realistic control benchmarks is termed *productivity judgments*. This analysis involves estimating the impact of various changes in each of the marketing variables under the marketer's control. For instance, if discounts are increased, or call frequency is reduced, how will sales be affected? Unless this type of analysis is either formally or informally undertaken, establishing control benchmarks will be difficult, for the marketer has no realistic estimate of what to expect from his or her actions.

Consider the case of a proposed increase in expenditures for advertising space in trade journals. The problem is to estimate a sales-response function such as that illustrated in Figure 14.6. The marketer must first obtain data relating purchases of advertising space to sales. This information might come from historical company records (secondary data), where the sales-response function is estimated by extrapolating the past relationship forward to forecast future trends. Or, some form of market experiment could be run, where different levels of advertising are used in different test markets.

Even with data on advertising expenditures and sales, however, it is difficult to determine the precise nature of the relationship—because sales are also affected by other variables, such as prices, competitor actions, and environmental change. Even in terms of the advertising variable itself, frequency of exposure is as much or more

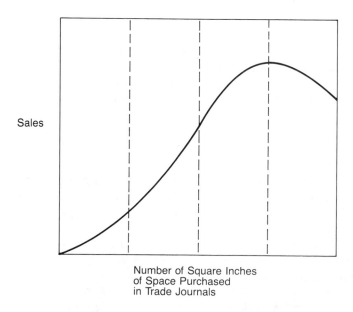

Figure 14.6 Sales-Response Function for Advertising Space in Trade Journals

a determinant of sales as is the amount of advertising space paid for. The analyst must either control for these other factors, or somehow weight their relative influence on sales. In addition, it is likely that the relationship between expenditures on advertising space and sales is nonlinear, as demonstrated in Figure 14.6. Certain levels of advertising may generate increasing returns in the form of sales, but other levels may produce diminishing returns. Simple extrapolations of past trends will tend to ignore the possibility of nonlinearity.

Once the productivity judgment has been made, the analyst can perform *sensitivity analysis*—a kind of *what if?* analysis. Consider the pricing area. Perhaps the productivity judgment has produced an estimate that demand for the company's product is somewhat elastic (e.g., elasticity coefficient of −1.5). Based on this estimate, the marketer has projected the level of revenues, contribution margins, and profits that will be achieved at a given price. However, sensitivity analysis could then be performed to see what would happen if the market proves to be more sensitive to price (e.g., a coefficient of −1.8). Revenues, contribution margins, and profit would be recalculated at this greater level of elasticity.

A spreadsheet software computer program is an increasingly popular tool for conducting such sensitivity analysis. A number of such programs are available for use on the personal computer. A spreadsheet is a blank sheet of paper divided into rows and columns, used by accountants and financial analysts to produce a wide range of reports. Electronic spreadsheets became available in 1979, and have achieved wide acceptance because of their simplicity, flexibility, and *what if?* capability (O'Leary and Williams 1985). They represent a useful method for illustrating numerical relationships, or models, which are valuable in evaluating marketing decision alternatives (Laric and Stiff 1984).

Data is entered in these rows and columns, and can then be manipulated. Columns and/or rows can be added, subtracted, multiplied, or divided. With a spreadsheet, the marketer can build basic models for use in evaluating each of the elements of the marketing mix. The spreadsheet is built upon certain assumptions. Sensitivity analysis can be performed, then, by varying these assumptions.

Figure 14.7 is a simple income-projection spreadsheet (using the Lotus 1-2-3 software) with assumptions regarding the percentage of sales represented by advertising and manufacturing costs. It is assumed that advertising is 20 percent of revenue, while manufacturing is 40 percent. Sales are broken down by quarter, and are projected to increase by 10 percent in each successive quarter. The result is the expected income for the year.

Now, if the marketer wishes to assess the impact of changes in any of these assumptions, he or she enters that change, and the program quickly calculates and enters the resulting changes in the data and in the expected income projection. Although the original spreadsheet can take considerable time to set up, changes can be made immediately. Figure 14.8 illustrates the results of modifying the assumptions regarding advertising as a percentage of sales, and the quarterly rate of sales increase. This outcome might reflect productivity judgments, such that if advertising is reduced (only 1 percent of sales instead of 2 percent), the effect on quarterly sales increases will be only half as much (i.e., sales will increase by 5 percent rather than 10 percent). Note that, in this case, while a reduction in advertising is expected to reduce annual revenue, the spreadsheet suggests that profitability will improve.

	A	B	C	D	E	F	G	H
1	INCOME							
2	ASSUMPTIONS:	Advertising as a Percent of Revenue =						20
3		Manufacturing Costs as Percent of Revenue =						40
4		Sales Percent Increase Expected in the Quarter =						10
5								
6			FORECAST INCOME FOR NEXT YEAR					
7								
8			1ST QTR.	2ND QTR.	3RD QTR.	4TH QTR.	TOTAL	
9								
10	REVENUE		40,000	44,000	48,400	53,240	185,640	
11	Advertising		8,000	8,800	9,680	10,648	37,128	
12	Mfg. Costs		16,000	17,600	19,360	21,296	74,256	
13								
14	INCOME		16,000	17,600	19,360	21,296	74,256	
15								
16								
17			SUMMARY: EXPECTED INCOME FOR NEXT YEAR IS 74,256					

Figure 14.7 A Marketing Model with Assumptions
(Source: M.V. Laric and R. Stiff, *Lotus 1–2–3 for Marketing and Sales,*
(Englewood Cliffs, N.J.: Prentice-Hall, 1984), 17. Reprinted with
permission.)

Spreadsheet analysis greatly enhances the marketer's ability to design a control system which is strategically meaningful. If actual income for the year deviates from that projected in the spreadsheet, there is a beginning point for determining the reasons why. Were the cost-to-sales ratios for advertising or manufacturing greater than expected? If so, were sales lower because the advertising was not as productive as expected? At the lower sales levels, were manufacturing costs higher because of a failure to achieve the anticipated experience curve effect? More complex spreadsheets would enable the marketer to perform detailed analyses of some of these questions.

Environmental Monitoring Systems

The control process is made much more difficult when the organization experiences change in its external environment. Such change may negate the marketer's assumptions, or make control benchmarks unrealistic. Scenario analysis can be useful in anticipating possible changes, but it is rare that scenarios will adequately capture all of the changes that take place. It becomes important, then, to stay on top of change.

	A	B	C	D	E	F	G	H
1	INCOME							
2	ASSUMPTIONS:	Advertising as a Percent of Revenue =						10
3		Manufacturing Costs as Percent of Revenue =						40
4		Sales Percent Increase Expected in the Quarter =						5
5								
6				FORECAST INCOME FOR NEXT YEAR				
7								
8			1ST QTR.	2ND QTR.	3RD QTR.	4TH QTR.	TOTAL	
9								
10	REVENUE		40,000	42,000	44,100	46,305	172,405	
11	Advertising		4,000	4,200	4,410	4,631	17,241	
12	Mfg. Costs		16,00	16,800	17,640	18,522	68,962	
13								
14	INCOME		20,000	21,000	22,050	23,153	86,203	
15								
16								
17			SUMMARY: EXPECTED INCOME FOR NEXT YEAR IS 86,203					

Figure 14.8   A Marketing Model with Altered Assumptions
(Source: M.V. Laric and R. Stiff, *Lotus 1 – 2 – 3 for Marketing and Sales,*
(Englewood Cliffs, N.J.: Prentice-Hall, 1984), 17. Reprinted with
permission.)

Data on each component of the environment must be regularly collected, processed, and interpreted. The environment includes everything external to the firm,
including the economy, regulation, technology, suppliers, creditors, customers, competitors, the political climate, and nature. Data on these environmental components
is evaluated to identify trends. If a clear pattern is recognized, then adjustments may
be required—both in marketing strategy and in control benchmarks.

Environmental monitoring should be part of the firm's *strategic intelligence
system* (SIS), a concept introduced in Chapter 5. To aid the control process, environmental monitoring should focus on three types of information gathering: defensive
intelligence, passive intelligence, and offensive intelligence (Montgomery and Weinberg 1979).

Defensive intelligence is concerned with helping to ensure that major surprises
are either avoided, or are recognized and responded to early on. Data is collected
to determine whether the assumptions upon which marketing strategies and tactics
were based are actually proving true. For example, current efforts may be predicated

on the belief that competitors will maintain current prices, or that energy costs will remain relatively stable. Defensive intelligence serves to send up a red flag if any of the assumptions are being violated.

Of course, some assumptions are not explicitly made, but are implicit. As a case in point, a major merger between a competitor and a large conglomerate may not have been expected. While no explicit assumption was made that a merger would not occur, the assumption was implicitly made to the extent that no merger was expected. Defensive intelligence would serve to pick up signs of a merger possibility.

Passive intelligence produces benchmark data against which to compare company policies. If competitors are using a particular sales force compensation program (e.g., 40 percent commission on sales to new accounts), or spending a sizable percentage of sales (e.g., 20 percent) on product development, then each of these figures might provide benchmarks against which to evaluate company policies in these areas.

Offensive intelligence seeks to uncover areas representing untapped opportunities the company can capitalize on. Here, the information collection might determine that competitors are over-leveraged, or are having problems with their distributors. From this information, the marketer might conclude that it will be at least eighteen months before the competitor can roll out a particular new product. As a result, heavy investments are made by the company to insure that the market is well-penetrated with its own product before the competitor gets there.

The strategic intelligence system can obtain information from a variety of sources, often at little or no cost. Table 14.9 provides a number of examples. It should be readily apparent that, in the so-called information age, a wealth of information is available to the company that takes a systematic approach to identifying and tapping usable sources, and demonstrates a degree of persistence.

A key problem in managing intelligence systems lies in the determination of which potential developments in the environment to focus on. The sheer volume of data suggests a need for priorities. The marketer must attempt to specify the relative extent of the effect different environmental events might have on the organization. Further, how quickly could the organization react? In addition, he or she must assess the probability of the development occurring. Clearly, some events are less relevant. Others are not really actionable. That is, the marketer can do little to prevent the development, and there is not much in the way of structure, policies, strategies, or tactics that can be done in response.

ANALYZING PERFORMANCE DEVIATIONS

This chapter has focused on the tools and techniques of value in monitoring the company's marketing efforts. Just as important is the need to conduct an analysis of the reasons for performance deviations, so that corrective action can be taken where necessary.

Having identified discrepancies between planned and actual performance, it often takes considerable skill and insight to pinpoint the exact causes. The challenge is, first, to come up with plausible explanations for sales, profits, contribution mar-

Table 14.9   Sources of Intelligence for Environmental Monitoring

Source	Examples	Comment
Government	Freedom of Information Act	1974 amendments have led to accelerating use.
	Government contract administration	Examination of competitor's bids and documentation may reveal competitor's technology and indicate his costs and bidding philosophy.
	Patent filings	Belgium and Italy publish patent applications shortly after they are filed. Some companies (e.g., pharmaceutical) patent their mistakes in order to confuse their competitors.
Competitors	Annual reports and 10Ks	FTC and SEC line of business reporting requirements will render this source more useful in the future.
	Speeches and public announcements of competitor's officers.	Reveal management philosophy, priorities, and self-evaluation systems.
	Products	Systematic analysis of a competitor's products via back engineering may reveal the competitor's technology and enable the company to monitor changes in the competitor's engineering and assembly operations. Forecasts of a competitor's sales may often be made from observing his serial numbers over time.
	Employment ads	May suggest the technical and marketing directions in which a competitor is headed.
	Consultants	For example, if a competitor has retained Boston Consulting, then portfolio management strategies become more likely.
Suppliers	Banks, advertising agencies, public relations firms, and direct mailers and catalogers, as well as hard goods suppliers.	Have a tendency to be more talkative than competitors since the information transmitted may enhance supplier's business. Can be effective sources of information on such items as competitor's equipment installations and on retail competitors already carrying certain product lines. Supplier biases can usually be recognized.

gins, market share, service levels, customer awareness levels, or expenditure levels being higher or lower than expected. Once these factors are clearly delineated, the marketer must distinguish between *symptoms* and *causes* of performance deviations.

To demonstrate the analytical task confronting the marketer, consider the situation where a meaningful discrepancy between the planned and actual total contribution of a product has been observed. While unit sales of this product were right on target, and the variable costs were as expected, the price charged was actually 10 percent lower than anticipated. Assume that company salespeople have a range within which they can negotiate prices with customers. The lower average price is not the real cause of the problem, however. The fact that prices were lowered may be reflective of a more fundamental or root development, such as aggressive sales efforts by a competitor. This competitor may have taken away some key accounts, leading company salespeople to go after new accounts, by offering lower prices— just to meet sales quotas. The underlying reason for the competitor's successes may be related to a new sales compensation program. Perhaps the real solution, then, is a modification of company compensation policies.

For control purposes, a symptom is a condition that indicates a more fundamental problem exists; a cause is an action that brings about the more fundamental problem. In the hypothetical situation described above, the problem was a loss in competitive position in the marketplace. The cause was the failure to respond effectively to a change in the competitor's sales program. The symptom was the fact that the sales force felt pressured to cut prices in order to meet unit sales goals, thus producing a lower contribution margin.

Analysis of problems, symptoms, and causes should be done in a logical and systematic fashion. Figure 14.9 provides another example, where a decision-tree type of procedure is used. Here, an unfavorable sales deviation has again been observed, and the marketer is anxious to make the necessary adjustments to prevent recurrence of the problem.

The first step is to determine whether sales were below expectations for uncontrollable reasons, such as a change in the environment. If the answer is yes, then objectives and/or marketing programs must be adjusted to reflect the new state of affairs. If the answer is no, then the analyst moves to an assessment of the specific objectives set out in the marketing program. These objectives might include the number of new accounts penetrated, sales by product type, the awareness levels created, or inquiries generated, among others. If the objectives were achieved, then the sales deviation suggests that the marketer has overestimated the productivity of the components of the marketing program. For example, he or she may have expected that two hundred inquiries from advertising would translate into fifty purchases, when the actual results suggest that a ratio of three hundred inquiries to fifty purchases is a closer estimate of productivity.

If the objectives were not achieved, then the marketer must investigate the design and implementation of the marketing programs. Is the level of program effort (e.g., sales effort, advertising effort, distributor support) equal to the intended level? If the answer is yes, then these levels apparently need to be increased in order to achieve objectives. This adjustment may necessitate increasing spending in certain areas (modifying the budget), or redesigning the program (e.g., changing the advertising media used or altering the distributor incentives provided). Finally, if the planned level of effort is not being achieved, then the problem lies in execution. The task now becomes identifying the obstacles slowing down program implementation. Possibilities might include communication problems, internal opposition to the program, holdups due to paperwork requirements, or employees who are poorly trained, unmotivated, or overworked.

The actual problems facing firms may be too complex to lend themselves to a simple solution. The questions in Figure 14.9 may have both yes and no answers.

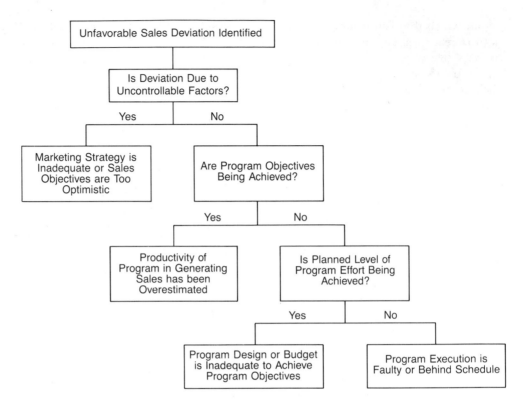

Figure 14.9   A Systematic Approach to Analyzing Performance Deviations
(Source: J. P. Guiltinan and G. Paul, *Marketing Management: Strategies and Programs,* (New York: McGraw-Hill Book Co., 1985), 398. Reprinted with permission.)

Sales deviations can occur in part due to controllable factors, but also due to uncontrollable factors. Multiple problems may exist, such as both overly optimistic objectives and behind-schedule program implementation. Problems at one level of Figure 14.9 may be contributing to the problems at another level. Faulty judgments of program productivity could lead to an improperly designed marketing program.

These complications only further emphasize the need for a systematic approach to evaluating why the company performed the way it did. The ultimate value of the control process lies here. Knowing how well goals and objectives are being achieved is vital, but an effective control process should provide inputs regarding future goals, and direction regarding future strategies and policies.

EVALUATING ETHICAL ASPECTS OF MARKETING PROGRAMS

A good control system looks not only at end results, but also at how the firm got there. Therefore, the control system should also monitor the ethical dimensions of the firm's marketing activities. Unethical actions are those that appear to be incon-

Table 14.10   Marketing-Related Practices That Involve Ethical Questions

---

Having less competitive prices for smaller buyers and for sole source buyers;

Using the firm's economic power to obtain price or other concessions;

Exaggerating vendor problems (e.g., in production, distribution, inventory, or financing) to customer;

Giving preferential treatment to buyers whom top management prefers;

Giving preferential treatment to good customers;

Allowing personalities to affect the terms of sale;

Providing free trips, luncheons, or gifts;

Seeking information on competitors' quotes or other competitive information from customers;

Promising delivery times, knowing they cannot be met;

Exaggerating claims regarding product quality, reliability, or service life;

Understating product safety risks;

Downgrading competitors to get a customer's business;

Announcing new products prior to their development;

Selling a customer a more expensive version of a product, withholding a cheaper version that would suffice;

Making excuses to customers about products that are not yet in stock or sold out;

Ignoring a prospective customer for one you believe will be better;

Refusing to accept returns of products that are clearly defective;

Replacing components in a currently available product with lower quality components without informing customers.

---

sistent with a sense of what is right. These actions are not necessarily illegal, but they violate generally accepted norms of behavior.

Ethics is frequently a gray area, because of differences in people's perceptions of what constitutes an unethical practice. For instance, in a study of attitudes regarding ethical behavior, salespeople and purchasing people differed significantly in their assessment of the ethical quality of every one of eleven business practices (Dubinsky and Gwin 1981). Examples of marketing-related practices that raise potential ethical dilemmas are summarized in Table 14.10.

The ability to monitor ethical performance, as with other areas of control, depends upon the establishment of objectives for ethical behavior. Charging fair prices, manufacturing safe products, and using truthful and informative advertising materials are worthy objectives. There is a need to "balance the motive of profit against other motives in order to improve a corporation's behavior" (Donaldson 1982). In fact, the blind pursuit of profit objectives typically leads to unethical behavior. For an organization to function efficiently over time, it must adhere to norms defined by more than its minimum required rate of return. This statement is especially true in the industrial market, where exchanges can be for considerable sums of money over long periods of time, and where relationships are predicated on trust as well as a contractual link. Nonetheless, ethical behavior sometimes comes at the expense of profits.

The real difficulty in the ethics area has to do with evaluation. How do managers measure whether their company's marketing and sales activities are ethical? Ethical goals are difficult to quantify, and performance evaluation is subjective at best. Management can develop a set of rules of conduct for issues such as those raised in Table 14.10. Rules are subject to individual interpretation, however, and will not apply to every circumstance that arises. Such rules may be incorporated into a corporate ethics handbook. Buying organizations will sometimes also prepare ethics handbooks, and distribute them to vendors.

Underlying the need for ethical control is the fact that corporations are legal entities with unlimited life and limited liability. Because of this fact, there is a tendency to view the actions of a corporation as separate from those of its members. Employees may find themselves doing things in the name of the corporation that they would not do in their own personal lives. Also, the members of society seem to expect less rigorous standards from organizations than from individuals.

Even so, ethics is a company-wide responsibility, and must be managed as such. Marketing managers are often caught in the middle by senior management who pay lip service to responsible behavior but reward short-term financial performance. Marketers are also pressured by competitors who successfully use tactics that clearly conflict with their own company's standards of conduct. Unless senior management explicitly includes ethical performance in the formal reward measurement system, it is probably unrealistic to expect those in marketing and sales to exhibit ethical standards beyond those which are pragmatic—defined in this context as behavior that is not somehow penalized in the marketplace.

SUMMARY

This concluding chapter has introduced the concept of marketing control. Control is a process which involves evaluating performance in comparison to objectives or benchmarks, uncovering variances and areas for improvement, identifying opportunities, and reallocating marketing resources. Control was presented as an integral part of marketing planning, and as applicable to the activities of the marketing department and the firm's overall marketing efforts. In the absence of the objectives, strategies, and action programs generated through formal or informal planning, control becomes a difficult, if not impossible, activity.

The control system represents a means to an end; control measures are merely indicators of whether or not things are on track. If the organization has many dimensions of performance on which measurements are taken and feedback is given, it is more difficult for managers to find ways of arbitrarily looking good while long-term company goals suffer (Cohen and Cyert 1973). Further, control measures are rarely perfect, making it critical that the manager continually evaluate the extent to which he or she is measuring the right things.

As a process, control incorporates four sequential activities: goal-setting, performance measurement, performance diagnosis, and corrective action. *Goal-setting* produces achievable and measurable standards of performance. *Performance measurement* is the comparison of actual performance to control benchmarks which reflect goals. If performance is outside an acceptable range around the benchmark, *performance diagnosis* attempts to ascertain the reasons why. Once the underlying causes of any deviations have been pinpointed, *corrective action* can be taken to adjust or change goals, benchmarks, strategies, action programs, budgets, or personnel.

In addition to the stages of the control process, four levels or categories of control were investigated. These included strategic control, annual plan control, profitability control, and efficiency control. These four levels are highly interdependent. A number of tools and analytical approaches for assessing performance at each level were presented. These tools included the marketing audit, variance analysis, the strategic profit model, the product evaluation matrix, marketing expense-to-sales analysis, attitude tracking, contribution analysis, and various efficiency indexes.

Effectiveness of the organization's control efforts can be enhanced by the quality of the inputs into the control system. Inputs can include the budget, an internal marketing data base, scenario analysis, productivity judgments, sensitivity analysis, and environmental monitoring systems. Computer spreadsheets were also presented as a helpful resource, especially in conducting scenario and sensitivity analyses.

The chapter next provided a discussion of the complexities involved in explaining the reasons for performance deviations—an undertaking that requires considerable skill and insight. The manager must be expected to explain any and all deviations in sales performance, marketing program performance, and marketing cost performance. The key to success in this area is the ability to distinguish among problems, symptoms of those problems, and the actual causes of those problems. Further, problems often exist at a number of levels, and interact with one another.

The industrial firm should also recognize that the focus of the control system must extend beyond measuring the bottom-line performance of marketing people and programs. Managers must ensure that these people and programs meet ethical guidelines. Toward this end, firms should establish ethical objectives which go hand-in-hand with financial and marketing objectives.

Finally, it is vital to recognize the extent to which a control system emphasizes efficiency versus effectiveness. Both qualities are important, but efficient operations are meaningless if those operations are not effective in achieving overall objectives. In this vein, Pinchot (1985, 310) argues that the years to come will increasingly bring control systems that are "based primarily on selecting and empowering the right people to manage resources, not on building elaborate controls to make sure inadequate people do what they are supposed to do."

QUESTIONS

1. Discuss the differences between efficiency and effectiveness in a control system. How could the control system encourage efficiency, while at the same time be ineffective?

2. The marketer must be wary both of undercontrol and overcontrol. Explain this statement and provide examples of the potential problems in either case.

3. How can annual plan control be used if the company has not prepared an annual marketing plan?

4. When using variance analysis, if *positive* variances are found for sales, prices, or profits, the marketer should basically do nothing. Do you agree or disagree? Why?

5. What are some of the pitfalls in relying on marketing expense-to-sales ratios in annual plan control?

6. Contribution analysis has been stressed throughout this book. Explain how contribution analysis can be a useful control tool in managing market segments, products, prices, advertising, and distributors.

7. What information would you need to use the following efficiency measures?
    —cost per sales call
    —advertising cost per inquiry generated
    —average order cycle time per customer
   How would you obtain such information?

8. Discuss some of the problems in performing productivity analysis on the likely effect on profits of adding a salesperson to the sales force. What is meant by *scenario analysis,* and how might this approach be useful in evaluating the effect of adding to the sales force?

9. Viceroy Valve finds that sales of its triple-flow valve used in heating and ventilating systems are 20 percent below target. Outline a systematic process for analyzing this performance deviation.

10. As a sales manager, you have a customer who critically needs one of your main products, and can find no other immediate source of supply. Would you find it unethical to charge this customer a higher price than you would charge other customers receiving the same product and delivery arrangements? Why or why not?

PART **V** CASES

The final section of the book consists of nineteen cases requiring the reader to analyze actual industrial marketing situations and make managerial decisions. These vary in length, and include both small and larger companies. There is, further, a mix of cases involving industrial products and services, and both domestic and international markets. In addition, cases are included dealing with commercial, institutional, and governmental markets.

The cases generally contain a number of problems, symptoms, and causes. However, most of them are focused around some central issue, and relate to one of the chapters in the text. The exhibit on the following page indicates the key chapter(s) associated with each of the cases.

All of the situations described in these cases are based on actual events. In some, company and/or product names are disguised, while in others, actual names are used.

	Related Chapter(s)	Basics of I.M. (1)	Market, Products, Purchasing Practices (2)	Marketing to the Org. Customer (3)	Org. Buying Behavior (4)	Marketing Research (5)	Demand Analysis (6)	Segmentation (7)	Strategic Product Management (8)	New Product Dev. (9)	Pricing (10)	Advertising and Sales Promo (11)	Personal Selling (12)	Channel of Distribution (13)	Control (14)
	Case Title														
1	Stevens Heat Treating Co.	X									X				
2	Diamond Door Co.	X												X	
3	Rema Ltd.		X						X						
4	Dyonix Greentree Technologies (B)			X	X										
5	Sunshine Electric (A)					X									
6	Sunshine Electric (B)					X	X			X					
7	Seanav Corp.						X	X	X						
8	Sunheat Inc.						X	X				X		X	
9	Eurocomm USA							X	X						
10	Across, Inc.								X						
11	HydroClean, Inc.								X						X
12	Dyonix Greentree Technologies (A)								X	X					
13	Sexton Energy Systems Division									X					
14	Aztec Chemical											X			
15	Zephyr Defence Systems, Ltd.		X									X			
16	Wall, Inc.											X			X
17	Gamma Business Systems			X		X						X			
18	United Tire												X		
19	Adapco													X	

THE STEVENS HEAT TREATING COMPANY[1]

HISTORY

The Stevens Heat Treating company was incorporated in November of 1975. The goal of Stevens was to offer quality service consultation at a fair price to the tool and die industry in the Los Angeles metropolitan area. The President and C.E.O., John R. Stevens, has been involved in the heat treating industry (SIC 3398) for 23 years. He has an excellent reputation, and is well respected in the heat treating community. He felt that there was a definite and substantial need for a heat treating company that would specialize in the processing of tools and dies. Sales doubled during each of the first three years, while at the same time the company's reputation as a high quality heat treating company became fairly widespread.

In mid-1978, the Stevens Heat Treating Company took an aggressive expansionary step and acquired the in-house heat treating facilities of the Kirby Corporation. At this time annual sales growth was projected at 20 percent. By acquiring the operations from the Kirby Corporation, Stevens was able to expand both its leverage and service in the Los Angeles area. It offered the service (for a reasonable charge) of picking up and delivering a customer's parts. This was promoted as a savings to the customers in terms of time and money. Although this division was doing quite well, irreconcilable differences with Kirby personnel caused Stevens to divest itself of these operations within a year. The company lost money on the sale of this operation. The loss was equal to 29 percent of Stevens's sales for 1979. At about this same point in time, a lengthy recession[2] hit the economy. The *Analysis of Industry Job Growth Sales* for the years 1979–1983 reflected a decrease in sales for the heat treating industry nationwide of about 50 percent. The southern California market in which Stevens operates was no exception, with an average decrease in sales per firm of between 40 and 50 percent.

---

[1]All names in this case are disguised.

[2]Could be considered a depression for the tool and die sector in Southern California with its reliance on aircraft, transportation, energy, etc. industries for the majority of its market.

Prepared by Steven Kowalski under the direction of Joseph W. Leonard, Miami University, Oxford, Ohio.

To combat high labor costs and high energy (electricity) costs, the Stevens Heat Treating Company fully automated its entire facility, reducing its labor force from 27 employees to 8. Stevens also installed energy saving devices on all of its high usage equipment. These measures resulted in a decrease in energy usage by about 20 percent, but total utility cost from 1978 to 1982 more than doubled. These energy-saving devices simply lessened the cost of the bill. At the beginning of 1983, Stevens began to experience a gradual lessening of the recessionary atmosphere. The question remains to be seen how long this general upturn in the economy will last. Stevens has experienced net losses in two of the last three years, but with the economy turning around, sales have shown strong increases, suggesting a brighter future.

PRODUCTION/QUALITY CONTROL

Production

The company production facilities consist of salt bath furnaces and supporting equipment. The furnaces used by Stevens are square steel containers that are lined with high temperature resistant bricks (much like a kiln used to fire clay). The furnace is then filled with molten chemical compositions known as salt (hence the name salt baths). These salts are maintained at specific temperatures ranging from 350°F to 2300°F by electrical current which flows through two electrodes that have been inserted in the furnace. The process is similar to the process used in basic plating, but for heat treating the electrodes are much larger. Stevens chose this type of furnace because of its outstanding ability to prevent distortion (i.e., warpage of intricate tools and dies during the heat treat process).

In simplified terms, the heat treating process is basically the placing of a piece of steel into a furnace at a specific temperature for a specific length of time. The metal is then quenched to a much lower temperature which causes the metal to harden. By hardening the metal, it increases its ability to withstand stress, corrosion, etc. The time and temperature of the process are dependent upon the type of steel, the size of material, and particular customer requirements. The furnaces used by Stevens are the most efficient of those on the market today. They can produce more output per hour at less cost than any other furnaces currently utilized in the heat treating industry.

Quality Control

The Stevens Company maintains a full complement of inspection equipment (machines used for testing hundred of parts), and dimensional inspection equipment (gauges and special fixtures to check warpage, flatness, and other dimensionality).

The quality control system used by the firm has the approval of military, nuclear, aerospace, and commercial industries. To maintain the quality assurance system, Stevens must maintain a complete set of records (on file for a minimum of seven years) on number of parts coming in and processes performed (charting of times and temperatures must be recorded). By continually upgrading and maintaining this Quality Assurance System, Stevens feels it will be able to attract larger accounts which will lead to increased revenues.

PERSONNEL

President

John R. Stevens, age 45, is the founder, President, and C.E.O. of Stevens. His experience and expertise have earned him a highly respected position in the heat treating industry. His knowledge of metallurgy (study of metals) has given Stevens a prominent reputation as a "state-of-the-art company." He has also shown effective insight in customer relations. John Stevens's training in law and finance has enabled the company to prepare proposals which permit future opportunities to become present realities. He is presently the driving force behind the growth of Stevens and has implemented long-term goals to ensure future growth will not be impeded by current managerial decision-making.

General Manager

Paul Lessard, age 25, has been with the company for five years. He has been trained in all facets of the company, thus enabling him to understand the limitations of equipment and time. Mr. Lessard gives Stevens strength in the managerial area. His current responsibilities include purchasing, production control, final quality control, and hiring of non-administrative personnel. In addition to his other managerial duties, Paul Lessard is presently being trained for the position of comptroller.

Marketing Manager

Scott Stevens, age 22, a senior at the University of California/Los Angeles, gives Stevens strength in the one area that they are currently relatively weak: marketing. He has been employed part-time for the past 3½ years, studying at U.C.L.A. and working full-time on holidays, breaks, and summers. He has proven to be quite successful in obtaining new business, but full follow-up has not been possible due to time constraints. These problems will be eliminated once he comes aboard full-time. His responsibilities will include all marketing functions, direction of the Quality Assurance System, and evaluation of future acquisitions. Scott Stevens will eventually take over as president of Stevens, but that is some years away.

Other Employees

All other Stevens personnel are hourly wage earners. Their wages are fairly high for low-skilled job requirements, but a high turnover rate exists because of the rigorous physical requirements of the work and the general lack of opportunities for advancement.

ADMINISTRATIVE

The Stevens Heat Treating Company presently uses net 30 days as terms for its accounts receivable. In the last two years it has seen this stretch to between 45–60 days due to market conditions. Although this may be seen as poor collection practices, the industry average is between 60–90 days. There has been very little the company could do to reduce accounts receivable since if customers can't get service—they'll go elsewhere. At the same time, Stevens has had to extend its payments to creditors from 30 days to between 45–60.

To handle expenses and ease the cash flow situation, Stevens invested in a computer in 1980. Since that time it has placed all accounts receivable, accounts payable, and payroll on the computer. This eliminated the need for one and a half secretaries. These savings have more than paid for the computer.

John Stevens handles all administrative functions. He has gradually turned controllable day-to-day operations over to Paul Lessard, thus enabling him to seek alternative financing and set long-term goals and objectives for the company. Stevens also employs an outside consultant who is presently advising Stevens on future acquisition and diversification opportunities.

John Stevens is currently spending more time consulting which is placing constraints on his time. Currently the limitations of Stevens Company are directly related to those time constraints on its president. At the present time, the company is moving more toward the decentralization of management activities. Paul Lessard and Scott Stevens are beginning to exert more influence in the areas of new markets and short-term goals thus freeing John Stevens to actively seek the additional capital needed to expand the company.

MARKETING

The company presently serves the greater Los Angeles metropolitan areas. In marketing its services, Stevens is selling an intangible. The process of Heat Treating is often the final stage in the manufacturing process. The changes that take place during this heat treat cycle are molecular and chemical, and thus cannot be directly observed by the unaided eye. Because of this Stevens has encountered the problem of a lack of appreciation on the part of its customers, making it difficult to estimate customer value. Often times these people feel that this process is relatively unimportant. A $25 drill bit costs about $.50 to heat treat, most of which is labor. But, unless a part is properly heat treated, it will fail in service, causing damage to equipment. Stevens has also had to contend with the generally poor reputation of its industry as a whole.

In an effort to try and eradicate these two problems, Stevens has designed and recently distributed a series of informative bulletins using the name "Stevens' Blacksmith's Journal". The name was used to project a trustworthy and high-quality image. To insure better reception for these bulletins, Stevens did not directly advertise anything about the company except that, if a customer had any questions, he should feel free to call. The objectives of the bulletin are two-fold—(1) to inform potential customers of the current technology available to them; and (2) to gradually cultivate a good reputation for the heat treating industry in general. In so doing, the company feels that it will benefit because it has put its name into the minds of customers. The initial responses of this campaign have been favorable. There is an indication that customers are remembering the information and thus enhancing the company's reputation. This campaign of assuring a constant flow of information to customers will be continued in the future and will act as an "ice breaker" for future sales calls.

COMPETITIVE STRATEGY

The Stevens Heat Treating Company operates in an extremely competitive market. In the greater Los Angeles market from which Stevens derives a majority of its revenues, there are over one hundred commercial heat treating companies. This number excludes the over one hundred twenty-five companies that have their own in-house facilities that also do some outside contracted work.

The majority of the companies are well established. When Stevens began operations (early 1976), the average age of these firms was 10 years. Stevens, however, was quickly able to capture a respectable share of the market through excellent service and fair prices. Stevens also had an advantage in that John Stevens had dealt with many of these firms in the past. Thus when the company was formed, many firms left their present sources and sent their work to Stevens.

At the present time, Stevens employs one part-time salesman. The average sales force in this market is about 3 to 5 sales representatives. As a result of this deficit, Stevens has been limited in its penetration of certain markets. The company feels that these problems will be rectified when Scott Stevens comes aboard full time (summer of 1984). With his background in metallurgy and "hands-on" knowledge, he will be able to answer many of the technical questions that potential customers may ask. In the heat treating industry, an effectively answered question often leads to an order. John Stevens considers Scott's "hands-on" experience and technical expertise helpful in his marketing activities.

Stevens, although not the largest heat treating company in its market, has become the industry leader. In the Los Angeles area, the quality of work and price charged by competitors are often compared to Stevens. It has earned this reputation in an industry that is notorious for overlooking quality and timely service to the customer.

Manufacturers have come to realize that if they need quick, reliable, and quality service, Stevens is the place to send their work. It has been said that word-of-mouth is the best salesman; Stevens annually gets 20 to 25 percent of its new customers that way. Since most of its competition cannot compete with Stevens's quality, they have begun to compete on the basis of price. The majority of its competition maintains prices within 5 percent of Stevens.

One area of concern is the recent formation of Heat Treat, Inc., a competitor who has virtually modeled itself after Stevens, from services offered to delivery schedules. Heat Treat has cut prices an average of 35 percent in the last two years, and has succeeded in attracting many of the smaller (and a few of the larger) accounts away from Stevens. Stevens realized a little too late that Heat Treat was a viable competitor. In July of 1983, Stevens responded with a drastic decrease in all prices, slashing them an average of 40 percent in a massive sales campaign which blanketed its control market. This was the largest campaign Stevens had undertaken in its history.

This price reduction gave Stevens the lowest prices of any commercial heat treater in the market. Feeling that it could no longer afford to let the smaller accounts be taken by Heat Treat, Stevens was fully committed to maintaining its high standards of quality and timely service to the customer. As a result of demand analysis, Scott Stevens had argued that revenue per order would decrease, but total revenue in the long-run would rise due to increased orders and larger volume. Scott based this change on the assumption that many companies preferred sending all their work to one place (thus if they can save money on smaller orders, they will send the larger volume orders). By lowering its prices, Stevens has given its potential customers every reason to change.

As of November 1983, the results of the aggressive pricing strategy have been good but not spectacular. Although total orders are up 35 percent, dollar sales have increased by only 18 percent (due to the lower price per order). After conducting a limited market survey, Stevens has found that many of its customers are still recovering from the recession and are waiting to make sure recovery is on its way before replenishing their inventories. This has had a substantial effect on the volume of business.

NEW MARKETS

The Stevens Heat Treating Company has not limited itself simply to standard commercial services. In the last 3 years, it has actively sought contracts from the military, nuclear, and aerospace industries. In spite of rigid quality standards and time-consuming administrative/contractual parameters, Stevens has secured contracts from all three industries. At the present time the company has not exploited these areas as fully as it would like to; currently only 5 percent of sales come from non-commercial sources. Some of the advantages seen in processing this work are higher prices and higher prestige.

The increased costs in administrative work, including record keeping, quality assurance systems, and adherence to specifications and standards, are seen as disadvantages. Often times these administrative costs are more than the cost of processing the material. Increased liability is another factor which must be considered as a disadvantage.

In the future non-commercial customers will be further analyzed by Stevens to determine if the benefits gained will outweigh the costs.

FUTURE PROJECTS

The company is presently involved in extensive negotiations for the acquisition of a large commercial heat treating company in San Francisco. If this acquisition is accomplished, the size of Stevens would triple. This acquisition would also enable Stevens to compete more economically on the large volume jobs that are above its present capacity. Its new market would range from San Diego to north of San Francisco and east to Sacramento and western Nevada. Given current available data, this new division would turn an estimated profit of 13% after tax within two years after acquisition.

Diversification

In late 1983, Stevens was contacted and requested to bid on the construction of four furnaces like those the company presently uses. If these bids are accepted, the sales from those furnaces would add about 8% to Stevens's sales. Stevens has recently initiated plans for a separate design and development division to handle the manufacturing of furnaces and related handling equipment. This project would require little additional management and costs would be absorbed by the customers.

With the national economy and demand for heat treating services both on the upswing, the company's favorable image and its strong commitment to production and management, and its diversification and acquisition opportunities, the Stevens Heat Treating Company anticipates financial success and continued growth in the future.

DIAMOND DOOR

INTRODUCTION

The Diamond Door Company is a medium-sized, regional manufacturer of molded fiberglass garage doors. The company was formed in 1977 by Clair B. Brown and his two brothers in response to what they perceived as a strong demand for cheaper, more efficient building materials. Clair Brown had previously managed a fiberglass pick-up topper manufacturer, and one of his brothers, Jerry, had worked for a steel garage door company.

During 1976 and 1977 prime interest rates were at their highest levels ever, and the crunch was being sorely felt by the building industry. Developers and contractors alike began scrambling for ways to keep cost down and quality up. Diamond Door's goal was to provide an inexpensive and durable garage door alternative to what was presently being used.

Initially Diamond Door had only one manufacturing facility. It was located in central Florida and served the Florida, Georgia, and South Carolina building industry. However, in 1981 a second operation was opened in Alabama, and Diamond Door began selling to five southeastern states: Florida, Georgia, South Carolina, Alabama, and Mississippi.

The garage door market consists of four types of doors: pressed board, solid wood, steel, and fiberglass. Of the four, the pressed board garage door was the most commonly used; the solid wood door was the most expensive; the steel door was perceived to be the most durable; and the fiberglass door was the most inexpensive.

DISTRIBUTION

Diamond Door had entered the market using a somewhat unusual distribution approach. They sold their doors to pressed- and solid-wood garage door manufacturers, providing them with a significant distributor discount, who in turn sold the

Case prepared by Bernard Tomasky under the direction of Michael H. Morris, University of Central Florida, Orlando, Florida.

product alongside their own line to local garage door dealers. Diamond dealt with two such companies; their Alabama plant sold to Raymoor Doors Inc., and the central Florida facility sold to Kislak Garage Door Co. Kislak serviced Florida, Georgia, and South Carolina and Raymoor handled Alabama and Mississippi. These two manufacturers sold to roughly 550 local garage door dealers in the southeast. These local dealers typically maintain about one month's worth of inventory, and work with building contractors on site to install the doors. Both manufacturing companies were considered number one in their respective areas. Diamond was currently the sole supplier of fiberglass garage doors sold in the southeast.

SOUTHEAST MARKET	Year	Sales
SALES OF GARAGE DOORS	1981	77.1
(all types, in $ millions)	1982	78.0
	1983	83.8
	1984	90.2

Diamond took this distribution approach because of lack of capital when they started out. They felt that it would be more cost effective to rely on the other companies' selling expertise and distribution channels instead of starting from scratch. Also, wood garage door companies were eager to diversify their product line. The industry as a whole believed that fiberglass doors had the potential to become the doors of the future.

PRODUCT CHARACTERISTICS

Fiberglass doors had many advantages over their counterparts. Both wood door models tended to rot over time, especially in the humid climate of the south. An average wooden door would last approximately 10–15 years, whereas a fiberglass door could last 30 years or more. Fiberglass doors were much lighter than wooden ones, and therefore many customers found that they did not really need a garage door opener. A housewife could lift a fiberglass door with one finger. Furthermore, fiberglass doors work on two simple stretch springs, versus wooden doors' bulkier and more expensive hardware.

SOUTHEAST MARKET (percentage of sales)

Type	1984	1983	1982	1981
solid wood	9.1	8.9	8.8	8.5
pressed board	60.1	60.4	61.7	62.0
steel	28.2	28.0	26.6	26.5
fiberglass	2.6	2.7	2.9	3.0

Although steel doors had some of the advantages of fiberglass, they tended to rust quickly. They were also used almost exclusively for commercial customers, due to the then direct competition with steel door manufacturers.

A major disadvantage of fiberglass doors was the inability to add dressings to them. Dressings would include such things as windows, decorator moldings, and cedar panels. At the same time, 60% of the total market for wood doors was plain paneled.

1984 Garage Door List Prices (RAYMOOR & KISLAK)

Type	Sizes			
	10×7	14×7	16×7	20×7
solid wood	528	589	685	799
pressed board	424	462	555	630
steel	509	549	669	789
fiberglass	277	298	322	367

FIBERGLASS DOOR SIZES (as percentage of fiberglass sales)

Size	%
10×7	.02
14×7	.315
16×7	.62
20×7	.045

THE CURRENT PROBLEM

While the business was profitable, recent financial performance raised some concerns. Although sales of fiberglass doors had moderately increased during 1983 and 1984, their share of the total door market had actually decreased over the same time. Further, this was a period in which interest rates had declined and a building boom had begun. Diamond did not appear to be sharing in that boom.

The company currently has had four marketing/sales representatives whose duties include: on going account servicing of Raymoor and Kislak, periodic checks on the Diamond product at the local garage door distributor level, and occasional small marketing studies. A marketing study had just been completed in response to the market share decline. The study attributed the problem to a lack of emphasis by local garage door dealers on fiberglass doors. It was believed that this was due to their limited knowledge of the product, and the need for justifications as to why they should be pushing it alongside the more expensive wooden doors.

DIAMOND DOOR INCOME STATEMENT
For the year ending
December 31, 1984

sales revenues	$1,638,709
cost of sales	992,676
gross margin	646,033 (39.4%)
other expenses	191,073
income before taxes	454,960
income tax expense (50%)	227,480
net income	$ 227,480 (13.8%)

The marketing reps had come to the conclusion that the solution was to start an annual direct mailing program to the local dealers, thus keeping them updated on their products. They had acquired a complete, detailed listing of these companies, and due to the lack of marketing manpower, felt this would be the best way to get the word out. The representatives believed that once the demand picked up on fiberglass doors, their distributors would start pushing the product more. The total cost of the direct mailing program was predicted to be $110,000 per year.

One of Clair's brothers, Jerry, objected to this line of reasoning. He felt that the problem would be better dealt with by adding another 5% across the board in discounts to Raymoor and Kislak, thereby encouraging the manufacturers to push Diamond Door's fiberglass garage doors harder.

DIAMOND DOOR
1984 DISTRIBUTOR DISCOUNTS

Size	Discount percentages
10×7	.25
14×7	.30
16×7	.30
20×7	.35

For his part, Clair Brown was somewhat at a loss. Despite an efficient, cost-saving door whose price was much below its competitors, the final market was still not buying the fiberglass door.

1984 Gross Profit Percentages (wood & fiberglass)

Type	Raymoor	Kislak
solid wood		
10×7	.15	.161
14×7	.163	.169
16×7	.165	.170
20×7	.168	.172
pressed board		
10×7	.201	.203
14×7	.207	.21
16×7	.209	.212
20×7	.215	.22
fiberglass		
10×7	.25	.25
14×7	.30	.30
16×7	.30	.30
20×7	.35	.35

REMA, LTD.
Evaluating a New International Market

REMA, Ltd. is located in Switzerland in a small town outside of Zurich. The company manufactures a highly developed machine tool system. Basically, the system is designed to adapt to boring, roughing, and cutting situations in designated industries.

REMA was founded in 1961, and began to produce the machine tool systems exclusively in the early 70s. REMA's growth from then on was attributable to the systems. In 1982 REMA employed 40 people and had an annual dollar sales volume of (Swiss Franc) 8.5 million. Even with the economy at a virtual standstill in Europe, the company was expanding at a rate of 20% a year in the early 1980s. Management anticipates even greater growth as economic pressures ease in European markets. The majority of REMA products are sold in Europe. Recently, the REMA management has begun to explore the possibility of expanding their markets to include the United States, an option previously avoided.

PRODUCTS (GENERAL)

Machine tools are components of power-driven metal working machines that shape or form metal by cutting, pressure, or impact electrical techniques, or a combination of these processes. Metal cutting machine tools shape metal parts to size and contour by cutting away unwanted portions. This can be done by turning on a lathe (the machine turns the part against the cutting edge), boring (which cuts cylindrically into a metal part), planing and shaping, drilling, or grinding.

Complete machine tool equipment includes expendable (and replaceable) parts such as boring tools, drills, taps, dies, reamers and chucks. When parts are replaced, or different components are attached, adaptors may be used to accommodate the new tool.

REMA manufactures cutting tools and adaptors. The REMA tool-system (see exhibit 1.1) has been designed for the highest production requirements and therefore guarantees accuracy due to its rigid and accurate construction. It has high cutting performance and a high boring precision. Other features of the system are shown in exhibit 1.2.

Case prepared by Michael H. Morris and Duane Davis, Department of Marketing, University of Central Florida, Orlando, FL

Boring range 7/8" - 6" Ø

Boring range 6" - 20"

*Many combination possibilities with standard elements for optimum rigid boring tools.

*On equipment with a different spindle system, tooling costs can considerably be lowered, since only the basic spindle adaptor has to be replaced.

*Wide adaptor faces and large pilots and threads transmit the cutting forces generated by high speed.

*Starting with a basic set, the tool assortment can be supplemented in line with changing needs.

*The comprehensive REMA ADAPTOR SYSTEM is available from stock: Order today, machining tomorrow!

Exhibit 1.1   There are important reasons why the REMA TOOL SYSTEM should belong in your tooling inventory.

Many combination possibilities with standard elements for optimum rigid boring tools.

On equipment with different spindle systems, tooling costs can be lowered considerably, since only the basic spindle adaptor has to be replaced.

Wide adaptor faces and large pilots and threads transmit the cutting forces generated by high feedrates and deep cuts.

Quality construction and precision tolerances guarantee stability. Eccentricity is held to a length-to-diameter ratio of 6:1.

Starting with a basic set, the tool assortment can be supplemented in line with changing needs.

The comprehensive REMA ADAPTOR SYSTEM is available from stock.

Exhibit 1.2   REMA System Features

REMA can deliver the products modified for the U.S. market when required. Approximately 90% of the tools are delivered from stock.

The REMA tool-system is specialized for NC (numerically controlled) machining centers. Numerical control automates machine tools and allows them to switch quickly from one job to another.

PRODUCTS (SPECIFIC)

The REMA Product Line consists of nine product groups: boring tools, carbide inserts, milling cutter adaptors, collet adaptors, Morse taper adaptors, tap holders, and miscellaneous items.

The boring tool group includes boring bars and attachments (i.e. adaptors, reducers, extenders, and cutting heads). The tool shank of the adaptors can be used with any existing equipment subject to ISO standards.

REMA adaptors with wide faces allow higher feedrates which translates into larger levels of torque and increased accuracy. A significant feature that adds to high cutting performance and high boring precision are insert holders that can be clamped to double cutter heads. These are mounted to a precision ground serration and supported by flats on each holder.

The REMA tool system offers many benefits to users of industrial machine tools. Advantages include the REMA system of double cutter and fine boring bars that allows the user to cover a wider range of diameter with only a few tools. The boring heads have graduated settings that permit high boring precision. The tools are made of case hardened steel, can use standard carbide inserts, and can be combined with any machine tool that does boring.

The REMA product line is distributed through technically qualified resellers and machine tool manufacturers' sales networks. Ninety percent of REMA's product line is standardized and available off-the-shelf. Sales people must be able to convince customers of the technical superiority of the REMA system. Knowledge of metal removal techniques is necessary to demonstrate the product line.

REMA coordinates its promotional activities with the resellers. They work with their distributors to train the sales force, and instruct the resellers on REMA product attributes before the products are introduced to new markets. The prices of REMA tools are higher than other machine tool manufacturers. This can be attributed to the superior quality, adaptability and high performance characteristics exhibited by REMA products.

MARKET ANALYSIS

The primary market for machine tools in the United States is the metalworking machinery industry. This industry can be separated into metal cutting (SIC 3541) and metal forming (SIC 3542) companies.

Total consumption of complete machine tools was equal to $6.34 billion in 1982 (see Table 1.1). Of this amount, consumption of NC-machine tools in the U.S. market was $259 million (Table 1.2). The demand for NC-machine tool equipment for 1980 was 500 percent higher than 1972.

Table 1.1   U.S. Machine Tool Consumption ($ Millions) 1982

	Cutting	Forming	Total
Shipments	4440.2	1428.7	5868.9
Imports	1271.3	228.5	1499.8
Exports	654.1	371.9	1026.0
Consumption	5057.4	1285.3	6342.7

Table 1.2   Multifunction NC Machine Consumption 1981

	Units	$ Millions
1981	1600	259

The principal buyers of metalworking machinery, machine tools and tooling equipment are found in the construction, oil field, auto and electrical equipment industries. These groups are also considered the major investors in machine tools according to *U.S. Industrial Outlook–1982*.

The general target markets for REMA machine tools and equipment are located in the northeastern and midwestern sections of the country. Table 1.3 gives the top 5 states and the value of their shipments for metal cutting machine manufacturers in 1982.

The U.S. tool producer is considered extremely price conscious. Nevertheless, the buyer is willing to pay a higher price for a product with the conditions that the tool life can be improved, the productivity is generally higher, or if tool inventories can be reduced (i.e. fewer tools used per time period, job, etc.). Using fewer tools

Table 1.3   Metalworking Machinery Manufacturers, Metal Cutting Type Concentration by State/Number of Companies

State	No. of Companies (more than 20 employees)	Value of Shipments 1982 ($ Millions)
Ohio	35	934.3
Michigan	83	1055.9
Illinois	30	357.8
Connecticut	17	326.0
Wisconsin	15	375.2
U.S. Total	293	4440.2

and the use of standardized tools is the most effective approach to saving inventory costs. The average prices of the REMA tool systems sold to resellers in Europe in 1982 were between $500–$1200 (U.S. dollars).

COMPETITIVE ANALYSIS

According to the Cutting Tool Manufacturers Association, which represents 70% of the companies producing cutting equipment, there are a total of 30 companies producing boring heads, 50 companies producing carbon-tipped boring tools, and 40 companies producing adaptors. Of these manufacturers of machine tool equipment, only 10 produce a full line of boring tools and adaptors. The leading machine tool

Table 1.4 *Leading Manufacturing States (SIC 3545) 1981 Shipments in Millions U.S. Dollars*

State	
Michigan	151
Ohio	92
Connecticut	84
Illinois	64
New York	40
	431

Exhibit 1.3 Competitors in U.S. Market

Competitor
Company Name
Criterion
Davis Tool
Ex-Cell-O
Carboloy
Fansteel
Greenleaf
Kennam.Erickson
Midwest Ohio
Sandvik
L-B Manuf.
Valenite
Chandler

Note: Boring tools for single purpose machining. None of them offers a multipurpose tool system with combination facilities.

Table 1.5 Sources of U.S. Imports of Machine Tools

Country	Imports in Millions U.S. $
Canada	8
Great Britain	3.5
West Germany	14
Other European countries	15
Japan	9
Other Asian countries	4
Rest of the World	1.5

accessory manufacturers in the U.S. are concentrated in the northeast, as shown in Table 1.4.

Direct competitors in the U.S. market can be found in Exhibit 1.3.

Competition in the market is composed of domestic and foreign manufacturers. Imports account for approximately 12% of the total machine tool accessory market. However, foreign producers supply 75% of the total NC machine tools market. Table 1.5 lists exporting countries and their sales.

Table 1.6 Comparison of REMA LTD. and Competitors (Rated from 1–10 points) for Performance

Competitor	Available Cutting Performance, Roughing	Precision Setting Accuracy, Reliability Standard of Fine Boring	Availability from Stock	Complete Boring Tool System
REMA	10	10	9	9
Wohlhaupter	7	9		7
De Vlieg	4	6		5
Kaiser	8	10	9	9
Criterion	4	6		5
Davis Tool				
Carboloy				
Ex-Cell-O	5	5		5
Fansteel				
Greenleaf		5		
Erickson	6	6		6
Midwest Ohio	special tools			
Sandvik	6	6		6
L-B Manuf.				
Valenite				
Yamazen				

REMA has recently compared and rated themselves to their competitors (See Table 1.6). The ratings were on a scale of 1–10 and the performance characteristics evaluated were customer oriented. REMA ranked highest with Kaiser second. The highest rated American manufacturer was Sandvik.

The distribution channels differ from one competitor to another. The channel used by the competitor depends especially on the size of the company. In general the larger companies are using their own exclusive distribution system, plus a large network of independent local distributors. The smaller manufacturers, and almost all importers, sell through resellers who also carry other products, including those of direct competitors (See Table 1.7).

Table 1.7 Channel Structure in U.S.

Name	Distributor	Number of Distributors	Location
Wohlhaupter	Dapra	over 20	east + west coast
De Vlieg	local distributor	over 50	all states
Kaiser	local distributor + 2 main offices	over 50	east + west coast
Criterion	local distributor	over 100	all states
Davis tool	—	—	—
Ex-Cell-O	independent local distributor	over 100	all states
Falcon	—	—	—
Fansteel	—	—	—
Greenleaf	local independent distributor	over 50	all states
Erickson	Kennametal sales network	19	all states (east + west coast)
Midwest Ohio	—	—	—
Sandvik	local independent distributor	—	all states
Valenite	own distribution network + independent resellers	over 100	all states

DYONIX GREENTREE TECHNOLOGIES, INC.
Part B

By June 1, Greentree's internal structure had been put in place and the software development program was well under way. Carey Mann, principal author of the Business Plan, had finished his M.B.A. and was retained on a full-time basis to oversee the day-to-day progress of the project. This would permit Dyment to concentrate his energies on attracting investment dollars and generating publicity for the company. David MacDonald was hired to head the software team which consisted of MacDonald, CKS software consultants, Calvin Smithson, and Kevin Gore. The three principals of the firm also decided that to truly address the needs of their vertical market, a retail outlet would have to be set up to provide the various hardware components, software packages (e.g., accounting, PERT, CPM, job costing, etc.) and peripherals required to completely computerize the LBM industry. In the initial stages this storefront operation would also double as national service headquarters for the Dataquote I. To take charge of setting this outlet in place, James Evans was hired. Finally, to assist Mann in researching the computer industry and source components for the Dataquote system, an M.B.A. student, Paul Crampton, was brought on board to work full time for the summer.

With the software development nearing completion and under the guiding hand of MacDonald, Mann decided to search the hardware market in an attempt to get a firm idea of what it would cost Greentree to put together a complete system. This would then put the firm in a good position to evaluate the desirability of marketing hardware with the software. He and Crampton went into Dyment's office to firm up the parameters:

> Dyment: "Well, gentlemen, we've sure got our work cut out for us. By the time we're finished, I want to have a complete picture of the North American computer market. Carey, I want you and Paul to get a file on everyone who makes anything that even remotely resembles the components we're looking for. I want to know where the company has been and where they're headed.
>
> "Have a short list of what you consider to be the final contenders ready for me

Case prepared by Paul Crampton and David S. Litvack, Department of Marketing, University of Ottawa, Ottawa, Ontario.

in six weeks. By the way, unless a supplier can deliver the product by October 1, you might as well cross him off the list. There are going to be a lot of people standing around that day waiting to see the Dataquote I in the final form and if we decide to market our own hardware configurations, the last thing we'll need is supplier delays."

Mann: "I think we should also place a premium on the ability to be flexible with orders. No amount of scanning and forecasting can generate accurate estimates of what our sales are going to be over the first six months. If a bug turns up in the software, we're going to want to put the sales program on hold until we get it cleared up. By the same token, if orders start coming in fast we will want to be able to deliver. We're going to have to have a supplier who stocks the component and who can handle order changes on short notice. This kind of flexibility and reliability is the key to our whole product launch."

Dyment: "Good point. Don't forget, quality is a big factor. I want the market to perceive the Dataquote I vis-a-vis the Dataline like a Cadillac compared to a Volkswagen. A big part of this, of course, is going to be our service network. I'd prefer it if our suppliers had Canadian service outlets. This would drastically cut down on the turnaround time for repairs."

Mann: "O.K.Mike. We'll have the short lists ready for you in six weeks."

Dyment: "Great. Oh, and guys, don't forget, we're looking to pay around $8,000 tops for all of our hardware. Say about $700 for the printer, $2,000 for the digitizer, $2500 for the microcomputer, $1000 for the workstation, $1500 for the hard disk and around $300 for cables and other peripherals."

As soon as they stepped outside Dyment's office and shut the door behind them, Mann and Crampton looked at each other while shaking their heads. $8,000! 6 weeks! How the hell are we going to pull this one off?

The logical starting point was the selection of the microcomputer Greentree would employ, since this was the base of the whole system. As it turned out this wasn't much of a problem at all. There was really only one big name in the business applications area of the micro market, and IBM was it. Dyment and Mann reasoned that these three letters would add an inestimable amount of credibility to their product. The only difficulty would be getting a value added remarketer (VAR) license from IBM. A quick call to the latter's Ottawa office indicated that there were only 51 in all of Canada. Dyment, however, was confident that IBM would see the great market potential in Greentree's product and would eventually approve his application. He was prepared to wait it out with IBM because the license would permit Greentree to obtain a 28–30 point discount off the $3,149.00 list prices on the IBM 256D version. If for some reason Greentree couldn't get a VAR, they could always apply for the VAD (value added dealer), which was supposed to be easier to obtain. Of course, in this latter case the discount would not be nearly as good.

THE DIGITIZER

The next component to be sourced was the digitizer. After the micro, this is by far the most important part of the configuration. Plainly speaking, the micro is the head of the Dataquote I, and the digitizer, its guts. This device enables an estimator or an IBM store employee to transfer data from a blueprint to the computer with an electronic pen or cursor pad. Typically, a digitizer is manufactured using one of two technologies, sonic and electromagnetic. The former is carried out by placing tiny microphones along the bottom of a metallic L-shaped device. An electronic pen then transfers an X-Y co-ordinate to the controller box of the digitizer by creating a spark which is picked up by the respective sets of microphones along the x and y arms of the L-frame. By contrast, electromagnetic digitizing is carried out by a tablet device over which the blueprint is placed. Inside of the tablet, thousands of tiny wires in a mesh-like structure enable a point above the digitizer to be given a two-dimensional representation accurate to within .001″. Like the sonic machine, points are digitized using an electronic pen or cursor pad. The software then transfers the points to scale and interprets the data to generate a bill of materials and a quotation for the job represented by the blueprints. Due to Greentree's unique requirements of a 24″ × 36″ digitizing area, Mann and Crampton quickly narrowed the market down to seven contenders. Looking over their "short list" as they had it in matrix form, they quickly realized that the story it told was full of details that Dyment was not going to like. To make matters worse, there really wasn't even a supplier whom they could recommend as being better than the others. Knowing that their boss was going to ask for such a recommendation, they slowly began to sweat as they mulled over their chart.

i. Science Accessories

Crampton: "The big plus with these guys, Carey, is the price - $2,060.* This is as close as we're going to get to Mike's $2000 target, and they're head and shoulders above the rest of the pack on this point."

Mann: "Ya, but look at the thing. This big L-frame has to sit on top of the work surface. The microphones won't permit it to be embedded or placed underneath the table like the electromagnetic tablets. You know that we'd really like to see the machine in a position where it's away from the potential damage and accidents that are inevitable in our end-user environment."

Crampton: "Well, you've got a point, but this is the product that Dataline is using and we know they're making money hand over fist with it. You can't overlook the fact that it's tried and proven in our market."

Mann: "That may well be true, but remember that our tests showed that the accuracy of this machine becomes impaired under high temperatures and when moisture accumulates on the blueprint."

Crampton: "True enough, but this hasn't hurt Dataline's sales or reputation. We can get over the awkwardness of the L-frame by bolting it to the table top and situating it in such a way that its intrusion onto the working area is minimal. I know of a distributor just down in Rochester who stocks these things by the dozen. The turnaround time on repairs would be only about 10 days and he'll give us a 90-day warranty."

Mann: "Why can't we get the thing here in Canada?"

---

*All prices are quoted at the 100 quantity level and have been altered for the purpose of academic exercise.

Crampton: "A company called Megatronix has an exclusivity contract with Science Accessories for Canada distribution. Science Accessories won't sell directly to us and Megatronix's price is about $3500. The best we can do is this Rochester guy Tony. He needs us to get his volume discount and, when you think about it, F.O.B. Rochester isn't that bad compared to some of the others. In any event, Mike's going to want to know about these guys."

ii. Summagraphics

Also located in Connecticut, Summagraphics is considered by many to be the industry leader in the "small tablet" end of the market. They also have what appears to be an advantage in the fact that they hold patent on the electromagnetic technology. A recent court recognition of this legal right forced other firms to either attempt an out-of-court settlement on a leasing arrangement or discontinue the manufacture of electromagnetic tablets. As Mann's eyes arrived at the "Industry Gossip" column of the matrix, his smile quickly faded.

Mann: "What's this about delivery problems?"

Crampton: "Just about everyone to whom I've mentioned Summa's name has made the same comment about Summa having big problems getting their product out to destination on time. In fact, I've even spoken with a few companies who buy from Summa and have the same complaint."

Mann: "What does Summa say about this?"

Crampton: "Well, the guys from Atelco (Summa's Canadian distributors) deny the charge. As for corporate headquarters, they don't seem to be too eager to return my calls. I'll tell you what. I'll call John Finlay*, the guy in charge of Canadian sales down there, and we'll listen over the speaker phone to what he's got to say."

Crampton: "Hello, John?"

Finlay: "Hi Paul. How y'all doin up there in Ottawa?"

Crampton: "Well, John, to tell you the truth, we've been having a hell of a time trying to get a demo unit out of Atelco, your Canadian reps up here. I can't understand what the problem is. Everyone else has gone out of their way to get us one."

Finlay: "Paul, I have to confess. I've been stalling the lads at Atelco because we're coming out with a new series, the Microgrid, that I know you're going to love."

Crampton: "You mean to say that you folks are discontinuing the I-D series?"

Finlay: "Exactly, Paul. But this won't be for some time. If you like, we'll still hold good on our promise to deliver you 100 of the I-D boards with a 13 button cursor for $3,000. You should, however, seriously consider this new line we're coming out with. Unlike the I-D tablet, the new one has the controller inside, and comes with a 16 button cursor."

Crampton: "Sounds great, but when will it be available?"

Finlay: "Paul, we had expected it to be out by now, but those guys over in production don't seem to be ready to give it to us. I can only say that we expect it any week now."

Crampton: "As good as this new machine sounds, John, it can't do us any good

---

*Some of the names have been changed.

if we can't get it up here to have a look at it or get a guarantee on delivery for Oct. 1st of the first 10 units."

Finley: "I understand your position up there, but I really can't give you anything more in the way of firm dates."

Crampton: "I tell you what. We really like the idea of a 16-button cursor pad as opposed to 13 buttons. It allows us to send more information to the software. While we'd prefer a tablet that has the controller inside, I'm sure we could live with having it in an external box for the first little while. So, why don't you send us up an I-D tablet with a 16-button cursor pad. Surely you've got the new cursor ready."

Finlay: "I know you're going to think that I'm being difficult, Paul, but we really can't mix and match like that. The folks down here just wouldn't go for it."

Crampton: "Tell them it could mean the whole deal. I know we're only talking 100 tablets right now, but the forecasts in our business plan call for 250 in '85 and almost double that again in '86. You should know that these estimates are conservative. We're not a rinky dink operation, John. I don't understand how you guys could be willing to throw a deal like this for the sake of a few little details."

Finlay: "My hands are tied Paul. The best I can do is to ask you to be patient and to wait until we get this microgrid line out."

Crampton: "Well, how about getting one of your I-D tablets up here in the meantime, John. We'd really like to get a hands-on look at the kind of work you guys do. Besides, we need to finish up some details on our software, and we can't do that until we get hold of a board that is going to be functionally similar to the final product. As I understand it, the I-D and the Microgrid are similar in all respects except for the controller being inside and the cursor having more buttons on the latter. If this is the case, then we'll be able to at least get moving on our software while we wait for the new line—if, indeed, we decide to go with it. How much is this new board going to cost?"

Finlay: "From what I know right now, all I can say is that it should be a little cheaper. Exactly how much I can't say. At the volumes you people are talking, it would probably be about $2,800."

Crampton: "O.K., John. Keep us posted on this new line and, in the meantime, send us up an I-D. When can we expect to receive one?"

Finlay: "I'll do my best to get you one up as soon as I can."

Crampton: "Fine. Oh, and one more thing John. I've heard from a few different sources that Summa's been having delivery problems. Normally I wouldn't pay much attention to such gossip, but the fact that it's been mentioned on different occasions leads me to ask you about it."

Finlay: "I don't know where you heard it Paul, but it's just not true. We didn't get to be the market leaders by having a reputation for late deliveries."

Crampton: "Fair enough. I just wanted to hear it straight from the horse's mouth. By the way, what's the accuracy on this new tablet?"

Finlay: "The same as on the I-D 0.001″. I understand that you folks only need 0.1″, so it's more than good enough. The warranty and service are the same as well—one year. Atelco in Ottawa will send the board to us for servicing. Oh, and don't forget, those prices are for f.o.b. Ottawa."

Crampton: "It's been nice talking to you John. Call me when you locate a board for us."

Finlay: "Will do, Paul. Bye now."

As Crampton hung up the phone he looked to Mann and shrugged his shoulders.

iii. Calcomp

An American firm with its Canadian office in Montreal, Calcomp appears to dominate the high end of the market, with the majority of its sales being to the government for mapping and defense applications. At a price of $5,860, the Calcomp tablet is evidently much more technologically advanced than its competitors. As Mann looked at this information, he remarked:

> *Mann:* "These guys really seem to market the cream of the board market. If it wasn't for the high price, I just know that Mike would love to have a machine like this that would blow Dataline right out of the water."
>
> *Crampton:* "Have you ever thought of paying the extra $2,500–$3,500 bucks for this product and then just tacking the premium on to the overall price of our Dataquote? If the product is really that much better, it might be worth going with it despite the cost. If it helps our Dataquote appear to the end-user to be visibly superior to the Dataline, then perhaps he won't mind paying an extra 10%.*"
>
> *Mann:* "You're sort of right, Paul, but Mike really wants to keep the price of the hardware under $8,000. I can't see him wanting to pay all of that extra money for bells and whistles that we can't use—even if they could be put to use in future generations of the Dataquote."
>
> *Crampton:* "You might want to remind him that we'd still come in way cheaper than the Dataline."
>
> *Mann:* "True enough."

If Dyment decided to go with Calcomp, he would get delivery and service from Montreal, a one-year warranty, and he'd be protected from fluctuations in the Canadian dollar, since the quoted price was in Canadian currency.

iv. Kurta

Located in Phoenix, Arizona, Kurta Corporation was started by a fellow named Jim Rogers, the same person who had built up a company called Talos before selling it to Calcomp. Kurta has been in the business of making customized digitizing tablets for about five years and has just recently begun to market standard stock lines. Upon receiving the tablet at Greentree, McDonald and Mann were quite excited.

> *McDonald:* "Hey, did you guys check this out? Not only is their controller inside the tablet, but so is the power supply."
>
> *Mann:* "Whoever thought of that was really using his head. An end-user who buys this tablet only has two cords to worry about instead of having a mess of wires running from the power supply to the tablet, from the tablet to the controller, and from the controller to the Micro. This product is a complete stand alone subsystem. What's the price?"
>
> *Crampton:* "When I first spoke with Janet Rice, the Canadian Sales Rep down in Phoenix, she quoted me $3,750. However, the V.P. of International Marketing, Steve Stain, told me the other day that if price was to be a major factor in securing the deal, then he'd be prepared to beat any price quoted to us in hard copy by a tablet manufacturer."

---

*The Dataquote will be sold for between $22,000 and $25,000.

Mann: "How the hell did you get him to say that?"

Crampton: "I just told him that we were looking at similar electromagnetic tablets by G.T.C.O., Altek, Numonics, etc., and that we were jockeying with everyone around the $2,500 mark. I asked him why he was so high. I think he got a little ruffled. He replied that he'd never been high in his life. That's when he gave us his last offer. I have to admit it sounds great, but I don't know if it's ethically kosher to be sending hard copies of other people's offers around. So far, it seems as though he'll settle for nothing less. He says that he has to protect himself."

As Mann thought over this last point his eyes browsed the matrix. The tablet, it seemed, also came with a built-in menu along the top which corresponded to the 10 function buttons of the IBM. Since Greentree was strongly leaning towards IBM as the supplier of its Micro, this was a nice feature. In addition, Kurta had its own patent. Apparently, its technology was different enough from Suma's that the authorities in the U.S. granted them this protection.

Nevertheless, it soon became apparent that the Kurta package was not to be without a hitch. It seemed that as Crampton began to lay the ground work for contract negotiations and deliveries with the Phoenix firm, he learned that the latter would not be in a position to market its products in Canada until it obtained USA approval. The reason for this was that the interiorized power supply required certification by the Canadian authorities. Kurta felt that such approval would not be a problem since the firm had already had certification by the USA authorities. However, Crampton was unable to get any firm estimation from either USA or Kurta as to when the board would be cleared. For insurance reasons, Greentree wouldn't consider marketing the board without such clearance, and it was common knowledge in the industry that CSA often took many months to clear a product. Other minor problems associated with the package were, firstly, that there was no Canadian or even northern U.S. distributor/servicer of Kurta. Secondly, the board was not perfectly square, but was about 1.5 inches thicker along the back than it was along the front, thereby giving the working surface a tilted appearance. This would be a slight problem when it came to embedding the digitizer into the working area of the work station table. Finally, the warranty was only 90 days.

v. Numonics

Just as the final phone calls were being placed with the other digitizer manufacturers to firm up the details of potential agreements, Greentree came across Numonics, a Philadelphia-based producer of electromagnetic tablets. Due to the fact that Dyment really wanted to make a decision on the digitizer before July 1 (in order to allow for time for customer alterations, C.S.A. approvals and whatever else might cause a delay), the research on and negotiations with Numonics had to be fast tracked and completed within one week. The process was assisted considerably by an Ottawa-based distributor of Numonics products, AIM Electronics. Paul Gibbons, president of AIM, brought over a tablet which was fairly similar to the one which would be the subject of negotiations, the model 2210.

Mann: "I must confess, Mr. Gibbons, your tablet looks quite nice. You were saying that it isn't quite the same as the one which we're interested in buying."

Gibbons: "That is correct. This is one of the 2200 series. The newer 2210 series is basically the same board, only there are less dip switches exposed on the back. This means less servicing since an overly eager do-it-yourself repairman end-user might flip the wrong switch and throw the whole board out of whack. Numonics will set the switches to your specifications at the factory now and box them in away from trouble."

Mann: "Not a bad idea. Is that the only difference between the two lines?"

Gibbons: "There's one more feature. The 2210 has a movable menu. This means that you don't have a permanent loss of area. When you want to use the area where the menu is for digitizing, you can simply move the menu. This effectively gives you the 24-inch by 36-inch digitizing area without having to buy a bigger board to accommodate such a menu."

Mann: "That would be a big help when it comes to designing our workstation. The smaller the tablet, the better."

Gibbons: "Of course, the warranty is the same on the 2200—90 days—and service would still be from us here in Ottawa, but at a premium. Like I said, I'm not making much here at all. In fact, I'm only acting as a rep, so, I'm not even getting a distributor's commission. If you want us to be competitive and come in around the $2,500 range, fine, but you'll have to bring the cards in from the U.S. your-selves and pay me a premium to service them because there just isn't much room to move at $2,500 to make it worth my while to do much more for you people than simply act as a rep."

Crampton: "So your people will come in at $2,500?"

Gibbons: "Close enough. Morris Bowles, V.P. Marketing down there, told me this morning that he'd be calling you to give you his best offer, $1,800 U.S. Depending on what conversion figures you use, the price comes in pretty close to $2,500 Canadian. I generally use a 1.35 factor on the exchange to protect myself. Since you'll be bringing the boards in yourself, you might as well just use today's bank rate of $1.33. That makes $2,394. Then, tack on 3.9 percent duty, that's $2,562. That's the best we can do. Don't forget our board is about 18 months ahead of the G.T.C.O., Altek, and Summa tablets in technology."

Mann: "We don't mind paying a little extra if we're getting something for it. I have to admit, the window option is nice."

Crampton: "The board's fine and dandy, Paul. We like it a lot. It looks nice and high techish—just what the president wants, but he's not going to like that rinky dink four-button cursor. It looks like it came out of a Cracker Jack box."

Gibbons: "What's wrong with it?"

Crampton: "Hell, Paul, just pick the damn thing up. This is the one part of the digitizer that the customer is actually going to have to put in his hands and use. When we sell the Dataquote, the customer is going to get a breakdown at the price per component. He's not going to want to shell out $3,000 to $4,000 for a machine that feels like it's worth fifty bucks. That thing looks like it would shatter the first time someone let it fall or dropped something on it. Besides, it's only got four buttons."

Gibbons: "I was talking to Morris Bowles yesterday and he said that they would be coming out with a nice 16-button cursor in about six to eight months. I really can't tell you any more than that it will be offered as an option."

Mann: "Would we have to pay extra for it?"

Gibbons: "It would, of course, be about $150–$200 more than the present one, but you'd get a credit on the four-button one that comes with the tablet."

Crampton: "What about power supply?"

Gibbons: "Numonics doesn't sell their tablets with a power supply, but I've got one that will do the job for CDN $80."

Mann: "It seems as though we're quickly rising above the $2,500 mark."

Gibbons: "Look, anyone who can sell you a board complete with a 16-button cursor and power supply at $2,500 f.o.b. Ottawa has got to have his pants down around his ankles."

As Gibbons left the office, Mann and Crampton winced. The product was quite nice except for the cursor—in fact, the nicest they had seen yet in the under $3,000 range. From a technical standpoint it did seem to have a lot on the other boards. The menu made the four-button cursor seem less of an issue since data could be sent to the computer via the menu to make up for the other twelve buttons.

All the same, there was something about Gibbons that rubbed them the wrong way. Sure, he was a nice enough guy, but there was something about him that made them wary. Perhaps it was his appearance, or his constant proclamations that he wasn't making a dime.

vi. Altek

The first company contacted by Greentree when they began their search for a digitizing unit was Gentian Electronics of Ottawa headed by Vic Popovich. When Vic brought his tablet over to Greentree for demonstration purposes, it became apparent that he did not manufacture the tablet at all. Rather, he sourced it from Altek in Maryland. The latter, it seems, is one of the "big three" in the industry, along with Summagraphics and G.T.C.O. The unit itself was nothing great to look at, and when remarks along these lines were made to Vic, he promised that he would have a board similar in functionality to the one presently at Greentree, yet much nicer in terms of aesthetic appearance. He acknowledged that he sourced some of the components of the tablet from Altek, but he claimed that he put the package together using a few different suppliers (i.e., one for the power, one for the controller box, and another for the 16-button cursor pad).

After McDonald tested the tablet for a few days, he came to the conclusion that it was functionally as good as he had hoped the final product would be. If the aesthetic shortcomings could be cleared up, he felt Vic's package would be a nice one to go with. However, Mann and Crampton felt that Vic was coming in way too high at $3,750. They had not yet seen another board or sourced another supplier; however, they felt that they would ultimately be able to find someone who would be willing to give them a 100 volume price much closer to Dyment's $2,000 target. Within weeks, they had negotiations under way with G.T.C.O., Summagraphics, Kurta, Calcomp, Hitachi, Hewlett Packard, and others.

Vic was quite perceptive and persistent. Phoning Greentree just about every day, he soon gained the impression that Crampton and Mann were moving toward another supplier. The latter acknowledged to Vic that there were better prices to be had than the one he was offering and indicated that he would have to try harder to convince them that this newer tablet that he had talked about would indeed be of nicer design. This latter point was of particular concern to Greentree marketing staff because, in configuring their product, a premium was placed on the overall system having an unmistakably state-of-the-art, high tech appearance. The ultimate end-users of their product would be lumber dealers and store owners who had worked hard all of their lives and knew the value of a dollar. They were going to want to see what they were getting for their $15,000, believe it was worth the price, and want to show it off to their friends and customers.

As the search continued, Crampton and Mann finally located Altek in Maryland. The international sales rep, Sandy Kobe, gave them prices on her firm's tablet, which converted to about $3,000 Canadian, including duty, shipping, and brokerage. Crampton identified Greentree as a Canadian firm and asked if Altek had any exclusivity agreement with a Canadian distributor. Kobe replied that Altek did not. With this important issue out of the way, Crampton then inquired whether a firm by the name of Gentian Electronics of Ottawa bought its tablets from Altek. Kobe replied that she knew the company well and that, yes, Gentian did buy the full digitizer configuration, including cursor pad and controller box, from them.

The next day, Vic was invited over for a chat.

> *Mann:* "We like the fact that you're located here in Ottawa, Vic, but we could bring in a board from Altek directly which has the same nice, 16-button cursor pad that you showed us for $3,000. In addition, Altek informed us that they are in the process of completing a new line of tablets which incorporates the controller inside the unit. To tell you the truth, Vic, we think we'd be better off going directly to Altek. We do, however, see a role for you here. In view of the fact that you know these boards, we'd like to strike up a service contract with you. That way we don't have to send the tablets down to the United States to get repairs."

Vic looked a little astonished.

> *Vic:* "So you have decided to go with the Altek board?"
> *Mann:* "No. We're still in the negotiation stages with five or six other companies. That's why we wanted to speak with you. If you will agree to the service contract, that will make the Altek option look a lot better."
> *Vic:* "Who else are you considering?"
> *Crampton:* "G.T.C.O., Numonics, Summagraphics, Kurta, Calcomp, to name a few."

Upon hearing this, Vic's face flushed.

> *Vic:* "Well, I don't care one way or the other. If you don't want to buy the boards off me, that's fine."
> *Crampton:* "Vic, we really haven't decided one way or the other yet. Why don't you think about our offer for a couple of days and get back to us?"

The next day, Vic called back and asked for a meeting between Greentree, himself, and Al Cameron, president of Altek. As Crampton drove out to Gentian for the meeting, he wondered what Vic was up to. As it turned out, Vic was an old friend of Al's.

> *Cameron:* "It's nice meeting you, Paul. Vic has told me all about your company's product, and I think it's just great. As I understand it, though, you people only need 1/10th accuracy. Is that so?"

Crampton: "Yes. First of all, blueprints shrink and expand according to room conditions. Secondly, our software has a built-in wastage factor. For these reasons, a resolution of 0.1″ will be all we'll need."

Cameron: "That's just dandy because we've got an offer I think you folks at Greentree are going to like. Altek is prepared to design a less expensive board for your application which will cost $2,600, cursor included. The only extra cost will be on the power supply, which I understand Vic can supply for $125."

Crampton: "I have to say, Al, that your offer sounds great, but I'm skeptical about receiving a cheaper product. What exactly are you going to take out of the stock tablet?"

Cameron: "Not to worry. We'll only be reducing the density of the copper wires. There's no point in your people paying for a 0.001″ resolution if you only need 0.1″. That's a whole lot of work and wires we can avoid putting into the board on our end, so we can afford to give you the board for $2,600 f.o.b. Ottawa. Vic here will bring the boards in for you and ship them either to your Ottawa location or anywhere else in Canada. He'll honor our one-year warranty and service the boards after that at a fee to be worked out between him and Greentree."

Crampton: "I must say, Al, you and Vic have come a long way."

Cameron: "So we have a deal?"

Crampton: "I wish I could say yes, Al, but it's really not my decision. I help Carey Mann source components and then the two of us present our findings to the company president, Mike Dyment. He's the guy who's going to make the final decision. To be quite honest, you are definitely in the running, but we've had a couple of firms who are willing to come in quite a bit cheaper than you."

Cameron: "May I ask who these companies are?"

Crampton: "Sure, G.T.C.O. and Kurta. In addition, Numonics has a price which works out to about the same as yours for a board which is definitely better."

Cameron: "Well, Paul, the best I can do is $2,500, and that's final. After that, it wouldn't be worth my while."

Crampton: "Al, I'll pass the information along to Mike. That's all I can do. You can be sure, though, that I'll do my best to convince him that you guys are the way to go."

After chatting for another few minutes, Crampton left. Driving away he knew he had bargained well, but now he and Mann would really have a hell of a time recommending a particular manufacturer to Dyment.

vii. G.T.C.O.

To complicate matters, Ken Dag, a salesman from Electralert, the Canadian distributor of G.T.C.O. Company of Maryland, phoned the day after the Altek meeting to announce that G.T.C.O., too, would beat any other offer. It wouldn't be by much, but they had a policy of not being undersold. Electralert, a Toronto firm, would handle the 90-day warranty and the servicing at the end of that period. The G.T.C.O. tablet had been at Greentree for about two weeks and McDonald and the others were quite fond of it. The nice, 16-button cursor and the shiny formica surface of the tablet gave the unit a very high-tech look. While Crampton and McDonald felt that the tablet, with its controller mounted under it, appeared to be too cumbersome-looking due to the three-inch thickness, Mann argued that this should not present an aesthetic problem since the digitizer would be mounted into the work-station from below, with a nice, smoked glass finish on top that would be flush with the surface of the table. As the others nodded in agreement with Mann, it seemed that the G.T.C.O. offer was just as good as any. In fact, the only shortcoming associated with the deal seemed to be that the contract price would be in U.S. dollars (about $1,800) and that this price was f.o.b. Maryland. Dag had come up from Toronto to visit Greentree three or four times and seemed like the kind of guy whom you could trust and who would go out of his way for you. When asked about the status of G.T.C.O. vis-a-vis Summagraphics, he put Greentree in touch with Eric Rodenberg, the sales manager for G.T.C.O. The latter asserted that the U.S. Court had removed G.T.C.O. from the general list of defendants named in the patent suit filed by Summagraphics in Washington two and one-half years prior. He also added that Numonics and Altek had settled out of court with Summa for the right to continue making tablets and infringing on the latter's patent.

TEACHER'S NOTES

The case was prepared as a teacher's tool for the "Industrial Suppliers" section of a marketing course. An effort has been made to make each of the seven components listed a supportable alternative. Depending upon the viewpoint and values of the reader, he or she will arrive at a different recommendation regarding which board to go with. There is evidently no right or wrong answer, however, some answers can be given more value in view of the fact that they conform to more of the selection criteria as set out at the beginning and at various points throughout the case. The traditional external/internal market analysis using the 4Ps and 6Os applies itself well to the case.

EXTERNAL

(i) Buyer Behaviour

Occupants—The buyers and the end users in this market are for the most part the same lumber store/home centre owners and employees, respectively. They are typically people who are over 30 and who are looking for a device that will save them time and therefore earn them money. The product offered by Greentree will generate earnings for 2 reasons. Firstly, because it will save the end user a great deal of time per quotation—hence, a labour saving. Secondly, it will enable the store to take in more quotes, thereby increasing sales.

Price—Since these consumers are for the most part people who've built up their businesses from scratch—either as their own operation or as a franchise, they know the value of a dollar. They will pay what they think the product is worth to them, but no more. They will certainly not want to think that they are paying for more than they need. For this reason, selling a high end product could be difficult. The price of the digitizer will be set out in the overall price breakdown of the Dataquote 1, therefore, the consumer will know exactly what he is paying for this component.

It is not likely that he will wish to pay over $6,000 for a digitizer, especially if he knows that he is paying for bells and whistles that he doesn't even need. In view of the fact that a lumber dealer could easily find out that he could get a good digitizer much cheaper, Greentree would risk tarnishing its credentials as a "good value" marketer if it decided to sell the Calcomp tablet. In addition, the $3,000 that this would add to the overall cost of hardware for the Dataquote would be hard to justify, considering the over-riding concern of Mike Dyment that the hardware components combined cost no more than $8,000. Remember, Greentree wants a Dataquote 1 in every Lumber and Building Supplies retail outlet, and the more expensive the end product becomes the less chance it has of being perceived as a worthwhile investment for consumers. This external downward pressure on the final price means that any additional component costs will have to be partially borne by investors—hence the return on investment will be reduced. The combined potential unhappiness of consumers and investors is therefore more than enough to preclude the Calcomp tablet from further consideration.

Place—The product will be launched in the Western provinces to people with a rural mentality. Lumber dealers all over the west will be watching this product closely through the eyes of their associations. The Dataquote 1 will therefore have to have perceived value. The pitch used by Greentree will be that the product will pay for itself within 2 months.

Extent of Demand—There are about 6,000 lumber dealers and home centres in Canada. Greentree feels that every one of these operations should eventually have their product.

Core Product—What the end user is really buying is a tool that will help him earn money. Greentree's product will enable him to save time and generate more quotations. In addition, the Dataquote 1 will enhance the perceived professionalism of his firm in the community.

(ii) Life Cycle

The digitizing method of quotation generation is in its introductory market stage. There is at present only one other company in the market and they are mainly confined to the States. For this reason, Greentree wishes to have its product perceived to be superior to that of its competitor. Furthermore, Greentree wishes to have state of the art components to assure the firm that a potential competitor will not enter the market with a superior product which makes the Dataquote 1 either redundant or cost ineffective.

(iii) Competition

As mentioned, there is at present only one other firm in the market. It is a U.S. based firm and sells a system that is well in excess of the $22,000 price that Greentree is planning to offer. As far as digitizers are concerned, the firm utilizes the L-frame sonic machine marketed by Science Accessories. Greentree should avoid going for this technology for a few reasons:

(a) This technology is quickly becoming redundant.

(b) S/A is the supplier used by Greentree's competitors. This point should not be underestimated. Dataline has a solid relationship with Science Accessories and could well influence S/A to either divulge information or cut Greentree off in the future.

(c) The price, its major advantage, isn't really much of an advantage at all. In fact it is only about $250–$300 cheaper than other machines of much higher quality that are available to Greentree.

INTERNAL

Skills of the Firm

Greentree is primarily a software development company. As a start up venture, it is heavily dependent on investment and this in turn forces it to be very concerned with marketing a product which is going to sell quickly, thereby generating fast returns which can be recycled back into the company and into the pockets of its investors. The product which Greentree should choose should be one which is of a high quality, hi tech appearance, at the lowest possible price. The higher the quality, the less likely the machine is to break down and the more likely it is that the end user will be happy and tell all of his peers about the product. The lower the price, the more convinced the end user will be that he is getting a good deal. For this reason, Summagraphic's price of $2,900 makes it difficult to go with them. Kurta, G.T.C.O., Altek and Numonics all sell tablets which are at comparable quality at a price anywhere from $200–$400 cheaper. In the first year alone, on projected sales of 100 units, this involves a saving for Greentree of $20,000 to $40,000. Furthermore, Summagraphics has been slow in getting a demonstration unit in and they have a reputation for late deliveries. These points created a large element of doubt in the minds of Dyment, Mann, and Crampton regarding Summa's ability to provide good service.

Marketing Plan

The marketing plan used to attract both investments and the services of a large merchandising company out west calls for the product to be launched on October 1, 1984. For this reason, Greentree places a large premium on the ability of a supplier to be ready by that time. In view of this, Kurta must drop out of the picture. CSA has a reputation for being slow and strict. There is no telling when the Kurta tablet will gain certification, and Greentree can't take the risk of relying on CSA. Executives at Kurta did maintain that they wouldn't begin marketing their product in Canada until it received CSA approval. In addition, there is always the possibility that the tablet will not pass the CSA tests. Finally, the firm has absolutely no distribution or service network in Canada.*

---

*It should be noted that these time requirements also work against Summagraphics. Greentree hasn't been given any firm commitment as to when the new Microgrid product offered by the former will be available. Since Greentree can get a table with a built-in controller from other manufacturers at better prices, this is another reason for not going with Summagraphics.

At this point 4 of the 7 contenders have been eliminated—S/A, Kurta, Summagraphics and Calcomp. The three left are G.T.C.O., Altek and Numonics. Of these finalists, G.T.C.O. promised to come in at the lowest price. They provide service out of Toronto, which isn't as good as the other two who offer service out of Ottawa, and their warranty is only 90 days. Numonics is also 90 days, yet it should be noted that these time requirements also work against Summagraphics. Greentree hasn't been given any firm commitment as to when the new Microgrid product offered by the former will be available. Since Greentree can get a tablet with a built in controller from other manufacturers at a better price, this is another reason for not going with Summagraphics. Altek's is one year. Another important consideration is whether the supplier stocks the tablets. This affects the manufacturer's reliability, as far as deliveries are concerned, and it gives Greentree the flexibility to alter orders on short notice. The 24″ × 36″ tablet is a stock item for G.T.C.O., as is the 2200 series for Numonics. However, the latter has not given any specific dates for the availability of the new 2210 series, and, as was mentioned, Altek will be customizing its board for Greentree—hence, it will not likely have the unit stocked in quantities over 10. Altek has promised to have the digitizer ready for mid-September. Regarding the cursor pads, Altek and G.T.C.O. sell an excellent 16-button model, while Numonics presently markets only a 4-button, cheap looking apparatus. Technically speaking, Numonics's board is slightly better than the other boards by virtue of the fact that it is sleek and has the movable menu. The 16-button cursor pads on the other two, however, compensate significantly for this shortcoming.

Looking at the pack at this point, it is still fairly difficult to make a clear decision; however, Numonics perceptibly trails the other two. The warranty is only 90 days, the cursor pad is cheap, and prices are f.o.b. Philadelphia, which means that Greentree must get involved in the administrative hassle of importing the components—i.e. arranging for shipping, brokerage, and having to deal with the uncertainty of Canada custom. There is another more important point which deals the death blow to Numonics. Greentree felt uneasy about Paul Gibbons, the President of Numonics's Canadian distributor. Business is, to a large extent, based on perceived trust, reliability, and confidence. For this reason, Greentree's management did not feel comfortable going with Numonics as a primary supplier.

Of the final two, the choice would have been hard since G.T.C.O. had offered to undersell anyone—at least, this is what Ken Dag, a salesman with Electralert, G.T.C.O.'s Canadian distributor, had intimated. As it turned out, Ken forgot to convert into American dollars when he told G.T.C.O. that Greentree was working around the $2,500 mark with other potential suppliers. This $2,500 turns out to be around $1,800 U.S. after duty, shipping and brokerage are taken into account, and Ken phoned one day to say that G.T.C.O. couldn't go any lower than $2,400 U.S.—about $3,450 Canadian. There was no way that Greentree would swallow this; hence, they decided to go with Altek at $2,500, with Numonics (about $2,800 with their newer 16-button cursor) as a secondary source.* It is true that Altek appears to have

---

*Numonic's price was $1,800 U.S. Converting this to Canadian currency using a 1.33 exchange ratio × 1.039 duty × 1.05 for shipping and brokerage = $2611. Add in about $200 for the new 16 button cursor they promised to have, and you get $2,800. As a bonus, Altek's price was quoted in Canadian dollars, which protects Greentree from currency fluctuations.

a great shortcoming in the fact that it will not have the finished product ready until September 15, two weeks before the scheduled product launch; however, the president of Altek, Al Cameron, assured Greentree that his firm would have the digitizer ready for shipment on that date. Mike Dyment was more than prepared to accept Cameron's word of honor on this point; and furthermore, Greentree's management as a whole were very impressed with Vic Popovich, president of Gentian, Altek's Ottawa supplier.

SUNSHINE ELECTRIC
(A)

Sunshine Electric (SE) provides electrical power to customers throughout one southern state. SE has shown great interest in the development and implementation of new energy-related technology. In particular, SE views Cool Storage technology as being potentially very valuable to many of its customers. For this reason, SE has decided to institute a marketing research project whose purpose is (1) to assess the likely rate of adoption of cool storage systems among its commercial and industrial customers; and (2) to assess which (if any) incentive alternatives should be implemented to increase market acceptance and the rate of adoption of the system.

SE management has submitted a Request for Proposals to a number of marketing research firms. The request contains some guidelines as to the crucial steps of the research project. The competing firms will be asked to bid on the project, describing what steps they would take in performing the necessary research and stating estimated costs. The selected firm will be responsible only for conducting the research, analyzing the results, and presenting the necessary reports (see below); they will not be responsible for actual implementation of a marketing program for cool storage if indeed the program is to be implemented.

COOL STORAGE TECHNOLOGY

In developing rate designs for utilities, there has been a trend toward peak load pricing. Resultingly, utilities such as SE have become increasingly interested in technologies which affect utilization of energy, especially during peak periods. Knowledge of the likelihood of adoption of such technologies in the future would help utilities determine both appropriate rate designs and required new electrical generating capacity.

The cool storage system is an application of thermal storage technology. Its operation is as follows: The air conditioning compressor in a commercial building is run at night to chill water, which is held in a storage tank until needed. During

Case prepared by C. Anthony di Benedetto, Department of Marketing, University of Kentucky, Lexington, KY. Copyright 1985

the day, the chilled water is circulated through the cooling coils in the building, while air is forced over the coils. In a variant of this system, ice and not chilled water is made at night and stored until needed.

A firm owning a cool storage system therefore may operate its refrigeration equipment at night (during off-peak hours), when energy charges and electrical demand are lowest. Also, less energy is required during the day (i.e., during high-cost peak hours).

Typically, the firm operating a cool storage system does not reduce its utilization level of energy. Rather, the major benefits obtained by the firm are in the form of cost reduction:

—Since the chiller refrigeration unit is operated over more hours of the day, a lower-cost unit of smaller capacity would be sufficient.

—Electrical connected load would be lower, resulting in cost saving to the firm.

—Energy usage would be shifted to off-peak periods and obtained at lower cost to the firm.

—The compressor operates at higher efficiency at night, due to lower outside air temperatures, improved condenser heat rejection, and lower compressor discharge pressures.

There are other minor benefits associated with the use of a cool storage system. The storage tank is a dependable standby source of water for the sprinkler system, thus the firm may obtain lower fire insurance premiums. Also, the system can be used directly to cool critical equipment during a power cut.

COMPANY BACKGROUND

Sunshine Electric is an electrical utility serving about 2.01 million active customers. Of these, about 1.76 million are residential customers, 237,000 are commercial customers and 13,000 are industrial customers. Although these two latter groups comprise just over 12% of the customer base, they account for over 40% of the generated revenue.

SE classifies its consumers according to rate class: residential, general service (industrial and commercial), and curtailable (also industrial and commercial). Customers in this latter rate class obtain electricity at a lower rate than general service customers, but are the first to have their electricity cut off in the case of a power shortage or other emergency. There is also a small number of consumers (only about 4,000) who do not fit into one of the above categories and are charged different rates. A listing of the rate classes, and the number of rate customers per class, appears in Table 1.

SE has an Energy Planning Department which performs four functions: it conducts Current Load Research, Consumer Research and Monitoring, Electricity Demand Planning, and engages in Load Forecasting. The Consumer Research and Monitoring Group (CRM) gathers statistically accurate data concerning the energy usage of the different customer groups. This information is primarily used in Load Fore-

Table 1 Customer Rate Classes

Rate Code	Description	Number of Customers
RS	Residential	1,761,571
GS-1	General Service—Non-demand, less than 20 kW	202,064
GSD-1	General Service—Demand 20 – 499kW	47,396
GSLD-1	General Service—Large Demand 500 – 1,999 kW	1,216
GSLDT-2	General Service—Large Demand—Time of Use 2,000 kW or greater	72
GSLDT-3	General Service—Large Demand—Time of Use 2,000 kW or greater (served at transmission voltage level)	9
CS-1	Curtailable (but otherwise similar to GSLD-1)	135
CST-2	Curtailable (but otherwise similar to GSLDT-2)	42
CST-3	Curtailable (but otherwise similar to GSDLT-3)	4
OL-1	Outdoor Lighting	3,234
OS-2	Sports Fields	320
SL-1	Street Lights	1,642
SL-2	Traffic Signals	309
Total		2,018,014

casting and Electricity Demand Planning, and in determining if governmental regulatory requirements are being fulfilled. The CRM group uses surveys to gather demographic, energy use and consumer attitude data in addition to the information obtained from magnetic tape meters installed in field locations.

For the most part, the CRM group has focused its attention on the residential consumer market: research and energy conservation activities for the commercial-industrial (C/I) segment have been comparatively limited. However, SE has undertaken a few activities concerning C/I customers in recent years. These include:

—Rate Load Research: magnetic tape meters have been used to monitor a sample of C/I customers from each of the major rate classes. This information has been used to study costs of electrical service and their relationships to rate load.

—C/I Energy Audits: For a fee, energy auditors employed by SE inspect a C/I customer's facilities and analyze the energy requirements of the customer's building and equipment. The auditor provides a report containing recommendations to the customer on potential energy savings. SE has performed well over 3,000 such audits for its C/I customers.

—Energy Conservation Studies: Participants in the Energy Audit Program have their energy consumption monitored for a year. Energy usage prior to the audit is compared to current energy usage.

—C/I Account Coding: SE is coding all of its C/I accounts with a nine-digit code based on the SIC classification system. The coding process began two years ago, with the largest accounts being coded first. All regular customers are now coded, with the exception of those belonging to the lowest-demand rate class (i.e., GS-1).

INCENTIVE PLANS

In order to speed up the rate of adoption of cool storage technology among this group of customers, SE could implement one of many incentive plans. Among these are:

—information programs, designed to make potential system users more aware of the kinds of cost savings available;

—financial assistance programs, designed to reduce costs of installation;

—replacement of the current rate structure by a Time-Of-Use (TOU) rate plan. SE is planning to phase in TOU rates for all its C/I customers over the next seven years, starting with the largest accounts. It would be advantageous to the user to distribute energy consumption more evenly throughout the day if a TOU rate plan were in effect.

Evidently, the list of possible incentives or inducements is not restricted to these three.

THE RESEARCH PROJECT

Sunshine Electric is currently seeking proposals from consulting firms to estimate the adoption rate of cool storage systems in the C/I segment. SE desires an assessment of market penetration of cool storage through "natural" (unaided) penetration as well as under the various incentive plans. In addition, SE requires an assessment of alternative inducement schemes as to their ability to increase market acceptance of cool storage systems.

SE has developed a two-level research task structure which is to be used as a guideline by the consulting firms in performing required research. Level 1 comprises an assessment of the characteristics of the C/I market with regard to the adoption of cool storage; Level 2 consists of the actual implementation of a survey of the market based on the results of Level 1 analysis. Each of these levels in turn is broken down into required tasks and subtasks as follow.

Level 1—Exploratory Assessment:

The consulting firm should begin with a literature review of cool storage technology, previous efforts in marketing this technology (including previously used inducement methods), and techniques for predicting rate of adoption of new technologies of this type.

Based on this analysis, the consulting firm must assess the market potential for the cool storage system, determine a sampling frame of potential users of the system, and develop a model for predicting the adoption rate of the system. At this point, an interim report should be delivered by the consulting firm for review by SE.

Level 2—Survey Implementation:

If the interim report is approved by SE, the consulting firm progresses to the survey implementation stage. The survey methodology has been specified in detail by SE: this task would entail the construction of a sample design and determination of appropriate sample size in addition to designing a suitable survey instrument. Once the field work is done, the consulting firm must carry out all required qualitative and quantitative analyses of the collected data. A final report should then be presented to SE upon completion of the study.

The next section describes each task and subtask in greater detail.

TASKS IN LEVEL 1—EXPLORATORY ASSESSMENT

The tasks comprising Level 1 are constructed to provide a basis for the survey implementation and data analysis tasks which make up Level 2.

Task A—Literature Review:

The consulting firm must demonstrate that it has sufficiently researched the existing literature for documentation of research relating to cool storage system design and engineering as well as for the methods of predicting market acceptance of new technologies of this kind. Other major issues to be researched include how incentives have been used to accelerate market penetration, how cool storage technology has been implemented by current C/I users, and what variables were significant in affecting the decision of these users to purchase a cool storage system.

The consulting firm should describe the facilities it has at its disposal for reviewing the literature (e.g., whether computerized literature search would be possible).

Task B—Assessment of Market Potential:

In completing this task, the consulting firm must identify the current users of cool storage systems in SE's service region. The firm must identify the factors which had the greatest impact in the decisions of these users to adopt the system: among these would most likely be psychological factors (such as perceptions of reliability of the technology); marketing factors (e.g., financial incentives from the public sector); economic factors (expected cost reductions in electrical bills); and probably many others.

The consulting firm should demonstrate its capacity to assess all factors pertaining to market potential, which would include at least the following:

—the identification of the key decision-makers in the current user firms (these may be purchasing managers, engineers, consultants, etc.);

—the nature of the current users of the technology (characteristics to consider here would be type of business, size of demand for electricity, and possibly geographic location within the state);

—The perceptions of current users regarding the reliability, economy and convenience of cool storage technology;

—The effects of different manufacturing processes, installation methods (new versus retrofit) and/or system type (ice versus chilled water) upon the purchase decision or manufacturer selection;

—The types of marketing programs and inducements to purchase employed and their effect upon the purchase decision.

The consulting firm is not restricted to these factors and indeed is encouraged to develop a list of additional factors (such as barriers to entry of new manufacturing firms, market sensitivity to economic changes or rate structures; sale of similar technology in other geographic locations) which have the potential at least indirectly to affect market acceptance of cool storage systems.

Task C—Determining the Sampling Frame:

Using the market potential considerations generated in Task B, the consulting firm must develop a sampling frame of all potential cool storage system users. It will be the consultant's responsibility to decide which C/I customers are the most likely purchasers of a cool storage system and also to develop a screening criterion for separating potential customers from unlikely users.

SE will make available to the selected consulting firm all customer billing account records, which contain data on electricity usage for each of the rate classes. The nine-digit SIC codes will also be made available to the consultant, who may want to use them in conducting a segmentation analysis of the market. Additional in-house data which the consultant may require for developing market penetration estimates (such as historical data for growth and energy use in the C/I segment) will also be provided if necessary.

The consultant should indicate how such data would be used in determining the sampling frame.

Task D—Developing a Framework for Predicting Cool Storage Penetration:

In this task, the consulting firm will clearly specify which variables are to be measured in the proposed survey of Level 2. Also, justification for the selection of the desired variables (based on related research and/or the analysis of Task B) must be provided, as must an adequate operationalization scheme for the selected variables. In developing this framework for prediction, the consulting firm should keep in mind the cost and time investment that would be required in gathering the data on the selected variables and in analyzing them. Another consideration should be how accurate the penetration estimates generated are likely to be.

The alternative inducement and incentive plans are also examined at this time. It will be useful to quantify the benefits obtained by firms investing in cool storage systems in terms of demand savings (for example, number of kilowatts saved per month); in fact, one approach the consultants could take would be to estimate the amount of systemwide demand saved under different estimates of market penetration rates.

Task E—Level 1 Report:

Once the first four tasks are completed, an interim report must be provided to SE. It would include, among other things:

—a listing of the findings of the market potential assessment (Task B), including the results of any informal interviews with representatives of C/I customers currently owning a cool storage system;

—a description of the recommended screening methodology designed to identify high-potential system purchasers;

—a report on the major variables isolated in Task D, including considerations of measurement.

The report should be preceded with a one-page summary and a two- to three-page management brief.

SE estimates that the consulting firm should produce its Level 1 report no more than twenty weeks after project commencement.

TASKS IN LEVEL 2—SURVEY IMPLEMENTATION

SE would recommend the continuation of the project if satisfied with the results contained in the Level 1 report.

Task A—Survey Methodology Development:

This task comprises all methodological issues involved in designing the sample, constructing the questionnaire, and collecting the data—that is, all aspects of data handling up to but not including data analysis.

This is a time-consuming task and may be broken down into subtasks. In subtask 1, *sample design,* the sampling method must be described and justified (e.g., probability sampling vs. nonprobability sampling). The consulting firm should make certain that the chosen sample of C/I customers is an accurate representation of the desired target population. Sampling design recommendations will be judged in terms of their statistical efficiency (standard error for a given sample size), and also their economic efficiency (the cost of each observation).

Subtask 2 is *sample size determination.* In deciding upon an appropriate sample size, the consultants should consider the maximum tolerable error, standard deviations, and confidence intervals (an acceptable confidence level for this project would be 90%).

Other factors determining sample size are: the likelihood of nonresponse occurrence, nonsampling error, and the possibility of biased results.

The third subtask, *instrumentation,* involves the development of an appropriate survey instrument. The instrument should naturally be pretested to improve interview quality, to verify clarity of instructions and the type of data gathered, and to estimate interview length and cost. Recognizing the critical importance of this step, SE will aid the consulting firm in the developing and testing of the survey instrument.

Organization of field work, subtask 4, includes the establishment of training requirements for the interviewers, estimation of the required number of researchers, and selection of the data collection method. The consulting firm should also indicate how the surveys will be validated (i.e., how missing data will be collected, which observations to omit due to incomplete responses, etc.).

Subtasks 5 through 7 are comprised of the actual *data collection,* the *coding and processing* of the obtained data, and the writing of a *status report* indicating the progress being made.

Task B—Data Analysis:

The specific data analytic techniques to be used are described by the consulting firm, with special attention being paid to the major assumptions underlying data analysis (e.g., assumptions of interdependence vs. dependence relationships).

Task C—Final Report (First Draft):

A draft of the final report is presented by the consulting firm to SE, which answers the research objectives stated by the latter.

Table 2 Anticipated Performance Timetable

	Period of Performance
Level 1	
Task A	4 weeks
Task B	8 weeks
Task C	2 weeks
Task D	3 weeks
Task E	3 weeks
	20 weeks
Level 2	
Task A	10 weeks
Task B	7 weeks
Task C	5 weeks
Task D	3 weeks
	25 weeks

Task D—Final Report (Final Draft):

The finished report would include all estimates of market penetration under all inducement conditions as well as a critical assessment of the effectiveness of the alternate marketing programs which SE could implement to facilitate penetration of the cool storage technology among its C/I customers.

The second level of tasks is estimated to require about 25 weeks; thus, SE would expect a finished report from the chosen consulting firm in a maximum of 45 weeks overall (see timetable in Table 2).

PROPOSED EVALUATION CRITERIA

The proposals received by SE from the respondent firms will be judged on five equally important criteria.

—Problem Comprehension;

—Technical Approach (completeness, practicality);

—Costs (consulting fees);

—Education and project-related experience of personnel;

—Experience of the firm with similar projects in the past.

SUNSHINE ELECTRIC
(B)

On the basis of the submitted proposals, Sunshine Electric awarded the cool storage research project to the consulting firm of John Miller and Associates (JMA). About ten weeks ago, JMA initiated the research process with an extensive literature review (Task A). At this point, midway through Task B: assessment of market potential, JMA has obtained from Sunshine Electric (SE) breakdowns of current commercial and industrial (C/I) customers by SIC code and by rate class, and have identified some of the current users of cool storage technology across the state. Based on this information, plus additional information concerning the marketing, economic and psychological factors likely to have an effect upon the adoption rate, JMA must now complete the task of assessing market penetration of cool storage technology and progress to Task C, the establishment of an appropriate sampling frame of potential adopters.

OBJECTIVES AND REQUIREMENTS OF CONSULTING FIRM

JMA believes that in order to estimate usefully the market for cool storage systems, the characteristics and perceptions of the potential user (in terms of opportunity perceived, ability of system to satisfy needs and wants, understanding of the system) must be analyzed, as well as the physical and technical aspects of the system. Some of the most important considerations in this regard are:

—perceptions of cool storage technology;

—beliefs that the technology is a worthwhile investment;

—financial resources;

—the firm's ability to operate, service and supervise such a system, and any additional cost considerations;

—expected benefit to the consumer of a relatively new, unknown *concept:* "freezing water to save money and energy."

Case prepared by C. Anthony di Benedetto, Department of Marketing, University of Kentucky, Lexington, KY

510

JMA has taken as its objective the quantitative prediction of the potential market for cool storage systems within the C/I segment of SE's customers, and the estimation of market penetration of the system either in the absence or presence of inducements.

The consultants are attempting to develop a market characteristic customer profile of the C/I segment. This would enable JMA to identify which customers would be likely to install a system under non-incentive conditions (i.e., "natural" adoption process); and which would react to an incentive plan, considering both sensitivity of market penetration rate to use of incentives and the cost effectiveness of the incentives.

JMA developed a more comprehensive list of incentives which could be employed by SE. These include:

—Financial incentives: time-of-use (TOU) rate, lease arrangements, third party financing, supplier subsidies, assistance from SE in quality control, post-installation cost analysis and comparisons, guaranteed positive cash flow, loan assistance, etc.

—Educational incentives and management, distribution, equipment-manufacturer seminars; design seminars, practical sessions on cool storage applications for engineers, equipment demonstrations, etc.

JMA hoped to recommend an incentive program which would enable SE to penetrate its C/I market most effectively (e.g., concentrate on high-potential rate classes, SIC codes, or geographic locations).

JMA would be required to perform all the tasks previously listed in order to fulfill its contract with SE. These include—conduct a literature review, design, test and implement a survey to estimate market potential, determine ability of alternative incentive schemes to encourage adoption of system, and recommend a course of action which would yield the optimal adoption rate. In turn, SE could use the results of the analysis in demand planning, load forecasting, and rate design.

LITERATURE REVIEW RESULTS

JMA has completed an extensive search of the literature dealing with both cool storage systems and the process of adoption of new technologies. The major results are described below.

Cool Storage Technologies

The literature review shows that very little market research has addressed the issue of user understanding and awareness of cool storage systems. Another issue which is relatively unexplored in the literature is the comparative effectiveness of various types of incentives. There is clearly a need for new market research which would identify market potential as well as characteristics of likely adopting customers. Until this kind of information is collected, utilities such as SE will have to rely on guessing and luck in designing an effective service package which would fulfill the desired customer needs and penetrate the market.

Also lacking is an adequate data base of current customer attitudes and beliefs concerning cool storage systems. This lack will make reasonably accurate assessments of future market presentation rate even more difficult.

However, due to their links with the state government's Information Service as well as a major local research institute, JMA was able to develop an extensive bibliography of the technical, marketing and feasibility aspects of cool storage technology, as well as a partial list of current users. For some of these users, a case history was available documenting the reasons for adopting the system; thus, JMA could draw some preliminary insights into the decision process to adopt such a system.

Estimating Market Penetration

The marketing literature deals extensively with the issue of new product adoption and penetration rate, as well as how to predict these occurrences. In general, the following variables have significant roles to play in the market penetration process: level of awareness of the new product; comprehension level of potential users; conviction and preference levels; outside influences such as opinions of perceived experts, and relative importance of variables (such as different elements of the marketing mix). Furthermore, in the case of organizational consumers purchasing high-tech equipment, other factors must also be considered: these include identification of the buying center or decision-making unit (DMU); attitudes of the DMU towards technology applicability in general; differences in relative importances across DMU's of different organizations.

Numerous internal and external constraints also affect the adoption process, such as technical ability, psychological attitudes, financial limitations, technological advances or constraints, etc. In studies of future adoption rates of other similar technologies by organizational firms, the relative importance of these constraints has been assessed, usually by interviewing current technology users as well as reviewing the literature.

By combining all of the above considerations and adapting them to the cool storage adoption situation, JMA was able to develop a framework for prediction of penetration rate which appears in Figure 1. A description of the specific variables which need to be assessed in applying this framework appears in Table 1.

MARKET POTENTIAL ASSESSMENT

Examination of Figure 1 indicates that definition of the macrosegments of the C/I customers with respect to their potential for adoption of cool storage technology is an important first step in this task. In particular, adequate macrosegmentation would be a crucial factor in the determination of the sampling frame and would thus have an impact on all later tasks in the study.

JMA obtained the following information on each of SE's commercial and industrial customers from internal company files.

—rate class

—three-digit SIC code (where applicable, nine-digit code was also provided

Figure 1   Framework for Prediction of Market Penetration

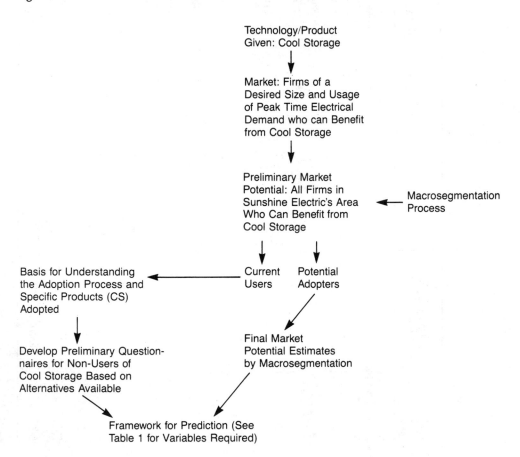

Table 1   Variables Required for Prediction Framework

Constraints

Internal	External
Technical	Technological
Physical	Economic
Psychological	etc.
Financial	
Equipment	
etc.	

Figure 2 Segmentation of Market by Rate Class and SIC Code

SIC Code	Description	RATE CLASS								
		GS1	GSD1	GSLD1	GSLDT2	GSLDT3	CS1	CST2	CST3	TOTAL
10–14	Mineral Industries	260	61	—	—	—	—	—	—	321
15	Building Contractors	13,422	3,148	10	—	—	1	6	1	16,581
16	Heavy Construction	1,503	352	2	—	—	—	1	—	1,857
17	Trade Contractors	37,650	8,832	29	—	—	1	—	—	46,512
6552	Developers	612	143	—	—	—	—	—	—	755
	Total Mineral and Construction	53,447	12,536	41	—	—	2	—	—	66,026
20	Food Products	458	108	112	9	2	14	6	1	710
21	Tobacco Products	15	4	9	1	—	2	1	—	32
22	Textile Mill Products	109	26	5	1	—	—	—	—	141
23	Apparel Products	974	228	18	1	—	4	1	—	1,226
24	Lumber Products	1,036	243	23	2	—	5	1	—	1,310
25	Furniture	531	125	5	1	—	—	—	—	662
26	Paper Products	81	19	49	4	1	5	2	—	161
27	Printing and Publishing	1,906	447	30	2	—	4	2	—	2,391
28	Chemical Products	86	20	280	24	4	32	12	2	460
29	Petroleum and Coal	49	12	—	—	—	—	—	—	61
30	Rubber and Plastics	427	100	13	1	—	2	1	—	544
31	Leather Products	68	16	—	—	—	—	—	—	84
32	Stone, Clay and Glass Products	551	129	72	6	1	7	3	—	769
33	Primary Metal Industries	63	15	40	3	—	5	2	—	128
34	Fabricated Metal Industries	907	213	32	3	—	4	2	—	1,161
35	Machinery, exc. Electrical	1,021	240	26	2	—	4	2	—	1,295
36	Electric Equipment	427	100	75	7	1	9	3	1	623
37	Transportation Equipment	534	125	30	2	—	4	3	—	697
38	Instruments	237	55	11	1	—	2	1	—	307
39	Miscellaneous Manufacturing	548	129	12	2	—	2	1	—	694
—	Auxiliaries	207	49	4	—	—	—	—	—	260
	Total Manufacturing	10,235	2,403	846	72	9	105	42	4	13,716

Figure 2 Continued

SIC Code	Description	RATE CLASS								
		GS1	GSD1	GSLD1	GSLDT2	GSLDT3	CS1	CST2	CST3	TOTAL
50	Durable Goods Wholesalers	10,351	2,428	8	—	—	—	—	—	12,787
51	Non-Durable Goods Wholesalers	5,457	1,280	4	—	—	—	—	—	6,741
52	Building Materials	3,693	866	33	—	—	4	—	—	4,596
53	General Merchandise Group	1,542	362	16	—	—	1	—	—	1.921
54	Food Stores	9,156	2,148	81	—	—	9	—	—	11,394
55	Automotive Dealers	4,958	1,163	4	—	—	—	—	—	6,125
554	Gasoline Service Stations	5,996	1,406	5	—	—	—	—	—	7,407
56	Apparel and Accessories	5,800	1,361	5	—	—	—	—	—	7,166
57	Furniture and Home Furnishings	5,401	1,267	4	—	—	—	—	—	6,672
58	Eating and Drinking Places	11,107	2,605	9	—	—	—	—	—	13,721
591	Drug Stores	1,597	375	1	—	—	—	—	—	1,973
59	Miscellaneous Retail	17,809	4,177	14	—	—	1	—	—	22,001
	Total Wholesale and Retail	82,867	19,438	184	—	—	15	—	—	102,504
70	Hotels and Motels	2,556	599	24	—	—	3	—	—	3,182
72	Personal Services	7,083	1,661	5	—	—	—	—	—	8,749
60–9,73	Financial and Business Services	9,658	2,265	87	—	—	9	—	—	12,019
75	Automotive Repair Service	4,658	1,092	4	—	—	—	—	—	5,754
76	Miscellaneous Repair Services	2,660	624	2	—	—	—	—	—	3,286
78–9	Recreation and Motion Pictures	2,542	596	2	—	—	—	—	—	3,140
80	Health Services	14,434	3,386	11	—	—	1	—	—	17,832
81	Legal Services	5,587	1,310	4	—	—	—	—	—	6,901
82	Educational Services	303	71	—	—	—	—	—	—	374
891–2	Engineers and Architects	2,072	486	2	—	—	—	—	—	2,560
893	Accountants	2,395	562	2	—	—	—	—	—	2,959
89,899	Social and Other Services	1,567	367	2	—	—	—	—	—	1,936
	Total Service Industries	55,515	13,109	145	—	—	13	—	—	68,692

—geographic location (northern, central or southern part of the state)

—load factor and average peak load

—application and uses of electricity

As a first attempt to analyze the obtained data, JMA constructed a data matrix which classified C/I customers according to what it felt were the two most critical variables: SIC code and rate class. This data matrix appears in Figure 2.

Choice of these two variables was easily justified by JMA. It was felt that firms operating in certain industries would by definition have much higher energy requirements (both in terms of average peak load and total monthly usage) and would therefore be more likely to be interested in a new energy- and cost-saving technology. Furthermore, the rate classes were clear indications of extend of demand and essentially broke C/I customers down into light, medium and heavy consumers of electricity. Rate class segmentation also indicated which customers were in the "curtailable" category, and JMA believed that a customer's choice of regular versus curtailable rates might also be related to potential for cool storage technology adoption.

JMA recognized that the other variables obtained might also have significant influence on the decision-making process. In particular, geographic location might be an especially important variable.

JMA had to perform a number of additional steps before completing the preliminary assessment task and progressing to Task C (determining the sampling frame).

First, the data matrix has not been reduced yet; i.e., no firms or groups of firms have yet been eliminated. Based on experience and on the literature search it would be possible to assess the economic benefits (and hence the potential for application) for the various segments. This would allow JMA to eliminate from the matrix those customers who would find it completely infeasible (from an economic point of view) to adopt the technology within the next five to ten years.

Second, some of the customers included in the data matrix are current users of cool storage systems and therefore should not be considered as potential adopters. Essentially, JMA will have to decompose this data matrix into two matrices—one listing current users, one listing potential adopters. Knowing who all the current users are is doubly important to JMA, as the chief member of the DMUs in these firms may be interviewed in later stages of the research project.

In short, JMA is currently in the midst of Task B. According to the prediction framework of Figure 1, it has for the most part completed the groundwork for the macrosegmentation process and is now at the "Preliminary Market Potential" stage. Following the pattern of Figure 1, JMA will now have to isolate the current users, understand their adoption processes and reasons for adoption of specific cool storage systems, and develop preliminary questionnaires for the current nonusers based on the available alternatives. JMA now also has to examine the list of current nonusers and identify potential adopters (develop final market potential estimates).

These may be developed from the literature search and from current cool storage system owners.

VARIABLES TO ASSESS AND OTHER PROCEDURES

(A) Awareness Level—the probability that potential adopters are aware of the existence, capability and/or usefulness of cool storage technology.

(B) Comprehension Level—the knowledge level possessed by potential adopters regarding technical capabilities of the technology as well as financial and operational benefits associated with its use.

(C) Conviction/Preference Level—The extent to which the potential adopter seriously considers cool storage as a possible alternative to current energy utilization.

(D) Buying Center Identification—The identification of the active decision-makers within the purchasing organization (i.e., the Decision-Making Unit).

(E) Identification of Outside Influences—Individuals or organizations such as HVAC (heating, ventilating and air conditioning) firms, architects, building consultants, etc., who may influence the DMU in its purchase decision.

(F) Engineering Requirements of Firm—as specified by the engineering department.

(G) Extent of Technology Applicability—A survey of the general flexibility of cool storage and related technologies as expressed by the DMU.

(H) Importance Analysis—Determination of the variables considered to be critical in the adoption decision—will differ from DMU to DMU. Also measured here is the responsiveness of each DMU to incentives either of a financial or of a marketing nature.

(I) Tradeoff Analysis—This analysis derives utilities associated by each DMU to each product attributes as well as any existing interaction effects. May be accomplished with LINMAP or some other psychometric optimization technique.

(J) Simulation—Using the above, profiles of each macrosegment as to its likely acceptance of the new technology may be through simulation.

SEANAV CORPORATION
Developing A Marketing Strategy

Paul Wilson was elated. He had just received word that Seanav Corporation had been granted $30,000 in start-up funds from the federal government. This, along with the financing supplied by the founders would enable the firm to survive until Seanav received a further capital injection from its private investors.

Paul was convinced that Seanav had unmatchable engineering strength and a head-start on potential competition. Private investors had also expressed interest in the newly formed high technology company. It seemed certain that Seanav would now become a viable firm in the marine electronics industry. Its product was navigation equipment that gave a ship's position with greater accuracy than had been previously available. The equipment also was usable world-wide, a significant advantage over earlier systems.

The initial feedback from the accounting firm assisting Seanav in obtaining funding was also good. The detailed (130 page) business plan that had been developed over the last four months had enabled the accounting firm to develop a financial model of the company covering the next seven years. The problems with the business plan were in the market analysis; there was a great deal of detail but Seanav's marketing strategy was not clear. Paul realized he had to re-examine the market information and develop a concise and realistic market plan, within the next week, in time for meeting with the accounting firm and potential investors. Paul sat back to review the market information before calling a meeting of his Board of Directors.

THE COMPANY

Born as an idea in the minds of a couple of engineers, Seanav was incorporated in August 1983. Using the expertise of one of the principals, an exhaustive business plan was developed that encompassed the engineering, marketing and administrative aspects of the company for a seven year period. By early January 1984, it had

© 1984, D. Joseph Irvine, Roger C. Bennett and David S. Litvack. This case was written by D. Joseph Irvine under the supervision of Roger C. Bennett, Associate Professor, McGill University and David S. Litvack, Assistant Professor, University of Ottawa. It is based upon the activities of a Canadian Corporation. Names and some data are disguised.

become apparent that Seanav had a great deal of potential and, based on the favorable reactions to the business plan by a major accounting firm, Seanav was able to open offices and a research laboratory in a high tech industrial park.

The Board of Directors of Seanav consisted of three engineers and a lawyer. Mike Ruby was an aerospace engineer with ten years of experience with navigation systems. Mr. Ruby had been involved in new product development in the high technology areas of the electronics industry, both as a product manager and, more recently, as the President of a marketing and engineering consulting firm. Mr. Ruby's entrepreneurial skills had been utilized by a number of international firms both in North America and in Europe. Mr. Ruby acted as the marketing consultant for Seanav.

Louis Hurteau had over twenty-five years of engineering experience in the avionics and electronics industries, with his main area of expertise in systems analysis and design. As Vice-President of Engineering, Mr. Hurteau was responsible for all engineering operations and program planning for Seanav.

John Richardson was a lawyer whose practice had focused on small and medium-sized businesses, for the purpose of patents and trademarks, taxation, letters of incorporation and shareholder's agreements. Mr. Richardson's experience in the private sector would assist him in his role as Secretary/Treasurer of Seanav.

Paul Wilson, the company's president, was a physicist with eight years of experience in the design and engineering of navigation systems. Mr. Wilson had been a key participant in several high technology engineering projects, both in North America and Europe.

The Navigation Industry

Electronic navigation systems had become standard by the early 1980s because they provided clear economic and safety benefits to their users. The most evident economic benefit of an accurate navigation system was the fuel savings generated. The need to conserve energy and to reduce costs had been powerful incentives for increased efficiency, some of which came from better navigation systems. An efficient navigation system reduced fuel consumption by allowing for frequent or noncontinuous position fixing, thereby enabling the most direct route to be utilized. In 1983 and 1984, fuel management packages were being developed to utilize the continuous position fixing data from satellites.

Another economic benefit of navigation systems was the time savings resulting from efficient route utilization and increased precision in position fixing. Additional economic benefits are generated by the reduced risk of environmental pollution (due to collisions, etc.) resulting from precise all-weather navigation information.

Navigation and positioning systems provided a number of safety benefits. It was, however, difficult to quantify the dollar savings resulting from these benefits. As transportation traffic increased, there was a greater need for accurate navigation and positioning information. This would facilitate traffic control and decrease the risk of collision to the user. As the need to minimize costs and to capture economies of scale in the transportation business grew, the size of the craft increased and the maneuverability of the craft decreased. Accurate positioning information was required to compensate for this disadvantage. In the marine transportation sector, hazardous cargoes (oil, gas, chemicals, etc.) were being carried in greater volumes. Casualties (such as collision, grounding and ramming) involving these vessels posed grave dangers to the environment and the public. Increased accuracy in navigation systems would offset this growing risk of environmental damage.

Historically, vessel navigation was performed by the observation of its course, or heading, relative to physical references. These references took the form of the heavenly bodies (e.g. Polaris, the sun) and the magnetic field of the Earth. During the eighteenth and nineteenth Centuries, worldwide navigation became possible through the use of sextants, chronometers (for longitude) and magnetic compasses. By estimating the direction and speed of the ocean current, the velocity of the vessel through the water, and the heading of the vessel relative to magnetic or true north, the captain could dead-reckon his position with acceptable accuracy for deep ocean navigation. As the ports and sea lanes became more congested, the importance of having more accurate information became apparent. In particular, the need to know one's true heading became vital.

The development of the ship's gyrocompass in the early 20th century was thus of such importance to the safety of the merchant fleet that many ships equipped themselves with the system immediately. By the 1980s most vessels had an electro-mechanical gyrocompass, providing an indication of true heading of the vessel on a continuous basis, and free of the anomalies and inconsistencies of traditional heading determination techniques.

Modern vessels still relied upon gyrocompasses for heading determination, and many high value vessels contained two for reliability reasons. At a cost of many tens of thousands of dollars per system, these electromechanical devices were still deemed necessary for navigation and control purposes.

Because of the self-contained nature of the gyrocompass, it was not possible to standardize and regulate the use of these devices. Hence, a proliferation of models has occurred over the preceding 40 years and this form of navigation system became the most widely accepted for merchant marine applications.

Many other navigation aids have been developed over the years in order to make transportation systems safer and more efficient, and to improve the overall effectiveness of military operations. This section discusses the major systems, in order to set the stage for an introduction to the NAVSTAR Global Positioning System.

The OMEGA system was established to meet U.S. Department of Defense requirements for a worldwide general navigation capability. The system consists of eight transmitting stations, situated at locations around the world. The system provided information that allowed a ship or other vessel to pinpoint its location with an accuracy of between two to four miles depending on location, the selection of the stations in current use, the validity of the correction through propagation delay and the time of day of operation. It was doubtful that OMEGA would be accepted as a primary navigational aid in domestic air traffic systems, because the accuracy would not provide navigation precise enough for narrow lanes.

LORAN C was a system that was developed to provide the Department of Defense with a capability for a greater range and accuracy. As with most radionavigation systems, LORAN C was developed by the DOD, but had found widespread acceptance with commercial users (more than 160,000 users in maritime applications). The range of operations was limited to the U.S. coast, continental U.S. and selected overseas areas.

TRANSIT was the major existing satellite navigation system in use in 1983. The system was originally conceived to provide accurate navigation updates to U.S. Navy ships' navigation systems. But by the early 1980s TRANSIT was a widely used commercial system as well (commercial users comprise 85% of the total user community). The system used six satellites placed in low polar orbits. Since the relative motion between the satellite and the user was used to determine position, the user had to know his own speed relative to the earth's surface. The main disadvantage of TRANSIT was the time required, to establish a low quality position solution. The process took six minutes. The user who moved a significant distance during those six minutes thus tremendously reduced the accuracy. TRANSIT provided world-wide coverage, but this coverage was periodic and the interval between positional fixes could be as much as ninety minutes. DOD planned to phase out the TRANSIT totally beginning in 1987 and ending possibly as early as 1992. This would have a major impact on civil marine users, of which over 50,000 operated TRANSIT receivers.

The NAVSTAR/GPS Program*

In the early 1970s, the U.S. DOD recognized the need for a global common grid positioning and navigation system to increase both the availability of current weapon

Exhibit 1   NAVSTAR Satellite Constellation

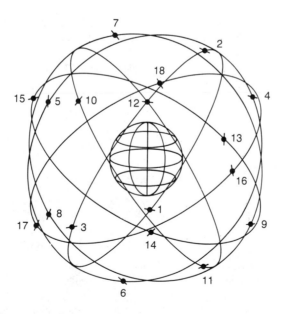

---

*NAVSTAR was the program's initial name. Later it became more generally referred to as GPS (Gloal Positioning Service).

systems, and their accuracy (particularly during adverse weather or at night). In response to these needs, the NAVSTAR program was in full scale development, with the initiation of production of 28 satellites by Rockwell International.

A competitive posture was taken by DOD for the development and production of NAVSTAR user equipment, because it was recognized as early as 1973 that continuation of the NAVSTAR program would depend largely on the availability of accurate, but inexpensive user equipment.

In 1982, the Pentagon announced that NAVSTAR's signals would be available at an accuracy level of 100 meters, instead of the previously announced 500 meters. This revised policy would attract thousands of civil users world-wide since civilian GPS would now attract thousands of civil users world-wide since civilian GPS would now meet all published civil navigation requirements except precision aircraft landing and maritime harbor entry.

Further, as a result of the Korean Airline incident in September 1983, the President of the United States announced that NAVSTAR satellite signals would be made available free of charge to the worldwide navigation community, in order to avert future airspace violations as a result of navigation error.

The value or utility of navigational signals depends on a number of technical and operational criteria of which coverage and positional accuracy are the most evident to the perception of the user. Exhibit 2 lists the features of the LORAN C, OMEGA, TRANSIT and NAVSTAR/GPS navigation systems. While no one system met all the accuracy requirements of all navigation users, NAVSTAR/GPS was clearly the optimal system. The continuous coverage and fix rate of GPS, along with the increased accuracy, assured that NAVSTAR would meet or exceed the requirements of most users.

The long term growth prospects for the NAVSTAR market were excellent. It was expected that NAVSTAR would be adopted as a navigation system at a similar

Exhibit 2 Navigation Systems Features[1]

Feature	LORAN C	OMEGA	TRANSIT	NAVSTAR/GPS
Predictable Accuracy	0.25 NM	2 – 4 NM	500 m	25 m Horizontal 30 m Vertical
Repeatable Accuracy	18 – 19 m	2 – 4 NM	50 m	25 m Horizontal 30 m Vertical
Relative Accuracy	18 – 19 m	1 – 2 NM	38 m	10 m Horizontal 8 m Vertical
Fix Rate	25/sec.	1/10 sec.	30 – 100 min.	Continuous
Coverage	U.S. Coast and Selected Areas	Near Global (90%)	Worldwide (Noncontinuous)	Globally Continuous
Availability	99 + %	99%	99% (when satellite in view)	99%

[1] Compiled from Federal Radionavigation Plan (March, 1982)

Exhibit 3   Growth of Transit System Users (1974 – 1982)

Year	Number of Users
1974	600
1975	860
1976	2,399
1978	5,820
1980	16,255
1982	45,555

rate to that observed for the adoption, by civilian users, of TRANSIT. Exhibit 3 displays the growth in commercial users of the TRANSIT system. In 1983, the TRANSIT market was still growing exponentially and there was no indication that this growth would slow in the near future. A similar growth curve, or rate of adoption for NAV-STAR technology, was forecast for the following decade. For example, the U.S. DOD had conservatively projected that the world marine market for NAVSTAR would grow to 10,000 users by 1990; 20,000 users by 2000; and would reach 80,000 users by the year 2020. NAVSTAR industry experts believed that realistic estimates would be three to four time these figures.

The Federal Radionavigation Plan (FRP) outlined plans and policies for the federal government's radionavigation services. The FRP reflected the unique combination or responsibilities of the U.S. Department of Transport and the Department of Defense: public safety, transport economy, and national security. The plan covered government operated systems having a high degree of common use (either military/civil or between different transportation modes). The radionavigation systems discussed included OMEGA, LORAN C, TRANSIT and NAVSTAR/GPS.

The FRP focused on three aspects of planning: the efforts to improve existing systems, the development required to improve existing systems, and the ability of existing and proposed radionavigation systems to meet future needs. The FRP included extensive descriptions of existing radionavigation systems and requirements. The Plan also included the criteria to be used in, and the process for, selecting future radionavigation systems.

The Federal Radionavigation Plan stated that, a National Radionavigation Policy should:

> "make NAVSTAR/GPS continuously available on an international basis for civil and commercial use at the highest level of accuracy consistent with national security interests."

The Federal Radionavigation Plan also included the following statements about the future of existing radionavigation systems:

> a. "The DOD currently uses LORAN-C; however, this use will phase down as NAVSTAR/GPS becomes operational."

b. "The military use of OMEGA will be phased out by the Army and by the Air Force by 1992. The Navy intends to re-evaluate its use of OMEGA . . . when NAVSTAR/GPS becomes fully operational."

c. "Phase-out by military TRANSIT users in favor of NAVSTAR/GPS is planned to begin in 1987 and end in 1992."

While the military would begin the phase-out of LORAN-C and other navigation systems as NAVSTAR/GPS became operational, the civilian use of these systems would be dependent on the cost of user equipment. The Federal Radionavigation Plan made the following statements about future civilian use of existing navigation systems:

a. "The LORAN-C system for coastal areas is expected to continue in operation at least until the year 2000."

b. "Use of OMEGA has been certified by the FAA for use on the North Atlantic by several airlines."

c. "Commercial vessel use of the TRANSIT system has far outpaced the DOD use."

d. "The degree of [NAVSTAR/GPS] acceptance for civil use will be especially sensitive to the successful design of low-cost user equipment . . ."

The Marine Market

The world marine fleet consisted of three major categories of ships; the merchant marine fleet, the coastal vessel fleet and pleasure craft. Exhibit 4 shows the five year fleet forecasts for each of these categories. The merchant marine fleet, which included tankers, bulk (and other) carriers and cargo vessels, operated under all weather conditions and in all four phases of marine navigation (open ocean, coastal, inland waterways and harbors). This class of vessel was larger than 100 gross registered tons (grt). The coastal vessel fleet included fishing and work boats of less than

Exhibit 4   World Marine Fleet Forecasts

Vessel Class	Thousands of Vessels (1988)	Average Annual Growth Rate
MERCHANT FLEET Large commercial ships (>100grt)	80	1–2%
COASTAL VESSEL FLEET Light commercial ships (<100grt)	1,300	2–3%
RECREATIONAL VESSELS Yachts and pleasure craft	27,000	2–3%
TOTAL WORLD MARINE FLEET	28,380	2%

100 grt. These vessels operated in coastal waters, harbors and inland waterways, mainly during acceptable weather conditions. The recreational fleet included yachts and small boats that could operate in all phases of marine navigation under good or acceptable weather conditions.

The merchant marine fleet consisted of large commercial vessels over 100 gross registered tons. This included tankers, bulk carriers and cargo ships, Exhibit 5 lists these vessels, and their numbers, as of mid 1982.

Navigation equipment could be purchased either when a ship was being constructed or it could be retrofitted. When a vessel costing tens of millions of dollars was ordered, the difference in price between the standard navigation equipment

Exhibit 5 World Merchant Fleet by Ship Type (Ships of 100 grt and over as of mid 1982)

Vessel Type	Number	Gross Registered Tonnage
Oil tankers	7,021	166,828,416
Liquefied gas carriers	722	8,785,230
Chemical tankers	774	2,963,886
Miscellaneous tankers (Trading)	128	279,669
Bulk/oil carriers (Including Ore/Oil Carriers)	418	26,030,013
Ore and bulk carriers	4,529	93,268,040
General cargo ships		
—Single Deck	11,005	19,579,023
—Multi Deck	11,237	59,898,492
Passenger/cargo ships	245	1,064,225
Container ships (Fully Cellular)	718	12,941,690
Lighter carriers	34	809,358
Vehicle carriers	245	2,485,130
Fish factories and carriers (Including Canneries)	866	3,672,380
Fishing (Including Factory Trawlers)	21,081	9,363,785
Ferries and passenger vessels	3,526	7,684,483
Supply ships and tenders	1,687	1,276,423
Tugs	6,939	2,106,708
Dredgers	721	1,428,918
Livestock carriers	106	370,593
Icebreakers	94	423,722
Research ships	596	696,358
Miscellaneous (Non-Trading)	2,459	2,785,140
Totals:	75,151	424,741,682

Compiled from Lloyd's Register of Shipping Statistical Tables (1982)

and state-of-the-art equipment was negligible and could readily be justified out of the 'new construction' budget. The retrofit decision, however, required that the purchase be justified over and above the current navigation equipment; and it required the funds to be removed from the owner's operations budget.

It could be quite difficult to convince a financial manager that a ship which had been navigating safely for years, now required a capital outlay of $30,000 to ensure that it navigated safely in the future. Therefore, the 'new construction' or shipbuilding segment of the merchant fleet was the most likely candidate for state-of-the-art navigation equipment.

There were other reasons why the most likely candidates for NAVSTAR Maritime Set acquisition were ships under construction. The merchant market was resistant to innovation and, as a result many shipowners would wait until NAVSTAR had proven itself in other commercial applications before considering its installation. The combination of the total construction cost and the lead time required prior to launch allowed for state-of-the-art technology to be used in navigation systems purchase. In late 1983, the world merchant fleet was growing at about 1% per year. However, this growth rate was expected to increase by 1986–87 when a post-recession shipbuilding boom was expected. This increase would be particularly noticeable in the tanker fleet. The shipbuilding market represented the largest single segment of the merchant market. Summarizing this analysis, Exhibit 6 indicates the possible total market for NAVSTAR equipment over the 10 year forecast period.

Aside from the increased accuracy and coverage of NAVSTAR, a $30,000 receiver could replace the systems currently in use (price in 1979: US $91,000).

The coastal vessel fleet consisted of light commercial vessels of less than 100 grt. This fleet included small fishing boats and small work boats that generally operated within 50 nautical miles of land. This group included all vessels which operated beyond the sight of land but which did not require the expensive installations of multiple navigation systems typical of the large ocean going vessels demonstrated in the preceding section. Expenditures on navigation equipment in the coastal vessel market were generally less than half of the capital outlay of the larger merchant ships.

The largest benefit to coastal vessels of a Maritime Set NAVSTAR GPS receiver was the improved performance/cost ratio. A receiver selling for approximately $25,000 would allow for worldwide positioning information to an accuracy of 100 m. This would enable more efficient operations and, perhaps, increased fishery

Exhibit 6 Merchant Fleet Market for NAVSTAR/GPS

Segment	Year					
	1984	1985	1986	1987	1988	1989–93
Retrofit	15	45	190	350	550	3330
New construction	10	75	200	400	500	2750
Total market (units):	25	120	390	750	1050	6080

yields due to this accurate positioning information. The largest potential market for NAVSTAR receivers was in the ocean-going Japanese and Korean fishery fleets; unfortunately, this market was not readily available to North American manufacturers. Japanese shipbuilders would subcontract navigation equipment out to Japanese manufacturers, unless they were given specific instructions to do otherwise. In the tradition-rich Japanese business world, this rarely occurred.

As with the larger merchant vessels, the new construction market for NAVSTAR receivers would be more significant than the retrofit market. As NAVSTAR came into operation, and was used by the merchant fleet, it was believed that a lucrative market would unfold. Although slower to develop, the coastal vessel market, due to its relative size, would represent a larger sales volume than the marine market by the early 1990s. Competition was expected to be fierce in this market as the NAVSTAR program would be fully implemented and the large merchant vessels would have demonstrated the reliability of this navigation aid. Exhibit 7 shows the estimated market size for the coastal vessel market, assuming less than 25% early adoption by the market segment within the 10 year forecast period. This is because most navigation system users would wait until the mid-1980s when lower cost second generation equipment would be made available.

The recreational vessel fleet consisted of all private pleasure craft—yachts and small boats. These craft generally operated in coastal areas, harbors and inland waterways, although some of the larger pleasure craft could be ocean-going. These vessels operated only under good weather conditions and seldom beyond sight of land. Many of these smaller craft would never install any more navigation equipment than a magnetic compass. However, as the cost of radionavigation equipment would decrease, some of the larger and more fully equipped of these craft were expected to become a significant market for radionavigation equipment during the next decade.

In the early 1980s, only a small percentage of these craft carried significant radionavigation equipment. This market, however, had an enormous potential for rapid growth. The expected availability of low cost navigation systems during the

Exhibit 7   Coastal Fleet Market Potential for NAVSTAR/GPS

Segment/Year	1984	1985	1986	1987	1988	1989–1993
Retrofit market	—	50	125	250	400	6,500
New construction market	10	20	50	100	250	5,000
Total coastal market	10	70	175	350	650	11,500

Exhibit 8   Recreational Fleet Market for NAVSTAR/GPS

Year	1984	1985	1986	1987	1988	1989–93
Market potential	—	—	25	50	100	750

early 1990s offered the owner of these small craft a navigation capability which he could use whenever he wanted or needed it.

The two main benefits of NAVSTAR/GPS to this segment would be safety and prestige. For the ocean cruising vessels in this fleet, NAVSTAR provided worldwide availability with 100 m accuracy at a relatively low cost. For a certain fraction of this market the prestige of using the state-of-the-art navigation equipment would encourage the purchase of NAVSTAR receivers.

Exhibit 8 is a forecast of the recreational vessel market for the following ten years. The segment would experience a great deal of growth. In earlier years many of these smaller craft would never install any more navigation equipment than a magnetic compass. However, as the cost of radionavigation equipment decreased, some of the larger and more fully equipped of these craft were expected to become a significant market for radionavigation equipment during the next decade.

Companies actively involved in developing and promoting radionavigation equipment for the Marine market were the slowest to commit to major GPS development programs at this time. A number of companies did have programs in the offing. For example, Magnavox was known to be spending approximately half a million dollars per year in the development of the Spartan set, a low-cost GPS Marine navigator, which would focus on merchant vessel and coastal vessel markets. Because of the success Magnavox has encountered with its other products in the marine market, the company would probably capture a large portion of the marine market as a result of its early development program. Some activities were taking place in Japan, with Mitsubishi and Japan Radio in the process of developing low-cost sets. Their emphasis would be placed primarily on the Japanese merchant and fishing fleets, although these companies were also reasonably successful in selling their products on an international basis. However, due to the size, financial backing and expertise of these firms, Seanav could expect fierce competition from established companies. Exhibit 9 lists the 22 major radionavigation equipment manufacturers in the marine market. Only four firms had established a GPS development program. The majority of the rest of the companies in the marine market were analyzing the GPS potential and its ramifications for their existing product lines.

The Board Meeting

Paul Wilson began the meeting by summarizing the events of the past few days:

> "I am happy to inform you that we have received our federal grant. We can now even afford to pay off some of our debts! However, the accountants have given

Exhibit 9 Radionavigation Equipment Manufacturers in the Marine Market

	Market Segment			Product Type				
	MERCHANT	COASTAL	RECREATIONAL	MARISAT	LORAN-C	SATNAV	RADAR	GPS
1. Anritsu Electronics	X	—	—	X	—	—	—	—
2. Data Marine International	—	X	X	—	X	—	—	—
3. Digital Marine Electronics	—	X	X	—	X	—	—	—
4. Dornier				X	—	—	—	—
5. Elektrisk Bureau				X	—	—	—	—
6. EPSCO Marine	—	X	X	—	X	—	—	—
7. Furuno U.S.A.	—	X	X	—	—	X	—	—
8. Internav Ltd.				—	X	—	—	—
9. Japan Radio Co. Ltd.	X	X	X	X	X	X	—	X
10. King (Marine) Radio				—	—	—	X	—
11. Kongsberg N.A. (Robertson)	X	X	—	—	—	—	X	X
12. Magnavox	X	X	—	X	X	X	—	X
13. Micrologic	—	X	X	—	X	—	—	—
14. Mitsubishi				—	—	—	—	X
15. Motorola				X	X	—	—	—
16. Navidyne	X	X	—	X	X	X	—	—
17. N.C.S.	X	X	X	X	—	—	—	—
18. Racal-Decca Marine	X	X	X	—	—	X	—	—
19. Raytheon Marine				—	X	X	X	—
20. Sperry Marine	X	X	—	—	X	—	—	—
21. Toshiba				X	—	—	—	—
22. Tracor	X	X	—	—	X	X	—	—
Number of firms in each area:	9	13	8	9	12	7	3	4

us a strict deadline for the revision of our marketing plan. All of the financial data, including our component cost estimates, our margins and our operating expenses are reasonable. The problem is that we now have only five days to develop our marketing strategy. Before I turn things over to Mike, I believe that John has a few words to say."

"As Paul has mentioned, we have a tight deadline. The reason for this is the federal government's changing of the R & D tax incentives. If our investors are to receive the maximum benefit from this change in legislation, they must act quickly. Seanav is not the only high tech company that is trying to woo these investors."

Mike Ruby wasn't really listening to what was going on. He still had not finalized his strategy for Seanav. A number of alternatives were going through his mind. He had just returned from a business trip for another of his clients and had only two hours to review the business plan and to develop alternatives. All of a sudden he realized that Paul was talking to him.

" . . . since we've got the budgets finalized. Now let's find out the best marketing strategy for Seanov's success."

SUNHEAT

Sunheat Inc. of Albany, New York, is a privately-owned company which designs, produces, and sells flat-plate collectors used in solar-energy heating. Despite its small size and recent formation (the firm being only ten years old), it has emerged as one of the major producers of flat-plate solar collectors in the Northeastern United States and has developed a reputation for high quality. The management feels that presently (September 1985) the company is experienced and reputable enough to expand its current business to other parts of the United States and abroad in a larger way. Their current task is to develop a marketing plan for the short and long run which would indicate which products ought to be emphasized, which markets (both geographical and by type of purchaser) hold the greatest potential, what promotional programs to employ, and how the distribution network should be improved, if at all.

INDUSTRY BACKGROUND

Solar energy is considered one of the most interesting alternative energy resource options for the future. Energy emanating from the sun is free and will virtually never run out. In addition, it knows no political bounds; a nation totally dependent on solar energy would never face a trade embargo or fuel shortage due to political turmoil.

These advantages have spurred development of various systems which harness the sun's rays. The most common, the flat-plate collector, is a simple panel-like device. The top part of the panel is black-colored metal covered by two or more sheets of glass. The black color causes heat absorption. Water, antifreeze, or some other "transfer medium" is fed through pipes attached to the panel and carries the heat to the desired location, where it may be stored for future use. Many variations on this basic flat-plate collector exist.

Non-flat-plate solar collectors have also been developed, but are much more expensive. Among these are parabolic collectors and glasstube collectors.

In the North American market, three uses of solar energy yield the greatest potential:

—heating swimming pools;

—hot water heating;

—space heating.

There are a number of secondary uses of solar energy: steam production, snow melting, distillation, etc. It is one of the desires of major solar engineering organizations to develop and promote other uses such as "solar cooling" (solar-powered air conditioning).

The equipment required for solar space and hot water heating is quite expensive. In addition to the collectors and storage tank, sensors, valves, circulators, and a complete control system must be installed. Also, "retrofitting" (converting conventional heating equipment in an existing building to solar equipment) is often difficult and costly. Installation in new structures is much easier; nevertheless, only an insignificant market share has been attained up to now by the solar manufacturers.

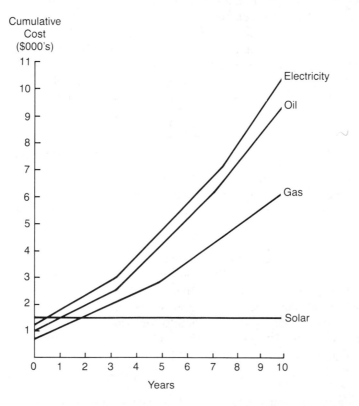

Figure 1   Comparative Cost Curves—Solar vs. Conventional Pool Heating

By contrast, flat-plate collectors are a very economical way to heat swimming pools. Although installation costs are slightly higher for solar than for conventional sources of energy, the difference is more than made up for after one year, with substantial savings to the consumer after a few years of use (since he or she never has to purchase gas or oil; see Figure 1). Retrofitting is also a much simpler operation for pool heaters than for space or water heating. As a result, about 4 percent of all swimming pools in North America (almost two million pools in total) have already been fitted with solar heating devices. The vast majority of these installations (about 80 percent) have been in pools owned by homeowners (the residential segment) with hotels and motels constituting the second largest segment.

GOVERNMENT ASSISTANCE

The Federal Government is a strong supporter of solar technology. Their objective is that by the year 2000, solar energy will supply 7 percent of American energy needs. Government support has taken many forms. Agencies (such as the Department of Housing and Urban Development and the Energy Research and Development Administration) have shown a strong commitment to solar energy. Programs (e.g., the National Program for the Demonstration of Solar Heating and Cooling of Buildings) have been established and congresspersons have supported private bills designed to promote solar energy (e.g., low-interest-rate loans or tax deductions for solar equipment).

The Canadian government has shown a similar interest in solar energy development. They have instituted the PUSH Program (Program to Utilize Solar Heating) which subsidizes purchasers of solar equipment.

State governments have also helped to further the development of solar technology. In some states (Florida, for example), it is required that all new single-unit homes must be designed to allow easy installation of solar water heating in the future. Other regional governments (e.g., Province of Ontario) have eliminated sales tax on solar equipment.

COMPANY BACKGROUND

Sunheat Inc. is not unusual in the solar energy business in that it is a very small firm: composed, in fact, of only three top managers. William Noland (President), Phil Franklin (Vice President of Marketing and Finance), and Carl Richmond (Vice President of Production) were college friends at the State University of Albany in the early 70s, went into business in late 1975, and still make up the core of the organization today (see Figure 2). Mr. Franklin was a business major, specializing in Marketing, while the others were engineers with extensive training in solar energy and other alternative energy sources. Indeed, Mr. Noland is regarded as a significant asset to the company as he is a nationally-renowned solar energy expert and consultant. In all, about 25 people work full time at Sunheat, including technicians, assembly workers and engineers in addition to management.

Although their field of expertise is the design and manufacture of solar flat-plate collectors, Sunheat management envisions the company as an important partic-

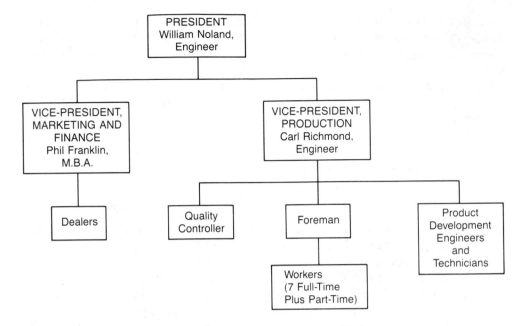

Figure 2   Organizational Structure—Sunheat Inc.

ipant in the development of all kinds of renewable energy in the future, including wind, geothermal, and tide power, to name a few. But, for the time being, they are concentrating their efforts on the solar energy business.

They feel it is important for all potential end-use customers to become more familiar with solar energy and, especially, the benefits associated with its use (Solar power is clean, efficient, inexpensive, and a renewable resource.) Thus, a major corporate objective is to increase consumer awareness of solar-power—on the part of homeowners, companies, governments, institutions, and all other potential users. Incidentally, it is a personal goal of Mr. Noland that the name "Sunheat" be perceived as being synonymous with "solar energy."

Sunheat's annual sales have been increasing at a dramatic rate, almost doubling every year for the past five years. The resulting cash inflow has permitted Sunheat to expand its production facilities greatly. For the first two years of operations, the company subcontracted out the manufacture of parts and assembled them at their Albany plant. At that time, output was approximately 80 flat-plate collectors (panels) assembled per month. In their third year, manufacturing equipment was bought and output increased to 800 panels per month. Today, monthly output averages about 3,000 panels per month. Although the plant is operating on average at only 40 percent capacity, Sunheat is already planning additional expansion.

Because of the nature of the business, monthly flat-plate collector production output varies greatly. Occasionally, a large contract with a major firm or foreign government is signed (see section on regional markets), which will require production of up to 7000 panels per month for one or two month periods. Thus, the number of workers required in the manufacturing plant can vary. During a normal month, seven full-time workers are sufficient; but when necessary, Sunheat has hired as many as fifteen part-time workers to augment its volume output (see Figure 2).

CURRENT PRODUCT/SERVICE OFFERINGS

Sunheat until now has concentrated on selling the following main solar energy systems, with the hope of expanding into other applications in the coming years:

Pool heating systems: consisting of six low-temperature flat-plate collectors and all required piping and controls. Installation is also available for a fixed charge.

Water heating systems: consisting of collectors, storage tank, control system, sensors, and additional equipment. Two variants of this system are in fact available: one which is designed to meet all domestic water heating requirements, and one which may be coupled to a conventional heating system.

Space heating systems: composed of the required number of collectors (number depends on size of structure and other considerations), all attachments and installation.

Sunheat products have been shown by independent engineering tests to be among the most efficient on the market. Some government contractors for solar pool heating, in fact, specify "Sunheat or equivalent," indicating that the government considers Sunheat the industry standard.

The company has also developed other solar energy applications of interest, mainly for irrigation projects in developing countries. These include solar power stations (in which solar energy is directly converted to electrical power) and solar pump stations (in which solar energy drives a motor which produces mechanical power).

Sunheat produces and sells a few low-cost "tie-in" products such as pool blankets (designed to minimize heat loss on cool nights and thus reduce heating expenses).

In addition to its line of products, Sunheat engineers and technicians (led by Mr. Noland) provide consulting services in the areas of solar system design for new homes and computer analysis of solar collector efficiency.

MARKET SEGMENTATION

Sunheat has found it useful to segment the market for solar pool heaters by purchaser type: the residential market, the commercial market, and the governmental and institutional markets. Mr. Noland and Mr. Franklin have been debating which specific target markets within these general segments hold the greatest immediate potential for expansion.

They feel that the residential segment could be further segmented by type of structure (single dwelling, row house, apartments, etc.), by type of ownership (owning versus renting), by demographic or psychographic makeup, by benefits sought in a pool heater, and others. They were able to compile a list of potentially useful criterion variables (see Table 1), which they felt could help them greatly in isolating important target markets.

Table 1   Segmentation of the Residential Consumer Market

Segmentation	Possible Criterion Variables
Demographic	Age, sex, education, income, occupation, social class, marital status, family life cycle stage, family size
Geographic	Urban, suburban, rural; warm vs. cool climate
Psychographic	Lifestyle, status-seeking personality, risk-takers, innovators
Benefits Sought	Economy, convenience, snob appeal, high technology interested in renewable energy sources
Type of Dwelling	Single dwelling, duplex, triplex, house, townhouse, condominium, apartment
Type of Ownership	Own, rent

The commercial segment for pool heaters includes such target markets as hotels, motels, apartments, health clubs, resorts, and so on; while the governmental and institutional segment is made up of government buildings (all levels), schools, hospitals, etc.

Among the most important consumer needs which could be fulfilled by solar pool heating would be: economy, ease of installation, adequate servicing, environmental concerns, prestige, and others (see Table 2). The relative importance of these needs depends upon the target market. For example, residential consumers may be most interested in satisfying prestige, economy and/or service needs, with preferences varying across individuals or target markets within the residential segment. For the commercial and governmental/institutional segments, service and economy

Table 2   Consumer Needs

Economy
Ease of Installation
Service and Maintenance
Reliability
Environmental Concern
Social Responsibility
Aesthetics
Prestige
Snob Appeal
Unique; Trend-setting
Innovative; Future-oriented; High Tech
Energy Saving
Etc.

would likely be more important needs, although for some such consumers, prestige might be a consideration as well (e.g., high quality image hotels, high-rent apartment buildings, etc.)

CURRENT CHANNELS OF DISTRIBUTION

Sunheat has organized the distribution of its products into four networks, each serving one of the following geographical markets: Northeastern United States (New York and surrounding states), the rest of the United States, Canada, and International. European and Sunbelt countries are viewed as being the most lucrative markets. The company's pool heater sales are currently concentrated in the Northeastern United States with homeowners (the residential market) making up the vast majority of these sales. The company is operating under the not unrealistic assumption that swimming pool heating is the end-use application with the best immediate potential (due to its obvious economic advantages to the user). They are also hoping that, if successful in expanding its pool-heater sales in the other regional markets, they will eventually be able to break into the national water- and space-heating market as well.

In the Northeast, Sunheat sells its pool heaters and related equipment either directly to end users or indirectly via about fifty swimming pool dealers, who then sell and install the products to residential or commercial purchasers. In order to reach more distant U.S. markets, Sunheat sells to independent regional distributors located all over the continental United States. These, in turn, seek out swimming pool dealers in their area. An additional level of distribution is added for sales to Canadian and international purchasers. For example, Sunheat has entered the Canadian market via a national distributor, located in Montreal, which represents many Canadian and American solar energy companies. The products are sold from national distributor to regional distributor to local swimming pool dealer. No extensive sales force is employed for sales outside the United States, as each national distributor signed up by Sunheat takes on full responsibility for the sale and promotion of the product. The channels of distribution used by Sunheat are schematically represented in Figure 3.

Despite the comparatively low sales levels outside the Northeast, Sunheat has been responsible for many installations of heating devices (both for pool and non-pool uses) in all parts of the United States and abroad. Table 3 lists some of the major Sunheat projects of recent times. The table shows that in addition to selling pool, water, and space heaters, Sunheat has been occasionally awarded contracts for solar power and solar pump stations from Sunbelt countries. The table also suggests that, given its small size and short history, Sunheat has been extremely successful in breaking into the solar energy market.

CURRENT PROMOTION AND PRICING

Sunheat is focusing its promotional efforts on all three major market segments (residential, commercial, and governmental), with emphasis on the pool heaters. Management believes that, for the moment, the cost of installation of space or water heating systems is still too high relative to electricity to justify promotion of these products to any great extent.

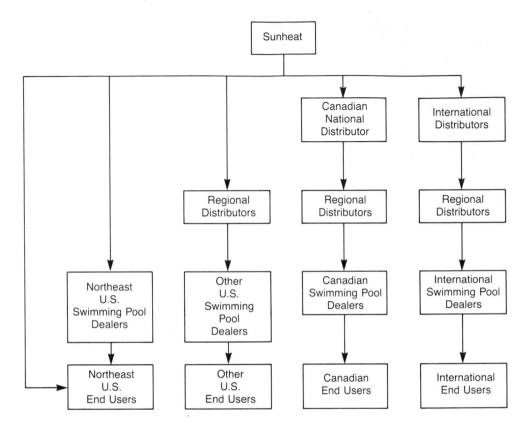

Figure 3   Channels of Distribution

Sunheat reaches the U.S. government market by advertising in purchasing guides used by government workers. In Canada and abroad, they advertise in export manuals which are made available to government agencies.

The company participates in trade shows dealing with renewable energy or environmental preservation. These shows are attended by architects, engineers, heating contractors, and various other industry representatives. They also advertise directly to industry using trade publications such as *Plumbing and Heating* and *Renewable Energy News* and have compiled a mailing list of engineers and architects to whom they send technical fliers.

The residential swimming pool segment is reached via cooperative advertising with swimming pool dealers in local home improvement magazines. However, the part of the promotional budget allocated to the residential segment is much smaller than the commercial or institutional portions. Sunheat is also a member of the U.S. Pool Institute and participates in many swimming pool exhibitions both in the United States and in Canada.

Cost of manufacture of one flat-plate collector is $60. Sunheat sells its collectors at a retail price of $150 each in the Northeastern market, regardless of whether the sale was made directly to an end user or through a swimming pool dealer. Due

Table 3   Major Sunheat Projects—Partial List

A.B.N.	One of the largest solar installations in the United States. 9,000 sq. ft. of high temperature Sunheat collectors used in hot water heating. Installed in 1979.
Cedar Food Processing, Troy, New York	3,200 sq. ft. of Sunheat collectors for heating process hot water in the food processing plant. Installed 1982.
Police Stations	Some Northeastern U.S. police stations have installed Sunheat heat pump assisted heating systems.
J.B. Black Shipping Inc.	6,000 sq. ft. of solar collectors installed for heating process hot water used in daily washing of trucks and tankers. Installed 1981.
North African Solar Power Station	Sunheat was granted one of the biggest export contracts ever tendered in solar power stations—over 20,000 sq. ft. of collectors for installation in a North African country.
Pleasant Court Hotel, Jamaica	2,200 sq. ft. of Sunheat collectors installed to provide heat for outdoor swimming pool during winter months. Not yet installed.
Bus Terminal West Germany	6,500 sq. ft. of collectors installed for process water heating. Sold through the West German licensed distributor Solarex.
Central African Solar Pump Station	Sunheat has just received the major share of a contract for a solar pump station to be installed within twenty-four months in Central Africa.

to the presence of additional distributional levels in reaching other markets, Sunheat offers its collectors at $180 each elsewhere in the United States and at the equivalent of $220 (American dollars) each in Canada. Table 4 gives full details of suggested dealer markups for each distribution channels.

A typical swimming pool installation requires six flat-plate collectors. Piping and other equipment, plus installation, usually costs about $600 per installation; thus, the total cost of installing a Sunheat swimming pool heater is about $1500 (slightly higher outside the Northeastern United States). Consumers who choose to install the heating system on a "do-it-yourself" basis save approximately $250; otherwise, the dealer or distributor installs the system. Sunheat only installs those systems which it sells directly to the final consumers in the Northeast.

CONSIDERATIONS FOR EXPANSIONS

This summarizes the situation currently facing Sunheat management. Mr. Noland now feels that the time is right for expansion: the company is well established as a high-quality pool-heater manufacturer in the Northeast. Ten years of operation have given the engineers and workers alike plenty of experience in the design and man-ufacture of equipment, and the Sunheat name is rapidly becoming synonymous with reputable, professional solar energy consulting. Mr. Noland believes that Sunheat can expand its current base of operations both by improving its pool-heater sales

Table 4   Prices of Flat-Plate Collectors for Pool Heaters

Cost of Manufacture:	$60.00	(U.S.)
Northeastern United States Market		
Direct Selling		
Price to End User:	$150.00	
Through Distributor		
Price to Dealer:	$ 98.00	
Price to End User:	$150.00	
Other U.S. Regions		
Price to Regional Distributor:	$ 85.00	
Price to Dealer:	$120.00	
Price to End User:	$180.00	
Canadian Market		
Price to National Distributor:	$ 70.00	(U.S.)
Price to Regional Distributor:	$105.00	
Price to Dealer:	$150.00	
Price to End User:	$220.00	

volume among non-residential segments and by rolling out into other geographic markets. He would now have to make decisions as to which target markets to reach and which geographic locations were the most promising.

PRODUCT CONCEPTS

Mr. Franklin was aware of the differences in consumer needs of the residential, commercial, and institutional segments and thought that Sunheat could use these differences to their advantage. Specifically, he was hoping to develop a few (perhaps five or six) high-potential *product concepts,* each suited to one of the desired target markets. He reasoned that product concepts designed for specific target markets could be developed by taking appropriate combinations of consumer needs from the list he had compiled earlier (see Table 2). For example, the same basic physical product (pool heater) could be marketed as a cost-efficient, low-maintenance product to the hotel chains and as a status/prestige object to the higher-income residential market. From this list of target market/product concepts, he could select the one or two combinations which appeared to hold the most potential.

The product concept method would help him not only to isolate the most lucrative target markets but, also, assist him in developing promotional and distributional campaigns (especially with regard to the responsibilities of Sunheat dealers and distributors). He realized that there may be relevant consumer needs to consider other than those from the list.

REGIONAL CONSIDERATIONS

Sunheat management would also have to decide which geographical regions would be entered. A number of factors would need to be considered in assessing the potential of different regions of North America:

— climatic conditions,

— intensity of competition, and

— economic and population factors.

Mr. Franklin believes that climatic conditions will play an important role in determining lucrative regional markets for Sunheat, since outdoor swimming pools are more numerous and used for more months of the year in warmer climates.

The regional competition would have to be considered as well, both in terms of how many competing solar energy companies distribute their products in the region (primary competition), and how many non-solar pool heater manufacturers are present in the market (secondary competition). Mr. Franklin believes that he would face the stiffest competition in the Southwest and along the Eastern seaboard (from Massachusetts to Florida), as most solar energy firms are established in these regions and probably concentrate much of their efforts on their home markets. Although he is not sure, he feels that secondary (non-solar pool heater) competition would be strongest in those areas as well.

Income per capita and amount of local industry are also considerations. For example, many states in the Southeast have relatively low per capita income levels compared to the national average. With the exception of Atlanta, there are relatively few major industrial centers. This may explain the small number of solar energy companies in this region (with the exception of Florida). However, in many less industrialized states, Sunheat would be able to apply for a development grant from either the federal or state government, so current economic conditions need not be a deterrent from entering such regions. Furthermore, the population density and the extent of the tourist industry might be important factors.

DISTRIBUTION CONSIDERATIONS

Mr. Noland was also concerned that some changes might have to be made in the current distribution networks for the regional markets. For example, establishing regional salesforces to deal with these markets would eliminate the national and regional distributors, but it might be expensive and difficult to implement and manage. Regional sales offices would have to be established. Companies involved in either the sale, installation, or maintenance of swimming pools are other possibilities, as are stores which cater to the "do-it-yourselfer." Sunheat would have to select a distribution method which would serve most efficiently the desired target markets. Certainly they would have to consider that, given its one Albany manufacturing plant, there are certain geographical limitations on their ability to distribute nationwide which must be overcome.

EUROCOMM USA
Developing a Comprehensive Marketing Strategy

"You simply must make sense of this American market," said Graham Clark, Managing Director of Eurocomm PLC, "and you haven't much time."

Marketing Executive Philip Bowers agreed. "It is critical to the long term viability of the Company that our U.S. market launch be successful." But not for the first time in the past weeks Mr. Bowers felt increasing pressure. With the responsibility of formulating the marketing plan for the U.S. launch of Britain-based Eurocomm's fiber optic product line, Mr. Bowers was faced with the most difficult task of his career.

The explosive U.S. telecommunication market for fiber optics was a dramatic deviation from the small and very conservative British market. Moreover, Mr. Bowers observed that it seemed to be comprised of multiple markets, each with its own distinct characteristics. With the limited resources budgeted for the product line launch, Mr. Bowers knew he had to determine how to approach the U.S. market to insure the best opportunity for success.

THE COMPANY

Eurocomm PLC is England's largest manufacturer of communications systems ranging from defense radar to satellite earth stations to telephone systems. The Company's primary line of business is telecommunications equipment, representing the majority of annual revenue. The Fibre Optic Division was the largest contributor to corporate revenue.

Eurocomm was founded in 1923 as the manufacturing arm of the British Post Office, which controlled the communications industry of the United Kingdom. In 1958, Eurocomm was incorporated as an independent, though highly regulated, company. Its primary business was supplying telecommunications equipment to its largest customer, British Telecom (BT), the English equivalent of A.T. & T. The equipment was built to BT specifications and partially funded by BT. This was an

Case prepared by Karen R. Zile under the direction of Michael H. Morris, Department of Marketing, University of Central Florida, Orlando, FL

excellent arrangement for both parties; offering BT a reliable source of custom-built equipment and providing Eurocomm a guaranteed return on investment at minimal risk.

But recently the British telecommunications industry, under pressure from other equipment suppliers, began to undergo a government-mandated deregulation. This served to break the BT-Eurocomm monopoly and open the door to suppliers from all over the world. Faced with flat sales growth and a potential decline for the first time in its history, Eurocomm PLC considered its positions.

The U.S. was determined to be the most attractive market to enter. With similar telecommunications standards, little product modification would be required. More importantly, there seemed to be no barriers to entry and the market itself was experiencing phenomenal growth. In the fiber optic area, demand clearly exceeded supply.

To enter this market, Eurocomm PLC purchased a small telecommunications company in early 1985 which had no fiber optic expertise. The strategy was to use this company as the Sales and Marketing outlet for the existing fiber optic product line, and ultimately for other equipment in the telecommunications product portfolio.

The new Eurocomm USA was located in Tampa, Florida. The Company had extensive previous experience in the U.S. telecommunications market, although not with fiber optics. Its main business had been Central Office equipment; the large-scale computers which are purchased by telephone companies to route calls from location to location. This equipment also maintains the database of telephone number assignment for a given community, as well as any custom calling features, such as call waiting. The Company had a 3% Central Office market share in the United States as of 1985.

Mr. Bowers was relocated to Tampa as Vice President of the new fiber optic organization. His immediate task was to recruit Marketing and Sales personnel for his department. Given a limited personnel budget, his resulting organization is shown in Appendix A.

Three salespersons were recruited from competitive firms. All had successful sales records, and were somewhat technically competent. John Hyatt, also recruited from a competitor, was the most technically skilled of the group. In addition to his responsibilities of coordinating bid activity and developing product brochures, Mr.

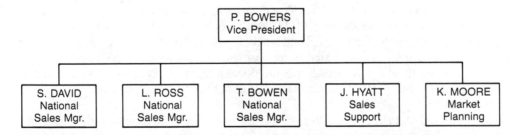

Appendix A Eurocomm USA Organization

Hyatt also provided technical presentations to customers when required by the salespersons. All planning and research activities were the responsibility of Karen Moore, who also gave technical presentations to customers.

With the fiber optic staff in place, the critical task was to develop an approach to the U.S. market.

THE PRODUCTS

Central Office equipment in the U.S. telecommunications network has been traditionally connected via large, buried cables containing many copper wires. Each copper wire transmits only one telephone conversation at a time, thus representing one major disadvantage of copper transmission. For high traffic routes, such as between two major cities, many cables containing many copper wires must be buried side by side at a very high cost. Secondly, phone calls which are transmitted over copper will "fade-out" after approximately one mile of transmission, thus the phone company must install and maintain expensive amplifiers every mile on the route.

Fiber optic systems were first introduced for telecommunications applications in the mid 1970s. These systems use a laser to convert telephone conversations into light pulses for transmission to a distant location via hair-thin glass fibers. The two primary advantages of fiber optic systems are the ability to transmit over 30 miles without amplifier equipment, and to transmit more than one conversation at a time over one glass fiber. In fact, current technology allows over 2,000 conversations to be transmitted simultaneously!

Eurocomm PLC is well respected in the fiber optic community, with an extensive research and development capability. Particularly in the area of laser research, Eurocomm PLC has been credited with many technological breakthroughs, and is thought to be a charter member of the fiber optic fraternity.

Eurocomm PLC currently has two fiber optic products which can be sold in the U.S. market, as shown in Appendix B. ALPHA 70 is a medium capacity system, able to transmit up to 2,016 simultaneous telephone conversations. It is primarily used to connect medium-sized communities. Representing the current state-of-the-art in fiber optics, ALPHA 70 is available for shipment twelve weeks after receipt of order.

ALPHA 200 is currently in the final stages of development. With the largest capacity of 8,064 simultaneous telephone conversations, ALPHA 200 is ideally suited for connecting major cities and for long distance network routes.

There is keen interest in ALPHA 200. Customers who require this type of capacity currently must purchase several smaller systems to achieve the same capacity. Thus ALPHA 200 represents a significant cost savings to telephone companies.

Eurocomm PLC has already begun development of its next product, which doubles the capacity of ALPHA 200. Designated ALPHA 1000, it is scheduled for early 1988 delivery.

Although ALPHA 200 would not be available to customers until June 1986, Mr. Bowers knew that some telephone companies typically took 4–6 months from initial request for proposal to subsequent equipment delivery. Privately, though, Mr. Bow-

ALPHA 70

ALPHA 200

Appendix B   Fiber Optic Product Line, Eurocomm USA

ers was counting on receiving a prototype in March for customer demonstrations. Customers were reluctant to commit to a new technology on written specifications alone, and there was some question as to which vendors were really close to having a viable product available.

THE MARKET

The U.S. market is a year ahead of the British market, in that deregulation occurred in America in January 1984. At that time A.T.& T. was divested of its local telephone companies, retaining its manufacturing company, Western Electric; Bell Labs, its research organization; and its long distance operations.

The Long Distance Market

Deregulation of A.T.& T. lead to an influx of competitors for the lucrative long distance market, which generated $40 billion in revenues in 1984. Most competitors plan to build their own transmission networks to compete with A.T.& T. Experts are skeptical, however. If all U.S. planned networks were implemented, then the network would grow to seven times its current size.

Typical long distance networks in the U.S. are 10,000 miles long. Most of the existing network is old, inefficient copper cable and must be replaced. Fiber optics, due to its capability to transmit long distances at a high capacity, is the preferred technology.

There is a tremendous demand for capacity. One long distance company, GTE-Sprint, recently ceased signing new customers due to straining their existing equipment capacity. Current and planned fiber optic networks are shown in Appendix C.

Most companies competing with A.T.& T. must look to outside investors to finance the enormous capital requirements to build their networks. Karen Moore, Market Planning for Eurocomm USA, believes that this will inevitably lead to a shake out in the long distance market due to a limited amount of available capital. She forecasts that in 2–3 years, only A.T.& T., and possibly two other companies, will offer long distance service. It is possible that some smaller companies may merge and serve small, regional niches.

But in the meantime, these long distance companies are primarily interested in delivery. They know that the first companies which put networks in service will be in a better position to attract investors. Consequently, their buying process is informal and decisions are made quickly, primarily based on delivery.

Ms. Moore cautioned Mr. Bowers that any substantial delay in ALPHA 200 would jeopardize Eurocomm's position in the long distance market. With several manufacturers actively promoting similar systems under development, coupled with a narrow market window, Ms. Moore believed this was a high risk market. She recognized that the rewards were equally high.

The Local Market

Organized into seven regional U.S. companies, the Bell Operating Companies (BOCs) comprise 80% of the local service telephone market. The newly divested BOCs, eager to show their independence from A.T. & T., are actively soliciting vendors other than the former Western Electric. Most BOC local networks are in place and relatively new, however BOCs are offering new services to their subscribers (such as video conferencing) which require increased network capacity. An aggressive expansion program was in progress and they were actively procuring small, medium and some large capacity fiber optic systems. Equipment is generally procured one year in advance of desired delivery.

While the BOC segment of the local market is not experiencing the rapid near term growth of the long distant market, it is nonetheless substantial and offers greater long-term stability.

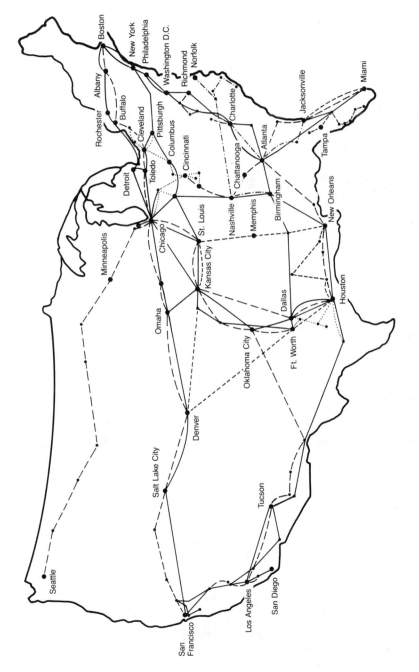

(Note: The various types of lines represent fiber optic links provided by different companies)

Appendix C Long-haul Fiberoptics Links Planned and in Place

547

Due to their regulated origins, the BOCs have a very formal procurement process. First, an evaluation document must be completed by the equipment vendor listing the results of an extensive test program specified by the BOCs. Next, a team of BOC representatives visits the vendor's facility and performs a lengthy test and evaluation procedure. The results are published and if the equipment has "passed" up to this point, a field trial of the equipment is scheduled. This is the final step in the process, whereby a BOC agrees to lease the equipment for a specified period (usually six months) to test the systems operation in a field environment. It is unusual for this entire process to take less than one year, although some BOCs will place orders after the first step, the written evaluation, is complete.

The remainder of the local service market is comprised of Independent Telephone Companies (ITCs). ITCs are of two types; large conglomerates such as United Telephone, and small "mom and pop" operations which are geographically dispersed. The large ITCs are typically organized into regions, each containing a regional headquarters office reporting to a national headquarters.

Appendix D   Revenue Forecast by Market & System Capacity, Fiber Optic Systems $(000,000)

	1985	1986	1987	1988	1989	Total
LONG DISTANCE:						
A.T.&T.						
small	23	26	22	20	17	108
medium	221	277	324	373	418	1613
large	115	123	146	181	226	791
Other						
small	39	43	43	40	29	194
medium	148	146	150	53	31	527
large	410	483	329	109	52	1383
LOCAL MARKET:						
BOC						
small	459	495	438	348	322	2062
medium	260	272	300	341	389	1562
large	83	101	176	257	287	904
ITC						
small	219	222	227	235	244	1147
medium	125	161	198	242	296	1022
large	42	68	105	141	156	512
TOTAL ALL MARKETS						
small	740	786	730	643	612	3511
medium	754	856	972	1009	1134	4724
large	650	775	756	688	721	3590

Source: Internal company records

The U.S. company which Eurocomm PLC acquired obtained the majority of its Central Office market share from the ITC segment. It sold directly to telephone companies with a large field sales organization. It had an established presence and an excellent reputation among the ITCs.

ITCs are currently replacing the majority of their networks and are committed to fiber optic technology. Their need is for small and medium systems, with some large ITCs requiring high capacity systems.

Unlike the BOCs, ITCs typically have very informal purchasing procedures. Popular telephone folklore has many a contract being written on a napkin over dinner!

The fiber optic procurement forecasts for the long distance, BOC, and ITC markets is shown in Appendix D, with a breakdown of market segment requirements by system capacity.

COMPETITION

Due to the massive construction plans in the long distance market, life could not be better for vendors of high capacity fiber optic systems. Not only does demand far exceed supply, but domestic capability is weak and market barriers are low.

Consequently, there is a massive effort by the Japanese and Europeans to be first in the market with the highest capacity system. This situation will change dramatically over the next 2–3 years as the first systems are delivered and production quantities are available.

In the local market, domestic suppliers have the situation much more in hand, and competition is crowded and intense. There are easily 8–10 major suppliers of small and medium fiber optic systems to the BOC and ITC segments of the local market.

Appendix E gives the fiber optic systems 1984 market share by supplier.

A.T.& T. Technologies

A.T.& T. Technologies, formerly Western Electric, supplies nearly all the fiber optic requirements of A.T.& T. Communications, the long distance company. Although A.T.& T. Technologies does not plan to release its high capacity system until 1988, it has a wide range of small and medium capacity systems. These systems have previously enjoyed success in the BOC market. But as the systems are highly featured and highly priced, A.T.& T. has lost market share in the deregulated environment.

Nippon Electric Company

NEC is a Japanese firm which has been very successful by solely targeting the BOC market. Its products are perceived as slightly less quality than A.T.& T., but at a lower price. NEC still, however, prices above most other competitors, and, like other Japanese firms, has competed based primarily on quick delivery.

NEC has a wide range of small and medium systems, and plans to have a high capacity system available late in 1986.

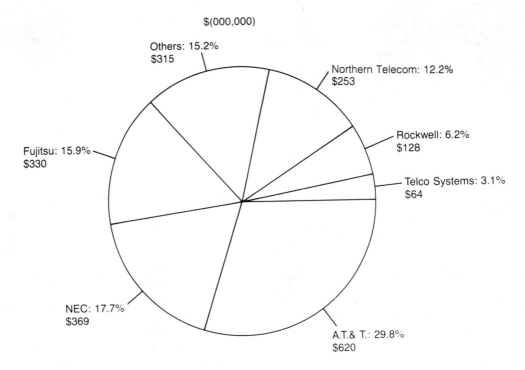

$(000,000)

Others: 15.2%
$315

Northern Telecom: 12.2%
$253

Rockwell: 6.2%
$128

Fujitsu: 15.9%
$330

Telco Systems: 3.1%
$64

NEC: 17.7%
$369

A.T.& T.: 29.8%
$620

Appendix E   1984 Fiber Optic Market Share by Supplier

Telco Systems

Telco Systems is a small fiber optic company with a limited product line; one small and one medium system. It has, however, had success in the BOC market with these products. Telco has relied heavily on its reputation of having the earliest planned delivery of a high capacity system—February 1986. Telco Systems has secured several multi-million dollar contracts from long distance telephone companies as well as BOCs based on this delivery.

There were rumors in the industry, however, that the high capacity system might be delayed. At a recent telephone convention, Ms. Moore confirmed via a Telco Systems engineer that the product was delayed until at least May 1986.

Fujitsu

Fujitsu is another Japan-based competitor with the same product and pricing strategy as NEC, except that Fujitsu markets solely to long distance telephone companies.

Northern Telecom

Northern Telecom, based in Canada, is the largest supplier of fiber optic systems to the ITC market. Currently with a wide range of small and medium systems, Northern has been rumored to have a high capacity system under development.

Appendix F Revenue Forecast Growth Rate, Fiber Optic Systems

	1985–86	1986–87	1987–88	1988–89	1985–89
LONG DISTANCE:					
A.T.&T.	0.19	0.15	0.17	0.15	0.84
small	0.11	−0.15	−0.12	−0.13	−0.28
medium	0.25	0.17	0.15	0.12	0.89
large	0.07	0.19	0.24	0.25	0.97
Other	0.13	−0.22	−0.61	−0.45	−0.81
small	0.10	−0.00	−0.06	−0.28	−0.26
medium	−0.02	0.03	−0.65	−0.42	−0.79
large	0.18	−0.32	−0.67	−0.52	−0.87
LOCAL MARKET:					
BOC	0.08	0.05	0.04	0.05	0.24
small	0.08	−0.12	−0.21	−0.07	−0.30
medium	0.05	0.10	0.14	0.14	0.50
large	0.21	0.74	0.46	0.12	2.45
ITC	0.17	0.18	0.17	0.13	0.80
small	0.01	0.02	0.04	0.04	0.11
medium	0.29	0.23	0.22	0.22	1.37
large	0.62	0.54	0.34	0.11	2.71
TOTAL ALL MARKETS	0.13	0.02	−0.05	0.05	0.15
small	0.06	−0.07	−0.12	−0.05	−0.17
medium	0.13	0.14	0.04	0.12	0.50
large	0.19	−0.02	−0.09	0.05	0.11

Source: Internal company records

Rockwell International

Rockwell, a government contractor specializing in defense communications, recently purchased a fledgling fiber optic company. With an infusion of research and development resources, Rockwell surprised the industry by unveiling a working high capacity system.

The remaining market share is comprised of various small vendors, primarily serving the ITC market. While European development activity is not reflected in current market share statistics, it should be noted that at least five international companies are planning to enter the U.S. market with a high capacity system in mid-1986.

ALTERNATIVES

Given the limited resources of Eurocomm USA, Mr. Bowers felt that they would be more successful if only one or two market segments were targeted. But each had

Appendix G   Competitive Market/Product Summary

Product	Market			
	A.T.&T.	Others	BOC	ITC
Small	A.T.&T.	Telco Sys. Fujitsu	A.T.&T. NEC Telco Sys.	Northern
Medium	A.T.&T.	Telco Sys. Fujitsu	A.T.&T. NEC Telco Sys. Rockwell	Northern
Large	A.T.&T. (1988)	Telco Sys. (May '86) Fujitsu (May '86)	NEC (late '86) Telco Sys. (May '86) Rockwell (early '86)	Northern (late '86)

Source: Internal company records

different buying processes, and varying near and long term potential; he was unsure of which segments were optimal to choose.

To make matters worse, Mr. Bowers just received a telex from England indicating that no ALPHA 200 prototypes would be available. Delays had been encountered, such that if ALPHA 200 were sold for delivery in June 1986, it would probably have to be drop shipped direct to the customer site.

Mr. Bowers knew one thing—Mr. Clark expected a fool-proof plan for entering the U.S. market, and he expected it soon.

Appendix H   Major Milestones for BOC Product Approval

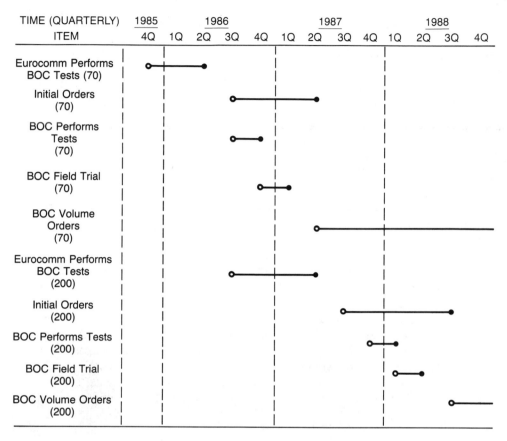

TIME (QUARTERLY)   1985   1986   1987   1988
         ITEM   4Q   1Q   2Q   3Q   4Q   1Q   2Q   3Q   4Q   1Q   2Q   3Q   4Q

Eurocomm Performs
   BOC Tests (70)

Initial Orders
     (70)

BOC Performs
    Tests
    (70)

BOC Field Trial
     (70)

BOC Volume
  Orders
   (70)

Eurocomm Performs
   BOC Tests
    (200)

Initial Orders
    (200)

BOC Performs Tests
    (200)

BOC Field Trial
    (200)

BOC Volume Orders
    (200)

KEY:

o = Start Date

● = Date Complete

ACROSS, INC.
Organizing the Marketing Efforts of a Small Industrial Firm

In the mid 1970s, the word for the future was "Plastics". By 1984, as the plastics industry continued to boom, that prediction had largely been fulfilled. American industries were continually discovering new, more efficient uses for plastic products, generating an ever-increasing demand for sources of supply.

Recognizing the potential demand for plastics, especially within the automotive sector, Ronald T. Noble incorporated a small manufacturing plant in 1978 within his hometown of Bellefontaine, Ohio. His initial product was to be a plastic dust tube for shock absorbers. Noble describes his corporate mission in a quote taken from the company's facilities list: "We are dedicated to quality, service, and profit. Our goals are to grow in a diversified manner into a medium-sized company with numerous fabricating and decorating secondary capabilities."

Noble chose the name of Across, Inc. with the help of his wife, Pat, the corporate secretary-treasurer, whose efforts enabled Ron to begin fulfilling his dream of self-employment.

COMPANY HISTORY

In March of 1978, Noble left his position as a marketing manager for Monte Plastics, Inc., in nearby Kenton, Ohio, to begin his own venture. Prior to his work with Monte, Noble had worked in sales for both the General Tire Company and Marmon Carbon Company. His education includes a 1960 bachelor's degree in Chemistry from Wooster College and a few graduate courses in business administration that he took during his first years of employment.

Since Noble had spent all but one year of his life in the Bellefontaine area, his established reputation as an honest, hardworking businessman, his business contacts, and family contributions proved to be key factors in the establishment of the corporation. The immediate Noble family includes three children: a daughter, who is a senior in college majoring in accounting, and two sons, one in college as a pre-

---

*This case was prepared by Laura Miller under the direction of Joseph W. Leonard of Miami University as a basis for class discussion rather than to illustrate either effective or ineffective handling of organizational practices.

med major and one in high school. At the time of incorporation, all three children lived at home and usually sacrificed Saturdays and summer vacation time to help with the production runs. Noble's father and father-in-law also volunteered help in running machines or in hand trimming products to meet customer specifications.

Through his past work experience, Noble not only learned how to successfully sell, but also became aware of the increasing demand for plastics within the automotive industry. By 1978, the major Detroit auto manufacturers were making headway in the switch from metals to plastics in order to reduce the weight of transportation vehicles and to comply with energy-saving regulations. Noble fabricated a mold for a dust tube and within several months, obtained a moderately large order from a supplier to one of these Detroit firms.

Acquiring sufficient bank loans to finance the corporation was a difficult process; the odds of Noble's success during the economy of the late 70s were slim. However, his persistence and confidence, as well as his contacts in the area, helped Noble to gain financial backing. With the funds, he installed production lines in a portion of a building which was situated in an area of the city with relatively low overhead costs. ACROSS leased a blow molding machine and various pieces of secondary equipment. Noble relied heavily upon the expertise and advice of long-time friends who also served ACROSS in the capacities of accountant, corporate lawyer, and insurance agent.

When they began, Noble and his family had no idea of when or if ACROSS would prove a successful venture. Normally, survival for a firm such as this one through the first three years of incorporation would signify eventual success. The unanticipated effects of the 1980 and 1981 automotive recession delayed the company's profitable efforts a few years. However, the subsequent economic recovery extended to ACROSS. By the end of the 1984 fiscal year (June 30), sales were expected to surpass the $1.0 million mark, with profits in excess of $120,000.

PERSONNEL

In 1978, the ACROSS payroll consisted of two people, Ron, the president, and Robert Benson, the only regular production worker. Noble served as "jack-of-all-trades" in fulfilling the roles of chief engineer, marketing manager, plant manager, personnel supervisor, financial planner, and president. His wife, Pat, worked out of their home as the secretary-treasurer on a volunteer basis.

ACROSS ran only one production shift in the first year of incorporation; Noble and Benson would alternate operating the main blow molding machine and hand finishing a product. Family members volunteered their time on those days when Benson didn't work or when three people were needed to meet production demands. Equipment breakdowns were a major concern; with only two people in the plant and Noble being the only expert repairman, if equipment malfunctioned, production halted indefinitely.

Presently, management continues to consist of only a few individuals, making for a simpler and more timely decision-making process. The payroll includes 28 full-time employees, Benson being the only current employee hired before 1980. Twelve part-time workers remain on call as substitutes for full-time employees on vacation

Exhibit 1   President's Time Expenditures (per month of working days)

Activity	Approximate Percent of Month
Production	10
Personnel & Employee Relations	20
Advertising/Promotion	1
Entertainment & Time with Clients	29
Engineering	20
Financing	20
	100%

or as additional labor during the peak production months. Only three of the full-time personnel are salaried, Ron, Pat, and Steve Gilbert, the general foreman who has been with ACROSS since December of 1980. Gilbert has authority over the supervisors of each of the three production shifts. (As orders for shipment increased, ACROSS gradually added shifts of production). The supervisors include Benson, Doug Clark and Mark Curran. Clark and Curran joined ACROSS in July of 1981 and August of 1980, respectively. All three were hired without experience in plastics manufacturing or a collegiate background.

Today, six years since the founding of ACROSS, Noble spends minimal time in the plant (see Exhibit 1). He relies on his foremen to supervise labor and on Gilbert to help interview prospective employees. However, Noble remains committed to maintaining effective employee relations. He has six month individual reviews with employees concerning bonuses, raises, and potential problems. When hired, each employee receives an employees manual which reflects ACROSS' commitment to open communication (see Exhibit 2). In this pamphlet, Noble expresses his and the company's responsibility to provide good working conditions, good wages, good benefits, and fair treatment for all. He believes that a union would be of no advantage to any of the employees; the business upon which each employee depends for

Exhibit 2   Excerpt from the *Introduction* to the Employee Wage and Policy Manual

> Dear Fellow Employee:
>
> Welcome to Across, Inc. I trust that this will be the beginning of a most beneficial association both for you and Across Inc. I intend to maintain that "personal touch" through close communication with each of you. It has been our employees who through their outstanding efforts have made our Company a competitive and respected business. From time to time, new or revised policies will be developed to insure the continued common good and mutual interest of the Company and its employees, and to keep in step with modern trends and philosophies which perpetuate harmonious employee-management relationships . . ."

his bread and butter would only be undermined by anyone who forces workers to pay dues. Expressing problems, suggestions, and comments need not be through a union, but through direct supervisors.

Office Personnel

ACROSS office personnel currently include Pat, who spends 3–4 days per week in the newly renovated secretary's office, and Julie Harden, whom Pat is training to take over her duties. Neither Pat, nor Julie, who joined ACROSS in 1982 as a production worker, have any significant business background. Because of the increased size of the payroll, ACROSS uses an outside EDP firm to process the payroll. Pat and Harden submit the ledgers and other pertinent work to a local CPA firm which quarterly compiles financial statements for ACROSS and offers Noble business and personal tax planning services.

Noble has investigated purchasing for the company a small business computer with spreadsheet and word processing software. However, neither Pat nor Julie claim to be able to find time to learn such a system. They rationalize that the time lost in learning how to operate the computer and convert from a manual system is not worth the benefits to ACROSS, such a relatively young business. Noble recently met with a systems consultant who estimates the cost for a complete spreadsheet system to be $18,000–$20,000. This consultant feels adaptation of the system is a must.

Production Personnel

With the exception of the aforementioned office workers, all of the labor is employed in direct production, which operates in three 8-hour shifts. These workers are in the plant six days a week and receive overtime pay at time-and-a-half for hours worked exceeding 40 per week. Except for an employee who is hired into ACROSS as a foreman, workers begin at minimum wage. Full-time employees have seniority; when hired, Gilbert informs them as to their positions on the list of seniority. Part-time workers stand in succession to full-time workers, a position to be desired for several reasons—better benefits, steady hours, and the opportunity to participate in the profit-sharing program. Noble outlined and, after consulting his lawyers, adopted the ACROSS Profit Sharing Plan in 1982. It extends to each employee after completion of 1 year of full-time hours.

In early years of production, employee turnover was a major concern. Often, Noble found himself working double shifts for workers who failed to report to duty. Now that ACROSS is "on its feet", this is no longer a major problem. If absenteeism becomes a concern, Gilbert takes responsibility; employees on the whole seem to be committed to a consistent schedule of working hours.

MARKETING

In 1978, ACROSS used one blow molding machine to produce one product sold to one supplier of one automotive company. In 1984, ACROSS operates five blow molding machines, produces 30 separate items, and sells to 19 companies which represent several industries. Dust tubes comprise 49% of production and reflect purchase orders from 3 suppliers, in the U.S. and Canada, who sell the tubes to 2 international automotive companies. Other products range from childrens' toys and plastic footballs to paint containers and birdfeeders (See Exhibit 3). Most customers are based in the Midwest. However, Noble anticipates that as the company's sales grow, ACROSS will need to find another location to not only house additional equipment, but also decrease freight costs. Having a balance of customers by industry has always been and will continue to be another concern for ACROSS.

Noble often finds himself traveling to the home offices of customers to meet with purchasing agents, engineers, or quality control managers in order to discuss complaints, to improve existing relations, or to acquire new business. As a result of the previous 2 years of increasing production orders, Noble has employed 2 manufacturer's representatives who aid in the establishment of a contract between ACROSS and a customer. These men spend a fairly insignificant amount of their time working with an ACROSS account. In fact, the growth in sales is attributable primarily to Noble's flexibility, reputation, and ability to undercut the larger bids of larger competitors, rather than an aggressive sales effort.

After an initial visit to a customer's place of business, Noble will receive an oral or written option from a customer to quote on a product price per piece (i.e., a "piece price"), a mold price, and costs of necessary secondary fixtures. Sometimes, a potential account will ask for a quote unexpectedly. In order to quote, Noble must consult several people: his moldmakers (2 independent contractors), his materials suppliers, and suppliers of secondary fixtures. He estimates, for each job, the costs of raw materials, direct labor, and factory overhead based on standard machine hours. Included in the overhead would be costs of operating equipment (i.e. drill

Exhibit 3   Breakdown of ACROSS Products

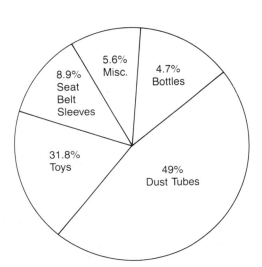

presses, flame treaters, conveyors, table saws) and secondary fixtures owned by ACROSS. Added to these costs is a margin which Nobel subjectively determines based on what he believes competitors would bid (Noble attempts to stay low relative to competitors). These inputs combine to determine the piece price, which is expressed in price per thousand pieces and sent to the customer with a detailed print of the product, matching customer specifications. Noble also must quote a mold and/or any additional secondary fixture cost, since the customer actually owns both his mold and any secondary fixtures that must be custom-made for a particular job. Noble adds a mark-up to the cost of fabricating the mold which covers such potential mold and tooling expenses as repair and maintenance or trial runs. ACROSS does not attempt to make a profit on mold and tooling income, but merely strives to break even.

The fact that customers own their own molds and, often, the secondary fixtures which are installed at the ACROSS plant, is not uncommon for the custom blow molding industry. (Noble does own one mold—the original dust tube design). A blow molder may choose to own his molds and amortize their costs over several years; however, such companies run the risk of a customer not accepting the mold design. In fact, most customers demand unique mold specifications and prefer to have their own molds, despite the initial capital outlay of purchasing the mold. Manufacturers in this industry, including ACROSS, must allow for the possibility of a customer's deciding to run production "in-house", i.e. not renewing an ACROSS contract, taking its molds and fixtures, and producing its own units.

PRODUCTION

The extent of the production process for each customer depends on that customer's specifications for dimension, color, and quantity. Dust tubes, for example, are of one color (black), and must be hand-trimmed once they are molded; toys come in various colors, and must be hand-trimmed and flame-treated to pass quality inspections.

A 17,000 square foot building, purchased by Noble and subsequently leased to ACROSS, houses the production area. Originally, ACROSS rented one part of the building to an independent party. Now, however, with the need for increased office space, production area, raw material and finished goods storage, and employee lunch and break rooms, ACROSS leases the entire structure. It does rent a small portion of the building to a third party with the plan of someday utilizing the complete floor space.

To meet production demands, ACROSS has leased 4 blow molding machines and last year purchased one used machine. Noble recently flew to New Jersey to inspect another machine being manufactured and to be delivered to Bellefontaine within a few months. The company also owns various secondary fixtures which it uses for several different jobs:

3 table saws;

1 radial saw;

3 conveyor belts; and

4 grinders.

Included in the production area are flame-treating stations, automatic handling equipment, and custom-made fabricating equipment. Raw materials are delivered to ACROSS in 40,000 lb. truckloads in the form of natural colored pellets. To fabricate a colored product, a color concentrate is added to the process. A 45 gram product would contain 45 grams of resin and approximately 3% of concentrate, by weight. The raw material price is between 40¢ and 42¢ per pound.

All incoming materials or subcontracted parts are inspected for damages and flaws by the receiving department. They are then segregated by lots according to material and source.

When a sales order has been accepted, the production control department delivers the proper blueprint and program sheets to the foreman who controls the computerized channels of the complex blow molding machines. He also installs and approves the proper machine tooling. Machine tooling consists of a bushing and mandrel through which the molten plastic passes and is shaped.

At the beginning of each new production run of either new or existing products, foremen conduct mandatory first-piece inspections to maintain compliance with predetermined dimensions and customer specifications. Once an hour, supervisors make sure these specifications are upheld; parts cannot proceed past any inspection station until accepted. If a discrepant part is discovered, the foreman and plant manager (Noble) review the item and either send it to a rework area or to the scrap area. Scrap may be successfully recycled into resin.

The impact on product quality of using recycled scrap depends on the type of product. Normally, a product may contain 20–30% scrap and still pass inspection. However, color may be one of the limiting factors—using recycled scrap may result in a color slightly lighter or darker than if pure resin were used. For some production runs of the black dust tubes, ACROSS has used 100% scrap and effectively maintained quality.

Finished products are boxed and tagged as one of the following:

1. Satisfactory and ready for shipment;
2. Held-over for reason on tag; or
3. Unsatisfactory for reason on tag.

These boxes remain in the finished goods storage area until shipment. Julie Harden maintains inventory control by indicating, through physical inspection, the finished good status on a daily basis.

In order to enhance employee performance and participation, Noble recently implemented quality control circles (See Exhibit 4). Similarly, to maintain productivity and job performance, employees rotate positions every 4 hours. Through an extensive study, Noble concluded that 4 hours was the optimal rotational basis; shifting before 4 hours would only decrease product quality.

PLANT RENOVATION

One portion of the ACROSS building is allocated to office space, a reception area, and an employee lunchroom. Casts, tools, and supplies are located in yet another

Exhibit 4

August 23, 1983

QUALITY CIRCLES

Periodically over the past few weeks, I have mentioned to many of you the desire to create "quality circles" amongst our people. What this means is that periodically each of our Class 1, Class 2, and Foremen groups would meet independently, the purpose of the meetings being to discuss ways to improve our operation. Anything can be brought up in these meetings and the only people attending would be the people in that particular job classification. The net result of these meetings should hopefully be to create a better channel of communication and to maintain or improve the quality standards of our products and company.

The meeting for our Class 2 workers, shifts 1 and 3, would be at 3:15 PM on a designated day. Shift 2 Class 2 workers could meet before their shift time. Regular hourly rates would be paid for your attendance at these meetings.

I have asked Cindy Magoline to be the spokesperson for shifts 1 and 3, Class 2 job description, and Carrie Carroll for Class 2 job description 2nd shift. Todd Miller will coordinate the Class 1 job description meetings and be their spokesperson. Robert Benson will be the spokesperson for the Foremen and will coordinate their meeting.

The spokespersons mentioned above should let me know ahead of time about their meeting times so there are no conflicts of space, people, etc. The spokesperson should put in writing (a few words) the recommendations resulting from their meetings. Remember, we're all looking for ways to better the quality of our product and methods of our production.

This "quality circle" concept is experimental for us—we'll see how it works out. Thanks for your cooperation.

Ron

room. Since July of 1982, ACROSS has undergone one-and-a-half phases of plant renovation. With the help of a local architect and long-time friend, Noble has divided renovation into 3 phases (see Exhibit 5). Phase I ended in early 1983; Phase II will extend through 1984. Pat is helping to furnish the offices and Noble's children help part-time to paint and wallpaper and with upkeep of the outside property (i.e. mow lawns, trim hedges).

Exhibit 5 Phases of Plant Renovation

July 28, 1982

Dear Ron:

As we discussed previously:

A. To repair, remodel, and expand the existing building to provide for present and near future needs of Across, Inc. and three rental units (approximately 20,000 sq. ft.).

B. This cost is detailed as follows:

Phase I

New dock and silo area
Interior wall changes
Partial office area
Toilet facilities $43,500
Heating and ventilation . . . .$ 3,500
New electrical power service—
    some plant and office lighting,
      service, etc. $24,000
Contingency . . . .$ 4,000
                                                                      $75,000

Phase II

Completion of office area, toilet area
Entry canopy and landscape
Parking pavement, etc. $32,000
HVAC offices . . . .$ 5,000
Electrical for offices and plant $10,000
Contingency . . . .$ 3,000
                                                                     $50,000

Phase III

Enclose additional storage space,
    dock, ramps, etc. at rear of bldg;
Move fence, plumbing, etc. $35,000
Heating and ventilation . . . .$ 2,000
Electrical, lighting service, etc. . . . .$ 9,500
Contingency . . . .$ 3,500
                                                                     $50,000

Sincerely,
R. Timothy James P.E.

CONCLUSION

Noble attributes the success of his venture to such factors as ACROSS's commitment to uphold effective subordinate/superior relations, ideal quality control and Noble's persistence and honesty in dealing with customers, bankers, accountants, and suppliers.

As the technology of the plastics industry continues to develop, and competition becomes more intense, Noble hopes to uphold the ACROSS image. His lifestyle as a member of top management is becoming more exclusive as he spends time entertaining clients, forecasting, analyzing organizational changes, investigating trends in technology, and making long-term plans. He has attended recent training seminars on employee motivation and on computer integrated manufacturing. As his products and markets have grown in size and complexity, Noble has also begun to realize a need for a more formal approach to his firm's marketing efforts.

Exhibit 6 Balance Sheets, 1979–83, Across, Inc.

Assets	Dec. 31, 1983	June 30, 1983	June 30, 1982	June 30, 1981	June 30, 1980	June 30, 1979
CURRENT ASSETS:						
Cash on Hand and In Banks	18,223	25,792	14,536	16,352	1,238	3,903
Accounts Receivable	195,165	140,214	83,327	32,235	4,576	14,932
Investments	70,055	30,357	52,973	—	—	—
Inventories[1]						
Raw Materials	21,968	45,508	10,724	8,479	2,491	1,611
Finished Materials	50,984	2,547	23,398	12,633	12,385	6,273
Work-in-Process	3,414		570	1,120		
(Total Inventories)	76,366		34,692	22,232	14,876	7,884
Supplies Inventories	3,775	67,552	1,250	228	170	1,306
Prepaid Expenses	345		43,082	17,089	21,444	22
(Total Current Assets)	363,939	311,969	229,860	88,135	42,304	28,048
CAPITAL ASSETS:[2]						
Equipment (at book value)	82,443	31,793	24,646	9,151	13,053	15,275
Leasehold Improvements[3]	101,574	89,368	—	87	433	780
Automotive Equipment[4]	17,336	3,431	6,955		—	—
Capital Lease Equipment	194,037	148,640	104,223	42,275		—
Office Equipment	2,373	465				
(Total Capital Assets)	397,763	273,703	135,824	54,513	64,954	16,056
OTHER ASSETS:						
Organizational Costs			165	330	494	659
Deposits	4,356	2,756	1,156	1,356	2,354	408
(Total Other Assets)	4,356	2,756	1,321	1,886	2,848	1,067
TOTAL ASSETS:	766,058	588,428	367,005	144,334	110,106	45,171
LIABILITIES AND STOCKHOLDER'S EQUITY						
CURRENT LIABILITIES						
Accounts Payable	60,225	34,329	26,785	3,774	3,251	14,470
Customer Deposits	76,139	2,550	—	—	—	
Notes and Capital Leases Payable[5]	29,400	52,988	35,006	25,045	21,842	2,640
Accrued Liabilities[6]	33,807	86,698	63,394	4,565	2,189	1,618
(Total Current Liabilities)	199,571	176,565	125,185	33,384	27,282	18,728
LONG TERM LIABILITIES:						
Notes and Capital Leases Payable[5]	229,330	174,818	127,240	58,349	74,594	20,116
Notes Payable—officer	58,940	48,870	11,937	11,937	11,753	11,692
(Total Long Term Liabilities)	288,270	223,688	139,177	70,285	86,347	31,808
STOCKHOLDER'S EQUITY:						
Capital Stock	500	500	500	500	500	500
Retained Earnings						
Beginning Balance	187,675	102,143	40,194	(4,022)	(2,174)	
Net Income for Period	90,234	85,632	62,617	44,216	(1,848)	(5,864)
Officer Life Insurance	(200)	(100)	(268)			
Dividends	—	—	(400)	—	—	—
(Retained Earnings)	277,708	187,675	102,143	40,194	(4,022)	(5,864)
(Total Stockholder's Equity)	278,208	188,175	102,643	40,694	(3,522)	(5,364)
TOTAL LIABILITIES AND STOCKHOLDER'S EQUITY:	776,048	588,428	367,005	144,334	110,106	45,171

[1] Inventories are stated at cost and reflect a FIFO system.
[2] Capital Assets are stated at cost.
[3] Leasehold Improvements represent outlays for both equipment and plant.
[4] ACROSS purchased a car for the president in 1982 and a truck in 1983.
[5] See Schedule of Notes and Leases for additional information.
[6] Accrued Liabilities represent items such as salaries, payroll tax, profit sharing contributions, and industrial insurance.

Exhibit 7 Income Statements, 1979–83, Across, Inc.

	Dec. 31, 1983	June 30, 1983	June 30, 1982	June 30, 1981	June 30, 1980	June 30, 1979
Sales	663,868	721,217	456,453	207,372	77,022	76,082
Cost of Goods Sold	493,682	442,193	228,552	118,734	56,076	68,147
Gross Income from Sales	170,186	279,024	227,901	88,638	20,946	7,935
Net Mold and Tooling Income	17,714	10,241	258	4,628	8,568	(15,986)
Gross Income from Operations	187,900	289,265	228,159	93,266	29,514	(8,051)
Administrative and Selling Expenses	80,623	171,828	147,474	40,465	24,476	
Net Income on Operations	107,277	117,437	80,685	52,801	5,038	
Other Income[1]	6,793	3,775	4,839	221	160	4,311
Other Expenses[2]	(11,136)	(16,896)	(10,392)	(8,806)	(7,046)	(2,126)
Net Income Before Tax	102,934	104,316	75,132	44,216	(1,848)	(5,865)
Provision for Federal Income Tax	12,701	18,684	12,516			
Net Income	90,233	85,632	62,616			

[1]Other Income includes such items as dividends and interest on investments, rental income from sub-leased property, and gains on disposition of equipment.

[2]Other Expenses include interest payments, penalties, and life insurance payments.

SCHEDULE OF NOTES AND LEASES

Long-Term Debt

The long-term debt as of December 31, 1983 consisted of the following:

1) A note payable to Fifth Federal Bank in the amount of $7,672.35. Monthly payments which include interest computed at 10.5% amount to $419.16 and are due through August 23, 1985.

2) A note payable to Fifth Federal Bank in the amount of $11,625.30. Monthly payments which include interest computed at 10.7% amount to $258.34 and are due through September 5, 1987. The note is secured by an automobile.

3) A note payable to Wizard National Bank in the amount of $12,773.61. Monthly payments which include interest computed at 13.5%. The note is secured by a blow-molding machine.

4) A note payable to Wizard National Bank in the amount of $6,837.37. Monthly payments of $250.51 include interest computed at 11.9%. The note is secured by a pickup truck.

5) A capital lease obligation to Fifth Federal Bank in the amount of $26,529.05. Monthly payments of $998.05 include interest and are due through November 1985. A final payment of $5,570.00 represents the purchase price of the equipment at the expiration of the lease.

6) A capital lease obligation to Leasing Corporation in the amount of $70,267.10. Monthly payments of $1,406.68 include interest and are due through December 1, 1987. A final payment of $6,996.50 represents the purchase price of the equipment at the expiration of the lease.

7) A capital lease obligation to Brewer Leasing Corporation in the amount of $92,136.92. Monthly payments of $1,467.24 include interest and are due through October 1, 1988. A final payment of $7,027.00 represents the purchase price of the equipment at the expiration of the lease.

8) A capital lease obligation to Brewer Leasing Corporation in the amount of $87,626.98. Monthly payments of $1,510.81 include interest and are due through October 1, 1988. A payment of $7,027.00 will be made at the expiration of the lease to purchase the equipment.

9) A note payable to an officer of the corporation in the amount of $58,939.62.

Lease Commitments

The annual rent amounting to $38,400.00 during the first year of the initial lease is payable in monthly installments of $3,200.00. Annual rent for each year thereafter is subject to the percentage increase of the Consumer Price Index. The principal lease, which commenced May 1, 1983 and extends through April 30, 1993, is renewable for two additional five year periods subject to the same terms and conditions as the initial term.

HYDRO CLEAN, INC.

On December 10, 1985, not long after breaking the $1 million mark in annual gross sales for the second straight year, the President and owner of Hydro Clean, Inc., Mr. Burke, held a general meeting with his three managers to discuss the upcoming year. They included Tom Davies, manager of production, Steve Babb, the manager of finance and accounting, and Jamie Stevens, the office manager. During the meeting he explained that, because of the size and rapid growth rate of Hydro Clean, it was imperative that they become more professional in their business decisions. He asserted that important management decisions were typically based on personal opinion and a concern for immediate profit, instead of on a market oriented basis. The company was considering the purchase of more equipment, but with the presently declining equipment utilization ratio, it was becoming increasingly difficult to decide for which of the company's three services more equipment should be bought. With decisions such as this to be made, and with the increasing number of tasks involved in the marketing function, Mr. Burke announced that it was time to open a position for marketing manager at Hydro Clean. This person was to be responsible for formulating and implementing marketing programs, and for managing the sales force.

One month later, the spot was filled by Mr. Johnson, an industrial marketing manager who had previously worked for FMC, Inc. in the Chemical Division. Mr. Johnson was quite familiar with industrial cleaning companies since they frequently serviced FMC, and since he also handled most of the chemicals that are used by these service companies.

After working at Hydro Clean for a month and a half, Mr. Johnson had a good handle on the structure and operations of both the company and the industrial cleaning industry. Presently, he was preparing for an important meeting to be held in one week at which he was to advise the rest of the management team, including Mr. Burke, on future company direction. More specifically, he was to discuss which services Hydro Clean should emphasize, how to improve the equipment utilization ratio, and to make recommendations regarding new equipment requirements.

Case prepared by Michael H. Morris, James Platis, and Scott Wilson, Department of Marketing, University of Central Florida, Orlando, FL.

COMPANY AND SERVICES

In 1979, after working for C.H. Hiest, an industrial cleaning firm, the nineteen year old Robert Burke obtained a $20,000 loan from his parents. With the money the young Burke bought a used water blasting machine, and incorporated Hydro Clean in his hometown of Richmond, Virginia. That first year he grossed $40,000. Since then the company has enjoyed rapid growth and has steadily been adding people and equipment (see Figure 1). Today Hydro Clean has two water blasting units, three vacuum units, and one chemical circulating unit.

Hydro Clean's main services are high pressure water blasting, vacuum services, and chemical circulating. With these three services Hydro Clean is considered to be a full service company.

High Pressure Water Blasting:

Consists of using a jet of water having pressure up to 10,000 pounds per square inch to clean industrial equipment such as boilers, heat exchangers, tanks, and pipelines. Water blasting seems to be more well known among manufacturers than the other two services, and is usually the first service that a new customer will request. Hydro Clean has made many innovations with this service in terms of new techniques and complementary equipment. The machine required for this operation costs $30,000 and requires three operators. Customers are charged $93.47 per hour for this service.

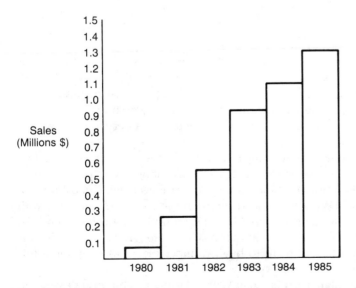

Figure 1 Hydro Clean's Growth

Vacuum Services:

Involves vacuuming large quantities of wet or dry industrial wastes or by-products. The vacuum unit costs approximately $50,000 and uses two operators. Customers pay $95.36 per hour including labor.

Chemical Circulating:

This service, which is not as well known as the other two, consists of circulating chemicals through the insides of industrial equipment in order to dissolve scale or other buildup. Except for set up, the operation cannot be seen, since all movement is enclosed within the machine and hoses going into and out of the equipment being cleaned. The machine for this service costs approximately $80,000 and requires two operators. Customers are charged $99.48 per hour including labor. Hydro Clean pays for all of its equipment on the basis of 2% of initial cost per month. Each piece of equipment for each service costs approximately the same to maintain and operate per hour, except for differences in the number of operators required.

The group of services that Hydro Clean provides is an integral part of the efficiency of many manufacturing plants. The technology for these services has been around for decades and was used to a limited extent by large corporations such as oil companies, who ran their own cleaning services. Only within the last 20 years has this technology been adapted by various firms, such as Hydro Clean, as a marketable service for increasing the efficiency of manufacturing plants. New applications are being found almost every day for all three services, and in turn, manufacturers are depending more and more on these service providers for reducing down time, replacing manpower, improving equipment productivity, extending equipment life, and many other efficiency measures.

CURRENT PERFORMANCE

Hydro Clean's 1985 sales were spread among its 3 services as follows: 37% water blasting, 48% vacuum services, and 15% chemical circulating for a total of $1.3 million. The total hours that each service was used throughout the year included 5,149 hours of water blasting, 6,543 hours of vacuum services, and 1,960 hours of chemical circulating. This averages out to six crews working five full days per week. However, a considerable amount of work was done on weekends.

Although Hydro Clean has known only sales growth in every year of operation, its equipment utilization ratio, measured in terms of operating hours per machine, fell in both 1983 and 1984. Burke considered this decrease acceptable, attributing it to the addition of a water blasting unit and vacuum unit in late 1982. But even with the addition of a second salesman, in mid 1985, the utilization ratio has increased only slightly. (See Table 1). With or without this problem, Burke recently was awarded two sizable contracts, and plans to buy two more pieces of equipment this year. He is still not sure for which services.

Vacuuming produces higher profits than water blasting or chemical circulating since it requires only two operators. It also is much easier to sell than chemical

Table 1a Equipment Utilization Rate

	1985			1984			1983		
	Total Hours	Units	Hours Per Unit	Total Hours	Units	Hours Per Unit	Total Hours	Units	Hours Per Unit
WATER BLASTING	5149	2	2574.5	4354	2	2177	3563	1	3563
VACUUM	6543	3	2181	5538	3	1846	4530	2	2265
CHEMICAL	1960	1	1960	1658	1	1658	1357	1	1357

Table 1b Equipment Capacity & Actual Usage, 1985

Hydro Clean Capacity	Total	Water Blasting	Vacuum Services	Chemical
100%	52,416	17,472	26,208	8,736
60%	31,452	10,484	15,726	5,242
40%	20,964	6,988	10,482	3,494
ACTUAL HOURS PER MACHINE		2,574.5	2,181	1,960
ACTUAL HOURS TOTAL		5,149	6,543	1,960

circulating, although not as easy as water blasting. In order to sell chemical circulating, salesmen usually have to push it aggressively while educating customers on its function and value. However, it is estimated that chemical circulating has up to 75% more market potential than vacuum services. At the same time, Burke does not want to lose ground in the vacuum services area to the new and aggressive Vacuum Services, Inc.

MARKET POTENTIAL

Hydro Clean estimates the current sales potential in its primary market area (the Richmond and Tidewater areas of Virginia) to be approximately $12 million. This includes an estimated $1.5 million from increasing service usage among existing customers, which can be taken advantage of by educating customers on industrial cleaning services and their numerous applications in different industries. Another $4 million of market potential is in untapped customers. These potential customers are very important to Hydro Clean and its competitors because once a cleaning service company attracts a customer, it is not that difficult for that company to maintain a relationship with the customer, regardless of how often they are serviced.

Table 2 Industry Composite

Industrial Cleaning Sales in Virginia by Service Type, 1985			
TOTAL SALES	WATER BLASTING	VACUUM	CHEMICAL
$6,550,000	$2,859,000	$2,496,000	$1,195,000

Hydro Clean also believes that large companies tend to account for a disproportionate share of sales potential.

The industrial cleaning industry has been growing rapidly over the past decade. Future market growth is expected to occur hand-in-hand with general industrial expansion. However, with the market not yet saturated, and with new innovations and applications being developed, the industry should grow much faster than the growth of manufacturing in general, at least for the rest of the decade. This is further supported by the fact that there are few substitutes and none foreseen in the future for any of the three major types of services offered by industrial cleaning companies.

THE CUSTOMER

The industry that Hydro Clean finds itself in is relatively young, and some or all of its services are new to many companies that could potentially use them. These companies do not realize all of the applications of Hydro Clean's services to their operations, or they do not know that these services exist. As a result, the salesman plays a large role in stimulating the demand for each service. Many times a customer will request one service, and during the job a salesman will suggest other beneficial services or applications of which the customer is unaware. This is especially true when a new customer requests water blasting, which is usually the first service requested. Eventually, as Hydro Clean and some of its more aggressive competitors attempt to educate potential customers about their services, industrial cleaning will be a standard among manufacturers.

The need for industrial cleaning usually starts in the manufacturing or power generation section of a company. Equipment common to these sections can malfunction, for example, from clogs or buildup of chemical or combustion wastes, which may call for an emergency action. Some companies have planned down periods for periodic cleaning. Company policy or government agencies, such as OSHA, may dictate cleaning certain equipment every so often. Also, salesmen may suggest ways in which a cleaning service could increase efficiency of equipment of which customers were unaware. Any of these examples may indicate to a potential or existing customer that there is a problem that calls for some type of cleaning service.

There are several sources that can be consulted in solving cleaning problems and determining which company or service to call upon. Customers can look in a phone book or industrial directory under industrial cleaning, tube cleaning, boiler cleaning, water blasting, vacuum services, chemical cleaning and other headings, depending upon their problem. They may learn of the service providers through ads in trade journals. If a similar problem has occurred before at the customer's plant or at another plant, then internal or external word of mouth may be very important for deciding both what it takes to solve the problem, (service, product, or technique), and which company they should use. Salesmen or previous mailouts from cleaning service companies may also be consulted. This information search may last from 10 minutes, or, if it is a very technical problem or if bids must be obtained for a continuous cleaning need, it may last up to a month.

Because of the diversity of industries that Hydro Clean serves, almost every job is different. Likewise, the time frame for each job varies. Although there is a 5 hour minimum charge, a job might last anywhere from 3 hours to around the clock for two months. This means that, unless the job is routine, a salesman must be sent in to see what is needed for each job, and to give the customer an estimate on the time and cost of the job. The salesman, if necessary, will go in with the crew and set the job up, and then check on the job while it is in progress, and again after it is completed. However, for routine jobs a crew can be sent in immediately when a customer calls.

Customers look for many qualities among service companies. Most of the larger customers prefer a full service company such as Hydro Clean. They find it easier to go through one company for all of their cleaning requirements, especially when two or more services need to be coordinated for one job, as is often the case. Also, emergencies can create enormous costs to customers. They require the 24 hour service which Hydro Clean and most other service companies provide. Other factors which are crucial during emergencies are ability to get in contact with a service company, promptness on the job, efficient workers, and minimal downtime. For some jobs, it may be more important to have knowledge of the customer's company and manufacturing processes in order to advise them on their problems.

THE SALES FORCE

Hydro Clean's two salesmen play a large communications role between the company and its customers. They fulfill a variety of functions and are viewed by customers as a representation of company quality. They advise customers on different techniques and applications of their services. After making estimates or bidding on jobs, they set the jobs up and check on them while they are in progress. Then comes follow up and checking with customers periodically for new business, as well as making calls on potential accounts. The two salespeople work quite well with each other, sometimes checking on jobs that the other has set up, or calling on the other's customers when he is busy. This can, however, have its drawbacks when the operators must explain the job to the second salesman, and he in turn to the customer. The salesmen visit customers by going down the list of present customers and talking over which customers they need to see that day. They then split the customers between themselves. An attempt is made to see each customer once a month unless they have done work with them recently, which is the case for most large customers. Calls are made on new customers at the end of the day if time permits. This method sometimes causes the salesmen to spend considerable time with small customers. Mr. Burke, to whom the salesmen formerly reported directly, had noticed that the salesmen were making friends with small company supervisors and socializing with them after work. This was good for customer relations, but did not produce much in the way of sales revenue.

After studying monthly sales data, Mr. Johnson, the new marketing manager, found that there was a trend for water blasting sales to be high during the beginning of the month and for most vacuuming and circulating to be done later in the month. Johnson noticed that early in the past month customers were waiting up to a week for water blasting services while the chemical circulator and a vacuum truck or two sat idle in the yard much of the time. Although there is almost always some waiting because emergency jobs have the first priority for equipment, this was usually minimal, and the equipment was traditionally used almost equally later in the month. Mr. Johnson found that water blasting was the easiest of the services to sell, and that Hydro Clean probably had the best quality among its competitors in water blasting. This is partially due to the many R & D innovations the company had adopted in this area. Johnson suspects that the trends in the sales of the different types of services over the course of a month may be due to the compensation plan for the salesmen, which is salary plus a monthly bonus for reaching a certain sales level. Johnson thinks that a fear of not reaching their sales quotas develops early in the month, leading salesmen to push water blasting, and then when they approach the quota in mid-month, they push the other services.

PRICING

Hydro Clean determines the price for each job separately. Also, each of the services has a different hourly rate. Quotations are based on predetermined hourly rates that are computed using a full cost system of pricing. The pricing process begins with an estimation of the time necessary to complete a particular job. This estimate is then used to quote a price to the individual customers. The prices are really ballpark figures, not firm quotes, due the variability of the time it actually takes to complete a job. Hourly charges are based on the costs listed in Table 3.

The variable costs other than labor are based on historical estimates of fuel consumption and equipment usage. Total overhead is allocated to the three services based on their respective percentage of total sales in the preceding year. The total overhead allocated to a given service is then divided by the estimated number of hours the machine will be operated during the coming year. The result is an hourly overhead charge for each service. The machine cost represents an amount equal to 2 percent of the original cost of Hydro Clean's equipment. So, 24 percent of the original cost of the equipment is allocated annually. This is divided by estimated machine hours used per year to arrive at an hourly charge. The markups are somewhat arbitrary, and can be reduced when Hydro Clean is especially anxious to get a particular account.

COMPETITION

Hydro Clean has four major competitors in the Virginia area. Table 4 includes estimated sales and market share data for each competitor.

Table 3 Cost and Price Data

	Water Blasting	Vacuum	Chemical
Fuel	$ 4.66	$ 4.58	$ 4.54
Equipment (maintenance)	12.04	11.91	11.73
Labor Cost	15.20	15.20	15.20
(required men per hr per machine)	(3)	(2)	(2)
Total Labor	45.60	30.40	30.40
Total V.C.	62.30	46.89	46.97
O/H	7.00	7.18	7.50
Machine Cost	2.80	5.50	9.80
Total F.C.	9.84	12.68	17.30
Total Cost	$81.94	$72.75	$81.57
Mark-up (profit)	$11.53	$22.61	$17.91
Total Charges (per hour)	$93.47	$95.36	$99.48

Halliburton and Powell are two sizable companies that operate in a diversity of industrial businesses, most of which are chemical related. BFI is a large waste disposal company. Industrial cleaning is a relatively small part of the business of each of these industrial giants.

Mr. Johnson sat in his office pondering how he was going to advise Hydro Clean at next week's meeting. He noted that the company's past growth performance had been superlative, and that it continued to do very well in the industry. But he was also well aware of Mr. Burke's high ambitions to be the biggest and the best in his market. His job was to find the best possible mix of the company's resources in order to achieve these ambitions.

Table 4 1985 Sales and Market Share by Competitor

Competitor	Market Share	Market Sales	Total Company Sales
Halliburton	27%	$1.75 mil.	over $6 billion
BFI	23%	1.5	over $3 billion
Vacuum Services, Inc.	12%	.8	$12 million
Powell	17%	1.2	over $1 billion
Hydro Clean	20%	1.3	$1.3 million
TOTAL	100%	$6.55	

Table 5   Income Statements by Service, 1983–1985

WATER BLASTING	1985	1984	1983
Sales	$ 481,000	$ 407,000	$333,000
Operating Costs	374,880	304,646	231,453
Profits	$ 106,120	$ 102,354	$101,547
VACUUM	1985	1984	1983
Sales	$ 624,000	$ 528,000	$432,000
Operating Costs	389,982	316,800	254,793
Profits	$ 234,018	$ 211,200	$177,207
CHEMICAL	1985	1984	1983
Sales	$ 195,000	$ 165,000	$135,000
Operating Costs	125,075	122,154	122,154
Profits	$ 69,925	$ 42,846	$ 12,846
CONSOLIDATED	1985	1984	1983
Sales	$1,300,000	$1,100,000	$900,000
Operating Costs	889,937	743,600	608,400
Profits	$ 410,063	$ 356,400	$291,600

Table 6   Hydro Clean Sales Relative to Industry Sales and Market Potential

	Total	Water Blasting	Vacuum	Chemical
INDUSTRY SALES ($)	$ 6,550,000	$2,859,000	$2,496,000	$1,195,000
HYDRO CLEAN SALES	$ 1,300,000	$ 481,000	$ 624,000	$ 195,000
MARKET SHARE	.198	.168	.25	.163
INDUSTRY HOURS		30,607	26,175	19,602
HYDRO CLEAN HOURS		5,142	6,543	1,960
ANNUAL MARKET POTENTIAL				
TOTAL $	$12,000,000	$4,000,000	$4,600,000	$3,400,000
HOURS		42,000	49,000	34,000

Table 7 Consolidated Income Statement, 1985

	Total	Water Blasting	Vacuum	Chemical
Sales %	100	0.37	0.48	0.15
Sales $	$1,300,000	$481,000	$624,000	$195,000
Variable Costs:				
Labor	$ 497,249	$238,680	$198,900	$ 59,669
Equipment	162,538	61,765	78,018	22,755
Fuel	63,159	24,000	30,316	8,843
Total V.C.	722,946	324,445	307,234	91,267
Contribution				
before F.C. & O/H	$ 577,054	$156,555	$316,766	$103,733
Overhead				
Bonuses	$ 8,397			
FICA Exp.	19,145			
Unemployment	7,034			
Advertising	13,782			
Travel	5,490			
Misc. Exp.	43,543			
Total O/H	$ 97,391	$ 36,035	$ 46,748	$ 14,690
Contribution				
before F.C.	$ 479,663	$120,520	$270,018	$ 89,124
Fixed Costs				
Machine Costs	$ 69,600	$ 14,400	$ 36,000	$ 19,200
Total Contribution	$ 410,063	$106,120	$234,018	$ 69,924
% Contribution	0.315	0.221	0.375	0.359

DYONIX GREENTREE TECHNOLOGIES, INC.

Part A. Planning for the Diffusion of an Innovation

THE OPPORTUNITY

In December of 1983, Michael Dyment was considering the approach he and his partners would take to launch their Dataquote I computer product to the Lumber and Building Materials Retailing Industry. The product would be marketed through a yet to be formed company, Dyonix Greentree Technologies, Inc.

The Dataquote I was a system designed to generate computerized estimates of the materials required to construct a house and was expected to be primarily used in Lumber and Building Materials (LBM) stores. Before a house can be built, the builder, buyer or contractor must determine what materials are necessary to build it and what the cost of those materials will be. It is a time consuming and tedious job, but without an estimate the materials cannot be sold. Since a typical house requires $30,000 in materials, estimates are very important to the retailers of lumber and building materials (LBM).

The Dataquote was conceived as a computer software product that would generate an estimate in twenty minutes. The software would include a bill of materials program that would calculate the breakdown of the total cost for the customer and a complete detailed list of components by quantity, type and price book that contained stock code numbers, brief product descriptions and prices at cost, wholesale, contractor and retail levels. In addition, the software would provide various reports on sales performance, inventory items, suppliers and customers.

Michael Dyment knew the system would be of high utility to LBM dealers and could be integrated into a complete LBM retail computer system with little difficulty.

THE PARTNERS

Michael Dyment was an engineer who had considerable experience in new product development, particularly in the satellite navigation industry. He was very familiar with the development and testing procedures necessary for computer hardware and

---

Case prepared by Carey Mann and David Litvack, Department of Marketing, University of Ottawa, Ottawa, Ontario.

software applications. One of his partners, Eric Olafson, was president of a firm that developed and distributed software accounting packages. Olafson was an expert as well in the capabilities and functionality of the various microcomputer systems available in the computer hardware market. The final partner, Mort Sparber, was owner and president of a Canadian LBM merchandising distribution company called PEPI. Sparber was well versed in the marketing issues, techniques and practices in the LBM industry. Perhaps equally significant for the launch of the Dataquote I was Sparber's extensive network of personal and business contacts throughout the Canadian LBM industry. In fact, Sparber's interest in developing the Dataquote I had come from discussions that Sparber had with United Retailers, a Western Canadian buying group of over 600 Canadian LBM and hardware dealers. United was very interested in a quotation system but did not feel that the buying group had the internal skills to develop it. United was prepared, provided that the product specifications met its requirements, to endorse the system to their members and to support sales of it through their organizational mechanisms.

The three partners felt that they possessed the skills necessary to put together an effective organization to develop and market the Dataquote I and that an initial sale of the systems to Merchants members would greatly facilitate the launch of the enterprise.

THE LBM MARKET

Before the partners could determine their market strategy, they felt it was essential to learn all they could about both the LBM and microcomputer markets. So in September of 1983, Dyment hired Carey Mann, an M.B.A. student from the University of Ottawa. Mann was given a general mandate to research all facets of the market including market potential for the Dataquote, market characteristics, potential approaches for the product and the cost and time frame necessary to bring Dataquote from an idea to a salable product. His findings were compiled for analysis by the end of 1983.

The research indicated that there were approximately 6,000 retail establishments in 1983 that sold lumber and building materials in Canada. Over two thirds of these stores were part of a chain buying group or franchise arrangement at either a regional or a national level. Michael Dyment looked at the market research before him and realized that although he knew the technical requirements for the project, he and the others would need to familiarize themselves more with the market characteristics and demographics of the LBM market if this venture were to be successful. He flipped the page and read more of the report.

Excerpts from RESEARCH FOR LUMBERTECH: THE LBM PERSPECTIVE

Market Segmentation (Cont.)

By geography, the market is somewhat difficult to segment. Each province and each region of each province differs both in construction methods and in the favored materials used to build. These differences are reflected in the merchandising of the materials as well. In segmenting the market geographically these two factors as well as local life styles, climate and building codes have to be considered. Even chains that operate nationally will vary their approach to adjust

Exhibit 1   LBM Dealers in the Canadian Market

Province	Number of LBM Retailers by Province			% of Stores
	Building-Home Centers	Cash and Carry	Total	Canadian Mrkt
British Columbia	327	67	394	9.1
Alberta	336	33	369	8.5
Saskatchewan	388	30	418	9.7
Manitoba	409	31	440	10.2
Ontario	1,451	152	1,603	37.0
Quebec	507	89	596	13.9
Nova Scotia	153	25	178	4.1
New Brunswick	153	15	168	3.9
Newfoundland	114	3	117	2.7
Prince Edwards Is.	39	—	39	0.9
Yukon	2	—	2	0.0
	3,879	445	4,324	

Note: There are approximately 1,500 to 2,000 Canadian independents not included in this chart.

to local market conditions. The ability to adapt to local market conditions allows many independent operators to compete quite effectively with the larger chains. The LBM industry is a very personable business and many LBM managers get to know their customers quite well. While the central buying of large chains may be somewhat of a disadvantage to an independent, an intimate knowledge of these customers and suppliers can help to offset it. Most independents, however, are members or affiliates of buying groups. These buying groups buy centrally and provide some of the same cost advantages to the members as do the chains.

Not all LBM stores concentrate solely on heavy building materials. The types of peripheral goods sold range from such building accessories as windows and window frames to home decorating items such as lighting fixtures. The exact mix of goods offered depends primarily on the served customer segments. There are several distinct types of customers: developers, contractors, renovators, do it yourselfers (DIYers) and home decorators.

Developers concentrate on large projects such as housing developments and tend to purchase their materials on a bulk basis to take advantage of volume discounts. Contractors primarily concentrate on smaller projects such as small buildings and houses. They buy for each project and unlike the developers are often unable to coordinate their purchases to favorable periods in the building materials commodity price cycle.

The renovators are either contractors or DIYers and tend to buy small amounts of several types of building materials and finish products such as paneling, flooring and bathroom fixtures. The DIYers will do small repairs right through to major renovations, in addition to buying various types of plumbing supplies and home decorating items.

The home decorator is primarily interested in items that cosmetically upgrade the living environment. He will purchase a wide variety of items such as paints, hardware, lighting and bathroom fixtures, and lawn and garden supplies.

The segment of the market that an LBM retail operation serves allows for some broad categorization along three types of LBM outlets; 1) Cash and Carry; 2) Building Centers; and 3) Home Centers.

Cash and Carry Outlets

The cash and carry outlets vary in approach but primarily sell only lumber and selected building materials such as steel, brick or concrete. Some will sell only to developers and contractors and will shy away from the market. These operators are more price than service oriented and therefore prefer not to deal in smaller orders. Moreover, when they deal in heavier building materials such as lumber or concrete, their target market for these items would be developers and contractors and not DIYers.

Most cash and carry outlets will orient their operations to a broader spectrum of buyers and will pursue the renovation—DIY market as well as the contractors. When a request for quotation is placed by a customer for building materials, these operations will provide some type of estimation service to their customers. However, the speed and quality of the estimation will vary greatly depending on the size of the potential order and the service policy of the retailer. Many cash and carry outlets are local independents and will sometimes be reluctant to provide an estimation service because of a fear that the client may use the materials breakdown to price shop elsewhere. A quotation for an average house can take anywhere from four to eight hours for a retailer to complete, depending on the detail and the speed the customer requires in the quotation to make his purchase decision.

Building Centers

The building center is really an upgraded cash and carry outlet, an outgrowth from the "lumber yard" into a more service oriented operation that offers a wider variety of complementary products to the basic LBM. These operations are located on the fringe of urban markets or in rural settings. They tend to have a limited amount of display space of 5,000–10,000 square feet and rely on small contractors, tradesmen and commercial accounts for 50% of their volume. They also depend upon the DIY and renovation market. A good portion of their business base is in housing starts and local economic conditions greatly influence results.

The building center is more service oriented but again the degree of service depends on the outlet. Some are reluctant to provide estimating services free of charge. It is fairly common to charge a nominal fee of around $50 and to refund this fee should the sale be finalized. Others offer estimating services free of charge but sometimes do a general estimate and follow that up with a detailed estimate once a sale is imminent. The full service building center will often offer up to twenty standard house designs from which the consumer can choose, in addition to providing a custom estimating service.

Home Centers

In most markets, retailing evolves from a strict exchange of unprocessed goods into a broad exchange of processed goods and specialized services. In the LBM market, then, the cash and carry outlets best typify an exchange of unprocessed goods, lumber and basic building materials. The building center exemplifies the next stage of the process where in addition to LBM, a good quality of service and an assortment of up to 15,000 items is provided. The home center completes the cycle. It offers far more extensive service, more elaborate packaging, many times the amount of product lines and a much more relaxed shopping environment than do either of its predecessors. Yet because this marketing effort requires higher margins on each item, an umbrella market is created for the building center and the cash and carry outlet which competes less on service and more on price.

The home center does 75% of its sales with DIYers and will usually have annual sales greater than $750,000. It will sell LBM as well as a wide assortment of products in hardware, electrical ware, plumbing supplies, flooring, tools, lawn and garden supplies and home decorating items. Home centers do not always serve the housing market directly with basic building materials. Some stores prefer to sell to the DIY and renovation market rather than the house builders and therefore do not provide elaborate quotation services for housing. However, most will sell the materials to a house builder when requested to do so. Some home centers offer a quotation service as an integral part of their market effort and often have several basic in-house designs as well as custom estimating.

One chain, the Beaver Lumber Company Ltd., exemplifies the diversified approach necessary to serve the LBM market. Beaver operates 143 cash and carry and building centers, 42 home centers and 30 affiliated stores under different names. Of the Beaver stores 8% are franchised, 33% are joint ventures and 59% are company owned.

MANAGEMENT STYLE IN THE LBM INDUSTRY

Management style in the LBM retailing industry naturally varies a great deal from firm to firm. All stock in commodity lumber and building materials are sold at current market rates regardless of the price that was paid to the supplier. Therefore, an inventory bought at high prices will be sold for a loss if the price drops. Managers buy heavily on low points in the price cycle and low on the high points. They find the best prices they can and stay in constant touch with their various suppliers. It is much like playing a commodities market. The larger chains, or home centers, carry less LBM and more items in hardware, home decorating, that need to be constantly monitored as do LBM goods. And although these items may not offer the same volume potential as LBM goods, their margins may be substantially higher.

The volatility of LBM prices is reflected in consumer buying habits. Price shopping by customers for large orders is common and some managers are therefore reluctant to provide detailed estimates to prospective home buyers. Some contractors and developers generate their own estimate and simply present a bill of materials to the LBM retailer. The consumer requires an estimate.

Most manual estimators follow the same procedure: the plans are reviewed for building details; the retailer establishes when the quote is needed; potential problem areas are identified; and finally an itemized quotation is developed, and presented to the consumer. As described earlier, the level of detail required and the restrictions on the time of employees who do the estimates can result in a quotation lead time of from one hour to over one day. Some managers treat quotations as peripheral to the sale and generally ignore the potential of the service as a marketing tool.

Generally, the use of control systems for management is much more prevalent in the consumer oriented, home-center chains. Monitoring of suppliers, accounts receivable, inventories and customers is common, but it is still largely done manually. Some chains have centralized computer services for their stores for generalized accounting along with some sales analysis. However, few chains or independents have installed computerized cash register systems or use computers for day to day in-store record keeping and sales analysis. Therefore, both the efficiency and the effectiveness of the control systems suffer. Some stores carry 30,000 items and track inventory manually. Obviously, a computer could do much to improve the inventory control of such an operation.

Dyment felt the market research was beginning to give him the feel for the LBM market that he and his partners would need to make a decision on how to market the Dataquote I.

THE COMPUTER INDUSTRY IN THE 1980s

In the 1950s and 1960s a computer was thought of as a wonderful thing—a weird but wonderful thing. The machines were huge, their operation complex. With the sixties began the spread of first transistor and ultimately integrated circuit technology. These new developments began to free the computer from its cumbersome beginning and allow the construction of much smaller and infinitely more powerful machines. The electronic calculator of the mid 1970s would have filled a large room with the tube technology of the 1950s. In addition to larger more powerful data processors, an umbrella market emerged for a smaller yet very functional processor, called the minicomputer, a computer in fact that went beyond the processing capability of its "mainframe" predecessors.

By the middle 1970s the minicomputer was established as the ideal computer to use in large inventory and accounting systems (more than 5000 items in inventory and more than 500 accounts in the Chart of Accounts). However, as new integrated circuits were introduced and better chip technology produced, the microcomputer began to emerge in certain applications as the replacement for the minicomputer in the same way that the mini had earlier displaced the mainframe. The general movement in processing power was upward, in fact, in every category of computer. In 1983, minicomputers ranged in cost from as low as $50,000 to as high as $250,000, depending on the supplier and the configuration. Software often had to be purchased separate from the hardware and could run into the tens of thousands of dollars, depending on the degree of customization necessary to integrate the software into the user's application.

Microcomputers on the other hand were much less expensive. Depending on the brand, in 1983 a 64K microcomputer with two drives could be bought for under $5,000. To outfit such a computer with business oriented word processing and basic inventory and accounting packages would require an additional investment of $2,000 to $4,000.

The king of the personal computer market in 1983 was without a doubt International Business Machines. After entering relatively late into the market in 1981, by mid-1983 IBM had already taken nearly 25% of the personal computer market with cumulative sales of close to 400,000 units. IBM had set standards for the PC market that had resulted in an outgrowth of IBM compatibility computer products. Hundreds of companies, from giants to startups, were churning out products that looked like, worked with, or plugged into the IBM desktop PC. Some of these PC-copycat computer makers had grown up almost overnight. Columbia Data Products Inc. had shot from $9 million in 1982 sales to an estimated $50 million for 1983, while Compaq Computer Corporation, which had zero sales in 1982 was expected to reach an astounding $100 million of sales in its first year of production in 1983.

In 1983 IBM was expected to build more than 600,000 PCs and even so would have to allocate the machines to PC-hungry dealers. The PC compatible models were selling so well as a result of the shortage of IBM PCs that industry analysts predicted that in five years this market would hit nearly $8 billion. Robert Harp, president of Corona Data Systems, said "We are struggling to get production up. The market is a bottomless pit."

Olafson was convinced that IBM compatibility would be the major market determinant in the microcomputing business. The cornerstone for the PC-compatible market was laid by IBM itself in 1981. IBM astounded everyone by publishing the PC's technical specifications, showing how the machine was built and how it was operated. This move allowed other manufacturers to write applications software based on the IBM operating system, MS-DOS. Before IBM entered the market, software and peripherals of one brand of computer rarely worked on another. Now, by allowing MS-DOS adaptations by other manufacturers, IBM began to create a standard technology in the business microcomputer market.

The price of a microcomputer began to drop substantially in 1983 and Olafson saw that as technological improvements occurred the gap between price and cost would continue to narrow. This trend would reduce the initial high margins and reduce the price flexibility of the smaller producers. It was thus clear that when dominant producers began to be affected by the competition, they would lower prices and a shakeout would begin. While the stronger IBM copycats like Corona and Compaq would be expected to survive, many of the marginal producers would not. Olafson felt that a better OEM deal could be arranged with a copycat producer than with an established computer company. He knew that IBM had both very high standards and fairly rigid terms for any firm that directly marketed its PCs. Even so, IBM strongly supported any firm that remarketed their personal computer products.

CHANGES IN THE COMPUTER SOFTWARE INDUSTRY

Eric Olafson knew only too well how dynamic the computer software market was in 1983. Recent advances in software technology and increased consumer demand gradually had shifted the industry into a new generation of micro programs, or software programs, that were considerably more powerful, reliable and easier to use than their predecessors. These new programs opened up the world of business and personal computing to many people who had thus far resisted computers because of the perceived unfriendliness of much of the early technology.

Initially the legions of companies that sprang up to write software for microcomputers divided neatly into two camps. So-called systems software companies supplied the basic programs that enabled the computer and its associated memories and terminals to work together. The second type of company wrote the applications programs that permitted computers to carry out specific tasks such as turning out a payroll or controlling an inventory.

Not only was software being used for many more tasks, it was increasingly being made easier to use. Software developed for the microcomputer was designed for the computer illiterate, so that users would need only a very rudimentary knowledge of computers to use micro based software.

EXISTING APPROACHES IN THE LBM COMPUTER SYSTEMS MARKET

Mann knew that the competition in the LBM computer system market was not substantial even though a huge number of firms could potentially enter the market. The existing dealers in software and hardware were numerous and included such large companies as NCR, Sperry and IBM as well as a host of smaller producers and software manufacturers. Very few of these companies had penetrated the large scale LBM retail environment to any large extent. Most of the present firms took a shotgun approach and designed general systems to be sold to many different types of large retail stores and warehouse operations.

No approach to computerization could be seen as a standard in the early 1980s. One method was to buy a system that seemed to fit one's requirements well enough, and then to modify the software and hardware which usually ran in the $125,000 to $250,000 range before modification or custom work, which could cost an additional $25,000 to $50,000 depending on the magnitude of the job. The second approach was to begin from scratch and design totally customized software to run on the chosen hardware system. A system could then be designed that precisely met the requirements of the end user. However, the time to design and write a typical inventory and accounting system for mid-sized and larger retail operations could run as long as 18 months. Obviously, the cost of such custom systems was much higher. As a general rule, the cost for a custom software system was double that of a canned or established generic system.

There was only one manufacturer in the 1983 Canadian market that offered systems specifically for LBM dealers although some firms did offer generic accounting and inventory packages to markets that spanned the LBM industry.

The one company that did specialize in computer systems for Canadian LBM dealers was LISCO of Belleville, Ontario. LISCO was a distributor for an American producer of LBM oriented computer systems called Dataline Inc. Its primary system was called the Dataline 2000 and retailed for over $200,000. It was offered on a modular basis and was primarily an accounting-inventory based system. The system had not yet been extensively marketed in Canada, nor did it appear that LISCO had the capability of achieving any significant rate of market penetration.

There were few Canadian companies specializing in the Lumber and Building Materials market. One firm, Rexon, was fairly successful in eastern Canada, particularly in Quebec. Rexon sold a variety of minicomputer processors and terminals and sold software in accounting, inventory and word processing applications. The only other distinctively Canadian LBM computer firm was Systemhouse of Ottawa, Ontario. Systemhouse had a variety of software products for many industries in addition to the LBM industry and also spent considerable time on custom software development. In fact, the LBM computer system that Systemhouse had developed was an outgrowth of custom work done for Orleans Building Supply of Orleans, Quebec. The system was minicomputer based and sold for more than $200,000 before installation and customization fees. Since Systemhouse had products and projects in many other markets, it was unclear how concentrated their effort would be in the LBM industry. Compounding matters for Systemhouse was the poor overall performance of the corporation in its 1982 and 1983 fiscal years.

Unlike the Canadian market there were several dedicated LBM computer companies in the United States. STC Systems, AID in Management and Triad were three of Dataline's main American competitors. Triad was, in fact, Dataline's toughest U.S. competitor, offering minicomputer based systems that sold in the $100,000 to $200,000 range, before installation and customization. Often their installations were elaborate and required custom software.

Dataline was the only firm in the market to offer an estimating product. Their "Estimatic" came complete with a sonic digitizer, a forerunner of the more advanced electronic digitizers that had begun to be used extensively in CAD applications. The sonic digitizer comprised two sonic arms in an L-frame that through tiny electrodes sent sonic signals intersecting across a plane. When a special pen or electrode broke the sonic signal, the digitizer was able to sense precisely where the sonic intersection of signals was broken. In this way, by touching the corners or points on a drawing with a special pen, the data necessary to generate an estimate could be stripped off the blueprint. The points could then be referenced as Cartesian coordinates. After a scale was set to the drawing, the lengths and areas necessary to calculate an estimate could be retained and a full take-off with materials calculated. Although Dataline's product saved time theoretically, there were fundamental structural problems in the software that did not give it the flexibility to mass procure estimates. Dataline seemed quite content to offer it as a tag on to their existing minicomputer based systems, although it could operate as a stand alone system. Dataline offered the "Estimatic" with an IBM PC, a cabinet style furniture system and a sonic digitizer. A hard disk was optional as the system was really designed to utilize the storage capability of a minicomputer. Dataline marketed the system as is for $18,000 U.S.

THE MEETING

On January 21, 1984 Dyment, Sparber, Olafson and Mann met in Ottawa to finalize how they intended to develop and market Dataquote I. The following are excerpts from their conversation.

Dyment: "Well gentlemen, I think we can say that it's high time we finalize the planning and start the Dataquote development under way. I think it is obvious that we should incorporate a business to develop the system. No matter how hard we try or how thorough we attempt to be, there will eventually be problems we didn't, or even couldn't, anticipate. Right now though we need a facility for operations. I'd estimate $15 a year per square foot and we should have 250 square feet per person. We should be able to find a facility that would last us the first couple of years quite easily. It's mostly software design anyway, at least until we gear up the market. We'll need an administrative assistant, of course, and that will run about $14,000.

"Nobody should be able to match our quotations software unless they match our development program. We'll need a software analyst at about $40,000 and two programmers at about $18,000 on average. Benefits will run about 10% of salaries. The software should only take 8 months to one year to develop, since we already have functional software specifications. We should retain the consulting firm we have hired to ease us into the software development program. They'll cost us $250 per day and I estimate we'll need them full time for four months and then one day a week after that."

Olafson: "I know the development part is a real headache—don't get me wrong—but it really is only the tip of the iceberg. We still have to decide on the hardware and who knows what else. I figure we can put together the necessary hardware at reasonable prices, but we still haven't decided on a distribution strategy. We do have several options and it'll all depend on whether we sell hardware with our software or just the software.

"We can always sell our software through a software house or distributor. Most of the software houses have a lot of clout in the market and can place our packages with the right retailers of software and hardware products. Typically we might expect 30% margin on a package such as ours. But the software industry is promotion intensive and I really think we need to support our package to our end users with the right kind of promotion or advertising program. If we didn't, these software houses won't even touch us.

"Another way is to place the package with one of the major software houses like MicroSoft. They develop their own packages but they also acquire a great many packages from inventive developers who just don't have the marketing expertise or the capital to market them themselves. We could sell it outright or obtain a royalty, maybe about 10%. For that matter, we could also sell it to one of the LBM computer companies, too.

"Another possibility is to take it straight to market, directly sell it to the LBM dealers. If we do that, though, we'll need a sales force of some type, whether it's a distribution company or our own people. 5% commission is about the going rate in the computer industry, in addition to a base salary of about $25,000. I guess we'd need to provide the hardware and some degree of installation and training support if we go the direct route."

Sparber: "Forty years a cowboy and never rode a horse. What you guys have to understand is that we're not selling computer products, we're selling a way of doing business. Estimates are part of their bread and butter. And these guys won't be impressed by fancy machines, not unless they do exactly what you say they will do. And our product won't run unless these guys know how to run the computers.

"And you guys seem to be throwing quite a lot of money around. We've got the software development well taken care of but I think we had better get organized on the marketing end of things before we break the bank. From some industry surveys that I've seen, less than 10% of all LBM dealers are presently using a computer. It almost seems from my experience that every LBM dealer that does have a computer has a different make and uses it in different ways. A lot of the users don't really understand the systems they've installed."

Mann: "Exactly. These devices work off of any computer and would work fine off a microcomputer. One thing we haven't discussed is future products. We know we're thinking of accounting because of the natural linkage between Dataquote and an inventory system. But if we ever decide to get into the design end of the housing market, these are the computer tools to do it. There are several digitizers we could recommend to our customers or if we choose to provide equipment, at 100 level pricing we can get about a 40% area that would be 36″ × 24″, although the tablet is actually 42″ × 30″ total physical size.

"If we sell a digitizer we might seriously look at housing it in computer workstation furniture. Otherwise, there will be cables and machinery all over the place. The proper way to use the digitizer would be by embedding it in a tilt table. The tablet can be read through as much as one inch of a non-metallic surface. We could purchase such a table at a cost of $650 and outfit a computer terminal table, arrange a piece to join the two components and a three drawer cabinet for an additional $600. A decent tilt and height adjustable chair can be purchased at about $200. Not only would the furniture enable us to use the equipment properly, but it would allow for the management of the cables as well."

Dyment: "If we do supply the equipment and the installation and training for it, we'll need to have people to do it. Eric, you've told me that such installations with training would take anywhere from three to five days to complete per site. And a qualified technician training type person would run us about $20,000.

"I think our overhead will run about $5,000 per month on top of rent in the beginning and should stabilize at about $10,000 six months from now. As members of the management team, I think our salaries would average out to about $40,000. I would think that in the next two years we won't grow beyond a management team of six, one of whom will be the system analyst mentioned earlier. But we'll need the three additional persons within the next nine months. We'll also need two marketing researchers on staff; that will be about $2,000 a month in legal and accounting fees.

"We've been able to raise $400,000 thus far, but I'm not sure how far that will take us out on our development program. We will have about $25,000 in prototype expenses and to keep the development team working. We can lease three microcomputers with printers at about $375 each a month and we'll also have about $1,000 per month in travelling expenses. I only hope that we have the kind of marketing dollars available to give the operation a proper market launch."

Mann: "The more I think about it, the more I feel that with the right approach we could be very successful in this market. The big players in the United States are really not that big at all. They concentrate on the $200,000 systems, but they can take 6 to 8 weeks to install, notwithstanding any additional custom work that may have to be done. Don't get me wrong, they do well as corporations—typical sales in the ten to forty million range—but they really don't take the market by storm. They really do have a maximum level of business they can handle. In Canada it's even more amazing. The market's been barely touched and even so, if we totalled the top players, including even the non LBM type companies, no one would have more than 5% of the computer sales in the LBM business in any one year. And to top it all off, all anyone offers is accounting, inventory, and point of sale systems and some very basic job costing.

"No one offers total solutions, not mass marketable ones anyway. We've got a new product, an innovative one too. There's no obvious way to approach the market, but we really have a foot in the door with this product."

Olafson: "I know what you're saying, but don't forget that those people are all using minicomputers for their systems. Micros are getting more and more powerful and from the rumors I hear, the market's close to introducing better ways of networking microcomputers. IBM apparently has a microcomputer coming out that will act as a central processor, and very effectively, for four or five PCs. It has less processing power than minicomputers, but we know it's the same idea. And instead of dumb terminals, each PC has its own processing power. Given the hard disk storage required, we could put together such a network for less than $35,000. We could even throw in a few cashboxes hooked up to the PCs."

Sparber: "You guys are giving me a mental hernia. Let's concentrate on Dataquote before you make me crazy. As I understand it then, the development of the software should take about six months before we begin to really refine the product. I guess that the best way would be to put the development . . . at the right stage smack into an LBM operation. I can arrange one in Winnipeg but we'll have to get the guys out for about three weeks and put them up at a hotel. As we gear up for the market we'll have to pull out the stops in the marketing end of things and that will cost as well. But we do have some time before the software is ready and that will give us the time to decide exactly how to approach the market.

"We've got many things to decide. Distribution, marketing approach, future products and I guess we also have to nail down exactly what the Dataquote should be. The software is the only part of the product we've decided on but what part of the product mix can we attribute to service, training, installation, or hardware for that matter. Or would we be better off seeking less costly means of distribution? We had better decide soon because that $400,000 won't last very long."

Dyment: "I think the task is pretty clear. We know the expenses we have to have to develop the Dataquote software. We'll have to see how far that will take us. Beyond that, the remaining money will go to marketing product development, or something along those lines, it all depends what strategy we pursue. We have to determine the best way to bring Dataquote to the market. I guess that depends on how we distribute the product. Whatever route we take will affect our budget and influence our future plans. So gentlemen, let's formulate a strategy to make Dataquote and Greentree a success and develop the financial plan to get us on our way!"

SEXTON ENERGY SYSTEMS DIVISION

Sexton Energy Systems Division (SES) is a division of a multinational conglomerate headquartered in New England. Its 3,000 employees are involved in designing, manufacturing and selling a wide variety of products related to energy technology: energy conversion systems, renewable energy systems, environmental control products and automotive emission detection equipment. One of the energy conversion systems to have been developed by SES is the Cattle Waste Processing System, which converts cattle manure to methane (a fuel gas) and a high-protein ingredient for cattle feed. Over the past decade, SES engineers and other key personnel have developed the technology, tested and improved the quality of the process outputs, and conducted extensive programs and other activities designed to evaluate market potential and process feasibility. SES was now charged with the task of deciding whether it would be advisable to market this product.

THE CATTLE WASTE PROCESSING SYSTEM

Three serious problems which plague cattle feedlot operators are:

—rising feed costs, especially high-protein feed;

—increasing price and scarcity of energy;

—pollution problems caused by cattle manure.

SES's Cattle Waste Processing System was designed to help the feedlot operator circumvent all three problems. The system is based on the process of anaerobic fermentation, as depicted in simplified form in Figure 1. The process is similar to that which occurs in the cow's digestive system. Conditions in the system allow for the growth of anaerobic micro-organisms through the process of fermentation. Three outputs are obtained from the micro-organism mass via a process known as "harvesting": methane (fuel gas), a high protein feed ingredient called HPFI, and carbon dioxide. The methane is used to supply energy to the farm and feedlot or

---

1985 C. Anthony di Benedetto, Department of Marketing, University of Kentucky, Lexington, Kentucky, USA 40506

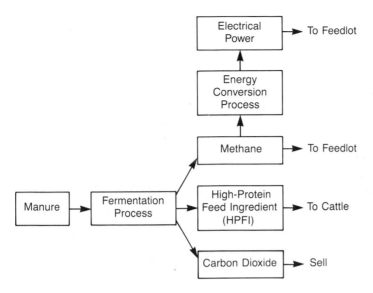

Figure 1   The Anaerobic Fermentation Process

converted to heat and power and used to drive the processing system. The HPFI may be used by the feedlot operator, in place of other high-protein ingredients in the cattle feed, or as fertilizer. HPFI contains about 60% of the protein content of an equivalent volume of cottonseed meal, while the methane produced contains about 600 British Thermal Units of energy (BTU) per cubic foot.

SES was the first company to investigate seriously the anaerobic fermentation process as applied to cattle waste conversion, commencing research about ten years ago. Since that time, about one million dollars has been invested in research and development, with some of this funding being obtained from Government sponsors. Highlights in the development of the process include the following:

—Development of the On-location Waste Conversion System, in which all process equipment and facilities were mobile (a converted tank truck and a house trailer were used). The On-location System treated small quantities of manure under realistic "field" conditions, and showed that laboratory results could be reproduced on the farm quite successfully.

—Design of the Large-Herd Environmental Feedlot System, suitable for use on a feedlot consisting of 10,000 head of cattle. Over 300,000 cubic feet of methane and 10 tons of HPFI could be produced per day by this system with a minimum of labor (only one operator required) and capital input (cost of operation estimated at $300 per day).

—Design of the Anaerobic Fuel and Feed Production Pilot Plant, sponsored by the U.S. Department of Agriculture. This facility would allow SES to make improvements to the waste processing system in order to upgrade the nutrient value and weight-gain stimulating ability of the HPFI, and also to adapt the system to the conversion of sheep and swine manure.

ECONOMIC FEASIBILITY

The investor's decision to own a cattle waste processing system will be dependent upon its economic value; that is, whether it can produce a reasonable return on investment capital. This would in turn depend upon the predicted volume of methane and HPFI produced, and the likely selling prices of these outputs (the third process output, carbon dioxide, would by comparison only generate a small amount of revenue).

Company figures (see Table 1) would seem to indicate that the economic value of the processing system is quite high: an 8,000-head system, for example, would produce 99,250 cubic feet of methane; at an average price of $1.60 per thousand cubic feet, this represents a value of $158,800 per year. The system would also produce 3,150 tons of HPFI, containing 60% of the protein of cottonseed meal. Since the latter sells for $190 per ton, the value of the HPFI (if sold as a cottonseed meal substitute) may be estimated at $190 times 60%, or $114 per ton; thus the system output would be worth a total of $359,100. Subtracting annual operating costs of $88,200 leaves an annual net income before interest and taxes of $429,700. Such a system would require an investment of $1,300.000.

In general, the larger the system size, the shorter the payback period (as is the case for most large farm investments of this type). The company estimates that the payback period for the waste processing system is approximately two to four years.

The economic feasibility of the process has also been studied by an independent marketing consulting firm. They are somewhat less optimistic about the sales potential for the processing system for a number of reasons.

Table 1 Economic Feasibility of System, Based on Company Figures

Head of Cattle	4,000	8,000	10,000	20,000
Annual Production of Methane (in thousands of cubic feet)	49,625	99,250	124,375	255,938
Annual Value of Methane ($)	79,400	158,800	199,000	409,500
Annual Production of HPFI (in tons)	1,580.7	3,150.0	3,868.4	7,736.8
Annual Value of HPFI ($)	180,200	359,100	441,000	882,000
Total Annual Value ($)	259,600	519,900	640,000	1,291,500
Minus Annual Operating Costs ($)	63,000	88,200	100,800	182,700
Annual Net Income before Interest, Tax, Depreciation and Insurance ($)	196,600	429,700	539,200	1,108,800
Installment Cost ($)	375,000	650,000	675,000	1,150,000

First, the cattle waste disposal problem is not as serious as it had been ten years ago when product research was first conducted. At that time, it was greatly feared by the feedlot operators that the Environmental Protection Agency would impose stiff legislation concerning the disposal of cattle waste. However, the regulations actually adopted by the EPA were not as harsh as had been anticipated, and most large feedlot operators had little difficulties complying with them. In fact, rather than being a liability, cattle waste has over the last two years emerged as an income source for many operators as it is profitably being sold as fertilizer. Since the processing system is a major cash investment for an operator (see Table 1), many might prefer to take the short-term profits accruing from the sale of fertilizer rather than make the long-term investment of capital.

A second point of concern was the expected volume of HPFI that would be generated by the process. Although the consultants agreed that the overall HPFI production volumes as reported in Table 1 were probably good estimates of the most likely volume, there was an approximately 10% probability that these volumes were overstated by 20%. They also believed there was a 10% chance that the volumes were understated by 20%. Nevertheless, they felt that the cautious feedlot operator ought to consider the possibility of lower-than-expected HPFI production.

A third and potentially very serious problem concerned the likelihood of approval of HPFI by the Food and Drug Administration as an ingredient in cattle feed. At the time, no FDA authorization existed for the sale of cattle waste in any form as an ingredient in feed. Recently the FDA has begun the procedure of establishing standards concerning the acceptability of HPFI; but difficulties have arisen in getting the standards finalized and published. Some of these difficulties have centered around the possible negative public perceptions of a system producing cattle feed from manure and the sanctioning thereof by the FDA. (Excerpts from the consulting report dealing with these issues appear in Appendix A.)

All would not be lost for the feedlot operator if he were not able to use or sell his HPFI as a feed ingredient, as it also can be used as fertilizer; however, the price he could get for HPFI as fertilizer would be only one-tenth the price he could obtain selling it as cattle feed (i.e., $11.40 per ton as opposed to $114.00 per ton). The consultants felt that, considering the economic conditions facing farmers, the approval for the sale of HPFI as cattle feed would probably go through eventually. Nevertheless, they estimated that there was a 10% chance that the feedlot operator who invested in a waste processing system would have no choice but to sell his HPFI at the drastically reduced fertilizer price. They also felt that there was a 10% probability that the market would bear a slightly higher price than expected ($125.40 per ton; that is, 10% higher than anticipated); but this was small compensation to the operator when compared to the downside risk.

Based on these factors, the consulting firm concluded that the potential market for the waste processing system was not as large as had been anticipated by SES. Interviews with feedlot operators and others in the industry did not reveal a high level of interest in the concept. This was partly due to the severe financial constraints being faced by the smaller, independent operators (many of whom had gone bankrupt or were on the verge of doing so). Too many independent operators were more concerned with short-term survival than with committing large sums of capital to this kind of system. Furthermore, operators were beginning to recognize the profit potential of selling unprocessed cattle waste as fertilizer. Thus, the independent operator was not a likely prospective customer; the recommendation the consultants made to SES was to concentrate its efforts on selling the processing system to larger operations: feedlot cooperatives or large agricultural companies, for example. This would reduce greatly the number of potential customers. The consultants suggested that the system would be economically feasible only for minimum 10,000-head feedlots; this represents about 150 sales opportunities in the U.S. If a system could be developed that was economically feasible for all feedlots with a minimum herd of 50 head, the potential market would increase to 100,000 operators.

Many other factors would influence the level of marketability of the waste processing system: among these, the most important are the cyclical nature of the domestic cattle market and the price of cattle feed.

THE DOMESTIC CATTLE MARKET

The United States raises about 10% of all the cattle in the world. Beef production is the agricultural activity which accounts for the greatest share of farm income (about one-fourth), utilizes the most land, creates the most market value, and accounts for the greatest consumption of feed.

Beef Supply and Demand:

As is typical in the agricultural industry, a small number of buyers dominate the demand side, while a large number of farmers and operators make up the supply side. Beef demand depends upon population size, its purchasing power, its tastes in food, prices of competitive products (pork, poultry, lamb, fish, etc.), and other factors. Beef export and import is comparatively insignificant. In the short run, demand is less likely to fluctuate than supply; thus market price of beef will depend to a large extent upon the supply of beef relative to other types of meat. However, a long-run trend toward greater per capita demand for beef is expected to continue.

Beef supply depends upon factors such as the size of the calf crop, the number of cattle feeding on grain, and the weight to which they are fed until slaughtered. The cost of feed and the condition of grazing land will have an important effect upon these factors. For example, when grazing conditions are good, the demand for range (grass) cattle increases and the supply of cattle feeding on grain (feeder cattle) diminishes. If a drought occurs in range areas, or in the Corn Belt which supplies the grain for feed, the grass cattle would be forced to market before being "finished" (fattened) on grain; thus beef prices would be depressed.

Cattle Consumption of Grain and Roughage:

Most calves are born around March or April, and weaned in September or October. The calf (weighing about 400 pounds) will be sent to a Southwestern range to graze for the winter, then is "summered" for about six months, perhaps in Nebraska. By this time it has gained over 300 pounds, and is ready to be sent to a feedlot to be "finished" on corn or other grain. The finishing period may last seven months, with the young steer gaining about two pounds a day. The steer might then be sent to Chicago, Kansas City or Omaha to be slaughtered and sold as a medium choice steer. Depending upon the region of the country, this basic pattern might vary.

The seasonal fluctuations in steer production cause variations in price levels of different grades of beef. The "fed" (fattened) cattle are more numerous in spring and summer; so during these months, "choice" and "prime" grade beef (the highest grades) are cheapest. Prices of "commercial" and "good" grade beef are at their lowest point in the fall when grass cattle (including stocker and feeder cattle which have not been fully fattened) are in greatest supply.

Up until the early 70s, about 70% of the cattle slaughtered for beef production were finished on feedlots, where they are fed rations containing high levels of grain. This proportion is now down to about 60%. The remaining cattle are sold at somewhat lower prices and marketed as "grass-fed," "forage-fed" or "baby" beef.

A feeder steer is only moved to a feedlot after it has been wintered and summered. Almost all of its feed intake prior to relocation to a feedlot consists of roughage. Furthermore, the feedlot ration is likely to contain only about 65% grain, with most of the remainder being roughage. Cattle, being ruminant animals, can digest roughage which man and other monogastric animals cannot. Because of this, they can convert roughage into food for humans. If not fed to cattle, most roughage (which produces millions of pounds of beef annually) would have to be discarded. Furthermore, much of the land used for producing roughage (grassland pasture, woodland, and cropland pasture) cannot be easily converted to grain-producing cropland. Almost 900 million acres of land unsuitable for grain production may thus be put to productive use as foraging region for cattle (see Table 2).

Even though a large proportion of the grain-fed cattle's ration is roughage, it is the grain-fed portion of the ration during the finishing period which is chiefly responsible for both the high quality and the high quantity of American beef. It is said that grain feeding "makes an excellent product out of a good one."

In recent times, however, shortages in feed supplies and increases in grain prices have caused a reduction in the amount of grain fed to cattle and subsequently a reduction in the percentage of cattle which are finished on feedlots. The proportion of grass-fed cattle in American beef production has been further increased by excess inventories of cattle in recent years. However, it should be noted that production of roughages and other inputs have also been rapidly increasing to the point where, for many producers, it costs as much (if not more) to produce grass-fed beef as grain-fed beef. Rising prices of both grain and roughages coupled with the excess inventories of cattle have forced cattlemen to sell beef at prices far below costs of production.

The Cattle Cycle:

Aside from the seasonal cycle mentioned earlier, a longer-term cycle also has great impact on cattle production: it is known as the cattle cycle.

The expansion phase of this cycle begins when beef producers believe beef prices will rise. They withhold their cows and heifer calves for use in herd expansion. Meanwhile, calves and steers are finished to an older age and therefore gain

Table 2 Uses of Land in the United States

Land Use	Number of Acres (millions)	
Cropland used for crops	333	
Soil improvement crops and idle cropland	51	
Cropland pasture	88	
Total cropland	472	472
Grassland pasture and range		604
Woodland grazed		198
Farmsteads, farm roads		9
Total agricultural land	1,283	1,283
Urban and other built-up areas	61	
Recreation and wildlife areas	81	
Public installations and facilities	27	
Forest land not grazed	425	
Other land	287	
Total nonagricultural land	981	981
Total land areas		2,264

much more weight. Continuing to finish these calves and steers rather than sending them to slaughter puts upward pressure on beef prices, which encourages still more withholding. Eventually, though, the point is reached when slaughter rate is forced to increase, since fully-finished steers must be marketed regardless of the stage of the cattle cycle. At this point, prices fall and the liquidation phase begins. Many feedlot operators may still be waiting vainly for higher prices and withholding their cattle. By the time they get their cows and calves to market, the prices have decreased even further and they may be lucky to recover their production costs. Finally, herds become so thin that beef is scarce and steer prices rise once again. Cows are once again withheld from market and another expansion phase begins. The entire cattle cycle usually lasts about ten years (although the duration has been decreasing in recent years), with the expansion phase typically being slow and liquidation rather rapid.

The last time the cattle cycle caused a difficult situation for the cattle-producing business (and the feedlot operators in particular) was during the mid-70s. Low grain prices, profits in the feedlot industry, and an increase in investment in feedlots from outside sources caused feeder cattle prices to increase sharply in 1972 and 1973. Primarily the large feedlots (1,000 head of cattle or larger) benefitted from these trends: they make up about 1% of all feedlots, yet increased their share of total feed cattle brought to market from 47% in 1968 to 65% in 1973. These trends caused expansion in herd size and further increases in feeder cattle prices.

However, by mid-1972, feed grain prices begain rising (partly due to increased grain exports reducing supply in the U.S.). Then in 1974, poor growing conditions reduced both grain and forage supplies, causing sharp increases in feed prices. Feedlot activity was substantially reduced and many investors who entered the industry during the late 60s pulled out, aggravating the situation. Additionally, the price of fattened cattle, though rising, could not match the inflated prices of feeder (not yet finished) cattle, causing many feedlot operators to face severe losses. All these factors combined forced operators to slaughter many cattle which had received little or no grain feeding, resulting in decreases in availability of grain-finished beef. The situation corrected itself in later years, with feeder cattle and grain prices returning to moderate levels.

Risk Taking and Responsibility:

Most feeder cattle are owned by farmers or feedlot operators. Because of rapidly rising feed and transportation prices, there has been a trend toward large, mechanized feedlots; benefits such as volume buying are achieved by lots of larger size. Many feedlots (especially those located in the West) are designed to produce "choice" grade beef; the "prime" grade (favored by top restaurants) is becoming scarce. The predominant source of feeder cattle is Texas, while Iowa and California have the best feedlots.

The feedlot operator assumes much of the risk of cattle production. He purchases calves or yearlings and therefore has the responsibility of finishing them to an appropriate weight, regardless of the flunctuations in feed prices or cattle herd sizes. He also faces costs of transportation, marketing, taxes, interest, insurance, veterinary services, and repairs, to name a few. He can reduce his risk somewhat by selling by "private treaty"; he sells his cattle a few months before being finished while making provision for a price adjustment depending upon the condition of the cattle at delivery time. Future trading is another alternative.

IMPACT OF GRAIN PRODUCTION

The preceding discussion illustrates the intimate relationship between beef cattle production and the production of corn, other grain, and roughages. The extent of this relationship is now examined.

Most of the corn produced in the United States is grown in the Corn Belt, which roughly encompasses the midwestern states. Almost 90% of the corn grown in the U.S. is fed to livestock or poultry; hence, the size of the livestock and poultry inventory determines to a great extent the demand for corn. The remainder of the corn is processed (into starch, sugar, syrup, corn oil, cereal, etc.), sold as is, or exported.

Corn makes up about one-fourth of feed concentrate supplies. During the mid-50s, acreage allotments caused reduced plantings of wheat and cotton, much farmland was converted to corn, and the amount of feed concentrate produced increased greatly. By 1963 production peaked, falling sharply in 1964 due to reduced acreage.

Since then, other feed concentrates (notably soybean meal) have increased in importance.

Most feed concentrate (made of corn, soybean meal, and other grains) is used to feed livestock. In the short run, the amount of feed concentrates utilized depends both on the number of animals fed and the amount fed to each animal. However, in the long run, the opposite causal direction takes precedence: that is, the amount of feed concentrate available determines the amount of livestock that can be raised. This is because, as production of feed concentrate increases, livestock producers adjust their inventories. This is called the primary shift in inventory size. Hog inventories, for example, can be adjusted rather quickly as feed concentrate supply increases. Cattle inventories take longer to adjust, especially downward; most cattle producers are reluctant to liquidate a costly breeding herd due to reduced feed concentrate supply. However, the primary shift in inventory size does eventually occur.

In the longer run, a secondary shift also occurs. As hog production increases, the price of hogs decreases, thus making it less profitable for the farmer to produce hogs. Hence, economic resources would be shifted from hogs to cattle and poultry. The net longer-term effect of an increase in food supplies, then, is a uniform increase in all livestock inventory.

Most recently, there have been upward trends in both the livestock inventory size and in the consumption per animal, resulting in increased demand for high-protein feeds. In addition to corn, production of soybean meal and cottonseed meal also increased in response to the increasing demand. Traditionally, soybean meal has been used as a high-protein feed for hogs and poultry, and cottonseed meal has been used for cows and beef cattle; but consumption of soybean meal by the latter has been increasing constantly in recent years. Other grains such as oats and barley make less satisfactory substitutes as they contain proportionately less proteins.

FUTURE TRENDS

As has been the case for some time, the type of beef produced, and the choice of cattle feed, will continue to depend upon the prevailing economic situation. For example, recent years have shown an increase in grain prices; hence the percentage of grain-fed cattle has been reduced.

The production of roughages from acreage not suitable for grain production is expected to increase, especially in light of recent technological advances in this area (e.g., the development of cattle feed from by-products of grain production such as corn stalks and straw). However, roughages cannot supplant grain as the chief fattening ingredient in cattle feed, nor can roughages produce alone the high-quality beef which can only be obtained from grain-fed cattle.

Some of the other current trends which are expected to carry on into the future include the following:
—Demand for high quality beef (requiring feedlot operations) will increase both in the U.S. and abroad.
—Manure prices will fluctuate, due to the increasing importance of its alternative use as a fertilizer.

—The average domestic feedlot size will continue to expand as the large operations continue to dominate the industry.

—The larger the feedlot, the more severe the problem of waste disposal becomes.

Perhaps an important factor to monitor in the future is the possibility that the Department of Agriculture may change the beef standards. Such changes would allow a shorter duration of time on the feedlot for a beef steer to be graded "choice" or "prime". The measure would be beneficial for the feedlot operators, currently in a profit squeeze, as it would lower their inventory costs of maintaining a steer on feed, without reducing the number of finished cattle delivered to market.

APPENDIX A

Excerpts from Market Study

High protein supplements have become increasingly sophisticated in recent years. Among the most common of these are soybean meal and cottonseed meal, each containing about 40–45% crude protein. HPFI has a protein content of about 25%, which is about twice the crude protein content of raw manure. Basic food ingredients such as corn have a far lower crude protein content (about 8%); thus the HPFI produced by the waste processing system could be used as a satisfactory food supplement from a strict protein-content point of view.

For some years now, feedlot operators have added composted manure to the feed ration of their cattle, up to concentrations of about 10%. Given that the crude protein content of unprocessed manure is about 12%, it is clear that operators have seen the economic benefits of using this basically free protein source. They also report that there are no negative effects due to the practice, and that the animals appear to assimilate feed containing manure quite well.

The Food and Drug Administration knows of the practice and has started procedures for the establishment of standards concerning the recycling of manure. They have no control over intra-state practices, thus cannot address themselves to the practices employed by a feedlot owner on his own feedlot. But, if the operator ships his beef over state lines, the use of recycled manure as a component of cattle feed could come under their jurisdiction.

The proposed standard would set maximum levels on the following: Salmonella, Drug Residues, Mycotoxins, Pesticide Contaminants, Heavy Metals. Such standards would define contamination limits in cattle feed additives and allow the feedlot operator to make use of the protein in manure, which currently is a wasted resource by many such operators. Given the recent plight of the feedlot operators, such a practice would likely be eagerly accepted and initiated once sanctioned by the FDA.

The normal FDA procedure for establishing a set of standards such as these is that the proposed standards are published and 60 days are allowed for response from the public. In the case of this product, however, the proposed standards should have published months ago. Apparently there is a feeling among the upper level FDA employees that the publishing of such a standard would cause negative public reactions and embarrassing complications for all concerned. The notion that manure was used in cattle feed and that the FDA had officially sanctioned its use as such was considered especially troublesome.

The product value (i.e. crude protein content) of HPFI would have to be verified via extensive tests. Even if the results were favorable, the product would likely be judged inferior to other feed supplements due to its association with manure.

The price at which the HPFI could be sold would depend upon many factors. Among these are: the manner in which the product form is introduced, the reputation of the launching company, the accompanying documentation and promotion, and the existence of other inexpensive treatments or processes which may be judged superior by the FDA.

It appears that eventually the FDA-proposed standards will be published, since articles in recent publications have indicated that the concept is feasible. For example, a 1974 *World Animal Review* article discusses the use of chicken excretions as an ingredient in cattle feed and also as the sole diet constituent. The conclusions were that chicken excreta were an economical protein supplement which was readily consumed by the cattle without health problems resulting.

AZTEC CHEMICAL COMPANY
Managing a Price Change

On May 10, 1985 the Lubricant Division of the Aztec Chemical Company of Houston, Texas, announced a price increase associated with its dry lubricant product line. The price increase would be effective as of June 9, 1985. Immediately after the announcement, only one competitor followed the Aztec Lubricant Division's price lead. As a result of the mixed competitive response, Aztec delayed the price increase another month. By the end of June, a few other dry lubricant producers had announced similar price increases. However, several producers had not done so. Consequently, the primary decision facing the Lubricating Division's management was whether to withdraw the announced price increases or to put them in effect on July 8, 1985.

The Lubricating Division of the Aztec Chemical Company was a large supplier of graphite based lubricants for use in the lubrication of various types of commercial rotating machinery. Sales associated with the dry lubricant product line accounted for approximately 40 per cent of the Division's annual sales volume. As of June 1985, the division offered three grades of lubricant in its dry lubricant product line: a low-grade graphite lubricant selling under the trade-name Graphtec General, a standard grade lubricant called Graphtec Standard, and a higher quality, more advanced graphite lubricant called Graphtec Plus.

THE COMPANY AND ITS PRODUCTS

Aztec Chemical Company had grown from a small, privately owned firm to a relatively large, public company since its inception in 1942. The company had started out as a chemical firm that specialized in producing various petroleum distillates for industry use. Through the years, it diversified its products to include lubricating oils and greases which were petroleum derivatives. They were available in various viscosities and grades for use in a multitude of applications that included internal combustion engines, electric motors, and many kinds of rotating machinery that required high quality oil or grease lubrication.

Prepared by Jeffrey C. Snyder under the direction of Michael H. Morris, University of Central Florida, Orlando, FL

Aztec Chemical's Lubricating Division expanded its research and development emphasis during the early 1970s in search of alternative production methods for its lubricants, as well as new lubricants that were based on primary chemical constituents other than petroleum. The price of petroleum had been increasing rapidly during the 1970s and Aztec executives did not foresee a relief in petroleum prices in the near future. The development of dry lubricants whose production was primarily based on raw materials other than petroleum, and that possessed costs that were more stable and predictable, was an important concern for the division.

In January 1973, the Lubricating Division completed development of its first graphite lubricants and began selling the Graphtec Standard and Graphtec Plus dry lubricants. The Graphtec Standard lubricant was a graphite based grease that was designed for use in rotating machinery associated with clean or closed systems (operating equipment where lubricated parts are not exposed directly to dirt or dust or other such open air contaminants). This product was known in the industry to be a high quality product that was virtually free of any undesired foreign matter. Because of this, it possessed superior lubricating ability, and a longer useful life. Many customers, therefore, employed the Graphtec Standard lubricant for use in electric motors and rotating machinery that had more stringent maintenance and operating standards. The Graphtec Standard currently sold for $48.00 per pound.

Graphtec Plus was introduced in August 1973 and by July 1974 accounted for roughly 30 percent of Aztec's dry lubricant sales. Graphtec Plus possessed higher quality standards than the standard grade. Moreover, it underwent additional treatment so that it was extremely resistant to chemical breakdown imposed by high temperature conditions. This made it very attractive for use in lubricating rotating machinery, motors, bearings, etc., that were subject to great heat through continuous operation, or equipment that was operated in high temperature geographic environments. Graphtec Plus, although of extremely high quality, was often used in open and unclean systems because of its heat resistant characteristics. This grade of dry lubricant was currently selling for $62.00 per pound.

The Graphtec General lubricant was a graphite-based grease that was designed for use in rotating machinery associated with open or unclean systems. This grade of lubricant was not offered by the company until January 1985, as a means of responding to the smaller lubricant companies' product and pricing tactics. Like the other products, it was available in various viscosities for different applications and was felt to be a good, all-purpose lubricant available at a competitive price. The Graphtec General grease has been sold for $36.00 per pound since its introduction.

Basic raw materials for all grades include graphite, glycerin, and petroleum distillates. The petroleum distillates comprise only 10 percent of the production input. The raw materials are available in ample supply, are standardized in quality, and are relatively uniform in price, with the exception of the petroleum distillates, which tend to have very erratic prices. The price differences between the General and Standard grades were primarily due to better quality control, a slower production process, and the additional refining and filtering needed to produce the higher quality Standard grade. The Plus grade employed additional refinement techniques in its production and also underwent production stages to incorporate heat resistant constituents to stabilize the product's chemical composition in high temperature environments.

A number of other companies became involved in the development of dry lubricants at approximately the same time as Aztec Chemical. Two in particular, Noble Oil Corporation and Johnston Chemical Corporation, introduced similar products at about the same time. Other competitors entered the market a few years later. The dry lubricant industry was a highly competitive one. About 40 percent of total sales were to large industrial users, either through direct channels or through jobbers, and the balance was sold primarily through chemical and lubricant jobbers to many small and medium-size users. Most sales, then, were to jobbers, who provided a variety of marketing and distribution functions in selling lubricants to end-users (see Table 1).

The majority of the large and medium-size dry lubricant producers advertised extensively in various trade journals to develop brand recognition and brand acceptance for their products. Their advertisements typically stressed factors such as lubricating ability, extended life of rotating machinery and equipment, reduced maintenance frequency, and product quality. Sales associated with the high quality, heat-resistant dry lubricant accounted for 55 to 65 percent of total dry lubricant sales for most producers.

Four major producers of the products accounted for almost 70 percent of industry sales and more than 10 other manufacturers accounted for the remaining industry sales. The four major producers were Aztec's Lubricant Division, Noble Oil Company, Johnston Chemical, and Coppers Corporation.

Noble Oil Company, with between 20 and 30 percent of total dry lubricant sales, was the largest supplier. About 50 percent of this company's output was sold in the Midwest, with the remainder being marketed in the northeastern United States and throughout the west coast. Noble produced and sold two grades of dry lubricant with specifications and characteristics similar to Aztec's Graphtec Standard and Plus

Table 1 Major End Users of Dry Lubricants

General grade lubricant	Standard grade lubricant	High quality grade lubricant
Oil Drilling Industry Equipment	Auto Industry Equipment	Commercial Power Equipment
Construction Equipment	General Manufacturing Equipment	Medical Equipment
Mining Equipment	Air Conditioning Equipment	Robotics
General Home Uses	Department of Defense (DOD) Equipment	Computers
		Airline Equipment
		DOD Equipment

brands. Because of its extensive advertising, the medium grade dry lubricant sold by Noble was probably the best known in the industry. Noble Chemical also used a jobber organization that was known to be the strongest in its field.

Aztec Chemical and Johnston Chemical vied for second and third place in the dry lubricant industry. Aztec Chemical sold most of its output in the Midwest with the remainder being marketed in the southeastern United States. Johnston Chemical carried only two grades of dry lubricant, one that was comparable to Aztec's Graphtec General, and a heat-resistant type that was considered by some customers to be slightly superior to Aztec's Graphtec Plus brand. Johnston Chemical emphasized what it felt to be superior product quality with its advertising. This emphasis on sales of the superior brand dry lubricant had discouraged Johnston's jobbers and caused some of them to carry other manufacturer's product lines.

Coppers' dry lubricant division was particularly strong in the East, selling 60 percent of its output in this area, with the rest being marketed in the Midwest. Coppers Corporation accounted for approximately 8 percent of the total industry sales.

The small producers of dry lubricants were important factors in the marketplace. Their products were typically unbranded and they promoted them on the basis of price by underselling major brands. A great percentage of their business was gained through direct sales to large industrial users, accounts that the major suppliers typically handled through their jobbers.

PRICING HISTORY

In 1983, a number of small manufacturers of dry lubricants, located primarily in the Midwest, began reducing their manufacturing quality control, employing lower quality raw materials in their production process, and then began cutting prices. Up until this time, the market for dry lubricants had been considered to be relatively mature and lubricant prices offered by different manufacturers were very consistent with one another. As the small producers reduced their prices associated with the product line, many jobbers handling branded dry lubricants began losing their customers to jobbers supplied by these small companies. As a result of the price cuts by the small producers, Noble Oil was the first major producer to reduce the prices of its dry lubricant product line. In order to remain competitive, all other producers subsequently followed this price reduction. However, price cutting by the small producers continued. Table 2 relates the price of dry lubricant per pound for various producers over the time period encompassing July 1983 to July 1985.

As major manufacturers reduced their prices, some of the small midwestern companies maintained a policy of keeping prices a predetermined percentage below average market prices. Aztec Chemical Lubrication Division jobbers began demanding a lower grade dry lubricant to compete with the small companies' products being offered at reduced prices. Aztec's Lubrication Division management reluctantly agreed to expand their product line to include such a lower quality dry lubricant. In January 1985, the company introduced its Graphtec General lubricant to the market place. Graphtec General was priced at $36.00 per pound. Within a few months, virtually all producers who did not previously offer a lower quality product that was

Table 2

| GENERAL GRADE DRY LUBRICANT (price per pound) | | | | |
	Small Cos. (avg. price)	Noble Oil	Johnston Corp.	Coppers Corp.	Aztec Chemical
July 83	37.00	39.00	37.60	39.20	—
Oct 83	37.30	39.30	37.60	39.20	—
Jan 84	37.15	39.10	37.60	39.30	—
Apr 84	36.90	38.40	37.20	39.00	—
July 84	36.65	38.10	37.00	39.00	—
Oct 84	36.20	37.40	36.80	39.00	—
Jan 85	35.90	37.10	36.65	38.60	36.00
Apr 85	35.20	36.60	36.35	38.20	36.00
July 85 (proposed)	35.00	—	—	38.00	39.60

| STANDARD GRADE DRY LUBRICANT | | | | |
	Small Cos. (avg. price)	Noble Oil	Johnston Corp.	Coppers Corp.	Aztec Chemical
July 83	46.80	49.80	47.20	48.60	48.90
Oct 83	47.00	50.10	47.20	48.60	49.80
Jan 84	46.90	49.90	47.20	48.40	49.80
Apr 84	46.60	49.20	47.00	48.00	49.30
July 84	46.50	49.00	46.80	48.00	49.10
Oct 84	46.30	48.75	46.40	48.00	48.60
Jan 85	46.10	48.30	46.30	47.70	48.20
Apr 85	46.00	48.10	46.10	47.20	48.00
July 85 (proposed)	45.80	48.10	50.61	51.90	52.80

| HIGH QUALITY DRY LUBRICANT | | | | |
	Small Cos. (avg. price)	Noble Oil	Johnston Corp.	Coppers Corp.	Aztec Chemical
July 83	62.00	65.40	62.60	63.80	64.10
Oct 83	62.60	65.40	62.60	63.80	64.80
Jan 84	62.40	65.20	62.60	63.60	64.40
Apr 84	62.10	65.00	62.40	63.10	64.10
July 84	61.90	64.60	62.10	62.70	63.80
Oct 84	61.60	64.30	61.80	62.70	63.20
Jan 85	61.40	64.10	61.50	62.60	62.60
Apr 85	61.20	64.00	61.50	62.30	62.00
July 85	61.00	64.00	67.65	68.50	68.20

not heat-stabilized did so. After the introduction of the Graphtec General brand, Aztec lubricant division's executives believed that many jobbers were using the lower grade lubricant as a "door-opener" and a way for establishing accounts with customers, but that they still tended to promote the standard and high quality, heat-resistant grades. Many customers continued to purchase the medium and high grade dry lubricants because of the inherent benefits stemming from their higher quality and heat resistance.

The price reductions associated with the dry lubricants had been made during a period of rising costs associated with manufacturing of the product. This acted to accelerate a profit squeeze that had been occurring due to declining sales prices. Aztec's executives believed that all producers in the dry lubricant industry were experiencing the same profit squeeze. Consequently, they believed that if Aztec Lubrication Division were to increase prices, other producers were ready to do the same.

On May 10, 1985, the Aztec Chemical Company announced new, higher base prices. The company afforded its current jobbers a 30-day period during which they were able to purchase the products at the old prices. This protection period was designed to reduce a possible unfavorable impact on Aztec's sales volume. Aztec's announced price increase was equal to 10 percent for each of the company's dry lubricant product grades.

Following the announcement of the price increase, only Johnston Chemical announced similar price increases. Consequently, Aztec extended the jobber protection period until July 8, 1985, an additional 30 days. Over the course of the next few weeks, Coppers Corporation and various small companies announced similar price increases. On July 1, 1985, Coppers Corporation introduced a new dry lubricant claimed to be superior to all of the industry's current high quality, heat-resistant brands. Coppers introduced the new lubricant at a price that was 30 percent above Aztec's Graphtec Plus brand after the proposed Aztec price increase.

Two of Aztec's primary competitors, Noble Oil and Johnston Chemical, decided to withdraw their low quality dry lubricant from the market place. Moreover, Noble Oil did not announce any price increases associated with its higher quality brands.

Aztec's Lubrication Division executives believed that they had to resolve the pricing dilemma immediately. The company's current jobbers could not compete with those jobbers who purchased their products from the small producers. Moreover, they would not be able to compete with the jobbers who purchased from larger companies like Noble whose dry lubricant prices would be below Aztec's. At the same time, the profit squeeze continued to threaten the firm's bottom line.

ZEPHYR DEFENCE SYSTEMS LIMITED

"Oh, just what I needed!" exclaimed Alastair McTavish, president of Zephyr Defence Systems Limited, as his secretary presented a telex marked 'urgent'. "What now?"

The telex was from an anxious distributor of Polyguide and Tellite, two products for which Zephyr had recently been forced to buy production rights. The distributor had a 'large' order in the works and wanted to know what prices to quote on by the end of the week.

"We don't even know how to produce the stuff yet," McTavish muttered, "how the hell are we supposed to figure out what to charge for it? Fay, muster the troops for a meeting this afternoon. We'd better act quickly on this. Tell them to think about production and marketing strategies so we can make a decision on prices this afternoon."

Fay reached for the phone to get in touch with marketing, finance and manufacturing.

In October 1985, Zephyr, a Canadian defence contractor, was faced with the unpleasant prospect of being thrown well behind schedule and over budget on several large contracts because an American company was stopping production of a small, but vital, component for Zephyr's electronic warfare systems. To avoid this, it quickly bought the production rights to the components, Polyguide and Tellite, from their American owners. Polyguide and Tellite are copper-clad, irradiated laminated circuit boards used in microwave transmissions.

COMPANY BACKGROUND

Zephyr was started in Ottawa wih six employees in 1982. A wholly-owned subsidiary of Stevens' Canada, Zephyr intended to become the electronic defence "centre of excellence" in Canada—designing, integrating and producing defensive electronic systems for naval, land and air use.

Defence was the fastest growing industry in Canada in the early 1980s, due to renewed commitment to improvement by the Canadian government. Several large contracts were awarded in this period and Zephyr hoped that the technology it provided would be part of many of those contracts. Winning the contracts was based on the best combination of technology, price, and delivery. Another important consideration was the home base of the supplier—the Canadian government far preferred to award contracts to suppliers who would create jobs in Canada, not elsewhere.

By the end of 1985, Zephyr had sales of $31 million in part payment on four major long-term contracts worth $20–30 million each. It had established good working relations with its customers and the government departments it worked with (Department of National Defence, Department of Supplies and Services, and the Department of Regional and Industrial Expansion). Zephyr had rapidly expanded to 97 employees, but even so was strained to provide enough engineers to meet commitments. Zephyr was outgrowing its office and production space literally as soon as it was built. In May, 1984, a 15,000 sq. ft. plant opened in the Goulbourn Industrial Park on the outskirts of Ottawa, and another 35,000 sq. ft. were added in June, 1985.

Although owned by Stevens' Canada, Zephyr's president, Alastair McTavish, reported managerially to the Managing Director of Scott Electronics in England, a company owned by the British branch of Stevens. Profit and loss results were reported to Scott and consolidated in its financial statements. Scott specialized in military systems and was the Stevens company most familiar with the electronic warfare product line. Prior to his appointment with Zephyr, McTavish had been Scott's Director North America. It was felt however, that a Canadian company, run from Canada but with access to Scott's technology and experience, would be able to crack the Canadian defence market far more easily than a foreign-owned company. With Zephyr therefore acting as the prime contractor on several contracts, Scott actually became a subcontractor to Zephyr.

THE PRODUCTS

Flat stripline transmission has been used in the microwave industry since the early fifties. There were initially three ways to produce economical, mass-produced stripline components, but there were several problems with these methods of production that made the technical characteristics of these materials unreliable.

A new process for producing circuit boards with irradiated modified polyolefin was developed and patented by Everest Chemicals Ltd. in the 1950s. This Polyguide process permanently imparted to the material a high degree of mechanical stability, making it highly resistant to variations in environmental conditions and therefore suitable for microwave applications. Polyguide was also widely used in the production of high-temperature-resistant insulated wire and cable and the production of shrinkable plastic tubings, harnesses and fittings for the electronics and aerospace industries, as well as classified high-frequency computer applications.

At the same time, a Dr. Tell had developed a similar product with the same degree of quality and consistency in his own laboratory. Tellite, as his product was known, was purchased by Everest in the sixties.

Exhibit 1   Product Classification

STANDARD SHEET SIZES— 2 square feet (12″ × 24″)
                  — 2½ square feet (16½″ × 22″)
                  — 5 square feet (22″ × 32½″)

DIELECTRIC THICKNESSES

STANDARD—1/32″   *NONSTANDARD*—3/16″
         —1/16″   —1/4″
         —1/8″   —3/32″

Finished Product Categories

Standard   —1/32″, 1/16″ or 1/8″ dielectric, standard sheet size with 1 oz. copper
                        cladding on two sides.
Slightly Non-Standard—Standard dielectric, sizing variations or unclad on one or both
                        sides.
Wholly Non-Standard—Aluminum cladding or non-standard dielectric.

GENERAL PROPERTIES

SUBSTRATE	*VALUE*
Tensile strength	3000 psi clad or unclad
Elongation %	500% min.
Density	0.942 + .003 −.007 clad
	0.949 + .005 unclad
Elastic Modulus	100 psi ave.
(150 degrees C)	
Dielectric strength	500 volts/mil
Surface Resistivity	10 ohms, min
Volume Resistivity	10 ohms
Water Absorption	less than 0.01%

CHARACTERISTICS

High dielectric homogeneity
Low loss tangent
Low thickness variation
High heat resistance
High mechanical strength
No adhesives used in lamination
Adequate peel strength
Flatness and little or no post-etching warpage
Inert to chemicals used in printed wiring board fabrication
Long term stability of electrical, physical and mechanical characteristics
Easily and accurately machined, punched and drilled
High uniformity from piece to piece and batch to batch

Polyguide and Tellite could be described as 'cheese sandwiches' which served as printed circuit boards. The slices of 'bread' were usually copper (½ oz., 1 oz. or 2 oz.) but it was also available with aluminum cladding or no cladding. The 'cheese' could be either Polyguide or Tellite, depending on the application. Both products could be produced in several sizes and thicknesses of dielectric. (See Exhibit 1)

Polyguide and Tellite were innovative in quality control and the guarantee that they would meet the telecommunications, electronics and aerospace industries' need for uniform high quality. Another major attraction for these industries was the quietness of the products. Competitive substances made electronic noises that made them unacceptable when used in radar or communication.

THE COMPETITION

There have been several competitive substances developed for economical stripline components. 3M, a large, diversified company who at one time owned the Polyguide process, had a similar but not interchangeable product in place. A European company, Rogers Limited, also produced a competitive substance. However, the most competition stemmed from the development of ceramics for use in microwave transmission and reception. Ceramics are considered to be the wave of the future and are the most common substance in applications presently being designed. They will probably replace Polyguide and Tellite within two years. Ceramics offer a new type of substrate which is smaller, cheaper, easier to produce in quantity and weighs less than Polyguide or Tellite. Although preferred to Polyguide or Tellite in new applications because of these characteristics, no competitive substance can immediately replace them in existing applications without incurring high costs.

There are two major cost barriers to substitution for Polyguide and Tellite customers. The first is the cost of redesigning equipment without Polyguide or Tellite, which Scott estimated would cost them 1 million pounds and several months. The second is the cost of acquiring approval for the new substance or design for existing contractual specifications and government requirements, entailing considerable engineering resources and production delays from 18 to 24 months.

PRODUCT OWNERSHIP

In 1982 Everest was bought by Henley Electronics to fill a gap in its product line. Everest was a very small operation, run by a couple of employees who worked on boat building in slow times, which varied throughout the year. (See Exhibit 2) Records from this time were ad hoc, designed more as memory cues for the employees than as data for business analysis. When Everest was taken over, the new ownership did not interfere with these patterns as long as orders were filled within a reasonable time.

Two years later Henley itself was bought by 3M, but the company was not interested in producing or marketing Polyguide or Tellite because of the small volume involved and because it had its own comparable product. Late in the summer of 1985, 3M put the Polyguide and Tellite processes up for sale, intending to cease production at the end of the year, regardless of demand. Distributors did not inform customers of the impending shutdown for fear of losing sales. They hoped a white knight would materialize at the eleventh hour to continue production.

In September 1985 Zephyr heard on the grapevine that its source of supply was in jeopardy. Without a guaranteed supply of Polyguide and Tellite, Scott would

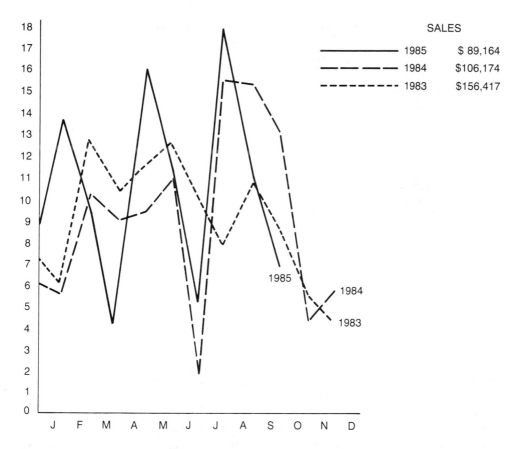

Exhibit 2   Sales Seasonality Chart

not be able to meet its subcontracting agreements with Zephyr, costing Zephyr its good relations with other contractors and government departments, as well as a whopping amount in late delivery charges. As Scott would not have been able to run an operation effectively from England, Zephyr had to buy the production rights to Polyguide and Tellite in October 1985. One of the clauses of the purchase agreement was to satisfy existing customers' orders for one year at "reasonable" prices. Although heated negotiations were expected between Zephyr and Scott over who should pay for costs incurred in purchasing these rights, Zephyr's first concern was to guarantee its ability to deliver on time.

THE MEETING

Early that afternoon the troops gathered in the boardroom—Alastair McTavish, President; Peter Mason, Finance; Geoffrey Pitts-Drake, Manufacturing; and Michael Walker, Marketing.

Exhibit 3   Zephyr Defence Systems Limited Organizational Chart*

```
                          President
                       Alastair McTavish
        ┌──────────────────────┼──────────────────────┐
     Director               Director                Director
   Manufacturing            Technical               Marketing
  (G. Pitts-Drake)                                  (M. Walker)

Materials Management       Hardware                Commercial
 Production Control        Software                  Naval
  Product Support          R & D                      Air
       Test                Quality                    Land

        ┌──────────────────────┼──────────────────────┐
     Director               Director                Director
     Programs             Administration             Finance
                                                   (P. Mason)
       PMS                 Personnel
       CPF                  Security               Accounting
    DELEX/280                 Plant                Estimating
   Development           Administration               MIS
```

Personnel Summary

McTavish, Alastair: M.A., Economics and Law, Cambridge University, Solicitor with Diploma in Management Studies from the U.K. Joined Scott in 1980 as Commercial Director and in 1982 became Director North America. In 1984, appointed President of Zephyr.

Mason, Peter: Joined Scott in 1961 in accounting. 1969–1984, served as Financial Controller in several Philips U.K. companies. Joined Zephyr as Controller in 1984.

Pitts-Drake, Geoffrey: M.A. Electrical Engineering and Physics, Cambridge University; M.B.A., St. Mary's University, Halifax. Experience in defence industry in engineering, production and management. Joined Zephyr in 1985 as Manufacturing Director.

Walker, Michael: B.A., M.B.A., Concordia University, Montreal, Marketing and Finance. Marketing experience in a variety of industries. Joined Zephyr in 1985 as Marketing Co-ordinator.

---

*From company records, January 22, 1986.

> *McTavish:* "Well, you all know the situation. We've been forced to purchase production rights for Polyguide and Tellite to ensure a supply for Scott so that we would not be forced into late delivery on our contracts. We now have to produce sufficient Polyguide and Tellite to satisfy existing customers for a year and provide our own lifetime supply. The most pressing concern is the price we are going to charge customers for Polyguide and Tellite. It depends on the production and marketing strategies we choose. I'd like each of you to run through what information you have on your area."

Production

Pitts-Drake: "On the production end, at least we're pretty sure we'll be able to produce the stuff. Some of our engineers have been down to the plant in the States to look at the operation and have a grasp of what needs to be done, but I don't know how much more time they can spare without putting their main tasks behind schedule. It shouldn't be hard to hire two people to actually do the production once it's set up—maybe a retired skilled labourer would be interested. I'm estimating I'll have to allot one day a week to running it. We are lucky to have the guy who has been running the Polyguide and Tellite operations for years willing to come up as a consultant and help us get started.

"With what we learned from past production, we can probably produce 30 sheets per week after we get the hang of production. It is a very delicate process in places and it may take a while to get it right. We've been working with finance to get estimates of what the production costs will be, on the assumption that we will produce for a year.

"Our major problem though is time. We need to order raw materials by the end of next week if we want to be in production in time for Scott to meet their commitments to us. It will take about eight weeks for delivery because we have to order from U.S. suppliers, and with our plant closed for two weeks at Christmas, we won't be in production until January. We have to do the trial runs and get enough Polyguide and Tellite to England by February at the latest or else they'll miss their deadline and that means we'll miss ours. But before we order supplies we need to know how much we're going to produce. I don't want to order more than once because it's so expensive to ship the stuff."

Finance

Mason: "I've put together a few numbers you will need. They're on the sheets I had passed out. Firstly, here's an estimate of the production costs. (See Exhibit 4) These costs are based on standard sheet sizes, but allowances have been made for non-standard sizes. With the present pricing structure, which was set up in January 1984, (See Exhibit 6), contribution margin is quite reasonable, but I'd like to look very carefully at projected volumes and prices, bearing in mind the fixed costs we have to cover. What I'm wondering is what costs do we want the revenues from Polyguide and Tellite to cover and how much do we want Scott to swallow? Between management time and engineers we've invested about 300 hours which hasn't been costed anywhere. At about $40 loaded labour cost per hour, that's not something we can easily hide in our budget. We are planning to expense all the purchase costs (See Exhibit 5). I think this ought to be strongly pointed out to Scott. They got us into this mess in the first place!"

McTavish: "Careful George, remember who decides our future."

Mason: "True. Anyway, the other point I wanted to make is what are we going to do with Polyguide and Tellite in the long term? Perhaps our long and short term goals will be different. By the way, there is a company who might be interested in buying the production rights and that could change the strategy we choose."

Exhibit 4   Cost per Sheet (Average Size, 3 Square Feet)

MATERIALS

Copper*	$2.86
Resin ½₃₂" dielectric needs 1½ lbs	
⅛₆" dielectric needs 2½ lbs	0.64 per lb.
⅛" dielectric needs 4½ lbs	
Nitrogen	1.00
Cleaning Materials	2.00
Crating Materials	1.00

LABOUR

Planning	$1.40
Lamination	4.58
Finishing	4.58

NON-STANDARD—average additional materials and labour costs for non-standard sheets are $3.00 per sheet.

OPERATING COSTS (annual figures represent contractual agreements)

Rental—property	$12,000.00 per annum
—planning equipment	90.00 per month
Utilities	600.00 per month
Security and Insurance	1,000.00 per annum
Maintenance	1,000.00 per annum

Administration costs are 5% of sales on average for this company.

---

*Owing to cutting patterns, the same amount of copper is used for all sizes.

Marketing

Walker: "Right. Now for the fun stuff. I've been plowing through the records we have from Everest for Polyguide and Tellite for the last few years. Their system was, shall we say, less than comprehensive. There is a lot of conflicting information, so I don't know how accurate my estimates will be. All the estimates have been based on worst case scenarios, taking the highest costs and lowest demand because I know how nervous Peter gets if we aren't conservative in our estimates.

"There are a couple of exhibits I'd like you to look at.

Exhibit 5   Costs Incurred to Date

Purchase	$26,700
Travel	7,600
Removal	13,150
Customs Duty	2,000
Total	$49,450

Exhibit 6   Price List

POLYGUIDE

	Price per Square Foot			
Dielectric	1 – 4	5 – 18	19 – 199	200 +
Thickness	sq. ft.	sq. ft.	sq. ft.	sq. ft.
1/32"	$45.60	$36.81	$34.95	$32.15
1/16"	53.58	42.45	40.18	36.97
1/8"	67.33	53.19	50.50	46.45

TELLITE

	Price per Square Foot		
Dielectric	1 – 99	100 – 499	500 +
Thickness	sq. ft.	sq. ft.	sq. ft.
1/32"	$30.03	$27.02	$25.48
1/16"	27.86	25.06	23.66
1/8"	32.76	29.40	25.00

SPECIALS—to regular prices add:

NON-STANDARD ITEMS	Additional Charge
Standard 2 oz. copper cladding	$4.75 per sq. ft.
Non-Standard	$7.25 per sq. ft.

"First, here's a breakdown of sales for the past three years. (See Exhibit 7) This was taken from Everest's invoices, but a computer printout from Henley's accounting department showed sales to be 15% higher for every year. It's impossible to tell whether we're short on invoices or if Henley bumped up the estimated sales when they were trying to sell the production rights. It makes a difference when you project demand.

"I have worked out conservative demand projections for the next year and listed the assumptions on the bottom of the page. (See Exhibit 8) I don't know how much effect the break in production will have on demand. It might be possible to drum up even more business, especially if there are other companies caught in the same bind we are. There seems to have been a good response to advertising placed in an electronics trade magazine last year. Henley got about two dozen inquiries, which isn't bad. However, there's no record of whether those leads panned out into sales.

"You already have a copy of Everest's price list, but I have to say I have my doubts about it. The invoices I looked at had price variations of up to $15 per square foot for the same product, sold to the same customer! There is *no* consistency. Customers would have a hard time proving our prices were less reasonable than past prices, no matter what we charged. There appears to have been a discount offered to distributors, ranging from 12 to 20% of the price list value, depending on the size of the order. The bigger the order, the bigger the discount

Exhibit 7 Sales Breakdown

Total Sales	1985		1984		1983	
Customers	$ Value	%	$ Value	%	$ Value	%
Auriema U.K.*	$26,000	30.2	$32,050	30.2	$38,565	24.7
Electro-Dynamics*	14,560	16.3	7,560	7.1	5,440	3.8
Auriema N/lands*	11,550	13.0	—	—	—	—
Westinghouse	8,010	9.0	—	—	10,170	6.5
Mitsubishi	6,600	7.4	—	—	—	—
Loral Electronics	3,770	4.3	—	—	11,370	7.3
Western Electric	—	—	20,100	18.9	38,440	24.6
Baytron Systems	—	—	4,570	4.3	—	—
Auriema France*	—	—	3,060	2.9	9,810	6.3
In-Speck Corp	—	—	2,990	2.8	—	—
Lother Sandford	—	—	2,870	2.7	—	—
Auriema Germany*	—	—	2,570	2.4	—	—
Krytar Corp	—	—	2,540	2.4	—	—
Hollande Signal	—	—	—	—	7,890	5.0
St. Research	—	—	—	—	6,610	4.2
		80.2%		73.7%		82.4%

usually was. I think the most important thing we have to do is to decide on a price structure and then stick to it.

"Here are a couple of odds and ends figures we might need.

	1984	1985
Average order size (sq. ft.)	30.4	34.6
Average order value	$740	$1013
% order by distributors	37%	47%
Sales by dielectric thickness		
Polyguide—1/32″	4%	9%
1/16″	33%	21%
1/8″	24%	7%
non-standard	39%	63%
Tellite— 1/32″	2%	2%
1/16″	15%	21%
1/8″	21%	25%
non-standard	62%	52%

"O.K., now a bit about the customers. Distributors account for a lot of past sales. They order on behalf of their customers, rather than buying from us on spec. You'll notice that the customer base seems to have been changing. About 22% of the 1985 customers were new, or at least they hadn't ordered since 1982.

Exhibit 8   Demand (1984 and 1985) and 1986 Projections (Square feet)

POLYGUIDE

Standard	1984		1985		1986	
¹⁄₃₂″ Dielectric	92		135		100	
¹⁄₁₆″ Dielectric	889		315		323	
⅛″ Dielectric	647		111		111	
		1,628		561		534

Nonstandard	1984		1985		1986	
¹⁄₃₂″ Dielectric	48		111		29	
¹⁄₁₆″ Dielectric	555		805		517	
⅛″ Dielectric	429		34		26	
		1,032		950		572

TELLITE

Standard	1984		1985		1986	
¹⁄₃₂″ Dielectric	25		25		25	
¹⁄₁₆″ Dielectric	150		338		251	
⅛″ Dielectric	210		403		240	
		385		766		516

Non-Standard	1984		1985		1986	
¹⁄₃₂″ Dielectric	258		145		188	
¹⁄₁₆″ Dielectric	90		183		133	
⅛″ Dielectric	282		490		414	
		630		818		735

ASSUMPTIONS

(1) Where figures for both years are close (one less than 3× the other), an average of the two previous years was taken.

(2) Where figures are much lower in 1985 than 1984, the 1985 figure is used.

(3) Where a large order was placed in 1985 it was assumed to be advance ordering for 1986 and an average of remaining orders was taken.

That's probably due to a long order cycle, since you can store these products for a long time with no problem—they're small and last forever. Interestingly enough though, the number of customers has been stable at 40–45 customers a year for the past three years. If we wanted to, it wouldn't be hard to get a mailing list together and get in touch with past customers, letting them know we're continuing production and see if we can drum up more business.

"Most of the customers seem to be large firms, so their Polyguide and Tellite purchases are probably insignificant to their total budgets. Not that it really matters anyway, because it's usually the engineers who order their own supplies directly. They realize that they need particular characteristics and that Polyguide and Tellite are the only things which will do the job.

"Besides this telex today, I've had a few queries from other customers who have heard we've taken over production, but there are no orders yet. On the

Exhibit 9   Manufacturing Process

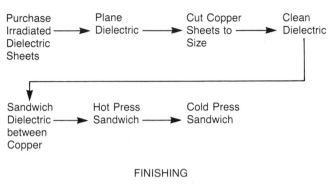

LAMINATION

Purchase Irradiated Dielectric Sheets → Plane Dielectric → Cut Copper Sheets to Size → Clean Dielectric

Sandwich Dielectric between Copper → Hot Press Sandwich → Cold Press Sandwich

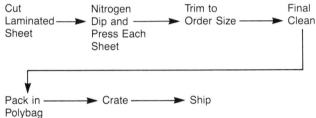

FINISHING

Cut Laminated Sheet → Nitrogen Dip and Press Each Sheet → Trim to Order Size → Final Clean

Pack in Polybag → Crate → Ship

subject of orders, I'd just like to point out that the customer's definition of "large" orders and ours are quite different. The average order is only a thousand dollars. How much do we really want to worry about that?

"The last question I have is what name are we going to sell this under? Electronics is a pretty small playing ground and I'm not sure we want our company name associated with something so small or something that doesn't really fit in with our product line. There might be other risks as well."

SUMMARY

McTavish: "Thank you, troops. That's a lot of information for us all to digest, so I propose a ten minute break.. Before we go, I'd like you to be thinking about our objectives and marketing strategies. Remember that whatever strategy we choose for production and marketing in the short term must be consistent with our long term plans. At the very least I want to be sure of covering all the costs we've incurred with Polyguide and Tellite from start to finish, and of course our traditional 20% profit margin on sales, and work out prices from there."

WALL INC.—MODERN FIXTURES DIVISION

In April 1985, Mr. Charles Williams was promoted to the position of Sales Manager of the Modern Fixtures Division of Wall Inc., a highly diversified corporation operating mainly in the Midwest. He had worked his way up through the sales ranks and most recently had been Assistant Sales Manager of the Ceramic and Tile Division, but the Fixture Division was relatively new to him.

He had been scanning some of the company and industry data left to him by his predecessor in the Modern Fixtures Division. He was particularly concerned about the advertising expenditure and sales revenue data—and about the effectiveness of Modern's advertising campaign. He realized that this was a function of at least two main factors: (a) the *per dollar* effectiveness of advertising expenditure (i.e., what level of sales or market share would be generated by a given dollar amount invested in advertising), and (b) the *qualitative* aspects of the advertising campaign, such as which media to use, which product features (if any) to mention, and so on.

INDUSTRY AND COMPANY BACKGROUND

Although Wall Inc. is highly diversified (producing and selling such goods as prepared foods, corrugated boxes, and handguns), much of its manufacturing is related to the construction industry. Among its operating divisions are the Cool-Air Division (specializing in air conditioners), the Ceramic and Tile Division, and Modern Fixtures Division. The latter makes and sells plumbing fixtures and many other kitchen and bathroom items.

The construction-related division sales were highly responsive to fluctuations in housing starts. Figure 1 indicates recent national trends in new private and public construction.

Modern Fixtures serves a twelve-state region in the Midwest (Ohio, Indiana, Illinois, Michigan, Wisconsin, Minnesota, Iowa, Missouri, North and South Dakota,

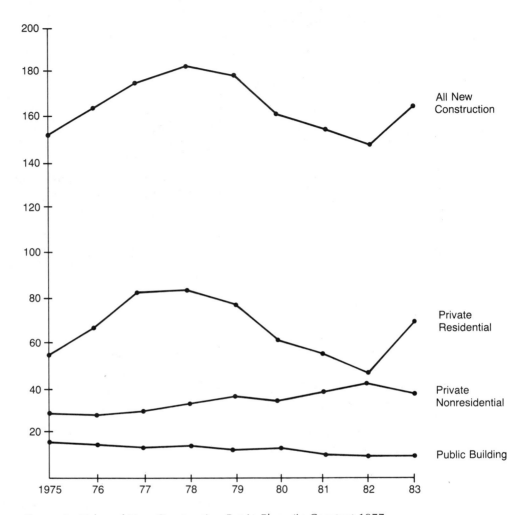

Figure 1   Value of New Construction Put In Place (in Constant 1977
Dollars; in millions of dollars)
(Source: *Statistical Abstract of the United States,* 105th ed., U.S.
Department of Commerce, Bureau of the Census.

Nebraska and Kansas). This region has usually accounted for about 13 to 15 percent
of nationwide industry housing starts. Additionally, housing trends in the Midwest
paralleled the national trends in recent years. Housing starts declined during the
late seventies, only to begin increasing again in 1983. Table 1 indicates investment
in new building construction in the Midwest since 1970, broken down by category
(residential, private nonresidential, and governmental).

Table 2 provides information on the total number of fixtures (kitchen and
bathroom combined) installed in the Midwest, also by category of building. The
figures in this table are self-explanatory, but it is worth noting that in the residential
market, more *fixtures per housing unit* are installed in one-unit houses (since many

Table 1 Midwest Region—New Building Construction (in constant 1977 dollars; in millions of dollars)

Period	New Private Residential Home Construction, by Type of Structure				Com-mercial (1)	Other Private (2)	Total Private	Govern-mental (3)	Total New Con-struction
	1 unit	2 – 4 units	5+ units	Total					
1970	11,660	720	2,015	14,395	3,569	4,354	22,318	7,812	30,130
1975	11,173	743	2,103	14,019	2,801	4,202	21,022	6,769	27,791
1976	13,344	1,072	2,911	17,327	2,852	4,196	24,375	6,604	30,979
1977	15,694	1,109	3,369	20,172	2,943	4,217	27,332	6,314	33,646
1978	15,433	1,137	3,737	20,307	3,593	4,463	28,363	6,807	35,170
1979	13,996	1,215	3,779	18,990	4,355	4,661	28,006	6,413	34,419
1980	10,873	1,188	3,167	15,228	4,377	4,484	24,089	5,516	29,605
1981	9,865	1,090	3,018	13,973	5,087	4,752	23,812	6,167	29,979
1982	8,054	838	2,917	11,809	5,475	4,993	22,277	5,525	27,802
1983	11,844	1,070	4,351	17,265	4,674	4,904	26,843	6,845	33,688
1984	13,501	1,291	5,063	19,855	5,827	5,188	30,870	6,452	37,322

(1) Includes offices and industrial buildings.

(2) Hospitals, institutions, schools, religious buildings, etc.

(3) Federal, state and local.

Table 2 Midwest Region—Number of new Plumbing Fixtures Installed (Total Industry)[1] (in thousands of units)

| Period | New Private Residential Home Construction, by Type of Structure | | | Comm-ercial | Other Private | Total Private | Govern-mental | Total Fixtures Installed |
	1 unit	2–4 units	5+ units	Total					
1970	480.0	25.9	88.1	594.0	39.0	47.6	680.6	85.4	766.0
1975	519.3	32.2	110.1	661.6	36.7	55.0	753.3	88.6	841.9
1976	529.7	38.4	112.8	680.9	29.1	43.7	753.7	70.4	824.1
1977	544.1	39.5	114.0	697.6	24.9	35.7	758.2	53.4	811.6
1978	537.5	40.7	127.0	705.2	30.5	37.9	773.6	57.8	831.4
1979	447.8	39.7	118.0	605.5	40.0	36.4	681.9	50.1	732.0
1980	319.7	35.6	91.0	446.3	31.4	32.2	509.9	39.6	549.5
1981	264.5	29.6	79.1	373.2	33.3	31.1	437.6	40.4	478.0
1982	248.6	26.0	87.9	362.5	41.2	37.6	441.3	41.6	482.9
1983	400.4	36.9	143.6	580.5	38.6	40.5	659.6	56.5	716.1
1984	406.7	39.5	149.6	595.8	43.0	38.3	677.1	47.7	724.8

[1]Includes kitchen and bathroom fixtures.

have two bathrooms) than in duplexes or apartments. On average, about 2.5 fixtures are installed in each one-unit house, about 2.3 fixtures per unit in two-to-four-unit houses, and approximately 2.1 fixtures per unit in apartments. These ratios have remained relatively constant through time.

SALE AND PROMOTION OF FIXTURES

There are four major groups of purchasers of plumbing fixtures for installation in new buildings. Modern has for some time now been servicing all four. They are:

1. Residential-tract contractors, who develop the majority of one-unit and two-to-four-unit structures in Modern's territory.

2. Small independent contractors and builders, who also construct some of the one-unit and two-to-four-unit structures. They usually construct about 20 to 30 percent of these buildings, but this proportion is highly variable.

3. Apartment building and townhouse contractors who, aside from being the major builders of apartment, townhouse, and condominium complexes, also construct a small number of four-unit structures.

4. Commercial contractors, who develop offices, shopping centers, hospitals, schools, and institutions, as well as government buildings (federal, state, and local).

Modern, like its competitors, uses a combination of personal selling and advertising to contractors in its promotional plan. Sales representatives call upon regular and prospective clients a few times a year (the exact number of times depends upon such factors as extent of past dealing and likelihood of high sales potential in the near future). The sales representatives distribute four-color brochures upon request.

Modern advertises to each of the major contractor segments. They employ both magazine advertising (in trade magazines such as *Progressive Builder* and *Plumbing and Heating*) and direct mailings, using mailing lists of contractors obtained from an outside agency. The advertising (which has not changed appreciably since the early 1970s) and the brochures place great emphasis upon the ease of installation and maintenance of the fixtures (this is due to their "washer-less" design, becoming increasingly prevalent in new installations, which eliminates dripping due to worn washers). Brochures, trade magazine advertising, and direct mail also stress the sleek design of Modern's fixtures. The same ad design and copy is used in advertising to all segments. Interestingly, very little is said about price in the ads. Mr. Williams's predecessor, who had been sales manager for twenty years until his retirement, always said, "Our customers know us . . . they know our reputation for quality. We don't have to sell our products cheap!"

THE SITUATION

Mr. Williams had been most concerned about the figures in Table 3. They had caused him to question the effectiveness of Modern's advertising program over the last decade.

Table 3   Modern Sales and Advertising Data

Period	Sales (in thousands of units)	Advertising (in thousands of dollars)	Market Share (%)	Advertising Share (%)
1970	158.0	49.1	20.6	20.2
1975	185.9	61.0	22.1	23.8
1976	184.0	59.1	22.3	22.6
1977	195.7	73.5	24.1	26.1
1978	190.3	62.9	22.9	24.3
1979	169.9	79.8	23.2	30.6
1980	128.1	66.7	23.3	24.1
1981	105.6	69.3	22.1	27.0
1982	105.8	73.7	21.9	28.9
1983	164.2	61.6	22.9	23.4
1984	162.7	58.1	22.5	21.5

Comparing sales dollars and advertising expenditure dollars, Mr. Williams noted that the most Modern ever spent in one year on advertising was $79,800 in 1979; but 1979 showed the lowest sales level since 1970. He also noted that Modern had cut back in advertising during 1983 and 1984 (down about 20 percent from 1982), but company sales showed a dramatic increase over this period (from 105,800 units in 1982 to 164,200 units in 1983; see Table 3).

Table 4   Producer Price Indices for Plumbing Fixtures (1967 = 100)

Period	All Plumbing Fixtures[1]	Modern Plumbing Fixtures	All Construction Materials[1]
1970	111.2	110.1	112.5
1974	149.1	148.1	160.9
1975	162.3	158.4	174.0
1976	174.1	171.1	187.7
1977	186.6	185.4	204.9
1978	199.1	193.2	228.3
1979	217.1	215.2	251.4
1980	246.7	246.6	266.4
1981	267.5	267.9	283.0
1982	278.7	280.1	288.0
1983	289.3	292.3	297.7
1984	—	303.1	—

[1]Source: *Statistical Abstract of the United States 1985,* 105th Edition, U.S. Department of Commerce, Bureau of the Census.

Mr. Williams was well aware of the downturn in construction activity between 1979 and 1982 and reasoned that this probably had a significant effect on Modern's sales. Therefore, he tried instead to find a relationship between market share and advertising share (percentage of total industry advertising expenditure) spent by Modern.

However, during the period under study, Modern's advertising share had varied from 20.2 percent (in 1970) to 30.6 percent (in 1979) while market share was almost invariant at about 22 to 23 percent.

Mr. Williams decided to investigate other likely explanations for these observations. It was possible, for example, that prices had been increased about the same time as advertising expenditures, possibly nullifying the effect of the advertising if the purchasers were highly price-conscious. He knew that prices had been rising sharply in fixtures (as well as other construction materials) for a number of years, partly due to inflation, partly due to raw material prices. Upon obtaining the information in Table 4, however, he realized that Modern's prices had not been out of line with those of the industry.

FURTHER ANALYSIS

Mr. Williams was able to obtain some additional information on the sale of Modern fixtures. The management information systems staff provided him upon his request with Modern's sales figures (grouped by category of structure) from 1970 to 1984. Knowing what industry sales were for these years enabled him to calculate market shares as well. The sales figures he obtained are provided in Table 5.

These figures revealed much more than the composite figures did. For example, Modern's share of the market in 1981 was approximately equal to its share in

Table 5 Midwest Region—Company Sales by Type of Structure (in thousands of units)

| Period | Private Residential Units | | | | All Commercial | All Governmental | Commer. & Gov't. Total | Grand Total |
	1-unit	2 – 4 units	5 + units	Total				
1970	108.0	5.3	16.3	129.6	14.4	14.0	28.4	158.0
1975	126.2	7.1	22.1	155.4	15.4	15.1	30.5	185.9
1976	129.8	8.4	22.4	160.6	11.9	11.5	23.4	184.0
1977	148.0	9.6	20.3	177.9	9.3	8.5	17.8	195.7
1978	136.0	9.7	23.4	169.1	11.8	9.9	21.7	190.8
1979	115.5	9.7	22.7	147.9	13.2	8.8	22.0	169.9
1980	87.6	9.2	16.7	113.5	9.1	5.5	14.6	128.1
1981	65.6	6.7	16.0	88.3	10.9	6.4	17.3	105.6
1982	61.7	6.0	17.4	85.1	13.7	7.0	20.7	105.8
1983	108.1	9.2	26.1	143.4	12.2	8.6	20.8	164.2
1984	109.4	9.9	25.6	144.9	11.1	6.7	17.8	162.7

Table 6 Midwest Region—Advertising Expenditure by Market Segment
(in thousands of dollars)

Period	Residential Contractors/Small Builders		Apt. Building and Townhouse Contractors		Commercial and Government Contractors		Totals	
	Industry Total	Modern	Industry Total	Modern	Industry Total	Modern	Industry Total	Modern
1970	110.5	22.2	21.2	4.3	111.5	22.6	243.2	49.1
1975	121.7	30.3	21.4	5.9	113.3	24.8	256.4	61.0
1976	124.4	31.1	22.1	5.3	114.8	22.7	261.3	59.1
1977	140.5	50.2	23.5	4.2	117.5	19.1	281.3	73.5
1978	125.3	34.6	21.2	4.3	112.5	24.0	259.0	62.9
1979	130.6	36.6	20.9	4.5	109.3	38.7	260.8	79.8
1980	140.6	47.7	23.6	4.5	112.4	14.5	276.6	66.7
1981	126.9	33.1	22.6	5.6	109.0	31.1	258.5	69.8
1982	122.4	31.5	21.9	5.8	110.7	36.4	255.0	73.7
1983	129.0	39.7	23.2	4.5	110.9	17.4	263.1	61.6
1984	131.5	41.6	24.1	4.1	114.7	12.4	270.3	58.1

1984 (22.1 percent as compared to 22.5 percent). But the expanded table clearly shows that over that time, Modern's market share increased appreciably in some segments (e.g., one-unit family dwellings), and decreased in others (e.g., commercial and government installations).

From the same source, he was also able to obtain estimates of overall industry and Modern advertising expenditures, broken down by targeted market segment. These figures are given in Table 6. In the past, Modern had experimented with different advertising dollar allocation schemes in attempting to develop an "optimal mix." For example, in 1977, the major share of the advertising budget was invested in reaching the residential contractors and small builders; while in 1979 and 1982, they made a strong bid to obtain the interest of the commercial and government contractors.

SALES REPRESENTATIVE ASSISTANCE

Mr. Williams knew that the sale and advertising figures were only a rough guideline for measuring advertising effectiveness. They might indicate the relative effectiveness of the advertising campaign through time, but they would not necessarily give any insight as to why ads were more or less effective or how effectiveness could be improved.

He reasoned that one potentially useful source of information would be the sales representatives themselves as they had to deal on a day-to-day basis with the contractors and would be the first to notice any discontent among the clientele. Some of the comments he received were as follows:

"Now that business is picking up again, I'm back up to quota, at least with old customers. But construction has really taken off here since '83; there are lots of new faces in the business, and they don't seem to know or care about Modern. Frankly, they're my toughest sale!"

"I'm disappointed with my sales—have been for some time. I work in a government town, and the state government has just cut back everywhere. They're making do with old, outdated buildings. I don't know when that's going to change."

"Those twenty-story apartment buildings are springing up all over downtown. The apartment contractors are somewhat style conscious, but I'll tell you what they want most—the lowest price they can get for dependable quality. They don't want cheap stuff, most of them anyway; but they want to avoid repairs, not that I blame them. You'd think they'd trust our brand name!"

"Fancy magazine ads and brochures and direct mailings may sell a lot of VCRs and patio furniture, but I don't think they sell a lot of bathroom fixtures. It's as if my clients don't even read the ads. I've really got to hustle to make a sale."

THE ISSUE

Just having taken over the sales manager's job, Mr. Williams has plenty to do, so he would like to take any required action regarding advertising quickly and efficiently. He has to decide how effective his division's advertising expenditures have been, where its strengths were, and what weaknesses ought to be improved. He must also make some sound recommendations for the future, especially in light of the apparent trends in the construction industry. He should decide upon a satisfactory advertising campaign which would fit well with Modern's promotional plan and, indeed, with the overall marketing strategy of the division.

GAMMA BUSINESS SYSTEMS, INCORPORATED

Gamma Business Systems, Inc. (GBS) was an authorized Canon copier dealer with its main headquarters located in Orlando, Florida. It had grown rapidly since its inception in 1976 through a strategy of strong personal selling and emphasis on the Canon name. The company's marketing decisions were controlled by Fred Cady, the Marketing Director, and Steve Dolan, the President. With the 1987–8 fiscal year (which begins in July) approaching, the two principals found themselves assessing the Central Florida market situation and the company's advertising needs for the coming year.

The geographic boundaries of the market corresponded roughly to the Orlando Metro Area (MSA), which included Orange, Seminole, and Osceola counties, as well as Volusia County (Daytona Beach) and Brevard County (Cocoa Beach and Melbourne). The area had experienced rapid economic growth from 1970 to 1986, initially as a result of tourism anchored by Disney World, but more recently in the form of light industry, construction, retailing, banking, high tech firms, government contractors, and a wide array of other medium and small-sized enterprises. An overview of the Orlando economy is provided in Tables 1 and 2.

The extremely rapid growth of the area had fostered some unique marketing circumstances. For instance, municipal building regulations had caused the downtown area to become a mixture of mostly financial services high-rise office buildings and original architecture refurbishments. Numerous suburban communities had become commercial centers networked and partially linked with a system of congested highways, including Interstate 4 running north-south, and the Orlando Expressway running east-west. Morning and afternoon traffic invariably clogged all major highways as business commuters sought to move to and from their places of work.

Orlando acted as a magnet to new businesses and a professional work force, drawing national headquarters relocations and a wide cross-section of branch offices seeking tax benefits, lifestyle gains, and growth opportunities stemming from the rapid expansion of the population and economy. The special situation was both a blessing and bane to Gamma. It insured constant growth in the need for copy ma-

---

Case prepared by Alvin Burns of the Department of Marketing, University of Central Florida, Orlando, FL.

Table 1 Employment by Industry, Orlando Metro Area (MSA)

	1970	1980	1983	1984	1985	Percent Change 1980–1985
Total, All Industries	144,500	288,000	339,600	385,100	410,600	42.7
Manufacturing	21,800	36,700	40,600	45,500	48,200	33.3
Construction	15,700	19,900	23,100	30,900	32,500	63.3
Transportation, Communications and Public Utilities	8,800	15,000	16,500	20,100	21,200	41.3
Trade	37,800	79,100	93,600	104,700	110,900	40.5
Wholesale Trade	N/A	(20,300)	(22,700)	(25,800)	(28,200)	40.0
Retail Trade	N/A	(58,800)	(70,900)	(78,900)	(82,700)	40.6
Finance, Insurance, and Real Estate	9,700	19,600	22,100	24,900	26,900	37.2
Services	26,900	76,300	98,800	113,700	122,300	60.5
Hotels/Lodging Places	N/A	(13,400)	(15,700)	(18,600)	(20,800)	55.2
Personal Services	N/A	(3,100)	(3,600)	(4,000)	(4,400)	41.9
Business Services	N/A	(12,000)	(20,100)	23,700)	(25,700)	114.2
Health Services	N/A	16,600)	20,500)	22,600)	(24,200)	45.8
Membership Organizations	N/A	N/A	(3,800)	(4,800)	(4,900)	—
Government	23,800	41,400	44,900	45,300	48,500	17.1

Note: Annual Average Employment. Figures in parenthesis are based upon estimates.

Source: Florida Department of Labor and Employment Security

chines, while, at the same time, bringing an ever-changing set of prospects who were unfamiliar with GBS, and also bringing a growing list of competitors.

GBS was a sales oriented company that had built its success on a young, eager sales force. Salespeople were expected to aggressively push the firm's products, usually with a mix of appointments and cold calls, and would sometimes join forces to "blitz" local office buildings. They were paid on a straight commission basis. Commissions were set as a percentage of gross margin, with the individual salesperson given some leeway in negotiating prices. Although a number of salespeople earned in excess of $50,000 per year, turnover among the sales force was fairly high. GBS provided the sales force with little formal training. They did provide sales leads, generated through a telemarketing service, and a variety of promotional support materials.

The company sold a line of twelve copiers, ranging in quality, price, and features from the most basic to the top of the line. GBS had also recently added a line of facsimile equipment. About 60 percent of company revenues came from servicing copiers after they were sold, as well as from parts and supplies. GBS offered customers a number of different service contract options, and paid salespeople a commission when they sold one of these contracts.

The basic philosophy at GBS was that "everybody's a customer." The firm had made sales to a wide cross-section of organizations in Central Florida, including

Table 2 Selected Economic Data on the Central Florida Market

	Brevard	Orange	COUNTY Osceola	Seminole	Volusia
Number of Establishments	7,465	15,550	1,458	5,407	7,683
Number of Establishments with more than 100 employees	119	393	34	75	98
Number of Employees:					
Total	124,706	293,254	21,938	61,816	93,421
Agriculture, Forestry, and Fishing	1,706	7,308	392	1,340	2,004
Mining	M /	36	L /	0	L /
Construction	8,023	21,560	1,646	5,911	6,341
Manufacturing	26,293	32,569	1,604	10,146	10,344
Transportation, Communication, and Public Utilities	6,063	19,764	429	2,554	3,877
Wholesale Trade	2,810	19,563	813	3,142	2,496
Retail Trade	24,534	51,823	5,411	15,934	24,662
Finance, Insurance, and Real Estate	4,394	20,755	824	2,713	5,347
Services	40,711	107,058	9,592	17,536	32,342
Government	10,117	12,797	1,222	2,522	5,988
Other	L /	21	L /	18	L /

Note: L / = 0–19; M / = 20–99

Source: County Business Patterns (1984), Florida, U.S. Department of Commerce, Bureau of the Census. Florida Statistical Abstract (1986), 20th ed., Bureau of Economics and Business Research, Gainesville: The University Presses of Florida.

hospitals, insurance agencies, hotels, legal firms, schools, municipal government offices, retailers, construction companies, and many more. No formal attempt had been made to track customer sales patterns, and only recently was a program instituted to coordinate copier sales with service sales.

The copier dealer competitive scene in Central Florida was dominated by one competitor, Copymasters, Inc., which was estimated to have almost 50 percent of the market, compared to 30 percent for Gamma. Cady and Dolan were uncertain of why Copymasters was the dominant company. In their analysis both companies offered equivalent copy machines at competitive prices. In fact, GBS offered more support services to customers than did Copymasters. Both had been in business for about twelve years. Mr. Cady claimed that much of the difference was due to Copymasters' radio advertising campaigns, which were launched four years ago and continued to be an important part of its promotional mix.

GBS had historically adopted a different promotional strategy. To support the personal selling effort, which relied on referrals and cold calls, GBS had invested heavily in billboard advertising all across the five counties constituting Central Florida.

Cady and Dolan agreed on the overall marketing objective for 1987: to increase market share from its current level of 30 percent to at least 35 percent. They disagreed, however, on the advertising objectives and strategy. Dolan contended that the billboard advertising had been successful in creating GBS name recognition and should remain the mainstay of the 1987–8 strategy. His rationale was based on the heavy commuter traffic patterns in Orlando and the obvious high exposure value of strategically placed outdoor ads. Cady, on the other hand, felt that Copymasters' radio advertising should be a model, since they had come to dominate the market. The advertising could have more impact, in his opinion, especially if a catchy jingle were used. He also felt radio would be useful in generating sales leads, especially if the ads emphasized Gamma's toll-free and local telephone numbers.

The two principals also disagreed on spending levels. Cady favored an aggressive program based on a $200,000 budget, which amounted to 5 percent of copier revenues earned in the Orlando market during the 1986–7 fiscal year. Gamma had never before spent more than $75,000 on advertising. Dolan was concerned that no more than $100,000 be spent, based on current sales projection and budget needs of other parts of Gamma's business. Also, Cady believed in a "blitz" approach, with saturation of the marketplace attained in a short period of time. Dolan felt uncertain about this.

Both men were in agreement that the time had come for an objective resolution of Gamma's advertising needs. Cady's daughter, Cassy, was a graduate student enrolled in a nearby university and had recently completed an advertising management course. She had agreed to do research on the relative virtues of billboard compared to radio advertising in the local market. Independent of Cassy's efforts, GBS commissioned a local marketing research company to conduct a survey of the copier market.

Within a month, Cassy's research was completed. Among other things, it detailed the characteristics of billboards and radio advertising in the target market area and provided an accounting of the specific advantages and limitations of each medium. These are summarized in Table 3.

The market survey sought answers to specific as well as broad questions. In particular, the objectives of the survey were finalized as follows: (1) to determine the relative effectiveness of different media in stimulating copier dealer name awareness; (2) to determine the present level of awareness of Gamma Business Systems in the target market; (3) to determine prospects' current copier needs; and (4) to determine prospective customers' buying behavior characteristics.

The survey method involved the design of a telephone questionnaire which was administered to 100 companies randomly selected from a master list of about 6,000 company names in Central Florida. This was purchased from a listing service. The interviews focused on " . . . person who makes the copier machine purchase or lease decisions . . . " in the company.

Table 3   Radio versus Billboard Advertising

Radio Advantages:

1. Excellent demographic selectivity
2. Good geographic selectivity
3. Negotiable costs
4. Short-term advertising commitment; Gamma Business Systems would not be restricted to a twelve-month contract with the same advertising message as would be the case with billboards.

Radio Limitations:

1. Because there are so many stations in Orlando, the audience is highly fragmented. It requires a number of stations to cover a particular market.
2. Many commercials per hour—it is difficult to position a product away from the competitor's product.

Billboard Advantages:

1. Largest and most colorful display for an advertiser's trademark or product.
2. Good geographic flexibility.
3. Broad customer reach.
4. This is the only medium Gamma Business Systems could dominate at this time.
5. Long-lasting presence in a given market.
6. Good at stimulating awareness of market presence.

Billboard Limitations:

1. Billboards make a broad sweep of the largest segment of the market; not a specialized segment.
2. Land values and zoning regulations.
3. Orlando roads are traveled by a large proportion of tourists.
4. The message must be told in a few words; the average viewing time is 6–10 seconds.

The final report contained many tables and figures summarizing the findings, but Cady and Dolan agreed that a few tables succinctly related to the basic questions addressed. These are presented as Tables 4 through 9 below.

Advise Gamma Business Systems.

Table 4   Familiarity with Copier Dealers in the Area

Dealer's Name	Percent Familiar
Copymasters	81%
Gamma Business Systems	48%
Electrocopiers	25%
Donka Shane, Inc.	10%

Table 5 Recall of Local Copier Company Advertising

Medium Mentioned	Percent Mentioning For Any Company	Percent Mentioning for Gamma
Radio	69%	59%
Direct Mail	55%	22%
Sales Call	52%	28%
Television	43%	11%
Word of mouth	30%	9%
Yellow Pages	28%	7%
Billboards	11%	4%
Newspaper	5%	11%
Magazine	5%	2%

Table 6 Plans to Buy, Lease, or Replace Copier in Next 6 Months

Response to Question	Percent
No	90%
Maybe	9%
Yes	1%

Table 7 Familiarity with Gamma Business Systems Services

Degree of Familiarity	Percent of Those Aware of Gamma
Not at all Familiar	53%
Somewhat Familiar	35%
Familiar	8%
Very Familiar	3%

Table 8 Decision Makers for Copiers: Number of Persons Involved

Number	Percent of Respondents
One	42%
Two or Three	53%
Four or Five	2%
Over Five	3%

Table 9   Title of Copier Decision Makers

Title	Percent of Respondents
Owner	45%
Office Manager	16%
Purchasing Agent	14%
Corporate Officer	13%
Secretary	3%
Other	9%

UNITED TIRE COMPANY
Adopting Telemarketing

Phil Hart, Vice President of Sales for United Tire Company, hung up the phone and heaved a sigh of fatigue. He had just concluded a conversation with Jay Johnson, a regional division sales manager in Atlanta. Johnson had described the growing morale problem among his field sales representatives. Many of them had heard about a new telemarketing program that was being adopted by the company which, in their opinion, would cause significant reductions in the sales force. Other rumors that were circulating indicated that those salespersons who did keep their jobs would find their compensation reduced significantly as a result of United's use of telemarketing to achieve sales.

BACKGROUND

United Tire Company, a manufacturer of a full line of automotive tires, sells on a nationwide scale to car manufacturers in the United States as well as retail tire dealers. The number of automotive and tire dealers that United serves is approximately 20,000. Among these retailers are a wide variety of types and sizes of businesses. Some of United's customers are chains like K-Mart and Target. Others are small garages owned and operated by one person. The customers of United are distributed across the United States in a pattern closely resembling the national population distribution. Sales figures for United Tire Company are listed in Table 1.

The sales force consists of 340 sales representatives managed by 20 district managers who, in turn, report to 5 division managers whose offices are in White Plains, New York; Atlanta, Georgia; St. Louis, Missouri; Denver, Colorado; and Los Angeles, California. The sales force is organized on a geographic basis with each person assigned a number of counties, an SMA (Standard Metropolitan Area), or a portion of an SMA that provided each salesperson with an approximately equal sales potential.

Compensation of the sales personnel is a combination salary plus commission. Commissions were calculated on the percentage of a gross dollar volume that a sales representative attains each month. Average compensation for the sales force is $38,000 per year. The lowest paid sales representative received $25,000 and the highest paid received $70,000. As a result of the above-average compensation and

Table 1   1986 Gross Sales for United Tire Company

$50 million—	Automotive manufacturers purchasing tires for use on new cars and trucks
$200 million—	Sales to retailers which included: $40 million—one thousand of the largest United customers $160 million—sales made to the remaining nineteen thousand customers
$250 million gross sales	

benefits package, the sales force turnover rate was low. Over the past four years the average was less than 10% a year.

United Tire Company is facing the same forms of pressure that confront other domestic tire manufacturers. Foreign brands such as Bridgestone and Michelin have entered the U.S. market during the past ten years. The foreign marketers have introduced high quality products while keeping prices at or below the U.S. tire prices. This factor coupled with rising sales costs (see Table 2) caused United's profits to slump by approximately 3% a year for the past 4 years. United's top management has embarked on a vigorous campaign to cut costs and raise employee productivity.

Mr. Hart sensed the need to adopt significant cost saving practices that would show that the Sales Department was aggressively attacking the problems of high costs. Therefore, when an invitation to attend a seminar on telemarketing was extended to Hart by the telephone company, he accepted it.

The leaders of the seminar emphasized several points which were new to most of the executives attending the program. First, the audience was told that telemarketing was much more than just selling over the telephone to private consumers. Some of the other telemarketing applications that were of immediate interest to Hart involved the qualification of sales leads prior to turning the leads over to a field representative for a face-to-face visit. One of the many diagrams shown to the audience illustrated how the sales lead qualification program worked (see Figure 1).

The average cost to qualify a lead through the telemarketing program was estimated at $5.00, which included all of the costs associated with paying salaries, telephone service and other overhead costs. An example the seminar leader pro-

Table 2   Average Cost of a Sales Call for a United Tire Representative

1975	$ 64.14
1977	$ 87.11
1979	$123.32
1981	$160.20
1983	$184.86
1985	$206.73

Figure 1 A Sales Lead Qualification Program Using Telemarketing

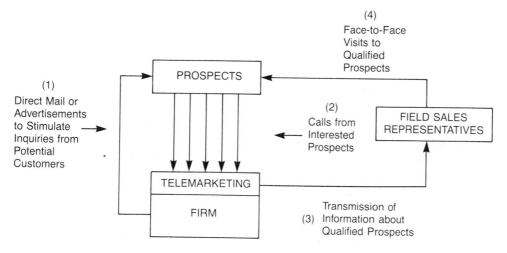

Sequence of Steps in Qualification Process

1. Firm sponsors advertising of various kinds to stimulate inquiries from people who may be prospective customers.

2. Prospects respond by using (in this case) an 800 number to acquire more information and are then "qualified" by a telemarketing specialist.

3. Prospects' names which have been acquired during the qualification process are passed to field sales.

4. Field sales representatives call on only those consumers or businesses that have been submitted as qualified prospects.

vided to support her claim about the effectiveness of this program involved an adopter of the program who had improved the sales-closed to sales-calls-made ratio from one in ten to five in ten. A .500 batting average is extremely impressive in the sales world.

In addition to the sales lead qualification possibilities, Hart was also intrigued by another application called "marginal account handling." The seminar example featured a situation in which a well known greeting card manufacturer used telemarketing to continue to serve the thousands of small retail establishments where greeting cards were sold. In this situation, the greeting card marketer had realized almost ten years ago that there was no way to economically continue to achieve intensive distribution and serve all of the small accounts through face-to-face contact. By turning the marginally profitable accounts over to the new telemarketing center to handle, more frequent contact was maintained with the small gift shops, drug stores, and grocery stores. Presently, the greeting card marketer served almost ninety percent of its customer base through the telemarketing center. Although Hart's firm sold tires, the parallel to his problem did not escape his attention.

Shortly after attending the seminar, Mr. Hart received a call from a telephone company representative who proposed a meeting to discuss the United Tire Company's situation. At the meeting, the telephone representative offered to work with Hart and his people to establish a telemarketing pilot program to test the feasibility of using telemarketing at United Tire Company. The initial test was designated for White Plains, New York. Three people were hired and trained to take in-coming calls from prospects who were making inquiries to various advertisements, brochures, and direct mail (i.e., the "raw material" for sales leads).

In addition, to maximize the productivity of the three telemarketing specialists, each specialist was given one hundred dormant accounts to contact. The telemarketing personnel were to attempt to sell tires that had been priced at a very attractive level for this situation. The purpose of this arrangement was to revive the accounts. The offer featured not only low priced tires but also a two day maximum delivery time plus a toll-free "hot line" for dealers to get instant service on any problems they were having with the United Tire Company's products or services.

The success of the pilot was apparent within three weeks. After tracking the success of the field salespeople who followed up on the qualified leads furnished to them, Hart discovered that their sales-closed to sales-visits-made ratio exceeded 3.3 out of 10. This was compared to the national average of United's sales force, which was 2 out of 10. The marginal or dormant account situation was also doing quite well. Twenty percent of the accounts contacted had responded favorably with purchases that averaged $2,000 per customer.

As a by-product of some of the conversations the telemarketing specialists had with customers, Hart learned that several customers indicated they had not been contacted by a field salesperson from United Tire in many months. Some of the customers revealed their desire to continue to do business via the telemarketing program rather than having a field representative call on them.

After witnessing the pilot program results in White Plains for two months, Hart submitted a request for $300,000 to develop a telemarketing program in each of the other regional offices. After reviewing the proposal, Hart's superiors approved the request.

During the weekly teleconference Phil Hart had with the regional sales managers, he announced that within the next three months each regional office would have a sales lead qualification program and a marginal account program. The division managers were told to come to White Plains for additional briefing on the telemarketing program that would be implemented at United Tire Company.

It was two weeks after the division managers' meeting in White Plains that Hart received the call from Jay Johnson.

ADAPCO, INC.

Adapco, Inc. is an exclusive sales agent for Luray Engineering, of Athens, Georgia. Luray manufactures fogging machines and chemicals for use by the mosquito control industry. With its strength primarily in product development and production, Luray relies on Adapco for its marketing and distribution needs.

Based in Lakeland, Florida, Adapco was founded in 1984 by Allen Woolridge, Pete Pederson, and Dan Boyd. The company possesses years of experience in mosquito control. Allen worked for seventeen years as a field research specialist with Dow Chemical. Pete spent twenty-six years with Chevron, the last few as regional manager of sales. Adapco relies on a network of nine distributors in the United States and five international distributors to sell most of the Luray line. The firm also employs three salespeople who deal with distributors as well as directly with customers, and earn a straight commission.

Although sales and profits have been steadily growing, Adapco has lately been searching for new products and markets. In early 1986, a line of biodegradable odor neutralizers was added. These are produced by the X-O Company of Knoxville, Tennessee. Adapco achieved only modest success in selling these products directly to waste treatment plants and limited success with patient care facilities. Further, distributors demonstrated little interest in the line. As a result, the line was dropped after one year.

THE MEDINA VERDE OPPORTUNITY

In continued efforts at diversification, Adapco recently began investigating opportunities which related its traditional expertise to the outdoor leisure industry, a market which has demonstrated rapid growth and strong potential in recent years. One of the most promising products is a new, high-performing, micro-nutrient fertilizer called Medina Verde, developed by the Medina Corporation of Austin, Texas. This is a product that, when applied, rapidly improves the health and fullness of grass, and has considerable greening power. Medina was interested in using Adapco as its sales

---

Case prepared by William Reynolds and Michael Morris, University of Central Florida, Orlando, Fl.

agent for the southeastern portion of the United States (North and South Carolina, Georgia, Florida, Alabama, and Mississippi).

To assess the potential of Medina Verde, Adapco test marketed the product in Florida for four months using its own sales force. The golf course industry was identified as the primary market for the fertilizer, while other markets include sod farms, athletic fields (e.g., schools), and city and county parks/recreational departments. One-third of the golf courses in the southeast are in Florida.

Sales response from the initial calls, which were directed at golf courses, was very impressive. Salespeople had little difficulty in getting a large number of prospects (60 percent of those contacted) to make a trial purchase, and a little over one-third of those trying the product placed larger orders within six weeks.

Based on the pilot sales program, the management team at Adapco put together some projections. Market potential for micro-nutrient fertilizers such as Medina Verde within the golf course market was estimated at $675,000 per year for the state of Florida (see Table 1). With sufficient sales support, Medina Verde can realistically expect to capture 10 percent of the total southeast market within its first year, and could conceivably capture 25 percent within three years.

THE SALES AND DISTRIBUTION QUESTION

Adapco management was enthusiastically in favor of formalizing the relationship with the Medina Corporation as sales agent for Medina Verde. Unresolved, however, was the question of whether to sell the product through their own sales force, or to

Table 1 Industry Sales Potential, Golf Courses in Florida

Number of golf courses in Florida	800
Average acres covered per golf course	3
Total potential acreage to cover	2,400
Quarts consumed per acre	3
Total quarts consumed per application	7,200
Applications per year	25
Total quarts forecasted	180,000
Quarts per gallon	4
Total gallons consumed	45,000
Price per gallon of Medina Verde	$ 15
Dollar Market Potential, Florida Market	$675,000

*ASSUMPTIONS

(1) Each golf course will only apply micro-nutrient to greens and tees. However, through field feedback, golf courses indicated they will use micro-nutrient (Medina Verde) on fairways through the winter.

(2) This market potential also assumes golf courses will only use 3 quarts per acre. On severely deficient soil the rate of application per acre will increase, resulting in increased sales of Medina Verde.

use a network of dealers who sell a wide range of products (including other micro-nutrient fertilizers) to golf courses, nurseries, municipal recreation departments, and small farms, among others. Even if dealers are used, however, Adapco would first have to get them to carry Medina Verde. These are dealers with which the company has had few direct dealings in the past.

To evaluate the alternatives, the following information has been compiled. Adapco's cost per gallon for Medina Verde is $8.50. The price per gallon to golf courses during the pilot sales effort was $15.00, and was accepted without resistance. Adapco would most likely sell the fertilizer to dealers for $11.00. Adapco's sales force has been receiving a straight 10 percent commission on direct sales, and a 5 percent commission on sales through distributors.

Inventory for a product such as Medina Verde should turn about five times per year, whether held by Adapco or dealers. If dealers are used, shipments would be made directly from Medina Corporation, and Adapco would only need to maintain enough inventory to make initial sales to dealers. The initial inventory requirements for direct sales within the State of Florida are estimated to be about five pallets, where each pallet holds 36 five gallon pails.

Credit costs are also likely to vary under the two forms of distribution. Experience with distributors selling mosquito control products suggests that accounts receivable usually average about 30 days of sales. Direct sales are more likely to average 45 days.

While the existing sales force was used in the test marketing of Medina Verde, their time is virtually entirely spoken for. As a result, Adapco would have to employ additional salespeople if the direct sales option is pursued.

Advise Adapco.

REFERENCES

CHAPTER 1 REFERENCES

Ames, B.C., and J.D. Hlavacek, *Managerial Marketing for Industrial Firms.* New York: Random House, 1984.

Calantone, R.J., and R.G. Cooper, "A Typology of Industrial New Product Failures," in Greenberg and Bellenger, eds., *1977 Educator's Conference Proceedings.* Chicago: American Marketing Association, 1977.

Choffray, J.M., and G.L. Lilien, *Market Planning for New Industrial Products.* New York: John Wiley & Sons, Ronald Press, 1980.

Corey, E.R., *Industrial Marketing: Cases and Concepts,* 3rd ed. Englewood Cliffs, N.J.: Prentice-Hall, 1983.

Drucker, P.F., *People and Performance: The Best of Peter Drucker on Management.* New York: Harper & Row, 1977.

Drucker, P.F., *Managing in Turbulent Times.* New York: Harper & Row, 1980.

Fern, E.F., and J.R. Brown, "The Industrial/Consumer Marketing Dichotomy: A Case of Insufficient Justification." *Journal of Marketing* 48 (Spring 1984): 68–77.

Levitt, T., *The Marketing Imagination.* New York: Free Press, 1983.

Levitt, T., "Marketing Success Through Differentiation—of Anything." *Harvard Business Review* 58 (January–February 1980): 83–91.

Marketing News, "AMA is Ready for Challenges in the Decade of Marketing." Sept. 28, 1984.

Mintzberg, H., *The Structuring of Organizations.* Englewood Cliffs, N.J.: Prentice-Hall, 1979.

Mullins, P.J., "Lasers Get Into the Eavesdropping Act." *Business Week* (July 12, 1982): 76.

Naisbitt, J., *Megatrends.* New York: Warner Books, 1982.

Peters, T.J., and R.H. Waterman, *In Search of Excellence.* New York: Harper & Row, 1982.

Porter, M.E., *Competitive Strategy.* New York: Free Press, 1980.

Toffler, A., *The Third Wave.* New York: William Morrow & Company, 1980.

Upah, G.D., and M.M. Bird, "Changes in Industrial Buying: Implications for Industrial Marketers." *Industrial Marketing Management* 9 (April 1980): 117–21.

U.S. Department of Commerce. *U.S. Industrial Outlook for 250 Industries with Projections for 1987.* Washington: GPO, 1983.

U.S. Department of Labor. Bureau of Labor Statistics. *Employment Projections for 1995,* No. 2197. Washington: GPO, March 1984.

Webster, F.E., Jr., *Industrial Marketing Strategy,* 2nd ed. New York: John Wiley & Sons, 1984.

CHAPTER 2 REFERENCES

Ammer, D.S., *Materials Management and Purchasing.* Homewood, Ill.: Richard D. Irwin, 1980.

Bornemann, A.H., *Essentials of Purchasing.* Columbus, Ohio: Grid, Inc., 1974.

Cateora, P.R., and J.M. Hess, *International Marketing*. Homewood, Ill.: Richard D. Irwin, 1983.

Corey, E.R., *Industrial Marketing: Cases and Concepts,* 3d ed. Englewood Cliffs, N.J.: Prentice-Hall, 1983.

Dobler, D.W., L. Lee, Jr., and D.N. Burt, *Purchasing and Materials Management*. New York: McGraw-Hill Book Co., 1984.

Forbis, J.L., and N.T. Mehta, "Value-Based Strategies for Industrial Products." *Business Horizons* (May–June 1981): 32–42.

Fram, D., *Value Analysis: A Way to Better Products and Profits*. New York: AMACOM, 1974.

Hahn, C.K., P.A. Pinto, and D.J. Bragg, "Just-in-Time Production and Purchasing." *Journal of Purchasing and Materials Management* 19(Fall 1983): 2–10.

Hillier, T.J., "Decision-Making in the Corporate Industrial Buying Process." *Industrial Marketing Management* 4 (May 1975): 99–106.

Hout, T., M.E. Porter, and E. Rudden, "How Global Companies Win Out." *Harvard Business Review* 60 (September-October 1982): 98–108.

Kotler, P., *Marketing Management: Analysis, Planning, and Control*. Englewood Cliffs, N.J.: Prentice-Hall, 1984.

McNally, G.J., "Global Marketing: It's Not Just Possible—It's Imperative." *Business Marketing* (April 1986): 64–70.

Sales and Marketing Management's Survey of Industrial and Commercial Buying Power (27 April, 1987): 22–29.

U.S. Bureau of Census. *Statistical Abstract of the U.S.: 1986,* 106th ed. Washington: GPO, 1985.

U.S. Bureau of Economic Analysis. *Survey of Current Business* 66. Washington: GPO, July 1986.

Waters, C.R., "Why Everybody's Talking About Just-in-Time." *Inc.* (March 1984): 77f.

Webster, F.E., Jr., *Industrial Marketing Strategy*. New York: John Wiley & Sons, 1984.

Zimmerman, L.W., and G.D. Hart, *Value Engineering: A Practical Approach for Owners, Designers, and Contractors*. New York: Van Nostrand Reinhold Co., 1982.

CHAPTER 3 REFERENCES

Bellizi, J.A., and P. McVey, "How Valid is the Buy-Grid Model?" *Industrial Marketing Management* 12 (February 1983): 57–62.

Bonoma, T.V., R.P. Bagozzi, and G. Zaltman, "The Dyadic Paradigm with Specific Applications Toward Industrial Marketing," in T.V. Bonoma and G. Zaltman, eds., *Organizational Buying Behavior*. Chicago: American Marketing Association, 1978: 49–66.

Cooley, J.R., D.W. Jackson, and L.L. Ostrom, "Analyzing the Relative Power of Participants in Industrial Buying Decisions," in B.A. Greenberg and D.N. Bellenger, eds., *Contemporary Marketing Thought*. Chicago: American Marketing Association 1977: 243–46.

Dichter, E.R., "Psychology in Industrial Marketing." *Industrial Marketing* 58 (February 1973): 40–43.

Giunipero, L.C., "Purchasing's Role in Computer Buying: A Comparative Study." *Industrial Marketing Management* 13 (November 1984): 241–248.

Hakansson, H., *International Marketing and Purchasing of Industrial Goods: An Interaction Approach*. Chichester: John Wiley & Sons, 1982.

Hillier, T.J., "Decision Making in the Corporate Industrial Buying Process." *Industrial Marketing Management* 4(1975): 99–106.

Laczniak, G., "An Empirical Study of Hospital Buying." *Industrial Marketing Management* 8, (1979): 57–62.

Lehmann, D., and J. O'Shaughnessy, "Decision Criteria Used in Buying Different Categories of Products." *Journal of Purchasing and Materials Management* 18 (Spring 1982): 9–14.

Levitt, T., *The Marketing Imagination*. New York: Free Press, 1983.

Robinson, P., C. Faris, and Y. Wind, *Industrial Buying and Creative Marketing*. Boston: Allyn & Bacon, 1967.

Tucker, W.T., "Future Directions in Marketing Theory." *Journal of Marketing* 38 (April 1974): 30–35.

Von Hippel, E., "Get New Products From Customers." *Harvard Business Review* 60 (March–April 1982): 117–122.

Webster, F.E., Jr., *Industrial Marketing Strategy*. New York: John Wiley & Sons, 1984.

CHAPTER 4 REFERENCES

Anderson, P.F., and T.M. Chambers, "A Reward/Measurement Model of Organizational Buying Behavior." *Journal of Marketing* 49 (Spring 1985): 7–23.

Bagozzi, R.P., "Exchange and Decision Processes in the Buying Center," in T. Bonoma and G. Zaltman, eds., *Organizational Buying Behavior*. Chicago: American Marketing Association, 1978: 100–125.

Bonoma, T.V., "Major Sales: Who Really Does the Buying?" *Harvard Business Review* 60 (May–June 1982): 111–119.

Bonoma, T.V., and G. Zaltman, *Organizational Buying Behavior*. Chicago: American Marketing Association, 1978.

Buskirk, R.H., *Principles of Marketing*. New York: Holt, Rinehart & Winston, 1970.

Choffray, J., and G. Lilien, "Assessing Response to Industrial Marketing Strategy." *Journal of Marketing* 42 (April 1978): 20–31.

Corey, E.R., *Procurement Management*. Boston: CBI Publishing Co., 1978.

French, J.R.P., and B. Ravens, "The Bases of Social Power," in D. Cartwright, ed., *Studies in Social Power*. Ann Arbor, Mich.: University of Michigan Press, 1959: 150–167.

Johnston, W.J., and T.V. Bonoma, "The Buying Center: Structure and Interaction Patterns." *Journal of Marketing* 45 (Summer 1981): 143–156.

Kiser, G.E., C.P. Rao, and S.R.G. Rao, "Vendor Attribute Evaluations of 'Buying Center' Members Other Than Purchasing Executives." *Industrial Marketing Management* 4 (1978): 45–54.

Kiser, G.E., and D. Rink, "Use of the Product Life Cycle Concept in Development of Purchasing Strategies." *Journal of Purchasing and Materials Management* 16 (Summer 1980): 12–17.

Laczniak, G., "An Empirical Study of Hospital Buying." *Industrial Marketing Management* 8 (1979): 57–62.

Lehmann, D., and J. O'Shaughnessy, "Difference in Attribute Importance for Different Industrial Products." *Journal of Marketing* 38 (April 1974): 36–42.

Manville, R., "Why Industrial Companies Must Advertise Their Products . . . and Consumer Companies Should Advertise Theirs." *Industrial Marketing* 63 (October 1978): 46–50.

Moriarty, R.T., and J. Bateson, "Exploring Complex Decision Making Units: A New Approach." *Journal of Marketing Research* 19 (May 1982): 182–191.

Morris, M.H., and J. Holman, "Source Loyalty in Organizational Markets: A Dyadic Perspective." *Journal of Business Research* (1987) (in press).

Patchen, M., "The Locus and Basis of Influence in Organizational Decisions." *Organizational Behavior and Human Performance* 11 (April 1974): 195–221.

Peter, J.P., and M.J. Ryan, "Investigation of Perceived Risk at the Brand Level." *Journal of Marketing Research* 13 (May 1976): 184–188.

Robinson, P., C. Faris, and Y. Wind, *Industrial Buying and Creative Marketing*. Boston: Allyn & Bacon, 1967.

Sheth, J., "A Model of Industrial Buyer Behavior." *Journal of Marketing* 37 (October 1973): 50–56.

Spekman, R.E., and L.W. Stern, "Environmental Uncertainty and Buying Group Structure: An Empirical Investigation." *Journal of Marketing* 43 (Spring 1979): 54–64.

Strauss, G., "Tactics of Lateral Relationships: The Purchasing Agent." *Administrative Science Quarterly* 7 (September 1962): 161–186.

Thomas, R.J., "Bases of Power in Organizational Buying Decisions." *Industrial Marketing Management* 13 (October 1984): 209–218.

Upah, G.D., "Applying the Concept of Perceived Risk to Buying Influence in Industrial Firms," J.C. Olson, ed., *Advances in Consumer Research* 7. Ann Arbor, Mich.: Association for Consumer Research, 1980: 379–384.

Vroom, V.H., *Work and Motivation*. New York: John Wiley & Sons, 1964.

Webster, F.E., Jr., *Industrial Marketing Strat-*

egy, 2nd ed. New York: John Wiley & Sons, 1984.

Webster, F.E., Jr., and Y. Wind, "A General Model for Understanding Organizational Buying Behavior." *Journal of Marketing* 36 (April 1972): 12–19.

Weigand, R.E., "Identifying Industrial Buying Responsibility." *Journal of Marketing Research* 3 (February 1966): 81–84.

Wind, Y., "Organizational Buying Center: A Research Agenda," in T.V. Bonoma and G. Zaltman, eds., *Organizational Buying Behavior.* Chicago: American Marketing Association 1978: 67–76.

Wind, Y., "Industrial Source Loyalty." *Journal of Marketing Research* 7 (November 1970): 450–57.

CHAPTER 5 REFERENCES

Cox, W.E., Jr., and L.V. Dominguez, "The Key Issues and Procedures of Industrial Marketing Research." *Industrial Marketing Management* 8 (1979): 81–93.

Katz, M., "Use Same Theory, Skills for Consumer, Industrial Marketing Research." *Marketing News* (January 12, 1974): 16.

Kotler, P., and R. Singh, "Marketing Warfare in the 1980's." *Journal of Business Strategy* 1 (Winter 1981).

Lee, D.D., *Industrial Marketing Research: Techniques and Practices,* 2nd ed. New York: Van Nostrand Reinhold, 1984.

Little, J.D.C., "Research Opportunities in the Decision and Management Sciences." *Management Science* 32 (January 1986): 1–13.

CHAPTER 6 REFERENCES

Hughes, G.D., *Marketing Management: A Planning Approach.* Reading, Mass.: Addison-Wesley Publishing Co., 1978.

Yesawich, P.C., "A Market-Based Approach to Forecasting." *Cornell HRA Quarterly* (November 1984): 47–55.

CHAPTER 7 REFERENCES

Bonoma, T.V., and B.P. Shapiro, "How to Segment Industrial Markets." *Harvard Business Review* (May–June 1984): 104–110.

Kotler, P., *Marketing Management: Analysis, Planning, and Control,* 5th ed. Englewood Cliffs, N.J.: Prentice-Hall, 1984.

Moriarty, R.T., and D.J. Reibstein, *Benefit Segmentation: An Industrial Application,* Report No. 82–110. Cambridge, Mass.: Marketing Science Institute, 1982.

Plank, R.E., "A Critical Review of Industrial Market Segmentation." *Industrial Marketing Management* 14 (1982): 79–91.

Wind, Y., and R.N. Cardozo, "Industrial Market Segmentation." *Industrial Marketing Management* 3 (1974): 153–166.

CHAPTER 8 REFERENCES

Aaker, D.A., and J.G. Shansby, "Positioning Your Product." *Business Horizons* 25 (May–June 1982): 56–62.

Brandt, S.C., *Entrepreneuring in Established Companies.* Homewood, Ill.: Dow Jones–Irwin, 1986.

Day, G.S., *Strategic Market Planning: The Pursuit of Competitive Advantage.* St. Paul, Minn.: West Publishing Co., 1984.

Ford, D., and C. Ryan, "Taking Technology to Market." *Harvard Business Review* 59 (March–April 1981): 117–126.

Guiltinan, J.P., and G. Paul, *Marketing Management: Strategies and Programs,* 2nd ed. New York: McGraw-Hill Book Co., 1985.

Jain, S.C., *Marketing Planning and Strategy.* Cincinnati, Ohio: South-Western Publishing Co., 1981.

Kotler, P., *Marketing Management: Analysis, Planning and Control,* 5th ed. Englewood Cliffs, N.J.: Prentice-Hall, 1984.

Lele, M.M., and U.S. Karmarker, "Good Product Support is Smart Marketing." *Harvard Business Review* 61 (November–December 1983): 124–132.

Levitt, T., "Marketing Success Through Differentiation—Of Anything." *Harvard Business Review* 48 (January–February 1980): 83–91.

Peter, J.P., and J.H. Donnelly, Jr., *Marketing Management: Knowledge and Skills.* Plano, Tex.: Business Publications, Inc., 1986.

Porter, M.E., *Competitive Strategy: Techniques*

for Analyzing Industries and Competitors. New York: Free Press, 1980.

Shanklin, W.L., and J.K. Ryans, Jr., *Essentials of Marketing High Technology.* Lexington, Mass.: D.C. Heath Co., 1987.

CHAPTER 9 REFERENCES

Bogaty, H., "Development of New Consumer Products—Ways to Improve Your Chances of Success." *Research Management* 17 (July 1974): 26–30.

Bonoma, T.V., "Marketing Subversives." *Harvard Business Review* 64 (November–December 1986): 113–118.

Booz, Allen, & Hamilton, *Management of New Products.* Chicago, (1968): 11–12.

Calantone, R., and R.G. Cooper, "A Typology of Industrial New Product Failure," in B.A. Greenberg, and D.N. Bellenger, *Proceedings,* Educators' Conference, Series No. 41. Chicago: American Marketing Association 1977: 492–497.

Cooper, R.G., "The Dimensions of Industrial New Product Success and Failure." *Journal of Marketing* 43 (Summer 1979): 93–103.

Cooper, R.G., "The Impact of New Product Strategies." *Industrial Marketing Management* 12 (November 1983): 243–256.

Crawford, C.M., "New Product Failure Rates—Facts and Fallacies." *Research Management* (September 1979):9–13.

Crawford, C.M., *New Products Management.* Homewood, ILL.: Richard D. Irwin, 1983.

Crawford, C.M., *New Products Management,* 2nd ed. Homewood, Ill.: Richard D. Irwin, 1987.

Morris, M.H., and G. Paul, "The Relationship Between Entrepreneurship and The Emphasis on Marketing in Established Firms." *Journal of Business Venturing* (1987) (in press).

Murray, J.A., "Marketing is the Home for the Entrepreneurial Process." *Industrial Marketing Management* 10 (May 1981): 93–99.

Peters, M.P., and M. Venkatesan. "Exploration of Variables Inherent in Adopting an Industrial Product." *Journal of Marketing Research* 10 (August 1973): 312–315.

Pinchot, G., *Intrapreneuring.* New York: Harper & Row, 1985.

Robertson, T., "The Process of Innovation and the Diffusion of Innovation." *Journal of Marketing* 31 (January 1967): 14–19.

Rousel, P.A., "Cutting Down the Guesswork in R&D." *Harvard Business Review* 61 (September–October 1983): 154–160.

Souder, W.E., "Effectiveness of Product Development Methods." *Industrial Marketing Management* 4 (November 1978): 299–307.

Warren, E.J., "The Interface Between R&D, Marketing, and Marketing Research in New-Product Development." *Journal of Consumer Marketing* 1 (Summer 1983): 80–90.

White, G.R., and M.B.W. Graham, "How to Spot a Technological Winner." *Harvard Business Review* 56 (March–April 1978): 146–152.

CHAPTER 10 REFERENCES

Anderson, F., and W. Lazer, "Industrial Lease Marketing." *Journal of Marketing* 42 (January 1978): 71–9.

Buzzell, R.D., B.T. Gale, and R.A.M. Sultan, "Market Share—A Key to Profitability." *Harvard Business Review* 53, No. 1 (1975): 97–106.

Corey, R.E., *Industrial Marketing: Cases and Concepts,* 2nd ed. Englewood Cliffs, N.J.: Prentice-Hall, 1976.

Corey, R.E., *Industrial Marketing: Cases and Concepts,* 3rd ed. Englewood Cliffs, N.J.: Prentice-Hall, 1983.

Dobler, W., L. Lee, Jr., D.N. Burt, *Purchasing and Materials Management,* 4th ed. New York: McGraw-Hill Book Co., 1984.

Guiltinan, J.P., "Risk-Aversive Pricing Policies: Problems and Alternatives." *Journal of Marketing* 40 (January 1976): 10–15.

Kotler, P., *Marketing Management: Analysis, Planning and Control,* 5th ed. Englewood Cliffs, N.J.: Prentice-Hall, 1984.

Maitlandt, P., "An Alternative to Transfer Pricing." *Harvard Business Review* 54 (March–April 1976): 81–6.

Monroe, K.B., *Pricing: Making Profitable De-*

cisions. New York: McGraw-Hill Book Co., 1979.

Stern, L.W., and T.L. Eovaldi, *Legal Aspects of Marketing Strategy.* Englewood Cliffs, N.J.: Prentice-Hall, 1984.

Sultan, R.A.M., *Pricing in the Electrical Oligopoly; vol.1: Competition or Collusion; vol.2: Business Strategy.* Boston: Harvard University, Division of Research, Graduate School of Business Administration, 1974.

Webster, F.E., Jr., *Industrial Marketing Strategy.* New York: John Wiley & Sons, 1984.

CHAPTER 11 REFERENCES

Bellizzi, J.A., and R.E. Hite, "Improving Industrial Advertising Copy." *Industrial Marketing Management* 15 (1986): 117–122.

Boyd, H.W., Jr., M. Ray, and E. Strong, "An Attitudinal Framework for Advertising Strategy." *Journal of Marketing* 36 (April 1972): 27–33.

Cahners Advertising Research Report No. 411.2, "What Percent of Purchasing Influences Read Specialized Business Magazines?" Boston: Cahners Publishing Co.

Cahners Advertising Research Report No. 450.4, "Do Recipients Refer To and Take Action As A Result of Seeing Advertisements And Manufacturer Listings in Annuals And Directories?". Boston: Cahners Publishing Co.

Cahners Advertising Research Report No. 551.9, "How Many Key Buying Influences Must Marketers Reach Through Industrial Advertisements?" Boston: Cahners Publishing Co.

Cavanaugh, S., "Setting Objectives and Evaluating the Effectiveness of Trade Show Exhibits." *Journal of Marketing* 40 (October 1976): 100–103.

Cox, J., "Trade Shows Provide Easiest Media Evaluation." *Marketing News* 19 (May 10, 1985): 13.

Dichter, E.R., "Psychology in Industrial Marketing." *Industrial Marketing* (February 1973).

Donath, B., "Show and Sell By the Numbers." *Industrial Marketing* (March 1980): 70–72.

Donath, B., "Q: What Makes the Perfect Ad? A: It Depends." *Industrial Marketing* (August 1982): 89–92.

Green, S., "Trade Shows Should Be Marketing Focal Point." *Marketing News* 19 (May 10, 1985): 12.

Lilien, G.L., *A Study of Industrial Marketing Budgeting, Descriptive Analysis-Final Report.* Sloan School of Management, M.I.T. (February, 1978).

Lilien, G.L., and J.D.C. Little, "The ADVISOR Project: A Study of Industrial Marketing Budgets." *Sloan Management Review* (Spring 1976): 17–31.

Manville, R., "Why Industrial Companies Must Advertise Their Products . . . and Consumer Companies Should Advertise Theirs." *Industrial Marketing* (October 1978): 46–50.

Marsteller, W.A., "A Conversation with Bill Marsteller." *Marketing Media Decisions* 19 (Fall 1984): 78f.

McAleer, G., "Do Industrial Advertisers Understand What Influences Their Markets?" *Journal of Marketing* 38 (January 1974): 15–23.

Mee, W.J., "Who Visits Your Booth and Why?" *Sales and Marketing Management* (August 20, 1979): 65–7.

Milmo, S., "Precise Data Makes Exact Markets Push." *Business Marketing* (November, 1984): 9f.

Milsap, C.R., "Make Your Customer's Customer Your Ally." *Business Marketing* (February 1986): 100–106.

Moriarty, R.T., Jr., and R.E. Spekman, "An Empirical Investigation of the Information Sources Used During the Industrial Buying Process." *Journal of Marketing Research* 21 (May 1984): 137–47.

Morrill, J.E., "Industrial Advertising Pays Off." *Harvard Business Review* (March–April, 1970): 4–14.

CHAPTER 12 REFERENCES

Bellizzi, J.A., and P.A. Cline, "Technical or Non-technical Salesmen?" *Industrial Marketing Management* 14 (1985): 69–74.

Bonoma, T.V., R. Bagozzi and G. Zaltman, "The Dyadic Paradigm with Specific Application Toward Industrial Marketing." *Or-*

ganizational *Buying Behavior.* Chicago: American Marketing Association 1978: 49–66.

Dalrymple, D.J., *Sales Management: Concepts and Cases.* New York: John Wiley & Sons, 1982.

Demirdjian, Z., "A Multidimensional Approach to Motivating Salespeople." *Industrial Marketing Management* 13 (1984): 25–32.

Enis, B., *Personal Selling: Foundations, Process, and Management.* Santa Monica, Calif.: Goodyear Publishing Co., 1979.

Evans, F.B., "Dyadic Interaction in Selling: A New Approach." Unpublished monograph, Graduate School of Business, University of Chicago, 1964.

Finn, D.W., and W.C. Moncrief, "Salesforce Entertainment Activities." *Industrial Marketing Management* 14 (1985): 227–234.

Fisher, R., and W. Ury, *Getting to Yes: Negotiating Agreement Without Giving In.* Boston: Houghton Mifflin, 1981.

Ford, N.M., G.A. Churchill, O.C. Walker "Differences in the Attractiveness of Alternative Rewards Among Industrial Salespeople: Additional Evidence." *Journal of Business Research* 13 (1985): 123–138.

Hackman, J.R., E.E. Lawler III, and L.W. Porter, eds., *Perspectives on Behavior in Organizations,* 2nd ed. New York: McGraw-Hill, 1983.

Johnson, M., "How Computerization Can Organize a Sales Force." *Business Marketing* (December 1985): 98–101.

Kent, D., "Sales Lead Management in the Computer Age." *Business Marketing* (March 1986): 60–69.

McGraw-Hill *LAP Report No. 8013.8,* "Cost of an Industrial Sales Call." New York: McGraw-Hill, Inc., 1986.

Moncrief, W.C., "Ten Key Activities of Industrial Salespeople." *Industrial Marketing Management* 15 (1986): 309–317.

Parasuraman A., and R. Day, "A Management-Directed Model for Allocating Sales Effort." *Journal of Marketing Research* 14 (1977): 22–23.

Porter, L.W., and E.E. Lawler III, *Managerial Attitudes and Performance.* Homewood, Ill.: Irwin, Dorsey Press, 1968.

Raiffa, H., *The Art & Sciences of Negotiation.* Cambridge: Harvard University Press, The Belknap Press, 1982.

Sales and Marketing Management's Survey of Selling Cost, February 16, 1987.

Vroom, V.H., *Work and Motivation.* New York: John Wiley & Sons, 1964.

Weaver, R.A., Jr., "Set Goals to Tap Self-Motivation." *Business Marketing* (December 1985): 54–62.

Zinkhan, G.M., and L.A. Vachris, "The Impact of Selling Aids on New Prospects." *Industrial Marketing Management* 13 (1984): 187–193.

CHAPTER 13 REFERENCES

Bobrow, E.E., *Marketing Through Manufacturers' Agents.* Sales Builders, New York (1976): 57–8.

Corey, E.R., *Industrial Marketing: Cases and Concepts,* 2d ed. Englewood Cliffs, N.J.: Prentice-Hall, 1976.

Corey, E.R., *Industrial Marketing: Cases and Concepts,* 3d ed. Englewood Cliffs, N.J.: Prentice-Hall, 1983

Hlavacek, J.D., and T.J. McCuistion, "Industrial Distributors—When, Who, and How?" *Harvard Business Review* (March–April 1983): 96–101.

Marketing News, "The Chain of Events in Industrial Distribution" (January 30, 1976): 7.

Marketing News, "Marketing Via Distributorships Requires Modernized Techniques," 19 (October 25, 1985): 24.

Milsap, C.R., "Conquering the Distributor Incentive Blues." *Business Marketing* (April, 1985): 50–56.

Narus, J.A., N. Reddy, and L. Pinchak, "Key Problems Facing Industrial Distributors." *Industrial Marketing Management* 13 (1984): 139–147.

Oresman, S.B., and C.D. Scudder, "A Remedy for Maldistribution." *Business Horizons* (June, 1974): 61–72.

Perreault, W.D., Jr., and F.A. Russ, "Physical Distribution Service in Industrial Purchase Decisions." *Journal of Marketing* 40 (April 1976): 3–10.

Peterson, J.W., " 'Before Product Users Can

Benefit, Industrial Marketer Must Offer Benefits to Distributor'." *Marketing News* (January 30, 1976): 7f.

Sabath, R.E., "How Much Service Do Customers Really Want?" *Business Horizons* (April, 1978): 26.

Sibley, S.D., and R.K. Teas, "The Manufacturer's Agent in Industrial Distribution." *Industrial Marketing Management* (November, 1979): 286–292.

Stern, L.W., and A.I. El-Ansary, *Marketing Channels*. Englewood Cliffs, N.J.: Prentice-Hall, 1982.

Webster, F.E., Jr., *Industrial Marketing Strategy,* 2nd ed. New York: John Wiley & Sons, 1984.

CHAPTER 14 REFERENCES

Beik, L.L., and S.L. Buzby, "Profitability Analysis By Market Segments." *Journal of Marketing* 37 (July 1973): 48–53.

Cohen, K.J., and R.M. Cyert, "Strategy: Formulation, Implementation, and Monitoring." *Journal of Business* (July, 1973).

Cook, R., "Conquering Computer Clutter." *High Technology* (December 1984): 61–71.

Donaldson, T., *Corporations and Morality.* Englewood Cliffs, N.J.: Prentice-Hall, 1982.

Dubinsky, A.J., and J.M. Gwin, "Business Ethics: Buyers and Sellers." *Journal of Purchasing and Materials Management* (Winter 1981): 9–15.

Dunne, P.M., and H.I. Wolk, "Marketing Cost Analysis: A Modularized Contribution Approach." *Journal of Marketing* 41 (July 1977): 83–94.

Grashof, J.F., "Conducting and Using a Marketing Audit," in E.J. McCarthy, J.F. Grashof, and A.A. Brogowicz, *Readings in Basic Marketing*. Homewood, Ill.: Richard D. Irwin, (1981): 347–58.

Kotler, P., *Marketing Management: Analysis, Planning and Control,* 5th ed. Englewood Cliffs, N.J.: Prentice-Hall, 1984.

Laric, M.V., and R. Stiff, *Lotus 1–2–3 For Marketing and Sales.* Englewood Cliffs, N.J.: Prentice-Hall, 1984.

Lorange, P., M.F.S. Morton, and S. Ghoshal, *Strategic Control.* St. Paul, Minn.: West Publishing Company, 1986.

Montgomery, D., and C. Weinberg, "Toward Strategic Intelligence Systems," *Journal of Marketing* 43 (Fall 1979): 41–52.

Mossman, F.H., P.M. Fischer, and W.J.E. Crissy, "New Approaches to Analyzing Marketing Profitability." *Journal of Marketing* 38 (April 1974): 43–48.

O'Leary, T.J., and B.K. Williams, *Computers and Information Processing with Business Applications.* Menlo Park, Calif.: Benjamin/Cumming, 1985.

Pinchot, G., *Intrapreneuring.* New York: Harper & Row, 1985.

Schiff, J.S., "Evaluate the Sales Force as a Business." *Industrial Marketing Management* 12 (April 1983): 131–137.

AUTHOR INDEX

SUBJECT INDEX